STRATEGIC MARKETING

HOLT, RINEHART AND WINSTON MARKETING SERIES

Paul E. Green, Adviser
Wharton School, University of Pennsylvania

Philip Kotler, Adviser
Northwestern University

James F. Engel, The Ohio State University
Henry F. Fiorillo, Canadian Breweries, Ltd. and University of Toronto
Murray A. Cayley, Imperial Oil Company
Market Segmentation: Concepts and Applications

James F. Engel, David T. Kollat, Roger D. Blackwell
All of The Ohio State University
Consumer Behavior
Cases in Consumer Behavior
Research in Consumer Behavior

Ronald R. Gist, University of Denver
Cases in Marketing Management
Marketing and Society: A Conceptual Introduction
Readings: Marketing and Society

Charles S. Goodman, University of Pennsylvania
Management of the Personal Selling Function

Paul E. Green, University of Pennsylvania
Vithala R. Rao, Cornell University
Applied Multidimensional Scaling: A Comparison of Approaches and Algorithms

David T. Kollat, Roger D. Blackwell, James F. Robeson
All of The Ohio State University
Strategic Marketing

Philip Kotler, Northwestern University
Marketing Decision Making: A Model Building Approach

John C. Narver, University of Washington
Ronald Savitt, Boston University
The Marketing Economy: An Analytical Approach
Conceptual Readings in the Marketing Economy

Vern Terpstra, University of Michigan
International Marketing

Thomas R. Wotruba, San Diego State College
Sales Management: Planning, Accomplishment, and Evaluation

Thomas R. Wotruba, San Diego State College
Robert M. Olsen, California State College, Fullerton
Readings in Sales Management: Concepts and Viewpoints

Gerald Zaltman, Northwestern University
Philip Kotler, Northwestern University
Ira Kaufman, University of Manchester
Creating Social Change

STRATEGIC MARKETING

David T. Kollat
Roger D. Blackwell
James F. Robeson
The Ohio State University

Holt, Rinehart and Winston, Inc.
New York Chicago San Francisco Atlanta
Dallas Montreal Toronto London Sydney

EDITORS' FOREWORD

The Advisory Editors of the Holt, Rinehart and Winston Marketing Series are pleased to publish this modern text on marketing by Kollat, Blackwell, and Robeson. *Strategic Marketing* is outstanding in several ways as a basis for educating present and future marketing and business executives. Its dominant theme is that marketing management is part of corporate management, not an isolated thing in itself. As such, marketing policy and practice must be constantly related back to the purposes and objectives of the firm. Within this framework, *Strategic Marketing* presents a comprehensive, well-organized, and up-to-date treatment of modern marketing. The chapters flow logically according to the major steps in the management process. Every topic of major importance to the marketing manager is presented with good conceptual and descriptive treatment. The text introduces the latest concepts in marketing analysis, planning, and control without becoming too mathematical or obscure. The Editors feel that this combination of virtues makes this book a distinguished contribution to the marketing literature.

Paul E. Green
Philip Kotler

PREFACE The expanding role and accelerating importance of marketing is one of the most significant developments in the business sector of the American economy since the Second World War. In an environment characterized by unparalleled technological advancements, intensifying competition, increasingly fragmented and discriminating customer markets, and massive and disruptive changes in distribution markets, business enterprises have relied more heavily on marketing than at any other time in the history of the Republic.

During the last quarter century a few firms have risen to the top of American industry, many have died, and most have achieved average results. These varying performance profiles are determined in large part by differing degrees of marketing competence. High-yield companies are usually proficient in marketing; the others typically have less expertise. Most enterprises now recognize the fantastic rewards of marketing competence and the devastative, often terminal effects of marketing incompetence. Corporate success is often synonymous with marketing success.

Marketing has become not only critical but also complex. Unlike production, accounting, finance, or engineering, marketing problems usually resist neat quantitative solutions. Designing products and services to satisfy customer needs is a hazardous process that often victimizes even the largest and most sophisticated companies. Marketing decisions must inherently be made with incomplete information, and the sales, cost, and investment consequences of these decisions are difficult to predict. The difficulty of making these important decisions makes marketing a critical determinant of corporate success.

This volume is dedicated to those who desire to understand marketing or who aspire to be marketing executives. It attempts to deal meaningfully with the marketing challenges that corporate and marketing executives face. Hopefully it reflects several themes and convictions.

First, this text is managerially oriented. It attempts to present an analytical orientation to the major marketing problems facing senior corporate and marketing executives. Description has been minimized in favor of this orientation.

Second, marketing has been subordinated to the overall interests of the firm. Like other functional areas of the business, marketing contributes to the development of corporate objectives and strategies. But the role of an enterprise is to achieve certain goals and objectives, and it can accomplish them most effectively and efficiently if it follows certain strategies that allow it to capitalize on its strengths and minimize its vulnerabilities. Thus marketing must contribute to the achievement of corporate objectives in ways that are consistent with corporate strategies and with the strengths and limitations of other functional areas of the business.

Third, we have attempted to present a practical framework that links corporate objectives and strategies to master marketing objectives and strategies, and then to objectives and programs for individual marketing activities. The linking mechanism is a general management-by-objectives system. Flow diagrams have been used to depict these relationships.

Fourth, the text has a strong empirical emphasis. We have reviewed books and articles appearing in major business publications since 1950, seeking to present a richly documented discussion that reflects the current state of marketing expertise. Literature reviews and theoretical concepts are rarely presented unless they have immediate or potential applications to the development of corporate and marketing strategies and programs. We have made liberal use of case examples to illustrate concepts and procedures, and heavy emphasis has been placed on research techniques and information systems.

Finally, this volume has a futuristic orientation. Since we are concerned more with the future than with the past, historical data and concepts are presented only where they shed light on the future. In an era of unprecedented change and discontinuity, the experiences of the past are often questionable guidelines for the future. Though the methods of futurology are imperfect and hazardous, we have nevertheless tried to present informed judgments about the future rather than ignoring it.

The twenty-two chapters that comprise the text are divided into six major parts. Part I is concerned with the development of corporate and marketing strategies. Chapter 1 discusses systems comprising the corporate environment and a management-by-objectives approach to managing a firm. A framework is then presented for developing a strategic plan—consisting of a corporate mission, objectives, and strategy. Chapter 2 first discusses the nature of marketing and the marketing concept and then presents a procedure for developing master marketing objectives and strategies that are consistent with, and that contribute to the achievement of, corporate objectives.

The seven chapters comprising Part II are concerned with identifying and assessing market opportunities. Chapters 3 and 4 present a managerial orientation to marketing research sources and techniques. Chapters 4 through 8 analyze the present and future structural and behavioral characteristics of consumer, industrial, institutional, and international markets. Procedures and techniques for selecting target market segments are presented in Chapter 9.

Part III consists of eight chapters dealing with marketing programs—discussing product programs (Chapters 10 and 11), pricing (Chapter 12), channels of distribution (Chapter 13), physical distribution (Chapter 14), advertising (Chapter 15), sales force (Chapter 16), and marketing personnel (Chapter 17) problems. Each of these programs is related to the master marketing objectives and strategy through the management-by-objectives system, depicted graphically via flow charts.

Techniques for pretesting the effectiveness of marketing programs are discussed in Part IV. Chapter 18 analyzes test-marketing procedures, and simulation techniques are discussed in Chapter 19.

Once implemented, marketing programs must be controlled and evaluated. In Part V, Chapter 20 describes the nature and content of marketing information systems that are necessary to utilize the control and evaluation procedures presented in Chapter 21.

The nature and role of marketing are likely to change in order to adapt to the problems and opportunities of the 1970s. Chapter 22 attempts to identify the moral and ethical responsibilities of business enterprises and corporate and marketing executives during this transitional decade.

Like most other books, this one reflects the ideas and experiences of many individuals. First and foremost are those authors who have generated perceptive ideas about corporate and marketing strategy and planning. Second, we are indebted to our colleagues at The Ohio State University: Robert Bartels, Theodore N. Beckman, W. Arthur Cullman, William R. Davidson, James H. Davis, Alton F. Doody, James F. Engel, John R. Grabner, Jr., Bernard J. LaLonde, Louis W. Stern, and Wayne Talaryzk. We are particularly grateful to the late Robert B. Miner for his understanding and assistance.

Many of the ideas and points of view have evolved from the authors' consulting experiences. We are particularly indebted to Management Horizons, Inc., especially Mr. Byron Carter, Dr. Bert C. McCammon, and Dr. Cyrus C. Wilson.

Several individuals reviewed various chapters. We particularly appreciate the suggestions made by Professors Bernard J. LaLonde, James F. Engel, John R. Grabner, Jr., and Lawrence Ritzman of The Ohio State University, and Mr. Charles Kimm of Battelle Memorial Institute.

We are also indebted to those individuals who reviewed the manuscript in the latter stages of its development: Professors Paul Green of Wharton, Philip Kotler of Northwestern, and Harper Boyd of Stanford.

We would also like to express our gratitude to Professor Beverly Anderson, now at Kansas University; Samuel Craig; and Dennis Garber for their assistance in collecting and synthesizing materials. Mrs. James Andrews did an outstanding job of typing the manuscript.

Finally, we are most grateful to our wives and families for accepting the deprivations and frustrations of living with writers. This book is dedicated to them.

Columbus, Ohio   D.T.K.
January 1972   R.D.B.
                                                                  J.F.R.

CONTENTS

PART I CORPORATE AND MARKETING PLANNING

Marketing's *raison d'être* is its contribution to the achievement of overall company objectives and strategies. These are initially developed and articulated in a corporate strategic plan, which then becomes the basis for the marketing plan. These planning procedures constitute the subject matter of Part I.

Chapter 1 is concerned primarily with the development of a strategic plan that will allow a firm to achieve above-average rates of growth and profitability by engineering a market position so advantageous that competitors can retaliate only over an extended time period at a prohibitive cost. Each stage in this planning process is examined in considerable detail.

Chapter 2 begins by discussing the nature of marketing and the contemporary marketing concept; then it presents a system for developing a marketing plan that makes the required contributions to the achievement of the strategic plan.

Chapter 1   Corporate Strategy

Marketing is perhaps the most dynamic, complicated, and challenging function of business. Indeed, more and more businessmen are recognizing that marketing success is a pivotal determinant of corporate success.[1]

While marketing is usually critically important, it is seldom the sole determinant of a company's success or failure. Like production, engineering, finance, and other functions of a business, it is judged ultimately by its contribution to the overall objectives and strategy of the firm. To be sure, marketing considerations together with those of other functional areas play an important role in framing corporate objectives and strategies. But once the latter are formulated, the role of marketing is to contribute to their achievement.

This chapter first discusses the firm and the environment in which it must operate; then it presents a management system that will be used throughout this text. The remainder of the chapter develops an operational framework for formulating a strategic plan. Marketing strategy is integrated into this framework in the next chapter.

THE TOTAL CORPORATE ENVIRONMENT

Historically there has been a tendency to think of the activities and boundaries of a company in terms of what the company owns. This perspective is too myopic to be of much value in strategic planning. Rather, we must take a much broader view of an enterprise by considering the total environment in which it operates.

[1] See, for example, Lee Adler, "Systems Approach to Marketing," *Harvard Business Review*, Vol. 45 (May-June 1967), pp. 105–118.

The Total Corporate System

Figure 1-1 is a schematic representation of the firm and major subsystems comprising its environment. The totality of these interacting subsystems comprises what has been termed the total corporate system.

These subsystems can affect a firm in two major ways. First, they may play a *constraining role* in limiting the success of an enterprise. They may also play an *opportunistic role* in presenting opportunities for improving its success. Many companies and much written literature emphasize the constraining role. While this perspective must be given careful consideration, companies enjoying above-average rates of growth and profitability *capitalize* on the opportunities presented by environmental forces.[2] With this opportunistic perspective in mind, let us examine the major subsystems comprising the total corporate environment.

Environmental Systems

Four major interacting systems comprise a firm's environment: (1) economic and technological systems; (2) political, legal, and regulatory systems; (3) cultural and life-style systems; and (4) other social systems. Each of these systems constrains the firm and also offers it opportunities.

Economic and Technological Systems. The size or level of the economy affects the opportunities available to an enterprise. The size of the economy affects the total market size for consumer and industrial goods and services. Higher levels of economic activity also create new business opportunities, as illustrated by the growth of firms offering various types of luxury goods and services.

Technological systems also affect a firm's destiny. When market opportunities exist but the necessary technology is absent, technology presents a limit. Conversely, technological innovations often create new business opportunities—as the development of synthetic fibers did in many fields, including apparel and carpeting.

Political, Legal, and Regulatory Systems. These systems restrain as well as create opportunities for perceptive companies. For example, the decision to rely heavily on monetary policy to combat the inflation of the late 1960s restrained the housing industry but created opportunities for apartments. Tax laws limit the profitability of many companies but they also create opportunities for individuals and firms having expertise in tax matters. Similarly, while many firms were restricted by Medicare (or viewed it as restrictive), others—such as nursing homes—organized to take advantage of the opportunities it created.

Cultural and Life-Style Systems. Cultural and life-style systems also limit and create opportunities for firms. For example, the weight consciousness of

---

[2] For corporate examples see Alfred D. Chandler, Jr., *Strategy and Structure* (Cambridge: The M.I.T. Press, 1962).

Figure 1-1 The total corporate system.

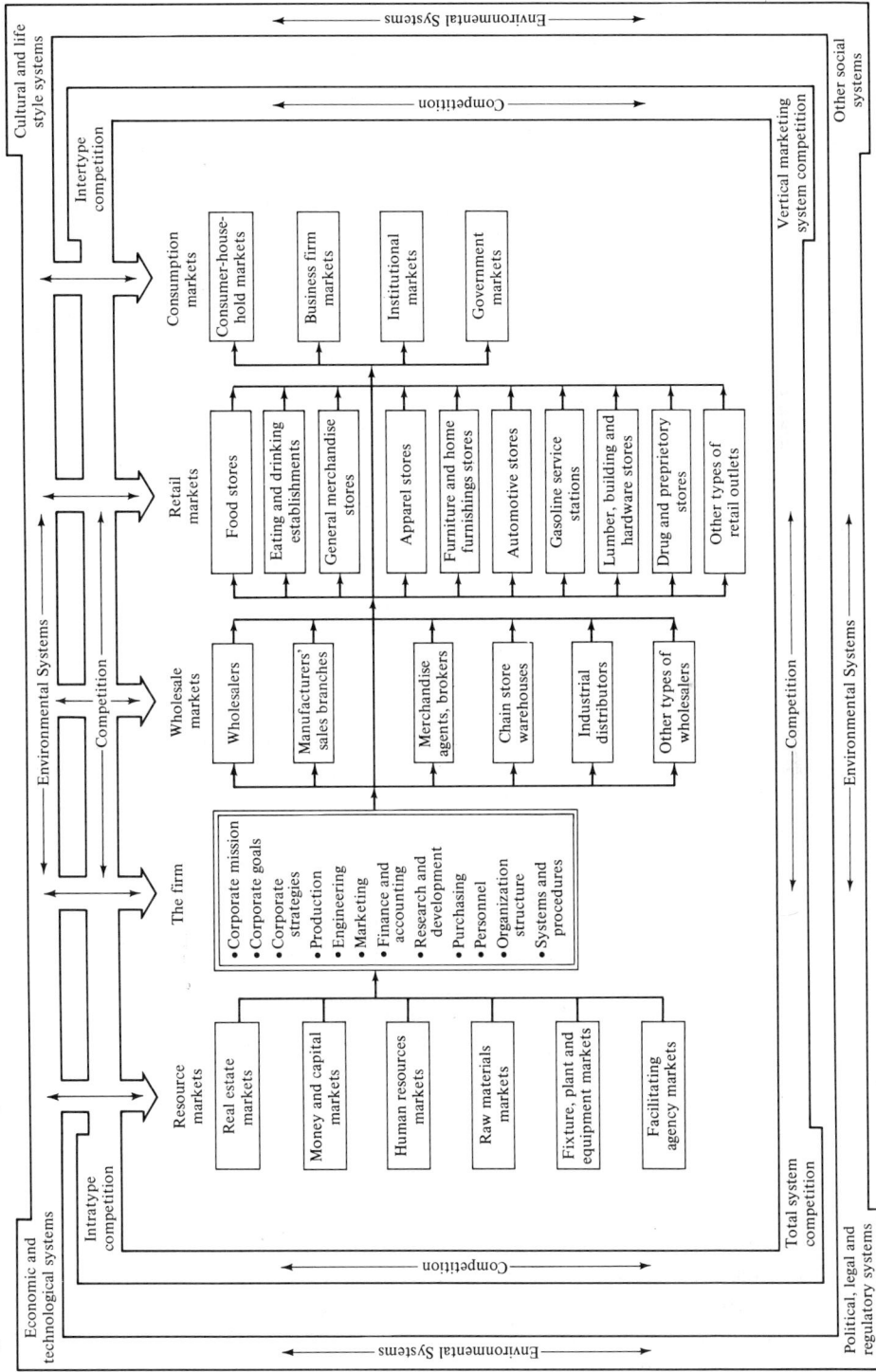

Environmental Systems (top)

Cultural and life style systems

Other social systems

Intertype competition — Competition

Consumption markets
- Consumer-household markets
- Business firm markets
- Institutional markets
- Government markets

Retail markets
- Food stores
- Eating and drinking establishments
- General merchandise stores
- Apparel stores
- Furniture and home furnishings stores
- Automotive stores
- Gasoline service stations
- Lumber, building and hardware stores
- Drug and proprietory stores
- Other types of retail outlets

Wholesale markets
- Wholesalers
- Manufacturers' sales branches
- Merchandise agents, brokers
- Chain store warehouses
- Industrial distributors
- Other types of wholesalers

The firm
- Corporate mission
- Corporate goals
- Corporate strategies
- Production
- Engineering
- Marketing
- Finance and accounting
- Research and development
- Purchasing
- Personnel
- Organization structure
- Systems and procedures

Resource markets
- Real estate markets
- Money and capital markets
- Human resources markets
- Raw materials markets
- Fixture, plant and equipment markets
- Facilitating agency markets

Economic and technological systems

Environmental Systems — Competition

Intratype competition — Competition

Vertical marketing system competition

Total system competition

Political, legal and regulatory systems

Environmental Systems (bottom)

5

many American consumers presents sizable business opportunities for companies offering products and services that assist in weight control, while it limits the opportunities of those offering products and services that result in weight gain. The trend toward suburban living adversely affected manufacturers and retailers relying on retail outlets in the central cities but has created fantastic opportunities for a variety of businesses, such as shopping-center developers, branch stores for retail outlets, and companies supplying goods and services involved in home and lawn maintenance.

As these few examples illustrate, a firm operates in an environment consisting of many interacting systems. The success of a business depends, in part, on how well it adjusts to the constraints and opportunities presented by these and other environmental systems.

Competitive Systems

In adapting to the restraints and opportunities of the various environmental systems and markets, a firm faces several potential types of competition (see Figure 1-1). The most obvious is *intratype competition*—conflict between firms of the same type. Thus, for example, Coca-Cola competes with Pepsi-Cola. This is the form of competition described in economic theory and stressed in economic studies.

Intertype competition occurs between different types of firms. Coca-Cola, for example, competes with such companies as Procter & Gamble, Kraft, and Kellogg for access to resource, retail, and consumption markets.

Another form of rivalry is *vertical marketing system competition*. This occurs between the firm and/or different levels of distribution; between manufacturers and wholesalers, wholesalers and retailers, manufacturers and retailers. Thus, for example, General Motors and its dealer network competes with Ford and its dealers. The vertical marketing system of Kentucky Fried Chicken competes with those of McDonald's and Burger Chef.

Total system competition, the most advanced form of rivalry, occurs between systems linking resource markets, the firm, and distribution markets. Sears Roebuck, for example, is an advanced total system linking resource markets, manufacturing facilities, and, of course, the largest distribution capability in the world.

Resource Markets

The ability of an enterprise to compete for resources is an important determinant of its success, because it represents its capacity to respond to threats and opportunities. Consequently, it is important for a business to manage its relationships with resource markets with as much sophistication as it manages its internal relationships.

The most common approach is an informal agreement. For example, a company deposits money in the bank, and the bank in turn provides a variety of services including, perhaps, an "open line of credit"—or an understanding that the company may borrow up to a stipulated limit for short-term needs.

A company may use legal contracts to assure access to certain resource markets. For example, a firm may enter into a long-term purchasing agreement with key suppliers of basic raw materials.[3]

Temporary partnerships and coalitions are other methods of gaining access to key resources. To illustrate, when the Birdseye division of General Foods lacked the capability to produce the freezer cabinets it needed to market its frozen foods, it entered into a coalition with a refrigerator manufacturer to make and sell (or lease) the cabinets to retail stores.[4]

Ownership is another method of gaining access to critical resources. It is common, for example, for steel companies to have at least a partial ownership in ore properties and mining companies. Large ore companies often invest in crude oil production enterprises.[5]

Every enterprise, then, must secure the continuing cooperation of various firms or groups comprising its resource markets. A combination of alliances must be developed to assure the company access to the goods and services provided by these firms—hopefully at competitive or preferred prices.

The Firm

The firm is, of course, the central part of the total corporate system. From a decision viewpoint, the overall task of an enterprise is to configure and direct the resource conversion process so as to achieve its objectives.[6] This task is the subject of this volume.

Wholesale and Retail Markets

In most situations a firm must obtain the continuing cooperation of various wholesaling and/or retailing firms in order to distribute its products to ultimate users. In seeking this cooperation it faces various types of competition alluded to above. Strategies and programs for competing in wholesale and retail markets are discussed in Chapter 13.

Consumption Markets

The success of any business hinges ultimately on how effectively it satisfies the problems of ultimate customers. All activities of a business can be justified only

---

[3] William H. Newman and Thomas L. Berg, "Managing External Relations," *California Management Review,* Spring 1963, pp. 81–86.

[4] William H. Newman, "Shaping the Master Strategy of Your Firm," *California Management Review,* Spring 1967, pp. 71–88.

[5] Newman and Berg, "Managing External Relations," p. 83.

[6] H. Igor Ansoff, *Corporate Strategy* (New York: McGraw-Hill, Inc., 1965), p. 5.

insofar as they are required to satisfy the demands of the markets the company is attempting to serve.[7] As Peter Drucker has stated:

It is the customer who determines what a business is. For it is the customer, and he alone, who through being willing to pay for a good or for a service, converts economic resources into wealth, things into goods. What the business thinks it produces is not of first importance—especially not to the future of the business and to its success. What the customer thinks he is buying, what he considers "value," is decisive—it determines what a business is, what it produces and whether it will prosper.[8]

The pivotal role of the customer in corporate and marketing strategy is the principal theme of this book and will be the subject of considerable discussion and analysis.

The Total Corporate System and the Corporate Imperative

Our discussion points up the danger of viewing a business as an independent entity. The decisive level of competition in the American economy is between systems, not individual firms. Hence the scope of management must be enlarged to include the management of resource, distribution, and consumption markets as well as the internal operation of the firm.

A Management System

Figure 1-2 summarizes a management system that is used by many successful companies. Each major component of this system is described below.

Strategic Management

The output of strategic management is the development of corporate objectives and strategies for the total enterprise. This includes the identification of the firm's mission, its specific objectives, and its strategies for achieving these objectives. The major input is the strategic audit. One element of the strategic audit is an analysis and assessment of what has been accomplished in the past; the other element focuses on what can be accomplished in the future. The latter involves an analysis of the environment or the total corporate system (what can be done) and the firm's resource base (what can the firm do).

The success of any business is influenced strongly by the extent to which its resources are kept in a profitable growth balance with environmental opportunities. Some firms have suffered because of an overly conservative attitude toward preserving the resource base; Montgomery Ward under Sewell Avery is a classic example:

---

[7] Robert W. Ferrell, *Customer-Oriented Planning* (New York: American Management Association, Inc., 1965), p. 19.

[8] Peter F. Drucker, *The Practice of Management* (New York: Harper & Row, Publishers, 1954), p. 37.

Figure 1-2 A total management system.

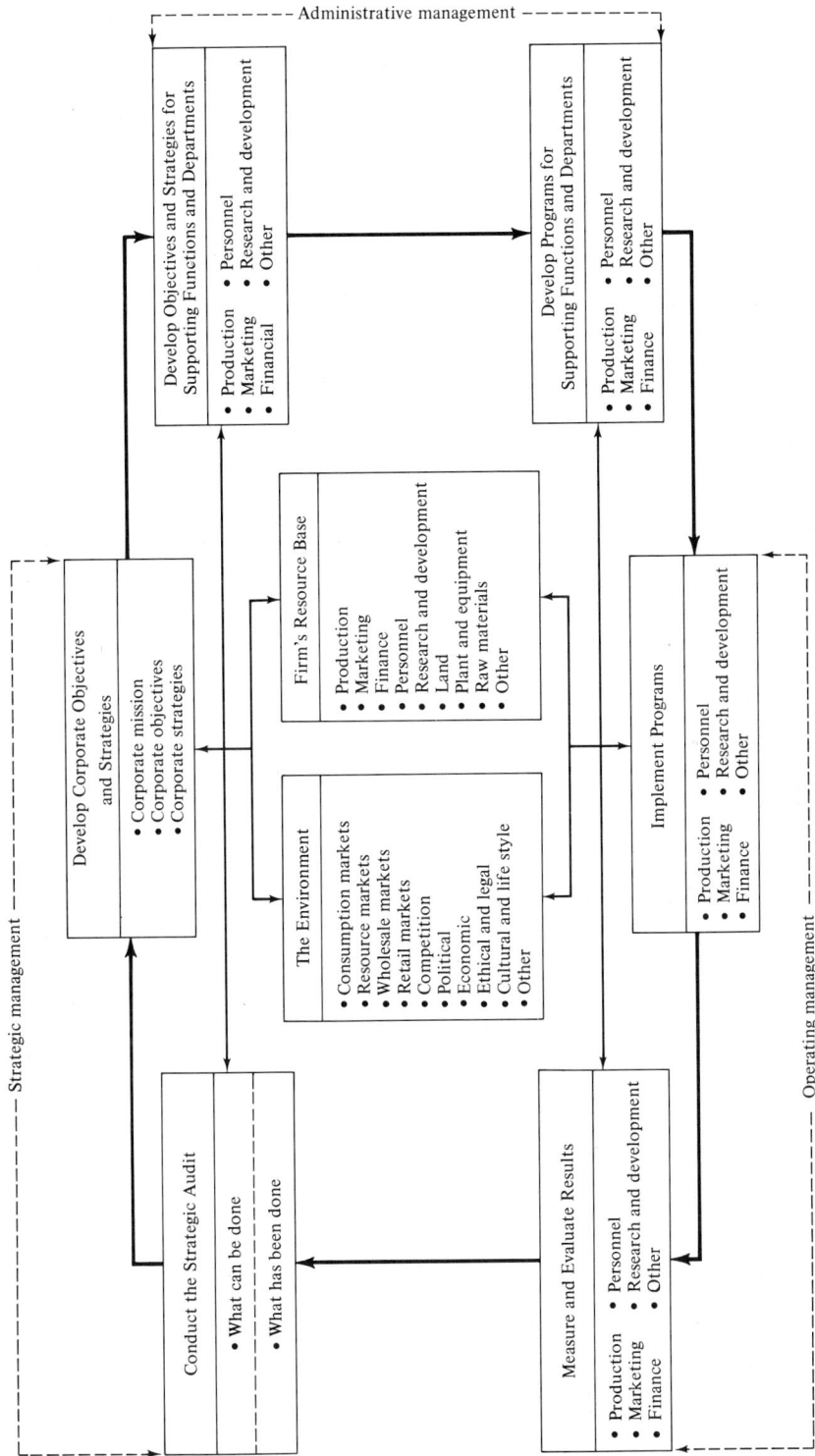

While Sears confidently bet on a new and expanding America, Avery developed an idee fixe that postwar inflation would end in a crash no less serious than that of 1929. Following this idea, he opened no new stores, but rather piled up cash to the ceiling in preparation for an economic debacle that never came. . . . By 1954 Ward was liquid all right, but it was also the shell of a once great company.[9]

In other cases, firms overestimate their resource capabilities. Consider:

In January 1956 Royal McBee and the General Precision Equipment Corporation formed a jointly owned company—the Royal Precision Corporation—to enter the market for electronic data processing equipment. This joint operation appeared logical because General Precision had computer production expertise but lacked distribution capability while Royal McBee had marketing experience but no production knowhow.

The venture was successful, but this caused Royal McBee serious problems. The success required more and more capital and Royal McBee soon found itself in a cash bind. In March 1962 it sold its interest to General Precision for $5 million —a price which represented a reported $6.9 million loss on the investment. Royal McBee simply did not have sufficient resources to stay with the new venture.[10]

Thus strategic management requires a balance between environmental opportunities and the firm's resource base. Since both are continually changing, the profitable growth balance of an enterprise also changes continuously. This dynamic situation challenges the survival of every business, but it can also be a renewing process for businesses that can identify environmental opportunities compatible with their resource capabilities.

Administrative Management

After corporate objectives and strategies have been identified and articulated, it is necessary to develop objectives and strategies, and then action programs, for all supporting functions of the business, including production, marketing, personnel, finance, and others (Figure 1-2). Stated differently, the task of administrative management is to: (1) develop objectives and strategies for all supporting activities that in toto will result in the achievement of the objectives of the total enterprise; and (2) develop detailed operating programs that will allow each functional area of the business to achieve its objectives most efficiently and effectively. This also requires balancing the firm's resource base with environmental opportunities.

Operating Management

The tasks of operating management are to manage the implementation of programs, to periodically measure and evaluate the results of operations against the

---

[9] "Montgomery Ward: Prosperity is Still Around the Corner," *Fortune,* November 1960, p. 140.

[10] Seymour Tilles, "How to Evaluate Corporate Strategy," *Harvard Business Review*, Vol. 41 (July-August 1963), pp. 111–121, at p. 118.

objectives and programs, and take whatever corrective action is necessary to make actual results correspond to planned results. Measuring results requires an information system that tracks the firm's environmental performance and its resource commitments.

The Criticality of Strategic Management

In the past, many firms have not excelled in strategic management. For example, most product and institutional innovations have been made by outsiders. Consider:

- Why did virtually no phonograph companies enter the radio field?
- Why did no theatrical companies enter the movie field?
- Why did no railroad companies attempt to establish airlines?
- Why did no buggy or wagon manufacturers attempt to enter the automobile business?
- Why did no steam-locomotive companies enter the field of diesel locomotives?[11]

A classic study by the Brookings Institution underlines the jugular role of strategic management. Of the 100 largest corporations in 1909, only 36 were left in 1948. The study notes:

The majority of the companies included among the 100 largest of our day have attained their position within the last two decades. They are companies that have started new industries or have transformed old ones to create or meet customer preferences. The companies that have not only grown in absolute terms but have gained an improved position in their own industry may be identified as companies that are notable for drastic changes in their product mix and methods, generating or responding to new competition. . . . There is no reason to believe that those now at the top can remain there any more than did their predecessors, short of alert participation in continuous product and market development.[12]

The explanation for these events is that for many companies strategic management is a painful and unnatural process. For one thing, it is likely to be subordinated to other activities, regardless of whether a firm is successful or is having problems. Success itself is often the justification for continuing the practices, policies, and patterns that brought it. On the other hand, when a company experiences difficulty, current problems enjoy the highest priority and occupy the attention of senior executives.[13]

---

[11] John Phillips, "The End Run," in Lee Adler, ed., *Plotting Marketing Strategy* (New York: Simon and Schuster, Inc., 1967), pp. 43–55, at p. 46.

[12] A. D. H. Kaplan, *Big Enterprise in a Competitive System* (Washington, D.C.: The Brookings Institution, 1954), p. 142.

[13] See, for example, *The Strategy Review* (Boston: The Boston Consulting Group, 1968).

In addition, the reward structure of most companies insures that current operations have a higher priority than longer-term strategic issues. Executive evaluations, bonuses, and other forms of compensation are usually based almost entirely on current operations rather than long-term results or prospects.

Another explanation is that strategic management requires a different set of skills than administrative or operating management. Among other things, strategy taxes conceptual skills, patience, and the ability to tolerate ambiguity. Administrative and operating decisions place a premium on other skills, including decisiveness and celerity. The promotion process in many organizations selects as top executives those who have demonstrated expertise in operating and administrative positions, even though strategic management requires a qualitatively different set of abilities.[14] Since executives, like others, tend to concentrate on things they do best, it is understandable why strategic management receives so little top-management attention.

In short, the evidence indicates that there is a decision imbalance in many business enterprises. Administrative and operating decisions preempt management's concern with strategic issues. As a result, the destinies of many firms depend more on momentum than on strategic planning—though past results indicate that this is a risky posture. Henderson has summarized the problems with extraordinary eloquence:

> For too many companies life consists of working very hard to make small differences in performance produce small differences in profitability. The really significant alterations in corporate fortunes, however, depend upon those relatively few major and basic decisions that determine the chances of success—decisions that enable the company to fight corporate wars with its best weapons, not those of competitors, and enable it to choose the time and place where competitive strength really counts.[15]

Formulating a creative corporate strategy is the most important and challenging task of senior executives. Companies pursuing obsolete strategies are rarely successful. More often they suffer a slow and grinding erosion of profits, markets, and vitality until they die of old age or are absorbed by a more imaginative competitor.[16] As the pace of environmental change continues to accelerate, strategic management will become an even more important determinant of profitability, growth, and survival.

THE STRATEGIC PLAN

The task of strategic management is to develop a long-run, time-phased plan that will produce an attractive growth rate and a high rate of return on investment

---

[14] For an interesting elaboration of this phenomenon see Laurence J. Peter and Raymond Hull, *The Peter Principle* (New York: William Morrow & Company, Inc., 1969).

[15] Bruce D. Henderson, "Strategy Planning," *Business Horizons,* Winter 1964, pp. 21–24.

[16] *Ibid.,* p. 22.

Figure 1-3   The strategic planning process.

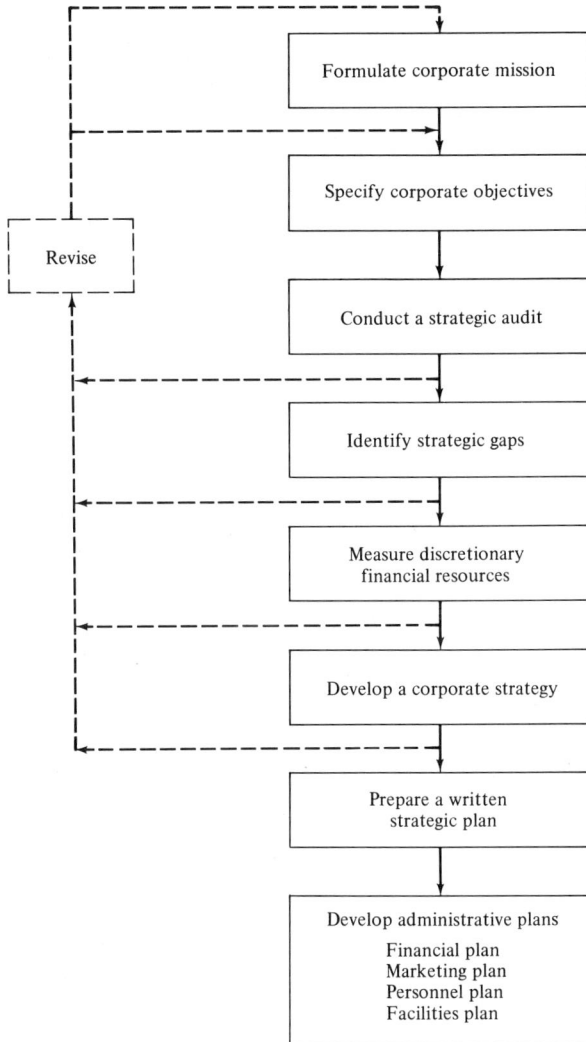

by achieving a market position so advantageous that competitors can retaliate only over an extended time period at a prohibitive cost.[17] This plan is the output of a strategic planning process. Unfortunately, little is known about this process, because it is not commonly discussed in public. The strategic planning model presented in Figure 1-3 attempts to integrate the written literature and documented company experiences. Each stage is discussed below.

[17] This approach was developed by Bert C. McCammon, Jr., Executive Vice-President, Management Horizons, Inc., Columbus, Ohio.

Formulating the Corporate Mission

A corporate mission is a long-term vision of what the business is or is striving to become. The basic issue is: "What is our business—and what should it be?" Nothing may seem simpler or more obvious to answer; but, in actuality, it is a most difficult question that requires serious thinking and studying. That the question is so rarely asked—at least in clear and sharp form—and so rarely given adequate study and thought, is perhaps the most important single cause of business failure. Conversely, outstandingly successful businesses almost always raise the question clearly and deliberately, and answer it thoughtfully and thoroughly.[18]

The techniques used to formulate the corporate mission or purpose are highly subjective. At the minimum, they require analyses of stakeholder expectations, the environment, and the distinctive competences of the firm.[19] If information on these influences is not already available, it can be obtained through the strategic audit.

STAKEHOLDER EXPECTATIONS. The stakeholders of a business are its owners; its customers; its managers and employees; its suppliers; its nonowner sources of capital, including brokers and underwriters, creditors and lenders; and society. These stakeholders are primarily concerned with certain characteristics of the company that affect their own interests. Thus, for example, owners are concerned with such things as dividends and stock prices. Managers and employees are interested in monetary rewards, recognition, advancement, challenge, and continuity. Profitability, stability, continuity, and growth are of concern to financial sources and suppliers.

While all stakeholders are important, an understanding of customer expectations is particularly important in defining the corporate mission. Historically many companies have made the mistake of thinking of customer expectations in terms of physical products or services rather than the underlying problems or needs. Consider:

The railroads did not stop growing because the need for passenger and freight transportation declined. That grew. The railroads are in trouble today not because the need was filled by others (cars, trucks, airplanes, even telephones), but because it was *not* filled by the railroads themselves. They let others take customers away from them because they assumed themselves to be in the railroad business rather than in the transportation business. The reason they defined their industry wrong was because they were railroad-oriented instead of transportation-oriented; they were product oriented instead of customer oriented.[20]

[18] Drucker, *The Practice of Management*, pp. 49–50.
[19] See, for example, Robert F. Stewart, J. Knight Allen, and J. Morse Cavender, *The Strategic Plan* (Palo Alto: The Stanford Research Institute, 1963).

Thus a detailed understanding of stakeholder expectations, particularly the needs of customers, is an important consideration in formulating the corporate mission.

ENVIRONMENT. The corporate mission should also consider the present and future environment of the firm. This includes an analysis of all environmental systems that have been discussed and summarized in Figure 1-1.

DISTINCTIVE COMPETENCE. Distinctive competence refers to those things that a firm does well—preferably better than its competitors. Some companies are particularly good in marketing, others in production, finance, or other functional areas of the business. To illustrate:

- The competence of *The New York Times* lies primarily in giving extensive and insightful coverage of events—the ability to report "all the news that is fit to print."[21]
- The distinctive competence of the Coca-Cola Company may be its remarkable distribution network consisting of over 1,600,000 outlets.[22]

EXAMPLES OF CORPORATE MISSIONS. Many companies have combined these considerations into an innovative corporate mission that has contributed to their success. For example, until the mid 1950s, The Carborundum Company offered a broad line of grinding wheels, coated abrasives, and abrasive grain. In the 1950s the company redefined its mission to that of offering a complete system for metal polishing, cleaning, and removal.

Westinghouse used to define its mission as "designing, producing, and marketing materials, products, equipment, systems and services, to create, distribute, apply and utilize controlled power." Now the company describes itself in terms of "opportunity-orientation," a willingness to invest in any area of suitable profit and growth potential in which Westinghouse has or can acquire capabilities.[23]

Formulating Corporate Objectives

Corporate objectives translate the corporate mission into operational terms. They are challenging guides to action that are specific enough to be measurable and be related to both the broader and more detailed objectives at higher and lower

[20] Theodore Levitt, "Marketing Myopia," *Harvard Business Review*, Vol. 38 (July-August 1960), pp. 45–56, at p. 45.

[21] Tilles, "How to Evaluate Corporate Strategy," p. 116.

[22] Lee Adler, "Marketing Vision," in Adler, ed., *Plotting Marketing Strategy*, pp. 11–39, at p. 17.

[23] *Ibid.*, pp. 18 and 24.

levels in the organization.[24] Most firms have several types of objectives, each of which is discussed briefly below.

PROFITABILITY OBJECTIVES. In most business firms, profitability is the single most important objective. The reason is simple: profit insures a supply of future capital for innovation and expansion, either directly by providing internal financing out of retained earnings, or indirectly by providing sufficient inducement for capital from outside sources.

The profitability objectives of most companies are expressed in terms of return on investment or some variation or refinement of it. Figure 1-4 is a schematic illustration of a basic return-on-investment model. The top half of the diagram charts the profit and loss statement, the bottom half the asset structure of the balance sheet.

As the model indicates, a firm's return on investment is the product of three key ratios—the profit margin, the asset turnover, and the leverage ratio. It follows that a firm can increase its profitability by improving its profit margin, by increasing its asset turnover, and/or by leveraging its operation more highly.[25]

What level of profitability should a company attempt to achieve? This will vary with the industry, the amount and level of risk that management is willing to accept, and other considerations. Historically, financial analysts have held that a 10 percent return after taxes is the minimum acceptable level. Some argue, however, that accelerated rates of inflation and the rising expectations of institutional investors make 15 percent the minimum. Another way of setting profitability objectives is to use the average for the firm's industry. Still another method is to adopt the levels achieved by the most profitable firms in the United States. Companies such as Avon, Gillette, and others consistently earn in excess of 30 percent after taxes.

Using these or other procedures, a firm should establish a specific profitability objective. To gain preferred access to resources, particularly capital, it is usually necessary to earn a return considerably in excess of 15 percent.

COMPETITIVE-STRENGTH OBJECTIVES. These objectives are often used as proxy measures of long-term profitability. It is useful to establish growth objectives stated in terms of specific annual rates of increase of sales, market share, and earnings per share. Since the economy has expanded at about 7 percent per year and is expected to continue doing so during the next decade, sales and earnings-per-share growth-rate targets should be considerably greater than 7 percent. Also common are stability objectives stated in terms of maximum fluctuations in sales, earnings, and capacity utilization.

[24] Charles B. Granger, "The Hierarchy of Objectives," *Harvard Business Review,* Vol. 42 (May-June 1964), pp. 63–74.

[25] For more sophisticated discussions see Stanley B. Henrici, "Eyeing the ROI," *Harvard Business Review,* Vol. 46 (May-June 1968), pp. 88–97; and John Dearden, "The Case Against ROI Control," *Harvard Business Review,* Vol. 47 (May-June 1969), pp. 124–135. Also see the bibliography on p. 134 of Dearden's article.

Figure 1-4 Return-on-investment model.

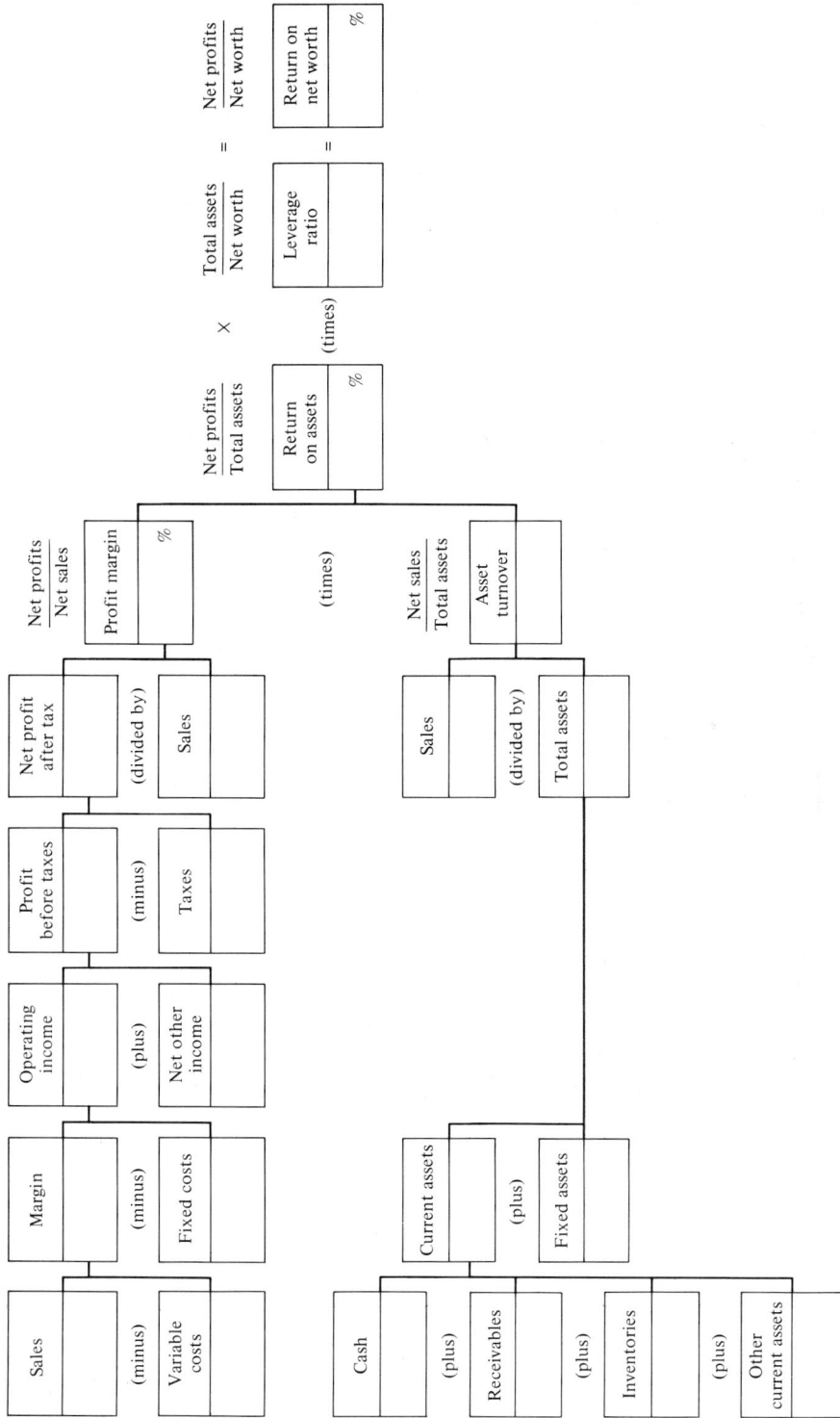

INTERNAL-EFFICIENCY OBJECTIVES. To achieve target levels of longer-term profitability, a firm must usually achieve certain levels of internal efficiency in the short run. Target turnover ratios are popular measures of internal efficiency. The key turnover ratio is return on sales, and supporting ones are turnover of working capital, net worth, inventory, and the debt/equity ratio.

Human and organizational resources are also key indicators of future profitability. Thus a firm may establish objectives concerning the depth of management, skilled personnel, and the age of plant, machinery, and inventory.

FLEXIBILITY OBJECTIVES. Since firms do not have the ability to predict the future precisely, they often buy insurance against catastrophes by maintaining certain types of flexibilities. For example, they may specify some maximum percentage of sales and/or profits that can be derived from a single customer or market segment. Similarly, maximum proportions of sales and/or profits may be specified for technological processes. Traditional objectives for internal flexibility are various liquidity measures. Common indices include the current ratio, the acid-test ratio, and the debt-to-equity ratio.[26]

The Strategic Audit

The purpose of this step in the strategic planning process is to evaluate the firm's current performance and identify the future realities upon which the strategic plan must be based. The major components of the audit are discussed below.

CURRENT MARKET ANALYSIS. This section summarizes the size of the firm's current markets, and the company's market shares in all consumption and distribution markets by each product category. In addition, it identifies the major factors contributing to the firm's success or failure for each product and market. An analysis of the actions necessary to improve future market shares is included, along with the costs of making these improvements.

DISTINCTIVE-COMPETENCE ANALYSIS. This section identifies the strengths, weaknesses, and problems of the company and its major competitors. This includes detailed and systematic comparative analyses in terms of:

1. *Human resources.* The number, breadth, and depth of skills of top management, managers, and employees in all functions and levels of the organization.
2. *Financial management.* Analysis of return on investment and all major financial relationships comprising it. Analysis of financial planning and control procedures and financial capacities to expand.
3. *Research and development and engineering.* Comparative analysis of

[26] Ansoff, *Corporate Strategy*, pp. 49–58. For a more detailed discussion of these and other objectives see William D. Guth and Renato Tagiuri, "Personal Values and Corporate Strategies," *Harvard Business Review*, Vol. 43 (September-October 1965), pp. 123–132; and Harper W. Boyd, Jr., and Sidney J. Levy, "What Kind of Corporate Objectives?" *Journal of Marketing*, Vol. 30 (October 1966), pp. 53–58.

the nature and depth of R&D capabilities, including major strengths and weaknesses.

4. *Manufacturing.* Comparisons of the nature of manufacturing processes, the facilities, the skills, and the adaptability to future conditions.

5. *Marketing.* Comparative analyses of the present product line and capability of developing new products and markets; pricing strategies and tactics including underpricing capabilities; advertising and sales promotion abilities; skill in doing business with distribution channels; and expertise in marketing research, testing, and market information systems.[27]

Significant differences between the company and its major competitors become potential distinctive competences that may be used in formulating corporate strategy.

ENVIRONMENTAL ANALYSIS. This component of the audit forecasts the environmental systems of the future. The forecasts estimate the extremes as well as the most probable economic, technological, political, legal, regulatory, and life-style conditions for the planning period.

RESOURCE-MARKET ANALYSIS. This section forecasts resource markets for the planning period. It includes estimates of the availability and prices of real estate, capital, raw materials, plant and equipment, personnel, and other critical resources.

DISTRIBUTION-MARKET ANALYSIS. This part forecasts the future size, structure, and economics of wholesale and retail markets. It may also identify specific firms within these markets that will be key outlets during the planning period.

CONSUMPTION-MARKET ANALYSIS. This section forecasts the future size of all of the firm's present and potential consumption markets and attempts to identify the future needs and buying behavior of the markets.

COMPETITIVE-STRATEGY ANALYSIS. Using the preceding components, this section attempts to identify the most likely moves that major competitors will make, when they will make them, and the impact that they will have on the company.

As Figure 1-3 indicates, the strategic audit may suggest changes in the firm's mission or objectives. If no changes are necessary, or after the modifications are made, the audit and objectives are used to measure strategic gaps.

Strategic Gaps[28]

Strategic gaps measure the difference between levels of performance specified in the firm's objectives and the levels attainable through the continuation and improvement of current operations. Figure 1-5 depicts a strategic sales gap.

[27] Parts of this analysis were adapted from Robert B. Buchele, "How to Evaluate a Firm," *California Management Review,* Fall 1962, pp. 5–15.

[28] Parts of this section were adapted from Ansoff, *Corporate Strategy,* pp. 141–149.

Figure 1-5   Strategic gaps: (a) original sales gap and (b) revised sales gap.

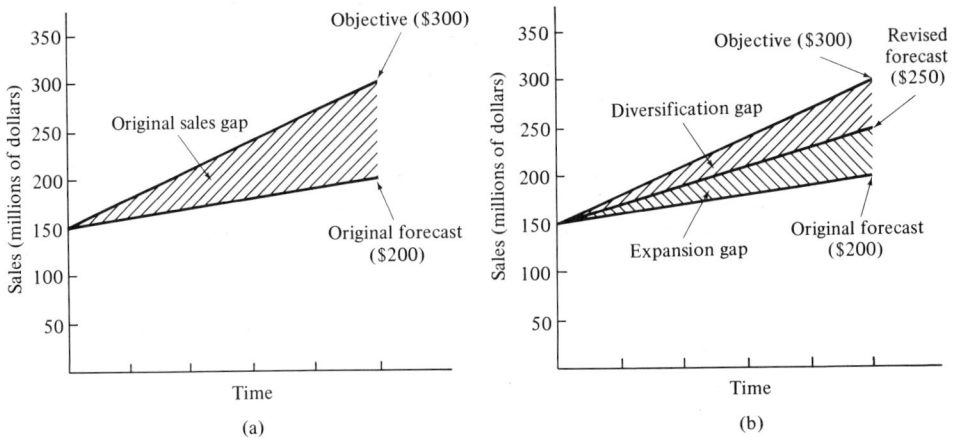

SOURCE: Adapted from Igor Ansoff, *Corporate Strategy* (New York: McGraw-Hill, Inc., 1965), p. 148.

Figure 1-5(a) illustrates an original sales gap for a hypothetical company. The objective is to increase sales from $150 to $300 million over the five-year planning period. The original forecast predicts the firm's future sales performance based on a continuation of current strategies and tactics. The difference between the objective and the original forecast is the original sales gap, which by the end of the fifth year amounts to $100 million.

Figure 1-5(b) depicts the revised sales gap. A new forecast projects the level of performance that the firm can attain if it corrects its weaknesses and capitalizes fully on the opportunities uncovered in the strategic audit. The difference between the original and revised forecast is termed the expansion gap, or the amount of the total sales gap that will be closed by more efficient and effective administrative and/or operating management. The difference between the revised forecast and objective is the gap that will be closed by new strategies.

Since most companies have several objectives, multiple gaps exist. That is, the same procedure should be repeated for all objectives—return on investment, earnings per share, and so on.

In some cases there will not be an original gap. This may suggest the need for an upward revision of objectives. Unless a firm is stretching, personnel and hence the company itself are likely to lose their vitality. In other cases gaps may be too large and management may decide to revise objectives downward.

Discretionary Financial Resources

The next step is to determine the resources available to the firm for closing strategic gaps. The resources available for growth and expansion can be estimated by use of the revised forecast. The primary determinants are the net cash flow and the equity base available for acquisition activity.

From this financial pool the amount required to close the expansion gap is subtracted. This includes all expenses and investments as specified in the strategic audit. The remainder is the initial amount available for developing and implementing new strategies. This amount needs to be revised if the new strategies involve acquisitions; because the acquired firm may have cash and/or unused debt capacity.[29]

Strategic gaps are then examined in relation to the available financial resources. If the pool of resources is not adequate, the objectives may again be revised downward. If the resources are available, the procedure moves to the next phase.[30]

Corporate Strategy

The role of corporate strategy is to indicate the general approach(es) that will be used to close the strategic gaps within the limitations imposed by the discretionary financial resources. There are various conceptualizations of strategy; the one used here consists of a product-market scope and growth vector, a synergy component, and a differential advantage requirement(s).

PRODUCT-MARKET SCOPE AND GROWTH VECTOR. This component of strategy specifies the general product and market entries and growth paths that the firm will use to close its strategic gaps. Figure 1-6 synthesizes an almost infinite number of possibilities into eleven basic alternatives.[31]

1. *Market-Penetration Strategies.* This strategy attempts to improve the company's position with its present products in its current markets. This can be achieved by improving the efficiency and/or effectiveness of any functional area of the business.
2. *Market-Development Strategies.* This alternative attempts to find new classes of customers that can use the company's present products. For example, some manufacturers of baby diapers now sell them to automobile manufacturers as polishing rags.
3. *Reformulation Strategies.* This strategy concentrates on improving present products to increase sales to customers currently being served by the company. Detergents with bleach and enzymes are an example of this approach.
4. *Market-Extension Strategies.* This approach is designed to reach new classes of customers by modifying the company's present products. DuPont has used this approach with many of its products, including Nylon and Teflon.

---

[29] Gordon Donaldson, *Corporate Debt Capacity* (Boston: Division of Research, Harvard Business School, 1961); and Alan J. Zakon and Bruce D. Henderson, "Financial Myopia," *California Management Review,* Vol. 11 (Winter 1968), pp. 87–94.

[30] Ansoff, *Corporate Strategy,* pp. 149–151.

[31] The strategy matrix presented in Figure 1-6 was influenced by several sources, the most important being Samuel C. Johnson and Conrad Jones, "How to Organize for New Products," *Harvard Business Review,* Vol. 35 (May-June 1957), pp. 49–62; Adler, ed., *Plotting Marketing Strategy;* and Ansoff, *Corporate Strategy,* pp. 122–138.

Figure 1-6 Product-market scope and growth vector alternatives.

Products Markets	Present Products	Improvements in Present Products	New Products with Related Technology		New Products With Unrelated Technology
			Assortment Manipulation	Expansion of the Variety of the Product Line	
Consumption Markets: Same markets	(1) Market-penetration strategies	(3) Reformulation strategies	(5) Replacement strategies	(7) Product-line extension strategies	(9) Horizontal diversification strategies
New markets	(2) Market development strategies	(4) Market extension strategies	(6) Market segmentation/ product differentiation strategies	(8) Concentric diversification strategies	(10) Conglomerate diversification strategies
Resource and/or Distribution Markets	(11) Forward and/or backward integration strategies				

5. *Replacement Strategies.* This strategy replaces current products with new products having better ingredients or formulations. Gillette, for example, has consistently replaced its razor blades—blue blades to super blue, to stainless steel, to platinum plus.

6. *Market-Segmentation/Product-Differentiation Strategies.* This alternative is designed to attract new customers by expanding the assortments of existing product lines. Bristol Myers, for example, offers Vitalis for men with older orientations, and Score for the youth-oriented.

7. *Product-Line Extension Strategies.* This approach uses related technology to broaden the line of products offered to present customers. For example, General Electric's appliance division markets TV, radio, phonographs, refrigerators, ranges, and a broad range of small electrical appliances.

8. *Concentric Diversification Strategies.* This strategy attracts new classes of customers by adding new products that have technological and/or marketing synergies with the existing product line. For example, in the 1960s, The Coca-Cola Company, through the acquisition of the Minute Maid Corporation, diversified into the citrus-processing and coffee industries.

9. *Horizontal Diversification Strategies.* This alternative broadens the line of products offered to present customers through technology unrelated to the company's present products. The National Cash Register Company, for example, diversified from cash registers into calculating machines and computers.

10. *Conglomerate Diversification Strategies.* The objective of this approach is to attract new classes of customers by diversifying into products that have no relationship to the company's current technology, products, or markets. To illustrate, International Telephone and Telegraph Corporation, originally an operator of telephone systems and manufacturer of telecommunications equipment, has diversified into hotels and motor inns, rental cars, homes, and heating and air-conditioning equipment for schools.

11. *Integration Strategies.* This strategy is intended to increase profitability, efficiency, and/or control by moving backward in the system to produce within the company those components which were previously purchased; or forward into additional fabrication, assembly, or distribution functions. An example of backward integration is steel companies' acquisitions of ore and transportation facilities, while the acquisition of retail outlets by clothing manufacturers is an example of forward integration.

SYNERGY. In addition to the product-market scope and growth vector, it is also desirable for the corporate strategy to specify desired synergy requirements. Synergy is concerned with the fit between the firm and its future product-market entries. It is a measure of joint effects, or of the mutually reinforcing impact that a product-market entry has on the firm's efficiency and effectiveness.

There are several potential forms of synergy. One is sales synergy. This can occur when a new product-market entry uses existing distribution channels, a common sales force, existing warehousing, and/or common advertising and sales promotion.

A second type is operating synergy. This can result, for example, when the new entry results in higher utilization of facilities and personnel, spreading of overhead, and purchasing economies.

Investment synergy is another important consideration. This can result from joint use of plant, common raw-materials inventories, carryover of research and development from one product to another, and/or common tooling and machinery.

Management synergy can be another important contribution to the total effect. If new product-market entries present strategic, administrative and/or operating problems similar to those management has encountered in the past, it is in a better position to provide effective leadership to the new venture.

Thus alternative product-market scope and growth vector alternatives have varying synergistic effects on the variables determining a firm's return on investment. For this reason, it is desirable to incorporate synergy requirements or goals in the strategic plan.

DIFFERENTIAL ADVANTAGE. This element of corporate strategy is of critical importance to the success of the strategic plan. It specifies the desired advantages that the company should have over competitors in consumption and/or distribution markets. A procedure for identifying differential advantage is:

1. Identify the consumption and distribution markets that have the highest growth potential.
2. Identify the success requirements for effectiveness in these markets.
3. Identify the distinctive competences of the firm and other businesses that are competing in these markets, both presently and in the future.
4. The firm is most likely to have a differential advantage in those markets where: (a) the success requirements correspond to the firm's distinctive competences; (b) other firms do not have these competences; and (c) other firms are not able to attain these competences except at a high investment and/or over an extended period of time.

The Strategic Plan

The results of these analyses are incorporated into a long-run strategic plan. The plan specifies the firm's mission and its specific objectives. It identifies the strategies to be used to achieve these objectives, including the product-market scope and growth vector, and the synergy and differential-advantage requirements.

This plan is then time-phased into annual objectives and strategies for all functions and departments of the business.[32]

Strategic Planning in Action: A Corporate Example

Philip Morris Inc. provides an example of the use of many of the concepts and procedures involved in strategic planning.[33] In 1954 it was a one-product, one-package company with a sales volume of $300 million, almost entirely in the United States market. Top management realized that the tobacco business had become a mature industry and that the growth rate was limited basically to the growth of the population.

The company felt that it had distinctive competences that would allow it to move into other products, markets, and industries. These competences were identified:

1. *Management savvy.* Management understood the "packaged, non-food, disposable, consumer product market," and the company knew in advance where the market was for what kind of products.
2. *Financial resources.* The company had a good cash flow and balance-sheet position.
3. *Manufacturing know-how.* The company knew how to manufacture consumer packaged goods at high speeds on automated equipment.
4. *Research and development.* They had built up a sizable reservoir of scientific talent in the process of developing different taste combinations for cigarettes.
5. *Advertising expertise.* They had considerable experience in managing large advertising budgets in many media.
6. *Distribution capability.* Salesmen had considerable experience in doing business with many types of retail outlets. Moreover, they could easily handle additional products, so that the efficiency of each sales call could be increased.

Given the desire to grow at a faster rate, and based on its distinctive competence analysis, the company identified the growth trends and success requirements of various markets; then it pursued four major strategies:

[32] In addition to previously cited sources, other views and dimensions of strategic planning can be found in Bruce Payne, "Steps in Long Range Planning," *Harvard Business Review,* Vol. 35 (March-April 1957), pp. 95–105; Mack Hanan, "Corporate Growth through Venture Management," *Harvard Business Review,* Vol. 47 (January-February 1969), pp. 43–61; Peter F. Drucker, "Managing for Business Effectiveness," *Harvard Business Review,* Vol. 41 (May-June 1963), pp. 53–60; and W. E. Hill and C. H. Granger, "Long-Range Planning for Company Growth," *The Management Review,* Vol. 45 (December 1956), pp. 1081–1092.

[33] Ross R. Millhiser and S. Harrison Poole, "Diversification as a Marketing Strategy," in F. E. Webster, ed., *New Directions in Marketing* (Chicago: American Marketing Association, 1965), pp. 108–121.

1. *Market development.* It moved into Canada with the acquisitions of Benson and Hedges and Tobacofina. It also further developed its position in Australia, Switzerland, Argentina, Mexico, England, India, Malaysia, New Zealand, and Pakistan.
2. *Market segmentation/product differentiation.* Since 1955, the company has introduced Marlboro, Benson and Hedges, Alpine, Galaxy, Parliament, and Virginia Slims.
3. *Concentric diversification.* The company acquired the American Safety Razor Company (Personna blades), the Birma-Vita Company (aftershave lotions and deodorants), and the Clark Brothers Chewing Gum Company, and has introduced Swiss chocolate Suchard bars. In 1969 it acquired controlling interest in the Miller Brewing Company.
4. *Conglomerate diversification.* The company acquired Milprint, a producer of finished packaging materials for many consumer-product companies; Nicolet Paper Company, which offers specialty paper products to packaging companies and packagers; and Polymer Industries, a technically advanced producer of industrial adhesives and specialty textile chemicals.

As a result of these strategies sales increased from $300 million in 1954 to $1,019 million in 1968. The company increased its share of the tobacco market, became more important in the razor-blade business, and made significant strides in the gum market.

SUMMARY

This introductory chapter has examined the anatomy of the strategic plan, the central document for formulating both long- and short-run marketing strategy and plans. Discussion began with an analysis of the total corporate environment, consisting of various environmental systems, competitive systems, resource, distribution, and consumption markets, as well as the firm itself. A management system consisting of strategic, administrative, and operating management was also discussed.

The bulk of the chapter was concerned with strategic management. Considerable emphasis was placed on the critical role that strategic management plays in the long-run success of a business enterprise. A strategic planning model was then discussed. The model begins with an identification of the corporate mission and objectives. The strategic audit appraises the firm's environmental and market opportunities and assesses its internal capabilities. Then strategic gaps and discretionary financial resources are measured. Corporate strategies—consisting of a product-market scope and growth vector, and synergy and differential advantage requirements—are then selected to close the strategic gaps within the limits imposed by financial resources. The results comprise the strategic plan.

QUESTIONS FOR REVIEW AND DISCUSSION

1. Why should strategic management be discussed in a marketing textbook?
2. Will strategic management become more or less important in the future? Why?
3. Distinguish between distinctive competence and differential advantage.
4. What steps can be taken to ensure that a firm devotes sufficient resources to strategic management?
5. Select a company and identify alternative corporate missions.
6. What are the success requirements in the carpet industry?
7. What are the distinctive competences of *Playboy*? What new product-market growth vector alternatives would allow *Playboy* to capitalize on these distinctive competences?
8. Identify new product-market growth vector alternatives that would be synergistic for Eastern Airlines.

Chapter 2   Marketing Strategy

Chapter 1 identified the systems comprising the firm's environment and discussed a total management system that can be used to capitalize on and adjust to dynamic environmental opportunities. The history of American industry clearly indicates that corporate survival, growth, and profitability hinge on strategic management and the development of a sound strategic plan, which becomes the central document for all long- and short-run corporate activities, including marketing. After discussing the anatomy of marketing, this chapter presents a system for developing a marketing plan that contributes to the achievement of the strategic plan.

THE ANATOMY OF MARKETING

There are various approaches to marketing, depending on the objectives of the writer and the time period considered relevant. This volume is concerned with marketing management; hence we are not primarily concerned with macroeconomic or societal views of marketing.[1] Since we are interested in marketing in the present and the future, we are concerned with historical views only to the extent that they help us understand the present and predict the future.[2] Thus, this section discusses

[1] For a societal view of marketing see *Statement of the Philosophy of Marketing of the Marketing Faculty of The Ohio State University* (Columbus: Bureau of Business Research, The Ohio State University, 1964). Republished in *Journal of Marketing*, January 1965, pp. 43–44.

[2] For illustrative historical views of marketing see Robert Bartels, *The Development of Marketing Thought* (Homewood, Ill.: Richard D. Irwin, Inc., 1962), and George Schwartz, ed., *Science in Marketing* (New York: John Wiley & Sons, Inc., 1965), pp. 1–98.

contemporary and futuristic views of marketing that are most relevant to the firm.

The Contemporary Marketing Concept

The contemporary marketing concept was originally articulated by The General Electric Company in 1946 and has since been adopted by a large number of firms. While the details vary from one company to another, in general the marketing concept has three major ingredients:

1. *Customer orientation.* The purpose of a business is to satisfy the needs of customers. Products and services are important only to the extent that they satisfy these needs—they are means rather than ends. Therefore, marketing starts with the determination of customer needs and ends with the repeated satisfaction of those needs.
2. *Profit orientation.* A business must satisfy the needs of its customers at an acceptable level of profitability. Therefore the purpose of marketing is not simply to generate sales or achieve a certain market share, but rather to produce profitable sales and a profitable market share.
3. *Integrated effort.* All activities of a business should be integrated and coordinated so as to satisfy customer needs at a satisfactory rate of profitability. Marketing must be coordinated with finance, production, personnel administration, engineering, and research and development. Moreover, all marketing activities must be effectively integrated and coordinated in order to achieve market impact.

A survey of the nation's 500 largest manufacturing firms as identified by *Fortune* magazine concluded that by 1965 the vast majority of companies having an annual sales volume in excess of $10 million had adopted the marketing concept.[3]

Corporate statements of marketing philosophy illustrate and enrich the marketing concept. A senior executive of The General Electric Company outlined the evolution of objectives of American industry:

. . . first from a focus on profit for the owner, to a striving for market position and success against competition, and most recently to a focus on growth in which there is a continuing planned effort to enlarge the size of the market. . . . So the principal task of the marketing function in a management concept is not so much to be skillful in making the customer do what suits the interest of the business as to be skillful in conceiving and then making the business do what suits the interest of the customer.[4]

[3] Richard T. Hise, "Have Manufacturing Firms Adopted the Marketing Concept?" *Journal of Marketing*, Vol. 29 (July 1965), pp. 9–12.

[4] J. B. McKitterick, "What is the Marketing Management Concept?" in Frank B. Bass, ed., *The Frontiers of Marketing Thought and Science* (Chicago: American Marketing Association, 1957), pp. 71–82.

A vice-president of Pillsbury Company described the evolution of the business philosophy of his company:

Production Orientation: 1896–1930. As professional flour millers, blessed with a supply of the finest North American wheat and with excellent milling machinery, we turn out flour of the highest quality. We know our product is good because it meets our professional standards of quality. Our function is to mill high quality flour and, of course, we must hire salesmen to sell it.

Sales Orientation: 1930–1950s. As a flour milling company manufacturing a number of products for the consumer market, we must have a first-rate sales organization which can dispose of all the products we can make at a favorable price. To accomplish this objective, our sales force must be backed up by consumer advertising and market intelligence. Our salesmen should have all the tools they need for moving the output of our plants to the consumer.

Marketing Orientation: 1950s–1960s. Marketing is viewed in our company today as the function which plans and executes the sale—all the way from the inception of the idea, through its development and execution, to the sale to the consumer. Marketing begins and ends with the consumer. The idea for a new product is conceived after careful study of her wants and needs, her likes and dislikes. With the idea in hand, the marketing department functions as a universal joint in the corporation, marshalling all the forces of the corporation to translate the idea into product and the product into sales.[5]

The General Foods Corporation adopted a similar point of view:

Instead of trying to market what is easiest for us to make, we must find out much more about what the consumer is willing to buy. In other words, we must apply our creativeness more intelligently to *people*, and their wants and needs, rather than to *products*.[6]

The marketing philosophy of the B. F. Goodrich Company has been described as:

The process of defining, anticipating, and creating customer needs and wants, and of organizing all the resources of the company to satisfy them at greater total profit to the company and to the customer.[7]

While there is some variation in these statements of marketing philosophy, in general they illustrate the pivotal roles of customer and profit orientation and

[5] Robert J. Keith, "An Interpretation of the Marketing Concept," in Lynn H. Stockman, ed., *Advancing Marketing Efficiency* (Chicago: American Marketing Association, 1959), pp. 105–106.

[6] Charles G. Mortimer, "The Creative Factor in Marketing," Fifteenth Annual Parlin Memorial Lecture, Philadelphia Chapter, American Marketing Association, May 13, 1959.

[7] Don C. Miller, "Total Marketing—Management's Point of View," in an address before the Third Regional Industrial Marketing Conference, American Marketing Association, Columbus, Ohio, March 31, 1960.

the need to organize company resources around these orientations. To a considerable extent this marketing concept has become a key ingredient of business philosophy.

Limitations of the Marketing Concept

Although the marketing concept originated as a guide for making market decisions, it has increasingly come to be proposed or described as a central guide for action and planning by general management.[8] Indeed, in some instances, marketing strategy and corporate strategy are viewed as synonymous. In many situations this is understandable, because corporate success is so strongly dependent on marketing success.

Without specific corporate experience that indicates otherwise, the marketing concept should not be the *only* guide for corporate strategy, because it is primarily concerned with the environment and does not give adequate consideration to other factors. It does not explicitly consider the firm's ability to compete for preferred access to resource markets—capital, land, raw materials and personnel. The marketing concept also does not explicitly consider the firm's internal capabilities—including manufacturing, engineering, research and development expertise as well as financial limitations. Moreover, it does not explicitly recognize the abilities, motivations, and predispositions of organizational personnel. To most organizations this human element adds dimensions of stability and complexity that make swift and drastic changes impractical.[9]

Thus a firm must strike a reasonable balance between its position in resource markets, its own capabilities and expertise, and the needs of its market including its channels of distribution. For these reasons the marketing concept and marketing strategy are not equivalent to corporate strategy; rather, they are simply a critical consideration in strategic planning.

An Ecological Concept Of Marketing

During the present century views of marketing have undergone significant revision in response to changes in economic conditions, environmental systems, and competitive conditions. Such changes will continue in the future, causing modifications and extensions of the marketing concept. Thus the marketing concept is an evolutionary, transitional view of marketing rather than a definitive one.

---

[8] See, for example, E. Jerome McCarthy, *Basic Marketing: A Managerial Approach* (Homewood, Ill.: Richard D. Irwin, Inc., 1964), p. 887; Robert L. King, "An Interpretation of the Marketing Concept," in Steven J. Shaw and C. M. Gittinger, eds., *Marketing in a Business Management* (New York: The Macmillan Company, 1963), p. 36; and Thomas A. Staudt and Donald A. Taylor, *A Managerial Introduction to Marketing* (Englewood Cliffs, N.J.: Prentice-Hall, Inc., 1965), p. 505.

[9] Charles B. Saunders, "Inappropriate Uses of the Market Concept," *Business Horizons*, Vol. 8 (Fall 1965), pp. 76–82; and Lee Adler, "A New Perspective For Marketing Strategy," in M. S. Moyer and R. E. Vosburgh, eds., *Marketing for Tomorrow . . . Today* (Chicago: American Marketing Association, 1967), pp. 3–5.

The marketing concept and the perspective it fosters may prove inadequate to the problems of the future. Future decades may require a marketing perspective that integrates profitability requirements with ecological or environmental considerations. Just as the problems of production gave way to the requirements of customer orientation, the latter may be displaced by the problems and opportunities of our social, cultural, and natural environment.[10] There is already evidence of this transition, and it is likely to accelerate during the 1970s.[11]

MARKETING PLANNING

A marketing plan is the central planning and control document for all marketing activities of the firm. It identifies marketing's contribution to the achievement of corporate objectives and spells out the strategies, plans, and programs that will be used. This section discusses the nature of marketing planning and presents a marketing planning and control system.

Scope and Purpose of Marketing Planning

Marketing planning began with informal efforts to cope with business problems and opportunities. Companies that first invested in a more systematic approach to organizing marketing activities were more successful than companies that did not. As these companies became aware of the competitive advantage they had acquired, they attempted to improve their planning performance. This resulted initially in greater formalization of organization and then in specialization of staff. Soon other aggressive companies adopted marketing planning systems. The systematic preplanning of the total marketing effort became a new management attitude and technique.

Formalized approaches to marketing planning first received widespread publicity in the early 1950s. Large companies in consumer-oriented industries were the innovators. Since that time marketing planning has been adopted and adapted by companies of every size and in every segment of industry. By the late 1960s an American Management Association survey of 163 companies found that 77 percent developed marketing plans.[12]

In general, a marketing plan is *a written document designed to provide the framework for a coordinated and integrated effort to implement marketing programs developed to achieve marketing objectives, which in turn make the necessary contributions to the achievement of corporate objectives.* Generally both long-range and short-run marketing plans follow this pattern. Short-term marketing

---

[10] See Patrick J. Robinson, "Whither The Marketing Concept? The Continuing Evolution of Marketing and the Emergence of Marketing Science," in Moyer and Vosburgh, eds., *Marketing for Tomorrow . . . Today*, pp. 6–10.

[11] For corporate examples see George Champion, "Creative Competition," *Harvard Business Review*, Vol. 45 (May-June 1967), pp. 61–67.

[12] Ernest C. Miller, *Marketing Planning* (New York: American Management Association, Inc., 1967), pp. 6, 9.

plans usually differ from long-range plans in that they are more comprehensive, detailed, and involve greater integration and coordination with other functional departments of the business.[13]

A Marketing Planning and Control System

The American Management Association survey referred to earlier found that while a few companies use highly sophisticated and unique approaches, even these companies first create a foundation by applying a "standard approach" to marketing planning.[14]

Figure 2-1 graphically depicts an approach to marketing planning and control synthesized from the approaches reported in the AMA survey,[15] a National Industrial Conference Board symposium,[16] and other sources.[17] The remainder of this chapter discusses the components of this system.

Strategic Plans

A strategic plan is a time-phased written document that specifies the mission of the firm and its objectives. It identifies the strategies to be used to achieve these objectives, including the general product-market scope and growth vector(s) as well as synergy and differential-advantage requirements. A procedure for developing this plan was described in Chapter 1 and will not be reiterated here.

From this point on, corporate planning systems and procedures vary with the diversity of products and markets and the firm's organizational philosophy and structure. Companies with limited or highly homogeneous product lines tend to develop only one strategic plan and one marketing plan at the corporate level. Companies that have diversity in product lines or in markets and industries served, as well as companies that have developed a divisional organization structure, tend to have several strategic and marketing plans integrated into a master strategic plan. In contrast, companies having markedly different products and heterogeneous divisions often will have only divisional marketing plans.[18] These variations are represented by the heavy lines in Figure 2-1.

[13] See, for example, *The Development of Marketing Objectives and Plans* (New York: National Industrial Conference Board, 1963).

[14] Miller, *Marketing Planning*, p. 27.

[15] *Ibid.*

[16] *The Development of Marketing Objectives and Plans.*

[17] John M. Brion, *Corporate Marketing Planning* (New York: John Wiley & Sons, Inc., 1967); Wroe Alderson, "Theory and Practice of Market Planning," *Cost and Profit Outlook*, Vol. 2 (July-August 1958), pp. 6 ff.; Andrall E. Pearson, "An Approach to Successful Marketing Planning," *Business Horizons*, Vol. 2 (Winter 1959), pp. 74–82; Clarence E. Eldridge, *The Role and Importance of The Marketing Plan* (New York: Publications Department, Association of National Advertisers, Inc., 1966); Leon Winer, "Are You Really Planning Your Marketing?" *Journal of Marketing*, Vol. 29 (January 1965), pp. 1–8; Everett C. Horne, "Developing a Marketing Plan," in Frederick E. Webster, Jr., *New Directions in Marketing* (Chicago: American Marketing Association, 1965), pp. 80–87.

[18] Miller, *Marketing Planning*, p. 10.

34

Figure 2-1 A market planning and control system.

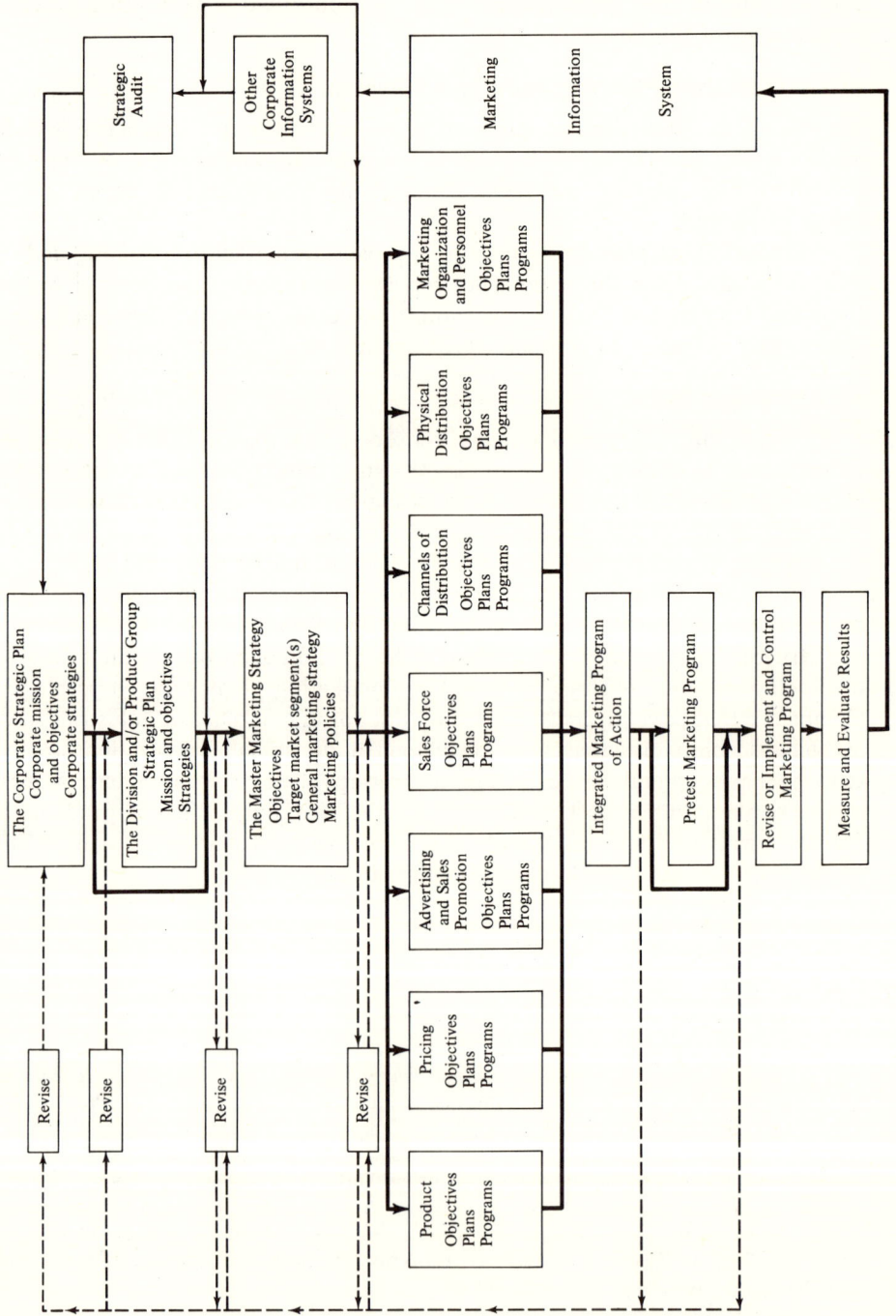

The Master Marketing Strategy

A master marketing strategy provides the linkage between the strategic plan and specific marketing programs. On the one hand, it should be consistent with, and contribute to the achievement of the objectives specified in the strategic plan. Simultaneously, it should provide an integrative focus and direction for all marketing activities. In order to perform these functions, a master marketing strategy usually includes marketing objectives, the specification of specific market targets, a general marketing strategy, and, in some instances, marketing policies.

MARKETING OBJECTIVES. In a planning sense, marketing objectives are selected qualitative and quantitative commitments that marketing makes to the strategic plan. They are usually stated either in terms of standards of performance for a given operating period or conditions to be achieved by given dates. Performance standards are commonly stated in terms of sales volume and various measures of profitability. The conditions to be attained are usually a certain percentage of market share[19] and various other commitments, such as a percentage of a given type of retail store stocking a product.[20]

In some companies the marketing planning process generates the company's corporate objectives; in others, marketing objectives are derived directly from the company's overall corporate objectives. In most companies both conditions are present. Marketing suggests objectives to top management. Top management reviews the marketing objectives in terms of the strategic plan, either accepting them or making countersuggestions. This negotiation process continues until marketing and top management accept specific marketing objectives that are consistent with the strategic plan, attainable within budget limitations, and compatible with the strengths, limitations, and economics of other functions of the organization.[21] This process is indicated by the "dotted revise lines" in the upper portion of Figure 2-1.

While this negotiation process is often onerous and time-consuming, it plays a critical role in corporate and marketing planning. McKinsey and Company, one of the largest consulting firms in the world, studied the effectiveness of the planning practices of 50 large industrial companies. A major reason for the planning ineffectiveness of many companies was the failure of top executives as well as executives of other functions of the business to participate in marketing planning. In contrast, companies that were successful marketing planners had a clear state-

[19] The term market share refers to: (1) a company's sales of a brand as a percentage of total brand sales; and/or (2) a company's sales as a percentage of the total sales of all companies classified as in the same industry category. Other measures of market share can be computed using alternative numerators and/or denominators.

[20] Alderson, "Theory and Practice of Marketing Planning," pp. 6 ff., and Miller, *Marketing Planning*, pp. 35–79.

[21] Miller, *Marketing Planning*, p. 15.

ment of corporate objectives, interfunctional coordination, and total company involvement in marketing planning.[22] The experience of other companies support the need for this type of involvement.[23]

TARGET-MARKET SELECTION. The success of a company hinges on how well it can identify customer needs and organize resources to satisfy them profitably. Hence a critical element of a marketing plan is the identification of the specific markets, or groups or segments of customers, that the company will serve. The markets or market segments that are selected are termed target markets.

The target-market selection process is critically important and complicated; hence it will be discussed in considerable detail in the seven chapters that comprise Part II of this volume. Previewing the process, it involves information contained in the strategic audit as well as more specific and detailed information obtained from the firm's marketing information system. Information from these sources is combined in creative ways to answer such questions as:

- What does the customer need?
- What must be done to satisfy these needs?
- What is the size of the market?
- What is the growth profile of the market?
- How profitable will it be to satisfy the needs of this market during each year comprising the planning period?

Provisional answers to these types of questions are estimated for present target markets and future target-market alternatives. Present and potential market segments can be rank ordered according to (1) profitability, (2) present and future sales volume, and (3) degree of match between the requirements for successfully appealing to the market segment and the firm's distinctive competence.

In order to estimate the sales-volume profile of market segments, it is necessary to decide on the scope of products that will be offered. For example, a single product or service can be offered to several market segments, or multiple products and services can be offered to a single segment. Several other combinations between these extremes are possible.

Taking all these factors into consideration, market segments can be selected in rank order until the marketing objectives are attained. These target-market selections are reviewed to make certain that they are compatible with the product-market scope and growth vector, differential-advantage, and synergy requirements of the strategic plan. If these requirements are met, the process continues to the next phase. However, if the requirements are violated, the strategic plan is reevaluated and revised. These processes are indicated by the dotted revise arrows in Figure 2-1.

[22] B. Charles Ames, "Marketing Planning for Industrial Products," *Harvard Business Review*, Vol. 46 (September-October 1968), pp. 100–111.
[23] *The Development of Marketing Objectives and Plans.*

The following example illustrates some of the most important dimensions of this process.[24] The overall corporate growth goal of Company A was an increase in earnings per share of 10 percent per year, a target that had been hit annually from 1965 through 1970. The company analyzed the sources of past profit growth, and it looked like this:

	Percentage points
Established Markets:	
Current Products	
Increased volume	4.0%
Increased margins (price increases and cost reductions)	4.0
New Products Established	2.0
Total	10.0%

The company forecasted its earnings-per-share growth rate from these sources over the next five years and came up with the following numbers:

	Percentage points
Established Markets:	
Current Products	
Increased volume	3.0%
Increased margins	1.0
New Products Currently Established	2.0
Total	6.0%

In order to maintain the 10 percent growth rate, senior corporate executives charged marketing with finding new opportunities that would produce 4.0 percentage points of profit growth annually within the guidelines specified in the strategic plan. After carefully analyzing the factors discussed above, marketing recommended the following course of action:

	Percentage points
Established Markets:	
New Products	1.0%
New Markets:	
Current Products	2.0
New Products	1.0
Total	4.0%

[24] This example has been adapted from "Shortcomings Predominate in Marketing Planning," *Industrial Marketing*, July 1967, pp. 60–62.

This target-market/product-scope course of action was accepted by top management, since it met corporate objectives and was consistent with the other requirements of the strategic plan. Other firms in other situations might have chosen a different course.

GENERAL MARKETING STRATEGY. After market targets have been selected, it is useful to spell out, in general terms, the marketing strategy that will be used to penetrate them. As used here, marketing strategy refers to the general procedure and central concept upon which the firm's entire approach to the market hinges.

Marketing strategy involves the appropriate use of marketing variables. These variables include:

1. *Total product*—policies and procedures relating to:
   (a) Product lines to be offered—qualities, design, and so on.
   (b) Brand policies—trademarks, individualized brands, family brands, private brands.
   (c) Packaging and labeling.
   (d) Other.

2. *Pricing*—policies and procedures relating to:
   (a) Price level to adopt.
   (b) Specific prices to adopt.
   (c) Margins to adopt.
   (d) Other.

3. *Advertising and sales promotion*—policies and procedures relating to:
   (a) Amount to spend.
   (b) Creative approach.
   (c) Media to use.
   (d) Displays to use.
   (e) Other.

4. *Personal selling*—policies and procedures relating to:
   (a) Emphasis to be placed on personal selling.
   (b) Sales approach.
   (c) Managing sales personnel.
   (d) Other.

5. *Channels of distribution*—policies and procedures relating to:
   (a) Channels to be used and relative importance of each.
   (b) Degree of selectivity among wholesalers and retailers.
   (c) Efforts to gain reseller support.

6. *Physical distribution*—policies and procedures for:
   (a) Warehousing.
   (b) Transportation.

(c) Inventories.

(d) Other.[25]

These variables can be varied and combined into an almost infinite variety of marketing strategies or marketing mixes. The goal is to design a marketing strategy that will appeal most profitably to the market target within the limitations imposed by available resources and the requirements of the strategic plan. It is common for companies to simultaneously pursue multiple strategies for multiple market segments.

Formulating marketing strategy is probably the most difficult and critical part of the entire marketing process. Strategy sets the limits of success; execution determines how closely marketing efforts will come to these limits. Stated differently, marketing strategy is concerned with the question: "Are we doing the right things?" while execution focuses on "Are we doing things right?"

As Figure 2-1 indicates, the marketing-strategy formulation process involves information inputs from the strategic audit, the firm's marketing information system, and information from functional areas of the business, particularly production, engineering, and finance. This information is combined to:

1. Identify the specific requirements that are necessary to successfully penetrate each target-market segment.
2. Identify the channels of distribution that are necessary to appeal to each market target.
3. Isolate the specific requirements that must be met to attain the active cooperation of these channels.
4. Using the distinctive-competence analysis, evaluate the relative capability of the firm and each of its present and potential competitors to satisfy each of these success requirements.
5. From step 4, identify the firm's differential advantage(s) and then classify according to (a) profitability and (b) sustainability (ability of competitors to duplicate and neutralize the differential advantage).

The general marketing strategy contains that mixture of marketing variables that exploits the firm's most profitable and sustainable differential advantage(s). Simultaneously a *contingency strategy* is formulated in the event the firm's differential advantage is erased through a change in success requirements and/or competitor's activities. Contingency strategies are often the difference between success and failure;[26] hence they should be planned in advance. This entire procedure should be repeated for each product entry in each target-market segment.

[25] Neil H. Borden, "The Concept of the Marketing Mix," in Schwartz, ed., *Science in Marketing*, pp. 386–397.

[26] See, for example, Ames, "Marketing Planning for Industrial Products," pp. 100–111.

Marketing strategy can emphasize any element of the marketing mix in an integrated marketing program of action. Consider the following:

- Historically most companies have offered a single product to a market segment. However, experience indicates that some customers will persist in buying a rival brand. Hence for some companies marketing strategy emphasizes multibrand entries. For example, in deodorants, Bristol-Myers has four brands and seven product variants: Ban (roll-on and cream), Mum (including Mum Mist and Mum Mist for men), Trig, and Discreet.[27]
- In the high-priced men's toiletries field it has been common to advertise in such "class" media as *The New Yorker, Holiday,* and the like. Yet when Swank introduced Jade East, their strategy involved the heavy use of spot TV in addition to conventional media. Jade East soon became one of the leading lines, despite entrenched competition.[28]
- The sales force of most cosmetics companies sells to retail outlets. Yet Avon's strategy uses house-to-house selling, and in the late 1960s it was the most profitable of the largest 500 industrial companies with a return on invested capital in excess of 40 percent. Recently Helene Curtis (through Studio Girl) and Bristol-Myers (through Luzier) have placed greater emphasis on this sales strategy.[29]
- Channels of distribution have been a critical element in the marketing strategy of many firms. In the 1920s General Motors established a franchised dealer system that has contributed much to the success and stability of G.M. ever since. Coca-Cola's distribution through more than 1,600,000 outlets allows it to achieve extensive distribution.[30]
- Sears has long dominated the catalog business with its eleven central order plants. Penney's is challenging Sears with only four distribution centers. Sears relies on truck and rail, Penney's on cargo jet. *If* transportation costs come down, Penney's will be able to compete with seven fewer distribution centers.[31]

[27] Lee Adler, "A New Perspective for Marketing Strategy," in Moyer and Vosburgh, *Marketing for Tomorrow* . . . Today (Chicago: American Marketing Association, 1967), pp. 3–10, at p. 5.

[28] John Phillips, "The End Run," in Lee Adler, ed., *Plotting Marketing Strategy* (New York: Simon and Schuster, Inc., 1967), pp. 43–55, at p. 51.

[29] Adler, "A New Perspective for Marketing Strategy," p. 5.

[30] William R. Davidson, "Distribution Breakthroughs," in Adler, ed., *Plotting Marketing Strategy,* pp. 257–283

[31] "Can the Last Be First?" *Forbes,* March 15, 1969. For a discussion of what marketing executives think are the most important elements of marketing strategy see Jon G. Udell, "The Perceived Importance of the Elements of Strategy," *Journal of Marketing,* Vol. 32 (January 1968), pp. 34–40.

MARKETING POLICIES. Marketing policies are formal guiding principles governing the course of management action. They are the broad, fixed guidelines that everyone in the organization must adhere to without exception.

Not all companies agree on the practical value of establishing formal policy guidelines for their companies' marketing operations. Nevertheless, a recent National Industrial Conference Board survey found that a substantial majority of companies feel that some fixed marketing policies are vital to marketing success.[32] The major benefits of marketing policies are:

1. *Guidance to decision makers.* They provide the framework for consistent, objective, on-the-spot decisions and actions and eliminate the need for time-consuming reviews and clearances by top management.
2. *Coordination and integration.* Policies are useful in clarifying the direction and focus of the company's marketing efforts.
3. *Protect the company's reputation.* Some companies view policies as a method of retaining the company's integrity in the market.

The major reasons some companies do not adopt marketing policies are: (1) they rely on personal communications instead of written statements; (2) policies reduce flexibility, speed, and initiative; and (3) policies change too frequently. These objections come primarily from small and medium-sized companies.[33] The subject matter of marketing policies differs from company to company. In general, policies cover most variables of the marketing mix. Figure 2-2 illustrates various types of marketing-policy statements.

Marketing Programming

As Figure 2-1 indicates, after the master marketing strategy has been formulated, marketing programs are developed by functional departments representing the elements of the marketing mix. These programs include specific objectives that are consistent with the master strategy and that make the necessary contribution to the achievement of the overall marketing objectives. They also include a detailed outline of the action steps to be taken to achieve specified objectives. These steps include what will be done, by whom, when, and the results anticipated from such actions. This involves inputs from the strategic audit, the marketing information system, and other corporate information systems. Market programming will be discussed in considerable detail in the eight chapters that comprise Part III of this text.

---

[32] Earl L. Bailey, *Formulating the Company's Marketing Policies* (New York: National Industrial Conference Board. 1968).
[33] *Ibid.*, pp. 1–10.

Figure 2-2 Examples of various marketing policy statements of selected firms.

On Product Quality:

"The company's greatest strength has been its reputation for quality products representing a sound value to the consumer. In order to ensure that this reputation continues: (1) Every product carrying the company name must operate well and perform its stated function; (2) every product carrying the company name must have a standard of quality which is equal to or exceeds the standard of quality commonly accepted in the industry for similar products, and these standards will not be sacrificed under any circumstances; (3) the company's products will continue to maintain design leadership in the industry—design being compatible with considerations of function and cost; (4) there will be an active program in effect at all times to produce a constant flow of fundamental new products and improvements to existing products."

On Protecting the Company's Reputation:

"Our long-range reputation for progress, fair dealing, quality products, stable trade relations, and generally respected management policies must be maintained above all else—even at the sacrifice of occasional short-range gains."

On Communications with Customers:

"To ensure that communications with our customers through the medium of advertising and by all persons within the company are being carried on with a tone of customer appeal, fairness, and a desire to be helpful in every relationship."

On Product Guarantees:

"All company merchandise is guaranteed against defects in workmanship and materials. This guarantee does not cover merchandise which has been damaged in transit or in use, nor does it cover merchandise returned without reason. All merchandise which is claimed to be defective should be returned to the factory, or to an authorized service office. It will be repaired and returned to the customer in used but good operating condition, or will be replaced with other merchandise at our option."

On Pricing:

"Every customer in a particular class of trade will be offered the same prices as every other customer in that class. Wholesale distributor prices, as shown on the distributor's price list, will be extended to specified classes of trade. Direct retail prices, as shown on the direct account price list, will be extended to selected key department stores, and certain other key retailers we choose to sell direct. In the event of a price decrease all customers will be protected on inventories purchased within 60 days prior to the date of the price decrease."

On Selective Distribution:

"It is the company's policy to distribute its line on a selective basis, reserving the rights (a) to choose the dealers through whom it will distribute its products, and (b) to sell or not to sell any specific part of its line to any individual dealer. This policy conforms to widespread and long-established industry practices and recognizes that the wide scope of the company's line makes it both impractical and unwise for any single dealer to attempt to display it in its entirety.

"It is the company's policy to distribute its products only to dealers who stock, pro-

Figure 2-2   Examples of various marketing policy statements of selected firms (*continued*).

mote, advertise, and service the company's products in a manner which the company deems to be in its best interests and which preserves the prestige and standing of the company name. It is the company's policy not to sell its products to any dealer who adopts policies of distribution or sales which are detrimental to the company's own interests, or methods of display, promotion, or advertising which bring discredit to the company's line.

"The company believes that each dealer must determine his own business policies as he sees fit. The company does not wish to impose its policies upon any dealer. If any dealer believes that the policies set forth in this statement are unsuited to his business, he may act differently or drop the company's line. However, the company intends to do business only with a dealer who: (a) respects the policies set forth in this statement; (b) does achieve the sales potential for the company line which the company feels exists in their area; (c) maintains a satisfactory credit standing; (d) sells the company's products at margins of profit consistent with general good business practice in his trading area so as to maintain the company's goodwill and public confidence and prestige; (e) resells only to consumers for their use and not for resale."

On Service:
"To provide dependable service, arrange for technical assistance, and assure product security to our customers, wherever they may be."

On Compliance with Antitrust Laws:
"One of the basic principles on which our nation was founded was faith in a competitive free enterprise system. The unmatched success of the economy of our nation is concrete evidence of the advantages of such a system. The antitrust laws were conceived and enacted as a means for helping to preserve that system by promoting healthy competition. It is the sincere belief of the company's management that, even in the absence of the requirements imposed by the antitrust laws, the interest of the company, its stockholders, and employees can best be served by a policy of vigorous and fair competition, such as those laws are intended to preserve. In addition, the penalties which may be imposed upon both the company and the individual employees involved in any violation of the antitrust laws are so heavy that good business judgment demands that every effort be made to avoid any such violations. For these reasons, *it shall continue to be the policy of the company to comply strictly in all respects with the antitrust laws.*"

On Cooperative Advertising:
"Direct retail accounts will be allowed [a specified percentage] of their net purchases for advertising of the company's branded products in daily newspapers only.

"The company logo must appear prominently in the ad. Proof of performance is required. A fixed line rate will be established by the company. Anticipation or overspending of accruals will not be permitted. Reimbursement will be by credit memo, with deductions from invoices permitted. A signed advertising agreement is required. Terms of the agreement must be adhered to, with no exceptions. There will be no other advertising or promotional funds available to the trade."

SOURCE: Earl L. Bailey, *Formulating the Company's Marketing Policies* (New York: National Industrial Conference Board, 1968), pp. 51–53. Reprinted by permission.

The Marketing Plan

The firm's master marketing strategy and the supporting marketing programs are summarized into a *written* marketing plan. The preparation of a sophisticated plan usually *saves* time, energy, and money. It provides, at the beginning of the planning period, basic agreement on the job to be done and the way to go about doing it. It lessens the chances of costly improvisation and changing of direction. It is the best available way to achieve the focusing and continuity of effort and direction that are so critically important to profitable marketing.[34]

In some cases marketing plans will be pretested by a variety of techniques, including test marketing and simulation. These methods are discussed in Chapters 18 and 19.

The original or revised marketing plan is submitted for top management approval. The approved plan—with whatever modifications are made by senior management—becomes the basic document for all marketing activities during the planning period.

Controlling and Evaluating Marketing Efforts

Sophisticated marketing management involves periodic measurements of actual results. This requires data input from the firm's marketing information system as well as other corporate information systems. Actual results are compared to planned results, and, if deviations exist, changes are made in marketing programs and/or planned objectives.

At the end of the planning period it is useful to evaluate the overall effectiveness of the marketing plan. Actual results should be compared against planned levels for all marketing objectives. A written evaluation of the reasons that objectives were achieved and/or not achieved becomes part of the marketing information system and strategic audit, and it is used in planning future corporate and marketing strategies. Procedures and techniques for controlling and evaluating marketing programs are discussed in Chapters 20 and 21.

SUMMARY

This chapter discussed the nature of marketing and the marketing planning and control process. The contemporary marketing concept has three major ingredients: (1) customer orientation rather than product or industry orientation; (2) profit orientation rather than sales or market-share perspectives; and (3) an integrated rather than a diffused combination of marketing efforts.

[34] Eldridge, *The Role and Importance of the Marketing Plan.*

The marketing plan was described as the central marketing planning and control document. It is the link between the strategic plan and day-to-day marketing activities. It identifies marketing's contribution to the achievement of corporate objectives by identifying specific marketing objectives and the strategies that will be used to achieve them. Detailed objectives and plans are then prepared for all elements of the marketing mix and integrated into a high-impact marketing plan of action. The plan may or may not be pretested. The final plan is submitted for top-management approval before it is implemented. Actual results are compared periodically with planned results, and remedial action is taken. At the end of the planning period a written analysis and evaluation of all marketing activities is prepared for use in future corporate and marketing planning.

The remainder of this volume discusses the major elements comprising the marketing planning and control system depicted in Figure 2-1. The seven chapters of Part II are concerned with identifying and assessing market opportunities and selecting target-market segments. In Part III, eight chapters discuss the development of marketing programs. Pretesting marketing programs is discussed in the two chapters of Part IV, while controlling and evaluating marketing programs is the subject of the two chapters comprising Part V. The social and ethical responsibilities of marketing are explored in the concluding chapter.

QUESTIONS FOR REVIEW AND DISCUSSION

1. What is meant by customer orientation? How does it compare with other concepts that it has displaced?
2. What is a marketing plan?
3. Is the marketing concept the same as a philosophy of business? Explain.
4. What is meant by marketing strategy?
5. How do marketing objectives differ from corporate objectives?
6. What are the differences between profit, sales, and market-share orientations?
7. Define or describe the term marketing mix.
8. What is the relationship between marketing programming and the master marketing strategy?

PART II IDENTIFYING AND ASSESSING MARKET OPPORTUNITIES

After tentatively identifying marketing objectives, management must identify target markets for the firm's present and future products and services and then study and come to understand the purchasing behavior of these markets. This is the subject matter of the seven chapters comprising Part II.

Chapter 3 and 4 present a nontechnical discussion of marketing research techniques that are used to investigate market opportunities. Chapter 5 examines the cultural and social dimensions of consumer markets and then summarizes the major socioeconomic changes that will occur in these markets during the decade ahead. Chapter 6 presents a framework for investigating the purchasing behavior of consumer markets. Chapter 7 examines the changing structure and purchasing behavior of industrial and institutional markets. International markets are becoming increasingly important to many companies; consequently, selected dimensions of key global markets are examined in Chapter 8. Finally, Chapter 9 discusses considerations and techniques in selecting target-market segments for the firm's marketing program.

Chapter 3   Analyzing Market Opportunities Through Research

The development of high-yield marketing strategies requires thorough, reliable analysis of market opportunities. In contemporary management practice, marketing research is ordinarily a necessary basis for adequate understanding of the structure and behavior of markets.

This chapter explains why management must increasingly rely upon research to analyze market opportunities. It helps develop a managerial philosophy needed to use research effectively, and it describes the four-stage process of using research for marketing decisions. It concludes with a brief introduction to some of the most important methods of analyzing data.

Chapter 3 is closely related to Chapter 4, which describes methods of obtaining data. It is important to determine the *objectives* of research before determining the methods for carrying out those objectives. Effective analysis is most likely to occur in a process where decisions about how data are to be used (including specific analytical methods) are made *before* rather than *after* data are collected. This conceptualization is presented in the next two chapters.

THE ROLE OF RESEARCH IN A COMPLEX MARKET STRUCTURE

Marketing research arises as a function of increasing complexity in the economic system. When market structure is uncomplicated, management has little difficulty in obtaining market information. Management is involved with the market daily on a face-to-face level, and so the ascertaining of market opportunity is direct and reasonably simple.

The need for marketing research also increases as a function of a "speeded-up" change in market characteristics. In the past, custom and prior usage dictated what products were produced, the prices typically charged, and distribution channels that were favored. Forecasting was not difficult; orders for a future season were, with only minor changes, likely to duplicate those for the previous one. Preferences for style, color, and form of products changed only at a glacial pace.

Modern conditions present other reasons for increasing emphasis on marketing research. Vast sums of discretionary income, rapid communications about product changes, and vastly more complex social structures sharply increase the pace of customer acceptance. There is also a necessity for long, automated production runs and increased sophistication in geographical specialization and logistics.

In prior decades, a reasonably intuitive businessman might satisfactorily understand and predict market opportunities. With the advent of large-scale specialization within the firm and separation from the market outside the firm,

Figure 3-1   Number of new marketing research departments formed in successive five-year periods (not cumulative).

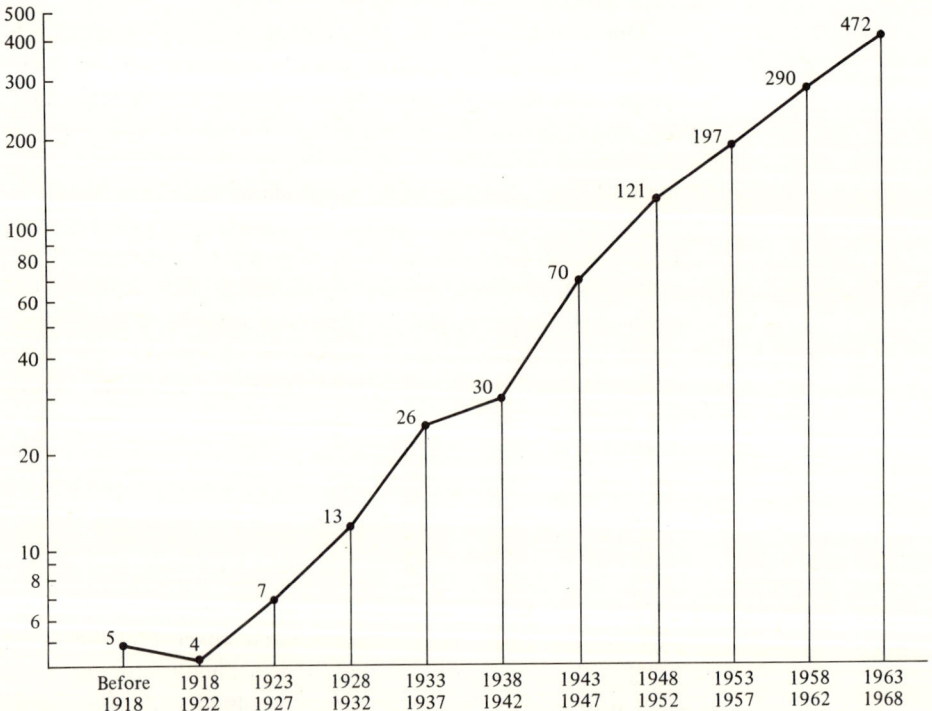

SOURCE: Reprinted from Dik Warren Twedt, *1968 Survey of Marketing Research,* published by the American Marketing Association, 1969.

the contemporary marketing strategist relies increasingly upon systematic and sophisticated methods of interpreting, predicting, and analyzing market behavior.

Rise in Marketing Research Expenditures

Corporate budgets for marketing research are estimated to be increasing three times as fast as America's GNP, three times as fast as marketing expenditures in general, and considerably faster than amounts spent on advertising.[1]

The rise in research expenditures is caused by the forces described above but is manifested in two forms: (1) expansion of research budgets in existing research departments, (2) creation of marketing research departments in firms where they did not previously exist. These trends are documented in Figures 3-1 and 3-2. Figure 3-2 also reveals that retailers and wholesalers, who have traditionally spent small amounts on research, are expanding marketing research more rapidly than any other group.

Figure 3-2   Survey of marketing research expenditures: 763 companies spent $197 million for marketing research in 1968.

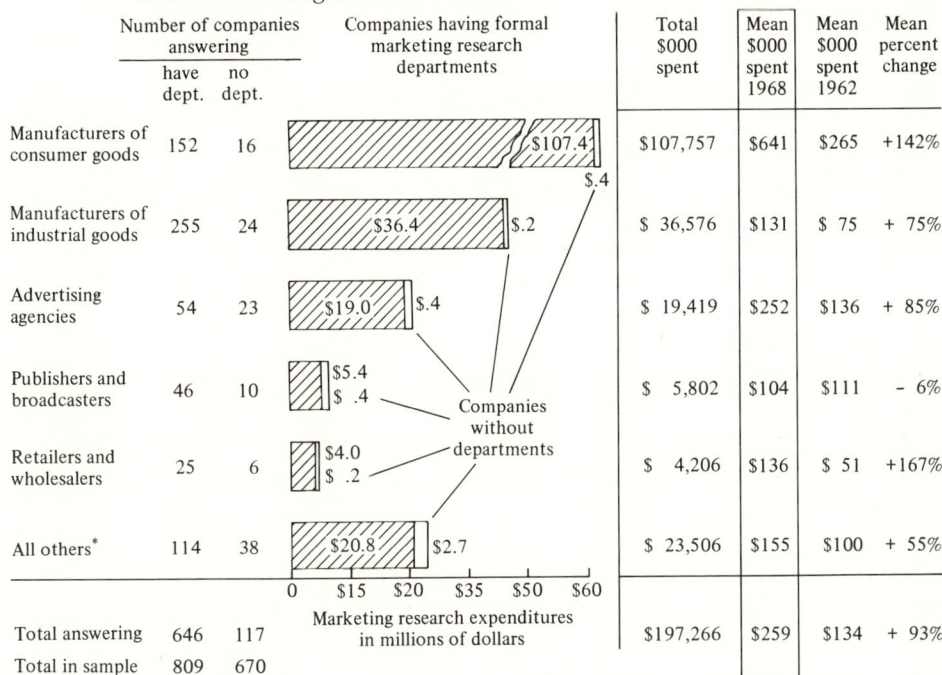

	Number of companies answering		Companies having formal marketing research departments	Total $000 spent	Mean $000 spent 1968	Mean $000 spent 1962	Mean percent change
	have dept.	no dept.					
Manufacturers of consumer goods	152	16	$107.4 / $.4	$107,757	$641	$265	+142%
Manufacturers of industrial goods	255	24	$36.4 / $.2	$ 36,576	$131	$ 75	+ 75%
Advertising agencies	54	23	$19.0 / $.4	$ 19,419	$252	$136	+ 85%
Publishers and broadcasters	46	10	$5.4 / $ .4	$ 5,802	$104	$111	– 6%
Retailers and wholesalers	25	6	$4.0 / $ .2	$ 4,206	$136	$ 51	+167%
All others*	114	38	$20.8 / $2.7	$ 23,506	$155	$100	+ 55%
Total answering	646	117		$197,266	$259	$134	+ 93%
Total in sample	809	670					

Companies without departments

0    $15 $20 $35 $50 $60

Marketing research expenditures in millions of dollars

*Includes: Trade associations, utilities, banks, insurance companies, and so on.

SOURCE: Reprinted from Dik Warren Twedt, *1968 Survey of Marketing Research*, published by the American Marketing Association, 1969.

[1] A. B. Blankenship and J. B. Doyle, *Marketing Research Management* (New York: The American Management Association, Inc., 1965), pp. 13–16.

Consumer-goods manufacturers spend more on marketing research, on the average, than any other type of firm. In 1968 consumer-goods manufacturers averaged $641,000 per firm compared to $259,000 for all types of firms.[2]

Establishing Research Budgets

The amount that an individual firm should spend on marketing research depends upon the firm's experience in using research results, the nature of the competitive situation, and the type of markets served by the firm. A recent survey of the American Marketing Association reveals that manufacturers of consumer products average .3 percent of sales for marketing research and that industrial marketers average .12 percent of sales (see Figure 3-3). The largest consumer companies spend the smallest percentage on marketing research.[3]

Analysis of market opportunities is the research activity most frequently observed among American business firms. Specifically, Figure 3-4 shows the most common research activities to be determination of market characteristics, development of market potentials, market-share analyses, sales analyses, competitive product studies, and research on new-product acceptance and potential.

A MANAGERIAL PHILOSOPHY OF RESEARCH

The purpose of marketing research is to aid management in making decisions about marketing strategy. Research has economic value *only* when it has the potential of changing the actions of managers. If managers will undertake the same actions regardless of the outcome of marketing research, the firm is wasting money on research expenditures!

Definition of Marketing Research

Research can be defined as "the systematic and objective search for and analysis of information relevant to the identification and solution of any problem in the field of marketing."[4] Two qualities in this definition serve to differentiate research from other forms of information gathering: research is *systematic* and *problem-oriented.*

SYSTEMATIC.   Haphazard questioning of a few customers or individuals about their reactions to a product is not research. Neither is a casual inspection of available data. Instead, the investigation must be *systematic,* even if only a few persons are to be questioned or only a few data examined.

A systematic approach prevents the analyst from including merely what is

---

[2] Dik Warren Twedt, *1968 Survey of Marketing Research* (Chicago: American Marketing Association, 1969), p. 28.

[3] *Ibid.,* p. 31.

[4] Paul E. Green and Donald S. Tull, *Research for Marketing Decisions* (Englewood Cliffs, N.J.: Prentice-Hall, Inc., 1966), p. 2.

Figure 3-3 Percent of sales spent for marketing research—by company type.

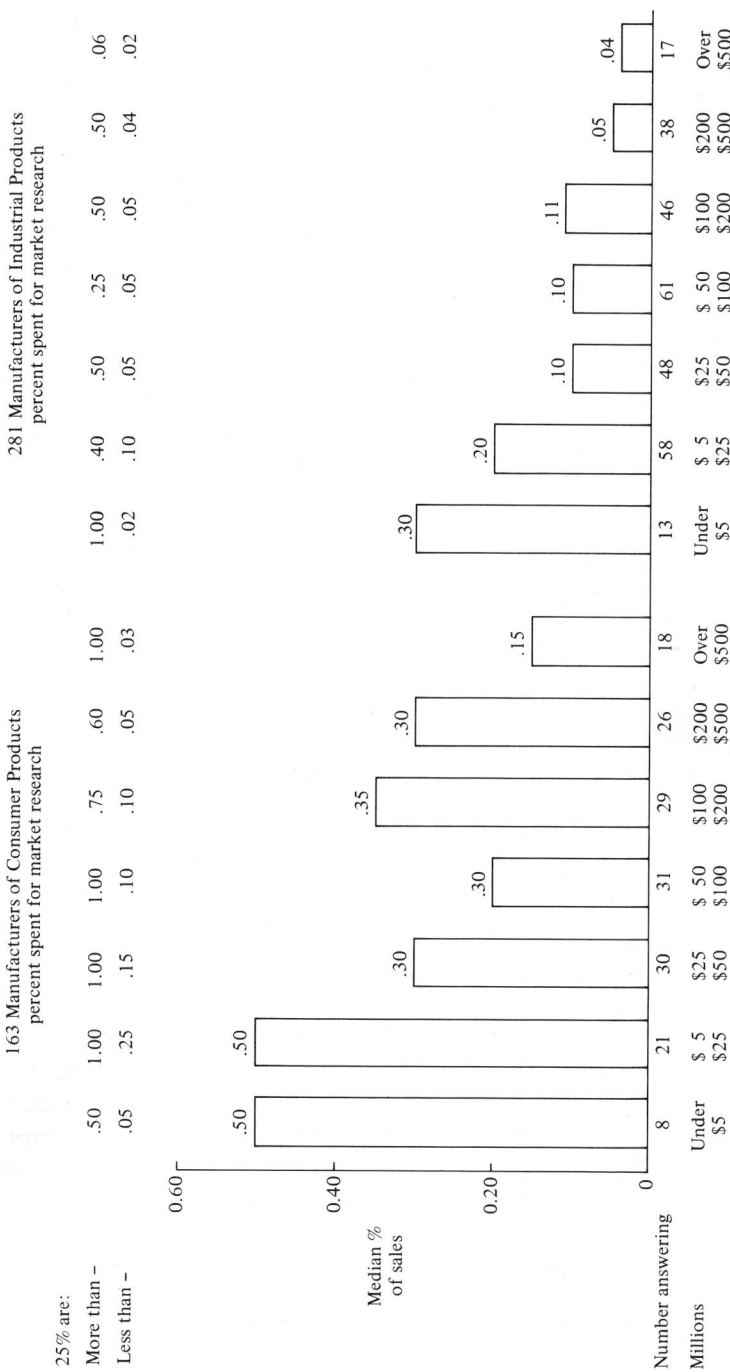

163 Manufacturers of Consumer Products
percent spent for market research

25% are:	Under $5	$5 $25	$25 $50	$50 $100	$100 $200	$200 $500	Over $500
More than –	.50	1.00	1.00	1.00	.75	.60	1.00
Less than –	.05	.25	.15	.10	.10	.05	.03
Median % of sales	.50	.50	.30	.30	.35	.30	.15
Number answering	8	21	30	31	29	26	18

281 Manufacturers of Industrial Products
percent spent for market research

25% are:	Under $5	$5 $25	$25 $50	$50 $100	$100 $200	$200 $500	Over $500
More than –	1.00	.40	.50	.25	.50	.50	.06
Less than –	.02	.10	.05	.05	.05	.04	.02
Median % of sales	.30	.20	.10	.10	.11	.05	.04
Number answering	13	58	48	61	46	38	17

(Millions)

Median % of sales axis: 0, 0.20, 0.40, 0.60

SOURCE: Reprinted from Dik Warren Twedt, *1968 Survey of Marketing Research*, published by the American Marketing Association, 1969.

53

Figure 3-4   Research activities of all respondent companies.

	Percent Doing	Done by Mkt. Resch. Dept.	Done by Another Dept.	Done by Outside Firm
Advertising Research				
a. Motivation research	32	19	2	15
b. Copy research	38	17	5	19
c. Media research	47	21	9	21
d. Studies of ad effectiveness	49	25	7	22
e. Other	13	7	2	4
Business Economics and Corporate Research				
a. Short-range forecasting (up to 1 yr.) ..	61	45	19	1
b. Long-range forecasting (over 1 yr.) ...	59	44	18	2
c. Studies of business trends	60	49	12	2
d. Profit and/or value analysis	53	18	37	1
e. Plant and warehouse, location studies ..	46	18	28	2
f. Diversification studies	49	28	25	2
g. Purchase of companies, sales of divisions	45	19	30	2
h. Export and international studies	41	21	21	2
i. Linear programming	33	8	25	2
j. Operations research	36	12	24	2
k. PERT studies	29	7	23	1
l. Employees morale studies	36	6	27	4
m. Other	7	4	2	—
Product Research				
a. New product acceptance and potential .	63	54	10	6
b. Competitive product studies	64	53	11	5
c. Product testing	53	31	22	6
d. Packaging research design or physical characteristics	45	23	19	7
e. Other	6	4	1	1
Sales and Market Research				
a. Development of market potentials	67	61	8	2
b. Market share analysis	66	61	6	3
c. Determination of market characteristics	69	63	6	3
d. Sales analyses	65	51	19	1
e. Establishment of sales quotas, territories	56	28	32	1
f. Distribution channels and cost studies ..	50	27	27	1
g. Test markets, store audits	37	26	7	7
h. Consumer panel operations	41	21	3	9
i. Sales compensation studies	43	15	29	2
j. Studies of premiums, coupons, sampling, deals	32	21	10	3
k. Other	5	4	1	1
Number of companies answering: 1703				

SOURCE: Reprinted from Dik Warren Twedt, *1968 Survey of Marketing Research*, published by the American Marketing Association, 1969, p. 41.

convenient to obtain or, even worse, only the data that confirm management's preconceived opinions about market opportunities.[5]

PROBLEM-ORIENTED. The accumulation of statistics or other data does not constitute research; it is merely fact finding. Fact finding may be an important part of the research process, but the process must be problem-oriented to be considered research.[6] In its most simplistic form, marketing research might be defined as "raising questions and getting answers that aid development of effective marketing strategies."

Effective research also helps to identify the most relevant questions to be answered. Management, however, must play the key role in the research process if research is to be directed to the *most relevant problems* or greatest market opportunities. Management should authorize only those research projects that are most likely to result in improved decisions about the most significant variables in a firm's marketing strategy.

In actual practice, selection of research projects is often based upon the interests of the researchers, previous experience, or the feeling that certain problems are "easiest" to study. Where research is not addressed to significant questions of strategy, administration, or recurring operations, however, it is worthless. It might be interesting for those who conduct it, but if it does not solve an important problem, it has no more value than the working of a crossword puzzle.

It is the conjoint responsibility of top management and qualified researchers to ask the *right* (most relevant) questions and to obtain *reliable* (adequate for decision making) answers.

The Risk-Reducing Nature of Research

Marketing research is a risk-reducing technique. Effectively practiced, research reduces (although it does not eliminate) some of the risk inherent in managerial decisions.

Huge risks typically accompany the exploitation of large-scale market opportunities. Customers may not accept the product. They may not accept it at profitable price levels. Competitors may bring out superior products. Distributors may be uninterested in handling the product. When such things happen in today's economy, the result may be losses in the millions of dollars. The function of research is to reduce (but not eliminate) some of these risks.

NO GUARANTEE OF SUCCESS. The best research available does not guarantee correct managerial decisions. Research does not usually analyze all elements of market opportunity and it cannot determine what has not yet occurred. Research techniques themselves are far from perfect. Executives sometimes wonder why

[5] A very useful introduction to what is meant by "systematic" or "logical" approaches to use of data (or research in general) is Abraham Kaplan, *The Conduct of Inquiry* (San Francisco: Chandler Publishing Company, 1964). Also see Norman Campbell, *What Is Science?* (New York: Dover Publications, Inc., 1952).

[6] For amplification of this idea, see Paul H. Rigby, *Conceptual Foundations of Business Research* (New York: John Wiley & Sons, Inc., 1965), pp. 4–9.

decisions made with high-quality research turn out wrong. It should be emphasized, therefore, that excellent research can still yield incorrect decisions. The criterion for good research should be that it *reduces* poor decisions—it does not eliminate them.

NO REPLACEMENT FOR EXECUTIVE JUDGMENT. Research does not replace executive judgment in decisions. Good research substitutes facts and objective evaluations for some of the hunches and guessing that have characterized much executive decision making. Research does not *make* marketing decisions, however. It is only an *aid* to executive judgment. "The predictions or recommendations which serve as an input to the decision maker must be complemented by his judgment and intuition. In no sense is the role of scientific analysis a substitute for experience or subjective analysis."[7]

When Research Fails

It should be clear that management personnel increasingly must understand the role of research and advanced analytical processes as an aid to decision making.[8] When use of research does not result in improved executive decision making, at least three explanations are possible:

1. The executives' intuition may be so good that research is merely confirming their judgment.
2. The research may be of such poor quality that executives cannot rely upon the results.
3. The research may be of reliable quality but the executives lack the sophistication required to understand it and therefore continue making decisions on a purely subjective basis.

If any of these situations continuously prevail, spending money for marketing research cannot be justified (other than for possible status or promotional values).

PLANNING EFFECTIVE MARKETING RESEARCH

Marketing research effective in determining marketing opportunity and the development of marketing strategy requires careful planning. The planning of effective research may be accomplished by attention to four basic elements or stages in the research process.[9] These four stages include (1) determining informa-

[7] William R. King, *Quantitative Analysis for Marketing Management* (New York: McGraw-Hill, Inc., 1967), p. 11.

[8] For persons with no prior background in using research for decision making, a useful introduction is provided by Irwin D. J. Bross, *Design for Decision: An Introduction to Statistical Decision-Making* (New York: The Free Press, 1953). This book also is unique among statistics books in that it is lucid.

[9] The identification of *four* stages rather than three, five, or some other number is arbitrary. For another approach, see Lyndon O. Brown and Leland L. Beik, *Marketing Research and Analysis* (New York: The Ronald Press Company, 1969), pp. 35–76. Almost the entire text

tion needs, (2) designing methods of information production, (3) modeling interrelationships between research and business decisions, and (4) communicating results to persons influential in implementation. This process is diagrammed in Figure 3-5.

Determining Information Needs

The first stage in planning marketing research is determining what information is needed by executives.[10] This requires *rigorous definition of the problem.* "A problem well defined is half solved," an old adage states. It is a useful adage because a frequent cause of wasteful research is inadequate conceptualization of the problem faced by management.

Figure 3-5   Planning effective research.

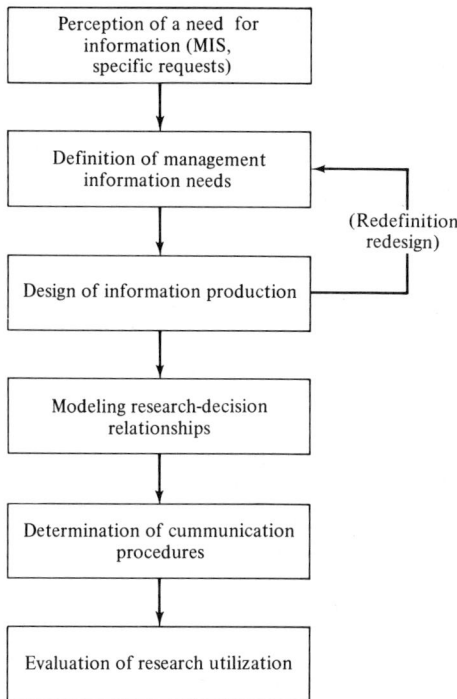

by Brown and Beik is useful for planning an effective research process. Also see Harper W. Boyd, Jr., and Ralph Westfall, *Marketing Research* (Homewood, Ill.: Richard D. Irwin, Inc., 1964), pp. 203–243. Another useful outline of the research process is in James H. Myers and Richard R. Mead, *The Management of Marketing Research* (Scranton, Pa.: International Textbook Company, 1969), pp. 68–69.

[10] A particularly good introduction to this topic is found in Robert D. Buzzell, Donald F. Cox, and Rex V. Brown, *Marketing Research and Information Systems* (New York: McGraw-Hill, Inc., 1969), pp. 20–32.

Specific types of information must be defined as most useful in answering the questions posed by management. Too often, executives simply ask for "information" on a problem rather than specifying exactly what would cause them to make a decision differently. Often then the research staff concludes that the executive wants "everything available" on a vaguely defined problem.

Many kinds of information *might* be relevant to a problem: consumer awareness of the product and the brand name, retail distribution and inventories, competitive-product availability and prices, and so on. When a problem is perceived only in very general terms, such as 'unsatisfactory sales volume,' there are likely to be many possible explanations and a correspondingly wide variety of potentially useful types of information. The manager, with the aid of his staff advisers, must somehow decide which kinds of information are most likely to shed light on a given problem. Seldom do time and resources permit the luxury of obtaining *all* classes of data that might be useful in a given situation.[11]

Designing Methods of Information Production

Planning methods of information production follows a clear definition of the problem that research is to solve. The temptation to design methods of maximum quality must be tempered by the need to minimize costs and time expended. Methods of obtaining data are described in a later chapter. In the planning phase, however, three criteria must be considered: confidence, precision, and costs.

CONFIDENCE. The executives who will use the research must decide how close to "perfect" results must be to be useful. The normal situation is to have something substantially less than perfect.

The more time and resources a research staff can devote to a project, the more confidently the results can be accepted. Yet if a firm must wait a long time or invest large amounts of money and people in the project, it may never be done. Should the research be expected to be correct 99 percent of the time, 90 percent of the time, or only 60 percent of the time?

The *user* of research should decide what confidence he must have in the research before acting on it. His desire is that the research be correct 100 percent of the time. As a practical matter, executives must usually accept much lower levels of confidence. Decisions about acceptable levels of confidence should be made *before* research is conducted *by the personnel who must use the results.*

PRECISION. The design of research methodology is also determined by the closeness with which estimates of market opportunities must conform to the actual situation. For example, if a researcher is estimating market share for a product that in truth will receive 40 percent of the market, how close to truth must the estimate be in order to be useful? Research might indicate a market share between 30 percent and 50 percent, between 39 percent and 41 percent, or

---

[11] *Ibid.*, pp. 22–23.

between 39.5 percent and 40.5 percent. The *user* of research must decide which level of precision is truly essential for the types of decisions to be made.[12]

Costs of Alternatives. Many alternative methods are usually possible in conducting research. Each has associated with it a cost as well as an estimated level of confidence and precision. The research plan must give careful consideration to a design that is the lowest cost for the level of confidence and precision required by the executive using the research results. Costs of alternatives are closely related to confidence and precision where probability sampling processes are used.[13] Increasingly, executives and their research staffs also are concerned with failure to accept correct conclusions about the market (type II statistical error) as well as failure to reject incorrect conclusions about market opportunities (type I statistical error).[14]

To solve a problem through research, one may usually choose among many alternative methodologies. If a high-cost alternative is chosen that yields a *higher* level of confidence or precision that is *acceptable for decision making,* the firm's resources are being wasted.

Modeling Research-Decision Interrelationships

The planning of effective research should include hypothetical models that specify interrelationships between research findings and decisions. This requires an executive or his staff to specify the interrelated decisions about such things as price, production scheduling, manpower requirements, advertising budgets, and other decision variables. In the past, research was often planned and carried out on a piece-by-piece basis, resulting in duplication, waste, and loss of information.

An overall model helps to establish priorities of research questions, determine the comprehensiveness of topics to be included in any specific research project, and interpret the results of research projects in terms of meaningful recommendations for the solution of overall business strategy problems.

In its simplest form, modeling of the research-decision process may be a simple, hypothetical description of the most important marketing variables and the information inputs that would be helpful in making decisions about them. It also includes a description of existing research findings about variables, execu-

---

[12] A discussion of some of the problems caused by overemphasizing precision is found in Kaplan, *The Conduct of Inquiry,* pp. 202–206.

[13] Most introductory statistics books describe procedures for determining sample size. See books such as Taro Yamane, *Statistics, An Introductory Example* (New York: Harper & Row, Publishers, 1964), Chap. 7, or Wilfred J. Dixon and Frank J. Massey, Jr., *Introduction to Statistical Analysis* (New York: McGraw-Hill, Inc., 1957), pp. 84–85. For a Bayesian extension, see Frederick A. Ekeblad, *The Statistical Method in Business* (New York: John Wiley & Sons, Inc., 1962), Chaps. 8 and 9.

[14] A good explanation of type I error (or significance) and type II error (or power) in a marketing research book is Brown and Beik, *Marketing Research and Analysis,* pp. 413–418. A slightly more detailed and excellent discussion is William L. Hays, *Statistics for Psychologists* (New York: Holt, Rinehart and Winston, Inc., 1963), pp. 250–287 and 299–300.

tive assumptions, and assessment of information gaps.[15] The research department may accomplish this with something as simple as a large flow chart showing research reports available on key decision variables. In more sophisticated applications, model building may be much more rigorous and accomplished in a variety of ways.[16]

Communicating Results

Research, if it is to be useful, must be communicated effectively. If the executive expected to rely upon a research report does not understand it or have confidence in it, the money spent on the report is probably wasted. Executives have a right to reports that contain no extraneous material, communicate with clarity, use appropriate levels of statistical terminology, and are presented with appropriate audio-visual materials.[17]

Management Involvement in Planning Research

The users of research should be involved in the very beginning of research plans. This develops interest in results and increases the probability that management personnel will understand the methodology. They will rely upon the outcome more than they would if a completed report were handed to them without their own inputs concerning questionnaire format, question content, and analysis. By involving executives in research throughout the process,[18] it is much more likely that the process will yield *useful information* rather than *useless data.*

When executives are not involved throughout the process, it causes the problem described below by Myers and Mead:

One of the primary problems of research is that it tends to present *data* to management, rather than *information.* Management is often not aware of what is wrong but they do know that what they have received is not quite what they are looking for. As a result, they begin calling on marketing research only when they want *data.* This tends to remove research more and more from the decision-making process to the point that management is not even able to discover that data are really not too useful in most decision processes. Thus it is that marketing executives often say (or think), "This is interesting, but it is not what I need to make my decision."[19]

[15] See James F. Engel, David T. Kollat, and Roger D. Blackwell, *Consumer Behavior* (New York: Holt, Rinehart and Winston, Inc., 1968), pp. 617–621.

[16] See Kenneth P. Uhl and Bertram Schoner, *Marketing Research* (New York: John Wiley & Sons, Inc.) Chap. 3.

[17] A guide for the preparation of research reports is George L. Morrisey, *Effective Business and Technical Presentations* (Reading, Mass.: Addison-Wesley Publishing Company, Inc., 1968).

[18] For an excellent discussion of this topic see Brown and Beik, *Marketing Research and Analysis,* Chap. 26.

[19] Myers and Mead, *The Management of Marketing Research,* p. 6.

METHODS OF ANALYZING DATA

Executives play an important role in determining the type of data collected and the methods of analyzing those data that will be useful to management. It is unrealistic to expect line executives to do much of the analysis themselves. That would be an inefficient use of their time. It is essential, however, that executives using information *understand* the methods of analysis used by the research staff and the process of choosing one method rather than another. In actual practice, it is the informed executive who can act with the most confidence in making decisions that rely heavily on research inputs.

This section describes a fundamental framework for categorizing and understanding the nature of alternative methods of data analysis. The purpose is not to provide sufficient detail to allow carrying out these methods; rather, it is to develop an understanding of why analytical methods must be chosen on the basis of their appropriateness for a specific research situation. The footnotes cite convenient sources for additional information.

Nature of Data

The *measurement strength* of data determines what types of analyses are permissible. The specific type of descriptive statistics, tests of significance, or measures of relationships to be used cannot be established until the level of measurement is determined. The relationships between measurement strength and analytical methods are summarized in Figure 3-6.

There are four primary types of data: nominal, ordinal, interval, and ratio.[20]

NOMINAL DATA. Nominal data represent measurement in its weakest form, concerned only with classification of a specified characteristic. Measurement of a characteristic is dichotomous or multichotomous; numbers assigned to the data are nothing more than "names" for characteristics. Examples of nominal data include telephone numbers, numbers to identify athletic contestants, social security numbers, and the like.

From a calculation perspective, it would be possible to compute the mean player number of one football team and compare it to another. Such a procedure would, of course, be meaningless. Unfortunately, managers are sometimes presented with computer output in which a researcher has made exactly such a mistake. Executives should be alert to such conditions in making their own decision about whether or not to rely upon research results. Admissible operations on nominal data can be based only on membership in a class, for example, frequency. Figure 3-6 displays these major permissible analytical procedures.

ORDINAL DATA. Ordinal data are pieces of information measured in such a way that the objects in one category are not just different from those in other

---

[20] For further discussion of measurement characteristics see Fred N. Kerlinger, *Foundations of Behavioral Research* (New York: Holt, Rinehart and Winston, Inc., 1966), pp. 422–424.

Figure 3-6 Common statistics and analytical procedures.

Level of Measurement	Descriptive Measure of Central Tendency	Type of Statistics	Tests of Significance			Measure of Relationship
			Single Sample	Multiple (K) Independent Samples	Multiple (K) Related Samples	
Nominal	Mode	Nonparametric	Binominal test Z for proportions chi square	Chi square	McNemar ($K=2$) Cochran Q	Phi Contingency Coefficient C Tschuprow's T
Ordinal	Median	Nonparametric	Runs test Kolmogorov-Smirnov	Median test Mann-Whitney U ($K=2$) Kruskal-Wallis one-way analysis of variance ($K=2$) Wald-Wolfowitz ($K=2$)	Wilcoxon ($K=2$) Friedman two-way analysis of variance ($K=2$) Sign test	Spearman rank Kendall tau Kendall W
Interval	Mean	Parametric[a]	Z t	Z t ($K=2$) ANOV with F test ($K=2$)	t_r ANOV$_r$	Pearson r Multiple R Eta

[a] Since the table should be interpreted cumulatively downwards along columns, interval and ratio data can employ the corresponding non-parametric tests as well.

Note: Most of these statistics are discussed standard sources such as William L. Hays, *Statistics for Psychologists* (New York: Holt, Rinehart and Winston, Inc., 1963) and Sidney Siegal, *Nonparametric Statistics for the Behavioral Sciences* (New York: McGraw-Hill, Inc., 1956).

categories but also stand in some kind of relation to them. In comparing two objects, one has "more" of some characteristic than another. In such cases, it is possible to *rank-order* several objects although not to decide "how much better" one is than another.

Nominal and ordinal data both permit methods of analysis limited to what is called *nonparametric* statistics.[21] These are statistics with much less relaxed theoretical assumptions than *parametric* statistics, which are appropriate for higher orders of measurement.

Marketing executives and even some researchers commonly have limited familiarity with nonparametric statistics. This may be due to the relative emphasis on parametric statistics in most university statistics courses, or perhaps to a longer history of usage for parametric statistics stemming from original physical and biological applications. Generally, there is a scarcity of standard computer programs for nonparametric tests, although this is changing rapidly. Nonparametric statistics are often easier to use. Frequently, they are the only kind that can be justified in marketing studies. Many of the innovative approaches to determining market opportunity involve nonmetric forms of multidimensional analysis. They must increasingly fall within the range of understanding of contemporary executives. (These methods are described in Chapter 9.)

INTERVAL DATA. Interval data contain information that a value (X) is not only greater than another value (Y) but also indicates the interval between X and Y is known. At this level of measurement, the ratio of any two intervals is independent of the unit of measurement and the zero point (both of which are arbitrary). A good example of interval data is temperature, which illustrates well the effects of an arbitrary zero point. If it were said that 50° F is twice as hot as 25° F, one would be in trouble when he converted to another scale with a different arbitrary zero point, such as centigrade. The conversion of 50° F and 25° F to centigrade would yield 10° C and −3.9° C, quite a different ratio. Although interval data have different ratios, it is significant that the differences between scores with interval measurement maintain the same ratios.

RATIO DATA. Ratio data have a true or "natural" zero point as their origin. The ratio of any two scale points is independent of the unit of measurement. Common examples include age, measures of length, and so on.

MANAGERIAL SIGNIFICANCE. In determining methods of analysis appropriate in a research project, one must consider the quality of the measuring instrument to be designed or used. If a test or analytical method requiring interval data is used when only ordinal data exist, the results can be misleading to the executives designing marketing strategy. Conversely, it would be a pity to employ an analytical technique that was less refined than the data measurement; that would

---

[21] Two easy-to-understand books on this subject are Merle W. Tate and Richard C. Clelland, *Nonparametric and Shortcut Statistics* (Danville, Ill.: Interstate Printers and Publishers, Inc., 1957), and Sidney Siegel, *Nonparametric Statistics for the Behavioral Sciences* (New York: McGraw-Hill, Inc., 1956).

be wasting information. The problem is to select an analytical technique thåt is appropriate to the quality of measure to be used in the project.

Some executives erroneously conclude that an elaborate statistical technique will compensate for poor-quality data. As a matter of fact, the more elaborate statistical procedures are usually more sensitive to aberrations in the data and require data of higher rather than lower quality.

Statistical Tests of Significance

The most commonly used form of statistical analysis in marketing research is probably the *test of significance*. Executives are constantly asked to review and act upon research results using terms such as chi square, *t* tests, *z* tests, and analysis of variance (ANOV). The following paragraphs describe the common purpose of such tests.

Tests of significance are used to help decide whether differences exist between two categories of variables, such as two market segments. Tests of significance are needed when sampling is involved. If a census is conducted, there is no need for tests of significance. If every member of a market group is counted and 32 percent prefer a product with an improved characteristic while 28 percent prefer the present form, the only question is one of managerial significance: is the difference large enough to justify product modification?

On the other hand, suppose the market measurement were made with a *sample rather than a census*. Assume again that market preferences are measured and that 320 persons in a sample of 600 are found to prefer the improved product while 280 persons prefer the existing product. In this situation, a *null hypothesis exists*: perhaps there is no difference in the market preferences as they truly exist in the entire group of market members—perhaps the difference obtained is due only to peculiarities of the sample selected for the market test. In a city of 1,000,000 consumers, for example, the observed differences of 320 persons and 280 persons could be obtained even though no difference existed in the whole market. The only *purpose of a statistical test of significance is to test the probability of such an occurrence*.

An executive may be told that a statistically significant difference exists on the basis of some statistical test such as chi square. He must still assess whether the difference in the entire market (universe) is *managerially significant*. The chi square or any other test does not answer this latter question. Frequently, results from market tests are statistically significant but not managerially significant.

Measures of Relationships

The planning of effective marketing strategy requires research techniques that enable an executive to establish the relationship between market *opportunity* and *strategy required to achieve that opportunity*. For example, it is important to establish relationships between reasons for buying a product and selling strategies that satisfy those reasons. It is important to understand the relationship between variables such as income, age, or attitudes and demand for specified products or brands. In sales forecasting, it is necessary to measure the relationship between economic conditions and demand for products or the relationship between sales-force activity and sales volume.

Many analytical procedures have been formulated to determine the nature and degree of relationship among variables. The simplest of these methods require little mathematical sophistication. One simple method of analysis is *cross-classification* or simple tabulation of data. Most studies classify market opportunities by income, age, geographical location, and other variables. Some other important methods are described briefly below.

REGRESSION AND CORRELATION. A basic technique used to predict one variable (such as sales of a product) with the knowledge of another variable (such as business condition, attitudes, social class) is regression.[22] In practical situations, it is seldom that only one item of prior information is used. Typically, management decisions are based upon the predictive relationship between one dependent variable and several predictors. The appropriate statistical procedure for accomplishing this aim is *multiple* regression. Assuming a linear model, the general multiple-regression equation is as follows:

$$Y = A + B_1X_1 + B_2X_2 + \cdots + B_nX_n$$

The predicted standard score value of Y is equal to the weighted sum of the predictors. The weights are found using a least-squares criterion. When the equation is expressed in standard score form, the weights are known as beta-weights. These weights are especially useful in obtaining the *coefficient of multiple determination*, R^2. Using the very same beta-weights, we define R^2 as the weighted sum of the correlation coefficients of each predictor with the dependent variable.

$$R^2 = b_1r_{1Y} + b_2r_{2Y} + b_3r_{3Y} + \cdots + b_nr_{nY}$$

This statistic gives the proportion of the total variance that is predicted by the independent variables employed. The *multiple correlation coefficient* is merely the positive square root of this R^2 value. Multiple regression is probably the most basic element used in *sales-forecasting applications* of market research.[23]

FACTOR ANALYSIS. Factor analysis is basically a technique for reducing a set of data into a more compact form and illuminating the underlying properties.[24] The functions delineating relationships can be linear or nonlinear, although linear functions are more usual and follow the least-squares criterion. Thus, weights and variables are represented as follows:

[22] A good exposition of regression and correlation is given in Ronald E. Frank, Alfred A. Kuehn, and William F. Massy, *Quantitative Techniques in Marketing Analysis* (Homewood, Ill.: Richard D. Irwin, Inc., 1962), pp. 56–104. This describes other analytical techniques also.

[23] For additional information on forecasting, see Norbert Lloyd Enrick, *Market and Sales Forecasting* (San Francisco: Chandler Publishing Company, 1969).

[24] See Jagdish N. Sheth and J. Scott Armstrong, "Factor Analysis of Marketing Data: A Critical Evaluation," in Philip R. McDonald, ed., *Marketing Involvement in Society and the Economy* (Chicago: American Marketing Association, 1969), pp. 137–144.

$$F = a_1X_1 + a_2X_2 + \cdots + a_nX_n$$

Ordinarily more than one factor is delineated. Combined, they represent or explain a part of the total variance in the original data.

Factor analysis is used in marketing in five principal ways:

1. Inference of dimensions that latently order products or brands in terms of consumer preferences.
2. Pattern or structural analysis of a set of attributes.
3. Separation and analysis of distinct groups or clusters of variables or individuals that exist in the sample.
4. Identification of key variables for further analysis from a large set of variables.
5. Summarization of correlated variables into a set of explanatory factor variables to remove collinearity in regression or discrimination analysis.[25]

OTHER MULTIVARIATE PROCEDURES. Many other analytical techniques are used to identify the structure of markets, and the breadth of techniques is enlarging with each passing year. Some of the other multivariate techniques becoming commonly accepted include linear discriminant analysis, canonical analysis, principal-components analysis, latent-structure analysis, and cluster or profile analysis.[26] All are closely related and evolve out of similar circumstances to provide adaptations to special problems that arise. Some other sophisticated methods are described in more detail in later portions of this book.

Management Attitudes Toward Analytical Methods

The range of analytical methods is so great that the typical marketing executive cannot be expected to be personally familiar with each. The executive emerging in contemporary practice, however, generally has some mathematical and analytical background, and he should be prepared, when he finds himself in a situation using a new or unfamiliar analytical procedure, to learn enough about the technique so to understand whether it is appropriately applied, what its limitations are, and why it is more useful than simpler or alternative methods. With the ability to understand analytical procedures, the executive is more likely to make decisions in a confident and strategic fashion.

SUMMARY AND CONCLUSIONS

The systematic development of a strategy to achieve market opportunities depends increasingly upon understanding research inputs and being able to base decisions upon them. This is a function of the increasing complexity of market structure, rapid communications, quick change in consumer tastes, and the rising magnitude of risk involved in important marketing decisions.

[25] Jagdish N. Sheth, "Applications of Multivariate Methods in Marketing," in Robert L. King, ed., *Marketing and the New Science of Planning* (Chicago: American Marketing Association, 1968), pp. 259–265.

[26] *Ibid.*

Marketing research is a *systematic* approach to *solve* important problems relating to marketing decisions. Research should not be expected to eliminate incorrect decisions; instead, it merely reduces some of the risks involved.

Planning effective marketing research involves four identifiable steps: (1) determining information needs, (2) designing methods of information production, (3) modeling interrelationships between research and business decisions, and (4) communicating results to persons influential in implementation of the research.

Decisions must be made about the types of analysis that will be performed before decisions are made about what data to collect. Figure 3-6 summarizes the major forms of descriptive statistics, tests of significance, and measures of relationships that are appropriate with different categories of data. Executives need not know how to conduct contemporary forms of analysis; instead, they need to understand the purpose and conditions of appropriateness sufficiently to act with knowledge and confidence on the results generated from marketing research.

QUESTIONS FOR REVIEW AND DISCUSSION

1. Marketing research has increased dramatically in recent years. Analyze the underlying factors that explain this rise.
2. Firms primarily involved in retailing and wholesaling spend considerably less than other types of marketing organizations. Why should this be true? In recent years, distribution enterprises have increased their marketing research expenses more rapidly than other types of firms. Why?
3. Within marketing research departments, certain activities are much more common than others. What types of activities are found most frequently? What explanation can be given for their predominance?
4. Some executives view research as threatening to their responsibility. They maintain that when decisions are constantly made with research reports, control of the firm may pass from the management to staff personnel from the research department, who probably have limited experience in important decisions. Comment on this view.
5. Some firms have spent rather large amounts on marketing research and have seen very little improvement in the firm's performance. What explanations would you offer?
6. Planning marketing research is described in this chapter as a four-stage process. Which stage appears to be the most critical? In each stage, identify whether top management or professional researchers should assume most of the responsibility and work load.
7. Describe the four types of data: nominal, ordinal, interval, and ratio. Give examples of each (other than those listed in the textbook). Why are they important in planning research?
8. Write a short essay on the purpose of statistical tests of significance in marketing research.

Chapter 4   Obtaining Market Data

Management personnel must trust the process for obtaining market data if they are to rely upon research results for decision making. This chapter describes the ways market data are collected and discusses variables to consider in the evaluation of alternative data sources. It also describes in general terms some of the more useful methods of data collection and suggests sources of information for additional information.

The criticality of quality data rests with two observations. First, analysis and conclusions based on research can be no better than the quality of data underlying the research. Second, if executives do not have confidence in the data at the most basic levels, the total research process is likely to be useless and wasteful.

SELECTING DATA-COLLECTION INSTRUMENTS

The breadth of assortment available in data-collection instruments is limited only by the creativity of the investigator in a research project. This means that if a problem has been defined by management that does not fit a standard type of data-collection instrument, it is reasonable to expect adaptation and innovation in the design of an instrument from the research organization. Described below are the principal types of instruments: (1) questionnaires, (2) projective techniques, (3) attitude scales, (4) multidimensional scales, and (5) physiological measures.

Questionnaires

Questionnaires are carefully planned methods of asking questions of respondents. The questionnaire consists of four basic elements:

1. Solicitation of the respondent's cooperation, while emphasizing the survey's importance.
2. Efficient presentation of questions about a marketing problem.
3. Requests for classification data that will permit stratification and analysis of the collected data by age, sex, location, occupation, economic status, etc.
4. Provisions for the coding operation to facilitate tabulation.[1]

Questions must be written very carefully, because a slight variation in wording may cause substantial variation in results. The purpose of the questionnaire is disguised in situations where the respondent might refuse to answer or might give biased answers if he understood the sponsor or purpose of the study. Questions may be open-ended in situations where the researcher is unsure of the range of responses that may be obtained or wants to capture the richness of verbatim comments. More commonly, fixed alternatives are specified for respondents to mark. An example of a carefully designed, large-scale, mail questionnaire is presented in Figure 4-1.

Projective Techniques

A major type of variation on standard questions is supplied by projective techniques.[2] In a *sentence-completion* test, respondents are given the beginning of a sentence as a stimulus and are asked to respond by completing the sentence. In a *thematic apperception test* (TAT) or pictorial test, consumers are given a picture and asked to imagine and report a story about what is happening in the picture. By analyzing consistencies, researchers may determine problems or frustrations and indicate market opportunities. Projective techniques are useful in yielding new insights or revealing "deeper" feelings about products. They depend heavily for usefulness upon the researcher's skill and creativity in interpreting the results.

[1] Adapted from John P. Alevizos, *Marketing Research* (Englewood Cliffs, N.J.: Prentice-Hall, Inc., 1959), p. 121. An excellent understanding of how to prepare questionnaires can be gained by study of Charles H. Backstrom and Gerald D. Hursh, *Survey Research* (Evanston: Northwestern University Press, 1963).

[2] One of the better discussions of the usefulness of projective techniques is contained in Lyndon L. Brown and Leland L. Beik, *Marketing Research and Analysis* (New York: The Ronald Press Company, 1969), pp. 295–310.

Figure 4-1   Mail questionnaire.

Clip and mail only the answer portion of each page. ⟶

FAMILY MONEY MANAGEMENT
QUESTIONNAIRE

These are the Official Rules for Better Homes and Gardens $25,000 Money Management Sweepstakes

1. Fully complete the Family Money Management Questionnaire.

2. Be sure to print your full name and address in the appropriate spot. Put the answer portions of the questionnaire into an envelope and mail it to: Money Management Questions, 1716 Locust, Des Moines, Iowa 50303.

3. In order to qualify for the prize money, you should try to fill out the questionnaire as completely as possible. There are no right or wrong answers. We want you to express your own honest preferences, ideas, and opinions.

4. The 50 winners will each receive $500. They will be selected on or about January 1, 1968, from a random drawing of all questionnaires submitted. Winners will be notified on or about January 15.

5. You are encouraged to submit a questionnaire from both the October and November issues. These questionnaires are different—thus, you are eligible to win $500 for each month's entry—total $1,000. Each entry must be mailed separately; they must be postmarked not later than December 4, 1967, and received no later than December 15.

6. All questionnaires, contents, and ideas therein become the property of Meredith Publishing Company, and may be used for whatever purposes the company deems appropriate. However, your name will be held in complete confidence—unless, of course, you are chosen as a winner.

7. A list of winners will be published in the May 1968 issue of Better Homes and Gardens. Sorry, but we cannot answer individual inquiries about the Sweepstakes or the winners.

8. Any resident of the United States may enter—except in states where sweepstakes are prohibited. Employees of Meredith Publishing Company, its subsidiary and affiliated companies, their advertising agencies, and their families are ineligible.

9. This Sweepstakes is subject to all federal and state regulations. Any liability for federal, state, or other taxes or duties imposed on a prize received will be the sole responsibility of the prize winner and not of Meredith Publishing Company.

DON'T MISS THIS CHANCE TO BE HEARD!

Want your opinions to count? Then spend a few minutes on this Better Homes and Gardens Money Management Questionnaire. You could be $500 richer, too, since 50 of our respondents will receive a $500 sweepstakes bonus. Because the survey spans several financial areas, from insurance to food-buying, you'll want this to be as much of a family project as you can. Then you will be giving us information vital to a sound editorial program —and by the time you finish, chances are you'll be looking at your own family money planning in a new light.

Your reply will be kept in strict confidence by our editors. No one will put your name on any list, or try to sell you something as a result of your reply. Be as frank as you wish, too. Winners are drawn at random, so your answers can't possibly influence your chances.

When you finish, you may have additional comments. Feel free to send them along on a separate sheet.

Questions   ## Answers

Please circle number next to the answer that comes closest to your opinion. Circle only one number unless question asks for several.

1. How do you feel about the availability of credit today—through credit cards, charge accounts, installment buying, and the like?

1. **1** Too easy for people to buy on credit
   2 Still not easy enough for people to buy on credit
   3 Credit availability is about right

2. How successful do you think American business has been in regulating itself through voluntary codes of ethics?

2. **1** Very successful   **2** Fairly successful
   3 Not too successful   **4** Not at all successful

3. How desirable do you feel it would be to have the federal government test and grade a wider range of consumer products?

3. **1** Very desirable   **2** Somewhat desirable   **3** Not desirable

4. The cost of living has risen in the past two years. Do you feel that prices of any of the following have risen far out of line from the others? Circle as many as apply.

4. **1** Clothing **2** Cosmetics **3** Furniture **4** Housing
   5 Taxes **6** Food products **7** Public transportation
   8 Medical expenses **9** Repair services **10** None of these

5. How do you feel advertising affects the price of most of the products you buy?

5. **1** Generally raises price   **2** Generally lowers price
   3 Makes no difference in price

6. As the cost of community services rises (for schools, street improvements, sanitation facilities, welfare services, etc.), what action would you *most* prefer? *Least* prefer?

6.

	Most Prefer	Least Prefer
New or higher sales taxes	1	2
New or higher income taxes	3	4
Increased corporation taxes	5	6
More federal aid for schools, urban projects	7	8
Further increases in property taxes	9	10
Reduce the community services	11	12

7. Do you feel that the cost of sending a youngster to college should be deductible from the parent's federal income tax?

7. **1** Yes **2** No **3** No opinion

8. Would you be willing to pay additional Social Security taxes to extend Medicare benefits to persons younger than 65?

8. **1** Yes **2** No **3** No opinion

BETTER HOMES AND GARDENS, OCTOBER, 1967

SOURCE: *Better Homes and Gardens Consumer Questionnaire*, October 1967. © Meredith Corporation, 1967. All rights reserved.

Figure 4-1   Mail questionnaire (*continued*).

Mail in this portion. Answers	Questions
9. 1 Always 2 Usually 3 Seldom 4 Never	**9.** Do you follow a consistent program of saving *before* bills are paid and other obligations or desires are met?
10. 1 Husband 2 Wife 3 Both husband and wife 4 Am single	**10.** In your household, who usually pays the bills?
11. 1 Increase cost 2 Decrease cost 3 Make no difference	**11.** How do you feel trading stamps affect the cost of food?
12. Husband Wife Both New refrigerator 1 2 3 New carpet 1 2 3 New sofa 1 2 3 New wall paneling 1 2 3 4 I do, because I'm single Your comment:_____	**12.** In deciding what specific brand to buy, who in your household makes the decisions when picking:
13. 1 Yes 2 No	**13.** Are you satisfied with the amount you are saving?
14. 1 Budget food only 2 Budget certain family expenses, but not all 3 Budget total family expenses 4 Have no budget of any kind	**14.** Do you have a spending plan or budget in which you allot a specified amount of money to food, household needs, clothing, car expenses, entertainment, etc.?
15. 1 Money is dribbled away in small amounts by careless, day-to-day spending 2 The family makes expensive purchases impulsively whether they need them or not 3 Just don't have enough income for their needs	**15.** Of the statements at left, which one is the most common reason families develop serious financial problems?
16. 1 Charge accounts lead to financial irresponsibility 2 Charge accounts teach financial responsibility	**16.** Which comes closest to your views on charge accounts for teen-agers?
17. 1 Fall behind the national trend in cost of living 2 Stay comparatively even 3 Move ahead of living costs	**17.** Do you expect your income in the next five years to:
18. 1 Better than ten years ago 2 About the same 3 Not as good as ten years ago	**18.** What do you think of the workmanship in today's new houses?
19. 1 Condition and appearance of the house itself 2 Quality of the neighborhood 3 Quality of schools	**19.** Which of the following would you rate as most important in establishing the sales price of an existing house?
20. 1 More expensive than buying on installment credit 2 Less expensive than buying on installment credit 3 Cost runs about the same for installment or package method	**20.** Would you say that financing major appliances by making them part of a new-house mortgage package is:
21. 1 Very difficult 2 Fairly difficult 3 Not too difficult Your comment:_____	**21.** Do you find it difficult to learn about new building products?
22. 1 Too low 2 Too high 3 About right	**22.** Many mortgage lenders use the formula of $2\frac{1}{2}$ times annual income to determine how much house the average family can afford. Do you feel this is:
23. 1 Yes 2 No 3 Am now renting	**23.** Comparing your present annual income and the approximate market value of your home today, are you living in *less* house than the $2\frac{1}{2}$-times formula allows?
24. 1 Already invest in common stocks 2 Not interested 3 Risk too great 4 Not familiar enough with stock market 5 Too much investment required 6 Too much time required 7 Still building up basic savings and life insurance 8 Don't believe in any speculative investment 9 Don't have money to invest	**24.** If you do not now invest in common stocks, what are your major reasons? Circle as many as apply
25. _____ _____ (make) (year) Your comment:_____	**25.** In your opinion, what was the best car you ever owned?

BETTER HOMES AND GARDENS, OCTOBER, 1967

Figure 4-1   Mail questionnaire (*continued*).

𝒬uestions

Mail in this portion.

𝒜nswers

26. Do you think you can get a better deal on a new car by shopping a number of dealers selling the same make?

26. 1 Yes 2 No

27. Do you figure you'll get about the same trade-in price for your present car whether it's in good condition or not?

27. 1 Yes 2 No 3 Don't own a car

28. Which do you feel usually charges you the lowest interest on the purchase of a new car?

28. 1 The auto dealer 2 A finance company 3 A bank 4 A credit union 5 All about the same 6 Don't know

29. How do you feel about new auto safety features beyond those presently required?

29. 1 Should be standard equipment with all buyers paying for them 2 Should be optional features at extra cost

30. National averages put the annual costs for owning a new medium-sized car at around $1,000 per year during the first three years. In your opinion, which of the following makes up the *largest* part of the $1,000 cost? The *smallest?*

30.

	Largest	Smallest
Depreciation and financing	1	2
Insurance, taxes, licensing	1	2
Gasoline, maintenance, repairs	1	2
Don't know	1	2

31. About how much would you estimate you pay for gas and oil to operate the car you drive?

31. 1 One-two cents per mile 2 Three-four cents 3 Five-six cents 4 Seven-eight cents 5 Nine-ten cents 6 Eleven-twelve cents 7 Don't know 8 Don't drive a car

32. Certain drivers with accident or violation records must pay higher premiums for their auto insurance. In writing these policies, the insurance companies:

32. 1 Perform a valuable and necessary service 2 Keep many dangerous drivers behind the wheel 3 Make large profits from the higher rates

33. How often do you shop at more than one grocery store to take advantage of "specials"?

33. 1 About every week 2 At least once a month 3 Almost never 4 Never

34. How do you feel nationally advertised brands usually compare in *price* to local brands or grocery chain brands? In *quality?*

34.

	Price	Quality
National brands higher	1	2
National brands lower	3	4
About equal	5	6

35. Many food and household products are sold in "fractional" quantities (such as 1 pound 13¾ ounces or 1 pint 6 ounces). What do you think is the main reason manufacturers do this?

35. 1 To serve customers with a wider choice of sizes 2 To make it hard to compare prices of different size packages 3 To permit use of standard-size containers 4 To allow for recipes which call for odd quantities

36. How do you usually choose among brands of canned, bottled, or packaged foods?

36. 1 Compare weights and volumes 2 Compare price 3 Compare labels 4 Normally stay with brands I know

37. Which of these characteristics of convenience foods (such as cake mixes, prepared complete dinners, instant mashed potatoes) is most important to you?

37. 1 Time saving 2 Work saving 3 Fewer ingredients to buy and stock 4 Decreases waste
Your comment: _____

38. Has the *percentage of your total income* spent for food changed during the past two years?

38. 1 Has increased greatly 4 Has decreased slightly 2 Has increased slightly 5 Hasn't changed 3 Has decreased greatly

39. Which would be more likely to influence your decision to buy a major appliance?

39. 1 The manufacturer's reputation and warranty 2 The local dealer's reputation for service

40. Which would be likely to have more influence on your decision to buy a major appliance?

40. 1 The place where I can get the lowest price 2 Reputation of manufacturer or dealer

41. How would you rate the durability of the majority of *small* appliances you have bought during recent years?

41. 1 Well-built, trouble-free 2 Fairly well-built, require occasional service 3 Poorly built, too often need repair 4 Haven't purchased any small appliances in recent years

42. You are about to make a credit purchase. Assuming the sales price is acceptable, which of these considerations would be most important to you?

42. 1 Total interest 2 Amount of down-payment or trade-in 3 Size of your monthly payments 4 Never buy on credit
Your comment: _____

BETTER HOMES AND GARDENS, OCTOBER, 1967

Figure 4-1   Mail questionnaire *(continued)*.

Mail in this portion.	
Answers	**Questions**
43. 1 A percentage rate 2 Total dollars of interest	**43.** In installment buying, is it more helpful to you to have the finance charge expressed as:
44. 1 A law requiring the same wording of finance charges on all credit contracts 2 Let each company decide on wording of finance charges that best suits the nature of its business	**44.** Which would you favor regarding interest and finance charges on credit contracts?
45. 1 None 5 $50,000 2 $5,000 6 $75,000 3 $10,000 7 $100,000 4 $25,000 8 Don't know	**45.** How much life insurance would you recommend for a typical 35-year-old father of two with income of $10,000 a year?
46. 1 Most life insurance coverage should be on the breadwinner 2 Term insurance is always the best buy in life insurance 3 Employer's group insurance is sufficient for most families 4 Life insurance doesn't keep pace with inflation 5 By shopping around, you usually can get a better buy	**46.** Following are six statements about life insurance. Circle the number of each statement you feel is *true*.
47. 1 Annually 2 When have increase in family income 3 When have increase in family 4 Let agent set up review 5 Don't have life insurance 6 Never	**47.** How frequently do you feel you should review your life insurance program with an agent?
48. 1 Much too high 2 High but justified by research costs 3 Not out of line with other medical expenses 4 Considering the benefits, price is reasonable Your comment: _____	**48.** How do you feel about the price of prescription drugs today?
49. 1 Almost always 3 Occasionally 2 Whenever possible 4 Never	**49.** When you purchase drugs prescribed by your physician, do you shop around for the best buy?
Now please answer these questions about you and your family.	
50. Ages:	**50.** Ages of children under 18:
51. ☐ Under 25 ☐ 25-34 ☐ 35-44 ☐ 45-54 ☐ 55-64 ☐ Over 65	**51.** Age of household head:
52. ☐ Man ☐ Woman	**52.** Household head is:
53. ☐ Grade school ☐ Some high school ☐ High school grad ☐ Some college ☐ College graduate ☐ Graduate work	**53.** Education of household head:
54. ☐ Full-time ☐ Part-time ☐ Not at all ☐ No wife in household	**54.** Is the wife employed outside the home?
55. ☐ Central city (50,000 or larger) ☐ Suburb of a large city ☐ Small city or town (less than 50,000) ☐ Rural	**55.** Where do you live?
56. ☐ Own ☐ Rent	**56.** Do you own or rent your home?
57. _____	**57.** What make(s), year(s) of car do you own?
58. ☐ Husband ☐ Wife ☐ Both ☐ Other member	**58.** Which member of the family filled out this questionnaire?
NAME... ADDRESS..................................... CITY...............STATE.......ZIP CODE.......	REMEMBER, if you have comments on any questions, please feel free to send them along on a separate sheet of paper. BETTER HOMES AND GARDENS, OCTOBER, 1967

Attitude Scales

There are many instruments designed to measure attitudes or related constructs. In marketing research, some of the more common are the semantic differential, the Guttman Scalogram, Likert summated scales, the Q-sort, and the Sherif method.

SEMANTIC DIFFERENTIAL. A semantic differential involves repeated measurements of a concept against a series of descriptive, polar-adjectival scales on a seven-point scale of equal-appearing intervals. For example, several products might be measured on a variety of characteristics in the manner portrayed in Figure 4-2. By scoring the responses of each respondent, we can construct a "profile" of the product. Thus a potential or present product can be evaluated against other products in a fairly simple and graphic manner that is useful to marketing executives in making decisions about the product.[3]

Figure 4-2   Profile from semantic differential.

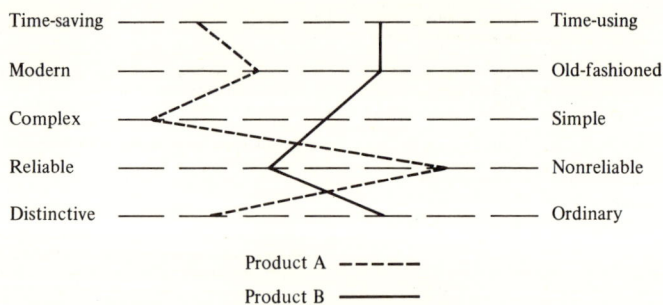

GUTTMAN SCALOGRAMS. The Guttman Scalogram measures both the content and intensity of an attitude. After a regular pattern of responses is observed, into which 90 percent of the individual answers fit, an attitude is said to exist toward the product and a Guttman scale can be constructed to analyze its nature.[4]

LIKERT SCALES. Likert summated scales contain items that are favorable or unfavorable to the product or concept being tested. Respondents indicate their agreement or disagreement with the statements and scores, either positive or negative. The scores are summated to obtain a numerical representation of the underlying attitude.[5]

[3] See William Mindak, "Fitting the Semantic Differential to the Marketing Problem," *Journal of Marketing*, Vol. 25 (April 1961), pp. 28–33. The basic reference work on the semantic differential is C. E. Osgood, G. J. Suci, and P. H. Tannebaum, *The Measurement of Meaning* (Urbana, Ill.: University of Illinois Press, 1957).

[4] L. Guttman, "Measuring the True State of Opinion," in Robert Ferber and Hugh Wales, eds., *Motivation and Market Behavior* (Homewood, Ill.: Richard D. Irwin, Inc., 1958), and Elizabeth A. Richards, "A Commercial Application of Guttman Attitude Scaling Techniques," *Journal of Marketing*, Vol. 22 (October 1967), pp. 166–173.

[5] R. A. Likert, "A Technique for the Measurement of Attitudes," *Archives of Psychology*, Vol. 140 (1932), p. 14.

Q-Sort. The Q-sort requires customers to specify the extent to which they agree or disagree with a series of statements arranged in such a way that extreme positions are weighted heaviest. The factor-analytic techniques used in analysis compare *individuals* rather than attitudinal statements. The method can provide some excellent insights into the underlying nature of a market situation but is costly to develop and administer.[6]

Sherif Scales. The Sherif method is useful in indicating the content and intensity of attitudes toward a brand. In comparing alternatives within the market, this method focuses upon those products that are within what the Sherifs call the *latitude of acceptance,* the *latitude of rejection,* and the *latitude of non-commitment.*[7]

Marketing researchers have tried to assess the relative merits of some attitude scales.[8] Kassarjian and Nakanishi conclude there is little intermethod variation in results:

The selection of a research method might best be determined by reasons other than concerns about intermethod differences, the method in fashion or acceptance by clients or colleagues. The numerous articles and discussions about a method's efficiency and about the acceptability of the research plan are illaudable when concerns about validity, accuracy, costs to the client, and psychological effects on the subject, interviewer, and researcher are more significant.[9]

Multidimensional Scales

Sometimes, in the assessment of market opportunity, executives need to assess the underlying factors that determine customers' preferences for products or brands. Multidimensional scaling or "mapping" is a method for delineating the dimensions or attributes underlying perceptions of products (or other objects).[10] A person's preference for products can be related to his perceptual judgments of similarity between products. When a person's preference data are combined with the dimensional configuration of products, viable market segments of the

---

[6] William Stephenson, "Public Images of Public Utilities," *Journal of Advertising Research,* Vol. 3 (Spring 1961), pp. 40–48, and Mary Jane Schlinger, "On Methods: Cues on Q-Technique," *Journal of Advertising Research,* Vol. 9 (September 1969), pp. 53–60.

[7] C. W. Sherif, M. Sherif, and R. E. Nebergall, *Attitude and Attitude Change* (Philadelphia: W. B. Saunders Company, 1965).

[8] G. David Hughes, "Selecting Scales to Measure Attitude Change," *Journal of Marketing Research,* Vol. 4 (February 1967), pp. 85–87.

[9] Harold H. Kassarjian and Masoa Nakanishi, "A Study of Selected Opinion Measurement Techniques," *Journal of Marketing Research,* Vol. 4 (May 1967), pp. 148–153.

[10] For an introductory treatment, see Lester A. Neidell, "The Use of Nonmetric Multidimensional Scaling in Marketing Analysis," *Journal of Marketing,* Vol. 33 (October 1969), pp. 37–43. Also, see Paul Green and Vithala R. Rao, "Nonmetric Approaches to Multivariate Analysis in Marketing," A Working Paper of the Marketing Science Institute, Cambridge, Mass. (April 1970). Also, see James R. Taylor, "Unfolding Theory Applied to Market Segmentation," *Journal of Advertising Research,* Vol. 9 (December 1969), pp. 36–46.

market are identified, and the possibility emerges of predicting how market shares might change if a new product were added to a market or there were a significant change in an existing product in the market configuration.

The methodology involved in multidimensional scaling has been improving rapidly and is described in more detail in later chapters of this book.

Physiological Measures

It is sometimes desirable to measure customer responses in a nonverbal manner. A reason for doing this is to measure response objectively. Biases in verbal responses may be caused by the respondent's trying to "outguess" or mislead the researcher. Another reason for physiological measures is the need to measure small changes in dependent variables that may be important in the communication process but too small to affect verbal responses.

Understanding of physiological measures is still embryonic, but the most important of them appear to be pupil dilation response (PDR), galvanic skin response (GSR), and various mechanical-interest measures such as CONPAAD. PDR appears to be a measure of information processing occurring in the minds of customers as they evaluate a product or communication stimulus.[11] GSR measures the arousal qualities of a product[12] and CONPAAD (which stands for conjugately programmed analyses of advertising) is a measure of interest in communications material.[13] All of these measures—and other related ones—are specialized in nature and are usually used in connection with other measures of market opportunity and response.[14]

SAMPLING DECISIONS

In analyzing market opportunity, decisions must be made whether to measure *all* members of a market or only a *portion* of the market. The former instance is a *census*. The latter instance requires decisions about how a representative portion of the market—a *sample*—is to be selected.

A census of the market is justifiable principally in two circumstances. First, a census is feasible where the total number of customers in the market is small. Many industrial markets follow this pattern. Second, a census may be possible

---

[11] Roger D. Blackwell, James S. Hensel, and Brian Stenthal, "What Does Pupil Dilation Measure?" *Journal of Advertising Research*, Vol. 10 (August 1970), pp. 15–18. Also, see Roger Blackwell, James Hensel, Michael Phillips, and Brian Sternthal, *Laboratory Equipment for Marketing Research* (Dubuque, Iowa: Kendall-Hunt Publishing Co., 1970).

[12] L. J. Kleinsmith and S. Kaplan, "Paired-associate Learning as a Function of Arousal and Interpolated Activity," *Journal of Experimental Psychology*, Vol. 65 (1963), pp. 190–193.

[13] Abraham Wolf, Dianne Z. Newman, and Lewis C. Winters, "Operant Measures of Interest as Related to *Ad Lib* Readership," *Journal of Advertising Research*, Vol. 9 (June 1969), pp. 40–45.

[14] See James S. Hensel and David T. Kollat, "Present and Projected Uses of Physiological Measures," a paper presented at the American Marketing Association Educators Conference, Boston, August 31, 1970.

where original data do not have to be gathered. Government statistics or data gathered by trade associations of sufficient quality may exist, so that sampling is not necessary. In many instances, however, measuring market opportunity requires either generating original data with a sampling process or evaluating data previously collected through sampling.

The purpose of sampling is to make inferences about the parameters of the market without measuring all members of the market. Sampling is successful when it reliably predicts the parameters of the entire group by measuring a subgroup. Since the parameters are unknown, the executive is constantly in a position of deciding whether or not to consider the information contained in the sample a reliable estimate of the entire market.

Sampling Process

The process of describing the total market based upon sample data is shown in Figure 4-3. This diagram shows the sampling process to be one of logical, systematic steps. The process depends upon careful definition of the market to be analyzed, careful collection of data through scientific procedures, and the application of statistical methodology to make the sample data useful in describing the universe or total market opportunity. Executives must be especially wary of using sample data as descriptions of the total market without application of appropriate statistical inference procedures.

Figure 4-3   Sampling process.

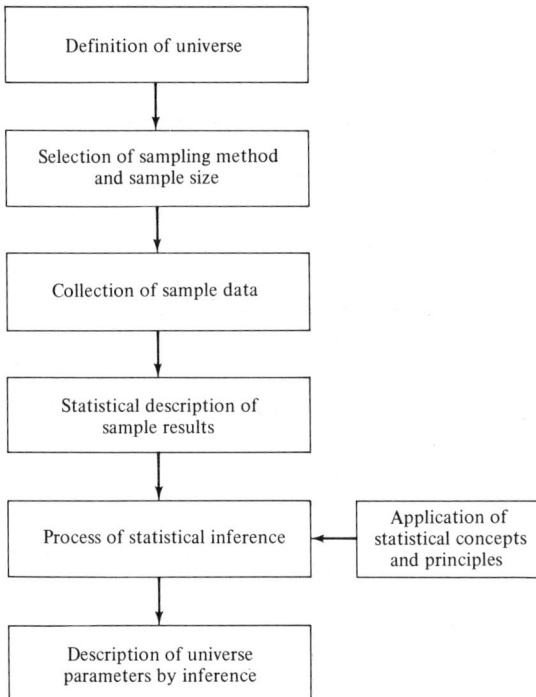

Probability or Nonprobability Samples

Executives must decide whether to rely upon probability or nonprobability samples. This, one of the most important decisions to be made about sampling, often leaves executives confused.

The process of statistical inference assumes that a sample has been selected on a probability or random basis. It is assumed that all elements of the universe have an equal or at least a known probability of being selected. The selection process must be carried out under rules that insure those probabilities.

Executives may believe that probability samples are always better than nonprobability samples. That is a false assumption. In any given study, a non-probability sample may be more representative than a probability sample. In actual practice, qualified researchers may consistently yield more representative samples at lower cost with nonprobability samples than with probability samples.

In view of these observations, the executive may wonder why there is so much emphasis upon probability samples. One reason is that probability sampling is taught extensively in most statistics courses because of the need to make clear the complexities of statistical inference.

The major problem in relying upon nonprobability samples is that the quality inherent in them is determined mostly by the *judgment* of the researcher conducting the sample. With probability sampling, quality is determined by statistical laws, especially the central limit theorem, and an executive has a known chance of being right or wrong in concluding that a sample represents the universe. With nonprobability methods, he is forced to rely on the judgment of his research staff or his own judgment to determine whether the sample accurately represents the market.

It is clear that the selection of probability or nonprobability samples should not be automatic. The decision should be based upon the amount of money that can be spent. (Nonprobability samples are frequently more reliable than probability when small samples are involved.) The decision should also be based upon the experience or ability of the individuals involved in obtaining and using data and upon the specific situation in which data are to be collected.

There are many forms of probability sampling, as shown in Figure 4-4. These are standard categories, but some are quite sophisticated.[15] Although executives normally depend upon professional researchers to design and conduct the plan, the executives should be familiar with each basic type. Decisions about

---

[15] Most marketing research texts describe the sampling plans discussed here. See especially Robert Ferber, *Market Research* (New York: McGraw-Hill, Inc., 1948). For more intensive discussions see William G. Cochran, *Sampling Techniques* (New York: John Wiley & Sons, Inc., 1963), or Leslie Kish, *Survey Sampling* (New York: John Wiley & Sons, Inc., 1965).

Figure 4-4   Classification of sampling techniques.

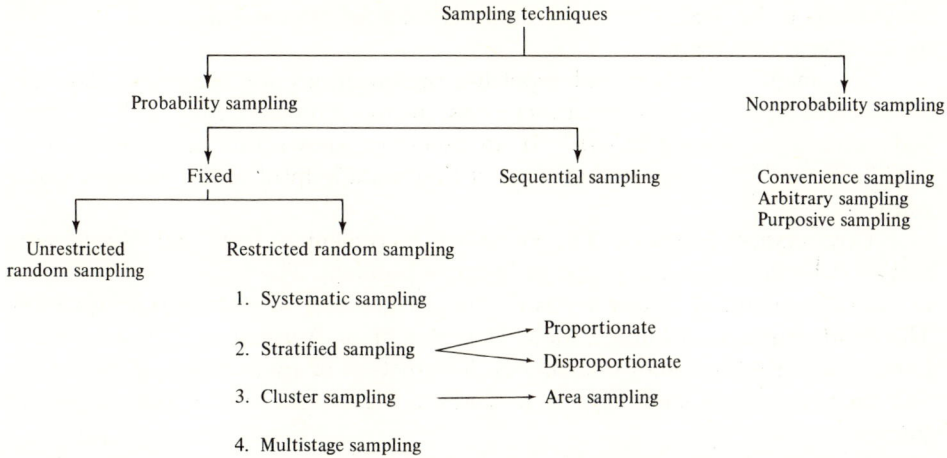

For description of these techniques, see Robert Ferber, *Market Research* (New York: McGraw-Hill, Inc., 1948).

type of sampling plan should be made jointly to yield the information needed by management with adequate reliability and precision at the lowest cost to the marketing organization.

DETERMINING SOURCES OF DATA

It is usually possible to obtain data helpful in making marketing decisions of any sort. The problem is *where* and *how much it will cost* to obtain the data. Executives should not be satisfied with reports from researchers that the data are not obtainable. Perhaps the cost of obtaining the data exceeds their value, but it is rare that data are truly unobtainable.

The pages that follow describe major sources of data. The purpose of the discussion is to provide marketing decision makers with understanding about the wide scope of data sources that exist and to examine some of the characteristics that might indicate preference for one source over another. The major sources of data identified below are (1) secondary sources, (2) internal records, (3) surveys, (4) observations, and (5) experiments.

Secondary Data Sources

The first place to begin in obtaining data is usually the library. Most large firms maintain a corporate library. University and public libraries are readily available in most urban centers. Great amounts of time and money can be saved by consulting secondary data sources before others. Previous studies indicate past successes and mistakes and are invaluable in the design of new studies. Frequently, past studies do not report the precise data desired by management.

Even though differences exist between the desired data and those available, the *conclusions* to be drawn from the data may not be altered sufficiently to justify the costs of a new study.

The major collection and reporting organizations for secondary data are government agencies, industry associations, media, commercial research agencies, and universities, among others.[16] If an executive knows the activities of these organizations, he is likely to find some of their data helpful in the problem under study.[17]

GOVERNMENT SOURCES. The Federal Government collects and disseminates market data on nearly every type of business problem. The Bureau of the Census in the Department of Commerce is the largest gatherer of statistical information. The Small Business Administration, Department of Agriculture, Department of Labor, and other agencies disseminate information of great value—*if* executives and their assistants know where to find it. Figure 4-5 lists a few important sources.[18]

INDUSTRY ASSOCIATIONS. Most industries and professions have a trade or professional association. Many of them collect useful data to be made available to the public or their members.[19] Executives must evaluate such data carefully, because they may be gathered from fragmentary (and biased) sources and may be gathered to "prove" some position held by the industry. In many instances, however, association data are comprehensive and reliable.

There is a trend in the direction of improved reporting by association members. In some industries this is taking the form of computerized data processing for individual firms, information retrieval systems being available for member firms that use both the industry's collective data and the firm's specific data. This type of information is invaluable in improving marketing strategy and decision making. The computers required for economical processing are often so large and the level of sophistication so high that members find the most efficient approach to be on a cooperative industrywide basis.

MEDIA SOURCES. Most large newspapers, magazines, broadcast stations, and

---

[16] A useful (and free) bibliography of readily available secondary data is the Small Business Administration's *Basic Library Reference Sources for Business Use* (Washington, D.C.: U. S. Government Printing Office), 1966. It is available at field offices of the Small Business Administration.

[17] One of the best reviews of secondary data sources is in Stewart Henderson Britt and Irwin A. Shapiro, "Where to Find Marketing Facts," *Harvard Business Review*, Vol. 40 (September–October 1962), pp. 44–50 and 171–178. Also see Dan Gaby, "How to Get Free Market Research," *Industrial Marketing*, May 1962, pp. 100–102, and "Market Research for the Asking from the Government," *Business Management*, May 1963, pp. 39–41 ff.

[18] For a more detailed description, see Erwin Esser Nemmers and John H. Myers, *Business Research* (New York: McGraw-Hill, Inc., 1966), pp. 1–14.

[19] The names, addresses, and other data of over 35,000 associations are published annually in *Directory of National Trade and Professional Associations of the United States* (Washington, D.C.: Potomac Books, Inc.). Also see *Encyclopedia of American Associations* (Detroit: Gale Research Company).

Figure 4-5   Important sources of government data for market analysis.

Census of Population (detailed information on sex, marital status, education, racial characteristics, occupation, and other demographic characteristics)

Current Population Reports (annual update of demographic characteristics)

Census of Manufacturers (output by SIC category of products by industry, number of firms, plant locations, and size of firm)

Census of Business (detailed information on retail, wholesale, and service trades classified by number of establishments, employment, receipts, geographic location, and other characteristics)

Census of Housing (structural and financial aspects for all political subdivisions)

Census of Agriculture (number of farms, types, acreage, land-use practices, value of products, employment, etc.)

Census of Mineral Industries

Census of Governments (annual Municipal Yearbook gives current data on population, areas, and finance)

Census of Transportation (commodity shipments, passenger travel, truck and bus inventory)

Statistical Abstract of the United States (more than 1,000 tables of economic, social, demographic, financial and other data)

Handbook of Economic Statistics

Economic Report of the President (very current data of various kinds)

Federal Reserve Bulletin (data on department stores, banking and monetary issues, industrial production, etc.)

Survey of Current Business (basic source for economic forecasting problems)

Monthly Labor Review, Economic Indicators, Business Cycle Developments, Construction Review, Quarterly Summary of Foreign Commerce, Statistics of Income, etc.

similar firms produce occasional or periodic studies on market opportunities. Sometimes these are invaluable basic studies, such as *Life* magazine's studies of consumer markets. Other studies are on specialized geographic areas (such as Los Angeles) or specialized markets, such as bridal markets, farm chemical markets, specialized steel markets, and many others. Radio stations with segmented audiences have prepared studies on the youth market, Black markets, and Spanish-speaking markets. Large advertising agencies also produce studies on specialized market opportunities.

Executives must be careful when relying on media data sources. Media consider such studies as selling tools, showing that the medium reaches important or growing markets. The data in media studies are ordinarily factual, but data that are not supportive of that particular firm or medium may be omitted. Also, executives should ask their own researchers to be especially alert for aspects of the research methodology that might result in built-in biases or misleading information.

COMMERCIAL RESEARCH AGENCIES. Many commercial agencies collect and disseminate market data on a regular basis. It is often far less expensive, and yields better data, to use a standardized data source than to collect new data. *Business Periodicals Index* and *Wall Street Journal Index* are the starting points to find published information. *Dun and Bradstreet* and *Moody's Manuals* are invaluable for industrial marketing research. Sales Management's *Annual Survey of Buying Power* is one of the most used sources of market data for all types of firms. There are many, many others.

UNIVERSITY AND OTHER RESEARCH SOURCES.   In-depth studies of market opportunities are published by university research bureaus and individual researchers.[20] Professional journals such as the *Journal of Marketing, Journal of Marketing Research*, and *Journal of Advertising Research* also carry some useful research reports.

The creative researcher will find many other sources of data in a variety of forms. For example, First National City Bank of New York issues a Monthly Economic Letter, and the April issue each year carries a report on the 3,800 largest publicly owned corporations, sales by industrial groups, and other valuable information on market opportunities and competitive positions.

All the foregoing discussion of sources suggests the following conclusion. Relevant data probably exist; it is merely a question of finding them. An aggressive and creative person working with a good library and industry sources can save a firm a great deal of time and money in obtaining helpful data.

Internal Sources

An underutilized source of market information often is a firm's internal records. Internal records may be used by themselves to indicate market opportunity, or they may be combined with other sources.

SALES RECORDS.   Past sales and other performance records of most firms are valuable sources of information in forecasting future markets and markets for related products. The first step in forecasting sales of related products is to establish an associative relationship between new products and the sales of existing products. If such a correlation exists, the firm's own sales records of existing products provide an excellent base for predicting success of the new product, since existing records reflect the firm's own marketing strengths and weaknesses.

Another use of internal records is for analysis in establishing territorial assignments and forecasting sales estimates. Sales records may not accurately describe the total market, but they reflect variations in the individual firm's ability to capture the total market. Internal records can also be used to predict the rate of acceptance of new products. Many firms assess market growth of new products on the basis of external and inadequate information. By examining the sales growth curves of similar products in the past, they might improve market forecasting substantially.

[20] See Associated University Bureaus of Business and Economic Research, *Index of Publications of Bureaus of Business and Economic Research,* 1950–1964, and Supplements (Eugene, Ore.: University of Oregon.)

GRASS-ROOTS RESEARCH. Most firms require a salesman to submit call and sales reports. These reports contain valuable information. When properly analyzed, they help locate market trends and opportunities. Salesmen may also be asked for additional inputs to the market data base. These can be used by the centralized marketing research staff and by decentralized managerial centers with immediate information needs.[21]

An extensive grass-roots system used by General Electric is described below:

Once we pulled together a complete picture of a competitor's distribution from reports turned in by 120 salesmen even up to and including its warehousing in the most strategic locations. It put us in a better position to plan and implement our own distribution needs. We have a planned program of sending questionnaires to our salesmen requesting information for a competitive analysis and we get a great deal of valuable information from them.

We get research into how our competitors are marketing their products, how many salesmen they have, and how their products compare as to service, function, and quality.[22]

Survey Data

Surveys are one of the most common sources of data for marketing decisions. They are frequently called *cross-sectional* studies, because often they are used to describe characteristics of a cross section of the market instead of the entire market. Executives should be reluctant to authorize a survey, unless it can clearly be shown that the data cannot be collected with less expensive and (often) more reliable methods.

There are three primary methods of collecting survey data: mail interviews, telephone interviews, and personal interviews. Two principal variations, the group interview and the panel, are also discussed below.

MAIL SURVEYS. Mail surveys are commonly used where a large number of respondents must be contacted. They are most useful where respondents have a good reason to return the questionnaires. They are also useful in situations where respondents must look up information in order to report it, as often they must in industrial marketing research. Compared to alternatives, mail surveys may be the only viable data source where visual material is required.[23]

There are many disadvantages to mail surveys. Foremost of these is the *nonresponse bias*. The proportion of people responding to mail surveys is often around 40 percent, although it frequently varies from 5 percent to as high as 95

[21] A thorough discussion of how to implement this type of system is contained in Louis W. Stern and J. L. Heskett, "Grass Roots Market Research," *Harvard Business Review*, March–April, 1965, pp. 83–96.

[22] Phillip Gustafson, "Let Salesmen Help You Plan," *Nation's Business*, July 1961, p. 62.

[23] For a comprehensive review of mail survey methodology see Charles Scott, "Research on Mail Surveys," *Journal of the Royal Statistical Society*, Ser. A, Vol. 124 (1961), pp. 143–205.

percent. Some users of survey data might conclude that the response rate is no problem, since the relatively low cost per questionnaire still allows a large sample to be collected. That is true *only if those who fail to return survey forms are not systematically different from those who return them.* In actual practice, people who return mail surveys are often not representative of the rest of the population.

Another disadvantage of mail interviews is that the *cost per completed interview* may approach or surpass the cost of interviews by telephone. Other disadvantages include limitations on sequencing of questions, lack of control over who completes the form, exclusion of illiterates, time required to obtain returned questionnaires (often three to four weeks or more), difficulty in obtaining responses suitable for optical scanning, and difficulty in obtaining answers to open-ended questions of more than a few simple words.

TELEPHONE INTERVIEWS. Telephone interviewing has become a primary way of obtaining data. Two reasons explain the recent increase in use of telephone surveys. First, a high proportion of U.S. consumers (and nearly all industrial buyers) have telephones. Second, telephone interviewing methodology has been vastly improved in recent years. Today, telephone interviewing is a flexible and reliable data source. It is also fast.

Telephone data may be less biased than mail or personal interviews. Some low-income people do not have telephones, but with mail interviews those people are often omitted because of mail theft and high resident turnover. With personal interviews it may be impossible to reach low-income persons in an unbiased way, especially in the evening hours. In addition, telephone interviewing has the very great advantage that several callbacks are possible at relatively low cost in a variety of time periods. This is also significant in reducing bias in obtaining data from high-income (and busy) families, factory shift workers, and working women.

Telephone interviews can collect data on nearly any subject, even those that are delicate or socially sensitive. Interviews can last a few minutes or much longer. There is evidence to indicate that unless visual materials or complex questions are essential, telephone interviews yield essentially the same results as personal interviews and at much lower costs.[24] For many reasons, telephone interviewing is becoming the standard mode of survey data collection.

PERSONAL INTERVIEWS. Personal interviews include a wide variety of face-to-face ways of collecting data from customers or potential customers. Personal interviews are most justifiable where complex data-collection instruments (such as attitude scales) are necessary, with projective techniques (and other visual materials), and where strict probability sampling is not required.

Executives sometimes ask whether consumers are alienated by surveys.

---

[24] A succinct review of studies of telephone interviewing is contained in Robert Ferber, Donald F. Blankertz, and Sidney Hollander, Jr., *Marketing Research* (New York: The Ronald Press Company, 1964), pp. 242–245.

Questionable practices do exist; sales organizations may deceive consumers, using the guise of marketing research to gain entry to make a sales presentation. In spite of an initial suspicion of surveys, most people do cooperate. After they are convinced of the authenticity of the survey as research, they usually enjoy being asked their opinions about products and marketing practices. One study found that 88 percent of consumers thought legitimate market surveys were useful activities and only 5 to 7 percent favored any legal restrictions on them.[25]

Personal interviews may yield biased results. One study revealed a completion rate of only one-third for the first call of personal interviews, with a range of 20 percent in large metropolitan areas and 42 percent in rural areas. Callbacks are necessary to raise the completion rate.[26] Furthermore, nonresponses vary systematically by categories. The most difficult to reach are high- and low-income families, males, and working wives.[27] The rising crime rates of most cities are practically eliminating evening interviews, since most interviewers are women.

The managers who expect to rely upon survey data should know enough about the quality of the data source to have confidence in the results. One study found that about one-third of the interviewers deviated frequently and markedly from their instructions.[28] Many other sources of bias are introduced by interviewers who cheat, lead respondents into misleading statements, and are not careful about procedures.[29]

The quality of data provided by interviewing firms varies so widely that a manager probably can justify a personal interview with key executives of the interviewing firm in order to satisfy himself about the firm's quality. Outstanding firms select interviewers carefully, train them thoroughly, and maintain systematic controls and supervision.[30] Many interviewing firms do not provide good data, however, and executives need to know just how much to trust the data.[31] If the

[25] Irving L. Allen and J. David Colfax, "Respondents' Attitudes Toward Legitimate Surveys in Four Cities," *Journal of Marketing Research*, Vol. 2 (November 1968), pp. 431–433.

[26] Charles S. Mayer, "The Interviewer and His Environment," *Journal of Marketing Research*, Vol. 1 (November 1964), pp. 24–31.

[27] For a thorough discussion of these and many related issues see Mildred B. Parten, *Surveys, Polls and Samples* (New York: Harper & Row, Publishers, 1950).

[28] William A. Belson, "Increasing the Power of Research to Guide Advertising Decisions," *Journal of Marketing*, Vol. 29 (April 1965), pp. 35–42. Also, see Bo W:son Schryberger, "A Study of Interviewer Behavior," *Journal of Marketing Research*, Vol. 4 (February 1967), pp. 32–35.

[29] See the classic article by Harper W. Boyd, Jr., and Ralph Westfall, "Interviewers as a Source of Errors in Surveys," *Journal of Marketing*, Vol. 19 (April 1955), pp. 311–324, and the same authors' follow-up review, "Interviewer Bias Once More Revisited," *Journal of Marketing Research*, Vol. 7 (May 1970), pp. 249–253.

[30] For an example see Charles S. Mayer, "A Computer System for Controlling Interviewer Costs," *Journal of Marketing Research*, Vol. 5 (August 1968), pp. 312–318.

[31] A useful checklist for evaluating research suppliers is found in Charles S. Mayer, "Evaluating the Quality of Marketing Research Contractors," *Journal of Marketing Research*, Vol. 4 (May 1967), pp. 134–141.

input is poor, no amount of sophistication in analysis is likely to produce the kind of information needed by management to act confidently on the research results.

GROUP INTERVIEWS. A specialized form of personal interviewing is the group interview or "focused group interview." An interview with a group of five to nine people focused on the topic under investigation is frequently more useful than the same number of individual interviews. The advantages stem from group synergisms, snowballing effects of ideas, interpersonal stimulation of thinking, willingness of respondents to speak more freely in a group than with a single interviewer, and spontaneity of solutions to problems.[32] Disadvantages of group interviews include difficulty in interpretation, the necessity of a highly skilled discussion leader, social inhibitions that may exist in a group, and the problems of transcribing and reporting group data.[33]

Group interviews are frequently among the most useful, rapid, and inexpensive sources of data, especially in the early stages of new-product development or the formulation of marketing strategy.

PANEL DATA. Panel data can be collected with any of the survey methods described earlier or a combination of several. Panels are ongoing groups of persons who periodically report purchasing behavior, attitudes, information sources, or any other variable of relevance to marketing strategies. Some panels merely report their normal activities. Others are asked to do something special, such as try a new product and report their reactions.

Panels have come into greater use in recent years because they offer some distinct advantages. At the same time, some peculiar problems exist in the interpretation of panel data. Some of the most important uses of panels are the following:

1. To determine *trends* in behavior.
2. To study underlying *causes* in opinion or behavior shifts over a period of time.
3. To obtain *involvement in the problem* by respondents to such an extent that they will take a special interest in the problems of the investigator.
4. To collect voluminous quantities of information that ordinarily could not be obtained in a single questionnaire.
5. To study fundamental *processes* rather than estimating the total proportion of the population possessing some characteristics.

The last-mentioned use of panels particularly intrigues researchers who hope to develop dynamic mathematical models to explain market behavior longitudinally.

---

[32] John M. Hess, "Group Interviewing," in Robert L. King, *Marketing and the New Science of Planning* (Chicago: American Marketing Association, 1968), pp. 193–196.

[33] A description of how to overcome these difficulties is contained in Alfred E. Goldman, "The Group Depth Interview," *Journal of Marketing*, Vol. 26 (July 1962), pp. 61–68.

The most significant problems of panels are noncooperation bias and aging effects.[34] These problems are analyzed by Green and Tull:

There is evidence to indicate that the characteristics of both those families who refuse to participate and those who later drop from the panel are different from those who agree to participate and remain. In the MRCA panel, it was found that a significantly higher percentage of nonurban households agreed to participate than did urban households. In another consumer panel, it was found that a larger proportion of nonusers than users of the products about which purchase data were being reported dropped out after the first interview.

An additional source of bias may arise from continued participation in the panel. Since the individual is undoubtedly conditioned to some extent by the fact that data on purchases are reported, panel members may become atypical in their purchase behavior as a result of being a part of the panel.[35]

SELECTING SURVEY METHODS. No single survey method of collecting data is appropriate for all situations. The interface between decision-making personnel and research personnel must be adequate to develop the appropriate arsenal in terms of reliability, timing, and cost efficiency. It is theoretically possible to complete most survey research with any of the alternative survey methods; the task of efficient management is to select the most efficient among these alternatives.

Data from Observations

There is growing interest in research methods that obtain data from direct observation of market behavior rather than relying upon buyers' retrospective reports of their behavior. In some instances panel data are similar to direct observation, in that consumers are required to record in a diary their purchases during the day or for the past week. Other forms of observation data include inventories and audits and direct observations of consumers.

AUDITS AND INVENTORIES. Assessment of market opportunity is frequently accomplished by measuring the size and trends in sales of related products or the product in question. Many commercial services provide detailed data concerning the shipments of consumer and industrial product lines, changes in retail inventories of products and brands, and sales changes by type of distributor or retail outlet. For example, in the drug industry it is possible to purchase very accurate and detailed breakdowns of sales of prescription drugs by generic name. A firm, through proper interpretation of the data, can assess the growth or decline of markets for specific drugs. By combining market data with internally generated sales

[34] For discussion of these problems see the following sources: Marion G. Solbol, "Panel Mortality and Panel Bias," *Journal of the American Statistical Association*, Vol. 54 (March 1959), pp. 52–68; J. D. Schaffer and G. C. Quackenbush, "Cooperation and Sampling in Four Years of M.S.U. Consumer Panel Operation," *Quarterly Bulletin*, Michigan Agricultural Experimental Section, Michigan State University, Vol. 38 (August 1955).

[35] Paul S. Green and Donald S. Tull, *Research for Marketing Decisions* (Englewood Cliffs, N.J.: Prentice-Hall, Inc., 1966), pp. 157–158.

data, the firm can assess its performance relative to competing products or brands. The growth in computerized information systems facilitates use of audit and inventory movement data.

DIRECT OBSERVATION. There are many ways to collect data by direct observation of consumer buying activities. The most common procedure is to station an investigator near a shelf containing the product being analyzed to record actions of buyers. Investigators record what people actually do, as distinguished from what people say. This may overcome problems of faulty memory, desires to impress the interviewer, or simple inattention to details of the shopping procedure. Direct observation can provide answers to questions such as these:

Who actually buys the product, and who influences the choice? To what extent are brand choices made before the shopper enters the store, and to what extent are they made at the point of purchase? How many people check the price? Do shoppers study the package before purchase?[36]

There are many ways of recording the observations, such as photographs, secluded microphones, cameras that measure eye movements, electric-eye counters, and so on.[37]

UNOBTRUSIVE MEASURES. Useful forms of direct observation include those that do not "intrude" into the consumer's behavior. Even when the investigator does not interact with the consumer, his presence and conspicuous recording of behavior on prepared schedules, and perhaps the presence of other technical aids, may change the behavior being observed.[38] The solution is to use unobtrusive measures to collect data.[39] These measures may range from the unique and imaginative (hiring garbage collectors to count liquor bottles in the refuse of various market segments—presumably to get an honest picture of actual consumption) to the mundane (counting the traffic that passes by a prospective retail outlet). Frequently, observational techniques can be combined with other forms of data collection to provide a richer understanding of buyer behavior.[40]

[36] William D. Wells and Leonard A. LoScinto, "Direct Observation of Purchasing Behavior," *Journal of Marketing Research*, Vol. 3 (August 1966), pp. 227–233.

[37] For a description of some of the equipment that can be used for observing behavior see Roger D. Blackwell, James S. Hensel, Michael Phillips, and Brian Sternthal, *Laboratory Equipment for Marketing Research* (Dubuque, Iowa: Kendall-Hunt Publishing Co., 1970).

[38] Claire Selltiz, Marie Jahoda, Morton Deutsch, and Stuart W. Cook, *Research Methods in Social Relations* (New York: Holt, Rinehart and Winston, Inc., 1961), p. 233. For an excellent discussion of observation techniques see pp. 200–234.

[39] The primary source for information on this method is Eugene J. Webb, Donald T. Campbell, Richard D. Schwartz, and Lee Sechrest, *Unobtrusive Measures* (Skokie, Ill.: Rand McNally & Company, 1966).

[40] Michael L. Ray, "Neglected Problems (Opportunities) in Research: The Development of Multiple and Unobtrusive Measurement," in Robert L. King, *Marketing and the New Science of Planning* (Chicago: American Marketing Association, 1968), pp. 176–183.

Data from Experiments

The most rigorous way of assessing market opportunity is through experiments that attempt to determine the effect of one variable (such as a new product, new taste, advertising) on another variable (such as sales, attitudes, dealer inventory reaction).[41]

PURPOSE OF EXPERIMENTS. Experiments are designed to produce an investigation in which the *causal variables are controlled* or measured so closely that the *effects can be attributed* to one or a group of causal variables. In the biological and physical sciences, it is (almost) possible to prepare two groups of variables in identical ways with the exception of the single isolated variable under study. If perfection is reached in this process, the only possible difference between the two groups is the independent or causal variable under study. Thus, all differences in effects must be attributed to the causal variable.

In behavioral sciences, it is not possible to control adequately all differences between two groups. For example, if the effect of a change in the marketing program is being investigated, it is impossible to select two groups of customers with characteristics that are identical (in every way). The alternative is to make sure that before the application of the experimental variable the two groups differ in only one way: by randomization or chance. Analysis of covariance is also used where test units differ. In a true experimental design, some customers are assigned by a random process to the group receiving the existing marketing program (control group) and other customers from the same universe are assigned by a random process to a group receiving the new marketing program. Thus, only two plausible hypotheses exist (in the perfect experiment) to account for any observed differences between the groups after the experiment. The first hypothesis is that the differences are due to effects of random (chance) variation in the assignment of customers to each group. That hypothesis can be investigated with statistical tests of significance; if the probability of occurrence of such differences by chance is less than the level executives have specified as acceptable for decision making, the second hypothesis is accepted: namely, that the observed differences between the two groups are attributable to the independent variable—the aspect of the marketing program being tested.

VALIDITY OF EXPERIMENTAL DATA. In the perfect experiment, the only hypotheses possible are that (1) the observed differences are due to chance variation or (2) they are due to the causal variable under investigation. Unfor-

---

[41] Two useful introductions to marketing experimentation are Seymour Banks, *Experimentation in Marketing* (New York: McGraw-Hill, Inc., 1965), and Keith K. Cox and Ben M. Enis, *Experimentation for Marketing Decisions* (Scranton, Pa.: International Textbook Company, 1969). For a more intensive discussion see D. R. Cox, *Planning of Experiments* (New York: John Wiley & Sons, Inc., 1958), or Allen L. Edwards, *Experimental Designs in Psychological Research* (New York: Holt, Rinehart and Winston, Inc., 1965).

tunately, marketing studies rarely meet this high standard. Other explanations of the observed differences between groups may rival the main hypotheses. These additional hypotheses are *rival plausible hypotheses.*

In determining whether the conclusions from an experiment are valid or not, an executive seeks to *rule out all rival plausible hypotheses.* Two basic types of hypotheses rival the causal and chance hypotheses: hypotheses about internal validity and hypotheses about external validity.

Internal validity refers to the condition in an experiment where no other hypothesis (except chance) is tenable except that the specific treatment in which the researcher was interested brought about the effects indicated by the measuring instruments. *External validity* refers to the condition in an experiment where the results in the experimental setting can be projected to the external world. This is called *generalizability* of results.

In evaluating an experiment to determine whether or not to rely upon the results, it would be difficult for an executive to think of every possible plausible hypothesis rivaling the main hypothesis. Fortunately, excellent checklists are available for use in this evaluation.[42] It will be impossible to achieve control for each rival plausible hypothesis, but an executive should satisfy himself that it is *unlikely that the uncontrolled rival hypotheses produced much of the reported results.*

SUMMARY AND CONCLUSIONS

There are many ways to obtain market data. This chapter described the more common and the more useful approaches for marketing executives. The approach has been to describe the nature of each method and some of the characteristics that might lead to a decision to choose one method over another.

Data-collection instruments may be of several types. Questionnaires are probably the most common. Attitude scales of many types are increasingly used. The use of multidimensional scaling and physiological measures is also increasing.

Executives decide whether or not to measure all members of the market (census) or to measure part of them (a sample). Since sampling is the most common, the chapter describes criteria for choosing between *probability samples or nonprobability samples.*

This chapter also describes basic characteristics and analyzes methods of determining where to obtain data. The major sources of data are secondary sources, internal sources, surveys, observational sources, and experiments. Criteria for choosing one instead of the other are analyzed under each category.

[42] Donald T. Campbell and Julian C. Stanley, *Experimental and Quasi-Experimental Designs for Research* (Skokie, Ill.: Rand McNally & Company, 1963).

QUESTIONS FOR REVIEW AND DISCUSSION

1. Analyze the questionnaire reprinted as Figure 4-1. What strengths or weaknesses are contained in it?
2. Select one of the attitude scales described in this chapter and prepare a report on current applications for this scale in marketing research.
3. Since the use of physiological measures is complex and the knowledge about them embryonic, many firms might be reluctant to use them. Develop a rationale that a major firm might apply in deciding to use physiological measures of market opportunity.
4. Why is probability sampling rather than nonprobability sampling emphasized in marketing research? Which do you believe is justified most often in the practice of marketing research?
5. Assume that you wish to obtain market data on the casket manufacturing industry. Where would you obtain data on this market? Be specific as to names of organizations, sources of data, and so on.
6. Describe how the *Business Periodicals Index* and *Wall Street Journal Index* might be helpful in a marketing research project.
7. What is "grass-roots research"?
8. Executives of a large automobile marketing organization wish to collect data about car ownership, income of owners, major appliances owned by car owners, number (and ages) of children in family, and a few other similar topics. How should these data be collected?
9. What is the purpose of marketing experiments? Why would a firm obtain data through experiments rather than less expensive methods?
10. What is meant by internal and external validity of marketing experiments? Do these concepts have relevance to the evaluation of other data sources or methods of analysis?

| Chapter 5 | Consumer Behavior: Cultural, Social, and Demographic Dimensions |

Many companies have risen to the top of American industry partly because they made a shrewd appraisal of changes that were occurring in consumer markets. Currently the great consumer market opportunities of tomorrow are taking shape. But what are they? How can they be recognized and understood?

One effective way to isolate future market opportunities is to analyze structural and behavioral dimensions of consumer markets. The present chapter discusses cultural, social, and demographic aspects of consumer markets, while the next chapter analyzes consumer decision processes.

CULTURAL DIMENSIONS OF CONSUMER MARKETS

Culture refers to the complex of values, ideas, attitudes, and symbols created by man to shape human behavior. Consumers can accept completely, accept partially, or reject these cultural norms. Cultural norms are important to marketing strategists because they are accepted by large numbers of people who constitute profitable market segments, and because variations in cultural norm acceptance are often a useful way to segment markets. Changes occurring in the basic values of many American consumers are discussed below.

Institutional Reliance

Traditionally most Americans believed that they controlled their own destiny, or at least they should. "Work hard," "make financial provisions for sickness, disasters, retirement, and death"—these are the traditional values. While many consumers feel this way, their behavior indicates that they are relying, to an increasing extent, on outside institutions—particularly government—to deal with these problems.

This trend has several important implications for marketing strategists. Consumers are becoming more concerned over the safety and purity of products and whether they are being marketed "fairly," "equitably," and in the consumer's best interests. Consequently, accelerated and more widespread government involvement in these issues is expected in the future.[1] Moreover, increasing numbers of consumers expect government to provide or insure the availability of a much wider range of products and services. Many segments of society, particularly the underprivileged and the Black community, feel they have a "right" to a reasonable standard of living and expect government and business to provide it.

In the longer run, government reliance may change the basic orientation toward consumption. As consumers rely more on government and other institutions for the basic needs of life, other, higher-order needs may become more prepotent. Pleasure, fashion, culture, and the other accoutrements of "gracious living" may gain importance.

Instant Standards of Living

While many may have wished otherwise, throughout the history of the United States there has been almost universal acceptance of the fact that it takes a considerable period of time to acquire the "standard package" of goods and services owned by most families. "Most families save for a long time to buy a home" and "most people buy only a few pieces of furniture at a time" are illustrative manifestations of this conventional value.

As consumers become increasingly affluent, they want to satisfy their desires now, not in the future.[2] While postponed gratification is still inevitable in many cases, increasing numbers of consumers are unwilling to forego present consumption for future consumption. In short, they want an instant standard of living, at least as good as their parents', although, of course, often qualitatively different.

Increasingly consumers are purchasing from firms that offer a complete package of goods and services rather than those who force them to assemble the package over a period of years. They want to buy a complete houseful of furniture; a complete, color-coordinated kitchen; and complete home improvement services, including the credit that is required to finance them.

---

[1] For illustrative developments and points of view see E. B. Weiss, "Marketers Fiddle While Consumers Burn," *Harvard Business Review*, Vol. 46 (July-August 1968), pp. 45–53; David L. Rados, "Product Liability: Tougher Ground Rules," *Harvard Business Review*, Vol. 47 (July-August 1969), pp. 144–152; and Frederick D. Sturdivant, "Better Deal for Ghetto Shoppers," *Harvard Business Review*, Vol. 46 (March-April 1968), pp. 130–139.

[2] Phillip E. Jacob, "Social Change and Student Values," *Educational Record*, Vol. 41 (1960), pp. 338–346; and Kenneth Keniston, "Social Change and Youth in America," *Daedalus*, Vol. 91 (1962), pp. 145–171.

The Credit Revolution

Most consumers no longer view credit as immoral or a sign of poor management of family finances. While some still accept credit reluctantly,[3] numerous data, studies, and polls indicate that most Americans use and accept credit as a normal instrument of the consumption process.[4] Easily available credit has become a basic marketing tool.

The Metaphysical Revolution

One of the strongest and most pervasive values of the past is the Puritan ethic with its emphasis on hard work, economy and thrift, on absence of credit, rugged individualism, and personal responsibility. There is growing evidence that substantial numbers of Americans are shifting their metaphysical orientation from the Puritan ethic and its concern with the future and the afterlife toward the present and existing life.

One indicator is the rise and fall of religiosity. During the 1930s and 1940s, Americans became more religious in terms of attitudes toward God and support of religious institutions. Beginning in the late 1950s, however, the influence of institutionalized religion began declining.[5] Whether the trend is away from religion *per se* or, rather, away from doctrines based upon authority and revelation and toward adoption of a modern set of theological constructs and institutional arrangements is unclear. However, it is clear that there is a decline in ecclesiastical influence on traditional behavioral norms.

The shift away from the Puritan ethic toward a new theology of pleasure is one of the fundamental changes in the marketing environment. Thus it is often effective for companies to stress the role of their products and services in aiding consumers to "have fun in life," "to live today," rather than "save for the future."

The Easy Life

Another major ingredient of the Puritan ethic is that work is good in and of itself. "Hard work is good for one," is a statement to which most older people would agree. The easy life was considered the sin of the bum or other social outcast.

---

[3] M. E. Brady, "The American Family and Consumer Economics," *Marriage and Family Living*, Vol. 25 (1963), pp. 448–451.

[4] Stuart Chase, "American Values: A Generation of Change," *Public Opinion Quarterly*, Vol. 29 (1965), pp. 357–367; and *A Graphic Guide to Consumer Markets* (New York: National Industrial Conference Board, 1968), pp. 36–39.

[5] For example, church membership has stabilized, church attendance has declined, and the influence of institutionalized religion has diminished. See *Yearbook of American Churches* (New York: National Councils of the Churches of Christ), annual editions; *Generations Apart* (New York: Columbia Broadcasting System, Inc., 1969), p. 10; and Eleanor Sheldon and Wilbert Moore, eds., *Indicators of Social Change* (New York: Russell Sage Foundation, 1968), pp. 349–449.

By contrast, several studies suggest that people, particularly younger consumers, are more inclined to easy-life values.[6] Marketers who perceive this change and design products and services to make life easier and more pleasurable will reap substantial rewards.

Creative Eroticism

There is also mounting evidence that growing numbers of Americans, particularly youth, have new values and attitudes about sex. Several studies have documented a widening gap in parent-child attitudes toward sex as well as increasing permissiveness and openness.[7] This change in sex values varies widely by age, sex, and geographical location. For example, a 1968 study of Georgia students found no increase in premarital coitus over Kinsey's 1948 figures.[8] However, a recent national probability sample did document some increases.[9] A 1969 study of five college campuses indicates that sex attitudes and behavior vary considerably from one geographic location to another as well as between males and females.[10]

The general consensus is that premarital coitus and sexual acts leading to coitus are increasing; that values toward sexual activity have become more permissive and open; and that sexual behavior is considered less of a community or religious issue and more of an individual decision.[11] This represents a substantial departure from the Judeo-Christian ethic of the past. An understanding of new attitudes toward sex is valuable in designing marketing strategies, particularly products and services and advertising.

The Changing Family

Traditionally the male has been considered the dominant family member in terms of power, authority, and influence. Whether this has ever really been true is debatable, of course, but nevertheless it has been the conventional image of the American family.

Studies conducted within the last decade document the trend toward an enlarged and more important role for the wife. In general there is a trend toward a more equalitarian family structure.[12] There are even occasional reports of com-

---

[6] See, for example, Robert Frumkin, "Scientific Millennialism as the Coming World Ideaolgy," *Journal of Human Relations*, Vol. 10 (1962), pp. 145–162.

[7] Ira L. Reiss, *The Social Context of Premarital Sexual Permissiveness* (New York: Holt, Rinehart and Winston, Inc., 1967); and Ira E. Robinson, "Changes in Sexual Behavior and Attitudes of College Students," *Family Coordinator*, Vol. 17 (1968), pp. 119–123.

[8] *Ibid.*

[9] Ira L. Reiss, "America's Sex Standards—How and Why They are Changing," *Trans-Action*, Vol. 5 (1968), pp. 26–32.

[10] "Sex in Academe," *Playboy*, September 1969, pp. 193 ff.

[11] Albert Ellis, "Sexual Promiscuity in America," *Annals of the American Academy of Political and Social Science*, Vol. 378 (1968), pp. 58–67.

[12] Robert O. Blood, Jr., "Impact of Urbanization on American Family Structure and Functioning," *Sociology and Social Research*, Vol. 49 (1964), pp. 5–16; Karen F. Geiken, "Expectations Concerning Husband-Wife Responsibilities in the Home," *Journal of Marriage and the Family*, Vol. 26 (1964), pp. 349–352.

plete abdication of home responsibilities to the wife, and of women moving toward the husband's role.[13]

Of particular importance is the fact that the wife generally plays the dominant role in child rearing. This may have an increasing impact on youth fashions, personal grooming, personal activities, and their roles in all activities.

Still other evidence suggests a movement from parent-centered to child-centered families.[14] Certainly many cookie and cereal companies, toy manufacturers, drive-in restaurants, and others have enjoyed considerable success in providing products and services that parents perceive as "right" for their children.

Peer-Group Dominance

During recent years peer-group influence has become more important in shaping behavior. When children enter school, early parental influence begins to be replaced by teacher and peer-group influence. As children become older, peer-group influence gradually overcomes the dominant role of adult influence, so that by the time an individual has become a young adult, peer influence generally dominates social, normative, and political opinions.[15]

Consumers' selections in such product and service categories as clothing, cars, movies, records, and home furnishings are often strongly influenced by peer-group attitudes.[16] Thus, for many product categories, the creative use of peer-group influence will become an increasingly important ingredient of successful marketing.

A Youth-Oriented Society

One of the most visible and fundamental developments in recent decades is the transition from an emphasis on seniority to a youth-oriented society. While society has always admired, and to some extent envied, youth and all that it involves, never before has it occurred to such a degree. The reasons for this transition are complicated and little understood in terms of rigorous, publicly available empirical documentation. Nevertheless, youth orientation, whether defined in terms of age or of attitude, is of fundamental importance to marketing strategists. Youth orientation in marketing strategy can take several forms, including the following:

---

[13] Urie Bronfenbrenner, "The Changing American Child—A Speculative Analysis," *Merrill-Palmer Quarterly*, Vol. 7 (1961), pp. 72–84; Margaret Mead, *The Meaning and Role of Culture in Foreign Language Teaching* (Georgetown University: Institute of Languages and Linguistics, 1961); and F. L. K. Hsu, *Clan, Caste, and Club* (New York: Van Nostrand-Reinhold Company, 1963).

[14] Mead, *Meaning and Role of Culture*; Hsu, *Clan, Caste, and Club.*

[15] Harvey Overton, "Youth and Their Values," *Clearing House*, Vol. 35 (1964), pp. 407–411; Russell Middleton and Putney Shell, "Student Rebellion Against Parental Political Beliefs," *Social Forces*, Vol. 41 (1963), pp. 377–383.

[16] See, for example, "A Motivational Study of the Apparel Buying Habits of High School Boys" (Study Prepared for The Boys' Apparel Buyers Association and Celanese Fibers Marketing Company by Gilbert Youth Research, February 1966).

1. *Designing products and services to meet the needs of youth-oriented consumers.* Manufacturers such as Bobbie Brooks in the apparel industry have enjoyed indecent success because of their ability to perceive the preferences of youth. Similarly many companies and individuals have become successful by developing dancing facilities, pizza parlors, and movie and drinking establishments for younger consumers.

2. *Developing transgenerational strategies.* The experiences of many companies indicate that it is possible to sell youth-oriented products to older consumers but not older products—in terms of age usage and image—to younger consumers. For this reason many products that have potential multiple-market-segment appeal are given a youth image. For example, both the Mustang and Javelin successfully penetrated multiple age segments by developing youth-oriented products and advertising campaigns. Budweiser, through Frank Sinatra, found a generation linkage between older and younger segments. In recent years, Sears, Roebuck and Company attempted to strengthen its market penetration through a transgeneration strategy captured in its advertising for swimwear ("Soak it to me time at the big boutique around the corner)."

Changing Cultural Values and the Corporate Imperative

Many cultural values are changing. These changes are creating new market and product opportunities and are changing the marketing requirements for many existing products. Consequently, it is important to monitor these changes and make certain that they are being used effectively in the firm's marketing strategy.

SOCIAL DIMENSIONS OF CONSUMER MARKETS

Social influences refer to the impact of social classes, reference groups, and the family on consumer behavior. These influences often have a profound effect on purchasing behavior and hence are sometimes useful in segmenting markets and designing marketing programs.

Social-Class Influences

Social classes are relatively permanent and homogeneous divisions of society into which individuals or families can be categorized when being compared with other individuals or families. The most important determinants of an individual's social class are his occupation, how well he performs within his occupational class, how frequently and intimately he interacts with other occupants of a particular social class, his possessions, his value orientations, and his class consciousness.[17]

[17] Joseph A. Kahl, *The American Class Structure* (New York: Holt, Rinehart and Winston, Inc., 1957), pp. 8–10; Robert W. Hodge, Paul M. Siegel, and Peter H. Rossi, "Occupational Prestige in the United States: 1925–1963," in R. Bendix and S. Lipset, eds., *Class, Status, and Power*, 2d ed. (New York: The Free Press, 1966), pp. 322–334.

There is no agreement about how many social classes exist in America or their size. One of the best estimates, and one that has been used extensively in the development of marketing strategy, is based on national studies by Social Research Inc. in Chicago. SRI's typology and the most important distinguishing characteristics of each class are discussed below.[18]

UPPER CLASSES (3 percent). This category is comprised of the upper uppers and the lower uppers. The upper uppers are the social elite that enjoy inherited wealth from socially prominent families. Lower uppers are the *nouveaux riches* comprised of very high-income professional people, the presidents of major corporations, and entrepreneurs who have made large amounts of money. For mass markets these two groups have little importance because of their small size; however, they may be important markets for certain specialized luxury goods.

THE UPPER MIDDLE CLASSES (12 percent). This category is comprised of successful professionals and businessmen. Education is an important value, and gracious living is the pattern of life that the family seeks. This represents the quality market for many goods and services. They consider it important to appear fashionable, to have an attractive home in a good area, and to have well-dressed, attractive children.

THE LOWER MIDDLE CLASS (30 percent). This is the "typical" American family, exemplifying the core of respectability, conscientious work habits, and adherence to culturally defined norms and standards. The home is very important and they usually adopt standardized home furnishings following the advice of medium-level shelter and service magazines. These women work more at their shopping. They acquire clothing and furniture one item at a time rather than as a coordinated unit, and most of their nonfood purchase decisions are demanding and tedious.

THE UPPER LOWER CLASS (35 percent). Consumers in this class exhibit a routine life. Males work at generally uncreative jobs requiring manual activity and only moderate skill or education. Because of unions and seniority, however, many of them enjoy considerable affluence. The housewife views her life as crowded and busy, but monotonous. She feels that her primary reason for existence is to raise her children. She has little social contact outside the home and is not a social climber. She enjoys buying little things for her children and has a strong tendency to be brand loyal and to buy national brands.

THE LOWER LOWER CLASS (20 percent). With some important exceptions, the average American wishes lower-lower persons did not exist, but the lower lower still feels that his social position is largely his own fault. He often rejects the standards associated with middle-class morality and behavior. He is likely to be poorly educated and have a low IQ. There is a tendency to neglect this class

---

[18] From Charles B. McCann, *Women and Department Store Newspaper Advertising* (Chicago: Social Research, Inc., 1957). Also see James M. Carman, *The Application of Social Class in Market Segmentation* (Berkeley: University of California School of Business Administration, 1965).

in marketing strategy because of its low purchasing power; however, it is a large market for food products and other types of products including durable goods.[19]

Marketers should be aware of the social class membership and/or aspirations of purchasers of their products and services. Product design, pricing, distribution, and advertising should be consistent with the values, attitudes, and life styles of the social class(es) involved. In many instances it is effective to communicate subtly that a product or service is appropriate for a particular social class.

Reference-Group Influences

A reference group is any interacting aggregation of people that influences an individual's attitudes or behavior. Reference groups are influential in forming and changing attitudes, in determining aspirations, in forming norms, in creating conformity, in self-evaluation, and in perceiving phenomena.[20]

Reference groups exert varying degrees of influence on product and brand decisions. Reference groups may have no impact or may influence product selection, brand selection, or both. "Product conspicuousness" appears to be the most important determinant of whether products will be strongly influenced by reference groups. There are two aspects of conspicuousness: (1) the product must be seen and identified by others; and (2) it must stand out and be noticed.[21]

Other studies have documented the importance of reference-group influences in purchasing behavior. For example, reference groups appear to influence the brands of bread preferred and the degree of brand loyalty.[22] Similarly, White has found that reference groups influence the purchase of air conditioners.[23]

Marketing strategists should determine whether reference-group influences are operative, and, if so, whether they affect product choice, brand choice, or both. Elements of the marketing program should be consistent with the values, attitudes, and life styles of members of the reference group. And "typical" reference-group members can be used in advertisements and other forms of communication.

[19] For further discussion of the consumption behavior of various social classes see Sidney Levy, "Social Class and Consumer Behavior," in Joseph Newman, ed., *On Knowing the Consumer* (New York: John Wiley & Sons, Inc., 1966), pp. 146–160; Lee Rainwater, Richard P. Coleman, and Gerald Handel, *Workingman's Wife* (New York: Oceana Publications, Inc., 1959), and David Caplovitz, *The Poor Pay More* (New York: The Free Press, 1963).

[20] See, for example, John W. Thibaut and Harold H. Kelley, *The Social Psychology of Groups* (New York: John Wiley & Sons, Inc., 1957), Chap. 8; and T. Shibutani, "Reference Groups as Perspectives," *American Journal of Sociology*, May 1955, pp. 562–569.

[21] Foundation for Research on Human Behavior, *Group Influence in Marketing and Public Relations* (Ann Arbor, Mich.: The Foundation, 1956), pp. 7–8.

[22] James E. Stafford, "Effects of Group Influences on Consumer Brand Preferences," *Journal of Marketing Research*, Vol. 3 (February 1966), pp. 68–75.

[23] William H. White, Jr., "The Web of Word of Mouth," *Fortune*, November 1954, pp. 140–143 ff.

Family Influences

Family members also affect individual consumption behavior. Other family members have consumption needs that may preempt or otherwise modify an individual's needs. In addition, their values and attitudes may alter a consumer's brand preference.

Of fundamental importance to marketing strategists is the influence of family members in purchasing decisions. Research in this area supports several generalizations. First, the role of family members in purchasing decisions varies widely from one product to another. The extent of joint husband-wife decision making tends to increase as the price of the product increases. For lower-priced products there is usually a tendency for the purchase decision to be delegated to the husband and wife according to their respective skills and knowledge.[24]

Second, typically there is substantial interfamily variation in the pattern of decision making. For example, the degree of joint husband-wife decision making usually declines over a family's life cycle. Joint decision making is least common among lower and upper social classes and most common among the middle social classes.[25] Finally, the influence of family members often varies with the specific decision that is being made. To illustrate, the husband may evaluate the mechanical aspects of different brands while the wife makes decisions on style and color options.[26]

Marketers need to determine the role and influence of family members when purchasing their type of product. This information is used in designing the product, in selecting the types of retail outlets that will handle it, and in designing advertisements and choosing the specific media vehicles that will carry the advertisements. Since there is so much variation, it is dangerous to rely on the results of general studies; instead, specific studies for the product in question should be conducted. Finally, it is important to be alert for interfamily variations, which, if pervasive and systematic, may be a useful basis for market segmentation.

DEMOGRAPHIC TRENDS IN CONSUMER MARKETS

The decade of the seventies will be a disruptive and dislocative era, for we will experience a transformation in our population's demography that is unparalleled

---

[24] See, for example, Elizabeth H. Wolgast, "Do Husbands or Wives Make Purchasing Decisions?" *Journal of Marketing*, Vol. 23 (October 1958), pp. 151–158; and Harry Sharp and Paul Mott, "Consumer Decisions in the Metropolitan Family," *Journal of Marketing*, Vol. 21 (October 1956), pp. 149–156.

[25] Mirra Komarovsky, "Class Differences in Family Decision Making on Expenditures," in Nelson Foote, ed., *Household Decision Making* (New York: New York University Press, 1961), pp. 259–264; Sharp and Mott, "Consumer Decisions in the Metropolitan Family," p. 152.

[26] See, for example, George H. Brown, "The Automobile Buying Decision Within the Family," in Foote, ed., *Household Decision Making*, pp. 193–199; and "A Pilot Study of the Roles of Husbands and Wives in Purchasing Decisions," *Life*, 1965, Parts I–X.

in the nation's history. These changes will generate tremendous opportunities for those firms that position themselves to capitalize on them. This section examines four socioeconomic changes in consumer markets: (1) population, (2) demography, (3) purchasing power, and (4) expenditure patterns.

The Population of the Seventies

Population growth is the net result of births, deaths, and migration. Since the 1920s, the rates of deaths and migration have been reasonably predictable. Consequently, the number of births is the key to accurate population forecasts.

Births are a function of the number of women in child-rearing ages (defined by the Census Bureau as 14–49) multiplied by the birth rate. Since women in the child-rearing ages are already alive, the birth rate is the key to accurate projections of the future population.

The birth rate has fluctuated widely during recent decades, reaching its highest level during the 1947–1957 period and declining ever since. As a consequence, most firms use a conservative birth-rate assumption—called Series C—in population forecasting. Series C, which assumes 2.775 children per woman, is used in the following projections.

BIRTHS. The number of births rose to a record of 4.3 million in 1956, 1957, and 1960, and then declined during the remainder of the decade. During the 1970's there will be the greatest birth boom in history. During the decade 46 million children will be born, compared to 40 million during the 1960s and 41 million during the 1950s. Moreover, a considerably larger proportion of births will represent the first child of a recently married couple.[27] The birth boom will occur because of the rapid increase in the number of women in prime child-rearing ages, not because of an increase in the birth rate. Thus there will be a rapidly expanding market for products and services involved in having babies and rearing young children.

MARRIAGES. Since the Second World War the annual number of marriages has continually increased. Even using conservative marriage-rate assumptions, the 1970s will experience the greatest marriage boom in history. During the decade there will be approximately 22.5 million marriages, compared to 17.4 million during the 1960s.[28] Thus goods and services involved in establishing households should enjoy above-average growth rates.

THE POPULATION BY AGE GROUPS. Table 5-1 presents projections of the total population by major age groups. The total population is projected to increase from nearly 206 million in 1970 to 235.2 million in 1980. The increase of 29 million will cause the total market for goods and services to expand dramatically.

Important changes will occur in the age structure of the population. Individuals less than five years of age will increase at a rate twice as fast as the total

[27] U.S. Department of Commerce, "Current Population Reports," Ser. P-25, No. 388 (March 14, 1968).

[28] *Ibid.*

Table 5-1 Estimates and Projections of the Total Population by Age Group, United States, 1960-1980 (Selected Years)

Age Group	1960		1965		1970		1975		1980		Change: 1970-1980	
	Number	Percent	Number	Percent	Number	Percent	Number	Percent	Number	Percent	Number	Percent
All ages	180,682	100.0%	196,842	100.0%	206,038	100.0%	219,365	100.0%	235,211	100.0%	29,173	14.2%
Under 5 years	20,364	11.3	19,851	10.1	18,740	9.1	21,211	9.7	24,298	10.4	5,558	29.7
5–9 years	18,825	10.4	20,806	10.7	20,591	10.0	18,903	8.6	21,366	9.1	775	3.8
10–14 years	16,910	9.4	19,402	9.9	20,668	10.0	20,741	9.5	19,056	8.1	(1,612)	(7.8)
15–19 years	13,467	7.5	17,895	9.1	19,100	9.3	20,807	9.5	20,879	8.9	1,779	9.3
20–24 years	11,116	6.2	14,047	7.1	17,261	8.4	19,299	8.8	20,997	9.0	3,736	21.6
25–29 years	10,933	6.1	11,611	5.9	13,878	6.7	17,449	8.0	19,475	8.3	5,597	40.3
30–34 years	11,978	6.6	10,956	5.6	11,437	5.6	13,974	6.4	17,522	7.4	6,085	53.2
35–39 years	12,542	6.9	11,789	6.0	11,061	5.4	11,464	5.2	13,980	5.9	2,919	26.4
40–44 years	11,681	6.5	12,436	6.3	11,900	5.8	10,995	5.0	11,396	4.8	(504)	(4.2)
45–49 years	10,926	6.0	11,636	5.9	12,223	5.9	11,692	5.3	10,812	4.6	(1,411)	(11.5)
50–54 years	9,655	5.3	10,695	5.4	11,103	5.4	11,840	5.4	11,335	4.8	232	2.1
55–59 years	8,465	4.7	9,330	4.7	10,040	4.9	10,552	4.8	11,262	4.8	1,222	12.2
60–64 years	7,162	3.9	7,931	4.0	8,451	4.1	9,279	4.2	9,770	4.1	1,319	15.6
65–69 years	6,264	3.5	6,378	3.2	6,883	3.3	7,470	3.4	8,223	3.5	1,340	19.5
70–74 years	4,769	2.6	5,190	2.6	5,214	2.5	5,721	2.6	6,234	2.6	1,020	19.6
75 and over	5,625	3.1	6,889	3.5	7,488	3.6	7,968	3.6	8,606	3.7	1,118	14.9

SOURCE: United States Department of Commerce, Current Population Reports, Series P-25, No. 388, March 14, 1968 (Series C projections), and authors' calculations.

population. The number of individuals 20 to 24 years of age will increase one and a half times faster than the total population. The key growth segment of the decade will be individuals 25 to 34 years of age, expanding at a rate three and a half times faster than the population as a whole. The number of persons 35 to 39, and 65 to 74, will also assume greater relative importance. All other age groups will experience below-average growth rates.

The nonwhite population will continue to grow more rapidly than the white population. Nonwhites will increase from 25.3 million in 1970 to 30.9 million in 1980. The number of individuals in the 15-to-34 age category will increase much faster than the total population, while the number of individuals in other age groups will experience average or below-average growth rates.[29]

HOUSEHOLDS. Since 1950 the annual net increase in households—which includes families as well as individuals living alone or with persons other than relatives—ranged from 900,000 to 1.0 million. The youth explosion of the 1960s will result in a dramatic increase in household formations during the 1970s. As Table 5-2 indicates, by 1980 the household population will total 74.7 million, representing a growth rate of 19.7 percent for the decade.

Critical changes will occur in the age structure of the household population of the 1970s. Households headed by individuals under 34 will be the key growth segment. The number of households with heads 25 to 34 years old will increase by about 6.2 million—an increase of 53.5 percent over 1970. As indicated earlier, this trend will generate a rapidly expanding market for goods and services involved in establishing and equipping new households and rearing younger children.

The Demography of the Seventies

Important changes will occur in the demographic characteristics of the population during the decade. This section examines the changing geography of the population, the new anatomy of the labor force, the changing education market, mobility, and housing patterns.

REGIONAL AND STATE POPULATIONS. For many corporate and marketing strategy decisions, national projections are too inclusive—regional, state, and metropolitan projections are needed. For these areas, the main difference in growth rates is due to migration because death and birth rates are similar.

The regional redistribution of the population will continue during the 1970s (Table 5-3). The Pacific, Mountain, and South Atlantic regions will grow at rates considerably faster than the total population. Other regions will experience below average growth rates, although the numerical increase will be substantial in certain regions (for example, South Atlantic, East North Central, and Middle Atlantic).

[29] *Ibid.*

Table 5-2 Estimates and Projections of Households by Age of Head, United States, 1965–1980 (Selected Years)

Households by Age of Household Head by Year (in thousands of households)

Age of Head of Household	1965 Number	1965 Percent	1970 Number	1970 Percent	1975 Number	1975 Percent	1980 Number	1980 Percent	Change: 1970–1980 Number	Change: 1970–1980 Percent
Total households	57,251	100.0%	62,425	100.0%	68,229	100.0%	74,728	100.0%	12,303	19.7%
Under 25 years	3,402	5.9	4,549	7.3	5,263	7.7	5,862	7.8	1,313	28.9
25–34 years	9,896	17.3	11,569	18.5	14,779	21.6	17,763	23.7	6,194	53.5
35–44 years	11,970	20.9	11,554	18.5	11,470	16.8	13,137	17.6	1,583	13.7
45–54 years	11,486	20.1	12,112	19.4	12,193	17.9	11,476	15.4	(636)	(5.3)
55–64 years	9,569	16.7	10,571	16.9	11,304	16.6	11,921	16.0	1,350	12.8
65–74 years	7,150	12.5	7,669	12.3	8,473	12.4	9,357	12.5	1,688	22.0
75 and over	3,778	6.6	4,401	7.1	4,747	7.0	5,207	7.0	806	18.3

SOURCE: United States Department of Commerce, *Current Population Reports*, Series P-25, No. 388, March 14, 1968, and authors' calculations.

Household: A household includes all of the persons who occupy a house, an apartment or other group of rooms, or a room that constitutes a housing unit under the 1960 Census rules. A household includes the related family members and all unrelated persons, if any, such as lodgers, foster children, wards, or employees who share the housing unit. A person living alone in a housing unit or a group of unrelated persons sharing the same housing unit as partners is also counted as a household. Accommodations such as institutions, large rooming houses, convents, staff quarters in hospitals, and so on are defined as group quarters rather than households.

Table 5-3   Estimates and Projections of the Population by Regional Divisions, United States, 1960–1980 (Selected Years)

	Region Population by Year (in thousands of people)										
	1960		1965		1970		1975		1980		Change: 1970–1980
Region	Number	Percent	Number	Percent	Number	Percent	Number	Percent	Number	Percent	Number	Percent
New England	10,509	5.9%	11,145	5.8%	11,634	5.7%	12,247	5.6%	13,006	5.5%	1,372	11.8%
Middle Atlantic	34,168	19.1	36,470	18.8	38,123	18.6	40,041	18.3	42,252	18.1	4,129	10.8
East North Central	36,224	20.2	38,232	19.7	39,702	19.4	41,730	19.1	44,382	18.9	4,680	11.8
West North Central	15,395	8.6	15,857	8.2	16,111	7.8	16,579	7.6	17,281	7.4	1,170	7.3
South Atlantic	25,972	14.5	28,746	14.8	31,018	15.1	33,557	15.4	36,447	15.6	5,429	17.5
East South Central	12,050	6.7	12,818	6.6	13,338	6.5	13,942	6.4	14,638	6.2	1,300	9.7
West South Central	16,951	9.4	18,540	9.6	19,735	9.6	21,060	9.6	22,488	9.6	2,753	13.9
Mountain	6,855	3.8	7,692	4.0	8,398	4.1	9,203	4.2	10,146	4.3	1,748	20.8
Pacific	21,198	11.8	24,291	12.5	27,082	13.2	30,234	13.8	33,854	14.4	6,772	25.0
Total United States	179,322	100.0	193,791	100.0	205,141	100.0	218,593	100.0	234,494	100.0	29,353	14.3

SOURCE: United States Department of Commerce, *Current Population Reports*, Series P-25, May 1968, and authors' calculations.

States along the southern rim of the United States—from Florida on the Atlantic to California on the Pacific—will grow at a much faster rate than other states. California, the Southern Mountain States, Arizona, Texas, Louisiana, and Florida will grow the fastest. California will have the largest absolute growth—adding about 6.0 million new residents.

Several states on the Atlantic seaboard from New Hampshire to Virginia will also grow rapidly. These states are adjacent to those containing the large metropolitan centers of Boston, New York, Philadelphia, and Washington, and their growth reflects the growth that is taking place at the perimeter of these metropolitan areas.

Low rates of growth are expected in the states between the Mississippi and the Rockies (except for Minnesota), and in Pennsylvania, West Virginia, and Kentucky. The projections also suggest an abatement of the shift from southern states to the Great Lakes observed prior to 1955.

These regional and state growth projections indicate a growing market potential for products and services associated with life styles in warmer climates. They are also useful in planning future plant and distribution center locations (see Chapter 14).

The Metropolitan and Nonmetropolitan Population

Since the Second World War the population of the suburbs has been increasing more than twice as fast as the total population, and over five times as fast as that of the cities. By the early sixties the population of the suburbs became greater than that of the central cities, and then during the latter years of the decade it became greater than the population of nonmetropolitan areas.

With growing urban problems, the increasing number of young families, and the proliferation of affluence, the United States will become even more of a suburban society in the 1970s. By 1980 the suburban population will reach about 96.8 million, or about 41 percent of the total population. In fact, about 70 percent of the population growth of the 1970s will be accounted for by the suburbs. While the population of central cities and nonmetropolitan areas will grow in number, they will decline in relative importance.[30]

It is anticipated that the population will become even more concentrated in large urban areas. In 1960 the largest 100 metropolitan areas contained 46 percent of the population. By 1980 the top metropolitan areas will account for about 57 percent of the population[31] and over 60 percent of the total purchasing power.

The difference between the residents of suburbia and the central city will continue to widen during the 1970s. The suburbs will house an increasing percentage of the young-married, college-educated, affluent market. Thus, the

[30] *The Consumer of the Seventies* (New York: National Industrial Conference Board, May 1969), Statistical Supplement.

[31] See Jerome P. Pickard, *Dimensions of Metropolitanism*, Research Monograph No. 14, Urban Land Institute, 1967.

suburbs will become an even more important market segment during the decade.[32]

The Labor Force

Significant changes will also occur in the age structure of the labor force. Growth will be concentrated primarily in the 20- to 34-year-old age groups, with smaller increases in the number of older people in the labor ranks. Stated differently, there will be only a small increase in age categories from which managers and experienced workers are drawn, and a large increase in those groups that historically have been viewed as comparatively inexperienced.

The female labor force will increase at a rate 20 percent greater than the male force. Females in the 20- to 34-year-old category will account for 57 percent of the total increase in the female labor force.[33]

The growing female labor force will have important implications for marketers. During the last decade the majority of families earning above-average incomes attained this status because the wife worked. Thus, working wives increase the spending power of their families, allowing them to purchase additional goods and services. Moreover, when a wife works, other changes occur in consumption patterns. The most pervasive change is an increased consumption of convenience foods, household maintenance products, and appearance-related products including clothing, cosmetics, and so on.[34]

In addition to changes in the size, age, and sex structure of the labor force, important changes will occur in the relative importance of different types of occupations. The last two decades have seen a dramatic occupational evolution. For example, at the end of the Second World War, the number of people holding blue-collar jobs exceeded the number holding white-collar positions by about 15 percent. By 1980 white-collar consumers will exceed the number in blue-collar pursuits by about 60 percent. Growth in the labor force will be heavily concentrated in white-collar positions, with an increasing percentage of consumers employed in professional, technical, clerical, and service occupations.[35]

These changes portend a growing market for dress clothing, health and beauty aids, and other appearance-related products. In addition, office equipment and furnishings and facilitating services should enjoy attractive growth rates.

EDUCATION. School enrollment will rise to about 61 million in 1980, an increase of about 5.1 percent over 1970. The most dramatic trend will be the continued rapid increase in college enrollment. The number of college students will increase by 2.7 million, or 37.9 percent. In fact, the increase in college

[32] *The Consumer of the Seventies.*

[33] United States Department of Labor, *Manpower Report of the President* (Washington, D.C.: U.S. Government Printing Office, 1967).

[34] See, for example, Ellis I. Folke, "Working Women," *Media Scope*, October 1968, pp. 28–32.

[35] *The Consumer of the Seventies.*

enrollment will account for 90 percent of the total increase in school enrollment. Thus college students will become a more important market segment.[36]

The United States will be a more highly educated society in the 1970s. In 1960 there were only 8.2 million college graduates, but by 1980 there will be almost 18 million. The percentage of the population having only an elementary education will decline from 28 to 18.4 percent.[37] This development may result in more exacting demands for product quality standards and warranties, and suggests that more sophisticated advertising may be needed. In addition, consumers may expect more competent point-of-sale assistance, unless they are plainly sacrificing this service in favor of lower prices.

POPULATION MOBILITY. Every year 18 to 20 percent of the population moves. About two-thirds of the movers make intracounty moves, one-sixth go to different counties in the same state, and one-sixth move to other states.[38] If these mobility rates continue, the number of people moving each year will reach 44 million in 1975 and 47 million in 1980.

The rate of mobility varies widely by age group. The 20–24 age group has the highest mobility—about 42 percent move each year. About 33 percent of those 25 to 29 years old and 23 percent of those 30 to 34 move annually. Older individuals have a below-average tendency to move.[39]

Mobiles have certain unique consumption patterns. A study of long-distance mobiles revealed that 34 percent purchased major appliances; 43 percent purchased furniture; 34 percent purchased clothing; 61 percent purchased draperies and slipcovers; and 12 percent purchased minor appliances.[40]

Studies reveal that with certain provisions, mobiles have a strong tendency to carry store and brand loyalty from one community to another. Credit plays a major role in maintaining this store loyalty. Mobiles frequently go to chain organizations where they shopped in their former community and/or where they hold national charge plates. Locally identified retail outlets are typically included in the shopping pattern only after a number of chain-store visits. Mobiles, then, will become an increasingly important market segment of the 1970s. Firms desiring to capitalize on the mobile market should make certain that their products are distributed through outlets having multiple locations offering credit privileges.

HOUSING PATTERNS. It is estimated that 26 million new housing units will be needed during the period 1968–1978. Despite skepticism concerning the

[36] United States Department of Commerce, *Current Population Reports*, Series P-25, No. 388 (March 14, 1968).

[37] *The Consumer of the Seventies.*

[38] United States Bureau of the Census, *Current Population Reports*, Ser. P-20, No. 171 (April 30, 1968).

[39] United States Bureau of the Census, *Current Population Reports*, Ser. P-20 (December 9, 1966).

[40] See, for example, Alan R. Andreasen, "Geographic Mobility and Market Segmentation," *Journal of Marketing Research*, Vol. 3 (November 1966), pp. 341–345; and James E. Bell, Jr., "Mobiles—A Neglected Market Segment," *Journal of Marketing*, Vol. 33 (April 1969), pp. 37–44.

supply capability of the industry, there is general consensus that a housing boom will occur during the decade. The primary stimuli will be the unfilled demand of the 1960s and the explosive growth of younger households between ages 20 and 39. Another stimulus is growing government involvement, as illustrated by the HUD Act of 1968, which calls for some form of aid in the construction of six million public-aided units during the period 1968–1978.[41]

During the early years of the decade, a large proportion of total housing demand will be triggered by young singles and marrieds in search of apartments.[42] Hence it will become increasingly important for companies attempting to capture this market segment to increase their market penetration in suburban shopping centers and other locations strategically positioned to appeal to this market.

Housing choices during the remainder of the decade are less certain. There may be an accelerating demand for conventional single-family homes, or the trend may shift to housing, including modular units, in planned communities and cities. Marketing strategists should monitor these trends carefully to make certain that their marketing strategies are capitalizing on changing housing trends.

Purchasing Power

During the 1970s critical changes will occur in the level and distribution of income. This section summarizes these anticipated changes.

HOUSEHOLD INCOME. Each year millions of Americans enjoy higher earnings. During the 1950s this improvement involved primarily the shift of families from lower earning levels into the middle-income brackets. This trend continued during the 1960s, with increasing numbers of middle-income families moving into upper-middle-income brackets. By the late 1960s the average family had an annual before-tax income of $9,300. By 1980, it is estimated that the average family's before-tax income will be $13,800 (in constant 1967 dollars).[43]

The first column of Table 5-4 summarizes the changes that are expected to occur in household income during the decade. The number of families in every income class under $15,000 will decline. The percentage of households earning over $15,000 will increase from 28.5 percent in 1967 to over 48 percent by 1980. Thus it is anticipated that a remarkable proliferation of affluence will occur, which will increase consumers' ability to elevate even further their standards of living and life styles.

DISTRIBUTION BY HOUSEHOLDS. During previous decades, households with heads between 35 and 54 years of age have been the prime market segment in terms of purchasing power. As shown in Table 5-4, as recently as 1967 this age group captured 49 percent of all before-tax income. By 1980 their share of purchasing power will decline to 40.5 percent. In contrast, households under 35 will

---

[41] *1980 Construction Market Outlook* (New York: F. W. Dodge, 1969).
[42] *The Consumer of the Seventies.*
[43] *Ibid.*

Table 5-4   Percent Distribution of Before-Tax Income by Age of Household Head, United States, 1967 and 1980

Year and Income Class	Total	Percentage Distribution by Age of Household Head (based on constant 1967 dollars)					
		Under 25	25–34	35–44	45–54	55–64	65 and Over
1967							
All Households	100.0%	4.7	18.4	23.9	25.0	17.5	10.5
Under $3,000	3.7	.2	.3	.3	.3	.6	1.9
$3,000–5,000	6.5	.7	1.0	.9	1.0	1.3	1.7
$5,000–7,000	11.2	1.1	2.5	2.2	2.0	1.9	1.4
$7,000–10,000	21.9	1.4	5.5	5.3	4.5	3.5	1.7
$10,000–15,000	28.3	.9	6.0	8.0	7.5	4.3	1.5
$15,000–25,000	18.6	.2	2.3	5.0	6.2	3.6	1.3
$25,000 and over	9.9	.1	1.0	2.2	3.4	2.3	.9
1980							
All Households	100.0%	6.2	26.0	21.2	19.3	16.4	10.9
Under $3,000	2.0	.2	.2	.1	.1	.3	1.1
$3,000–5,000	3.6	.4	.6	.3	.3	.6	1.5
$5,000–7,000	5.2	.7	1.1	.6	.6	.9	1.2
$7,000–10,000	12.7	1.5	3.7	2.2	1.7	2.0	1.6
$10,000–15,000	27.9	2.2	9.3	6.0	4.4	3.9	2.1
$15,000–25,000	33.3	1.0	8.8	8.9	7.7	5.1	1.8
$25,000 and over	15.3	.3	2.5	3.0	4.4	3.5	1.7

SOURCE: *The Consumer of the Seventies* (Statistical Supplement), National Industrial Conference Board, May 1969.

increase their share of income from 23 percent in 1967 to 32 percent in 1980. Thus the under-35 household market will become considerably more important, although the 35-to-54 group will remain dominant.

GEOGRAPHIC DISTRIBUTION. Since average family earnings in the suburbs are about 20 percent higher than in the central cities, and because the suburbs are growing much faster than other places, a rising share of total personal income will flow to suburban families in the 1970s. By 1980 about 48 percent of before-tax income will go to suburban residents, compared to 26 percent to central-city residents and 26 percent to people living in other areas.[44] This is further evidence that the suburbs will become an even more important market during the decade.

[44] *Ibid.*

Expenditure Patterns

Changes in the size, structure, demography, and purchasing power of the population will affect the level and pattern of consumer expenditures during the decade. This section summarizes these changes.

THE ECONOMY. Most forecasters agree that the 1970s are endowed with a substantial growth potential. Gross National Product is predicted to increase from $980 billion in 1970 to approximately $1.9 trillion in 1980. Disposable Personal Income is expected to increase from $665 billion at the beginning of the decade to about $1.2 trillion in 1980. Finally, Personal Consumption Expenditures are expected to reach $1.1 trillion in 1980 compared to $608 billion in 1970.[45] These projections portend market opportunities unprecedented during any previous decade.

CONSUMPTION PATTERNS. As Table 5-5 indicates, by the middle of the decade the United States will evolve into a services economy, as consumers spend more on services than on durable or nondurable goods. During the 1968–1980 period, expenditures on services are predicted to expand at a 7.8 percent average annual growth rate, compared to 6.5 percent for durables and 5.6 percent for nondurables.

Expenditure categories predicted to increase at above-average rates include personal business, private education and research, medical care, recreation, housing, and personal care. These and the product categories previously mentioned will be the key consumer growth markets of the decade.[46]

SUMMARY AND CONCLUSIONS

This chapter has examined cultural, social, and demographic dimensions of consumer markets. Cultural influences are important to many firms because they often affect the consumption behavior of profitably large segments of consumers. Many cultural values are changing, and these changes offer opportunities for new products and for improvements in the effectiveness of marketing programs for existing products.

Social-class, reference-group, and family influences on consumer behavior have also been examined. Marketers need to relate these influences to their specific products and services. These insights can then be used to increase the effectiveness of product, pricing, advertising, and channel programs.

[45] Authors' estimates based on projections of Office of Business Economics, The Conference Board, and The National Planning Association.

[46] For other estimates see *Economic Projections to 1980: Growth Patterns for the Coming Decade* (Washington, D.C.: National Planning Association, March 1970); Ronald E. Kutscher, "1980 Projections in an Input/Output Framework," in Keith Cox and Ben M. Enis, eds., *A New Measure of Responsibility for Marketing* (Chicago: American Marketing Association, 1968), pp. 302–305; and *The Consumer of the Seventies*.

Table 5-5 Personal Consumption Expenditures by Major Component, United States, 1968–1980 (Selected Years)

Expenditure Component	Expenditures by Year								Average Annual Growth Rate, 1960–1968	Average Annual Growth Rate, 1968–1980
	1960		1968		1975		1980			
	Billions of Current Dollars	Percent	Billions of Current Dollars	Percent	Billions of Current Dollars	Percent	Billions of Current Dollars	Percent		
Durable goods	$ 45.3	13.9%	$ 83.3	15.5%	$132.1	15.3%	$ 178.3	15.2%	7.9%	6.5%
Nondurable goods	151.3	46.5	230.6	43.0	342.1	39.6	443.2	37.8	5.4	5.6
Services	128.7	39.6	222.8	41.5	389.3	45.1	549.9	46.9	7.1	7.8
Total personal consumption expenditures	$352.2	100.0%	$536.6	100.0%	$863.5	100.0%	$1,171.5	100.0%	6.5%	6.7%
Food and tobacco	$ 87.5	26.9%	$124.7	23.2%	$179.9	20.8%	$ 227.9	19.5%	4.5%	5.2%
Clothing and accessories	33.0	10.2	55.5	10.3	83.7	9.7	109.7	9.4	6.7	5.9
Personal care	5.3	1.6	9.1	1.7	15.6	1.8	21.4	1.8	7.0	7.4
Housing	46.3	14.2	77.4	4.4	137.2	15.9	183.5	15.7	6.6	7.5
Household operation	46.9	14.4	75.9	4.1	119.9	13.9	160.4	13.7	6.2	6.4
Personal business	19.1	5.9	38.6	7.2	70.3	8.1	104.6	8.9	9.2	8.7
Medical-care expenses	14.9	4.6	29.6	5.5	54.6	6.3	82.4	7.0	9.0	8.9
Transportation	43.1	13.3	72.2	13.5	111.9	13.0	152.9	13.1	6.7	6.5
Recreation	18.3	5.6	33.6	6.3	57.6	6.7	82.2	7.0	7.9	7.8
Private education and research	3.7	1.1	8.4	1.6	15.5	1.8	23.0	2.0	10.8	8.8
Religious and welfare activities	4.7	1.5	7.9	1.5	12.4	1.4	17.2	1.5	6.7	6.7
Foreign travel and other, net	2.2	0.7	3.8	.7	4.9	.6	6.1	.5	7.1	4.0
Total	$352.2	100.0%	$536.6	100.0%	$863.5	100.0%	$1,171.5	100.0%	6.5%	6.7%

SOURCES: Office of Business Economics; National Planning Association; and authors' calculations.

The last half of the chapter discusses major socioeconomic trends that will occur in consumer markets during the 1970s. This type of analysis is an important prerequisite to the development of corporate and marketing strategies. In the chapter and/or throughout the remainder of this book, we will examine how this type of analysis can be used to: (1) identify new-product opportunities; (2) estimate future market potential; (3) develop advertising campaigns, including media and creative strategies; (4) design channel strategies; and (5) develop physical distribution systems. However, as will become apparent as we proceed, an enormous amount of creative managerial expertise is required to combine this with other information into effective marketing strategies.

QUESTIONS FOR REVIEW AND DISCUSSION

1. Why should a marketing strategist be interested in cultural influences on consumer behavior?
2. What are the major implications of changes in cultural values for a major apartment builder?
3. What is meant by reference-group influences?
4. Identify the major ways that a manufacturer of teenage boys' apparel could use reference-group influences to improve the effectiveness of his marketing strategy.
5. Why could a marketer be interested in social class? Select a firm and show how it can use social-class insights to improve its marketing program.
6. How can a brewer use family influences to increase the effectiveness of his marketing efforts? Give specific examples to support your position.
7. Assume you are a market analyst for a large furniture manufacturer. Interpret the relevance of changes that are predicted to occur in consumer markets during the 1970s.
8. What would be the consumption consequences of zero population growth?

Chapter 6   Consumer Decision Processes

Understanding the cultural, social, and demographic dimensions of consumer markets is a necessary but not a sufficient condition for identifying market opportunities and developing marketing strategies. Why do some consumers decide to buy a vacation home while others choose a trip to Europe? Why do some drink Coke while others prefer Pepsi? In order to answer these types of questions, a marketing executive needs a reasonably accurate view of how consumers perceive, evaluate, and respond to marketing programs.

A variety of perspectives and models of consumer behavior have emerged in marketing, economics, psychology, sociology, and anthropology.[1] This chapter synthesizes and integrates these insights into a framework that can be used by marketing executives to analyze consumer behavior for their products and services. Figure 6-1 summarizes the framework that will be used.[2]

INDIVIDUAL PREDISPOSITIONS AND PERCEPTUAL PROCESSES

This section is concerned with the central control unit and the processes involved in receiving and processing inputs, such as

[1] See, for example, Francesco Nicosia, *Consumer Decision Processes* (Englewood Cliffs, N.J.: Prentice-Hall, Inc., 1966); John A. Howard and Jagdish N. Sheth, *The Theory of Buyer Behavior* (New York: John Wiley & Sons, Inc., 1969); and James F. Engel, David T. Kollat, and Roger D. Blackwell, *Consumer Behavior* (New York: Holt, Rinehart and Winston, Inc., 1968).

[2] This model first appeared in Engel, Kollat, and Blackwell, *Consumer Behavior*, Chap. 3.

114

Figure 6-1　A complete summary model of consumer behavior.

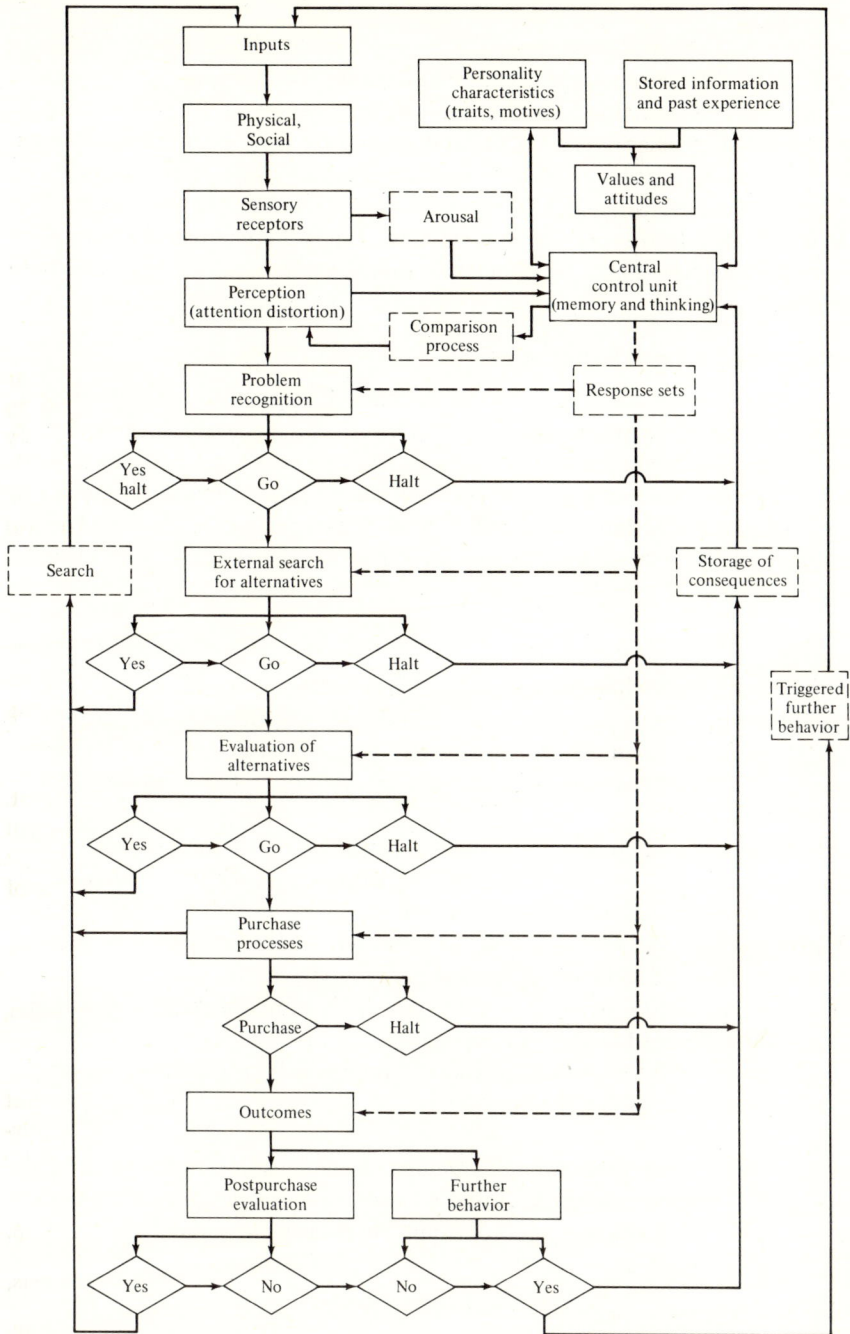

SOURCE: James F. Engel, David T. Kollat, and Roger D. Blackwell, *Consumer Behavior* (New York: Holt, Rinehart and Winston, Inc., 1968), Chap. 3. Copyright © 1968 by Holt, Rinehart and Winston, Inc. Reprinted by permission of Holt, Rinehart and Winston, Inc.

advertisements and other stimuli from the outside world (Figure 6-1). The central control unit is the psychological command center, so to speak, for it includes both memory and the basic facilities for thinking and behaving. Stored in memory are various personality characteristics or predispositions, past information or experience, and values and attitudes. These components are illustrated separately in Figure 6-1 so that relationships can be made clearer; *this does not mean, however, that they stand outside the central control unit.* Each is an integral component with its own unique function, as will become more apparent as we examine them in greater detail.

Past Information and Experience

Nearly everything we do and experience is retained in the central control unit as either conscious or unconscious memory. As a result, we learn to respond to stimuli of all types in consistent and predictable ways. These tendencies to classify and respond to stimuli correctly are sometimes referred to as *stimulus influences* in perception. Other information is retained in less organized fashion, but, as will be pointed out shortly, it is of central importance in what the individual thinks and does.

Motives

A consumer is motivated when his system is energized or made active, and behavior is directed toward some type of goal. Generally it is possible to find groups of consumers with common motives.[3] Maslow's research suggests the following classification, proceeding from the lowest order of motives to the highest:

1. *Physiological*—the fundamentals of survival, such as hunger and thirst.
2. *Safety*—concern over physical survival, ordinary prudence, which might be overlooked in striving to satisfy hunger or thirst.
3. *Belongingness and love*—striving to be accepted by intimate members of one's family and to be an important person to them.
4. *Esteem and status*—striving to achieve a high standing relative to others, including desires for mastery, reputation, and prestige.
5. *Self-actualization*—a desire to know, understand, systematize, organize, and construct a system of values.[4]

It has been verified that prepotency is reflected in consumer buying, in that previously ignored desires are often found to exert themselves only after a purchase has satisfied a predominant (and perhaps lower-order) motive.[5]

---

[3] David C. McClelland, *Personality* (New York: William Sloane Associates, 1951), p. 474.

[4] A. H. Maslow, *Motivation and Personality* (New York: Harper & Row, Publishers, 1954).

[5] George Katona, *The Powerful Consumer* (New York: McGraw-Hill, Inc., 1960), p. 132.

Consumers behave in a consistent and purposeful manner because motives are integrated into a meaningful whole. The organizing mechanism is the *self-concept* or *the individual as perceived by that individual in a socially determined frame of reference*. Through the self-concept, social values and controls become integrated into the individual's psychological makeup, thereby becoming internalized behavioral standards.[6]

Personality Traits

Personality traits are the third component of the central control unit (Figure 6-1). Personality refers to the characteristics that determine the *general* pattern of behavior, especially as it makes the individual distinctive in relations with others.[7]

Many studies have attempted to relate various personality characteristics to product, brand, or store preference. Martineau, for example, postulated that three basic personality types underlie variations in automobile purchasing behavior: (1) conservatives, (2) moderates (sociables), and (3) the attention-getters.[8] Evans, however, found that personality is of little value in differentiating owners of Chevrolets and Fords.[9] The Edwards Personal Preference Schedule has been administered to 5,000 members of the J. Walter Thompson panel, and the results indicate that personality is of limited value in explaining the types of toilet paper purchased or in predicting beer, coffee, or tea purchases.[10] Tucker and Painter found some relation between product use and personality traits, but it was not found to be strong.[11]

These and other studies indicate that *general* personality traits are usually of limited value in predicting purchasing behavior. However, *tailor-made* personality variables are often very useful. For example, White designed a series of measures relating specifically to household cleaning. He found two distinct market segments: (1) housewives that do not judge their worth by cleaning and do not consider it an expression of love, and (2) housewives who feel that their worth is judged by cleaning and rigid schedules. White's company, a detergent manufacturer, was able to increase its market share by modifying packaging and brand names to adapt to these two segments.[12]

[6] See, for example, Carl R. Rogers, *Client-Centered Therapy* (Boston: Houghton Mifflin Company, 1951), p. 492.

[7] See, for example, D. O. Hebb, *A Textbook of Psychology* (Philadelphia: W. B. Saunders Company, 1966).

[8] Pierre Martineau, *Motivation in Advertising* (New York: McGraw-Hill, Inc., 1957).

[9] Franklin B. Evans, "Psychological and Objective Factors in the Prediction of Brand Choice: Ford versus Chevrolet," *Journal of Business*, Vol. 32 (1959), pp. 340–369.

[10] A. Koponen, "Personality Characteristics of Purchasers," *Journal of Advertising Research*, Vol. 1 (1960), pp. 6–12; *Are There Consumer Types?* (New York: Advertising Research Foundation, 1969); and Ronald E. Frank, "Is Brand Loyalty a Useful Basis for Market Segmentation?" *Journal of Advertising Research*, Vol. 7 (June 1967), pp. 27–33.

[11] W. T. Tucker and J. J. Painter, "Personality and Product Use," *Journal of Applied Psychology*, Vol. 45 (1961), pp. 325–329.

[12] Irving S. White, "The Perception of Value in Products," in Joseph W. Newman, ed., *On Knowing the Consumer* (New York: John Wiley & Sons, Inc., 1966), pp. 90–106.

The White study, as well as others that could be mentioned, points up the need for marketers to determine the personality traits that relate specifically to their products or services. These can be used to segment markets and design more effective marketing strategies and programs.

Values and Attitudes

Each of the characteristics discussed so far is a general pervasive predisposition of the individual, basic to his whole mode of behavior. These predispositions become stored in memory, as illustrated by the arrows in Figure 6-1, and thus they affect behavior in their own right. They also interact with stored past experience and information to form *values and attitudes*—or "an organization of concepts, beliefs and motives associated with a particular object."[13] Values differ from attitudes only in the sense that they are generally considered to be more basic, or central, to the individual's cognitive structure.

Considerable progress has been made in recent years using psychographics, which is a broad spectrum of measurements of life style or "daily activity, interest, and opinion" (AIO). Wilson, for example, found that homemaker living patterns can account for up to 30 percent of the variance in product consumption and for 25 percent of the variance in media readership levels. AIO analysis led Wilson to introduce such consumer types as "the happy homemaker," "the special shopper," "fashion consciousness," "the weight watcher," "beauty consciousness," and so on.[14] More recently Wells and Tigert have successfully used AIO measures in product segmentation analysis.[15]

These and other studies, including those conducted by private companies, indicate that AIO scales are often useful. The most common procedure is to first segment the market according to usage patterns—heavy, light, and nonusers of a product or brand—and then construct psychographic, as well as demographic and other product- and media-usage, profiles for each segment. This type of analysis is then combined with other data to select market segments and develop marketing programs for them.

Inputs to the System

Everyone is continually bombarded with physical and social stimuli (Figure 6-1). They are received by the five senses (sensory receptors) in the form of a physical sensation from the firing of a retinal cone or other physiological reactions. Physical stimuli include such factors as temperature, humidity, traffic conditions, and marketing stimuli (advertising, salesmen, point-of-purchase displays, and so on).

[13] Wilbert J. McKeachie and Charlotte L. Doyle, *Psychology* (Reading, Mass: Addison-Wesley Publishing Company, Inc., 1966), p. 560.

[14] Clark Wilson, "Homemaker Living Patterns and Marketplace Behavior—A Psychometric Approach," in John S. Wright and Jac L. Goldstucker, eds., *New Ideas for Successful Marketing* (Chicago: American Marketing Association, 1966), pp. 305–331.

[15] William D. Wells and Douglas J. Tigert, "A Consumer Attitude Inventory," working paper, Graduate School of Business, University of Chicago, 1969.

Social stimuli refer to the impact of cultural, social-class, reference-group, and family influences discussed in Chapter 5.

Arousal

The system must be "turned on" before behavior can occur, and this is the function of arousal. Arousal can occur internally through *need activation*, in which case the individual becomes alert, responsive, and vigilant because of a feeling of discomfort triggered by his sensory receptors. Similarly, arousal can be achieved through an outside stimulus of some sort.

It is generally assumed that a need must be activated or aroused before behavior can occur. This is not necessarily true, but there is no question that physiological and psychological needs perform this function. The result is arousal of a state of *drive*, which, in turn, provides for an energizing of need-satisfying action. The consumer, for example, becomes hungry; his system now is activated because of this state of felt discomfort.

Arousal can also occur through awareness of an external stimulus. Assume that a consumer is thumbing through a magazine and sees an advertisement for a German chocolate cake mix. The picture of the cake, in itself, can make him feel hungry and thereby initiate behavior. This will not happen in all situations, however, because the incoming stimulus could also conflict with his preference and lead him to distort or ignore what he sees or hears.

Perception

Let it now be assumed that the system is active and vigilant (that is, attentive to relevant incoming stimuli), since this is the "normal" state of affairs. How does a person make sense out of what he sees, hears, or senses in other ways? Clearly, he cannot consciously attend to all stimuli that reach him, for such stimuli could easily number into the millions during the course of a day. Rather he perceives, or "sizes up," inputs selectively through a process of *comparison*, whereby inputs are compared with all that is stored in memory. The individual thus will be highly selective and under most circumstances will not attend to irrelevant stimuli. The comparison process is illustrated in Figure 6-1.

If the individual is aroused by a state of need, he will be highly selective in what he sees, hears, touches, feels, and smells. He is now especially alert to those inputs that are relevant in satisfying the aroused drive. To continue the previous example, those stimuli that are known from past experience to be relevant to hunger satisfaction are likely to be attended to. For example, a picture of a juicy steak in a restaurant window or of a big piece of chocolate cake in an advertisement are now likely to be noticed, whereas previously they were largely ignored.

Meaning is attributed to incoming inputs through a decision process in which the individual evaluates input cues and selects the most appropriate category of meaning. All of the components of the central control unit become relevant by serving as categories in their own right or by enhancing the probability that a given category will be chosen.

Perception is selective, however, even in the absence of aroused drive. Consumers resist a challenge to their values and attitudes. When one occurs, perhaps through an advertisement challenging their brand preference, they tend to avoid a state of dissonance or imbalance, which would probably result if the message were consciously weighed and evaluated. Over 400 empirical studies indicate that perception is selective in three major ways:

1. *Selective exposure.* Consumers attend to stimuli that are relevant and consistent with their values and attitudes and tend to ignore stimuli that do not meet those conditions.
2. *Selective perception.* Consumers interpret stimuli in a manner consistent with their values and attitudes. Selective perception has been found to take the form of: (a) distortion and misinterpretation of message content to make it consistent with motivational predispositions, (b) rejection of the source and message content as being biased, and (c) retention of the factual information but rejection of the behavioral-recommendation component of the stimuli.
3. *Selective retention.* Consumers remember stimuli that are consistent with their values and attitudes longer than if the stimuli are inconsistent.[16]

Thus consumers' psychological processes function, in part, as perceptual screens that filter out and/or otherwise change the meaning of incoming information. For these and other reasons, it is usually more profitable to try to convert light users into heavy users than it is to convert nonusers into users. However, this is a generalization; in some cases it is not possible to convert light users into heavy users and sometimes it is possible to convert nonusers into light or heavy users. The key variables seem to be the knowledge-base and centrality of predispositions. More specifically, the greater the experience and knowledge with and about the brand, and the more central the behavior pattern is to consumers' cognitive structures, the less the chance of changing their purchasing behavior.

In attempting to convert nonusers to users and/or increase the usage rates of current users, it is usually most effective to design marketing strategies that are consistent and compatible with the conversion markets' values, attitudes, personality traits, and other predispositions. In other words, the chances of success are greater if the marketer shows how his product or brand is compatible with the way consumers feel than if he tries to change how they feel.

---

[16] For supporting evidence see James F. Engel, "The Influence of Needs and Attitudes on The Perception of Persuasion," in Stephen Greyser, ed., *Toward Scientific Marketing* (Chicago: American Marketing Association, 1964), pp. 18–29.

PROBLEM RECOGNITION

Figure 6-1 illustrates the outcomes of the comparison process. Problem recognition results when a consumer perceives a difference of sufficient magnitude between the actual and the desired state of affairs. If such a difference is not perceived, the process halts at this point. If a difference is perceived but the consumer is unable and/or unwilling to do anything about it, a problem is recognized but the process halts.

The desired state is the result of complex and little-understood interactions of motives, personality traits, values, attitudes, group influences, financial resources, future expectations, and perhaps marketing efforts. The actual state is the result of past behavior and is determined by the interactions of the same phenomena.

Decision to Stimulate Problem Recognition

Whether it is advantageous to attempt to stimulate problem recognition requires an analysis of three basic factors. First, it must be determined whether it is possible to stimulate problem recognition. In many cases the key determinants may be isolated from marketer influence. For example, a home builder may find that the decision to buy a home usually occurs as the result of new or growing children or a change in the husband's place of work. In this case there is limited opportunity to evoke this process.

The second step is to determine the cost involved in stimulating problem recognition. For example, while it may be possible to form or change the determinants of the desired state, the level of investment may be so high that it is unprofitable.

Finally, it may not be to the company's advantage to evoke problem recognition. For example, if a firm has a small market share, it is probably not wise to follow the strategy, since the probability that consumers will ultimately purchase the firm's brand is very low.

Methods of Stimulating Problem Recognition

If a firm decides to try to evoke problem recognition, it then must decide which approach to use. The three alternatives are: (1) change the determinants of the desired state, (2) adapt to the determinants of the desired state, or (3) change the determinants of the actual state. Since the specific determinants of both states vary from one situation to another, it is impossible to advance recommendations applicable in all instances. However, the following generalizations should be given careful consideration:

1. Of the three approaches, changing the determinants of the desired state is usually the most difficult and expensive, since it is most likely to fall victim to the processes of selective exposure, perception, and retention.

2. Changing the determinants of the actual state is usually the second most difficult approach, since it is also likely to be vitiated by the processes of selective perception. However, it has often been successful, as illustrated by the many companies that have increased the number of users and uses for their products.

3. Of the three approaches, it is generally more effective to demonstrate how the company's brand is consistent with what consumers perceive to be the determinants of the desired state. This approach is least likely to be diluted by selective perception.

Several studies have concluded that marketing efforts have very little effect on stimulating problem recognition. In many cases, some degree of problem recognition must already exist before marketing efforts are even perceived by consumers.[17] In these instances a common strategy is to maintain brand awareness, so that when consumers perceive a problem, the company's brand is among those considered as possible problem solutions.

INFORMATION SEEKING

Information seeking refers to the processes and activities whereby consumers learn about the number of alternative solutions to the perceived problem, the characteristics and attributes of these alternatives, and their relative desirability. In *external search* consumers use such sources of information as mass media, personal sources, advertisements, and dealer visits. *Internal search* differs from external search in that all the information used is stored in memory, having resulted from past experiences.

Search will continue until it appears that enough is known to proceed. This is shown in Figure 6-1 as a "go" decision. In other situations the information gained will result in halting of the process, because: (1) the information gained causes the consumer to reevaluate the differences between the desired and actual states—that is, the problem is erased; or (2) the information causes the consumer to postpone the solution to the problem. In still other situations the alternatives will be known and a decision will be made to "go" without search. Where the purchase is based on habit, this step is completely bypassed without thought or consideration—that is, a "go" decision is made almost automatically.

Determinants of External Search

Whether or not external search occurs, and the extent to which it occurs, appear to depend on the consumer's perception of the *value* of the results of search and

[17] See, for example, Robert W. Pratt, Jr., "Understanding the Decision Process for Consumer Durable Goods: An Example of the Application of Longitudinal Analysis," in Peter D. Bennett, ed., *Marketing and Economic Development* (Chicago: American Marketing Association, 1965), pp. 240–260.

the *costs* involved in searching. When perceived value exceeds perceived cost, search is most likely to occur.[18]

Research in this area indicates that the probability of search increases: (1) the shorter the length of time the consumer has been purchasing the product, (2) the greater the dissatisfaction with past purchases, (3) the higher the price and/or the greater the length of time the consumer is committed to use the product, (4) the greater the degree of physiological or social risk, and (5) the greater the frequency of price and style changes.[19]

Utilization of Information Sources

This section outlines how consumers obtain information from the mass media, personal sources, and marketer-dominated channels.

MASS MEDIA. Some media, such as *Better Homes and Gardens, Mademoiselle, Charm, Esquire,* and *Playboy,* often serve as a type of reference group for certain market segments.[20] Moreover, some mass-media personnel and certain newspaper and magazine columnists are often used as information sources, apparently because of their reputations for impartiality and knowledge. In general, the influence of celebrities varies widely by product, depending, in part, on consumers' attitudes about the competence of the celebrity to give advice about the product in question.[21]

PERSONAL SOURCES OF INFORMATION. Many studies show that consumers commonly seek information about the attributes of products and services from friends and neighbors. These advice-giving consumers are called opinion leaders, and they have been found to be very important in the purchase of a wide variety of products, including food items, soaps and cleaning agents, motion pictures, hairdo styles, makeup techniques, clothing styles, dental products and services, farming practices, physicians, drugs, man-made fabrics, and major household appliances, to mention just a few.[22]

Opinion leaders tend to have certain distinguishing characteristics. First, an

---

[18] See, for example, Louis P. Bucklin, "Testing Propensities to Shop," *Journal of Marketing,* Vol. 30 (January 1966), pp. 22–27; and John U. Farley, " 'Brand Loyalty' and the Economics of Information," *Journal of Business,* Vol. 37 (October 1964), pp. 370–381.

[19] See George Katona, *The Mass Consumption Society* (New York: McGraw-Hill, Inc., 1964), pp. 289–290; William P. Dommermuth, "The Shopping Matrix and Marketing Strategy," *Journal of Marketing Research,* Vol. 2 (May 1965), pp. 128–132; and Wesley C. Bender, "Consumer Purchase Costs—Do Retailers Recognize Them?" *Journal of Retailing,* Spring 1968, pp. 1–8.

[20] See, for example, *Better Homes and Gardens Impact and Action* (Des Moines: Research Division, Meredith Publishing Company, 1964).

[21] *Building Reliability into Communications* (New York: The Interpublic Group of Companies, Inc., 1966).

[22] See Elihu Katz and Paul F. Lazarsfeld, *Personal Influence* (New York: The Free Press, 1955); Sidney P. Feldman, "Some Dyadic Relationships Associated with Consumer Choice," in Raymond Haas, ed., *Science, Technology, and Marketing* (Chicago: American Marketing Association, 1966), pp. 758–776; and Katona, *The Powerful Consumer,* p. 157.

individual is not usually an opinion leader in several areas; that is, opinion leaders are usually monomorphic or confined to an area that is of interest to them. Second, opinion leaders are usually found in approximately equal proportions in all strata of society, rather than being confined to any one social class. Opinion leaders are also perceived as personifying certain values that are relevant to those they influence and as being competent to give advice. They are more gregarious than other individuals and are usually, though not always, more exposed to mass media.[23]

MARKETER-DOMINATED SOURCES. The extent to which consumers use marketer communications as a source of information unfortunately defies simple generalizations, because it varies widely by product category as well as across consumers. Typically, less than 25 percent of purchasers say that they obtained information from advertisements, circulars, and other sources of marketer information.[24]

Relative Importance of Information Sources

Although subject to methodological criticisms, studies generally indicate that consumers usually have a greater tendency to be *exposed* to marketer-dominated sources of information but personal sources are usually the most *effective*. Information seeking tends to be a cumulative process; that is, those who seek information from mass media and/or marketer-dominated sources also usually seek information from personal sources, and vice versa.[25]

A marketing executive needs to determine the relative importance of sources of information consumers use in purchasing his products or services. These data can be used in planning media strategies (Chapter 15). Where opinion leaders are important, three strategies can be used: (1) develop satisfied customers, hoping that they will communicate their opinions to other consumers; (2) direct communications to non-opinion leaders, encouraging them to seek information from opinion leaders and other information sources; and/or (3) direct communications to opinion leaders, stimulating them to engage in favorable word-of-mouth advertising.

In many instances the third strategy is not practical, because opinion leaders cannot be identified and/or reached by advertising at a reasonable cost. However, when they can be identified and reached economically, the third strategy may be useful.

[23] Alvin J. Silk, "Overlap Among Self Designated Opinion Leaders: A Study of Selected Dental Products and Services," *Journal of Marketing Research*, Vol. 3 (August 1966), pp. 255–259; Robert Mason, "The Use of Information by Influentials in the Adoption Process," *Public Opinion Quarterly*, Vol. 27 (1963), pp. 455–466.

[24] John G. Udell, "Prepurchase Behavior of Buyers of Small Electrical Appliances," *Journal of Marketing*, Vol. 30 (October 1966), pp. 50–52; George Fisk, "Media Influence Reconsidered," *Public Opinion Quarterly*, Vol. 23 (1959), pp. 83–91; and George Katona and Eva Mueller, "A Study of Purchase Decisions," in L. H. Clark, eds., *Consumer Behavior: The Dynamics of Consumer Reaction* (New York: New York University Press, 1955), pp. 30–87.

[25] See sources identified in footnotes 22, 23, and 24.

ALTERNATIVE EVALUATION

Alternative evaluation refers to the processes and activities involved in evaluating the desirability of products, various brands, or attributes of products and brands. Alternative evaluation will continue until it appears that enough is known to proceed. This is shown in Figure 6-1 as a "go" decision. In other situations the process will halt, because the information gained during alternative evaluation: (1) causes the consumer to conclude that the problem doesn't exist after all; or (2) results in his postponing the decision to solve the problem. In other instances, when the purchase is based on habit, this step will be bypassed without thought or consideration—that is, a "go" decision is made automatically.

Determinants of Alternative Evaluation

The tendency to evaluate alternatives increases as the consumer's education, income, and occupational status increase and as attitudes toward shopping become more favorable. Conversely, the tendency to evaluate alternatives decreases as the amount of past experience and the perceived urgency of the need increase and when there are special opportunities to buy.[26]

Alternative Evaluation Processes

Alternative evaluation involves three variables: (1) evaluative criteria, (2) characteristics of alternatives, and (3) comparison processes. Alternative evaluation, then, consists of processes whereby the consumer compares the characteristics of alternatives with evaluative criteria.

EVALUATIVE CRITERIA. Some of the more common evaluative criteria are price, brand, size, appearance, style, material, color, label, image, and maintenance costs. The role of price deserves special comment.

The importance of price as an evaluative criterion is frequently misunderstood. Many studies indicate that a significant percentage of consumers do not use price as an evaluative criterion. Moreover, the importance of price varies considerably from one product to another. In many product categories there is a *range* of acceptable prices; and as long as price falls within the acceptance zone, it is not a criterion.[27]

PERCEIVED CHARACTERISTICS OF ALTERNATIVES. Notice in Figure 6-1 that alternative evaluation becomes an input into the system, thereby involving perception, values, attitudes, and personality characteristics. Consequently, what a

[26] Katona and Mueller, "A Study of Purchase Decisions," pp. 60–63, 72, 74.

[27] See, for example, George Haines, "A Study of Why People Purchase New Products," in Haas, *Science, Technology, and Marketing,* pp. 665–685; William D. Wells and Leonard A. LuSciuto, "Direct Observation of Purchasing Behavior," *Journal of Marketing Research,* Vol. 3 (August 1966), pp. 227–233; and A. Gabor and C. W. J. Granger, "Price Sensitivity of the Consumer," *Journal of Advertising Research,* Vol. 4 (December 1964), pp. 40–44.

consumer evaluates is what he perceives, and whatever this is, it may differ considerably from what *other* consumers and marketers perceive.

COMPARISON PROCESSES. Comparison processes can take two major forms —direct and indirect. Under the direct technique, alternatives are compared directly in terms of product attributes. For example, a housewife may be looking for green wool carpeting for under $20 a square yard. In this case, alternatives can be compared directly against these criteria.

Indirect comparison processes are more complex and subtle. For example:

- An experiment conducted by a large dairy found that customers considered a cream-colored, 14 percent butterfat ice cream to be richer in flavor than white-colored, 16 percent butterfat ice cream.
- Detergent manufacturers have found that housewives tend to judge the cleaning power of a detergent on the basis of suds level and smell. Similarly, the color of a detergent and its package are cues often used to judge mildness.[28]

These examples indicate that consumers often compare alternatives by using certain cues that they feel predict whether alternatives have certain desired attributes.

In some instances alternative evaluation involves a point-by-point comparison of product trait and evaluative criterion. In other cases the comparison is not divisible into specific product traits. For example:

- A study of sugar coating added to an old well-accepted cereal told us that the difference was not merely one of perceiving the presweetening and liking it or not liking it. . . . Add presweetening and you no longer have corn flakes at all. . . . The addition of a sugar coating to corn flakes does not make the emerging product super corn flakes capable of maintaining the previous market segment while adding a new one. . . . The new difference meant the perception of a whole new user group.[29]

In some cases, then, it may be dangerous to view alternative evaluation as involving separate evaluations of product characteristics. The whole may be greater than the sum of the parts.

Marketing Implications

In the context of their specific products, marketers need to determine the extent to which alternative evaluation occurs; the numbers, type, and relative importance

---

[28] Donald H. Cox, "The Measurement of Information Value: A Study in Consumer Decision Making," in William S. Decker, ed., *Emerging Concepts in Marketing* (Chicago: American Marketing Association, 1962), pp. 413–421.

[29] White, "The Perception of Value in Products," p. 94.

of evaluative criteria that are used; how alternative brands are perceived; and the type and content of the comparison process. Appropriate techniques for making these determinations are discussed in Chapter 9. This information is then used to design product, promotion, and sales-force strategies.

PURCHASING PROCESSES

The consumer may or may not have visited retail outlets as he passed through the previous stages in the decision-making process. However, with few exceptions, consumers typically visit retail stores at some time during the decision-process period. This interaction between customer and store environment, called purchasing processes, is of vital importance in understanding consumer behavior.

Figure 6-1 illustrates the relation between purchasing processes and the concepts and variables previously discussed. Purchasing processes result in two types of outcomes—purchase, or halt (no purchase). The process may halt because the information obtained in the store environment may erase the problem or result in a decision to postpone the purchase.

Purchasing processes encompass many dimensions of consumer behavior, of which several illustrative examples are discussed below.

Store Choice

Research indicates that store choice involves the same major variables as alternative evaluation—evaluative criteria, perceived characteristics of stores, and comparison processes. Studies indicate that the evaluative criteria used in selecting stores include location, depth and breadth of assortments, price, advertising and sales promotion, store personnel, and store services. The relative importance of these factors varies by consumer and according to the type of product or service being purchased.[30]

The way consumers perceive a store often varies from what it is in an objective sense. For example:

- One of the major mail-order chains talks about expanding its market upward, attracting the middle-class customer. Yet when the ads from stores of this chain were tested in three different cities where women did not know their actual identity, in every case the stores were seen as having a lower-class appeal.[31]
- Their (consumers) personality concept is not primarily the result of physi-

---

[30] For illustrative studies see "The Movers," *Progressive Grocer*, Vol. 44 (November 1965), p. k-47; Stuart U. Rich and Bernard D. Portis, "The Imageries of Department Stores," *Journal of Marketing*, Vol. 28 (April 1964), pp. 10–15; and William Lazer and Eugene J. Kelly, "The Retailing Mix: Planning and Management," *Journal of Retailing*, Vol. 37 (Spring 1961), pp. 34–41.

[31] Martineau, *Motivation in Advertising*, p. 174.

cal features of the store—it is rather the result of the group of customers who have come to shop there. Customers associate themselves with a social group, shop where that group shops, and attribute to the store, characteristics of the group.[32]

These factors are important in designing a channel strategy. Marketers need to determine the factors that influence where consumers shop for their products. In addition they need to analyze store patronage by socioeconomic, psychographic, and other variables used to specify their target-market segment, to make certain that their distribution is reaching that segment. Since consumers usually have varying shopping patterns, it is often most effective to program distribution through multiple types of retail outlets.

Store Layout

DISPLAYS. In self-service outlets, such as supermarkets and super drug-stores, point-of-purchase and end-aisle displays typically increase sales. The greater the attention-attracting capability of the display the greater the sales increase. However, the degree of sales increase usually varies considerably across products—that is, products have differential susceptibility to sales increases from displaying.[33] Product characteristics that account for this differential susceptibility have yet to be isolated.

SHELVING. The shelf location of an item in self-service outlets also influences consumer behavior. For example, shelf-facings—the number of rows of a product that are displayed—sometimes have no effect on sales, while for other products, sales increase by varying rates. In other words, the effect of increasing the number of shelf-facings is heavily influenced by the type of product.[34]

Shelf height can also influence consumer behavior in retail outlets. Studies usually indicate shelf locations are most effective in increasing sales in the following order: (1) eye level, (2) waist level, and (3) knee or ankle level.[35]

MARKETING IMPLICATIONS. It is possible to increase the sales of many products by strategically locating them in the store and by using displays and appropriate shelving. A marketing executive should determine whether it is profitable to

[32] John Wingate, "Developments in the Supermarket Field," *New York Retailer,* October 1958, p. 6.

[33] See, for example, *Drugstore Brand Switching and Impulse Buying* (New York: Point-of-Purchase Advertising Institute, 1963); *Motion Moves More Merchandise* (New York: Point-of-Purchase Advertising Institute, undated); Mary L. McKenna, "The Influence of In-Store Advertising," in Joseph Newman, ed., *On Knowing the Consumer* (New York: John Wiley & Sons, Inc., 1966), pp. 114–115; and George J. Kress, *The Effect of End Displays on Selected Food Product Sales* (New York: Point-of-Purchase Advertising Institute, undated).

[34] See Keith Cox, "The Responsiveness of Food Sales to Shelf Space Changes in Super-markets," *Journal of Marketing Research,* Vol. 1 (May 1964), pp. 63–67.

[35] "Shelf Merchandising Strategy: A Key to Increased Sales," *Progressive Grocer,* March 1964, pp. C-121–C:125; and "Shelf Attitudes Affect Buying Attitudes," *Progressive Grocer,* March 1964, p. C-126.

pay the additional costs usually required to obtain this type of preferred treatment in retail outlets.

Type of Purchasing Decision

By comparing preshopping purchase intentions with actual shopping behavior, it is possible to determine whether a purchase was: (1) specifically planned—the consumer purchased the product and brand intended; (2) generally planned—the consumer intended to purchase the product but decided on the brand while in the store; (3) a brand substitution—the consumer purchased a different brand than originally intended; and (4) unplanned—the consumer decided to purchase both the product and brand while in the store.

The relative importance of these types of purchasing decisions varies widely by type of product and retail outlet. In drugstores, for example, about 56 percent of purchases are specifically planned, 22 percent unplanned, and the remainder in the other two categories. By contrast, in supermarkets only 31 percent of purchases are specifically planned while 50 percent are unplanned.[36]

Marketers need to determine the relative importance of these types of purchasing decisions for their specific products. The greater the magnitude of unplanned purchasing, the greater the importance of attractive packaging and of in-store locations, displays, and shelving that increase the probability that consumers will be exposed to the product.

POSTPURCHASE BEHAVIOR

Behavior does not cease once a decision is made to purchase or not to purchase, because, as shown in Figure 6-1, two additional things can happen: (1) perceived doubt about the wisdom of the action can trigger a search for information to justify the decision; and (2) the outcomes may change circumstances sufficiently to serve as a stimulus for further behavior. Postdecision evaluation is represented by an extension of the "search loop," and the triggering of further behavior is shown as a new input.

Triggering New Behavior

A decision to buy often necessitates or produces many other decisions. For example, the financial outlays involved often require further decisions as to whether the item can be afforded and, in many instances, the amount, type, and source of credit that should be used. Marketing strategy should accommodate these problems through appropriate types of credit plans offered by retailers, financial institutions, or, in some cases (such as durable goods), by the manufacturer.

---

[36] *Drugstore Brand Switching and Impulse Buying* (New York: Point-of-Purchase Advertising Institute, 1963), p. 29; *Package Stores Brand Switching and Impulse Buying* (New York: Point-of-Purchasing Advertising Institute, 1963), p. 7 (categories have been adjusted to correspond to those used in this text); and *Consumer Buying Habits Studies,* E. I. duPont de Nemours and Company, 1965.

In addition there is often the need to assemble, install, and/or learn to use the product or service. This can be extremely frustrating, as anyone who has ever attempted to assemble children's toys will attest. Techniques designed to simplify and "pleasurize" these activities may increase the effectiveness of marketing efforts.

The purchase of an item often generates interest in others. For example, the purchase of a new sofa or carpet may trigger an awareness that other items of furniture are inadequate. In such situations, much can be gained by developing a coordinated product line and preparing literature that illustrates possible accessories, companion products, and so on.

Postdecision Dissonance

In many purchase situations, conflict remains after purchase. The buyer may recall favorable attributes of unchosen products or may be upset by an awareness of the importance of alternative expenditures. The result can be a state of tension referred to as postdecision dissonance.[37]

To allay this dissonance, consumers may search for information that reinforces the wisdom of their actions. Among other things, they may consult advertising, return to the store or showroom, or study product literature.

Attempts to understand the nature of postpurchase evaluation have produced more questions than answers, but there is evidence that manufacturers may be able to strengthen the probability of repurchase by helping customers overcome postpurchase doubt.[38] For example, in the automobile industry it is common to send new purchasers letters and aim advertisements at them.

Unconfirmed Expectations

There is also evidence that consumers form performance expectations about a product or service before purchasing it. If use of the item confirms these expectations, no imbalance is created. An unconfirmed expectation, however, generates a state of dissonance, and the individual may be motivated to overcome the resulting imbalance.[39]

Marketing strategy, particularly advertising, must arouse realistic expectations that are completely fulfilled by the product. This requires a strong foundation of research that identifies in detail consumer expectations, not only for the product itself but for its relationship to other products in the consumer's style of life.

[37] Leon Festinger, A Theory of Cognitive Dissonance (New York: Harper & Row, Publishers, 1957), Chap. 1.

[38] D. Ehrlich, I. Guttman, P. Schonbach, and J. Mills, "Post Decision Exposure to Relevant Information," Journal of Abnormal and Social Psychology, Vol. 54 (1957), pp. 98–102; and James F. Engel, "Are Automobile Purchasers Dissonant Consumers?" Journal of Marketing, Vol. 27 (1963), pp. 55–58.

[39] For representative studies in this area see W. D. Ward and K. D. Sondvold, "Performance Expectancy as a Determinant of Actual Performance," Journal of Abnormal and Social Psychology, Vol. 67 (1963), pp. 293–295; and P. A. Goldberg, "Expectancy, Choice, and the Other Person," Journal of Personality and Social Psychology, Vol. 2 (1965), pp. 895–897.

BRAND LOYALTY

Referring to the model of consumer behavior in Figure 6-1, we are now concerned with the pattern of purchasing over time. Brand loyalty is one aspect of this temporal pattern. Although brand loyalty is measured in a variety of ways, in general it refers to the relationship between brands purchased at different points in time. When consumers purchase the same brand on every purchase occasion, perfect or total brand loyalty exists. By contrast, if a different brand is purchased every time, then there is no brand loyalty. In most situations, of course, the degree of brand loyalty is somewhere between these extremes. This section presents some findings concerning the degree of brand loyalty, the correlates of this type of behavior, and a brief overview of brand-loyalty models.

The Degree of Brand Loyalty

The first major study of brand loyalty was published by Brown in 1952 and 1953. He found that a majority of consumers are brand loyal when buying frequently purchased household items. The percentage of households demonstrating loyalty varied from 54 to 95 percent, depending on the product involved.[40]

Cunningham has also documented the existence of brand loyalty for six common grocery products and headache tablets. He found that in each product category 50 percent (or more) of the families studied concentrated at least 43 percent of their purchases on the brand most often bought. Other researchers have documented the existence of brand loyalty for many other products.[41]

Most studies have found that the degree of brand loyalty varies considerably across both products and consumers. Brown, for example, found that 54 percent of the respondents exhibited some degree of loyalty when purchasing cereal, while the comparable figures for margarine and coffee were 73 and 95 percent, respectively. Similar degrees of variation have been found for other products by other investigators.[42]

---

[40] George Brown, "Brand Loyalty—Fact or Fiction," *Advertising Age*, Vol. 23, June 19, 1952, pp. 53–55; June 30, 1952, pp. 45–47; July 14, 1952, pp. 54–56; July 28, 1952, pp. 46–48; August 11, 1952, pp. 56–58; September 1, 1952, pp. 80–82; October 6, 1952, pp. 82–86; December 1, 1952, pp. 76–79; January 26, 1953, pp. 75–76.

[41] Ross Cunningham, "Brand Loyalty—What, Where, How Much," *Harvard Business Review*, Vol. 34 (January–February 1956), pp. 116–128; Ross Cunningham, "Customer Loyalty to Store and Brand," *Harvard Business Review*, Vol. 39 (November–December 1961), pp. 127–137; Frank, "Is Brand Loyalty a Useful Basis for Market Segmentation?" pp. 27–33.

[42] Brown, "Brand Loyalty—Fact or Fiction," January 26, 1953, p. 75; Cunningham, "Brand Loyalty—What, Where, How Much," p. 122; and William F. Massey, "Brand and Store Loyalty as Bases for Market Segmentation," in Newman, *On Knowing the Consumer*, pp. 169–172.

Brand Loyalty Correlates

Attempts to identify the variables that account for variation in brand loyalty across products and consumers have not been particularly successful. For example, numerous studies have shown that brand loyalty is unrelated to: (1) attitudes toward brand similarity, (2) personality characteristics, (3) most economic and demographic variables, (4) frequency of purchase, (5) social class membership, and (6) brand preference patterns of family members.[43]

Studies do indicate that brand loyalty increases: (1) with age, (2) as the amount used increases, and (3) as the time between purchases decreases.[44] The effect of special deals and price variations is uncertain, but the extensiveness of distribution and the market share of the leading brand exert an important influence on loyalty.[45]

Most brand-loyalty studies have concentrated on grocery products. The results indicate that brand loyalty is not a particularly useful basis for segmenting these markets, because brand-loyal customers do not differ from other customers in operational ways.[46] Whether or not brand-loyal customers will be identifiable for other product categories is an important question that has yet to be resolved.

Brand-Loyalty Models

Since 1958, a variety of mathematical models have been designed or adapted from other sources by researchers attempting to understand brand-loyalty behavior. These include Bernoulli models, homogeneous first-order Markov models, quasi-heterogeneous first-order Markov models, higher-order Markov models, the learning model, and the learning-Markov model. Since many of these models have severe shortcomings, and space here is limited, we shall consider only the learning model.[47]

A LEARNING MODEL OF BRAND LOYALTY. In order to explain the model, assume that a market consists of three brands—A, B, and C. Assume further that a

---

[43] John S. Coulson, "Buying Decisions Within the Family," in Newman, *On Knowing the Consumer*, pp. 59–66; and Advertising Research Foundation, *Are There Consumer Types?* (New York: Advertising Research Foundation, Inc., 1964).

[44] Cunningham, "Brand Loyalty," p. 127; and Frank, "Is Brand Loyalty a Useful Basis for Market Segmentation?" p. 30.

[45] William F. Masey and Ronald Frank, "Short-term Price and Dealing Effects in Selected Market Segments," *Journal of Marketing Research*, Vol. 2 (May 1965), pp. 171–185; and John U. Farley, "Why Does Brand Loyalty Vary Over Products?" *Journal of Marketing Research*, Vol. 1 (November 1964), pp. 9–14.

[46] Frank, "Is Brand Loyalty a Useful Basis for Market Segmentation?," p. 33.

[47] For a description and critique of these models see John U. Farley and Alfred E. Kuehn, "Stochastic Models of Brand Switching," in George Schwartz, ed., *Science in Marketing* (New York: John Wiley & Sons, Inc., 1965), pp. 446–464; and Engel, Kollat, and Blackwell, *Consumer Behavior*, Chap. 26.

consumer has a probability of .7 of purchasing A, .2 of purchasing B, and .1 of purchasing C. These probabilities can be expected to fluctuate up and down as the result of the passage of time, exposure to advertisements, and the specific brand that is purchased on a given occasion.

In order to make the model dynamic, a procedure is needed for revising the set of purchase probabilities for the next time period $(t + 1)$ given the behavior during the immediate past period (t). The approach is shown in Figure 6-2. The revised purchase probability for each brand after each purchase is determined by two functions, or operators. The *purchase operator* is operative only if the consumer purchased the brand in question, in this case A. If the consumer does not purchase the brand in question, the *rejection* operator takes effect.

The probability of purchasing brand A is indicated on the horizontal axis of Figure 6-2. If the consumer does not purchase brand A, the probability of buying the brand on the next occasion is read from the intersection of a vertical line from the initial probability (P_1) with the rejection operator—resulting in this case in P_2. The 45-degree line is then used to project P_2 back to the horizontal axis for the next trial. On the second purchase occasion the consumer purchases brand A, hence the probability of purchasing A again on the third trial is obtained from the intersection of the vertical line through P_2 with the purchase operator, resulting in P_3.

Thus purchase probabilities are revised after every purchase situation. Purchasing brand A at time t increases the probability that the brand will be purchased at time $t + 1$. Conversely, failure to purchase A at time t decreases the probability that A will be purchased at time $t + 1$. The degree to which purchase

Figure 6-2   A learning model of brand loyalty.

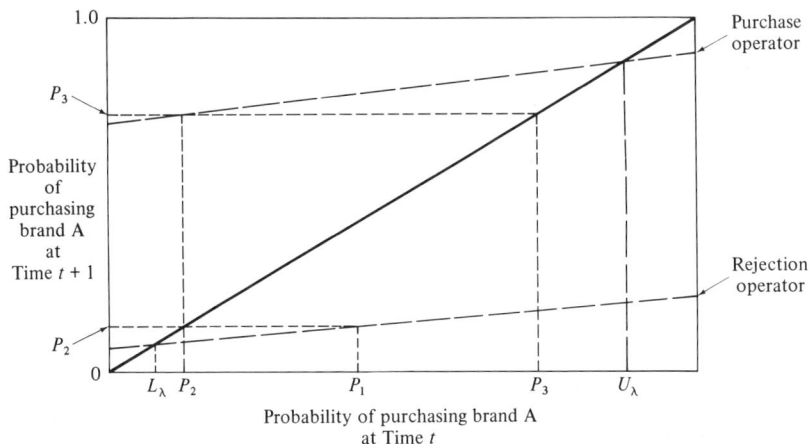

Probability of purchasing brand A at Time t

SOURCE: John U. Farley and Alfred E. Kuehn, "Stochastic Models of Brand Switching," in George Schwartz, ed., *Science in Marketing* (New York: John Wiley & Sons, Inc., 1965), p. 453. Used with the permission of the publisher.

probabilities are revised after each purchase depends on the slopes and intercepts of the purchasing and rejection operators. These are estimated from consumer-panel data on the basis of purchase sequences of three and four purchases. The model has been tested and is consistent with brand loyalty for grocery and drug items.[48]

USES. After the effect of time between purchases is understood for a product class, the model can be used to study the effects of several types of marketing activities. For example, the model has reportedly been useful in evaluating the effects of special promotions or deals such as merchandise packs and "two for the price of one" coupons. It has also been of theoretical value in analyzing the effects of advertising.[49]

LIMITATIONS. Problems of data collection and handling constitute the model's major limitation. For example, complicated problems are encountered in obtaining estimates of the parameters of the model.[50] Other problems—which also plague other models—lie in determining the most appropriate methods of reflecting variations in interpurchase time, the amount purchased, and in the way to handle mixed-brand purchases.

Overall, then, the model needs considerable refinement and extension before it can attain its full stature. Nevertheless, it is one of the most promising approaches to the modeling of brand loyalty that has been developed to date.

SUMMARY

This chapter has integrated and synthesized traditional perspectives, viewpoints, and models of consumer behavior into a comprehensive and practical model. The elements and relationships of the model were illustrated by the findings of representative empirical studies. These concepts will be used throughout the remainder of this volume to identify and assess market opportunities and to design marketing programs to capitalize on them.

The individual's psychological makeup was conceptualized as consisting of stored information and past experience, motives, personality traits, values, and attitudes. The consumer is subjected to two types of stimuli—physical and social. It was shown how these stimuli must arouse the consumer before behavior can occur. Only a limited number and type of stimuli have this effect, however, be-

[48] Alfred E. Kuehn and Ralph L. Day, "A Probabilistic Approach to Consumer Behavior," in R. Cox, W. Alderson, and S. Shapiro, *Theory in Marketing* (Homewood, Ill.: Richard D. Irwin, Inc., 1964) pp. 380–390.

[49] Alfred E. Kuehn and Ralph L. Day, "Probabilistic Models of Consumer Buying Behavior," *Journal of Marketing*, Vol. 28 (October 1964), pp. 27–31; and Alfred E. Kuehn, "How Advertising Performance Depends on Other Marketing Factors," *Journal of Advertising Research*, Vol. 2 (March 1962), pp. 2–10.

[50] For a discussion of some major problems in applying the model to advertising see James F. Engel, Hugh G. Wales, and Martin R. Warshaw, *Promotional Strategy* (Homewood, Ill.: Richard D. Irwin, Inc., 1967), p. 132.

cause of the perceptual screening that results from selective exposure, perception, and retention.

The outcome is the decision-making process, consisting of problem recognition, information seeking, alternative evaluation, purchasing processes, and postpurchase evaluation. Each of these stages was described, and illustrative studies showed their importance to marketing strategists. The chapter concluded with an overview of brand loyalty, including its nature, extent, and correlates, and a discussion of an illustrative model.

QUESTIONS FOR REVIEW AND DISCUSSION

1. How should personality variables be used in market analysis?
2. In what types of situations should a company attempt to evoke problem recognition?
3. What types of consumers are most likely to pay attention to Buick advertisements?
4. How can a marketer use an analysis of information-seeking behavior?
5. Assume you are a market analyst for a soft-drink manufacturer. What dimensions of purchasing processes would be of interest? Why?
6. Prepare a list of questions that a marketer should ask about consumer behavior.

Chapter 7   Industrial and Institutional Markets:
             Structure and Behavior

What are the greatest opportunities for marketers of industrial
products? To answer that question, it is necessary to understand
the relationship between the structure of consumer demand
(discussed in previous chapters) and the structure of industrial
demand. Industrial products are used in producing consumer
goods. Thus, ultimately the structure and behavior of industrial
markets must be a function of the structure and behavior of
consumer markets.

   Industrial marketing organizations are increasingly conducting research and investigations on consumer markets and
their relationship to industrial markets. An example is E. I.
duPont de Nemours, one of the largest industrial marketers in
America. DuPont is also a major force in research on consumer
behavior and executive education programs on consumer
trends. The purpose of these programs is to develop understanding of the complex relationships among consumer markets,
retail distribution patterns, markets for manufactured goods,
and markets for basic materials—the latter sometimes being the
only one to which DuPont directly sells.

   This chapter examines some of the patterns and behavior
found in industrial markets, especially with a view to forecasting the most attractive profit opportunities for industrial and
institutional marketing organizations.

MARKET CHARACTERISTICS OF
INDUSTRIAL PRODUCTS

Industrial goods are those products (including services) sold
to industrial, business (commercial), institutional, or govern-

ment buyers to be incorporated into their manufactured products, resold, or used in the conduct of their own activities. In many instances the same physical product can be classified as either an industrial or a consumer good, depending on the end use. For example, a typewriter sold to a business firm or to the United States Department of Defense would be classified as an industrial product. If it were sold to a student for preparation of term papers, however, it would be a consumer good. Similarly, an accountant's services sold to a business firm would be classified as an industrial product, but his services sold to an individual preparing the family's income tax would be a consumer product.

Principal types of industrial products include basic materials, components and subassemblies, capital goods and other equipment, and facilitating goods and services.[1] The relationship of these types of goods to consumer markets (which are fundamentally supported by consumer demand) is shown in Figure 7-1. That diagram also shows that marketers of industrial goods often sell to each other.

Figure 7-1   Markets for industrial products and services.

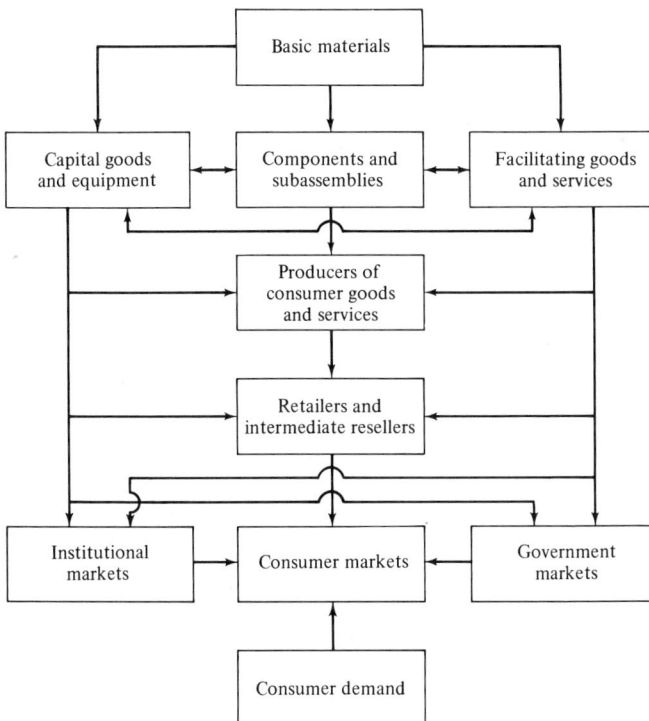

[1] For a more detailed description and classification, see Ralph S. Alexander, James S. Cross, and Ross M. Cunningham, *Industrial Marketing*, rev. ed. (Homewood, Ill.: Richard D. Irwin, Inc., 1961), Chap. 1.

Basic Materials

Basic materials are usually sold on a contractual basis, with product characteristics precisely specified. In the case of "commodity" types of materials, specifications are established by the industry, and sales are determined mostly by competitive pricing, delivery schedules, credit terms, and geographical influences on transportation costs. For semimanufactured goods, specifications may be standardized in the industry (such as certain chemicals, steel) or they may be highly individualized to meet the needs of the buyer and the capacities of the seller. In the latter instance, a firm's reputation for technical ability and service may dominate sales activities, replacing emphasis upon pricing and transportation costs. In either case, the buyer is usually influenced in his choice of a supplier by his desire to eliminate problems of production (and related customer acceptance) that would develop if the source of supply were not dependable in quality or availability.

Distribution structure typically consists of direct sales by the producer of basic materials to the manufacturers. This is facilitated by a market structure typically consisting of a few buyers, well known to the seller, and the need for a close working relationship in the schedule of deliveries and anticipation of price fluctuations. If the basic material is sold to a market with many small manufacturers, however, the chances for encountering middlemen are great. In agricultural or other industries where there are many small producers, middlemen commonly perform *sorting out* and *accumulation*[2] activities.

Components and Subassemblies

Markets for components and subassemblies have many of the characteristics of basic-materials markets. Marketing activities may be more extensive, however, because of less standardization in components. Also, because components are usually more complex than basic materials, more opportunities exist for the product to fail to operate in the hands of the final user. Thus buyers of components are especially interested in the part's giving dependable service, so that part failure will not cause the customer to transfer his disgust to the assembled product.

Channels of distribution tend to be fairly direct because of the need for the manufacturer of the component part and the assembler to cooperate closely in matching their specifications. Price is important as a buying motive, but most successful marketing strategies are dominated by ability to give dependability of quality and supply or an enhanced competitive position due to product improvement.

---

[2] For amplification of these terms see Wroe Alderson, *Market-Behavior and Executive Action* (Homewood, Ill.: Richard D. Irwin, Inc., 1957), pp. 195–206. Chapter 7 of this book contains a classic analysis of the logic of exchange as it applies to both industrial and consumer markets.

Opportunities exist for aggressive marketers occasionally to follow a strategy whereby the component part becomes better known and accepted than that of the assembler. An example might be the British-produced Garrard record changers and turntables, which some lesser-known manufacturers of stereo equipment advertise in (apparently successful) attempts to generalize the quality of the Garrard changer to the rest of the audio system.

Opportunities also exist for marketers of components and subassemblies in the repair and replacement market—for example, for such items as automobile tires and spark plugs, television tubes, and record-player needles. Marketers of components must decide whether opportunities are greater in selling to original producers of the equipment (as depicted in Figure 7-1) who act as distributors for the replacement part or in circumventing the original producer and selling through wholesalers and retailers.

Capital Goods and Equipment

Markets for installations tend to require high technical competence from sellers. Consequently, marketing strategies tend to include salesmen who are technically trained or work closely with the firm's engineering and customer service personnel. Marketing organizations best equipped to exploit marketing opportunities frequently take a "team" or "systems" approach and work closely with the buyer through negotiations extending over months or years.

Criteria for selecting a seller often center upon the *cost per unit of output* from the production process rather than the *input cost* of the installation. All of these factors usually result in a direct-to-buyer form of distribution. The demand for capital goods is highly influenced by the general state of the economy, with demand slumping greatly in a recession. (See Figure 7-2.) Buying is often influenced by a firm's top executives.

Accessory equipment tends to be more standardized than installations, and buying activity tends to take place at lower levels of management. Selling organizations tend to exploit opportunities best by allocating resources less to technical training and more to professional selling skills. Markets tend to be more *horizontal* than vertical—that is, the products are sold to companies in a wide variety of industries instead of being limited to a single industry. Consequently, various forms of middlemen are frequently encountered in the marketing strategies for accessory equipment. If industrial distributors are not used in the channel, manufacturers often need numerous sales offices or branch organizations.

Buyers of accessory equipment tend to be price-conscious, and frequently there are numerous suppliers of equipment with reasonably similar operating characteristics. Because of this situation and because of market dispersion, it is not unusual for market opportunity to be realized by a strategy that uses advertising to deemphasize direct price comparison by communicating special features that differentiate one brand of equipment (such as typewriters, drills, and so on) from another.

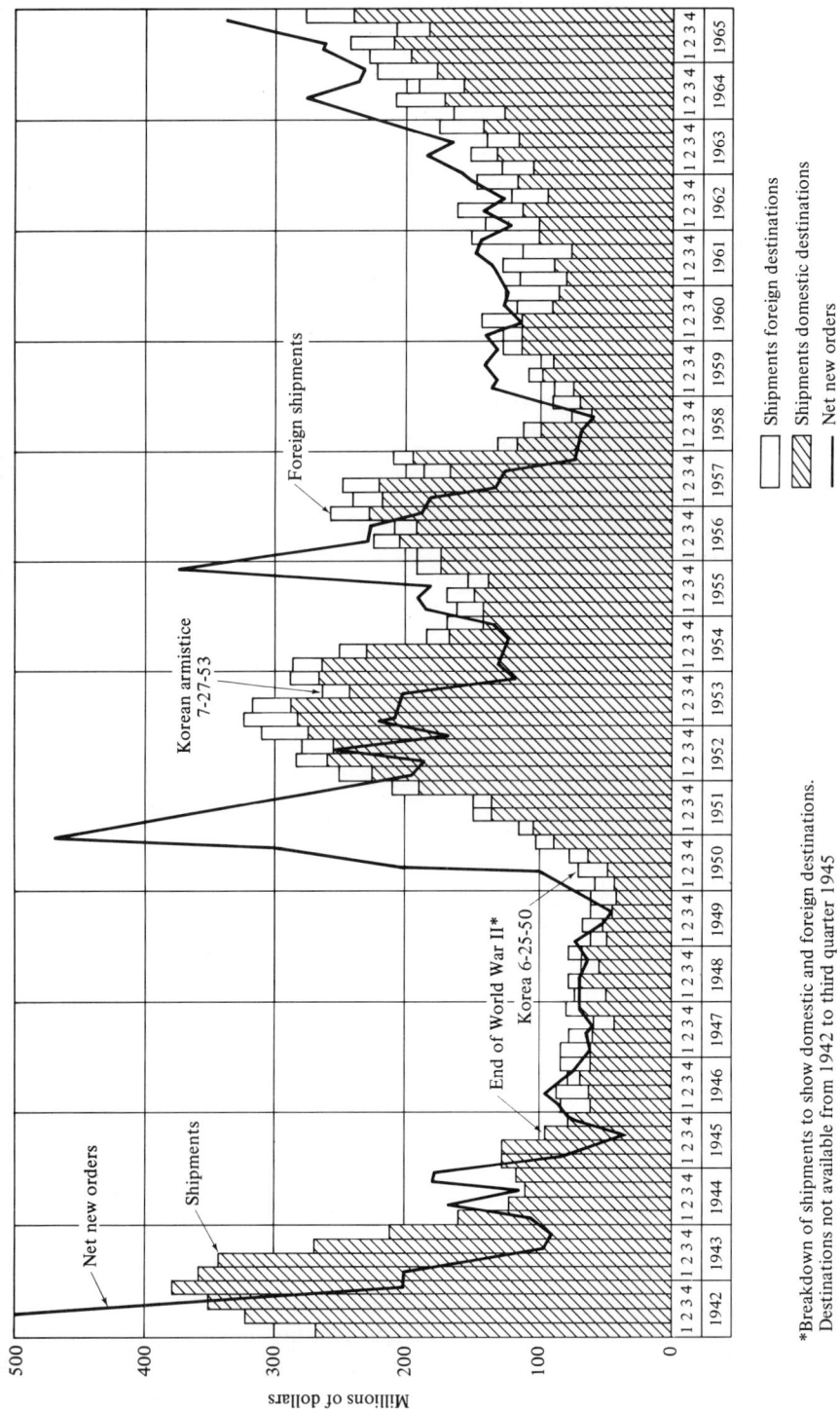

Figure 7-2 Quarterly shipments and net new orders of machine tools (metal-cutting types only).

*Breakdown of shipments to show domestic and foreign destinations.
Destinations not available from 1942 to third quarter 1945

SOURCE: National Association of Machine Tool Builders, Washington, D.C., April 21, 1965.

140

Facilitating Goods and Services

Facilitating goods and services include many types of items that facilitate rather than enter directly into the production or distribution of goods and services. A large proportion of these products are called MRO (maintenance, repair, operating) items. Services include a wide variety of items and are increasing in importance; examples include advertising-agency services, banking services, drayage and delivery services, elevator repair services, credit bureaus, employment agencies, and business consulting services.

MRO items are found in both vertical and horizontal markets. They tend to be distributed through middlemen, though by direct sales to very large buyers. Price is usually important in the selection of one supplier over another, although the influence of the distributor can also be important. The emphasis on price creates market opportunities for firms with exceptional production capabilities.

Market opportunities for services are very great, but knowledge of market structure and buying behavior is still embryonic. Services usually constitute a relatively minor part of total cost, yet quality is of major importance. Consequently, the tendency is for selection of a service supplier to be made at higher levels of management and to be less sensitive to price than to perceived quality or reputation. Successful strategies for selling services often give considerable emphasis to special training programs for employees, research reports, and other efforts to provide and establish a reputation for high levels of client attention. Marketing is almost always done in a direct-to-buyer manner.

FORECASTING INDUSTRIAL MARKETS

The relationship of industrial markets to consumer markets is clarified by two concepts, derived demand and joint demand. These concepts are fundamental in developing techniques appropriate in forecasting industrial-market opportunities.

Derived Demand

The demand for industrial goods is *derived* from the demand for consumer goods rather than existing by itself. In principle, therefore, the forecasting of industrial markets involves simply an extension of consumer-market research plus the establishment of a relationship between consumer markets and the derived industrial demand. This "simple" relationship, however, produces some complex and difficult-to-manage aberrations in the structure of industrial demand, felt most intensely in the markets for capital goods and equipment.

Derived-Demand Opportunities

Trends in consumer markets (described in Chapter 6) will have a profound effect on derived industrial markets. By studying trends in consumer markets, a marketing analyst can forecast the kinds of natural resources that must be extracted and refined, the kinds of capital goods that must be purchased and produced, and the new kinds of services and equipment that must be developed. The rise in relative importance of durable consumer goods and services in this decade (see Chapter 6), for example, will produce above-average growth for industrial goods involved in the production and distribution of sporting equipment and toys, airline travel, radio, TV and other entertainment equipment, hospitals, educational institutions, and housing. The shifting distribution of the population to younger age groups is resulting in a splurge in multifamily housing units. This also creates markets for new types of building materials, construction equipment, architectural and land-development services, and capital expansion for the production of such far-ranging products as carpeting, air-conditioning systems, swimming pools, furniture, and a host of others.

Joint Demand

Demand for industrial products is not only derived from *consumer* products but also is derived from other *industrial* products. More precisely, the demand for products in various industrial markets *varies jointly* with consumer demand. One of the most rigorous and useful methods of expressing the nature of these relationships and forecasting for strategic planning is called input-output analysis.

Input-output Forecasting

Input-output is a powerful tool for analyzing joint or interindustry demand and transaction flows. The relationships between national income and product accounts (GNP) and sales of each major industry are shown in a large matrix or table. These relationships are determined through careful analysis, and final product flows are shown as sales by each industry to the same final markets. The analysis, accomplished by tracing these flows among producers and users, covers the flows of raw materials, semifinished products, and services *among* industries. In the United States, information is collected by the Office of Business Economics and made available for business use.[3] Other industrialized countries provide similar information on their economies.

Input-output tables are revised to reflect changing relationships and additional information and analysis.[4] The first tables reflected 1958 data and contained data for 86 industries, but the 1963 tables provide interindustry relationships for 350 industrial categories as well as 10 final-demand categories. Even finer detail is given in the specific information the Office of Business Economics uses to build

---

[3] See Janet B. Riddle, "Input-Output as an Analytical Tool with Emphasis on Recent Development," in Raymond M. Haas, ed., *Science, Technology, and Marketing* (Chicago: American Marketing Association, 1966), pp. 89–93.

[4] See, for example, Anne P. Carter, "How to Handle Changing Technical Coefficients in Input/Output Tables," in Keith Cox and Ben M. Enis, eds., *A New Measure of Responsibility for Marketing.* (Chicago: American Marketing Association, 1968), pp. 310–311.

up the data for the 350 classifications.[5] All of the data are available on computer tape or punch cards. (This is important, since the 1963 matrix contains 122,500 cells describing interindustry relationships.)

An example of interindustry demand relationships is presented in Figure 7-3. This figure is similar to the OBE data but compiled by *Fortune* magazine. The cells at the intersections of 106 rows and columns contain two figures. The top of the cell shows the direct purchases of the row industry from the column industry, or the row-industry sales to the column industry. The bottom part of the cell shows the sales of the row industry to all industries supplying the column industry. The total of all that each row industry sold to all column industries is shown in the intermediate output column. The six "final demand" columns show the source of industrial demand as well as the share of the gross national product accounted for by each industrial sector. The sum of total intermediate outputs and total final demand is shown in the final column of the matrix.

STRATEGIC USES OF INPUT-OUTPUT. Input-output analysis is useful in the development of marketing strategy for many types of organizations; it is especially useful for analyzing industrial demand. Some typical applications are listed below:

1. *Forecasting of market potential and future sales.* National Steel has used a modified input-output approach to forecast steel tonnage reliably and to simulate the effect of changes in market conditions.[6]

2. *Determination of company market share in specific industries.* A commercial service offered by IBM allows companies to measure their market penetration with sufficient depth to suggest needed changes in market strategy.[7]

3. *Determination of regional sales in an industry.* Input-output can be used in a variety of ways to determine the volume of sales in a geographic area.[8] For example, a printing organization wished to know its share of total printing sales in its state in various industries. Its own sales could be determined, and through input-output analysis of printing purchases for its state, the firm made an estimate of its present market share with sufficient accuracy to undertake a revised marketing strategy.

4. *Determination of foreign-domestic market relationships.*[9]

[5] Eugene P. Roberts, "The New 350 Sector 1963 I/O Tables," in Cox and Enis, *A New Measure of Responsibility for Marketing*, pp. 310–312.

[6] Andre B. Celestin, "How National Steel Uses I/O to Forecast Annual Steel Opportunities to 1975," in Cox and Enis, *A New Measure of Responsibility for Marketing*, pp. 313–316.

[7] Jay M. Gould, "The Use of Input-Output in Industrial Marketing," in Haas, *Science, Technology, and Marketing*, pp. 105–114.

[8] R. C. Haring, "Use of Input/Output Analysis in Developing Measure of Regional Marketing Activities," in Haas, *Science, Technology, and Marketing*, pp. 100–104.

[9] John A. Sawyer, "Forecasting Industry Output and Imports in an Open Economy: Some Experiments for Canada, 1950–1958," Unpublished Ph.D. Thesis, University of Chicago, 1966.

Figure 7-3 Input-output matrix: dollar flow.

Read down columns for Input — Final Demand

Read along rows for Output		1 Livestock and livestock products	2 Other agricultural products	3 Forestry and fishery products	4 Agricultural, forestry and fishery services	5 Iron and ferroalloy ores mining	6 Nonferrous metal ores mining	7 Coal mining	8 Crude petroleum and natural gas	9 Stone and clay mining and quarrying	10 Chemical and fertilizer mineral mining	11 Residential buildings	12 Private industrial buildings	13 Other private nonresidential buildings	14 Other private construction	15 Public nonresidential buildings	16 Highways	17 All other public construction	105 Inventory valuation adjustment	106 Scrap and by-products adjustment	Total Intermediate Outputs	Personal consumption expenditures	Private fixed capital formation	Net inventory change	Net exports	Federal government purchases	State and local government purchases	Total Final Demand (GNP)	Total Gross Output	
Livestock and livestock products	1	5851.3 3271.8	2374.1 600.1	109.8 16.7	274.8 11.9	– 0.5	– 0.7	– 1.4	– 0.2	– 0.7	– 0.2	– 121.0	– 23.1	– 47.8	– 14.3	– 21.2	– 29.5	– 19.9	–	64.7	35502.7	2388.2	–	213.5	35.1	14.4	18.4	2567.8	38170.3	1 Livestock and livestock products
Other agricultural products	2	10434.2 1105.2	1074.3 6439.4	229.6 31.7	761.3 27.1	– 0.9	– 1.2	– 2.5	– 0.3	– 1.2	· 0.3	176.8 445.7	7.8 48.9	8.9 107.1	– 29.9	6.1 49.4	87.9 131.9	1.0 37.3	–	–	27220.6	3020.7	–	154.7	3205.1	-476.1	23.8	5928.2	33148.8	2 Other agricultural products
Forestry and fishing products	3	– 1	– 4.3	37.0 229.7	– ·	– 0.2	– 0.2	– 1.1	– ·	– 0.1	– ·	· 427.6	– 26.5	– 108.8	– 12.7	– 49.6	– 14.7	– 18.4	–	–	2120.8	60.5	–	14.8	49.3	100.7	0.7	226.0	2346.9	3 Forestry and fishery products
Agricultural, forestry and fishery services	4	792.7 10.6	1332.2 271.8	30.5 4.6	2.8 67.5	– 0.1	– 0.1	– 0.2	– ·	– 0.1	·	– 36.1	– 4.9	– 11.1	– 2.6	– 4.9	– 7.7	– 3.6	–	–	2378.0	–	–	–	7.8	58.5	-132.4	-66.1	2313.7	4 Agricultural, forestry and fishing services
Iron and ferroalloy ores mining	5	– 1.9	– 5.7	– 0.1	– ·	152.3 192.4	22.9 5.3	– 1.6	– ·	0.7 1.0	0.8 0.3	– 151.0	– 50.5	– 86.3	– 96.9	– 34.3	– 33.7	– 57.6	–	–	2113.8	–	–	88.4	90.9	–	–	179.2	2283.0	5 Iron and ferroalloy ores mining
Nonferrous metal ores mining	6	– 1.8	– 5.7	– 0.1	– ·	71.3 7.2	397.2 412.9	– 1.6	– ·	1.5 0.7	0.5 0.2	– 160.3	– 71.3	– 95.3	– 97.5	– 34.3	– 23.7	– 42.9	–	–	2249.0	–	–	-53.0	7.8	394.3	–	349.1	2598.1	6 Nonferrous metal ores mining
Coal mining	7	9.7 1.5	0.8 10.8	– 0.3	– -0.1	10.2 1.5	2.4 1.7	867.1 829.4	0.2 0.1	4.4 2.1	0.8 0.4	– 136.5	– 43.7	– 79.2	0.1 56.0	– 33.5	– 40.0	– 50.9	–	–	2992.7	325.0	–	-58.8	317.4	13.3	80.2	877.0	3688.7	7 Coal mining
Crude petroleum and natural gas	8	– 42.4	– 172.9	– 3.0	– -0.9	– 2.2	– 4.0	– 8.1	441.5 57.3	– 7.4	1.8 2.0	– 439.2	– 122.1	– 199.9	0.1 84.3	– 102.2	– 288.4	– 161.5	–	–	16842.2	–	–	29.4	25.8	–	–	55.4	16897.6	8 Crude petroleum and natural gas
Stone and clay mining and quarrying	9	0.1 5.1	95.2 24.2	– 0.2	– -0.1	– 0.1	0.1 0.4	1.7 0.9	– ·	18.8 348.2	14.9 1.7	89.8 233.8	17.3 64.0	31.2 126.3	20.0 35.5	28.0 72.0	515.5 579.6	168.8 233.1	–	–	2231.5	24.2	–	264.6	37.6	–	-12.3	344.1	2575.8	9 Stone and clay mining and quarrying
Chemical and fertilizer mineral mining	10	– 5.1	40.8 24.3	0.1 0.2	– -0.1	– 0.2	2.1 1.0	0.1 0.8	– ·	1.0 0.8	81.6 104.2	– 29.1	– 8.3	– 15.7	– 10.3	– 7.1	– 13.0	– 16.2	–	–	886.5	2.0	–	–	83.1	–	12.3	97.4	963.9	10 Chemical and fertilizer mineral mining
Residential buildings	11	– –	– –	– –	– –	– –	– –	– –	– –	– –	– –	– 25990.0	– –	– –	– –	– –	– –	– –	–	–	–	–	25500.0	–	–	42.0	448.0	25990.0	25990.0	11 Residential buildings
Private industrial buildings	12	– –	– –	– –	– –	– –	– –	– –	– –	– –	– –	– –	– 7086.0	– –	– –	– –	– –	– –	–	–	–	–	6700.0	–	–	110.0	276.0	7086.0	7088.0	12 Private industrial buildings
Other private nonresidential buildings	13	– –	– –	– –	– –	– –	– –	– –	– –	– –	– –	– –	– –	– 14075.0	– –	– –	– –	– –	–	–	–	–	14075.0	–	–	–	–	14075.0	14075.0	13 Other private nonresidential buildings
Other private construction	14	– –	– –	– –	– –	– –	– –	– –	– –	– –	– –	– –	– –	– –	– 7775.0	– –	– –	– –	–	–	–	–	7775.0	–	–	–	–	7775.0	7775.0	14 Other private construction
Public nonresidential buildings	15	– –	– –	– –	– –	– –	– –	– –	– –	– –	– –	– –	– –	– –	– –	– 6342.0	– –	– –	–	–	–	–	–	–	–	538.0	5804.0	6342.0	6342.0	15 Public nonresidential buildings
Highways	16	– –	– –	– –	– –	– –	– –	– –	– –	– –	– –	– –	– –	– –	– –	– –	– 7951.0	– –	–	–	–	–	–	–	–	191.0	7760.0	7951.0	7951.0	16 Highways
All other public construction	17	– –	– –	– –	– –	– –	– –	– –	– –	– –	– –	– –	– –	– –	– –	– –	– –	– 8285.6	–	–	–	–	–	–	2.6	3357.0	4926.0	8285.6	8285.6	17 All other public construction
Maintenance and repair construction	18	411.8 86.3	525.2 194.5	0.5 2.6	2.8 -1.2	1.3 3.1	2.1 3.9	3.1 6.6	8.5 1.0	3.1 3.9	0.5 1.1	3.9 310.1	1.2 88.2	2.2 164.5	0.8 86.4	1.0 71.9	1.3 104.9	1.2 88.9	–	–	19998.4	–	–	–	–	1615.4	3398.6	5014.0	25012.4	18 Maintenance and repair construction
Ordnance and accessories	19	– 0.4	– 1.0	– ·	– ·	– ·	– 0.1	– 0.1	– ·	– 0.1	– ·	– 10.6	– 4.9	– 9.8	4.7 7.7	– 5.6	– 3.0	– 2.6	–	–	2414.7	274.5	–	372.7	175.5	4697.8	8.9	5529.4	7944.1	19 Ordnance and accessories
Meat products	20	10.2 9.9	– 5.5	– 0.3	– -0.1	– 0.1	– 0.2	– 0.5	– ·	– 0.3	– 0.1	– 32.6	– 10.2	– 18.9	– 6.4	– 8.3	– 9.4	– 9.0	–	–	5062.8	22075.1	–	487.5	373.0	494.1	38.9	23468.6	28531.4	20 Meat products
Dairy products	21	– 4.2	– 3.6	– 0.1	– ·	– 0.1	– 0.2	– 0.4	– ·	– 0.2	– 0.1	– 24.5	– 7.9	– 14.5	– 5.1	– 6.3	– 7.6	– 7.2	–	–	3498.5	14143.0	–	1.0	309.2	-5.2	187.5	14615.5	18115.0	21 Dairy products
Canning, preserving fruits, vegetables and sea foods	22	– 2.7	– 1.9	– 0.1	– ·	– ·	– 0.1	– 0.1	– ·	– 0.1	– ·	– 6.3	– 1.9	– 3.5	– 1.5	– 1.5	– 2.1	– 2.1	–	–	1302.9	7170.9	–	77.1	356.8	167.8	32.9	7805.5	9108.4	22 Canning, preserving fruits, vegetables and sea foods
Grain mill products	23	4605.1 428.2	– 82.7	3.4 3.2	10.3 -1.9	– 0.1	– 0.3	– 0.5	– ·	– 0.3	– 0.1	– 39.5	– 10.4	– 19.8	18.0 23.9	– 8.8	– 10.6	– 9.4	–	–	8214.2	2753.4	–	28.4	563.6	172.1	81.6	3597.1	11811.3	23 Grain mill products
Bakery products	24	– 1.5	– 1.2	– ·	– ·	– ·	– 0.1	– 0.1	– ·	– 0.1	– ·	– 9.3	– 2.9	– 5.3	– 1.6	– 2.3	– 2.5	– 2.3	–	–	495.2	7892.8	–	13.3	13.2	28.7	23.0	7968.8	8464.0	24 Bakery products
Sugar	25	34.0 16.8	– 4.4	– 0.2	– -0.1	– 0.1	– 0.1	– 0.2	– ·	– 0.1	– ·	– 12.9	– 4.0	– 7.4	– 3.0	– 3.2	– 3.8	– 3.6	–	–	2381.5	977.0	–	7.1	30.4	41.2	10.0	1065.7	2457.3	25 Sugar
Confectionary and related products	26	– 1.3	– 0.7	– ·	– ·	– ·	– ·	– 0.1	– ·	– ·	– ·	– 3.9	– 1.2	– 2.2	– 0.8	– 1.0	– 1.2	– 1.1	–	–	833.5	2442.5	–	28.4	40.5	38.8	7.0	2557.2	3390.7	26 Confectionary and related products
Beverage industries	27	11.8 9.4	– 8.7	– 0.3	– -0.1	– 0.3	– 0.6	– 1.2	– 0.1	– 0.7	– 0.2	– 72.8	– 23.5	– 43.1	– 14.7	– 18.6	– 21.3	– 20.6	–	–	3158.9	9280.4	–	20.4	67.8	–	–	9368.7	12527.6	27 Beverage industries
Miscellaneous food and kindred products	28	369.5 91.9	4.4 24.0	33.2 4.3	– -0.4	– 0.1	– 0.3	– 0.6	– ·	– 0.3	0.1 0.1	– 46.9	– 11.2	– 21.8	– 9.3	– 9.5	– 11.0	– 11.4	–	15.8	4834.4	4779.0	–	29.4	714.6	31.3	31.9	5648.2	10280.6	28 Miscellaneous food and kindred products
Tobacco manufacturers	29	– 0.5	– 1.1	– ·	– ·	– ·	– 0.1	– 0.2	– ·	– 0.1	– ·	– 10.7	– 3.5	– 6.4	– 2.1	– 2.3	– 3.1	– 3.0	–	–	2048.4	6714.8	–	50.1	624.7	–	–	7389.6	9438.0	29 Tobacco manufacturers
Broad and narrow fabrics, yarn and thread mills	30	– 11.8	10.4 24.9	– 1.0	– -0.3	0.5 0.2	3.4 1.2	2.5 2.0	– 0.1	– 0.9	0.3 0.2	– 103.0	– 29.3	– 53.8	– 14.4	– 21.9	– 19.5	– 20.4	–	-15.8	16799.5	1175.7	–	147.3	275.4	87.7	12.3	1878.4	18477.9	30 Broad and narrow fabrics, yarn and thread mills
Misc. textile goods and floor coverings	31	9.8 6.8	48.8 20.4	21.5 2.6	20.8 -0.8	– 0.1	– 0.2	– 0.8	3.5 ·	0.1 0.7	– 0.1	1.7 52.0	0.8 17.8	1.1 32.4	0.0 8.0	0.4 13.4	0.5 11.3	0.5 11.5	–	–	2869.8	1286.7	92.5	265.1	85.8	24.2	1.4	1755.7	4525.5	31 Misc. textile goods and floor coverings
Apparel	32	– 1.1	– 2.3	– 0.1	– ·	– 0.1	– 0.1	– 0.3	– ·	– 0.2	– ·	– 26.8	– 8.3	– 15.4	– 5.2	– 6.6	– 5.3	– 5.6	–	-1.3	4981.8	17800.7	–	220.9	387.3	105.4	144.0	18658.3	23840.1	32 Apparel
Misc. fabricated textile products	33	13.4 11.0	59.4 16.8	– 0.2	– -0.1	– 0.1	– 0.1	– 0.2	– ·	– 0.2	– ·	0.1 18.4	0.1 5.7	0.1 10.6	– 3.9	· 4.7	· 5.9	0.3 6.0	–	-0.3	1803.3	1880.3	–	117.8	29.9	89.5	0.7	2118.2	3821.5	33 Misc. fabricated textile products
Lumber and wood products, exc. containers	34	3.1 11.3	2.4 32.3	– 0.8	– -0.2	13.4 1.9	2.8 1.2	27.2 9.9	9.7 0.1	0.1 1.2	0.4 0.3	3007.8 4242.0	145.8 255.8	718.2 1070.5	58.4 119.1	328.5 488.2	76.5 137.2	101.1 172.6	–	–	12074.5	235.2	11.8		193.5	-8.1	1.3	435.7	12510.2	34 Lumber and wood products, exc. containers
Wooden containers	35	– 5.9	139.7 29.0	– 0.2	0.1 -0.1	– ·	– 0.1	– 0.1	– ·	– 0.1	– ·	– 26.8	– 5.9	– 12.9	– 2.4	– 5.2	– 5.1	– 4.4	–	–	672.5	–			3.8	3.2	0.7	7.6	880.3	35 Wooden containers
Household furniture	36	– 0.3	– 0.7	– ·	– ·	– ·	– ·	– 0.1	– ·	– ·	– ·	289.8 291.1	– 6.1	15.8 27.1	– 2.1	– 5.1	– 2.5	– 2.5	–	–	1058.0	3843.3	251.3	103.1	18.3	50.5	112.6	4379.1	5437.1	36 Household furniture

SOURCE: Reprinted by permission from *Fortune Magazine's Input-Output Folio.*

5. *Discovering potential markets.* Firms can trace sales distributions of their own output compared with those of the industry of which they are a member, and thus they can discover potential markets previously unknown to them.[10]

6. *Developing understanding of market structure and total business environment.* Scudder, Stevens, and Clark use input-output analysis to identify the demographic, technological, and political (especially government expenditures) variables that affect demand; these variables are used in simulating alternative marketing strategies under varying assumptions about the future.[11]

FORECASTS OF JOINT MARKET OPPORTUNITIES. Forecasts of high-growth and low-growth industrial markets through 1980 have been made using input-output analysis. These illustrate the use of input-output analysis for long-run market planning and strategy.[12]

Using growth rates for the period of 1965 to 1980, the following industries are projected to have the highest growth rate in real output:

1. electric components
2. computing machines
3. photographic and optical equipment
4. service-industry machines
5. synthetic fibers
6. communication equipment
7. electric, gas, and water utilities
8. rubber and plastics products
9. chemical and fertilizer mining
10. communications

Reversing the criteria but using the same forecasting procedures, the industries that are projected to have the slowest growth rates are:

1. leather products
2. wooden containers
3. shoes

[10] George Fisk, *Marketing Systems* (New York: Harper & Row, Publishers, 1967), pp. 206–207. Also see pp. 197–211 for an excellent introduction to input-output analysis.

[11] R. F. Mathieson, "Input-Output Analysis in a Changing World," in Bernard A. Morin, ed., *Marketing in a Changing World* (Chicago: American Marketing Association, 1969), pp. 129–131. Also, see Roberts, "The New 350 Sector I/O Tables," p. 311.

[12] The following projections are from Ronald E. Kutscher, "1980 Projections in an Input/Output Framework," in Cox and Enis, *A New Measure of Responsibility for Marketing*, pp. 302–305. These projections are derived from the Interagency Growth Project representing the U.S. Council of Economic Advisors, Bureau of the Budget, and the Departments of Labor and Commerce.

4. agricultural services
5. coal mining
6. iron and steel manufacturing
7. forestry and fishery
8. tobacco manufacturing

GOVERNMENT MARKET OPPORTUNITIES

Market opportunities created by sales to government-related institutions are expected to be among the high-growth markets in this decade. Even without the assumption that an increasing percentage of GNP will be allocated to the federal government, the U.S. administrative budget is expected to rise to $209 billion by fiscal year 1977.[13]

The problems of a society frequently create market opportunities for firms selling to state and local governments. High-growth markets in the future are expected to be for products and services to solve problems of:

1. population growth
2. poverty
3. urbanization
4. air and water pollution
5. congested transportation
6. agriculture

Each of these is analyzed in more detail in the pages that follow.

Population Growth

Immense population growth produces large-scale industrial and institutional markets. Products demanded include, among other things, vast quantities of natural resources and energy. Some resource needs will have to be met with man-made basic materials, perhaps yet undiscovered. Energy requirements will rise from 52 quadrillion BTU's in 1964 to 161 quadrillion BTU's in 2000. Much of this will be purchased or distributed by various levels of governmental units. The nation's daily consumption of water will rise from 325 billions in 1965 to 900 billion gallons in 2000, producing large markets for water filtration equipment, chemical purifiers, pumps and pipes, and many related products and services.[14]

Poverty and Urbanization

The problems of poverty and urbanization will provide huge markets for educational services of all types, municipal services such as fire protection and law

---

[13] George R. Morrissey and Phillip L. Oster, "Impact of Growth: Government Social Markets 1967–1977," in M. S. Moyer and R. E. Vosburgh, eds., *Marketing for Tomorrow . . . Today* (Chicago: American Marketing Association, 1967), pp. S-7 to S-83.

[14] *Ibid.*

enforcement, and housing. The rising need for law enforcement opens up new markets for many types of enforcement and detection equipment. Representative of the programs that apply to housing are FHA programs 235 and 236, which allow the financing of single-family residences or multifamily apartment projects with subsidies for mortgage interest. When government assistance accounts for about half of all housing units, marketing organizations must understand strategies appropriate for such an environment. One firm in Alabama profitably markets new single-family residences to "anyone who earns $50 a week" by adapting its marketing strategies to be compatible with government programs; the company has experienced phenomenal growth in sales and profits.

Successful marketing strategies of the future will often need to incorporate selling to or through the government. Immense markets will be provided by efforts to renovate America's cities:

The cost of renovating the nation's cities has been estimated to be of such magnitude that it will require $250 billion of federal funds for the next decade alone. The federal government, through 15 separate agencies, has already invested just short of $100 billion over the past decade in aid to state and city governments. This does not include federal expenditures for Social Security, the Federal Housing Administration, or the Veterans Administration. Current federal government expenditures on the nation's cities is running at a $13 billion annual rate.[15]

Air and Water Pollution

The eye-searing problem of air pollution will be met by private business firms selling automotive exhaust-control systems, pollution-free gasolines, and industrial exhaust systems rather than by direct governmental purchase of these systems. However, the impetus in their marketing is likely to come most strongly from governmental regulation of pollution. In London, for example, very strict laws have been enacted in the past decade that virtually eliminate air pollution. The laws tell people what kinds of products they must purchase and what kinds of fuel they must (not) purchase. Although some people dislike having their "rights" restricted, the net effect is both to provide immense markets for pollution-equipment marketers and, more importantly, to eliminate air pollution.

Water pollution is an equally serious problem providing, perhaps, even greater markets for business firms. Water pollution is a by-product of a rising population and an advancing technology. The rising population density has simply overtaxed the natural cleansing ability of streams and lakes. Technological development has also produced new types of pollutants less susceptible to natural cleansing processes. Research indicates the size of markets resulting from pollution control:

If the nation's rivers and streams are to be kept available for recreational use, the cumulative cost for the remainder of the century will exceed $100 billion. Simi-

[15] *Ibid.*, p. S-79.

larly, a solution to the problem of air pollution will also require an investment of $100 billion by the year 2000. The cost of effective solid waste disposal systems, including provision for rubbish, garbage, and junk automobiles, will be at least $50 billion. The federal government has taken several initial steps towards a solution to the problem of solid waste disposal. Last year Congress enacted the Solid Waste Disposal Act, and research and equipment demonstration programs have been sponsored in both the Department of Health, Education, and Welfare and in the Department of the Interior.

The cumulative private industrial market for pollution control systems and hardware will amount to a minimum of one-quarter of a trillion dollars over the remaining 34 years of this century.

Transportation

The rapidly expanding volume of automobiles in America (and other industrialized countries) is not a solution to transportation congestion—it is the cause of it; the result has been a plea for massive expenditures on public transportation. San Francisco has recently instituted a Bay-area mass-transportation system. In Aukland, New Zealand, planning is underway for a metropolitan area mass-transit system. The planning includes extensive marketing research to insure that the system meets the needs of area population and to plan effective communications to persuade residents to use the system rather than alternative forms of transportation. The great problem is not designing or producing or even financing mass transportation; the problem is *marketing it* in such a way that commuters will give up the door-to-door convenience of the private automobile (even with massive highway congestion) for public mingling in mass transit.

Over the next 20 years, at least 25 metropolitan areas in the United States alone are expected to install rapid transit systems, raising needs for industrial sales of equipment, planning and research services, financing, and operational products and services. Over the next decade, federal, state and local expenditures for rapid transit are expected to reach $12 billion. At the same time, the nation needs to spend over $55 billion in new highway construction. Some of this probably must include high-technology products such as controlled-guidance systems for automobiles and computerized traffic control. Needs are also rapidly expanding for alternative forms of transportation and the central systems needed to support them—mostly sold in government markets.

Agriculture

Traditionally, the federal government has provided substantial markets for products such as fertilizer, financing services, and the services of agricultural specialists. In recent years, however, *reduction* of farm output has rivaled *production* for federal dollars; the result has been the withholding of 56 million acres of crop land or about one-sixth of the total. In sharp contrast to the hunger of some parts of the world, the United States (and some other countries such as Canada, Australia, and New Zealand) have as their most severe agricultural problem *over*supply. Economic conditions among U.S. farmers are frequently poor because no markets exist for their output—so the goal of many federal programs has been to reduce supply.

People ask why a benevolent society doesn't give the surplus supply to countries that need it. There is a persistent belief, however, that to give or sell below cost large amounts of grain (except in abnormal situations such as a drought) would so seriously disrupt economic conditions in the receiving country that more damage than benefit would result.

The world needs the grain that countries such as the United States have the capacity of producing. A *need* exists for U.S. agricultural output but no *market*. The problem is one of *marketing* rather than *production* of food products. When a firm or coalition of firms figures out how to solve this marketing problem (presumably through governmental programs), the effects on markets for agricultural products and related products such as farm equipment and fertilizers will be staggering.

Defense

Defense-related expenditures have traditionally provided markets for many products and services. In 1971, military expenditures totaled $71.9 billion officially. When defense-related expenditures of other areas of Federal spending are included, the total in 1971 was approximately $106 billion.[16] In general, poor marketing practices have been common among defense firms, with the government identifying product needs and firms following orders. In recent years, however, space/defense firms have increasingly emphasized the marketing concept, improved selling practices, and more efficient marketing organization and planning for market development.[17]

Although defense firms often are weak in strategic marketing ability[18] there continues to be great interest in diversifying into nondefense markets. Areas identified as most likely markets for strategic growth by defense companies are surface transportation, hydrography or water systems, communication systems, atmospheric research and control, and area development.[19]

[16] This estimate was made by Arthur Burns, Chairman of the Federal Reserve Board, in public speeches. See "Nixon's Economic Dilemma," *Time*, July 5, 1971, p. 62.

[17] See the following articles: Arthur P. Felton, "Management Attitude and the Marketing Concept"; Victor W. McMahill, Jr., "The Marketing of High Technology Products: Historical Perspective and Implications"; L. D. Richardson, "Defense/Space Management Looks at Marketing"; and Peter E. Skerrett, "Market Planning—Accomplishments and Possibilities"; all in Frederick E. Webster, Jr., ed., *New Directions in Marketing* (Chicago: American Marketing Association, 1965). Also, see Blair A. Simon, "Government/Defense Industry Takes on the Marketing Concept," in John S. Wright and Jac L. Goldstrucker, eds., *New Ideas for Successful Marketing* (Chicago: American Marketing Association, 1966), pp. S-13 to S-20.

[18] Herold A. Sherman, "Marketing Organizations in the Defense/Space Industry," in Webster, *New Directions in Marketing Management*, pp. S-23 to S-37.

[19] Murray L. Weidenbaum, "Strategies for Diversification of Defense/Space Companies," in Moyer and Vosburgh, *Marketing for Tomorrow . . . Today*, pp. S-29 to S-34. For another useful description of a method for identifying diversification see James Alcott, R. E. Roberts, Jr., and William Park, "Identifying Diversification Potentials," *ibid.*, pp. S-8 to S-12.

Government Purchasing

Government markets include a wide variety of products and a wide variety of purchasing practices and organizations. The government is also a massive distributor of consumer products. The U.S. military, through post and base exchanges, ranks as the world's third or fourth largest retailing organization.

There is no one federal agency buying for the federal government, and no single buyer in any agency purchases all that agency's needs for any single item of supplies, equipment, or service. Less than 15 percent of purchases are made in Washington; the rest are dispersed throughout the world through specialized agencies and buying organizations.[20] It is often necessary, however, to coordinate actual buying at the local level with Washington influences.

GENERAL BINDING CORPORATION. An example of governmental selling is provided by General Binding Corporation, a producer of paper-punching and plastic-binding machines and plastic-binding elements. The company experienced limited success in selling to local branches and through a distributor until, in 1955, it established a Washington branch. The company spent two years "knocking on doors" of influential persons in the buying process, convincing them through demonstrations and analyses that the GBC products met or exceeded government specifications and had special advantages that justified changing existing specifications so that GBC could efficiently bid on projects at the local level. The company tried to find needs of the customer—the government—that could be met better by GBC's products than by competitors'. GBC communicated this information to all agencies through GBC's regional sales network. Throughout the two years GBC was getting started in government markets, they were actively determining the *specific individuals* who influence a decision:

> . . . we discovered that a salesman can spin his wheels in approaching a military reservation unless he has some idea of whom he is going to see. We've visited huge military bases where thousands of military and civilian personnel were working in acres of office space and yet we knew there were only four people on that base who were in a position to make a purchasing decision on our line of products. . . .[21]

Successful strategies for satisfying government market opportunities require increasing levels of understanding of institutional buying influences. Price is important in most government contracts but probably much less important than marketers often assume. In high-technology markets where a relatively few com-

---

[20] An elementary introduction to the diversified buying sources of government is provided in Stanley E. Cohen, "Looking Into the U.S. Government Market," *Industrial Marketing,* September 1964, pp. 129–138.

[21] This case and quote are summarized from Paul Jason, "How We Learned to Sell the Federal Government," *Industrial Marketing,* September 1964, pp. 146–148.

panies dominate contract awards, it is known that general reputation is of much greater significance than price.[22] Thorough knowledge of buyer's needs, timing, and personal sale abilities are important in most of the other government markets also. Strategies involving today's government markets require more sophistication than in the past in the skills of market intelligence and proposal preparation,[23] bidding,[24] negotiation,[25] sales-accountability and profit-planning procedures,[26] and systemic approaches to preparing marketing plans.[27]

OTHER INSTITUTIONAL MARKET OPPORTUNITIES

Hospitals, welfare organizations, educational establishments, restaurants and in-plant cafeterias, and other institutions represent vast and growing market opportunities. Some of these are governmental or quasi-governmental in nature, others are autonomous.

Hospitals

Hospitals represent huge market opportunities for food service, equipment, and supplies of many types. In 1967 there were over 1,300,000 beds in the nation's 7,000 hospitals and well over a billion meals a year were being served. The nonpayroll expenses of hospitals (presenting direct markets for equipment, capital, and commodity purchases) totaled nearly $6 billion.[28] Hospitals represent outstanding growth markets because of consumers' willingness to spend whatever is necessary for the best possible medical care.

Welfare and Charitable Institutions

Welfare and charitable (including religious) institutions tend to be understaffed, underfinanced, and, in the case of religious groups, faced with declining budgets. Consequently, they tend to be very price conscious and not as attractive as some other markets. Welfare agencies that are government financed may not fit this

[22] Murray L. Weidenbaum, "Competition in High Technology Government Markets," in Reed Moyer, ed., *Changing Marketing Systems* (Chicago: American Marketing Association, 1967), pp. 134–142.

[23] See John J. Kennedy, "Defense-Aerospace Marketing: A Model for Effective Action," *Business Horizons,* Volume 8 (Winter 1965), pp. 67–74.

[24] Kenneth Simmonds, "Measuring the Effectiveness of Marketing Expenditure in Bidding for Defense Contracts," in Wright and Goldstrucker, *New Ideas for Successful Marketing,* pp. S-149 to S-167.

[25] John Kennedy, "Practice and Theory in Negotiation: A Conceptual Model for Negotiation," in Webster, *New Directions in Marketing,* pp. S-85 to S-103.

[26] Salvatore F. Divita, "Government Marketing: An Appraisal," in Moyer and Vosburgh, *Marketing for Tomorrow . . . Today,* pp. S-41 to S-44.

[27] Sylvania's approach to selling government markets—see Lawrence J. Straw, "Corporate Review and Management of Divisional Sales Campaigns," in Webster, *New Directions in Marketing,* pp. S-119 to S-137.

[28] Joseph H. McNinch, "The Hospital Buying Decision and How it is Made," in Morin, ed., *Marketing in a Changing World,* pp. 36–38.

pattern, however. Successful marketing strategies to these markets often depend upon a high degree of understanding and empathy with the organizations' goals.

Educational Institutions

Educational-institutions markets are very large and attract many marketers. Many marketers have found it difficult to be profitable because of complexities, traditionalism and decentralization within educational institutions' buying groups. The Audio-Visual Products Division of Bell and Howell found the following conditions to characterize educational markets:

1. Buying is heavily influenced by locally determined political influences which are disruptive to product development, sales forecasting, and marketing planning.
2. Educators are by nature slow to accept anything new and consider new products risky to their tenure, reputation, and work load; consequently the pay-out of new product development is often spread over a long period.
3. School systems are decentralized and autonomous and *resist strongly* federal or state control or recommendations; this often requires a large, localized (and therefore expensive) sales organization.
4. Many different persons influence the buying decision: teachers, curriculum specialists, AV director, the principal, the superintendent, the business agent, and the school board. This complicates the selling task.
5. School buyers are more receptive to product demonstrations than other industrial buyers.
6. School officials are *very* fond of and influenced by *teacher workshops* done at the expense of the selling organization.[29]

Indirect Institutional Opportunities

Institutions are frequently the testing market for new products, techniques, and approaches. Their drive for efficiency and their relatively captured audiences often allow them to be innovators in the acceptance of new technology. Microwave ovens, convection cooking, and other new heating and reconstitution methods found their first acceptance in school cafeterias and in-plant feeding markets. The military paved the way for acceptance of instant apple sauce, orange juice, and sweet potatoes and freeze-dried cottage cheese. Dehydrated foods, including onions, pie apples, cheddar cheese, green pepper, and soups, are examples of assaults on perishability that were first successful in institutional markets.

The $18 billion freeze-dried food market is an illustration of the institutional market's attempt to eliminate people to reduce costs. The seventies will see the

---

[29] These conclusions are summarized from Roger W. Coomer, "Selling the Educator: Keys and Caveats," in *ibid.*, pp. 39–42.

common use of textured soy products that simulate beef, chicken, ham and bacon.[30] One meat processor tested soy-protein products that looked, tasted, and were textured like hamburgers. They were served without comment in a cafeteria to university students, who remained unaware that they contained absolutely no meat. In tests comparing normal hamburgers with the soy products, the school's dieticians also were unable to choose which were the meat and which were the soy products.

These examples emphasize the importance of institutional markets not only for their volume[31] but for their indirect encouragement of innovative product policies by firms seeking high-yield marketing strategies.

ORGANIZATIONAL BUYING BEHAVIOR

Industrial and institutional markets are composed of organizations of many types. Yet, in developing marketing strategy, it should be realized that sales are not made to organizations; sales are made to *individuals* within organizations. One key to analyzing organizational behavior is determining *which individual* or *individuals* influence buying.

Multiple Buying Influence

Multiple buying influence refers to situations where more than one person influences purchases of a specific product.

The marketer must develop a strategy to determine which individuals hold the decisive influence in each potential customer firm and make sure that effective contact is established with those persons. Where several persons influence the decision—including satisfaction with the decision after the sale—a marketer may need to use a variety of communication tactics (including advertising)— some to reach secretaries, some to reach purchasing agents, some to reach office managers, and some to reach top management.

Buying Authority

Some generalizations can be made about authority for buying decisions. Placing an order is usually the responsibility of a purchasing agent, regardless of who influences the decision, but the purchasing department tends to have authority mostly on standardized, established products that entail no great technical complexity or commercial uncertainty.

When buying influence is centralized in a purchasing department rather than the using department, the inherent assumption is that knowledge of *market* characteristics is more important than knowledge of *product* characteristics. Pur-

---

[30] See Richard W. Brown, "Food Service in the 1970's," *ibid.*, pp. 43–44.

[31] For a useful approach to forecasting institutional volume, see John C. Hofer and Russell L. Jones, "Forecasting Institutional Market Potential Through Socioeconomic Analysis of the Patron/Consumer," in Cox and Enis, *A New Measure of Responsibility for Marketing*, pp. 329–333.

chasing agents tend to be regarded as having more authority where price negotiations, vendor performance, delivery, and similar variables are determined by market and competitive pressures rather than by the technical and physical aspects of the product.

A purchasing department's authority will vary somewhat depending on the department's history, the skill and technical knowledge of individual purchasing agents, and the relationship and standing of the purchasing department with user departments and general management. Some general observations about buying authority, however, can be summarized as shown in Figure 7-4. Similar propositions emerge from research by Frederick Webster.[32]

Experts on the subject of organizational buying, however, increasingly advocate an expanded influence for professional buying individuals:

. . . the procurement executive is to an increasing extent a member of the top management group that makes the decisions, and many procurement executives are the primary decision-makers in an increasing number of buying decisions. One result is that the nature of the inputs to the procurement process from suppliers may be more complex and sophisticated than is recognized in the classical and neoclassical models. . . . The (new) model views procurement executives' major activity not as purchasing but as problem-solving. The model regards these activities as analytical and intellectual, rather than simply clerical in nature.[33]

This view may be more idealistic than realistic, but it is probably accurate to state that the trend is toward the "procurement executive." This should have a significant impact on industrial and institutional market opportunities in the seventies.[34]

[32] Frederick E. Webster, "Modeling the Industrial Buyer," *Journal of Marketing Research*, Vol. 2 (November 1965), pp. 370–376.

[33] Charles W. Faris, "Market Segmentation and Industrial Buying Behavior," in Moyer and Vosburgh, *Marketing for Tomorrow . . . Today*, pp. 108–110.

[34] For additional research on the roles of the purchasing agent, see the following books: Tamlin K. Lindsay and William F. Kinnard, *How Small Manufacturers Buy*, Vol. I (Storrs, Conn.: University of Connecticut School of Business, 1964); *Small Sellers and Large Buyers in American Industry* (Syracuse: Syracuse University Press, 1961); J. H. Westing and I. V. Fine, *Industrial Purchasing* (New York: John Wiley & Sons, Inc., 1955)); and the following articles: George Strauss, "Tactics of Lateral Relationships: the Purchasing Agent," *Administrative Science Quarterly*, Vol. 27 (1962), pp. 161–186; George Strauss, "Work-Flow Frictions, Inter-functional Rivalries and Professionalism: A Case Study of Purchasing Agents," in George Fisk and Donald Dixon, eds., *Theories for Marketing Systems Analysis* (New York: Harper & Row, Publishers, 1967) pp. 46–57; Robert Weigand, "Identifying Industrial Buying Responsibility," *Journal of Marketing Research*, Vol. 3 (1966), pp. 81–85; J. C. Denton and Erich P. Prien, "Defining the Perceived Functions of Purchasing Personnel," *Journal of Applied Psychology*, October 1963, pp. 332–338.

Figure 7-4   Determination of buying authority.

Commercial uncertainty[a]	Product Complexity[b]	
	Low	High
Low	Purchasing-department emphasis	User emphasis
High	General management or policy-maker emphasis	Total involvement

[a] Factors in commercial uncertainty:

Low	High
Little investment	High investment
Small order	Large order
Short-term commitment	Long-term commitment
No consequential adjustments	Substantial consequential adjustments
Small potential effect on profitability	Large potential effect on profitability
Easy to forecast effect	Hard to forecast effect

[b] Factors in product complexty:

Low	High
Standardized product	Differentiated product
Technically simple	Technically complex
Established product	New product
Previously purchased	Initial purchase
Existing application	New application
Easy to install	Specialized installation
No after-sales service	Technical after-sales service

SOURCE: Adapted from Lawrence Fisher, *Industrial Marketing* (London: Business Books Limited, 1969), p. 25.

BEHAVIORAL NATURE OF INDUSTRIAL BUYING

In recent years the behavioral nature of industrial buying has become generally recognized. Older textbooks often described industrial buying as "rational" or economic in nature, in contrast to consumer buying, and generally neglected the socio-psychological factors that are important in understanding how industrial buying decisions actually occur. Shrawder observes:

Industrial customers, like household consumers, must often act on impressions, on feelings, and on attitudes the origins of which they cannot entirely explain. He is no more irrational than the housewife is irrational for selecting and sticking with Betty Crocker Cake Mix without trying all the other brands. There is just not the time either for her or for the industrial purchasing agent to trying everything.[35]

[35] J. Edward Shrawder, "Popular Misconceptions About Industrial Marketing Research," in Wright and Goldstrucker, *New Ideas for Successful Marketing*, pp. 487–498.

Although industrial buyers may be *motivated somewhat more by economic influences* than consumers, an extensive review of the literature verifies the strong influences of behavioral variables.[36] Levitt's study of industrial buying revealed that communications approaches effective in consumer markets also are effective with industrial buying.[37] Concepts such as role theory[38] and perceived risk,[39] which are useful in analyzing consumer behavior, also appear useful in analyzing industrial behavior. The adoption process of new products by an industrial buying group fits the Rogers paradigm used to analyze diffusion of consumer products.[40]

Techniques used to assess consumer markets are often appropriate for assessing industrial markets.[41] In general, however, research methods used to assess industrial buying have relied more on traditional approaches. Large-scale sampling approaches and more recent developments in mathematical models are more difficult to apply to industrial buying. Some techniques, such as buyer simulation models[42] and Latin-square experimental designs,[43] have been used successfully to study industrial buying processes.

Models of Buyer Behavior

Attempts to model the behavior of industrial buyers appear much like attempts to model consumer behavior. That should not be surprising, since models of both types are extensions of basic human behavior as it is understood from socio-psychological research. Since psychology and a comprehensive model of behavior are discussed in Chapter 6, it is suggested that the reader review that material. The model discussed there serves as an adequate model for analysis of industrial buying behavior, with certain amplifications and modifications discussed below.

IMPORTANCE OF GROUP BEHAVIOR. Industrial buying behavior often is influenced more by group behavior than is consumer buying behavior. Consumer

[36] Frederick E. Webster, "Industrial Buying Behavioral: A State-of-the-Art Appraisal," in Morin, *Marketing in a Changing World*, p. 254–260. Also, see Philip Kotler, "Behavioral Models for Analyzing Buyers," *Journal of Marketing*, Vol. 29 (October 1965), pp. 44–45.

[37] Theodore Levitt, *Industrial Purchasing Behavior: A Study of Communications Effects* (Boston: Division of Research, Graduate School of Business Administration, Harvard University, 1965).

[38] Jerome B. Kernan and Montrose S. Sommers, "The Behavioral Matrix: A Closer Look at the Industrial Buyer," *Business Horizons*, Vol. 9 (Summer 1966), pp. 59–72.

[39] Richard N. Cardozo, "Segmenting the Industrial Market," in Robert L. King, ed., *Marketing and the New Science of Planning* (Chicago: American Marketing Association, 1968), pp. 433–440.

[40] Urban B. Ozanne and Gilbert A. Churchill, "Adoption Research: Information Sources in the Industrial Purchasing Decision," in King, *ibid.*, pp. 352–359.

[41] Shrawder, "Popular Misconceptions About Industrial Marketing Research," and J. L. Logan, "Motivation Research: An Aid to Industrial Advertisers," *Business Review*, Spring 1965, pp. 15–27.

[42] Yoram Wind and Patrick J. Robinson, "Simulating the Industrial Buying Process," in King, *Marketing and the New Science of Planning*, pp. 441–448.

[43] William E. Cox, Jr., "An Experimental Study of Promotional Behavior in the Industrial Distributor Market," in Haas, *Science, Technology, and Marketing*, pp. 578–586.

behavior is influenced by family members and other groups, but behavior models still focus upon the *individual,* as he is *influenced* by groups. In developing strategies for industrial marketers, it sometimes is useful to consider the collectivity of the individual members of a group as a separate unit of analysis. Such a unit of analysis is called a decision-making unit (DMU).[44] Some research in industrial buying behavior has centered upon identifying the constituents of the DMU and analyzing the roles of each.[45] The purpose is to isolate the decision-forming factors in industrial and institutional purchases.

In analyzing the collectivity of the group, however, one should not underrate the importance of the individual. His motives and his learning and perception process—even though a part of the organizational process—are still essential.

The industrial buyer does not cease to be a human being in his work situation. He has similar psychological drives, desires, urges and biological needs. So the classical conception of industrial buying as wholly rational and dispassionate must be qualified.[46]

MSI INDUSTRIAL BUYING MODEL. The Marketing Science Institute is responsible for one of the most comprehensive published studies of industrial buying behavior."[47] Its morphological approach closely resembles the one to which the reader was exposed in Chapter 6, except for differences in the context of decision making. This study concluded (as consumer analysts have concluded) that buyer behavior must be considered as *problem solving in a social context.*

The MSI study described industrial-buyer behavior in terms of stages of decision making ("buyphases") occurring in three types of buying situations ("buyclasses"). The eight buyphases and three buyclasses may be combined into a matrix for analysis of buyer behavior (see Figure 7-5), called a "buygrid." The eight buyphases presented in Figure 7-5 are the critical decision points of industrial buying situations. The reader should turn to page 115 in Chapter 6 and compare the "lower" portion of the model of consumer decision making with the eight buyphases of the model of industrial buying behavior. It should be apparent that specific stimuli and responses differ in industrial buying[48] but that both types of models are extensions of knowledge relating to fundamental human behavior.

[44] Aubrey Wilson, "Industrial Marketing Research in Britain," *Journal of Marketing Research,* Vol. 6 (February 1969), pp. 15–27.

[45] Ron Gorman, *An Empirical Analysis of Role Conception: A Study of Purchasing Behavior.* Unpublished Ph.D. Dissertation, The Ohio State University, 1970.

[46] Wilson, "Industrial Marketing Research in Britain," p. 20.

[47] Patrick J. Robinson, Charles W. Faris, and Yoram Wind, *Industrial Buying and Creative Marketing* (Boston: Allyn and Bacon, Inc., 1967).

[48] Two good elementary descriptions of buyphases can be found in Theodore N. Beckman and William R. Davidson, *Marketing,* 8th ed. (New York: The Ronald Press Company, 1967), pp. 204–208, and Stewart H. Rewoldt, James D. Scott, and Martin R. Warshaw, *Introduction to Marketing Management* (Homewood, Ill.: Richard D. Irwin, Inc., 1969), pp. 96–107.

Figure 7-5   The buygrid framework.

	BUYCLASSES		
BUYPHASES	New Task	Modified Rebuy	Straight Rebuy
1. Anticipation or recognition of a problem (need) and a general solution			
2. Determination of characteristics and quantity of needed item			
3. Description of characteristics and quantity of needed item			
4. Search for and qualification of potential sources			
5. Acquisition and analysis of proposals			
6. Evaluation of proposals and selection of supplier(s)			
7. Selection of an order routine			
8. Performance feedback and evaluation			

SOURCE: Patrick J. Robinson, Charles W. Faris, and Yoram Wind, *Industrial Buying and Creative Marketing* (Boston: Allyn and Bacon, Inc., 1967), p. 14.

SUMMARY AND CONCLUSIONS

Industrial products are items that are consumed in or used to produce other goods. Opportunities in industrial markets depend on an underlying demand for the consumer good. Analysis of industrial markets, therefore, must be based on adequate understanding of consumer demand and of derived and joint demand relationships.

The principal types of industrial goods may be identified as basic materials, capital and equipment, components and subassemblies, and facilitating goods and services. The demand for each has distinct characteristics, and normally, therefore, each has its own typical marketing practices and institutions.

A principal procedure for analyzing industrial markets is input-output analysis, which is useful in forecasting demand, determining market shares, and discovering the nature of market relationships and untapped potential markets. When input-output analysis is used as a forecasting technique for a period ending in 1980, it appears that the greatest growth in industrial markets will be in the areas of electric components, computing machines, photographic and optical equipment, service-industry machines, and synthetic fibers.

Government and other institutional markets are increasing rapidly in the seventies; government markets are expected to be well in excess of $200 billion by 1977. Markets are expanding rapidly for products used to solve the problems of population growth, poverty, urbanization, air and water pollution, congested transportation, and agriculture. Defense continues to be a huge market for industrial products, but defense marketers are also displaying a desire for diversification in their efforts to sell to governmental markets.

A fundamental model of buying is appropriate for analyzing both consumer and industrial buying, although group influences may be more significant in organization buying. Multiple buying influences are also common in industrial marketing. A study by the Marketing Science Institute reveals that the industrial buying process involves buyphases or stages similar to those found in the analysis of human behavior, as described in Chapter 6.

QUESTIONS FOR REVIEW AND DISCUSSION

1. Distinguish between the basic materials, capital goods and equipment, components and subassemblies, and facilitating goods and services. Outline major demand characteristics for each.
2. What is meant by "derived" demand? Why is it important for a firm?
3. Describe the most important growth markets of the seventies and identify the underlying factors that explain the growth of these markets.
4. Analyze market opportunities in the seventies for an industrial firm with which you are familiar. Prepare an analysis of the opportunities in the markets the firm now serves, and identify opportunities for the firm to profitably serve additional markets in the next few years.
5. Describe input-output analysis. What are some of its major uses for an industrial firm?
6. Using material in Chapters 4 and 7, analyze the effects of population growth in the seventies on markets for industrial products.
7. Prepare a research report on institutional programs designed to assist in solving the problems of your city or another city you know. Prepare the report in terms of the products that will be purchased in connection with these programs and the types of firms most likely to supply the products.
8. Analyze the need of a city for mass transportation and describe the conditions that must exist for the city's *need* to be converted into a *market*.
9. Analyze and prepare a report on how the *oversupply* of agricultural products in the United States (and other countries such as Canada, New Zealand and Australia) could feasibly be used to meet the *undersupply* of other countries without impoverishing the farmers in the undersupplied country.
10. Describe the factors that determine *which individuals* in an organization are the key influences on buying decisions.

Chapter 8   Global Markets: Structure and Behavior

With operations in 106 countries around the globe, IBM World Trade Corporation recently produced sales of $2.0 billion, almost double their global sales only three years earlier. IBM maintains 17 manufacturing plants in 13 countries, 7 development laboratories in foreign countries, and hires 87,000 employees for world trade. IBM had consolidated sales of $6.9 billion in 1968, but its business outside the United States was growing faster than domestic sales.

Several of the 500 largest U.S. corporations report that 50 percent of their profits come from their overseas operations. DuPont has major production operations in Holland, Belgium, and Northern Ireland. The Campbell Soup Company anticipates $30 million of sales in the growing European food market. In the mid-1950s Pepsi-Cola began accelerating global marketing activities; at one point they were opening a new bottling plant someplace in the world every 11½ days. By 1966 their 465 bottling plants were located in 110 countries, and worldwide Pepsi sales were exceeding a *billion cases of soda a year.*

Standard of New Jersey, Sears Roebuck, American Cyanamid, Ranco, NCR, Union Carbide, Coca-Cola, SCM, Charles Pfizer, Caterpillar, W. R. Grace, First National City Bank, and a host of other firms, both large and small, have moved aggressively in recent years to tap the ebullient sales growth and often attractive profit margins generated in global markets.

160

EMERGENCE OF GLOBAL MARKETS

Massive global trade has flowered especially in recent years, and it is useful to analyze how this has developed.

Emergent Markets

Since the first explorer set foot on what is now the United States, this country has been involved in global marketing in one way or another. Initially, the United States provided raw materials, particularly timber, for the more developed countries. To a limited degree it also provided a market for commodities and manufactured products of the developed nations.

Not until the First World War did extensive development of global markets by American firms occur. After that war, American firms increasingly began to serve foreign markets. Even then, however, the typical American businessman was totally American. In his mind, other countries usually were exotic places, characterized by inadequate plumbing and confusing train schedules, that were sources of occasional export orders. A few manufacturing firms had branches abroad, most notably in England, Canada, and Continental Western Europe. Mining and petroleum companies frequently had exploitative enclaves, complete with American-style villages for their senior executives, scattered around the world. In Latin America, a few agriculturally oriented American firms operated in tropical environments.

The more typical American investment in foreign markets during the 1920s was a portfolio investment—the acquisition of securities of foreign governments and firms without managerial involvement. The collapse of the 1930s soured these investments as many fell into default. Exports took on more interest for the most efficient American companies. Except for a few quick profits to be made in mining and petroleum exploitation, investments abroad by American firms virtually ceased during the 1930s.

The period from 1940 to 1950 was hardly better. Wars and reconstruction meant uncertainty abroad. Booming demand at home diverted attention from distant and risky markets. The inability of most countries to restore full convertibility to their currency after 1945 seemingly indicated and emphasized the riskiness of such foreign investment ventures.

Accelerating Global Markets

Starting with the 1950s some basic changes occurred. Western Europe was repairing its war damages, expanding investments, establishing exports, and increasing imports because of increasing incomes. Less developed countries were making and carrying out plans to expand their low per-capita incomes. In the United States economic growth continued, but at a slower pace than abroad. Relatively slow American economic growth meant, among other things, that the rather rapid accumulations of capital by stronger firms could not be immediately invested in the United States to earn adequate returns. As wartime shortages and sellers' markets diminished, many firms found diminishing rates of return on new investments in domestic markets. At the same time, adventuresome managers noted the rapid growth and apparent new stability of Western Europe—and American direct investments in European countries increased.

Between 1956 and 1958, six nations bound themselves together by forming two new unions—The European Economic Community (EEC), to remove trade barriers within the six countries, and the European Atomic Energy Community (EURATOM), to develop the use of nuclear energy for peaceful purposes. Many economic barriers were eliminated in these countries to permit freedom of financial and marketing functions, although political unification—another goal for the EEC—was not accomplished. The result has been a continued growth in the gross national product of the Community: from 1958 to 1966 it rose by 52 percent, as compared with rises of 35 percent in the United States and 30 percent in Britain. Industrial output grew faster still: by 68 percent in the Community, compared with 71 percent in the United States and 33 percent in Britain.[1]

Competitive Global Markets

The growth of mass markets in many countries provided a new impetus to American investments overseas, including the investment of abilities in strategic marketing and management. The task of competing on a global basis, however, has become less of an automatic selling situation; instead, it demands even greater sophistication in strategy than in domestic marketing. The American business firm is no longer a "sole source" of many goods. It must compete in the areas of price, quality, technology, and service with aggressive and able foreign firms.

Thus the situation that prompted many business firms to seek foreign markets—intensive competition—became just as prevalent in foreign markets. In addition, the global businessman has to contend with tariffs, nationalistic foreign regulations, alien cultural and business practices, and often distinctive situations such as cartels to put him at a further disadvantage.

Today a tempered expectation exists toward global business. Sophisticated U.S. business strategists have learned it is no longer a seller's market and that if their firm is to compete in global markets, it must be prepared to do so with all the skill and strategic planning that would be needed in domestic markets.

One reason for today's tempered attitudes of expectation in tapping global markets is the hard fact of declining profitability. Table 8-1 shows that although American investments have increased steadily at about 10 percent a year through the past two decades, return on investment in foreign markets has decreased substantially and is now below average domestic profitability. At the same time, the investments of foreign firms in United States markets have increased substantially, although they still experience less profitability than American firms experience in other countries (see Table 8-2).

[1] *The European Community: 1950–1967*, European Community Information Service, 1967.

Table 8-1   American Private Direct Investments Abroad, Earnings and Yields, 1950–1968

	Book Value (millions of dollars)	Earnings (millions of dollars)	Yield on Investment (percent)
1950	11,788	1,766	15.0
1951	12,979	2,236	17.9
1952	14,721	2,327	15.8
1953	16,253	2,258	13.9
1954	17,631	2,398	13.6
1955	19,395	2,878	14.8
1956	22,505	3,298	14.7
1957	25,394	3,561	14.0
1958	27,409	3,014	11.0
1959	29,827	3,241	10.9
1960	31,815	3,566	11.2
1961	34,667	3,815	11.0
1962	37,226	4,235	11.4
1963	40,686	4,587	11.3
1964	44,343	5,118	11.5
1965	49,328	5,460	11.0
1966	54,711	5,702	10.4
1967	59,267	6,017	10.1
1968	65,700 est.	n.a.	n.a.

SOURCE: Survey of Current Business, U.S. Department of Commerce, Washington, D.C.

Table 8-2   Foreign Private Direct Investments in the United States, Earnings and Yields 1950 and 1962–68

	Book Value (millions of dollars)	Earnings (millions of dollars)	Yield on Investment (percent)
1950	3,391	n.a.	n.a.
1962	7,566	397	5.2
1963	7,944	485	6.1
1964	8,363	596	7.1
1965	8,797	642	7.0
1966	9,054	695	7.6
1967	9,923	804	8.1
1968	10,900 est.	n.a.	n.a.

SOURCE: Survey of Current Business, U.S. Department of Commerce, Washington, D.C.

Table 8-3   American Private Foreign Direct Investments, Sales of U.S. Subsidiaries
Abroad, and Total U.S. Exports
(Projections for 1968 to 1975 in Billions of Dollars)

	Foreign Investments	Sales of U.S. Subsidiaries	Total U.S. Exports
1968	65.7	130.0	34.0
1969	71.5	143.0	36.4
1970	78.6	157.2	39.0
1971	86.5	173.0	41.7
1972	95.1	190.2	44.6
1973	104.6	209.2	47.7
1974	115.0	230.0	51.0
1975	126.5	253.0	54.6

SOURCE: N. William Hazen, "Overseas High Stakes of Multinational Firms," in Bernard A.
Morin, ed., *Marketing in a Changing World* (Chicago: American Marketing Association, 1969),
p. 50.

In spite of decreasing return on investment in foreign markets, it appears
that expansion into these markets will increase in the seventies. Table 8-3 shows
projected direct investment by U.S. firms in subsidiaries abroad and projected
U.S. Exports.

In the face of declining profitability, it might be asked why American firms
are still interested in foreign investment and exports. The answer is simple.
Dynamism in contemporary markets is a global phenomenon, and a major diversified firm must share in the normal growth of the world's markets if the firm
expects to maintain internal corporate growth. Making sales in foreign markets
is no longer an easy way to make excessive profits. Instead, firms are shifting to a
global marketing concept in which there are many markets comparable in
dynamics and opportunity to markets formerly found mostly in the United States.

A shift to globalization of marketing strategy can also be observed as a
result of the shifting nature of the global market structure. This is illustrated by
the experience of a global office-equipment firm:

SCM corporation has disbanded its international division. Responsibility for marketing SCM products overseas has reverted to the domestic marketing department.
The idea is to make no distinction between selling a product in this country and
abroad. SCM currently gets from 15 percent to 18 percent of its sales from abroad.
In five years the company is hoping to split domestic and foreign sales 50–50.[2]

[2] John Fayerweather, *International Marketing* (Englewood Cliffs, N.J.: Prentice-Hall,
Inc. 1965), p. 7.

EVALUATING GLOBAL MARKET OPPORTUNITIES

Market opportunities have as their most basic determinants *people, economic resources,* and a *propensity* to spend those resources on products of the marketing system. Basic trends in these determinants are described in the pages that follow.

World Population Trends

There were 3.3 billion people in the global market in 1965, and this figure has been projected to slightly exceed 4 billion by 1975. In 1985 the world market is projected to be about 5 billion people and 6.4 billion in the year 2000.[3] The continents of Africa and South America are experiencing the greatest rise in population (2.7 percent per year), although Asia retains the major proportion of the world's population (58 percent) and will continue to do so in the foreseeable future. Experts believe that world population is beginning to stabilize itself and presumably must do so in the next *few* centuries—perhaps at a level somewhere between 10 and 50 billion. A leading demographer believes that the stabilization of world population may occur as early as the year 2000.[4]

Projected population of the major countries of the world is shown in Table 8-4. This table shows population *growth rate* is declining in most major countries —including China and India. Of the 10 major countries in the world, only the United States and Canada are expected to have an increase in population *growth rate.*

The significance of population statistics lies in the latent demand represented for food, shelter, and basic consumption needs in countries such as China and India. These largely unfulfilled needs present an exceptional challenge to marketing and production technology. The development of solutions in the nature of low-cost, mass-marketed products for the basic consumption needs of these countries provide immense profit opportunities for firms of any nation with the sophistication to develop solutions. Even more important is the potential for marketing institutions to relieve human suffering and deprivation in those countries.

World GNP Trends

There are many measures of a nation's economic power. One of the more uniform ones is gross national product. In itself, GNP is not a measure of the purchasing or trading power of a nation in the markets of other nations, nor is per-capita GNP a measure of the purchasing power of a particular consumer. GNP and

[3] Herman Kahn and Anthony J. Wiener, *The Year 2000* (New York: The Macmillan Company, 1967), p. 139.

[4] D. J. Bogue, "The End of the Population Explosion," *The Public Interest,* No. 7 (Spring 1967).

Table 8-4   Population and Population Growth Rates, 29 Major Countries
(Millions of People)

	1965	Rates	1975	Rates	1985	Rates 1985–2000	2000
China	755	1.8	903	1.5	1,052	1.3	1,271
India	487	2.4	616	2.1	761	1.8	988
U.S.S.R.	231	1.3	260	1.3	296	1.2	352
U.S.	195	1.3	222	1.5	256	1.5	318
Japan	98	.8	107	.8	116	.4	123
W. Germany (with W. Berlin)	59	.4	61	.4	64	.3	67
U.K.	55	.3	57	.2	58	.2	60
Italy	52	.5	54	.3	56	.4	60
France	49	1.0	54	.7	58	.7	64
Canada	20	1.8	23	1.9	28	2.0	38
Pakistan	115	3.2	157	2.9	209	2.2	288
Indonesia	105	2.6	131	2.4	168	2.4	239
Brazil	82	3.1	112	2.9	149	2.4	212
Nigeria	58	3.1	78	3.2	108	3.3	176
Mexico	42	3.4	60	3.4	84	3.1	133
Poland	32	1.1	35	1.1	39	1.0	45
Thailand	31	2.9	41	2.6	52	2.4	74
U.A.R.	30	3.0	40	2.9	53	2.6	79
Argentina	22	1.4	26	1.2	29	1.0	33
Romania	19	0.8	21	0.8	22	0.8	25
S. Africa and S.W. Africa	18	2.7	24	2.8	31	2.7	48
Colombia	18	3.2	25	3.3	34	3.2	55
E. Germany (with E. Berlin)	17	0.3	17	0.3	18	0.2	18
Czechoslovakia	14	0.8	15	0.6	16	0.5	17
Taiwan	12	2.3	16	2.2	19	1.9	25
Australia	11	1.5	13	1.6	16	1.5	20
Sweden	8	0.5	8	0.4	8	0.4	9
New Zealand	3	1.9	3	2.2	4	2.0	5
Israel	3	2.0	3	1.6	4	1.3	5

SOURCE: Reprinted with permission of The Macmillan Company from *The Year 2000* by Herman Kahn and Anthony J. Wiener. Copyright © 1967 by The Hudson Institute, Inc.

per-capita GNP, however, are highly correlated with statistics that are more directly relevant if available.

The gross world product was $2.1 trillion in 1965. With an annual estimated growth rate of 4.8 percent, this would yield a gross world product in the year

2000 of $6.0 trillion.[5] In per-capita terms, the world per-capita figure of $630 in 1965 was about one-sixth of the United States figure. In the next 25 years, per-capita world product should triple, although there will be highly disparate relationships among regions of the world. Even in less-developed continents there is a projected increase in per-capita GNP of from $135 to $325 per year between 1965 and 2000.[6] The industrialized continents, plus Japan, will perform remarkably better, with a projected gain in per-capita GNP from $1,675 to $5,775.[7]

Table 8-5 presents projections of per-capita GNP for the 29 largest countries, underscoring the potential of consumer markets in many areas of the world. Among the 10 largest countries, the United States and Japan lead the way in projected increases, and the Soviet Union, Italy, mainland China, and India trail. The most notable change is that Japan, between 1965 and 2000, is projected to move from eighth place to *second place in per-capita GNP* among the world's largest nations. The opportunities for strategically planned marketing programs in Japan are remarkably attractive. Table 8-5 also indicates that Sweden, although not one of the largest nations, is second only to the United States in present and projected per-capita GNP.

Analysis of the global market structure reveals problems as well as opportunities. The development of marketing strategies implies exploitation of optimum profit opportunities—which would be expected to direct most attention to the industrialized world. In 1965 the per-capita GNP of the industrialized world exceeded that of the less-developed nations by about 12 times. By 2000, however, this factor will be close to 18 times. This means that the prosperity gap will increase by 50 percent in favor of the prosperous world. One might conclude that the less-developed countries will be satisfied because they are so much better off than before. However, it is probably more reasonable to assume that the expectations of improved living standards—awakened by significant economic progress—will increase faster than the actual improvement. Whether consumers of the less-developed nations will be satisfied in their absolute progress or whether they will increasingly envy and resent the discrepancies between rich and poor is one of the most significant questions of the approaching years. It is one of the questions that marketing analysts and strategists must be concerned with in the planning of corporate activity in those countries.

Geographical Distribution of World Exports

The emerging market trends described above can be observed in their effects upon geographical distribution of world exports. Comparative figures for 1955 and 1966 illustrate how analysis of market opportunities results in allocation of world markets. Table 8-6 shows that industrialized nations with rapidly expanding purchasing power—Japan and EEC countries—are the markets that are

---

[5] Kahn and Wiener, *The Year 2000*, p. 138.

[6] *Ibid.*, p. 142.

[7] *Ibid.*

Table 8-5   GNP Per Capita, 29 Major Countries (1965 U.S. Dollars)

	1965	1975	1985	2000
United States	3,557	4,850	6,510	10,160
Canada	2,464	3,360	4,550	7,070
France	1,924	2,710	3,920	6,380
W. Germany				
(with W. Berlin)	1,905	2,850	4,230	7,790
United Kingdom	1,804	2,580	3,750	6,530
U.S.S.R.	1,288	1,850	2,660	4,650
Italy	1,101	1,620	2,440	4,450
Japan	857	1,620	3,080	8,590
India	99	128	169	270
China	98	134	186	321
Sweden	2,497	3,535	5,078	8,679
Australia	2,009	2,250	2,544	3,195
E. Germany				
(with E. Berlin)	1,574	2,529	4,065	8,355
Czechoslovakia	1,554	2,357	3,638	7,046
Israel	1,334	1,949	2,978	5,839
Poland	962	1,396	2,054	3,680
Romania	757	1,143	1,717	3,224
S. Africa and				
S.W. Africa	503	598	699	906
Argentina	492	629	831	1,300
Mexico	455	503	588	680
Brazil	280	319	372	506
Colombia	277	298	322	359
Taiwan	221	314	456	837
U.A.R.	166	221	295	480
Thailand	126	170	239	402
Indonesia	99	107	112	123
Pakistan	91	109	134	200
Nigeria	83	94	107	125

SOURCE: Reprinted with permission of The Macmillan Company from *The Year 2000* by Herman Kahn and Anthony J. Wiener. Copyright © 1967 by The Hudson Institute, Inc.

absorbing increasing shares of the world's products. Areas of the world with slower increases in economic resources are declining in their absorption of products.

The Changing Trade Mix

Of the manufactured products that are marketed around the globe, the most important sales occur in exports of machinery and transport equipment. This is shown in Figure 8-1. Products experiencing increases in sales are generally those

Table 8-6   Geographical Distribution of World Exports and U.S. Exports
(Millions of dollars)

Market	World Exports[1]	Percent of Total	U.S. Exports	Percent of Total	U.S. Exports as Percent of World Total
		1955			
Canada	4,180	5.1	3,140	20.4	75.1
Latin America	6,920	8.5	3,170	20.5	45.8
Japan	2,120	2.6	650	4.2	30.7
EEC	18,070	22.2	2,100	13.6	11.6
EFTA	16,890	20.7	1,650	10.7	9.8
All other[2]	33,250	40.8	4,730	30.6	14.2
Total	81,430	100.0	15,440	100.0	19.0
		1966			
Canada	9,070	5.1	6,530	21.8	72.0
Latin America	10,410	5.8	4,170	13.9	40.1
Japan	8,080	4.5	2,350	7.8	29.1
EEC	51,020	28.5	5,460	18.2	10.7
EFTA	30,930	17.3	2,970	9.9	9.6
All other[2]	69,390	38.8	8,520	28.4	12.3
Total	178,900	100.0	30,020	100.0	16.8

SOURCE: United Nations, *Monthly Bulletin of Statistics,* in Morton Ehrlich and John Hein, *The Competitive Position of United States Exports* (New York: National Industrial Conference Board, Inc., 1968), p. 15.
[1] Excluding exports to the United States.
[2] Africa, Asia (except Japan), Eastern Europe, other Western Europe, and Oceania.

requiring a rather high level of production and marketing sophistication. The declining market opportunities—as reflected in actual world exports—are in the area of manufacturing classified by the basic material (such things as leather or wood products).

Manufacturers in the United States, Figure 8-1 also shows, have been successful in raising substantially their exports of machinery and transport equipment in the areas of highest growth. Products of IBM and SCM in office equipment and Boeing in air transport are good examples of marketing offerings for global markets that appear to be most responsive. America's share of this rapidly expanding world market, however, is not keeping pace with the overall growth of the markets or the growth of non-U.S. firms.

BEHAVIOR OF GLOBAL MARKETS

Global markets in their simplest categorization are of two types: *domestic* and *foreign.* The satisfaction of markets within one's own country is called domestic marketing, that of markets in another country is foreign marketing. However,

Figure 8-1   Composition of world exports and U.S. exports of manufactures, 1955 and 1966.

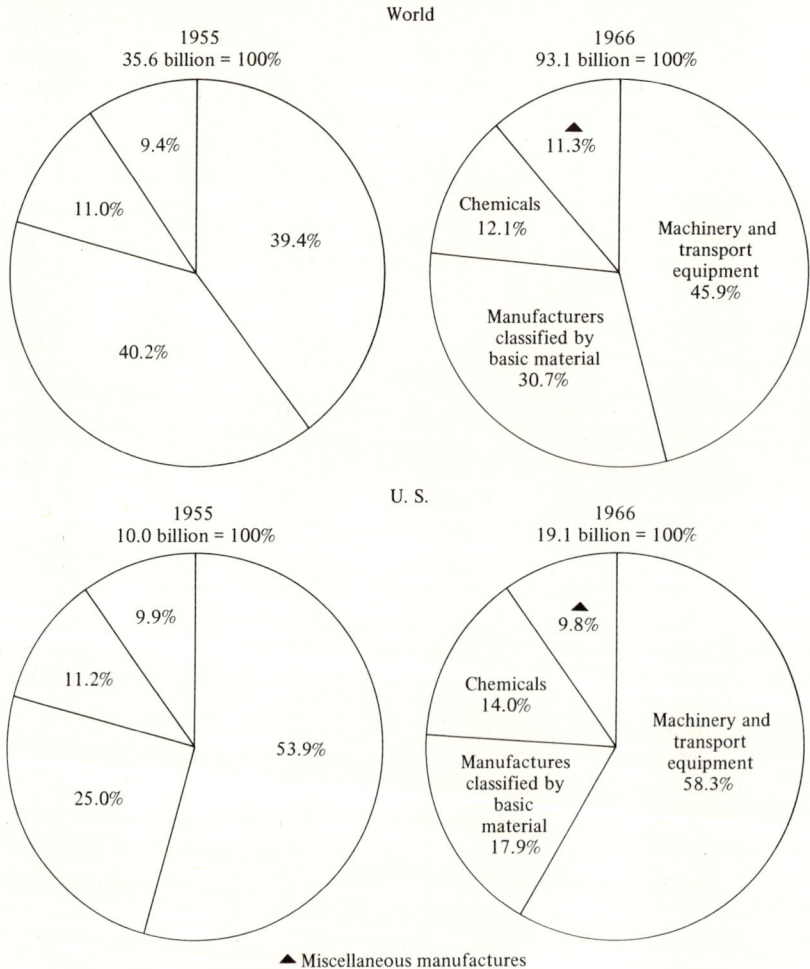

World

1955
35.6 billion = 100%

9.4%

11.0%

39.4%

40.2%

1966
93.1 billion = 100%

▲
11.3%

Chemicals
12.1%

Machinery and
transport
equipment
45.9%

Manufacturers
classified by
basic material
30.7%

U. S.

1955
10.0 billion = 100%

9.9%

11.2%

53.9%

25.0%

1966
19.1 billion = 100%

▲
9.8%

Chemicals
14.0%

Machinery and
transport
equipment
58.3%

Manufactures
classified by
basic
material
17.9%

▲ Miscellaneous manufactures

SOURCE: United Nations, reprinted in Morton Ehrlich and John Hein, *The Competitive Position of United States Exports* (New York: National Industrial Conference Board, Inc., 1968), p. 12.

what is "foreign" to the individuals of one nation is "domestic" to the individuals of that other nation. Both might be called "*national*" marketing.[8] The planning of marketing strategy in foreign markets is not an entirely different problem from the planning of domestic marketing; rather, it simply requires understanding the

[8] For amplification, see Robert Bartels, *Theory and Metatheory* (Homewood, Ill.: Richard D. Irwin, Inc., 1970).

national markets of the other country and developing competence to satisfy those markets.

When marketing is carried on within a free-trade area without artificial political or other restrictive barriers, the process may be so similar to domestic marketing that no major changes in analytical procedures are required. It is when marketing becomes subject to the promotive and restrictive interests of both the home and host countries, as well as international constraints, that the marketing environment becomes distinct from that of national marketing and can be termed "international" marketing.[9]

Global Markets as Behavioral Systems

The knowledge that underlies planning of management strategy for global markets stems from what is usually called comparative marketing. Comparative marketing is concerned with the identification, interpretation, and analysis of different yet comparable elements of different marketing concepts, systems, and techniques among various societies, including nations. Its ultimate concern is to provide a basis for related practice and for working effectively in various national settings.[10] The comparative-systems approach characterizes much of contemporary global-marketing analysis[11] and research.[12]

SYSTEMS COMPONENTS. Many attempts have been made to define and describe the primary determinants of global marketing systems. A typical list of the factors or system inputs to be considered includes variables such as size and topographical characteristics, urbanization, population shifts, concentration of wealth and population, economic growth, production, programs for economic development, nature of civilization, cultural transmission, society systems, religion, achievement syndromes, social relationships, pressure of political forces, and many other factors.[13] Attempting to evaluate the interrelationships between these variables and systems responsive to them is extremely difficult. One international scholar finds that the variables can be analyzed in their interrelationships under the topics of market characteristics, marketing problems, competitive environment, market maturity, distribution requirements, marketing costs, logistics problems, and other factors.[14] It is not unusual in current practice, however, for top management to analyze the nature of potential partnerships, con-

---

[9] *Ibid.*, p. 8.

[10] David Carson, "Comparative Marketing—A New-Old Aid," *Harvard Business Review*, Vol. 45 (May-June 1967), pp. 22–24, 32 ff.

[11] See, for example, M. S. Sommers and J. B. Kernan, eds., *Comparative Marketing Systems: A Cultural Approach* (New York: Appleton-Century-Crofts, Inc., 1968), and David Carson, *International Marketing: A Comparative Systems Approach* (New York: John Wiley & Sons, Inc., 1967).

[12] J. Boddewyn, "A Construct for Comparative Marketing Research," *Journal of Marketing Research*, Vol. 3 (May 1966), pp. 149–153.

[13] Carson, "Comparative Marketing—A New-Old Aid," pp. 233–278.

[14] M. Y. Yoshino, "Marketing Orientation in International Business," *MSU Business Topics*, Vol. 13 (Summer 1965), pp. 58–64.

Figure 8-2   A theory of world marketing—structural components.

NATIONAL MARKETING (Domestic and Foreign)	INTERNATIONAL MARKETING

1. Physical Environment
  (a) Geography—latitude, longitude, altitude, topography, climate, population size, resources
  (b) Predominant economic activity
  (c) Quantity of products
  (d) Variety of products
  (e) Market—size, income, age, standard of living
  (f) Transportation facilities
  (g) Storage facilities
  (h) Capital availability
2. Social Environment
  (a) Family types
  (b) School
  (c) Church
  (d) Type of economy
  (e) Government
  (f) Military
  (g) Leisure
3. Technical Marketing Systems
  (a) Institutions
  (b) Channels
  (c) Organization
  (d) Function allocation
  (e) Price
  (f) Tempo
  (g) Scale
  (h) Information systems
  (i) Identification systems
  (j) Flows
4. Social Marketing Systems
  (a) Social roles—manager, employees, owners, other financiers, consumers, intermediate customers, resources, competitors, government, community
  (b) Social behavior patterns
	1. Private Sector
	   Exporters—importers,
	   Direct—indirect investors
	   Abroad
	   Direct investors—portfolio investors
	   Sole—majority—minority ownership
	   U.S. incorporated—foreign incorporated
	2. Public Sector
	   Industrialized countries—less developed countries
	   Export surpluses—import surpluses
	   Trade deficit—payments deficit
	3. Home Country
	   Surplus producing—import dependent
	   Payments deficit—receipts surpluses
	   Aid giving—aid receiving
	   Raw materials supplying—finishing goods supplying
	4. Host Country
	   Industrialized—industrializing
	   Independent—colonial ties
	   Prosperous economy—depressed economy
	   Independent—trade area affiliate
	   Strong currency—weak currency
	   Strategic industries—nonstrategic industries
	5. Constraints
	   Enabling—restricting
	   Subsidies—taxes
	   Promotive—prohibitive
	   Protective—competitive
	   Arbitrary—negotiated
	   Unilateral—multilateral
	   Monopolistic—competitive
	   Trade-freeing—trade-restricting
	   Owner induced—labor induced
	   Fiscal—commercial
	   Legislated—administrative

SOURCE: Adapted from Robert Bartels, *Theory and Metatheory* (Homewood, Ill.: Richard D. Irwin, Inc., 1970).

tracts, government clearances, plant locations, and so on and then to visit a country on an inspection trip, "fall in love" with it, and neglect the objective evaluative factors.

The search for an analytical framework with which the marketing analyst can understand the markets of the world takes many forms.[15] One of these conceptual schemas, by Professor Robert Bartels,[16] is outlined in Figure 8-2.

RESEARCHING FOREIGN MARKETS

Global marketing strategy is increasingly based upon research rather than intuition. Increased need for hard data in global management decisions is due partly to involvement in foreign markets in ways that carry greater risk. Occasional export sales to a foreign market, for example, entail relatively little risk and a corresponding limited need for research. Figure 8-3 shows that as a firm increases the intensity of its involvement in foreign markets, risk also increases. As risk increases, the marketing organization can justify investing greater amounts of

Figure 8-3   Risk in entering foreign markets.

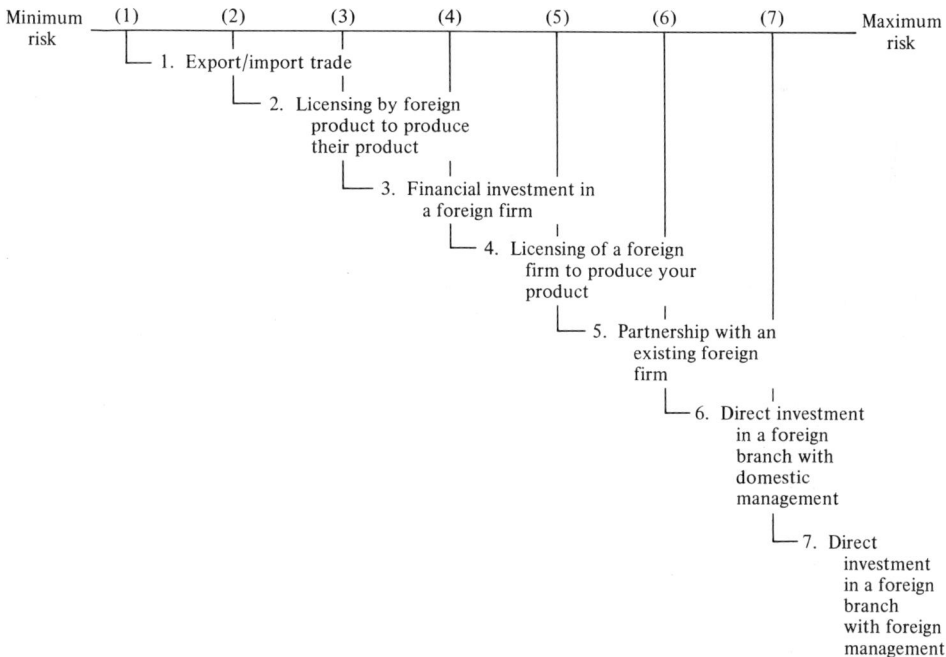

Minimum risk   (1)   (2)   (3)   (4)   (5)   (6)   (7)   Maximum risk

1. Export/import trade
2. Licensing by foreign product to produce their product
3. Financial investment in a foreign firm
4. Licensing of a foreign firm to produce your product
5. Partnership with an existing foreign firm
6. Direct investment in a foreign branch with domestic management
7. Direct investment in a foreign branch with foreign management

[15] C. A. Hamilton, "Opportunities for International Market Development," *Business Horizons*, Vol. 8 (Summer 1965), pp. 23–30, and M. Reed, "International Market Analysis," *Journal of Marketing Research*, Vol. 5 (November 1968), pp. 353–360.

[16] Robert Bartels, *Theory and Metatheory* (Homewood, Ill.: Richard D. Irwin, Inc., 1970).

resources to research the foreign market before committing itself. A procedure for using research in management decisions about foreign markets is shown in Figure 8-4.

Problems with Secondary Data

Researching foreign markets through the use of secondary data generally involves three major problems that can mean misleading results.

Figure 8-4   Using research for foreign-market decisions.

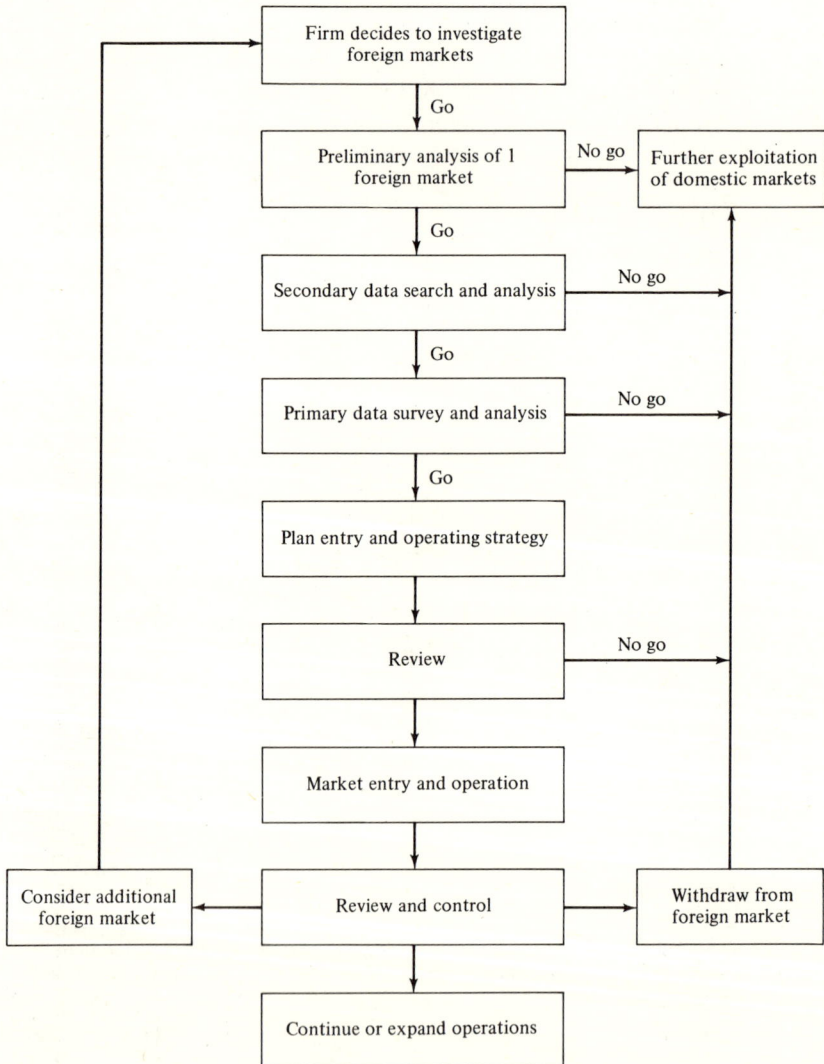

The first, and most critical, shortcoming is the unavailability of detailed data on specific market areas. Data may exist for the country as a whole, but little breakdown on rural-urban or regional variation may be available.

A second problem is the unreliability of some of the secondary data that are available. In many countries, national pride comes before statistical accuracy.

A third problem involves the comparability and currency of the available data. Especially in less-developed countries, data are often collected on infrequent and unpredictable schedules and may be years out of date. In many of the less-developed countries the most rapid changes in socioeconomic features are occurring, making the problem of recency or currency a critical one. Furthermore, even though many countries are currently gathering reliable data, there may be no historical series with which to compare the current information.

Problems with Primary Data

Cross-cultural methods for collecting primary data are becoming more available. The purpose of a cross-cultural analysis is to determine the similar and dissimilar behavioral and material aspects of specified cultures. In marketing research, the purpose specifically is to determine to what degree consumer decision processes, institutional structures, and other components of behavior systems are alike or different in varying cultures.[17]

Culture can be studied by most of the methods already familiar to marketing researchers. It is possible to use sophisticated attitude scales, projective techniques, standardized interview forms and questionnaires,[18] psychodrama, clinical analysis, and many other methods of collecting data.[19]

The problems in collection of primary data differ in foreign markets only in degree from those encountered in researching domestic United States markets. Some of the more significant problems are summarized below:

1. *Unwillingness to respond.* In many cultures, personal information is inviolably private and absolutely not to be discussed with strangers.
2. *Sampling in field surveys.* The greatest problem here is the lack of ade-

[17] James F. Engel, David T. Kollat, and Roger D. Blackwell, *Consumer Behavior* (New York: Holt, Rinehart and Winston, Inc., 1968), pp. 236–240, 252–258.

[18] See, however, Lucy L. Webster, "Comparability in Multi-Country Surveys," *Journal of Advertising Research*, Vol. 6 (December 1966), pp. 14–18, and Harper W. Boyd, Jr., Ronald E. Frank, William F. Masesy, and Mostafa Zoheir, "On the Use of Marketing Research in the Emerging Economies," *Journal of Marketing Research*, Vol. 1 (November 1964), pp. 20–23.

[19] Introductions to methodology for cultural research and descriptions of specific technique can be found in B. K. Stravianis, "Research Methods in Cultural Anthropology," *Psychological Review*, Vol. 57 (1950), pp. 334–344; Gardner Lindzey, *Projective Techniques and Cross-Cultural Research* (New York: Appleton-Century-Crofts, Inc., 1961); Bert Kaplan, ed., *Studying Personality Cross-Culturally* (New York: Harper & Row, Publishers, Inc., 1961); and R. L. Carneiro and S. F. Tobias, "The Application of Scale Analysis to the Study of Cultural Evolution," *Transcript of the New York Academy of Science*, Ser. II, Vol. 26 (1963), pp. 196–207.

quate detail of universe characteristics and the unavailability of lists from which to draw meaningful samples. In many countries, telephone directories, cross-indexed street directories, census tract data, and detailed social and economic characteristics of the universe are not available on a current basis, if at all.

3. *Language and comprehension.* The most universal problem of survey sampling in foreign countries is the difficulty with language. Differences in idiom and the difficulty of exact translation create problems in obtaining the desired information and in the interpretation of the respondents' answers. The obvious solution—that of making certain that all questionnaires are prepared or reviewed by someone fluent in the language—is frequently overlooked. Literacy, of course, poses another problem; in some lesser-developed countries with low literacy rates written questionnaires are completely useless. Within countries, too, the problem of dialects and different languages can make a national questionnaire survey impractical. In addition, some respondents with a minimum of education may have difficulty in comprehending the meaning of the questions asked.[20]

Sources of Information

There are many sources of publications and secondary data on foreign markets.[21] Those described below are published by the U.S. government, international organizations, governments of foreign countries, chambers of commerce, and trade service organizations.

U.S. GOVERNMENT. The Department of Commerce issues many publications that are useful in assessing foreign markets. These include:

1. *Trade lists*—for specific countries, the names and addresses of companies classified by commodity, including, for principal firms, relative size, type of operation, products handled, and sales territories.
2. *World Trade Directory Reports*—descriptions of operations of specific companies (prepared by Foreign Service commercial officers), products handled, U.S. manufacturers from which the company buys, size and reputation of company, its capital and annual capital turnover, and other facts.
3. *Marketing handbooks*—specific marketing information relative to selected

---

[20] Adapted from John H. Hess and Phillip R. Caeteora, *International Marketing* (Homewood, Ill.: Richard D. Irwin, Inc., 1966), pp. 394–397.

[21] Several useful papers on this topic are reprinted in C. Robert Patty and Harvey L. Vredenburg, *Readings in Global Marketing Management* (New York: Meredith Corporation, 1969), pp. 105–191. This book also has a number of useful reports on specific markets including communist countries.

foreign countries in two series, *The Market for U.S. Products in (selected country)* and *Investment in (selected country)*.

4. *International Commerce*—a weekly news magazine of up-to-date news and developments in world commerce.
5. *Overseas Business Reports*—a four-part report containing a wide range of marketing information on specific countries or areas. Part 1 contains basic economic and marketing data plus guidelines to business establishment and insurance information. Part 2 provides information on copyright and trademark protection, property rights, the mechanics of export shipment, export-import regulations, and living costs and conditions. Part 3 is a statistical section dealing with U.S. trade in aggregate and specific countries on a monthly basis and with the foreign trade of the countries of the world. Part 4 gives information on development of foreign shipping, railways, aviation, highways, and electric power.

INTERNATIONAL ORGANIZATIONS. The United Nations is a primary source of relatively comparable statistics on basic economic, social, and business-related data. *The Statistical Yearbook*, an annual publication of the United Nations, is a comprehensive source of data for more than 250 countries. Many regional organizations, such as the Organization for Economic Cooperation and Development (OECD), the Pan American Union, and the European Economic Community, publish statistics and market studies relating to their respective regions.

GOVERNMENTS OF FOREIGN COUNTRIES. Britain, Japan, and a number of other European and Asian countries publish information generally designed to increase the international trade flow and foreign investment in the country. Many of the less-developed countries also are now actively promoting the collection and dissemination of market information. Information about such publications is usually available from each country's consulate-general.

CHAMBERS OF COMMERCE. Many foreign countries maintain chamber-of-commerce offices in the United States that function as a type of permanent trade mission. They generally have research libraries available and are helpful in finding other sources of information on specific products or marketing problems. Another useful source of information is the American Chamber of Commerce operating in a foreign country. There are American chambers in many major trading cities of the world, which are often capable of giving very up-to-the-minute information on that city or region. A listing of these offices and other agencies in each city is contained in *A Directory of Foreign Organizations for Trade and Investment Promotion* (published by U.S. Department of Commerce).

A useful yearbook is the *Foreign Commerce Handbook*.[22] Its four sections deal with foreign trade services and activities of organizations concerned with

---

[22] Foreign Commerce Department, *Foreign Commerce Handbook: Basic Information and a Guide to Sources* (Washington, D.C.: Chamber of Commerce of the United States, 19th ed., 1968).

foreign trade, sources of basic data on specific markets, information on facilitating agencies and instruments (including copyrights, credit information, insurance, and advertising), and an annotated bibliography of up-to-date reference works, books, and periodicals on foreign commerce and international operations.

TRADE, BUSINESS, AND SERVICE ORGANIZATIONS. Creative marketing analysts can find information on global markets by intensively searching diverse types of organizations. Foreign trade associations may be good sources of information on specific products or product lines. Commercial banks and investment houses, international advertising agencies, foreign-based research firms, economic research institutes, and foreign carriers and shipping agencies usually maintain information services, and frequently they are better suited to the actual information needs of businessmen than are official agencies. If the organization maintains a separate research department, as many do, it often will make individualized information searches for interested firms. The Chase Manhattan and other banks have over the years developed the ability to provide reasonably reliable, firsthand analyses of the economic situation of specific foreign countries.

In recent years, a number of research agencies have developed that provide information on global markets either on a subscription basis or for specific projects. These vary greatly in quality and usefulness. The Department of Commerce's *Directory of Advertising Agencies and Market Research Organizations* is useful for its list of names and addresses of professional research and advertising organizations throughout the world.

GLOBAL MANAGEMENT INPUTS

There is a rapidly expanding literature analyzing management inputs for the planning and execution of global marketing strategies.[23] Underlying much of it is a trend toward a more global view of marketing management—toward the position that management strategies are most efficient when they are standardized rather than localized for each foreign market that is entered.

Additional clarification is needed about the nature of global standardization of marketing strategy. In a pure sense, global standardization might mean the offering of identical product lines, at identical prices, through identical channels of distribution, supported by identical promotional programs, in several different countries. This is the opposite of strategies that are completely localized—that is, containing no common elements whatsoever. Neither of these extremes is feasible

---

[23] In addition to texts mentioned elsewhere in this chapter, see David Carson, *International Marketing: A Comparative Systems Approach* (New York: John Wiley & Sons, Inc., 1967); Bertil Liander, Vern Terpstra, Michael Yoshino, and A. A. Sherbini, *Comparative Analysis for International Marketing* (Boston: Allyn and Bacon, Inc., 1969); Edward M. Mazze, *International Marketing Administration* (San Francisco: Chandler Publishing Company, 1967); Michael J. Thomas, *International Marketing Management* (Boston: Houghton Mifflin Company, 1969); Endel J. Kolde, *International Business Enterprise* (Englewood Cliffs, N.J.: Prentice-Hall, Inc., 1968).

or desirable.[24] The practical question is: which elements of the marketing strategy can be standardized and to what extent? To what extent can channels of distribution, pricing, advertising, packaging design, and so on be standardized?

Pepsi-Cola, for example, found that with careful planning of filmed commercials, the advertising could be used in most (but not all) of the 110 markets they serve. According to company estimates, the added cost of producing separate films with a localized approach for each market would have been $8,000,000 per year.[25]

There are many examples of management's success in finding a "great idea" to permit standardization of some element of marketing strategy. In 1965 Esso's campaign, "Put a Tiger in Your Tank," was used throughout the world. The same slogan and artwork could be found in many European countries with only the language changed. As another example, Avis Rent-a-Car Company used its theme, "We try harder," in the United States and throughout Europe. The layout, concept, and copy (translated) were always the same. The Avis "uniform" of a red jacket—an uncommon color in Europe—is another example of how standardization can work if carefully controlled. Some campaigns are not totally similar. An example is a campaign of Goodyear International Corporation that was based upon "prototype" campaigns developed from consumer research of markets around the world. The basic evaluative criteria for tires, the research discovered, were the same: safety, durability, and road-holding. Goodyear expressed these criteria in appeals appropriate to the region and in a lively format designed to create interest universally.[26]

Obvious examples of standardization exist in advertising strategy, but it can permeate other elements of strategy. In evaluating opportunities for American retailers, Yoshino found common analytical elements to use in assessing market opportunity.[27] In another study, Cundiff found that various nations' distribution systems are at different stages of development. In societies with high discretionary income and abundant goods, there are pressures for improvement in retailing

[24] See Robert D. Buzzell, "Can You Standardize Multinational Marketing?" *Harvard Business Review*, November–December 1968, pp. 102–113. An argument for global approaches to advertising is presented in Erik Elinder, "How International Can European Advertising Be?" *Journal of Marketing*, Vol. 29 (April 1965), pp. 7–11, Arthur C. Fatt, "The Danger of 'Local' International Advertising," *Journal of Marketing*, Vol. 3 (January 1967), pp. 60–62, and (for package design especially) Walter P. Margulies, "Why Global Marketing Requires a Global Focus on Product Design," *Business Abroad*, August 22, 1966, pp. 22–23. For a contrasting view see C. Larry Botthof, "One Common Market or Six Markets," *Journal of Marketing*, Vol. 30 (April 1966), pp. 16–18.

[25] Norman Heller, "How Pepsi-Cola Does it in 110 Countries," in John S. Wright and Jac L. Goldstucker, *New Ideas for Successful Marketing* (Chicago: American Marketing Association, 1966), p. 700.

[26] Allen R. Dodd, Jr., "Goodyear Gets Global Look," *Printers' Ink*, Vol. 292 (May 13, 1966), pp. 56–59.

[27] M. Y. Yoshino, "International Opportunities for American Retailers," *Journal of Retailing*, Vol. 42 (Fall 1966), pp. 1–10, 76.

efficiencies. The degree of retailing efficiency and innovativeness depends on several influential factors, various input effects, and the stage of development in the nation.[28]

Standard product-line strategies can be developed with considerable sophistication in global markets. In some cases adaptation of the product is necessary, as with products designed for 60-cycle, 120-volt power going into 50-cycle, 220-volt markets. In other cases adaptation is not mandatory but is useful in managing the phasing in and phasing out of models, price lines, material inputs, and so on in the firm's overall product strategy (see Figure 8-5). On a global basis, management can choose from strategic alternatives for different markets of the world.[29]

The essential management input for global marketing strategy is adequate planning. This requires study of the structure and behavior of global markets coupled with an analytical approach to such things as marketing and promotional investment.[30] Yoshino, who studied executives of 25 major North American corporations with large international branches, concluded that despite much current interest in international business, an overall policy to guide a company's entry into global markets, long-range goals, and thorough global planning prior to entering into overseas markets has generally been lacking.[31] When entering global markets, Yoshino found five elements of managerial strategy to be essential:

1. Definition of the basic perimeter-time span and commitments.
2. Selection of the markets.
3. Exploring alternative routes of market entry.
4. Evaluating alternative methods of direct investment.
5. Determine ownership policy.[32]

When these elements of planning were successfully completed, the global firm might have reasonable expectations for the successful execution of its strategy. "So does American marketing strategy work abroad? Of course it does—when as much time, trouble and expense are spent on preliminary planning abroad as at home."[33]

---

[28] E. W. Cundiff, "Concepts in Comparative Retailing," *Journal of Marketing*, Vol. 29 (January 1965), pp. 59–63.

[29] W. J. Keegan, "Multinational Product Planning: Strategic Alternatives," *Journal of Marketing*, Vol. 33 (January 1969), pp. 58–62.

[30] H. G. Lawyer, "How to Make Marketing Techniques that Work at Home Boost Sales and Profit Abroad," *Business Abroad*, Vol. 94 (January 1969), pp. 19–20.

[31] M. Y. Yoshino, "International Operations: What's the Best Strategy?" *Management Review*, Part I in Vol. 55 (November 1966), pp. 62–67; Part II in Vol. 55 (December 1966), pp. 50–55; Part III in Vol. 56 (January 1967), pp. 58–61.

[32] *Ibid.*

[33] D. Dutton, "Does American Marketing Strategy Work Overseas?" *Management Review*, Vol. 56 (October 1967), pp. 43–46. In addition to this quote, see J. Groves, "An Old Marketing Model: American and European Trends," *European Business: The International Management Review*, October 1967, pp. 47–55, and A. C. Nielson, Jr., "What Lies Ahead for Marketing Management," *Sales/Marketing Today*, Vol. 14 (January 1968) pp. 18–19.

Figure 8-5   Product life cycle in global marketing competition.

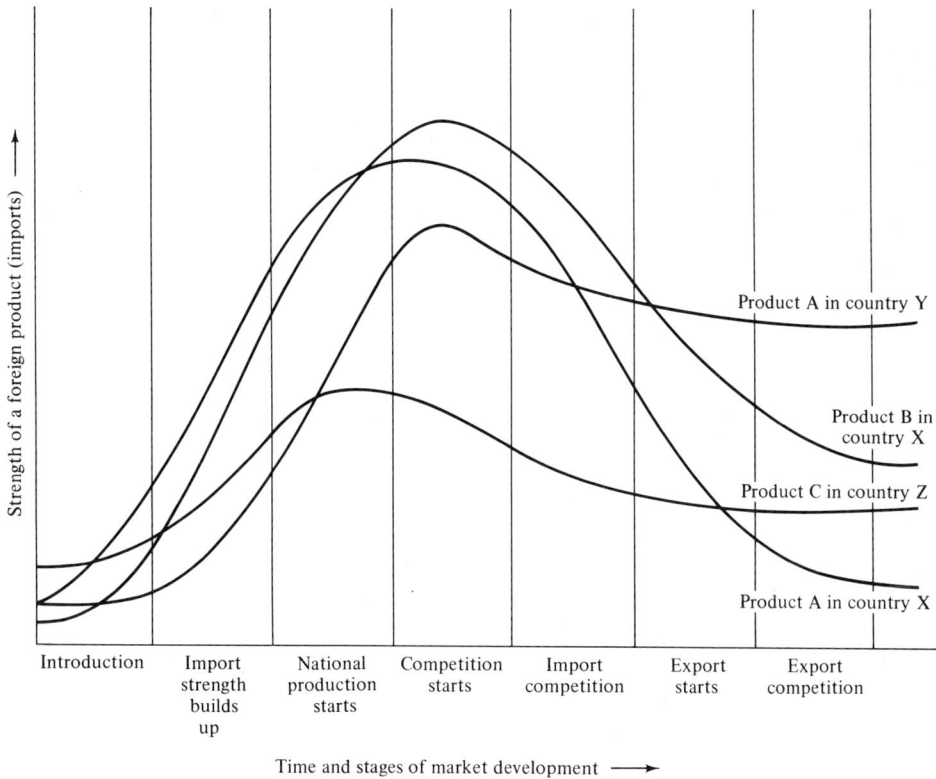

Product A in country Y

Product B in country X

Product C in country Z

Product A in country X

| Introduction | Import strength builds up | National production starts | Competition starts | Import competition | Export starts | Export competition |

Time and stages of market development ⟶

Note: The strength of a foreign product in a nation is the level of import for that product in that nation.

SOURCE: Adapted from ideas presented in W. J. Keegan, "Multinational Product Planning: Strategic Alternatives," *Journal of Marketing*, Vol. 33 (January 1969), pp. 58–62.

SUMMARY

There is great interest in capturing a portion of the markets of the world. In recent years interest in foreign markets has experienced unprecedented growth.

World markets are expanding rapidly, but so is competition for those markets. Consequently, it is difficult to make excessive or easy profits in foreign markets. Methods of satisfying foreign markets today require a more substantial investment of resources and marketing analysis than was typical in the past. Also called for is a much more sophisticated understanding of the structure and behavior of markets of the world.

The future should bring continued expansion of prosperity in world markets and some leveling of population growth. At the same time, there will be greater disparity between the rich nations and the poorer. The most dramatic rise in relative economic power on a per-capita basis will occur in Japan.

A basic principle of researching foreign markets is that additional research can ordinarily be justified as a function of the intensity of market involvement or risk. Although there are serious problems in using both secondary and primary data from foreign markets, the creative researcher can find numerous helpful sources, including the United States Government, international organizations (principally the United Nations), governments of foreign countries, chambers of commerce, and trade and service organizations.

QUESTIONS FOR REVIEW AND DISCUSSION

1. Analyze the importance of global marketing strategy for a major firm. Is it increasing or decreasing in importance for that firm? Why?
2. A major marketer of consumer appliances is considering entry into several foreign markets. Prepare a decision model to be used in his decisions about whether to enter foreign markets and which markets to enter if he does.
3. Choose a major domestic marketing organization and prepare from secondary sources an evaluation of opportunities for foreign-market expansion for that company. Include in your analysis a ranking of entry priorities for each market.
4. Define the following terms: global markets, world markets, national markets, foreign markets, domestic markets, international markets.
5. Write a term paper assessing future growth in population and economic power of the markets of the world. Analyze the implications of these trends for a major business firm such as IBM or NCR.
6. Assume you are employed in the planning department of a major marketing organization. Prepare a position for top management on the implications for this firm of growing disparity in prosperity levels of major countries in the world.
7. Analyze the major difficulties in collecting and analyzing primary and secondary data in foreign markets.

Chapter 9   Selecting Market Targets

After discovering the vast markets that exist for products of all types and the accelerating rate of change that characterizes many of these markets, a marketing manager expressed a major task faced by his firm:

Internally, in the succeeding five years we shall have to devise a procedure to evaluate our customers and markets from a profitability viewpoint and externally seek those markets and customers who offer us the greatest possible return on employed capital.

This also will include marketing studies to identify those specific industry groups that will offer the most profitable potential. Saying it another way: We must direct our marketing efforts to selective selling.[1]

The importance of market-target selection is also emphasized by Professor Frederick Webster of Dartmouth College:

The most critical decision made by marketing management is the definition of market targets—the segmentation decision. This decision requires careful analysis and a high order of creativity.[2]

---

[1] Roger M. Pegram and Earl L. Bailey, *The Marketing Executive Looks Ahead* (New York: National Industrial Conference Board,. 1967), pp. 24–25.

[2] Quoted in Milton Shapiro, "The Basics of Industrial Marketing Management," in Bernard A. Morin, ed., *Marketing in a Changing World* (Chicago: American Marketing Association, 1969), pp. 205–209, at 207.

NATURE OF MARKET SEGMENTATION

Selecting market targets can be defined as a *balancing of organizational capability (either existing or reasonably attainable) with market opportunities.* This might be done with a strategy that seeks to penetrate the entire market for a product. Such a strategy is called a *mass-marketing* strategy. The alternative is a market-segmentation strategy.

Market Segmentation Defined

Market segmentation is *the process of so designing or featuring a product or service that will make a particularly strong appeal to some identifiable subpart of a total market.* It is increasingly employed as an alternative to mass-market targets.[3] Market targets identified in the master marketing strategy of the firm may be *single segments,* or a firm may simultaneously pursue the profit opportunities in a variety of segments; the latter is a *multiple-segment* strategy.

Logic of Market Segmentation

If all humans were identical in their preferences, there would be no need for market segmentation among products. But no two people's preferences are exactly alike. Consequently, if products were to be produced and marketed in a way that would yield *maximum satisfaction* to customers, every product would be custom-tailored to the needs of each user of the product. Some products are in fact custom-tailored to each customer's preferences; most, however, are to some degree standardized to achieve economies in production or distribution—even though customers must then accept a product that does not meet their individualized preferences as well as it might.

In a developing economy, it is normal to find *mass-market* strategies that require all customers to buy the same product. In the early history of automobile marketing in the United States, for example, an automobile manufacturer typically produced only one model and one color of car. "Give the customers any color they want," Henry Ford reportedly stated, "so long as it is black."

As a nation rises above the economic subsistence level or as market volume becomes large, the nature of the product can be changed to satisfy groups of people whose desires and uses of products differ. The challenge of developing segmentation strategies is "how far to go" in adapting to the customers' various uses and desires for products. Defining segments, therefore, involves balancing desire for individual preference and desire for economies of standardization. Myers and Nicosia succinctly summarize these relationships: "Marketing managers have always had to cope with the heterogeneity of buyers. As society becomes

---

[3] See Nelson N. Foote, "Market Segmentation as a Competitive Strategy," a paper presented at Consumer Market Segmentation Conference, American Marketing Association, February 24, 1967. Also reprinted in J. Howard Westing and Gerald Albaum, *Modern Marketing Thought,* 2nd ed. (London: The Macmillan Company, 1969), pp. 269–278.

increasingly affluent, as discretionary income allows this heterogeneity to be more fully expressed, the problem of determining useful typologies of consumption patterns has attained paramount importance for marketers."[4]

MARKET SEGMENTATION AS A COMPETITIVE STRATEGY

In developing high-yield corporate strategy, the marketing approaches include satisfying mass markets, a single segment, or multiple market segments.

The process of developing a competitive market strategy can be described in terms of an example, drawn from the cake-mix market. Assume that darkness is an essential variable in determining which brand of chocolate cake mix customers will purchase. A heavy chocolate flavor is preferred by one group of purchasers, a light chocolate is preferred by purchasers at the other end of the spectrum, and the majority of consumers are located in between. This hypothetical distribution of cake-mix preferences is shown in Figure 9-1. The total cake-mix market is described as six million units distributed unequally among six brands, as shown in Figure 9-1. Using strategy 1—a mass-market approach—all six firms produce a cake mix with the same amount of chocolate or darkness. This is a logical development, since, of the six million consumers, four million prefer an "average" amount of darkness. If a company were directing its marketing resources to the largest market, it would do as all six firms in this example are doing and pick the average as the target.

Product Differentiation

Using a mass-market strategy, a firm may try to differentiate its product in the minds of consumers while retaining its basic physical similarity to other products. The company does not wish to alter the basic product very much; to do so would create a product not preferred by most of the market. Through advertising, packaging, reseller support, or some other marketing activity, however, the company may create a preferred position among basically similar brands. Brands A and B appear to have been successful in the case displayed in Figure 9-1, attaining two million units each compared to only 500,000 for each of the lesser brands. Strategies that emphasize a single product, attempting to satisfy with it all or much of the distribution of product preferences, are called product-differentiation[5] or market-aggregation[6] strategies. These terms apply to the situation resulting from strategy 1 in Figure 9-1.[7]

[4] John G. Myers and Francisco M. Nicosia, "On the Study of Consumer Typologies," *Journal of Marketing Research*, Vol. V (May 1968), pp. 182–193, at 182. This article also describes how to develop a typology and presents a new empirical approach.

[5] Wendell R. Smith, "Product Differentiation and Market Segmentation as Alternative Marketing Strategies," *Journal of Marketing*, Vol. 21 (July 1956), pp. 3–8.

[6] Allan R. Roberts, "Applying the Strategy of Market Segmentation," *Business Horizons*, Vol. 4 (Fall 1961), pp. 65–72.

[7] For a discussion of how to select between product-differentiation and market-segmentation strategies, see R. William Kotrba, "The Strategy Selection Chart," *Journal of Marketing*, Vol. 30 (July 1966), pp. 22–25.

Figure 9-1   Distribution of customer preferences by darkness of cake mix (hypothetical).

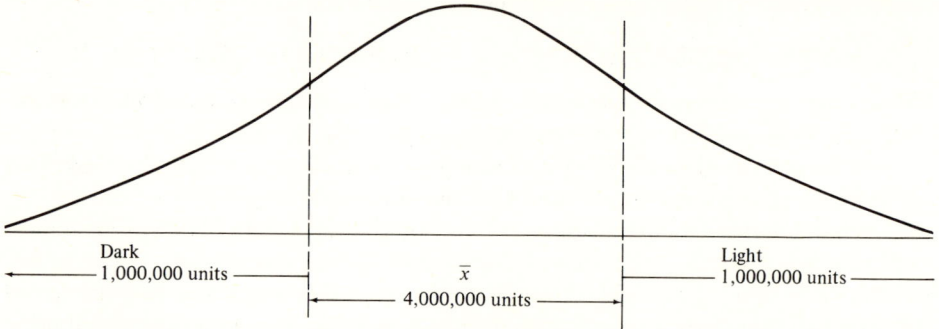

Dark
← 1,000,000 units ─────────┤ $\bar{x}$ Light
                           ├──── 4,000,000 units ────┤   ├─ 1,000,000 units ──→

Strategy 1

Mass-market results: Brand   A = 2,000,000 units
                                 B = 2,000,000 units
                                 C =   500,000 units
                                 D =   500,000 units
                                 E =   500,000 units
                                 F =   500,000 units

            All brands   = 6,000,000 units

Strategy 2		Original	From dark segment	From mass market	New volume potential
Single-segment market potential:	A =	(2,000,000	− 333,333	+ 151,515) =	1,818,181
	B =	(2,000,000	− 333,333	+ 151,515) =	1,818,181
	C =	(500,000	+ 916,667	− 416,667) =	1,000,000
	D =	(500,000	− 83,333	+ 37,879) =	454,546
	E =	(500,000	− 83,333	+ 37,879) =	454,546
	F =	(500,000	− 83,333	+ 37,879) =	454,546
All brands		6,000,000			= 6,000,000

Strategy 3

Multiple-segment
market potential: Not calculated

Single-Segment Strategy

Suppose that the brand C management, after careful assessment of the market, determines that some people prefer dark chocolate cake mixes strongly enough to switch away from their present brand with an average amount of chocolate to a new brand featuring dark chocolate. Brand C had 500,000 units of sales with a mass-market approach, but if it switches to a new product mix (either by changing the existing brand or by replacing it with a new brand), it now has an opportunity to sell one million units. In addition, less effort might be required (and less expense entailed) to sell to the new segment, where brand C would enjoy a clear preference rather than fighting severe competition of all other brands. Profits might, therefore, increase because of lower selling expense as well as increased volume.

By switching to a segmented product, brand C has lost the preference of most of the market. The results under strategy 2 in Figure 9-1 show brand C *losing* all of its previous customers except 83,333 (those in the dark segment before the switch); the lost customers want a mix with less darkness. However, brand C has gained 916,667 units from the dark segment at the expense of all other brands. Clearly, the change in market strategy is advantageous for brand C.

Actually, the single-segment strategy has many more complexities than are described in this example. Among these, first, preference for darkness is a continuous variable rather than discrete; thus, regardless of the darkness of brand C, there will still be many customers in the "dark segment" who would like the mix more or less dark. Second, even though brand C now satisfies the dark segment better than other brands, there is no assurance that this can be effectively *communicated* to that segment or that distribution channels will adequately supply it to that segment. Third, an assumption was made that darkness is important enough to cause purchase of the new product. Actually, brand A or B may have some other characteristic that induces preference over brand C even among the dark segment.

Multiple-Segment Strategy

If the single-segment strategy of brand C is effective, several other shifts in strategy might occur. Perhaps brand C will decide to bring out another new cake mix, brand X, designed for the light-chocolate segment. This multiple-segment strategy might be expected to yield another million potential customers. The company may have introduced the dark and the light mix *in addition* to retaining the original brand C for the average customer. If these strategies have been successful, they will probably stimulate competitive reaction among the other brands.

This process is typical of what has happened in markets during recent years, and the trend toward multiple-segment strategies can be expected to increase rapidly. High-yield management will increasingly require the capability of competing in a number of markets, with a variety of brands, offering an optimally satisfying mix of product characteristics and promotional methods. Today, success in multiple-segment strategy requires a constant search for groups of customers with relatively homogeneous demands, selected out of an area of consumer use that is heterogeneous in the aggregate in a manner that is profitably matched with the company's feasible pattern of resources.[8]

IDENTIFYING MARKET SEGMENTS

The identifying of market segments is a process of discovering groups of consumers who will respond similarly to a firm's marketing program. The analysis of

[8] Wroe Alderson, *Dynamic Marketing Behavior* (Homewood, Ill.: Richard D. Irwin, Inc., 1965), Chap. 8.

markets is a process of constructing customer typologies with similar *behavior* rather than similar static characteristics.[9]

The distinction between behavior and static characteristics can be illustrated with an example. An airline might identify groups of passengers by the characteristic of usage. The conclusion might be made that customers flying over 10,000 miles a year are most valuable. At the same time a market study would probably reveal that people who fly over 10,000 miles a year respond very differently to the marketing program of the airline. The heavy-user category might include businessmen, college students flying on youth fares, and retired couples on a trip to Hawaii. The group might have only a single characteristic in common —amount of air travel. They probably fly for different reasons, react differently to airline personnel, expect different meal standards, and are exposed to different media. Perhaps the airline might develop a multiple-segment strategy appealing to the heavy users in *each* category but a strategy for *all* heavy users would be ineffective.

The goal in identifying market segments is to identify groups of customers with behavior resemblances so strong, clearly marked, or obvious that the distinction between one group and related groups cannot be questioned. In practice, a firm must usually accept something less than the ideal.

The identification of market segments involves classifying consumers in groups that will allow the following information to be discovered about customers in the group:

1. The kinds of things that affect customer behavior.
2. The channels through which customers can be reached by a firm.
3. The strength of their need or desire for the product.
4. The appeals to which they are most responsive.
5. Their responsiveness to different types of sales devices (that is, their ability to be influenced by price considerations, availability of credit, sales talks from salesmen, and so forth).
6. Their location.[10]

Methods of Segmenting Consumer Markets

Consumer market segments are usually identified by static characteristics even though the goal is behavioral typologies. The reason this occurs in actual practice is because elements of the marketing program (such as advertising) usually are based upon characteristics such as geographic location, income, or family size.

The rationale used in developing strategy is an assumption that behavioral characteristics and static characteristics coincide. Where this assumption is true, the methods of segmenting markets described below may work well. Where the

---

[9] For amplification of this concept, see Alfred R. Exenfeldt, *Executive Action in Marketing* (Belmont, Calif.: Wadsworth Publishing Company, Inc., 1966), pp. 92–135.

[10] *Ibid.*, p. 107.

assumption is false, new bases for segmentation are needed. It is the latter condition that is forcing marketing strategy increasingly to adapt multidimensional approaches. Multidimensional approaches are discussed following the analysis of traditional methods of segmenting consumer and industrial markets.

Primary methods of segmenting consumer markets include *geographic location, demographics, individual characteristics, benefits,* and *volume of usage.* These are analyzed below.

GEOGRAPHIC SEGMENTS. Geographic variation arises when buyer preferences and usage varies by location. For products such as swimming pools, air conditioning, and snowmobiles, marketing programs obviously must be built in part on a geographic-segmentation strategy.[11]

A more subtle example is provided in the coffee market. Consumers in the western part of the United States appear to behave differently in coffee consumption than other consumers. Among other things, they drink "black" coffee in higher proportions. Procter & Gamble segmented the market with a "Western Blend" of Folger's coffee. P&G was able to prepare regionally segmented advertising themes and media schedules for market segments where it was possible to achieve high acceptance of Western blend coffee.

DEMOGRAPHIC SEGMENTS. Demographic variables are the most used but not necessarily the most useful approaches to segmentation strategies. Age, sex, income, and education are frequent bases for identifying market segments and developing a matching marketing program.

Some evidence disputes demographic methods as a useful basis for segmentation strategies. The Advertising Research Foundation concluded there was no basis for segmenting the toilet-tissue market on 15 socioecenomic variables.[12] Frank, Massey, and Boyd compared 57 product categories such as food and other household products and found little variation among demographic variables.[13] Many other studies have come to similar conclusions.

On the other hand, some companies find that demographic-segmentation strategies are successful. One large builder of condominiums in Chicago suburbs carefully researched the high-income, over-55 group and found a segment with distinctive behavior patterns. The company sold condominiums in the $50,000–$85,000 bracket and was exceptionally successful using special types of salesmen, specialized media, and unique product design features.

YOUTHFUL SEGMENTS. Young people in recent years have provided valuable

---

[11] A useful discussion on how to use geographic variation for marketing programming is contained in James F. Engel, Hugh G. Wales, and Martin R. Warshaw, *Promotional Strategy* (Homewood, Ill.: Richard D. Irwin, Inc., 1967), pp. 82–86.

[12] Ingrid Hildegaard and Lester Krueger, "Are There Customer Types?" in Frank M. Bass, Charles W. King, and Edgar A. Pessemier, eds., *Application of the Sciences in Marketing Management* (New York: John Wiley & Sons, Inc., 1967).

[13] Ronald E. Frank, "Market Segmentation Research: Findings and Implications," in Bass, King, and Pessemier, *Application of the Sciences.*

market segments for some firms. Youth may be better defined, perhaps, as a life style or attitudinal variable than a demographic variable; nevertheless, many firms have designed products and programs specifically for youthful markets.[14] The once staid firm, Yardley of London, combined the appeal of British products after the Beatles with a mod advertising program and a distribution strategy emphasizing youthful information and educational programs in key retail outlets. The net result of their segmentation strategy was a dramatic sales increase and a leadership role in the youth-oriented segment that later evolved to dominate other segments. It is important to realize that identifying this segment was successful because the *segment possessed behavioral characteristics permitting a coordinated marketing program to be developed for that segment.*

In the past, demographic variables were often predetermined as the variables with which to develop segmentation strategies. There is no doubt that they are sometimes useful, but future marketing executives will demand much more rigorous approaches[15] to demographic groups in an attempt to identify typologies that are behaviorally congruent instead of groups that only have the same demographic classification.

INDIVIDUAL BEHAVIORAL SEGMENTS. Markets may be segmented on the basis of individual behavioral variables such as *attitudes*,[16] *personality*,[17] or *life styles*.

One of the most pervasive attempts at individual behavioral segmentation has been with personality variables. Some products—such as cigarettes—are reported to correlate highly with personality variables. However, the successful cases of personality segmentation are often, upon closer analysis, found actually to be examples of combination variables that are more accurately defined in terms of some other variable such as life style. Personality appears to be an intervening or moderating variable in affecting consumer choice.[18]

Numerous other individual behavioral variables may be used for identifying segments. *Brand loyalty* has been analyzed in a variety of ways for segmentation

[14] For case analyses of a number of firms successfully selling to youthful markets and fundamental forces affecting youthful market segments see Roger D. Blackwell and David T. Kollat, *Marketing to Youth in the Seventies* (Columbus, Ohio: Management Horizons, Inc., 1970).

[15] For example, see Henry Assael, "Segmenting Markets by Group Purchasing Behavior: An Application of the AID Technique," *Journal of Marketing Research*, Vol. 7 (May 1970), pp. 153–158.

[16] *Ibid.* Also, for an intriguing development in segmentation by activity interest and opinion items, see William D. Wells, "Segmentation by Attitude Types," in Robert L. King, ed., *Marketing and the New Science of Planning* (Chicago: American Marketing Association 1968), pp. 124–126.

[17] For a comprehensive review of research in this area, see James F. Engel, David T. Kollat, and Roger D. Blackwell, "Personality Measures and Market Segmentation," *Business Horizons*, Vol. 12 (June 1969), pp. 61–70.

[18] *Ibid.*

strategies, though with limited usefulness.[19] Other methods of individual segmentation are possible. There is, for example, an emerging view that *highly mobile* families constitute a segment useful in marketing segmentation strategy.[20]

BENEFIT SEGMENTATION. Market segments may be effectively identified by the *benefit derived* in the product or brand. Segmentation strategies of this type often do not fit precise categorization and may be identified by variables such as patterns of usage, aesthetics, and reasons for buying products.[21]

Sony, a Japanese television marketer, found a market segment based upon *patterns of usage.* In the midst of a brutally competitive American television-set industry, Sony shrewdly staked out the segment of the market that used and could afford miniature TV sets—a segment that the U.S. giants had abandoned. By concentrating on this segment of market usage, Sony built up a $37-million market, half of it in straight-on competition with the U.S. market.

Benefit segmentation depends upon reliable and valid research describing the benefits desired by groups of customers. It then requires the ability to tailor products closely to those benefits. The benefit is designed into the product, causing customers to seek the product with desired benefits rather than the converse.[22] An example of a successful strategy using benefit segmentation is described below.

Macleans toothpaste. Over 70 percent of the United States toothpaste market was controlled in the 1960s by two giants, Colgate and Procter & Gamble (through Crest and Gleem).[23] The rest of the market was shared by other well-known brands including Stripe, Ipana, and Pepsodent. Toothpaste advertising amounted to over $40-million a year when an overseas company, Beecham, decided to enter the United States market.

The benefit stressed by nearly all existing brands at the time of Beecham's entry was *decay prevention,* especially among children. Crest stressed their endorsement by the American Dental Association and emphasized commercials around the theme, "Look, Mom, no cavities." Furthermore, when Beecham ran blind taste tests with existing brands, Macleans showed no special strength. Market research did show, however, that among the small minority who did like

[19] For examples, see John Farley, "Brand Loyalty and the Economics of Information," *Journal of Business,* Vol. 37 (October 1964), pp. 370–381; Ronald Frank and Harper Boyd, Jr., "Are Private-Brand Prone Food Customers Really Different?" *Journal of Advertising Research,* Vol. 5 (December 1965), pp. 27–35; Ross M. Cunningham, "Brand Loyalty—What, Where, How Much?" *Harvard Business Review,* Vol. 34 (January-February 1956), pp. 127–137.

[20] James E. Bell, Jr., "Mobiles—A Neglected Market Segment," *Journal of Marketing,* Vol. 33 (April 1969), pp. 37–44.

[21] Norman L. Barnett, "Beyond Market Segmentation," *Harvard Business Review,* Vol. 47 (January-February 1969).

[22] A very helpful discussion of benefit segmentation is found in Russell I. Haley, "Benefit Segmentation: A Decision-Oriented Research Tool," *Journal of Marketing,* Vol. 32 (July 1968), pp. 30–35.

[23] This case is adapted from Maurice E. Bale, "Market Segmentation," in Lee Adler, ed., *Plotting Marketing Strategy* (New York: Simon and Schuster, Inc., 1967), pp. 100–102.

Macleans, preference and loyalty were very high. They were, in fact, crazy about it. They were extremely and vocally enthusiastic about Macleans.

Market research showed that the most effective advertising themes—preferred overwhelmingly by the majority—were those of decay prevention, particularly in reference to children's teeth. A very substantial *segment,* however, were not so much interested in decay prevention and child themes as the *benefit of whiter teeth.* Whiter teeth—with the implications of attractiveness to the opposite sex—was a far more important benefit to *some* customers than the benefit of, "Look, Mom, no cavities." Macleans had stressed whiteness in some other markets and had product qualities to substantiate their claim.

Macleans introduced their *whiteness-benefit strategy* in 1962 and by 1965 had gained 7½ share points of the American market. Their product became the fourth largest seller, established a healthy trend toward additional growth, and defined a new area for competition in the toothpaste market.[24]

SOCIAL-SEGMENT CHARACTERISTICS. Cultural, ethnic, and social class groups frequently display differential consumption behavior patterns useful for marketing programming. Black consumers, for example, are attractive as market segments for petroleum companies because they purchase a much higher percentage of premium gasoline than do non-black consumers. In addition, black customers tend to be much more cohesive and concentrated as market segments than non-black customers. This provides a practical base for segmentation in distribution facilities and communications media.[25]

Social class appears to make considerable difference in product preferences, media observation patterns, and preferences for retail establishments.[26] Other social characteristics can be significant in market segmentation strategies.

USAGE SEGMENTS. It is often useful to identify and satisfy *heavy users* of the product.

In some product categories, such as car rental, air travel, hair coloring, and dog food, less than 20 percent of the population accounts for more than 80 percent of usage. Even among widely used products such as soft drinks and coffee, 50 percent of the U.S. households account for almost 90 percent of usage.[27]

The problem with usage variables is that *reasons for usage may vary greatly*

---

[24] For a list of the kinds of benefits that can be used for segmentation strategies, see C. R. Wasson, F. D. Sturdivant, and D. H. McConaughy, *Competition and Human Behavior* (New York: Appleton-Century-Crofts, Inc., 1968), pp. 12–13.

[25] For a comprehensive review of behavior patterns and characteristics of black market segments, see Ray Bauer and Ross Cunningham, *The Negro Consumer* (Cambridge, Mass.: Marketing Science Institute, 1970).

[26] One of the most comprehensive descriptions of the use of social class in marketing strategy is Sydney Levy, "Social Class and Consumer Behavior," in Joseph Newman, ed., *On Knowing the Consumer* (New York: John Wiley & Sons, Inc., 1966), pp. 146–160.

[27] Norton Garfinkle, "How Marketing Data Can Identify Your Target Audience," paper presented to the Eastern Annual Conference of the American Association of Advertising Agencies, October 25, 1966. Also see Dik Warren Twedt, "How Important to Marketing Strategy is the 'Heavy User'?" *Journal of Marketing,* Vol. 28 (January 1964), pp. 71–72.

among people who are all heavy users. Consequently, brands preferred, buying patterns, and media exposure vary greatly. If usage is to be a workable basis for segmentation strategy, heavy users must have the same behavioral patterns. Table 9-1 shows how certain group characteristics correlate with usage of common consumer products.

Methods of Segmenting Industrial Markets

Industrial-market segments are identified in a variety of ways. Many of the methods of segmenting consumer markets apply to industrial markets, though industrial-market segmentation often places more emphasis on the nature of the buying situation.[28] Some of the most common ways of segmenting industrial markets are described below.[29]

INDUSTRY SEGMENTATION. The most common form of segmentation is by industry. An illustration is provided by National Cash Register. When entering the computer market NCR had the difficult task of competing with IBM and other companies producing computers for all industries. NCR concentrated its marketing efforts on distribution industries and financial industries. It could compete successfully in these industries because of its long history of supplying equipment to them and its familiarity with the problems faced by their buyers. NCR also already had successful marketing organizations in those industries. This segmentation strategy has been successful in establishing NCR as a major competitor in the computer industry, facilitating expansion into other industries.

As another example, printing firms formerly sold to all types of industries and their salesmen were primarily knowledgeable about printing rather than the problems of the industries to whom they were selling. In recent years, however, some printing firms have begun specializing in certain industries. Some firms have hired ex-bankers to sell printing. These salesmen do nothing but call upon banks, thus allowing them to specialize in the problems and behavior of financial institutions.

CUSTOMER-SIZE SEGMENTATION. Industrial market segmentation may be identified by size of customer. Large customers can receive specialized attention such as direct sales effort and direct shipment. Smaller customers can receive a different type of marketing program.

APPLICATION SEGMENTATION. A basis for identifying segments is sometimes the application for which the products are designed. For example, equipment produced for research and development by a buyer may be very different from similar equipment purchased by the buyer for production purposes. R&D instruments may be made to much finer tolerances and have supplementary features for

[28] See Charles W. Faris, "Market Segmentation and Industrial Buying Behavior," in M. S. Moyer and R. E. Vosburgh, eds., *Marketing for Tomorrow . . . Today* (Chicago: American Marketing Association, 1967), pp. 108–110, and Richard N. Cardozo, "Segmenting the Industrial Market," in King, *Marketing and the New Science of Planning*, pp. 433–440.

[29] See Lawrence Fisher, *Industrial Marketing* (London: Business Books Limited, 1969), pp. 19–20.

Table 9-1 Light and Heavy Buyers by Mean Purchase Rates for Different Socioeconomic Cells

Product	Description		Mean consumption rate ranges		Ratio of highest to lowest rate
	Light buyers	Heavy buyers	Light buyers	Heavy buyers	
Catsup	Unmarried or married over age 50 without children	Under 50, 3 or more children	.74–1.82	2.73–5.79	7.8
Frozen orange juice	Under 35 or over 65, income less than $10,000, not college grads, 2 or less children	College grads, income over $10,000, between 35 & 65	1.12–2.24	3.53–9.00	8.0
Pancake mix	Some college, 2 or less children	3 or more children, high school or less ed.	.48–.52	1.10–1.51	3.3
Candy bars	Under 35, no children	35 or over, 3 or more children	1.01–4.31	6.56–22.29	21.9
Cake mix	Not married or under 35, no children, income under $10,000, T.V. less than 3½ hrs.	35 or over, 3 or more children, income over $10,000	.55–1.10	2.22–3.80	6.9
Beer	Under 25 or over 50, college ed., nonprofessional, T.V. less than 2 hrs.	Between 25 & 50, not college grad., T.V. more than 3½ hrs.	0–12.33	17.26–40.30	∞
Cream shampoo	Income less than $8,000, at least some college, less than 5 children	Income $10,000 or over with high school or less ed.	.16–.35	.44–.87	5.5
Hair spray	Over 65, under $8,000 income	Under 65, over $10,000 income, not college grad.	0–.41	.52–1.68	∞
Toothpaste	Over 50, less than 3 children, income less than $8,000	Under 50, 3 or more children, over $10,000 income	1.41–2.01	2.22–4.39	3.1
Mouthwash	Under 35 or over 65, less than $8,000 income, some college	Between 35 & 65, income over $8,000, high school or less	.46–.85	.98–1.17	2.5

SOURCE: Reprinted from Frank M. Bass, Douglas J. Tigert, and Ronald T. Lonsdale, "Market Segmentation: Group Versus Individual Behavior," Journal of Marketing Research, Vol. 5 (August 1968), pp. 264–270, at 267, published by the American Marketing Association.

flexibility in usage. Since R&D instruments are purchased by different individuals in the buying organization and in a different time frame, the selling methods may be radically different. Some companies may establish a favorable market position for one segment of the market on the basis of technical quality and availability, while another company may establish itself in a different market segment of the same product on the basis of technical service of installing engineers and planners.

REGIONAL SEGMENTATION. As in consumer markets, regional segmentation is often a feasible strategy. The ability to give prompt and individual service in a small geographic region, for example, is a strategy used by some burial-vault and casket companies to sell to local funeral directors in competition with national firms selling throughout the United States. Building-materials firms selling to manufacturers of mobile homes find that regional variation is so significant in material requirements that they must segment their selling and distribution strategies by regions of the country. Steel companies and other marketers of products with significant transportation costs find regional segmentation a necessity for some products.

The purpose in each of the segmentation alternatives described above is to find a basis on which to adapt the marketing program of the selling firm to the needs of a subpart of buying firms in such a way that the seller has a differential advantage over the firms that are left in the total market. The adaptation must be accomplished with sufficient advantage that relatively higher yields from management are attained than with a nonsegmentated strategy.

Multidimensional Segmentation

A single variable is often inadequate as a basis for developing segmentation strategies. Recognition of this inadequacy has led to new methods based upon a multidimensional segmentation of markets. They may be applied to either consumer or industrial markets, although most research originated in consumer marketing.

PSYCHOGRAPHICS. One way of identifying market segments is to measure users and nonusers of a product on multiple dimensions of activities, interests, attitudes, buying behavior, and media behavior. Such an approach is called psychographics. A leading theorist of this approach explains the attempt to determine common explanatory variables that underlie a segment:

Another way to analyze consumer behavior is to start with the behavior itself. If heavy users of X are also heavy users of Y and Z, there is a reason to suppose that heavy users of X, Y, and Z constitute a special type of consumer, a group of consumers with some specific set of needs, dispositions and experiences in common. For example, if heavy users of headache remedies are also heavy users of cold tablets and stomach remedies, there is reason to suspect that this group of consumers has in common an unusual number of ailments, a particular attitude about what should be done about ailments, or both. Similarly, if heavy users of oven cleaners are also heavy users of window cleaners, scouring pads and furniture polish, there would be reason to suspect a common attitude among this group toward dirt and disorder.[30]

From this type of segment identification arise important strategic implications. Attitude and buying characteristics are sorted along with important programming dimensions such as product attributes and media preferences. The traditional question of "what to do" with market segments after they are identified is therefore partially answered. For example, behavioral segments have been shown to be correlated with media preference patterns.[31] Psychographic approaches are gaining in acceptance, and the methodology upon which they are built has been shown to be reliable.[32]

PREFERENCE AND SIMILARITY MAPPING. Preference and similarity mapping encompasses a variety of methods designed to identify and "map" (describe visually) consumer and product characteristics on more than one dimension.[33] Some methods are *metric* (interval or ratio data), but some of the most attractive are *nonmetric* (nominal and ordinal data).

Preference and similarity mapping is based upon the premise that buyers (or potential buyers) may perceive objects (brands or products) as being similar to each other. When products are perceived to be similar or occupy the same (multidimensional) product space, they may compete for the same segment.

Examination of customer judgments about which products are more or less similar to others not only yields a map of the product space but can be used to determine the number of dimensions or attributes underlying these perceptions. The addition of preference data to the dimensional configuration permits the identification of viable market segments. There is also the possibility of predicting how market shares might change, given the entry of a new product or the movement of an existing product in the configuration to conform more closely to the preferences of an identified market segment.

THE MARKET FACTS BEER CASE. The blending of segment identification and marketing strategy through multidimensional methods is illustrated by a case reported by Market Facts, Inc. The study is based upon the beer market in Chicago.[34]

[30] William D. Wells, "Patterns of Consumer Behavior," in Moyer and Vosburgh, *Marketing for Tomorrow . . . Today*, pp. 134–138, at 134.

[31] See Seymour Banks, "Patterns of Daytime Viewing Behavior," in *ibid.*, pp. 139–142, and Charles E. Swanson, "Patterns of Nighttime Television Viewing," in *ibid.*, pp. 143–147.

[32] Douglas J. Tigert, "Psychographics: A Test-Retest Reliability Analysis," in Phillip R. McDonald, ed., *Marketing Involvement in Society and the Economy* (Chicago: American Marketing Association, 1969), pp. 310–315.

[33] For an introduction to this subject, see P. E. Green and F. J. Carmone, *Multidimensional Scaling and Related Techniques in Marketing Analysis* (Boston: Allyn and Bacon, Inc., 1970).

[34] This case is adapted from B. Sherak, "Consumer Segmentation and Brand Mapping: A Methodological Study," a paper delivered at the International Conference on Market Segmentation, March 1969, and Richard M. Johnson, "Market Segmentation: A Strategic Management Tool," *Journal of Marketing Research*, Vol. 8 (February 1971), pp. 13–18.

This study was designed primarily for the development of advertising and product-positioning strategies based upon multidimensional identification of market segments. Two types of information were sought: (1) the benefits desired in a beer, (2) perceptions of the brands of beer according to benefits. This provided the basis for analysis of interrelationships among brands.

A list of 35 benefits or product descriptions was compiled, and 499 beer drinkers were asked to rate how well the words described their "ideal" brand of beer. A factor analysis of the 35 items revealed seven basic dimensions: quality, prestige, smoothness, mildness, dryness, robustness, and youthfulness.

Beer drinkers were also asked to provide information about themselves, including their self-image (or life style), reasons for drinking beer, beer usage (quantity and brand), and demographic characteristics. Market segments of beer customers were determined by a nonmetric, clustering technique.

Eight brands of beer were rated on the same 35 characteristics used to rate the "ideal" brand of beer, and a multidimensional map was constructed of the brands, using multiple-discriminant analysis. The results show four significant dimensions: quality or "premium" characteristics, mildness-lightness, smoothness, and youthfulness. The first two dimensions accounted for 90 percent of the discrimination. They are graphed in Figure 9-2.

Figure 9-2 shows eight "ideal" points (in large circles) and the number of persons in the sample that were clustered in that market segment. The small dots show the perceptions of actual brands. The analysts described strategy implications from this segmentation study:

First of all, an inspection of the mapping will help pinpoint target population. For example, it would appear that price prospect segments for Schlitz are clusters 1, 2, 7, 9 and possibly 6; but most likely not 4, 5, and 8.

From knowledge of the clusters, the brand positions and the dimensions we can begin to infer the appropriate positioning strategies. For example, it would appear that a quality and lightness appeal should be effective in advertising to the men of Cluster 7 and that an appeal of a hearty beer for rugged individualists might be effective for Cluster 6.

In the development of a new product strategies, we may be interested in spatial locations which are near clusters of ideal points but far enough away from the existing major brands so as not to compete with them too directly. The mapping suggests opportunities for a mild, popular-priced beer (near Clusters 5 and 8), a mild, extra-premium beer (to capture Cluster 7), and possibly a very robust beer positioned between the current popular and premium-price beers.[35]

MANAGEMENT EXPERIENCE WITH MAPPING. A number of companies have used mapping or similarity research in the planning of marketing strategy.[36]

[35] Sherak, *ibid.*, pp. 21–22.
[36] These cases are adapted from James R. Taylor, "Management Experience with Applications of Multidimensional Scaling Methods," Working Paper of Marketing Science Institute, Cambridge, Massachusetts, 1970.

Figure 9-2   Distribution of ideal points in product space.

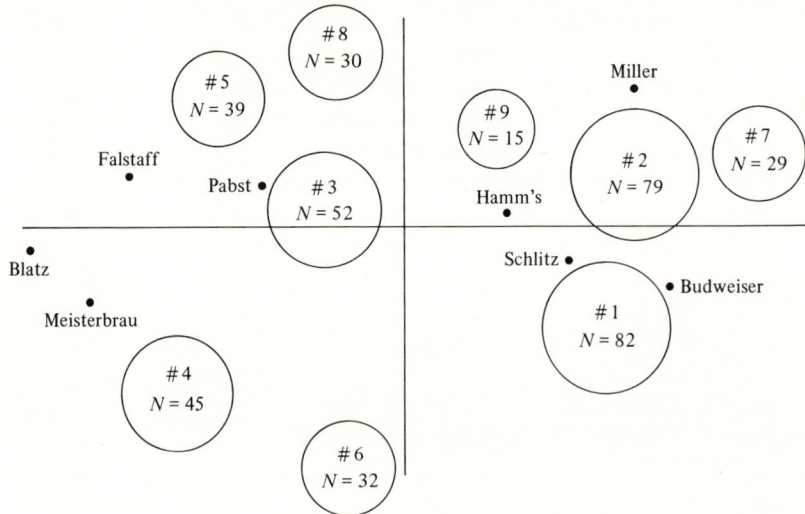

SOURCE: B. Sherak, "Consumer Segmentation and Brand Mapping: A Methodological Study," paper delivered at International Conference on Market Segmentation (March 1969), p. 21. Reprinted by permission of B. Sherak, President, Market Facts—New York, Inc.

E. I. DuPont de Nemours used it on over 45 projects between 1963 and 1970. At DuPont, preference data are related to perceptual maps of customers constructed from customer data, the aim being to develop a density distribution of ideal points in the configuration in order to determine viable market segments and the idealized nature of products. Mapping is used to assess where DuPont stands relative to competition, to measure progress as the product is varied (in form, package, or advertising), and to estimate market shares at the conclusion of the development.[37]

At Procter & Gamble, mapping is used to determine market segments and to position brands in segments. In one study of detergents, housewives evaluated brands in terms of several relevant attributes. The various attributes of detergents were found to correlate highly with two basic dimensions, "sudsiness" correlating highest on one dimension (.97) and "harshness" having the highest correlation with the second dimension.[38] This information was used to analyze and plan the positioning of the eight brands of detergent on the market.

Mapping, which is generally used in conjunction with other approaches, ap-

[37] See David H. Doehlert, "Similarity and Preference Mapping: A Color Example," in King, *Marketing and the New Science of Planning*, pp. 250–258.

[38] Marshall C. Greenberg, "Some Applications of Nonmetric Multidimensional Scaling," paper presented at the 129th Annual Meeting of the American Statistical Association, New York, August 19–22, 1969.

pears to hold much promise for the future. The following questions about market opportunities are appropriate for analysis of new products:

1. What are the salient product attributes perceived by buyers in a market?
2. What combination of attributes does the buyer most prefer?
3. What products are viewed as substitutes, and which are differentiated?
4. What are the viable segments in a market?
5. Are there "holes" in the market that can support a new-product venture?[39]

For analysis of *established markets*, mapping is generally used to answer the following questions:

1. Is my brand positioned where I think it should be?
2. How can I move my product to make it more profitable?
3. How has the market changed over time?
4. How did a new competitor position itself in the market?
5. Did this new entry change the positioning of other brands?[40]

EVALUATING AND CHOOSING MARKET SEGMENTS

Evaluating and choosing market segments toward which a firm's resources are to be directed is fundamentally a process of matching market opportunities with marketing programs. The criteria for evaluating market segments must always be: can an effective market program be developed by the identification of market segments?

It may be useful to review the case examples described earlier in this chapter. Sony, Macleans, and NCR all chose their market-segmentation strategy because of the *implications for achieving a differential advantage with their marketing program*. In each case, definite strategic and tactical implications result for advertising, sales, distribution, and product development.

The evaluating of market segments involves three basic steps: (1) accumulating information about the characteristics and behavior of market segments, (2) establishing criteria for comparing and choosing alternative segments, and (3) matching the firm's objectives and programming resources with opportunities and constraints of a segmentation strategy.

Accumulating Information

The marketing information system of a firm should yield information with which to *evaluate present market segmentation strategies* and continuously *evaluate new segment opportunities*.

---

[39] Taylor, "Management Experience with Applications of Multidimensional Scaling Methods," p. 28.

[40] *Ibid.*, pp. 28–29. Also see James R. Taylor, "Unfolding Theory Applied to Market Segmentation," *Journal of Advertising Research*, Vol. 9 (December 1969), pp. 39–46.

Segmentation data are collected basically in two ways.[41] The first approach involves investigation of existing products or usage categories to distinguish between buyers of different brands. The bases for collecting segmentation data are empirically determined. The second approach is from the opposite direction. Data are collected on the basis of theoretical variables believed to be relevant to behavior, such as those analyzed in Chapter 5. Data may also be collected on the basis of traditional variables believed related to behavior, such as education, sex, income, and family structure. The preceding section contains examples of both, and the trend is toward the inclusion of both types of data.

Criteria for Choosing Market Segments

Criteria to be used in choosing market segments are those which are most useful in the development of high-yield strategy. Four criteria to help make this objective operational are *measurability, accessibility, substantiality,* and *congruity.*[42]

MEASURABILITY. Measurability refers to the degree to which information is available or obtainable about the size and character of a market segment. While this criterion, in itself, is of less importance than the other three, it is important in the development of marketing plans and control procedures. A customer group that smokes a particular brand of cigarette because of parental influences during youth might be very important. Yet, if there is no way of *measuring* this segment, it is not useful and probably will not rank high in a market-target evaluation process.

ACCESSIBILITY. Accessibility refers to the degree to which a given segment can be differentially reached. Perhaps, for example, it is known that persons with a certain type of personality are very important for a proposed product. If there are no media that reach these people as a group and there is no other way of reaching them differentially, it is unlikely that these segments can rank high in desirability for a segmentation strategy.

SUBSTANTIALITY. Substantiality refers to the degree to which segments are large enough to be worth subdividing for separate marketing activity. Since the revenue generated from substantial segments and the high expenses (typically) generated from nonsubstantial segments so directly affect profitability, substantiality is a major determinant of the desirability of a market segment.

CONGRUITY. Congruity refers to the degree to which the members of a market segment *fit together.* Congruity is a measure of the appropriateness of the classification in explaining the *behavior* of the group, and so it is crucial in predicting the nature of response to marketing programs by segments.

Formal systems for weighing these four criteria are appropriate in the con-

---

[41] John C. Bieda and Harold H. Kassarjian, "An Overview of Market Segmentation," in Morin, *Marketing in a Changing World* (Chicago: American Marketing Association, 1969), pp. 249–253.

[42] The first three of these criteria are from Philip Kotler, *Marketing Management* (Englewood Cliffs, N.J.: Prentice-Hall, Inc., 1967).

text of a specific company's objectives and strategies, although in any case the last two criteria are of critical importance.

RANKING MARKET SEGMENTS. Market segments that have survived an initial screening should be ranked in order of desirability as market targets. A numerical scoring system should be used to rank segments on the basis of contribution to the firm's profit and growth objectives, compatible with the company's corporate development strategies (described in Chapter 1).

After unexploited market segments compatible with the firm's core strategy are identified, the analyst should prepare a list of the best estimates of profitability of each segment using best possible assumptions of costs, competitive position, revenues, and opportunity costs over appropriate time frames. The numerical evaluations should be done under varying assumptions about the levels of resources devoted to exploiting a market and buyer response to each level. The final selection of market targets (and thus strategy) is a balancing of risk, profitability, and growth with the objectives of the firm.

Segmentation Analysis for Marketing Programming

Segmentation analysis is basic to programming of marketing activities. (Marketing programming is the subject of Chapters 10 through 17 of this text.) Specifically, however, segmentation analysis can be used for the following purposes:

1. Allocating appropriate amounts of promotional attention and money to the potentially most profitable segments of the market.
2. Designing a product line that truly parallels the demands of the market instead of one that bulks in some areas and ignores or scants other potentially profitable segments.
3. Identifying the first sign of a major trend in a swiftly changing market, providing time to prepare to take advantage of it.
4. Determining appeals that will be most effective in the company's advertising, and, where several different appeals are significantly effective, quantifying the segments of the market responsive to each appeal.
5. Choosing advertising media more wisely and determining the proportion of budget that should be allocated to each medium in the light of anticipated impact.
6. Correcting the timing of advertising and promotional efforts so that they are massed in the weeks, months, and seasons when responsiveness is likely to be at its maximum.
7. Understanding otherwise seemingly meaningless demographic market information and applying it in scores of new and effective ways.[43]

[43] Daniel Yankelovich, "New Criteria for Market Segmentation," *Harvard Business Review*, Vol. 42 (March–April 1964), pp. 83–90.

Managerial Attitudes and Market Opportunities

Executives often are overly cautious; they appear to be more attuned to the constraining than to the opportunistic role of changing markets. The opportunistic role of markets involves systematically evaluating opportunities for profitability. The problem of enterprise survival and profitable growth is one that demands top management's increased attention toward changing market opportunities. Unfortunately, the reward system of most business firms still places primary emphasis upon executing strategies for existing markets rather than searching out new market opportunities and designing strategies for reaching them.[44] Few firms have programs designed to insure marketing programming to be ready for *future* market opportunities.

A continuous attitude of identifying market opportunities is a managerial resource that can provide a substantial profitability advantage for a firm.

SUMMARY AND CONCLUSIONS

Essentially, the challenge facing marketing executives today is based upon the need (1) to discover, define, understand, and isolate significant customer segments of a total mass market, (2) to develop quality products that can be produced at a profit in serving those market segments, and (3) to mount carefully planned programs for exploiting these opportunities. In balancing organizational capability with market opportunities, the marketing executive frequently employs a market-segmentation strategy.

Market segmentation is defined as the process of so designing or featuring a product or service that it will make a particularly strong appeal to some identifiable subpart of a total market. Market-segmentation strategies derive their existence from the fundamental fact that all human individuals are different. When the economic base of a society is sufficient, these desires are satisfied by "custom-tailoring" products to the special needs and preferences of customer groups.

Efficiency in segmentation strategy depends upon the determination of typologies that classify customers in terms of behavioral resemblances rather than descriptive static characteristics. The complexity of customer preferences makes this a difficult task.

There are numerous alternative methods of segmenting consumer markets. These include segmentation based upon geographic variations, demographics, individual behavioral variations, benefits, social groups, volume of usage, and multidimensional variations among segments. Psychographics and similarity map-

---

[44] See Robert L. Clewett, "Market Opportunity and Corporate Management," in Peter D. Bennett, ed., *Marketing and Economic Development* (Chicago: American Marketing Association, 1965), pp. 187–199.

ping are techniques of rising importance in the design of multidimensional segmentation strategies.

Strategies for industrial market segmentation may be developed along lines similar to those used for consumer segmentation. Additionally they are often based on purchasing characteristics or on variables such as type of industry, customer size, type of application, and geographic region.

Many firms have reward systems structured primarily to encourage outstanding performance in the *execution* of strategies for existing markets, often giving little attention to the need to continuously monitor and select dynamic market areas for adaptive strategy development. This chapter emphasizes the need for developing and rewarding executives' abilities to define strategic targets upon which the company should be focusing its valuable resources.

QUESTIONS FOR REVIEW AND DISCUSSION

1. Describe the purpose and role of defining market targets in the marketing strategy of a business firm.
2. Why does market segmentation exist? Would not everyone be better off if companies produced just a single model or style of a product instead of so many colors, styles, and other variations?
3. Differentiate between mass-market, single-segment, and multiple-segment strategies. Under what conditions would you recommend each one be employed?
4. Select a specified product area with which you are familiar or about which you can obtain data. What basic information would you specify as needed for making decisions about segmentation strategies for the product line?
5. Describe what is meant by each of the following terms as criteria for market segments: measurability, accessibility, substantiality, congruity?
6. Describe the major methods of segmenting consumer products. Identify a consumer market about which you have information; analyze which alternative method would be most useful for planning marketing strategy for that product.
7. Describe the major methods of segmenting industrial products. Identify an industrial product about which you have information; analyze which alternative method would be most useful for planning marketing strategy for that product.

PART III   DEVELOPING MARKETING PROGRAMS

After marketing objectives have been identified and target-market segments selected, it is necessary to develop a coordinated marketing program that will achieve marketing objectives and make the required contribution to the achievement of corporate objectives. Part III is concerned with the development of marketing programs that have these characteristics.

Chapter 10 considers the development of product objectives, how a firm can modify its present products or market them differently, and when and how it should eliminate products. New products are the sustaining force of many companies; consequently, the management of new-product programs is discussed in Chapter 11. Chapter 12 examines considerations and procedures in developing pricing programs. Distribution channels are undergoing a series of profound changes; Chapter 13 summarizes these changes and presents a procedure for developing a channel program.

A significant proportion of total marketing costs is consumed in the distribution of products from manufacturing to consuming sites. Chapter 14 discusses changes in physical distribution systems and presents a framework for developing a physical distribution system. Advertising has become an increasingly important determinant of corporate success; a procedure for developing a high-market-impact advertising program is presented in Chapter 15. Techniques and procedures for managing salesmen are discussed in Chapter 16. Finally, organizational-structure alternatives and personnel considerations are outlined in Chapter 17.

Chapter 10   Product Programs

Without products and services there would be no need for business firms or marketing. A company's product/service offer defines the boundaries of its business and is the most important determinant of its growth, profitability, and survival. Product programs are central to the corporate and marketing planning process and are the first consideration in developing an integrated marketing program.

NATURE AND SCOPE OF PRODUCT PROGRAMS

Sound product programs are based on a realistic understanding of the nature of products and the array of product variations available to the firm. These basic concepts are discussed in this section.

Product Concepts

There is a tendency to think of a product in terms of its physical characteristics and what it does. Often overlooked are its social-psychological dimensions, including aesthetic qualities, symbolic meanings, and other subjective and intangible factors. For example, we often form judgments about people on the basis of what they wear, what kinds of music they like, what books and magazines they read, how they furnish their homes, and so on. Thus products and services should be viewed from the customer's perspective, because the reality of a product or service is what customers think they are buying, not necessarily what executives think they are selling.

In the United States most firms offer many products and/ or services. Multiproduct firms have to make several basic product-scope decisions. First, they have to determine the *variety*—or number of generically different types—of goods and services that will be offered. They need to decide whether to offer industrial and/or consumer products and the number of different types of each.

Second, marketing executives make *assortment* decisions concerning the range of alternatives to be offered within each variety classification. RCA, for example, has to determine how many screen sizes and cabinet styles it will offer in its color television line.

Finally, product decisions need to be made for each *item* comprising the assortment. What should the cabinet look like? What tuning features should be included? During any planning period, product programming may involve additions, modifications, and/or deletions at the variety, assortment, and/or item levels.

A PRODUCT PLANNING AND CONTROL SYSTEM

Figure 10-1 summarizes the major elements of a product planning and control system. This system is a continuation of the one developed in Chapter 1 and expanded in Chapter 2. The remainder of this chapter discusses product objectives and programs for product-market modification and product elimination. New-product programs are discussed in the next chapter.

DEVELOPING PRODUCT OBJECTIVES

Product objectives serve as the connecting link between corporate and marketing objectives and strategies on the one hand, and detailed product programs on the other. Properly utilized, they provide the mechanism to insure that product programs make the appropriate contribution to the achievement of corporate and marketing objectives in ways that capitalize on the firm's distinctive competences. This section integrates the product life cycle with other considerations into a framework for formulating product objectives.

The Product Life Cycle

The "product life cycle" is a generalized model of sales and profit trends for a product class or category over a period of time (Figure 10-2).[1]

PHASE I: DEVELOPMENT. This is the period of time before the product is brought to the market. Customer needs are analyzed, product concepts tested, engineering and production techniques developed, and marketing strategy and programs prepared.

---

[1] For illustrative discussions of the product life-cycle concept see Theodore Levitt, "Exploit the Product Life Cycle," *Harvard Business Review*, Vol. 43 (November-December 1965), pp. 81–94; and Robert D. Buzzell, "Competitive Behavior and Product Life Cycles," in J. S. Wright and J. Goldstucker, eds., *New Ideas for Successful Marketing* (Chicago: American Marketing Association, 1966), pp. 46–67.

Figure 10-1   A product planning and control system.

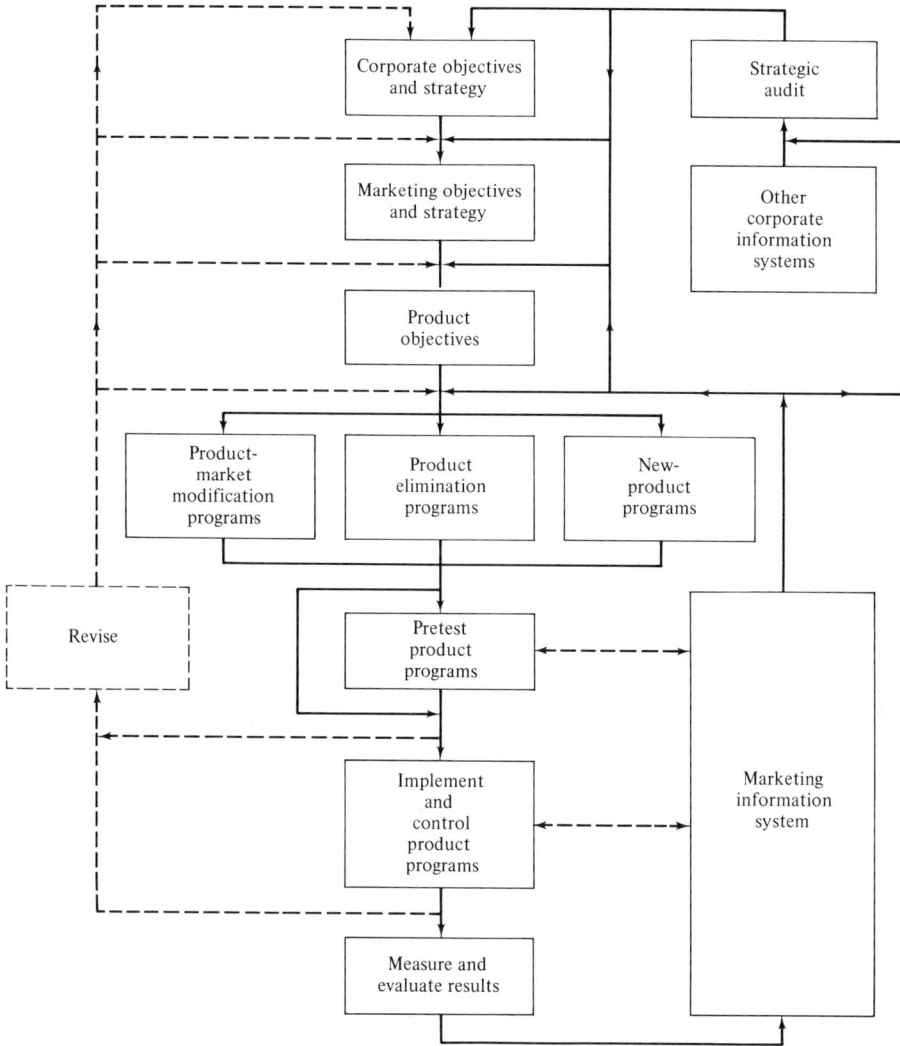

The time required to develop products varies widely. One study found that the range was from six months for Sinclair Power-X gasoline to 55 years for television.[2] Management often underestimates developmental time, and this is a prime cause of product failure.[3]

[2] Lee Adler, "Time Lag in New Product Development," *Journal of Marketing*, Vol. 30 (January 1966), pp. 17–21.

[3] Clarence F. Manning, "Principles of Product Strategy," speech before the 12th Annual Marketing Conference, National Industrial Conference Board, October 28, 1964.

Figure 10-2   The general product life-cycle model.

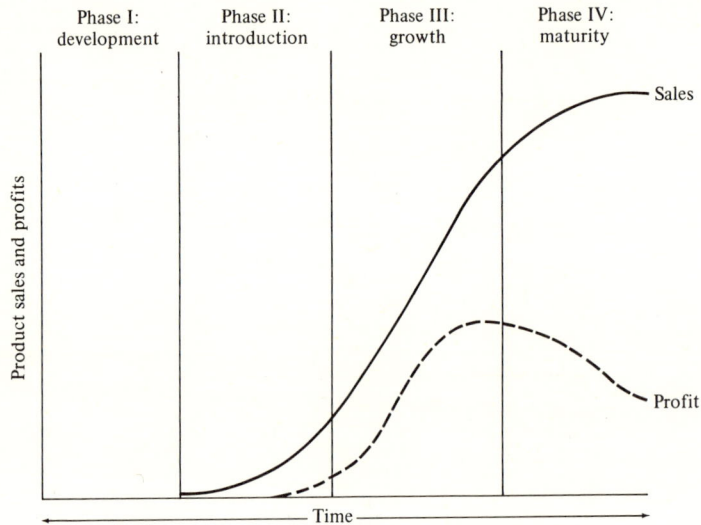

PHASE II: INTRODUCTION. This stage begins when a new product is first brought to market. Sales usually are low and increase at a modest rate. The marketing effort required to introduce the product usually eliminates profit margins until the latter part of this stage.

PHASE III: GROWTH. During this phase demand begins to accelerate and the size of the total market expands rapidly. Other firms enter the market with competing products. The nature of the originator's problem shifts from trying to persuade customers to try the product, to getting them to prefer his brand. The number and types of retailers handling the product generally increase, and they build inventory. This often causes manufacturers' sales to increase more rapidly than retail sales, which in turn creates an exaggerated illusion of profit potential and thus attracts additional competitors.

PHASE IV: MATURITY. Market saturation is the first sign of market maturity. Most prospective customers own the product, and the rate of sales increase declines to a par with population growth. Price competition intensifies, and competitive efforts focus on increasingly finer differentiations in the product, in customer services, and in advertising claims.

PHASE V: DECLINE. When market maturity ends, the product enters the final stage—decline. The product begins to lose customer appeal. Overcapacity becomes endemic, and prices and margins continue to decline. Eventually the product is replaced by better products or by substitutes.

QUALIFICATIONS AND ELABORATIONS. The general product life-cycle model should be viewed as a useful idealization rather than a definitive description.[4] There is a great deal of variation in the length of the product life cycle and its various stages. Fad and fashion products typically have a life cycle that is shorter and more pronounced, in terms of both growth and decline, than the general model.[5] Other products, such as men's shoes and industrial fasteners, have a life cycle that remains in the maturity stage for generations, with per-capita consumption neither rising nor falling. In other cases, a product experiences a gradual but steady per-capita decline, as in the case of beer and steel.[6]

Product Life Cycles and the Corporate Imperative

Despite the qualifications that must be attached to it, the general product life-cycle model suggests several valuable insights for corporate and marketing strategies. First, all products have a finite, limited life. Unless management takes appropriate action, the sales and profit margins of all products eventually decline and disappear. While there are undoubtedly exceptions to this mode, it is nevertheless a critically important planning premise.

Second, the death of products can be postponed in many instances through effective marketing strategies. Consider the classic case of nylon:

. . . if there had been no further product innovations designed to create new uses for nylon after the original military, miscellaneous, and circular knit uses, nylon consumption in 1962 would have reached a saturation level at approximately 50 million pounds annually.

Instead, in 1962 consumption exceeded 500 million pounds. . . . Had it not been for the addition of new uses for the same basic material—such as warp knits in 1945, tire cord in 1948, textured yarns in 1955, carpet yarns in 1959, and so forth—nylon would not have had the spectacularly rising consumption curve it has so clearly had.[7]

These observations indicate the importance of maintaining a balanced product life-cycle portfolio mix.[8] The President of Smith-Corona Marchant explains why his company follows this strategy:

[4] Arch Patton, "Top Management's Stake in the Product Life Cycle," *The Management Review*, June 1969, pp. 9–14, 67–71, 76–79.

[5] See, for example, Chester R. Wasson, "How Predictable Are Fashion and Other Product Life Cycles?" *Journal of Marketing*, Vol. 32 (July 1968), pp. 36–43; and Dwight E. Robinson, "Fashion Theory and Product Design," *Harvard Business Review*, Vol. 36 (November-December 1958), pp. 126–138.

[6] Levitt, "Exploit the Product Life Cycle," p. 83.

[7] *Ibid.*, p. 89.

[8] For further discussions of the product portfolio-mix concept see Seymour Tilles, "Strategies for Allocating Funds," *Harvard Business Review*, Vol. 44 (January-February 1966), pp. 72–80; and Donald K. Clifford, Jr., "Leverage in the Product Life Cycle," *Dun's Review and Modern Industry*, May 1965, pp. 62–70.

One of our objectives is to be a multi-product company, enjoying a normal rate of growth. The sale of practically any product will eventually reach a peak. Our strategy is to predict that peak in terms of time or other factors such as competitive developments, and to have additional products ready for marketing as close to that peak as possible.[9]

Identifying Product Objectives

Since product objectives should be derived from corporate and marketing objectives, and since the latter vary from company to company, it is not possible to identify specific product objectives here. Instead a procedure for developing product objectives will be presented.

THE PRODUCT LIFE-CYCLE AUDIT.[10] The first step is to determine the life-cycle positions of all the company's major products. Unfortunately this is difficult, and, as Tilles has pointed out, labeling a product in a particular stage often tends to become a self-fulfilling prophecy because products perceived to be in the growth stage may be heavily backed while products perceived to be in the decline stage may receive limited financial support.[11] Hence it is critically important to identify life-cycle positions correctly. A common procedure is as follows:[12]

1. Developing historical information for a three- to five-year period. This usually includes such data as unit and dollar sales, profit margins, total profit contribution, return on investment, market share, and price.
2. Tracking trends in the number and nature of competitors; the number and market-share rankings of competing products, and their quality and performance; shifts in distribution channels; and the relative advantages of competitive products in each channel.
3. Monitoring developments in short-term competitive strategy, including competitors' announcements of new products and additional plant capacity.
4. Developing historical information on the life cycles of similar and/or related products to help suggest the shape and length of the life cycle for the product under analysis.
5. Estimating, by use of the information developed in the previous steps, the number of years remaining in the product's life cycle, and assigning it to one of the positions in the life cycle.

This analysis should not require additional research, since all required information is part of the strategic audit that was used to formulate corporate and marketing objectives and strategies.

[9] "Smith-Corona Marchant, Inc. (AR)," a case copyrighted in 1964 by the President and Fellows of Harvard College.

[10] This section is adapted from Clifford, "Leverage in the Product Life Cycle," pp. 62–70.

[11] Tilles, "Strategies for Allocating Funds," p. 77.

[12] For an alternative approach see Levitt, "Exploit the Product Life Cycle," p. 87.

After the life-cycle positions of all of the company's major products have been determined, a life-cycle profile of the entire product line is constructed. This profile specifies the percentages of sales and profits that fall within each stage of the life cycle.

THE TARGET PRODUCT-LIFE-CYCLE PROFILE. The next step is to construct the target product-life-cycle profile. This profile specifies the percentage of sales and profiles that *should* fall in each stage of the life cycle.

Several factors should be considered in designing a target profile. One is the average length of product life cycles, including the rate of new-product introductions and the rate of obsolescence. These rates vary significantly across industries, but product life styles in general seem to be shrinking. The shorter the life cycle, the greater the proportion of sales that should be in the introduction and growth stages.

Growth objectives are another type of consideration. Generally, the more ambitious the growth objective, the greater the proportion of sales that should be in the introduction and growth stages.

Cash flow is a third consideration. Cash-flow life cycles should be constructed for all products. The pivotal consideration is the rate and level at which a product generates or consumes cash as it proceeds through the life cycle. Some products— such as computers—require a continually growing commitment of funds; others —some pharmaceuticals—require one major investment in research, after which they generate cash flow that can be used to fund other products.[13] The greater the cash-generation capabilities of products, the greater the proportion of sales that can be in the introduction and growth stages of the life cycle.

Risk is another important consideration. Products have varying degrees of risk, depending on the stability of the technological environment, the volatility of consumer demand, the degree of dependence on limited numbers of customers and markets, and other considerations. An increasingly popular strategy is to maintain a portfolio of products encompassing different degrees of risk.[14]

PRODUCT OBJECTIVES. By comparing the target profile with the current or actual life-cycle profile, preliminary product objectives can be identified. These objectives indicate the amount and timing of resources that will be allocated to product-market modification programs, product-elimination programs, and new-product programs.

These preliminary objectives are subjected to further analysis to make certain that they are consistent with corporate and marketing objectives and strategies. They are also evaluated in terms of their compatibility with the requirements of all other functional areas of the business. The finalized objectives constitute the basis for establishing individual product plans.

A CASE EXAMPLE.[15] The XYZ Company is a well-diversified company in the

[13] Tilles, "Strategies for Allocating Funds," p. 76.
[14] *Ibid.*, p. 76.
[15] Adapted from Clifford, "Leverage in the Product Life Cycle," p. 70.

packaging business. The company conducted a life-cycle audit, constructing sales and profit profiles of its entire line. Only 6 percent of its current sales were represented by products in the introduction and growth stages. This was considerably less than the target profile of 25 percent desired—an objective based on the expected length of life cycles in the business and on growth and profit objectives. As a result, management decided to accelerate its acquisition and new-product development programs and to eliminate two obsolescent products. These steps reduced the share of total volume represented by obsolescent products from 15 to 11 percent—close to the target profile of 10 percent.

PRODUCT-MARKET MODIFICATION PROGRAMS

This section discusses objectives for product-market modification programs and the major types of modification that can be made. These modifications include changes in quality, features, style, and market positioning.

Objectives of Product-Market Modification Programs

Theoretically, any product in any stage of the life cycle can be modified. In most instances, however, modification programs are confined to relatively new products that have not attained performance expectations, and products that are clearly in the maturity and decline stages of the life cycle. Modification objectives specify sales, profits, and other requirements for these products.

Selecting Products for Modification

Studies indicate that it is possible to accelerate the sales and profits of some products, but not others.[16] Consequently, it is necessary to have some procedure for selecting those products that should be modified as well as those that should be eliminated and those that should not be changed during the planning period. This selection procedure is facilitated by the use of a product audit. This audit uses information contained in the strategic audit and the marketing information system.

Figure 10-3 presents an illustrative product audit form. This, or another type of procedure, can be used to evaluate all products in the product line. The illustrative form rates each product according to several measures of profitability, life-cycle position, product position, market position, and dependency of other product lines on the product under analysis. The criteria used to measure each of these factors can, of course, be expanded or contracted to meet a company's unique situations.

Each criterion is assigned a weight to reflect its relative importance in determining whether a product should be modified or eliminated. Each criterion is also assigned a rating from 1 to 10, or some other interval, according to its present and/or future performance on the criterion in question. The weight is multiplied

---

[16] Buzzell, "Competitive Behavior and Product Life Cycles," pp. 46–48.

by the rating to arrive at a total point score. Total points can then be determined for each criterion and summed to yield a total score. A written explanation of the reasons for the ratings and other supporting documents should accompany the form.

The major advantage of this procedure is that all products will be reviewed annually on the same criteria. The major problems lie in selecting the criteria and weights and assigning realistic ratings.

Based on corporate and marketing objectives and strategies as well as experience with the technique, decisions to modify or eliminate a product can be made on the basis of a product's total score and its rating on criteria that are viewed as critical.

Products selected for modification can be changed through various product-modification and/or market-stretching strategies. The choice of specific strategies is dictated by the product audit analysis, which identified the major problems in marketing the product.

Product Modifications

Since products have a multitude of physical dimensions, such as size, shape, color, material, functional features, and styling, there are almost an unlimited number of ways that products can be changed. Quality, feature, and styling modifications are particularly popular.

QUALITY MODIFICATION. Quality modification can be achieved through the use of better materials, construction, and/or engineering. Certain conditions improve the probability that this strategy will accelerate and extend a product's life cycle. First, and most obviously, quality modification must enlarge the market and/or increase the firm's market share. This means that quality must be an important evaluative criterion to a sufficient number of customers (see Chapter 6).

Second, quality is defined by the customer, not the manufacturer. In some cases customers can judge quality directly, but in many instances surrogate indicators are used. For example, some consumers judge the quality of carpeting on the basis of thickness; so that, without the appropriate thickness, fiber and other improvements may not be viewed as quality improvements.

In some cases it is desirable to improve the quality level without increasing the price to the consumer. This may require reducing the quality of some components of the product and increasing the quality of others. Whenever possible, quality reductions should be confined to components that do not impair product performance, are not visible to customers, and/or are not critical evaluative criteria.

A related consideration is that quality improvement should be visible and easily promotable for maximum effectiveness. Aspirin advertising is a good example of promotional difficulties encountered when quality and performance characteristics are hidden and difficult to demonstrate convincingly.

FEATURE MODIFICATION. Feature modification involves physical product

Figure 10-3   A product audit form.

> Product No. _____
>
> Model No. _____
>
> Date _____

I. Profitability   Weight × Rating = Total Points
   1. Dollar profit
   2. Profit margin
   3. Return on invested capital
   4. Cash flow
   5. Other   _____
   Total   _____

II. Life-Cycle Position
   1. Current position
   2. Projected position assuming no product
      modification   _____
   Total   _____

III. Product Position (Rate in terms of
   importance to end-users)
   1. Performance Characteristics
      a. Efficiency, sensitivity, accuracy,
         capacity
      b. Operating cost
      c. Reliability
      d. Durability
      e. Length of life
   2. Features
      a. Potential new users
      b. Range of use
      c. Devices that may be added to product
      d. Ease of use
      e. Safety
      f. Packaging
   3. Attractiveness
      a. Styling
      b. Compatibility with surrounding
         products in end-use
      c. Design and workmanship   _____
      Total   _____

Figure 10-3   A product audit form *(continued)*.

IV. Market Position
    1. Percentage of market during past
       five years
    2. Technological threats to market
    3. Possible new technological approaches
       by one company
    4. Number of present competitors
    5. Potential number of competitors
    6. Advantages of major competitors
    7. Probable costs of surpassing or adequately
       matching leaders in industry
    8. Conditions that mitigate against
       leadership by our company   _____
       Total   _____
V. Dependency of Other Company Lines
    1. Effect on sales of other products
    2. Effect on dealers and distributors if
       line were eliminated
    3. Importance of this product to major
       competitors of other lines in company   _____
       Total   _____

SUMMARY

	Total Points
1. Profitability	
2. Life-cycle position	
3. Product position	
4. Market position	
5. Dependency of other lines	_____
Total	_____

Disposition

Modification   ☐
Elimination   ☐

SOURCE: Adapted from V. P. Gregg, *Developing Sound Company Policies for a New Product Program* (New York: American Management Association, Report 8, 1958).

modifications designed to increase the number of uses, the situations in which the product can be used, the ease of use, safety, and similar product benefits.

Feature modification has several competitive advantages. First, new features are an effective method of developing an image of progressiveness. Second, they are a flexible competitive weapon because they can often be adapted quickly, dropped swiftly, and made optional, often at very little expense. Optional features allow a firm to adapt a basic product to meet the needs of multiple market segments. Finally, functional features can bring the company free publicity and generate a considerable amount of salesman and dealer enthusiasm.[17]

These advantages can be realized only if the feature modification is appealing to a significant segment of the target market. Hence the feature must already be an important evaluative criterion or have the potential of becoming one. In addition, the company must have the promotion and distribution capabilities to capitalize on the features quickly, since successful features are usually quickly duplicated by competitors.[18]

STYLE MODIFICATION. A strategy of style modification attempts to create an acceptably different version of a product or service that is distinctive in terms of appearance, performance, or other dimensions. This type of competition has been used in many industries, perhaps the most conspicuous being automobiles and women's clothing. During the last two decades, style modification has been adopted or used more extensively in many other product categories. Examples include such diverse products as furniture, lawn mowers, men's clothing, footwear, pots and pans, and garment bags.

There are several reasons why style modification is such a popular product strategy. Most importantly, if successful, it dramatically accelerates sales opportunities. Consider:

In 1964 a "well-dressed" woman wore her skirts just below the knee. Suddenly skirts shot up as much as three inches above the knee. Many woman felt that all their skirts were obsolete! But that's just the beginning.

The spike heel looked funny with short skirts so women's shoes were obsolete. Woman's shoes are a $2.5 billion business a year. Boots looked good with short skirts—this added another $140 million of volume a year at retail. The short skirt placed a new emphasis on legs. Hosiery became colored and textured and sales increased by as much as 70 percent. Certain types of "concealment problems" also existed. The answer was body stockings and panty hose. For a retailer, body stockings meant a $5 or $10 selling price as compared to $.69 or $1.25 for a pair of nylon hose. Of course hair styles had to be changed and beauty shops began doing land-office businesses. Wigs became popular and grew to a size of $500 million a year. Makeup had to have a new look too. Bright colors were replaced with a natural makeup that enhanced the feeling of natural skin. The

---

[17] John B. Stewart, "Functional Features in Product Strategy," *Harvard Business Review*, Vol. 37 (March-April 1959), pp. 65–78.
[18] *Ibid.*

cosmetics industry is a $3.5 billion business a year. Handbags were out. Jewelry was changed. Belts came back. It goes on and on. . . .[19]

This example, as well as others that could be given, illustrate the sales opportunities available to companies that have an effective style-modification program. It also illustrates the interrelated nature of some forms of consumption; style modifications in one product category create modification opportunities in other categories.

Another advantage of styling emphasis is that a firm has the ability to create a unique image that helps in capturing an important segment of the market. Examples include Villager and Levi Strauss in the apparel field, Volkswagen in automobiles, and Baker in furniture.

A product strategy emphasizing styling has several problems. The most difficult challenge is usually to predict the acceptability of a new style. The Hudson and Packard are some automotive examples of what happens when styling is not accepted by a sufficiently large segment of the market. In 1970 Villager was in serious trouble, partly because it retained the styling that made it famous when it was apparently no longer acceptable to many consumers.

Styling is usually not as flexible as functional features. It can be adapted or dropped quickly, but it usually cannot be made optional as easily as functional features. With functional features it is often possible to fit features to specific market segments; with styling it is usually more difficult to predict what kind of people will prefer the style.[20]

Market Stretching

In many instances the life cycle of a product can be extended through market stretching.[21] This can be achieved through any one or combination of the following strategies: (1) promoting more frequent usage of the product among current users; (2) developing more varied usage of the product among current users; (3) creating new users for the product by expanding the market; and/or (4) finding new uses for the basic material.

MORE FREQUENT USAGE. Many companies in a wide variety of industries have successfully extended product life cycles by persuading current users to use the product more frequently. The rate of consumption of soft drinks, for example, has increased dramatically since the 1920s. Many food products have also enjoyed substantial increases in per-capita consumption rates.

VARIED USAGE. More varied usage of the product is one of the most powerful ways of increasing the frequency of usage. The key is to increase the number of use situations for a product or service. For example, the life cycle of women's

---

[19] Adapted from Richard L. Knight, "Fashion: Generator of Retail Profit," an address to the Society of Security Analysts, Columbus, Ohio, October 17, 1968.

[20] Stewart, "Functional Features in Product Strategy," p. 74.

[21] Levitt, "Exploit the Product Life Cycle," pp. 87–91.

slacks has been accelerated partly because many women feel that pants can be worn on a greater number of occasions than before.

NEW USERS. Creating new users is another market-stretching strategy. For example, one reason for the growth of carpet sales is their more frequent use in offices, schools, stores, and hospitals.

NEW USES. Manufacturers of basic materials are often able to extend product life cycles by finding new uses for the basic material. DuPont followed this strategy with nylon, Corfam, and Teflon.

MULTIPLE STRETCHING. Quite often, market-stretching techniques are used in concert. Frequently multiple stretching will have a more profound impact on sales and profits than stretching with only one technique.

PRODUCT-ELIMINATION PROGRAMS

Some products cannot be revitalized through modification programs. Sometimes this occurs because the basic problem has vanished, as when frozen orange juice largely replaced sales of orange-juice squeezers. In other cases better and/or cheaper products are developed to fill the same need; for example, plastics are replacing wood, metal, and paper in products ranging from dry-cleaning bags to aircraft parts. In still other cases the demise occurs because a competitive product gains a decisive advantage via superior marketing strategy, as when the American Dental Association publicly endorsed Procter & Gamble's decay-prevention claims for Crest toothpaste.[22]

The ability to eliminate products successfully is often just as important as knowing when and how to introduce new ones and modify existing ones. After discussing some of the problems that impede effective elimination, this section outlines a procedure for selecting candidates for elimination and then identifies elimination strategies and programs.

The Challenge of Product-Elimination Programming

Weak products exert a cost pressure on a company that is often not fully recognized by executives. For example:

- The weak product tends to consume a disproportionate amount of management's time.
- It often requires frequent price and inventory adjustments.
- It generally involves short production runs in spite of expensive setup times.
- It requires both advertising and sales-force attention that might better be diverted to making "healthy" products more profitable.

[22] These illustrations were taken from Clifford, "Leverage in the Product Life Cycle," pp. 62–70.

- Its very unfitness can cause customers misgivings and cast a shadow on the company's image.
- It delays the search for replacement products, creating a lopsided product mix that depresses profitability and weakens the company's future position.[23]

Despite these costs, in many companies there appears to be an aversion to product elimination. Sometimes it is expected that sales will pick up when economic or market factors become more propitious, or after the new marketing strategy is implemented. In other cases a weak product may be retained because of the alleged contribution it makes to the sales of other products, or because its sales volume covers more than actual costs and the company has no better way of keeping its fixed resources employed.[24]

In specific situations some of these factors are legitimate reasons for retaining products. In many instances, however, they are simply convenient rationalizations. The challenge is to identify objectively products that should be eliminated and dispose of them efficiently.

Selecting Products for Elimination

The central source of information in selecting products for elimination is the annual product review that is summarized in product audit forms and their accompanying documents (Figure 10-3). Products become candidates for elimination when their total score falls below a specified level and/or when their ratings on certain key criteria fail to meet expectations.

The criteria and cut-off points must be specified by management on the basis of company objectives and strategies. Consequently, it is not possible to specify cut-off levels that are appropriate for all companies. However, it is possible to outline a general procedure that can be modified to meet the requirements of individual companies.

IDENTIFYING CANDIDATES FOR ELIMINATION.[25] Certain indices and trends generally indicate that a product should be considered for elimination. One warning sign is a *downward sales trend*. This does not necessarily mean that a product should be eliminated. However, if the trend has continued over several years, the product warrants further examination.

A *declining price trend* is another warning signal. This does not always mean a product should be eliminated, because it may simply reflect a product's stage in its life cycle, and/or the pricing strategy, or other considerations. But when the price of an established product whose competitive pattern has been stabilized

[23] Philip Kotler, "Phasing Out Weak Products," *Harvard Business Review*, Vol. 43 (March-April 1965), pp. 107–118, at p. 109.

[24] *Ibid.*, p. 110.

[25] This section adapted from R. S. Alexander, "The Death and Burial of 'Sick' Products," *Journal of Marketing*, Vol. 23 (April 1964), pp. 1–7.

shows a downward trend over a period of time, the future of that product should receive careful scrutiny.

Another warning sign is a *declining profit trend*. This trend may be in terms of dollars, profit margin, and/or return on investment.

The successful introduction of *substitute products* by the firm or competitors is another signal that a product should undergo elimination analysis. This is particularly crucial when new products satisfy the same customer need more effectively and/or at a lower cost.

A final indicator is the *amount of executive time and attention* that is devoted to each item in the product line, because declining products typically consume a disproportionate share of executive attention. Care must be taken, however, to differentiate the "growing pains" of a new product from the disorders of established products that have matured and are declining.

SELECTING SPECIFIC PRODUCTS FOR ELIMINATION. Products identified in the preceding analysis should be evaluated on the basis of several additional criteria.

1. *Profitability Analysis*. Products consistently failing to achieve what has been established as a minimum acceptable rate of return on investment should be eliminated, unless there are extenuating circumstances of the types indicated below. In multiproduct firms, profitability calculations are difficult because a significant proportion of costs are joint—or applicable to several products. Consequently, it is useful to estimate the effect of the deletion on: (a) total company profitability and (b) the profitability of each of the remaining products.

2. *Asset-Deployment Analysis*. Product deletion has several potential types of effects on the asset structure of a business. In the long run, eliminating a product will usually not distort the overall current asset position, since inventories and receivables will gradually be converted into cash. However, short-run effects should be noted.

Product deletion presents no fixed-asset problem, provided that the equipment and facilities used to produce the product being considered for elimination: (1) can be used for other purposes that satisfy company objectives, or (2) can be sold at an acceptable price, or (3) are fully depreciated. If none of these conditions exists, it is usually desirable to retain the product so long as the cash inflow from its sales covers out-of-pocket costs and contributes to depreciation and other overhead expenses.[26]

3. *Marketing Considerations*. Several marketing considerations suggest product retention even though a product fails to meet profitability requirements and does not impair the asset structure:[27]

- The product is necessary to fill out the product line in accordance with

---

[26] *Ibid.*, pp. 3–4.

[27] See, for example, John M. Brion, *Corporate Marketing Planning* (New York: John Wiley & Sons, Inc., 1967), p. 230; and Alexander, "The Death and Burial of 'Sick' Products," p. 5.

company product strategy with respect to consumers, wholesalers, or retailers.

- It makes an important contribution to the company's leadership image and this type of image is considered critical to the company's success.
- It is used as a loss leader.
- Salesmen consider it an important selling tool.
- If deleted, the company would suffer a significant decline in sales and/or profits as a result of customers' deciding not to buy other company products.

Care should be taken to make certain that these reasons are really applicable rather than convenient rationalizations. If the stakes are high enough, marketing research may be conducted to ascertain the validity of these marketing considerations.

4. *Social Responsibility.* Another issue is the firm's responsibility to its employees, its customers, its suppliers, and the communities in which it operates. How far management can go in retaining sick products in order to retain employees and suppliers, and avoid disrupting a community is a question of balance that has never been resolved. Fortunately, employees can often be transferred to other products, and product eliminations rarely have a terminal effect on suppliers or a community.[28]

ALTERNATIVES TO ELIMINATION. Products identified through the foregoing procedure should be evaluated in terms of several alternatives to elimination. One alternative is the various types of modification options that have already been discussed. Management should be satisfied that they are not a viable alternative before it makes a final decision to drop a product.

In some cases, manufacturing problems may be the chief cause of unsatisfactory performance. One way of circumventing this problem is to reduce factory costs through improved processes that either eliminate manpower or equipment time, or else increase yield.[29] If factory costs cannot be reduced, then possibly someone else can be contracted to manufacture the product. One form is a cross-production contract where firm A agrees to produce the entire supply of product X for itself and firm B, and B reciprocates with another product. This approach is useful when a company has marketing expertise but small production runs make costs prohibitive.[30]

Product-Elimination Strategies

Products remaining after the above alternatives have been exhausted should be eliminated, using one of the strategies discussed below. These strategies differ in

---

[28] See Conrad Berenson, "Pruning the Product Line," *Business Horizons,* Vol. 6 (Summer 1963), pp. 63–69.

[29] Alexander, "The Death and Burial of 'Sick' Products," p. 5.

[30] *Ibid.,* p. 6.

terms of the number of products that are eliminated, and the time period, revenue, and costs involved in the elimination.

PRODUCT-LINE PRUNING. It is often possible to improve the profitability of a declining product line by selectively eliminating certain products in the line. For example:

After a study one company with annual sales of $40 million eliminated 16 different products with a total volume of $3.3 million. It also made a number of improvements in methods of handling the products retained. Over the next three years the company's total sales increased by one-half and its profits by some 20 times. Among the many factors contributing to these spectacular increases, top executives stated that dropping unsatisfactory products was one of the most important.[31]

One of the major reasons why substantial savings and profits can result from pruning is the "20-80 rule"—which means that it is common for 20 percent of a company's products to account for 80 percent of its sales. The remaining 80 percent of the products contribute only 20 percent of sales but consume a disproportionate share of costs. By eliminating products that are making marginal contributions, the dramatic effects noted above can often be achieved.

THE RUN-OUT. Running out means cutting back all support costs on a product to the minimum level that will optimize the product's profitability over its foreseeable limited life.[32] A run-out may involve product pruning, and/or reductions in advertising and sales effort, and/or reductions in delivery time and minimum acceptable order size. For example:

A soft-drink manufacturer noted that one product had been declining steadily in sales for several years despite advertising and marketing efforts that were equivalent to those maintained at the peak of its sales. Faced with a loss operation in the coming year on this product, the company analyzed the situation and decided to eliminate all advertising, shorten the product line, and tighten marketing backup support in the form of sales and product management. Five years later sales were up 50 percent more than at the time of the cutback and the product has become one of the most profitable in the company's line.[33]

Several developments account for the growing popularity of the run-out. First, fewer companies are able to make increasing contributions to their profits from the growth of established products in established markets.[34] Hence new ap-

---

[31] Charles H. Kline, "The Strategy of Product Policy," *Harvard Business Review,* Vol. 33 (July-August 1955), pp. 91–100 at p. 100.

[32] See Walter J. Talley, Jr., "Profiting from the Declining Product," *Business Horizons,* Vol. 7 (Spring 1964), pp. 77–81.

[33] *Ibid.*, pp. 77–78.

[34] J. Roger Morrison and Richard F. Neuschel, "The Second Squeeze on Profits," *Harvard Business Review,* Vol. 41 (July-August 1962), p. 53.

proaches must be found to take advantage of untapped potentials, and this often lies in optimizing the profit on declining products.

Second, as stated previously, in many industries product life cycles are shrinking. Therefore it is becoming increasingly important for companies to maximize the profits of products in the decline stage of the life cycle in order to generate research and development funds for new products.

Finally, a run-out often permits a company to capitalize on its strengths and challenge competition where it is weakest. This applies not only to the run-out product but also to other products, because the funds released by a run-out can be invested in other products in ways that capitalize on competitors' weaknesses.[35]

CONTRACT MARKETING. Another elimination alternative is to continue manufacturing the product but contract other firms to market it. This strategy is often appropriate where a product's decline is due to marketing ineffectiveness, and where alternative remedial strategies are not viable. In some cases it is possible to negotiate cross-marketing contracts, where company A agrees to market one or more of company B's products and B reciprocates by marketing one or more of A's products.

ABANDONMENT ALTERNATIVES. There are two basic abandonment alternatives: (1) sell or license the product to someone else, or (2) drop it.

Sometimes it is possible to sell or license a product to another firm that has the capability to make it successful. There are several reasons why a product may be profitable for another firm. For example, their manufacturing facilities may be better geared to handle the product's production requirements. Their marketing organization may be able to cover the specific areas needed, while the costs required to achieve the needed coverage may be prohibitive to the potential seller. In other cases, the original firm may not have the necessary financial resources while another firm has.[36]

If there are no remaining alternatives, a product should be dropped. This often happens to even the largest and most sophisticated companies. For example, DuPont discontinued their rayon line, partly because it hindered aggressive nylon merchandising. In the silicone field, W. R. Grace, Foote, Eagle-Picher, and DuPont pulled out because of industry overcapacity and steadily falling prices.[37]

PROGRAMMING PRODUCT ABANDONMENT.[38] Once a decision is made to abandon a product, it is necessary to prepare a plan that identifies the most efficient method of withdrawal. Timing is one of the most important considerations. It is desirable to time the deletion so that the released manpower, facilities, and capital can be immediately used for other purposes. Customers should be informed far enough in advance so they can make arrangements for replacement, if any are

---

[35] Talley, "Profiting from the Declining Product," pp. 79–80.

[36] For further discussion see James G. Kuester, "Recover Your Loss on Unprofitable Products," *Business Management*, May 1964, pp. 91–93.

[37] Talley, "Profiting from the Declining Product," p. 78.

[38] This section is adapted from Alexander, "The Death and Burial of 'Sick' Products," pp. 6–7.

available, but not so far in advance that they will switch to new suppliers before inventory is exhausted.

In some situations parts and replacements are an important consideration. In those instances where parts and replacements are used—durable goods are examples—it will be necessary to maintain stocks of these items for the expected life of the units most recently sold.

Finally, the abandonment program should provide for clearing out the stocks of the dying product and materials used in its production so as to recover the maximum amount of working capital. This is usually accomplished by gradually tapering off purchasing, production, and selling activities.

The complexity of abandonment programming varies considerably. In situations where the product has enjoyed a substantial sales volume and has been widely distributed, and if there are significant savings to be realized by efficient abandonment, it may be desirable to prepare a critical-path program.

SUMMARY

This chapter has been concerned with product programs that are central to the corporate and marketing planning process and are the first consideration in developing an integrated marketing program. Products have both physical and social-psychological dimensions, and their real meaning lies in what the customer thinks he is buying rather than what the manufacturer thinks he is selling.

Product programming begins with the development of product objectives, which are derived from corporate and marketing objectives and strategies. By comparing a firm's actual life-cycle profile with the target profile, product objectives are identified that indicate the amount and timing of resources that will be allocated to product-market modification, product elimination, and new-product programs.

The purpose of product-market modification programs is to accelerate and extend the life cycles of selected products. These programs involve product modifications—quality, feature, and style modification—and market stretching—more frequent usage, varied usage, new users, and new uses.

Products that cannot be extended through product-market modification become candidates for various types of product-elimination programs. These are products shown by the product audit analysis to have downward trends in sales, price, and profits, as well as those being challenged by substitute products and those that consume a disproportionate share of executive time. Products having these characteristics are then subjected to profitability and asset-deployment analyses, and screened against certain marketing and social-responsibility considerations. A final check is made to make certain that alternatives to elimination cannot rescue the product. Products remaining after this series of analyses are eliminated through pruning, the run-out, contract marketing, or abandonment. A plan is then prepared outlining the most efficient method of abandonment.

QUESTIONS FOR REVIEW AND DISCUSSION

1. "Product programs are central to the corporate and marketing planning process and are the first consideration in developing an integrated marketing program." Explain.
2. Identify five possible social-psychological dimensions of furniture.
3. Discuss the major managerial implications of the product life cycle. Do these implications hold for all companies? Why or why not?
4. Identify five specific market-stretching techniques that a soft-drink manufacturer could use.
5. In what situations does a firm have a social responsibility to retain a sick product?
6. Style modification has typically been more effective for women's apparel than for men's wear. Why?
7. The automobile industry is often criticized for its planned obsolescence policy. Do you agree or disagree? Why?
8. Select a product and show how feature modification can be used to market the product to multiple market segments.
9. Some products, such as clothing and cars, have social-psychological dimensions; others, such as nails and screwdrivers, do not. Why?
10. What are the warning signs that indicate that a product should be considered for elimination?

Chapter 11   New-Product Programs

Effectively managed programs of product modification and elimination can greatly alter a firm's success profile. However, exclusive use of these two product programs is usually risky. Sales and profits lost through product elimination must be replaced, and the existing product line is threatened by technological advances, changing consumption patterns, competitors' activities, and other forces. For these and other reasons, most firms rely heavily on new products to sustain and revitalize the company.

This chapter first discusses the scope of new-product programs and the critical role they play in corporate and marketing success. A new-product planning and control system is introduced and each component of the system is examined. The chapter concludes with a discussion of legal considerations in product programming.

THE CRITICALITY AND SCOPE OF NEW-PRODUCT PROGRAMS

The Criticality of New Products[1]

New products are important because they have a profound impact on the two major performance imperatives of a firm —growth and profitability.

CORPORATE GROWTH. Historically, growth industries in the American economy have had new products as a major propellant. A study of the 200 largest United States corpora-

[1] This section has been adapted from *Management of New Products* (New York: Booz, Allen & Hamilton, Inc., 1968), pp. 4–5.

tions found that a major factor differentiating fast-growing companies from others was the amount of reliance on new products. The study also suggests that new products will increasingly affect growth as competition continues to intensify and the flood of new products shortens the life cycle of existing products.[2]

PROFIT PERFORMANCE. As indicated in Chapter 10, products have characteristic sales and profit margin curves over their life cycle. Profit margins peak during the latter stage of the growth phase and then continuously decline during subsequent stages. This means that profits can be sustained in the long run only by a continuing flow of successful new products, not only to replace sales volume, but also to sustain and increase profit margins.

New Products and the Corporate Dilemma

The record indicates that most new products are failures. The incidence of failure depends on how it is defined. Booz, Allen, and Hamilton's study places the failure rate at 33 percent.[3] A study of products introduced by 200 leading packaged-goods manufacturers indicates that the failure rate runs as high as 80 percent.[4] An analysis of 9,450 new products introduced to supermarkets in 1968 found that 80 percent failed to meet their projected sales goals.[5] Another study places the rate as high as 89 percent.[6] These failures are expensive—a single product failure can cost from $75,000 to several million dollars.[7]

Studies indicate that individual companies vary widely in the effectiveness of their new-product programs. Between major companies in the same industry, efficiencies range from less than 6 percent to 84 percent. ("Efficiency" means the percentage of the company's new-product expenses devoted to successful rather than unsuccessful products.)[8] Thus new-product programming has tremendous improvement potential for many companies, and this improvement is critically important.

A New-Product Planning and Control System

Any approach to new-product planning must be tailor-made to meet the unique characteristics of each company. However, this tailoring is most effective when it represents a necessary modification and adaptation of proven techniques. Figure 11-1 summarizes a basic approach adapted from Booz, Allen, and Hamilton's experience with several hundred companies.[9]

[2] Joseph O. Eastlack, Jr., and Philip R. McDonald, "CEO's Role in Corporate Growth," *Harvard Business Review*, Vol. 48 (May-June 1970), pp. 150–162.

[3] *Management of New Products*, p. 9.

[4] John T. O'Meara, Jr., "Selecting Profitable Products," *Harvard Business Review*, Vol. 40 (January-February 1961), p. 83.

[5] Theodore L. Angelus, "Why Do Most New Products Fail?" *Advertising Age*, March 24, 1969, pp. 85–86.

[6] Burt Schorr, "Many New Products Fizzle, Despite Careful Planning, Publicity," *Wall Street Journal*, April 5, 1961.

[7] Angelus, "Why Do Most New Products Fail?" p. 85.

[8] *Management of New Products*, p. 2.

[9] *Ibid.*, p. 7.

Figure 11-1   A new-product planning and control system.

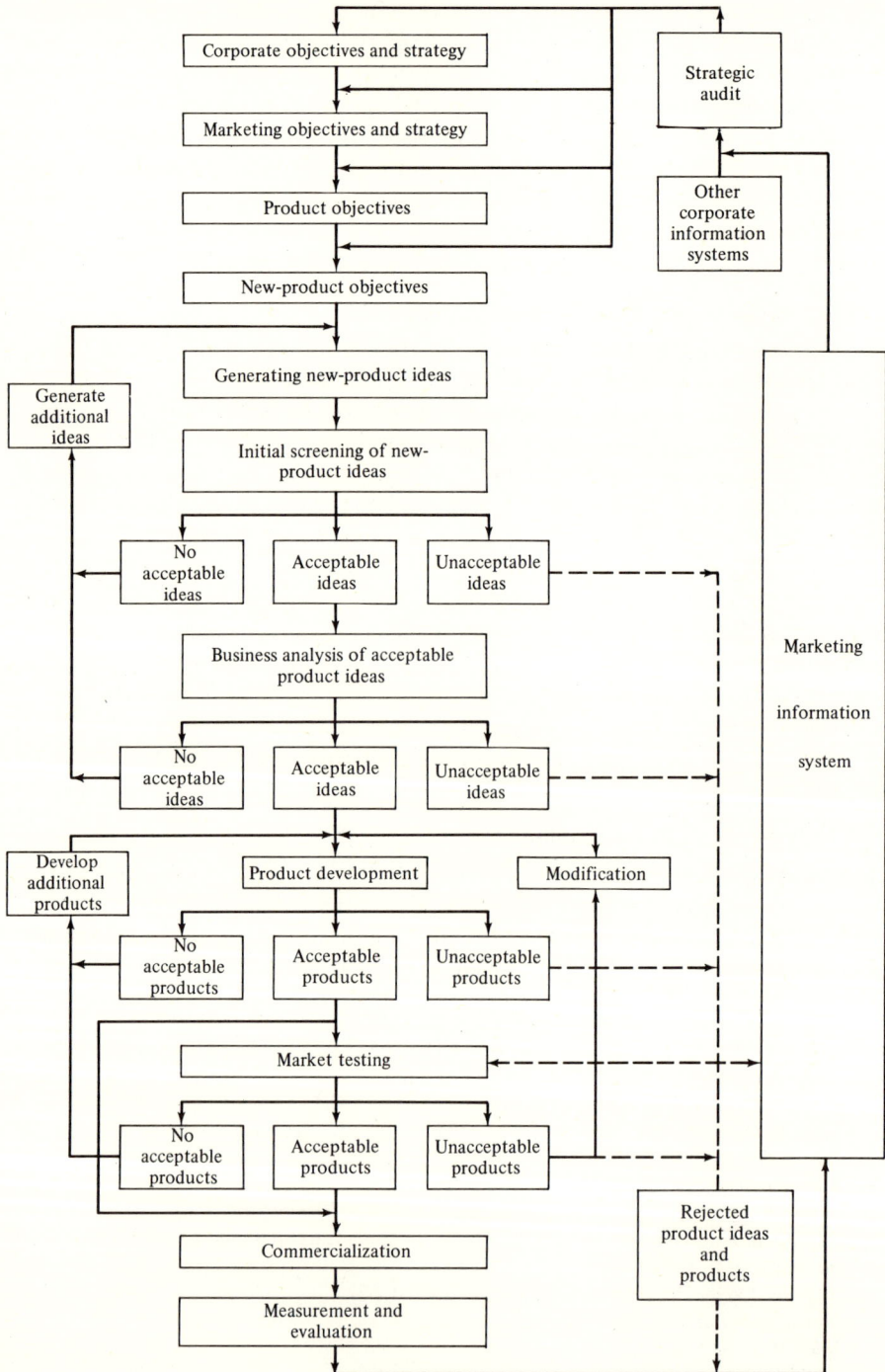

The process starts with the development of corporate objectives and strategies. These are translated into marketing objectives and strategies and then into product and new-product objectives as described in Chapters 1, 2, and 10. The development of new products is a seven-stage process, involving (1) exploration of new-product ideas; (2) the initial screening of new ideas to determine which ones deserve detailed study; (3) a business analysis to determine whether expensive product-development activities should be initiated; (4) turning the product idea into a demonstrable and producible product; (5) testing the product to verify market acceptance; (6) commercializing the product—that is, launching it in full-scale production and sale; and (7) periodic measurement and evaluation of the product's performance.

KEY CHARACTERISTICS OF THE SYSTEM. The new-product development process has certain properties that must be understood if it is to be managed effectively. First, product ideas have a severe decay curve. While the rejection rate varies between industries and companies, on the average it takes about 58 ideas to yield one successful new product.

Second, each stage of the process is progressively more expensive in terms of time and money. In general, more than 90 percent of total expenditures occur in the development, testing, and commercialization stages.[10] Collectively these two characteristics suggest that considerable attention should be focused on the first three stages of the process—idea generation, initial screening, and business analysis—to reduce the mortality of new-product ideas during the latter stages and hence lower the cost of new-product programs.

Additional Success Requirements for New-Product Programs

In addition to the caveats already mentioned, studies of new product successes and failures have isolated other clues for improving the effectiveness of new-product programs.

TOP-MANAGEMENT DIRECTION AND INVOLVEMENT. The key problems in the management of new products require top-management attention. Responsibility for direction must rest at the highest operating level in the company. This requires a clear statement of company objectives, effective organization, careful planning, and provision for rigorous analyses and control. When these conditions are absent, problems usually result.[11]

PROPER ORGANIZATION FIT. In many instances products fail partly because firms do not have the experience to generate a feeling for the business, or they overestimate their production, marketing, or financial capabilities. This happens to even the largest companies. Consider:

- Procter & Gamble failed on two occasions to successfully introduce a hairspray product (Hidden Magic and Winterset/Summerset).

[10] *Ibid.*
[11] *Ibid.*

232   Chapter 11   New-Product Programs

- Colgate failed in the men's aftershave lotion and cologne market with "007" in 1965.[12]

There are two basic ways to satisfy the organizational-fit problem. One is to develop new products that utilize and capitalize on the capabilities of the organization. This usually means sticking to the kinds of products that can be marketed through existing channels of distribution by the company's sales force.[13] The other approach is to acquire the capabilities required to make the product successful. For example:

- Louis Sherry Co. decided to introduce "Shimmer," a low-calorie gelatin dessert. The key man behind the product was an ex-General Foods executive who knew and understood the gelatin dessert business, having been intimately involved with Jell-O. Technical development was conducted by an ex-Jell-O research and development specialist, who joined Sherry specifically to develop Shimmer.[14]

DEVELOPMENT AND PRODUCTION. Product defects are often cited as the prime cause of failure. This results from poor product engineering in the design phase, or failure of the product in operating conditions. A common problem is to meet quality and performance requirements at a cost that will allow the product to be priced properly to earn satisfactory profits.[15]

MEANINGFUL PRODUCT DIFFERENCES. Many packaged goods fail because of the lack of a real customer point of difference. Most failures have a point of difference, but the difference is not important to customers in the target market. Consider these examples:

- When Menley & James introduced Duractin they had a sustained release analgesic which gave pain relief for eight hours. This difference proved unimportant to the major market segment because they wanted speedy relief.
- American Home introduced Easy-Off Household Cleaner. Easy-Off's point of difference was an aerosol foam formulation in a market dominated by liquids—Formula 409 and Fantastik. Consumers could not see any advantage to the aerosol foam. The company lost $850,000.[16]

PROPER POSITIONING. In some cases new products have meaningful points of difference but they fail because marketing strategy does not position them correctly. Marketing strategy often confuses the consumer. Thus:

[12] Angelus, "Why Do Most New Products Fail?" p. 86.
[13] "Why Many New Products Fail," *Printers' Ink*, October 23, 1964, pp. 40–42.
[14] Angelus, "Why Do Most New Products Fail?" p. 86.
[15] "Why Many New Products Fail," p. 40.
[16] Angelus, "Why Do Most New Products Fail?" p. 85.

- Revlon introduced Super Natural Hairspray and lost millions. Super means "more holding power"; natural means "less holding power." The consumer really didn't know what the product represented.[17]

Mismatched positioning is another problem. This occurs when the most effective combination of consumer appeal and product performance has not been achieved. To illustrate:

- Right Guard deodorant was positioned as a man's deodorant until 1963. Then a switch in advertising was made with the claim, "The perfect family deodorant because nothing touches you but the spray itself." Sales increased by $20 million annually.[18]

PROPER TIMING. Many new products fail partly because they were introduced at the wrong time. Sometimes this happens because the market changes during the period between product conception and debut, resulting in a product designed for a market that has vanished. The Edsel is the classic example of this problem. In other cases new products fail because they are trapped in a market explosion when several new entries are introduced simultaneously. For example:

- In the middle 1960s the mouthwash market explosion resulted in a combined loss of over $40 million from brands like Fact, Vote, Cue, Reef, and others.
- In the late 1960s the household cleaner market exploded with 17 new brands in nine months. The result was an estimated $5–7 million loss from failures like Easy-Off, Clean & Kill, Whistle, Power-On, Crew, and others.[19]

THE RESEARCH IMPERATIVE. Product failures from insignificant product differences, poor positioning, and improper timing occur primarily because of inadequate research. Thus it is important that new-product programs be based on appropriate research that has been correctly analyzed. This includes general economic research, customer research, product-performance research, packaging research, and knowledge of competitors' likely moves. Effective management of these areas will improve the success rate of most firms' new-product programs.

NEW-PRODUCT OBJECTIVES

As indicated in Figure 11-1, new-product objectives should be derived from product objectives that in turn are derived from marketing and corporate objec-

[17] *Ibid.*
[18] *Ibid.*
[19] *Ibid.*

tives and strategies. New-product objectives should specify the level of new-product activity and the general types of new products that are considered appropriate.

Level of New-Product Activity

This component of new-product objectives specifies the results required of new products during the planning period. The procedure begins with corporate sales, profits, and other objectives for the period. The forecasted performance of the existing product line is then subtracted from each relevant corporate objective to yield new-product requirements during the planning period.

Next the amount of discretionary financial resources available for new-products programs is identified. The level of new-product activity becomes the amount necessary to make the required contribution to sales, profits, and other appropriate objectives, within the limits imposed by available financial resources.

New-Product Guidelines

New-product objectives should also specify the types of new products that will be viewed as acceptable, and any other requirements that new products are expected to achieve, or conform to. These should have been articulated in the corporate objectives and strategy. Thus new-product objectives should:

1. State both the level, or range, of profitability that is acceptable, and the appropriate payback period.
2. Specify the product-market scope and growth vectors that senior management desires to pursue.
3. Identify the synergy expectations for new products.
4. Articulate the differential-advantage expectations for new products.
5. Specify any other guidelines that are considered appropriate in channeling new-product development activities.

New-product objectives containing these elements provide the basic foundation upon which new-product programs can be developed. They provide the mechanism that can help achieve part of the top-management direction and involvement required for new-product success.[20]

EXPLORING AND GENERATING NEW-PRODUCT IDEAS

Every new product begins as an idea. Progressive companies do not sit back and wait for these ideas; rather they organize to seek them out on a continuing,

---

[20] For other views of new-product objectives see R. C. Rives, "What Is Your New Product Policy?" and J. J. Flynn, "Top Management Responsibility for Product Development," in Elizabeth Marting, ed., *New Products New Profits* (New York: American Management Association, 1964), pp. 41–47 and pp. 54–58, respectively.

systematic basis. This is facilitated by an organized network for identifying and collecting new-product ideas and a systematic search of new idea sources.

An Organized Network for New-Product Ideas

New products can be generated and explored more efficiently and effectively if some individual, committee, or organizational unit is given responsibility for the activity. This procedure lessens the chances that good ideas will be lost and, by providing one central point of contact, usually increases the quantity and quality of new ideas.

Those responsible for new-product ideas should also stimulate and direct the process. This can be achieved by making certain that those involved are aware of the new-product objectives for the planning period. It is particularly important that participants understand the general types of new-product ideas that are of primary interest to the company. Based on the level of new-product activity required, and the company's new-idea mortality rate, those responsible for new product ideas should make certain that enough ideas are generated to produce a sufficient number of new products to satisfy sales, profits, and other requirements during the planning period.

Sources of New-Product Ideas

Major sources of new-product ideas are itemized in Figure 11-2.[21] Those responsible for new ideas can obtain them from those sources that are most applicable to the company. As increasing numbers of companies have adopted the marketing concept, added emphasis has been placed on customer-oriented sources of new-product ideas. Sources and concepts for these ideas were discussed in Chapters 5 through 8, and techniques for identifying them were discussed in Chapter 9 (see particularly discussions of preference distribution analysis and multidimensional scaling).

SCREENING NEW-PRODUCT IDEAS

The screening stage eliminates product ideas that are not consistent with corporate and marketing objectives and strategies. The objective is to separate those few basic product ideas that show enough promise to warrant further conceptual and/or product development from the many that have no future. The product idea—rather than the physical product or the execution of the idea—is evaluated using data and informed opinion that are already available. More detailed and costly evaluation of product ideas occurs during the business-analysis stage.

[21] For a detailed discussion of new-product ideas see Gustav E. Larson, "Locating Ideas for New Products," in Thomas L. Berg and Abe Shuchman, *Product Strategy and Management* (New York: Holt, Rinehart and Winston, Inc., 1963), pp. 420–430; Charles G. Ellington, "Sources of New Product Ideas," in Marting, *New Products New Profits,* pp. 61–74; and E. Janet Berry, "Patents and Their Importance in the New Product Effort," in Marting, pp. 93–99.

Figure 11-2   Major sources of new-product ideas.

I. Internal Sources
1. Marketing research department
2. Salesmen
3. Customer suggestions, inquiries, and complaints
4. Employee suggestions
5. Research, development, and engineering personnel
II. Distributors
1. Brokers
2. Manufacturers' agents
4. Retailers
III. Competitors
1. Customers of competitors
2. Competitors' products
3. Catalogs
4. Exhibits and trade shows
5. Foreign products
IV. Government
1. United States Patent Office, Department of Commerce
   (a) Register of patents available for licensing or sale
   (b) Government-owned patents
   (c) Dedicated patents
   (d) Official Gazette, United States Patent Office
2. Office of Technical Services, Department of Commerce
   (a) Bibliography of Scientific and Industrial Reports
   (b) The National Inventors Council
   (c) U.S. Government Research Reports
   (d) Technical Reports Newsletter
3. *Foreign Commerce Weekly*
4. National Bureau of Standards
V. Miscellaneous
1. Inventors
2. Patent attorneys and brokers
3. University and institute laboratories
4. Commercial laboratories
5. Industrial consultants
6. Management and product consultants
7. Market research agencies
8. Manufacturers of parts and accessories
9. Advertising agencies
10. Trade associations
11. Trade magazine writers and editors

SOURCE: Adapted from Gustav E. Larson, "Locating Ideas for New Products," in Thomas L. Berg and Abe Shuchman, *Product Strategy and Management* (New York: Holt, Rinehart and Winston, Inc., 1963), pp. 420–430; and Charles G. Ellington, "Sources of New Product Ideas," in Elizabeth Marting, ed., *New Products New Profits* (New York: American Management Association, 1964) pp. 61–74.

A Screening Procedure

The first step is to determine whether each new-product idea will satisfy corporate objectives. Using information that is easily and inexpensively attainable, each new-product idea should be evaluated according to the probability that it will: (1) achieve profitability objectives; (2) attain an acceptable rate of increase in sales, market share, and profits; (3) conform to maximum acceptable fluctuations in sales, capacity utilization, and profits; (4) achieve an acceptable turnover of working capital and inventory; and (5) not exceed the maximum acceptable proportion of sales to a single customer or market segment. A strong negative evaluation on any of these, or other, objectives can eliminate the product from further consideration.

The next step is to evaluate the probability that each new product idea: (1) is consistent with product-market scope and growth vector requirements; (2) will satisfy synergy requirements; and (3) is capable of satisfying differential-advantage requirements. A negative answer to any of these strategy requirements can also disqualify the new-product idea from further consideration. In some cases a product idea that has a negative strategy evaluation may still qualify for further consideration if it has a high probability of exceeding profitability objectives by a substantial margin. Ideas that satisfy these requirements proceed to the next stage—business analysis.

BUSINESS ANALYSIS OF NEW-PRODUCT IDEAS

In the business-analysis stage, each new-product idea surviving the screening phase is subjected to a more sophisticated and detailed analysis. The business-analysis stage is critical because new-product development costs accelerate sharply after this step. Thus it is imperative to eliminate inappropriate ideas at this point, and it is usually justifiable to commit substantial resources to this evaluation stage.

A Business-Analysis Procedure

There are a variety of ways of conducting a business analysis. Rating devices are a popular and useful technique. The criteria comprising the rating instrument vary between industries and companies, since a rating system must be tailor-made to fit a company's objectives and strategies.

Figure 11-3 presents an illustrative rating device. Each idea is evaluated on the basis of financial, market, competitive, research and development, production and engineering, and marketing considerations. Each criterion is assigned a weight to reflect its relative importance in the success of a new product. Factors comprising each criterion are assigned a rating on a scale—for example, from 1 to 10. Next a probability from 0 to 1.0 is estimated for each rating to indicate

Figure 11-3   An illustrative business-analysis chart.

Product Description _____
Estimated Annual Sales Volume _____
Annual Earnings (Before Taxes) _____
Total Capital Investment _____

Criteria	Relative Weight (1)	Rating (2)	Proba-bility (3)	Expected Value (2×3) (4)	Evalu-ation (4×1) (5)
I. *Financial Analysis*					
1. Return on investment					
2. Estimated annual sales					
3. Fixed capital payout time					
4. Time to reach estimated sales volume					
5. Other					
6. Total					
II. *Market and Competitive Analysis*					
1. Trend in sales					
2. Cyclical and seasonal demand					
3. Fashion stability					
4. Life-cycle position					
5. Time to reach maturity stage of life cycle					
6. Competitors' control of market share					
7. Market-share fluctuations					
8. Price stability					
9. Other					
10. Total					
III. *Research and Development Analysis*					
1. R&D investment time					
2. Compatibility with proven R&D capability					
3. Technological stability					
4. Potential "spin-offs"					
5. Patent status					
6. Other					
7. Total					

IV. *Production and*
    Engineering Analysis
    1. Competitor's capability
    2. Raw-material availability
       and costs
    3. Process familiarity
    4. Additional plant and
       equipment required
    5. Other
    6. Total
V. *Marketing Analysis*
    1. Market development
       requirements
    2. Number of potential
       customers
    3. Marketability to
       present customers
    4. Product competition
    5. Product advantage
    6. Similarity to present
       product line
    7. Effect on present products
    8. Suitability of present
       sales force
    9. Promotional requirements
    10. Channel-of-distribution
        requirements
    11. Physical distribution
        requirements
    12. Technical service
        requirements
    13. Other
    14. Total

SUMMARY   Total Points

    1. Financial analysis
    2. Market and competitive analysis
    3. Research and development analysis
    4. Production and engineering analysis
    5. Marketing analysis
             Total
                    Disposition
    Proceed to development stage   ☐
    Reject   ☐

SOURCE: Adapted from John S. Harris, "The New Product Profile Chart: Selecting and Appraising New Projects," in Elizabeth Marting, ed., *New Products New Profits* (New York: American Management Association, 1964), pp. 113–131, particularly pp. 118–119.

how certain the rater is that the rating assigned is true or will be realized. Ratings are then multiplied by probabilities to yield an expected value. Finally, expected values are multiplied by relative weights to arrive at evaluation scores. Evaluations are determined for each criterion and then summed to yield a total score. A written explanation of the reasons for the ratings and other supporting documents should accompany the analysis chart.

Like the product audit form presented in Chapter 10, this procedure offers the major advantage that all new-product ideas are evaluated on the same criteria. The difficulties lie in selecting the criteria, determining weights and rating scales, and assigning accurate ratings and probabilities.[22]

In order to pass the business-analysis stage, a new idea should display several characteristics. First, it should have a "satisfactory" total score. Second, it should have a "satisfactory" score for each criterion. Finally, it should receive "above average" ratings on factors that are critical success requirements.

What constitutes "satisfactory" and "above average"? These terms must be defined by each company on the basis of its objectives, strategies, and past experience. A useful procedure is to try out a rating device on some actual products for which the results are already known. By taking several products, some of which have succeeded and some of which failed, it can be determined whether the mechanism would have distinguished between them at the business-analysis stage. In some cases it is also possible to construct success and failure rating profiles. These past experiences can be valuable in increasing the validity and reliability of the procedure in future applications.[23] New-product ideas passing this or some other form of rating procedure are ready for development.

PRODUCT DEVELOPMENT

Up to this point new-product ideas have existed only as concepts, perhaps as drawings or rough models. The product-development process identifies a basic marketing strategy and transforms the concept into a physical form. This involves decisions concerning brand positioning, brand strategy, packaging, preference testing, and other developmental activities.

---

[22] One study has concluded that the decision to market new products is relatively insensitive to changes in the scores and weights of factors in this type of analysis. See Marshall Freimer and Leonard S. Simon, "Screening New Product Ideas," in Robert L. King, ed., *Marketing and the New Science of Planning* (Chicago: American Marketing Association, 1968), pp. 99–104.

[23] See, for example, John S. Harris, "The New Products Profile Chart: Selecting and Appraising New Projects," in Marting, *New Products New Profits*, pp. 113–131; Charles H. Kline, "The Strategy of Product Policy," *Harvard Business Review*, Vol. 34 (July-August 1955), pp. 91–100; and Barry M. Richman, "A Rating Scale for Product Innovation," *Business Horizons*, Summer 1962, pp. 37–44.

Brand Positioning

There are three requirements for effective brand positioning: (1) the difference(s) between the product and alternative choices must be meaningful to customers comprising the target market; (2) differences must be understood and believed; and (3) the physical product should demonstrate these differences. Brand-positioning strategy is the central theme guiding a new-product idea through product development.

Branding

A manufacturer has a choice of three major branding strategies: (1) *manufacturer's brand,* where the firm does not produce brands for any other organization; (2) *reseller's brand,* where the manufacturer produces only brands for resellers; and (3) *a mixed brand strategy,* where the firm produces both its own brand and brands for resellers.

MANUFACTURER'S-BRAND STRATEGIES. Historically most manufacturers have relied almost entirely on their own brands. As firms have grown and their products proliferated, two major manufacturer branding strategies have grown in importance—multibrand products and multiproduct brands.

1. *Multibrand Products.* A multibrand strategy refers to the practice of offering more than one brand in a product category. The major reason for this strategy is that two or more brands commonly capture more sales and profits than one. Multiple brands are sometimes used to leverage a product breakthrough into a dominant market position. For example, Procter & Gamble used synthetic-detergent technology developed during the Second World War to introduce both Tide and Cheer after the war. They also introduced additional brands, thereby capturing a dominant position in an expanding market.

Multibrands are also used to market new forms, flavors, colors, or odors, allowing a firm to expand its sales volume. Campbell's soup brands illustrate flavor variation. Revlon effectively uses color variation in its nail polish and lipstick lines.

Multibrands can also be used to adjust to behavioral variations in consumer demand patterns. For example, Lever Brothers offers Lux with Dermasil to women primarily interested in their hands, and Swan to women more concerned with the cleaning efficiency of a dish detergent.

In some instances multibrands are used as a defense against new brands introduced by competitors. The Toni Company, for example, responded to the threat posed by hair sprays to the home-permanent market by introducing Adorn.[24]

Multibrands are also used to combat low-priced brands offered by competitors, so that the manufacturer can compete with other firms in helping resellers

[24] Angelus, "Why Do Most New Products Fail?" p. 85.

build store traffic. This is usually called a *fighting brand*. In other cases a manufacturer desires a legal way of cultivating important retailers without offering a
private brand. One technique is through *derivative brands* that differ in some
way(s) from the manufacturer's other brands. This practice is used by some appliance manufacturers.[25]

2. *Multiproduct Brands.* This branding strategy—sometimes called family
or blanket brands—refers to the use of a single brand for a group of products.
These products may have a similar base (evaporated and powdered milk), or a
use relationship (batteries and tires), or some type of technical relationship
(motors and turbines). This strategy has been used successfully by many companies. To illustrate:

- Following the defeat of Gene, Colgate used the multiproduct brand
  strategy to enter the all-purpose liquid detergent market. Colgate used
  one of its best-selling brands—Ajax, a powdered cleanser—and called its
  new product Ajax liquid all-purpose cleaner with ammonia. A Colgate
  product manager stated: "The combination of the Ajax name and the
  ammoniated formulation allowed us to enter the market without spending the amount of money our competition did."[26]

There are several reasons why a manufacturer may decide to use an existing
brand name for a new product. Specifically, an established and respected brand
name often (1) increases customer acceptance of a new product, (2) reduces the
promotional cost of introducing a new product, and (3) makes it easier to
achieve wholesaler and/or retailer acceptance of a new product. Finally, the
strategy sometimes permits a manufacturer to promote other brands. A line of
related, low-volume items, no one of which generates sufficient sales to support
a brand name, in combination may produce adequate funds for promotional
support of the brand.[27]

These advantages must be balanced against several risks. For example, if
the new product does not meet customer expectations, it may reduce consumer
confidence in other products marketed under the brand label. Or the brand name
may have an image that is inconsistent with the success requirements for the
new product.

These advantages and limitations suggest that no definitive conclusions can
be drawn about the use of existing brand names for new products. Rather, each
situation must be examined on its own merits.

---

[25] For further discussion see Robert W. Young, Jr., "Multibrand Entries," in Lee Adler,
ed., *Plotting Marketing Strategy* (New York: Simon and Schuster, Inc., 1967), pp. 141–164.

[26] "Why Certain New Products Survive," *Printers' Ink,* February 8, 1963, pp. 21–28,
at p. 22.

[27] Theodore R. Gamble, "Brand Extension," in Adler, *Plotting Marketing Strategy,*
pp. 165–178, at p. 167.

Reseller-Brand Strategies. An alternative is to offer a new product under a reseller brand label. Most commonly this will be a brand for a retailer, although in some instances reseller brands are for wholesalers.

Private brands have increased in importance during the last two decades. One study found that reseller market shares range from an average of 7 percent in portable appliances to over 50 percent in shoes.[28] A study of supermarket sales found that retailer-brand market shares ranged from .4 percent for some product categories to over 60 percent in others.[29]

Few manufacturers engage exclusively in reseller brands. Profits are usually lower and there is less control, because sales are concentrated in fewer buyers. If a reseller fails to renew a contract for his brand, the effect on the manufacturer can be terminal.

Mixed-Brand Strategy. In recent years there has been a growing tendency for manufacturers to pursue a mixed brand strategy, offering both manufacturer and reseller brands. Several developments explain the growth of this strategy. First, some manufacturers fear that resellers will establish their own brands through other sources, causing them to suffer substantial sales losses. Second, some firms offer a reseller brand in return for greater reseller support of the manufacturer's brand. Finally, both brands can often be produced with the same plant and equipment, thereby increasing the utilization of capacity.[30]

No definitive conclusions can be advanced concerning the desirability of these branding alternatives. Each company must formulate its own branding strategy. However, as will be discussed in Chapter 13, the future will probably witness increasing concentration at the retail level and accelerated growth of integrated distribution networks. One consequence of this trend will be a growing demand and opportunity for reseller brands, hence it appears likely that more manufacturers will adopt multiple branding strategies to capitalize on the opportunities of multiple reseller and customer markets.

Packaging

The traditional role of packaging has been to provide product protection and economy. Today progressive companies view packaging as a major marketing tool. Increasingly packages are designed by committees, or design groups, consisting of merchandising and marketing specialists as well as graphic experts. This group interacts and coordinates with others involved in new product development so as to achieve an integrated and coordinated physical product and package that has market impact.

[28] Thomas F. Schutte and Victor J. Cook, "Branding Policies and Practices," in Raymond M. Haas, ed., Science, Technology, and Marketing (Chicago: American Marketing Association, 1966), pp. 197–213.

[29] Harper W. Boyd, Jr., and Ronald E. Frank, "The Importance of Private Labels in Food Retailing," Business Horizons, Vol. 9 (Summer 1966), pp. 81–90.

[30] Schutte and Cook, "Branding Policies and Practices," p. 203.

Packaging is a detailed and technically complicated process. Although a marketing executive is usually not a packaging expert, he does have to determine how a product will be packaged, and whether packages designed by others will be effective. The following criteria are useful in making these types of judgments.[31]

VISIBILITY. Visibility is a measure of how easily a package can be located in its place of sale, commonly a mass display. It includes measures of the legibility of the brand name, the product name, and any other elements that are important.

These criteria can be measured by the use of various laboratory devices or more informal methods. Laboratory instruments include a *distance meter* (how far away can the elements be identified); *tachistoscope* (how long does it take to identify the elements); *threshold illumination meter* (how much light is required for identification); *angle meter* (at what angle can the elements be identified); *apparent size meter* (which package appears larger at an equal distance); as well as others.[32] These devices can be simulated informally. For example, a row of packages can be approached from an angle to determine which ones are most visible. Similarly, by walking backward in a hall, one can evaluate differences in brand-name visibility.

INFORMATION. This criterion is concerned with how quickly and clearly a package communicates what it contains. One way to measure this is to expose a sample of customers to the package and then ask them to describe what they saw. Brief visual exposure can be achieved through a tachistoscope, or a split-second exposure of slide films of packages in mass display.

WORKABILITY. The workability criterion includes protection, ease of opening and reclosing, adequacy of information about product use, storability of the product, and, perhaps, use for other purposes after it has served its original purpose. These factors can be measured by allowing company personnel and/or a sample of customers to experiment with and use the product and package.

HANDLING AND STOCKING REQUIREMENTS. A study of resellers' methods and needs is essential if a package design is to be effective. The package should facilitate product and brand identification, and it should have size and other dimensions that facilitate handling, stacking, and storage.

EMOTIONAL APPEAL. A package should have an image that reinforces the major product benefits and is consistent with the attitudes and preferences of customers in the target-market segment. This can be measured through the semantic differential and projective techniques discussed in Chapters 3 and 4.

PROMOTIONAL IMPACT. Packaging is the largest of all advertising media, reaching far more people than any type of conventional advertising a product

---

[31] Dik Warren Twedt, "How Much Value Can Be Added Through Packaging?" *Journal of Marketing*, Vol. 32 (January 1968), pp. 58–61.

[32] For a description and evaluation of these and other laboratory instruments see Roger D. Blackwell, James Hensel, Michael Phillips, and Brian Sternthal, *Laboratory Equipment for Marketing Research* (Dubuque, Iowa: Kendall-Hunt Publishing Company, 1970).

can afford. For this reason, all visual surfaces of the package should be used, and the design should be clearly related to, and reinforce, other elements of the company's communication tools, including the trade mark, logotype, and advertising.[33]

Preference Testing

The objective of preference testing is to determine whether the physical product that has been developed is perceived by customers as having the desired characteristics. Both experience and formal research indicate that there is no simple answer to what method of preference testing should be used on any given occasion.[34] Rather, the choice depends on the specific objectives of the test.

BLIND AND IDENTIFIED TESTS. New products may be tested blindly—that is, without any brand or company identification—or they may be identified with the proposed brand name and package. A blind test should be used when the objective is to obtain customer evaluations of product characteristics free from any influences or associations resulting from brand or company identification. On the other hand, if it is desirable to test the total product, including its brand name and package, identified tests should be used. Still another approach is to combine blind and identified tests, using separate, comparable samples. Properly controlled differences in evaluations may then be attributed to the brand and package.[35]

SINGLE AND COMPARATIVE TESTS. It is also necessary to decide whether a new product should be tested independently or relative to other competitive products. There are three major testing alternatives:[36]

1. *Monadic test.* Respondents use the new product under circumstances as normal as possible and evaluate it by completing a questionnaire and/or some type of rating instrument.
2. *Direct Comparison Tests.* Respondents use the new product and one or more other products. The most common form is the paired comparison type where two products are evaluated concurrently, but it is also possible to test three or more products with triangle or ranking tests.[37]
3. *Staggered Tests.* Respondents use the new product and one or more other products, but use them at different points in time and evaluate them independently.

[33] For case examples of how these and other criteria have been used to design effective packaging see J. Gordon Knapp, "10 Things to Look For in Your Package Design," *Industrial Marketing*, February 1964, pp. 84–89.

[34] See, for example, Roger Bengston and Henry Brenner, "Product Test Results Using Three Different Methodologies," *Journal of Marketing Research*, Vol. 1 (November 1964), pp. 49–52.

[35] Ralph L. Day, "Preference Tests and the Management of Product Features," *Journal of Marketing*, Vol. 32 (July 1968), pp. 24–29.

[36] *Ibid.*

[37] See, for example, Albert J. Byer and Dorothy Abrams, "A Comparison of the Triangular and Two-Sample Taste Methods," *Food Technology*, Vol. 7 (April 1953), pp. 185–187.

The major advantage of a monadic test is that it introduces less artificiality into the testing situation because respondents use the new product in the usual way and then report their experiences.[38] In the absence of benchmarks or norms of performance, it is useful to compare the new product against others. In order to accomplish this with the monadic method, it is necessary to employ two or more separate samples. This creates problems of matching samples and increases research costs. Monadic tests are recommended when there are existing performance norms and where there are product differences that might be magnified out of proportion to their commercial importance in a paired comparison test.[39]

Direct comparison tests are more sensitive to product differences than are the other two tests. Consequently they are useful in determining whether a new product has the customer benefits specified in the product concept. If the benefits do not stand out clearly in these test results, the new product probably should be redesigned. The major problem is that this type of test requires an artificial situation because customers do not customarily use more than one brand at a time. Thus, even if the new product's benefits emerge from this type of testing, it is not clear that they will be perceived in realistic use situations.

Staggered tests, sometimes called comparative monadic tests, are a compromise. They avoid the artificiality of direct comparisons by having the new product and other products tried at different times. They also overcome the problems and costs of matching samples. On the other hand, they can only identify the relative preference for a new product; it may in fact be relatively better but absolutely poor.[40] This potential disadvantage can be overcome by using leading brands for comparison and/or by constructing norms of performance on the basis of previous test results.

In tests of this sort it is often necessary to eliminate from the sample those individuals who are unwilling and/or unable to reliably discriminate between brands. These individuals can be identified through double preference tests.

If these, and/or other tests[41] isolate problems, the product may be redesigned and then subjected to further testing. Simultaneously, a preliminary advertising and sales promotion program is formulated, applications are made for patents and copyrights, a pricing plan is formulated, distribution and sales organization requirements are identified, and preliminary plans are drafted.

---

[38] A. B. Blankenship, "Let's Bury Paired Comparisons," *Journal of Advertising Research*, Vol. 6 (March 1966), pp. 13–17.

[39] Bengston and Brenner, "Product Tests Results Using Three Different Methodologies," p. 52.

[40] This is also a potential disadvantage of direct comparison tests.

[41] See Alin Gruber and Barbara Lindberg, "Sensitivity, Reliability and Consumer Taste Testing," *Journal of Marketing Research*, Vol. 3 (August 1966), pp. 235–238; and Allan Greenburg, "Paired Comparisons vs. Monadic Tests," *Journal of Advertising Research*, Vol. 3 (December 1963), pp. 44–47.

MARKET TESTING AND COMMERCIALIZATION

After a new product has proceeded through product development, it may or may not be subjected to market testing. This type of testing *supplements and complements* testing procedures already described, because it attempts to measure customer acceptance of the total marketing program for the new product. Because market testing measures other marketing variables as well as the product, it will be discussed in Chapter 18.

Commercialization

After a new product passes test marketing—or, if it is not test marketed, after it emerges from product development—many other activities are required before it is ready for full-scale introduction to the market.

Production capacity and inventories must be built. Production facilities must be completed, the quality-control system must be operationalized, inventory levels established and attained, and warehousing and shipping patterns established. Distribution and sales-force plans must be finalized; this may include sales training and incentive programs and a "kick-off" sales meeting. Product presentations may be made to members of key distribution channels. The advertising and sales promotion program must be completed. Budgets must be finalized, advertisements must be selected, and space or time must be purchased in advertising vehicles. There may be general and trade press conferences and a trade-show exhibit.

Planning and Scheduling New-Product Programs

PERT (Program Evaluation and Review Technique) has proven to be a successful tool for planning and controlling the development of new products. In fact, new-product planning has become the third largest use of PERT and the fastest-growing one.[42] This growth has occurred because the timely introduction of new products is a key factor for successful marketing. New-product development imposes difficult coordination and scheduling requirements on all organizational units of the business. The dangers of time and cost slippage are always present, and failure to maintain schedules can stretch out the process sufficiently so that selling opportunities are missed, the advantage over competition is dissipated, and profitability is reduced.

PERT in new-product management provides a number of advantages: (1) it assures that a new-product program is thoroughly planned before execution; (2) it identifies individual responsibility and coordination requirements; and (3) it identifies activities that can delay the project and provides a practical means of evaluating costs and risks of changing the program to maintain or accelerate

[42] *Management of New Products*, p. 12.

schedules. PERT applications to new-product programming are discussed in the references cited.[43]

LEGAL CONSIDERATIONS IN PRODUCT PLANNING

Many legal restrictions affect product programs. These are complex, and few marketing executives know, or can be expected to know, all their details. However, a general familiarity is necessary so that one can avoid obvious legal violations and know when to consult legal counsel. This section summarizes major legal considerations affecting product design and quality, packaging, and labeling.

Product Design[44]

Certain product attributes are protected by patents and copyrights. A patent is a government-granted 17-year right to exclude others from making, using, or selling anything that infringes upon any claims of the patent. Copyrights allow authors or composers or their publishers to prevent the republication of, or the public use of, their works for a 28-year period, renewable for an equal period. Of the two, patents most often influence product design decisions.

A patent holder can license others to use the patented product and may require the licensee to pay royalties on the good produced and restrict sales to specified territories or to specified kinds of customers. The licensee may also be required to sell at prices established by the patent holder. Consequently, substantial restrictions can be placed on the way a firm can use a patented product. A patent holder can also exercise considerable control over the amount of competition he desires to face.

There are, however, restrictions on licensing. It cannot be used as part of an industrywide scheme to fix prices. If a competitor of the patent holder also intends to accept licenses under the same conditions, the courts will generally hold that the patent is being used to restrain trade illegally.

If companies in an industry each own patents that they all need, they may enter into agreements to cross-license their patents, or form a pool in which all place their patents. The pool then licenses each company to use any or all of the patents. These agreements are generally legal unless they are used to fix prices, restrict output, or otherwise restrain trade on an industrywide basis.

---

[43] See Warren Dusenbury, "CPM for New Product Introductions," *Harvard Business Review*, Vol. 45 (July-August 1967), pp. 124–139; Yung Wong, "Critical Path Analysis for New Product Planning," *Journal of Marketing*, Vol. 28 (October 1964), pp. 53–59; and Joseph B. Milgram, Jr., "How Pert and Critical Path Can Contribute to the New Product Planning Program," in M. S. Moyer and R. E. Vosburgh, *Marketing for Tomorrow . . . Today* (Chicago: American Marketing Association, 1968), pp. 37–48. For an excellent comprehensive approach to planning and scheduling new products see David B. Uman, *New Product Programs: Their Planning and Control* (New York: American Management Association, Inc., 1969).

[44] Much of this section was adapted from parts of John R. Grabner, Jr., "Legal Limits of Competition," *Harvard Business Review*, Vol. 47 (November-December 1969), pp. 4–24 and 182.

Product Quality

Many industries have laws relating to product quality. For example, the Pure Food and Drug Act outlaws product adulteration. The Meat Inspection Act, the Imported Meat Act, the Poultry Products Act, and the Wholesale Meat Act regulate the quality of meat and poultry products. The McNary Mapes Amendment to the Pure Food and Drug Act controls standards of quality for canned foods. The Food Additives Amendment controls the quality of food additives. The National Traffic and Motor Safety Act regulates motor vehicle safety standards. In addition to these and other federal laws, there are also numerous state and local laws—such laws are in fact too numerous to discuss here. Those responsible for product quality decisions must become familiar with the laws and regulations that apply to their products.

Packaging, Labeling, and Brand Names

There are also many legal restrictions on packaging and labeling. For example, the Food Additives Amendment specifies that labels must identify the manufacturer or distributor and the package contents and quality, and must contain warnings if the product is dangerous or habit-forming. The Flammable Fabric Act specifies that flammable fabrics must be labeled as such.

The recent Fair Packaging and Labeling Act (1967) has widespread effects covering products generally found in supermarkets (except such products as meats, poultry, tobacco, prescription drugs, poisons, seeds, and so forth). This act makes it mandatory for packages to bear labels specifying: (1) identification of the commodity, (2) name and place of business of the manufacturer or distributor, and (3) net quantity of contents; also (4) if the package weighs less than four pounds, its weight must be expressed in both pounds and ounces; and (5) statements about number of servings must include net weight, measure, or numerical count of each serving. In addition, administrative agencies have the discretionary authority to establish other regulations.[45]

Brand names have no legal status; they are simply a marketing designation for one type of trademark. The first user of a trademark may register it with the U.S. Patent Office for a period of 20 years, and renew it for comparable periods, thereby insuring the protection of his rights, and establishing the basis for legal remedies in the case of imitation. Over the years a company commonly invests millions of dollars in a brand name or trademark, so that it has almost incalculable value. Yet legal protection for these designations can be lost, as is illustrated by Aspirin, Lanolin, Shredded Wheat, Linoleum, and Cellophane, to mention just a

[45] See Dik Warren Twedt, "What Effect Will the 'Fair Packaging and Labeling Act' Have on Marketing Practices?" *Journal of Marketing*, Vol. 31 (April 1967), pp. 58–59.

few. In order to protect a brand name it must always be identified as such on labels, in advertising, and wherever else it may appear.[46]

SUMMARY

New products are the lifeblood of many companies. Without them it is difficult to survive, let alone achieve growth and profitability requirements. Yet the record indicates that most new products are failures. Hence new-product programming is an area of tremendous improvement potential for many companies.

The process of new-product planning and control begins with the formulation of new-product objectives. Derived from corporate, marketing, and then product objectives, new-product objectives specify the level of new-product activity required during the planning period and set forth general guidelines to be followed.

Responsibility for exploring and generating new-product ideas is assigned to an individual, committee, or other organizational unit. Those responsible serve as a collecting point and make certain that a sufficient number of new ideas are forthcoming.

The next two stages are concerned with evaluating new ideas. The screening stage uses available information to make certain the idea is consistent with objectives and strategy guidelines. The business-analysis stage goes considerably further and involves more rigorous analysis.

Ideas passing the evaluation stages move on to product development. Brand-positioning and brand strategies are formulated, packaging is developed, and engineering and production transform the idea from a concept into physical form. Preference tests may be conducted to make certain the physical product is perceived as having the desired attributes. Products passing this stage are test-marketed and/or readied for introduction.

QUESTIONS FOR REVIEW AND DISCUSSION

1. Why are new products a corporate dilemma?
2. In what types of situations would it be desirable for a carpet manufacturer to follow a multibrand strategy?
3. Prepare a short essay discussing general success requirements for new products.
4. A brewer wants to test a new beer. What type(s) of preference test should he use?
5. Historically many appliance manufacturers have avoided private branding. Is this a viable strategy for the future? Why or why not?
6. Assume you are the brand manager for a new cake mix, and the design group

---

[46] Sidney A. Diamond, "Protect Your Trademark By Proper Usage," *Journal of Marketing*, Vol. 26 (July 1962), pp. 17–22.

has just given you two packages. How would you determine which one is better?

7. Review Chapter 9 and discuss the major ways similarity and preference mapping can be used to identify new-product opportunities.

8. What is meant by brand positioning? How should a chewing-gum manufacturer go about determining whether his brand is properly positioned?

9. Why might a manufacturer of a line of household cleaning products follow a multiproduct brand strategy? What are the risks involved?

Chapter 12   Pricing Programs

Authors, businessmen, and theoreticians alike recognize the importance of pricing. However, almost without exception these same people openly admit their inability to deal with the subject clearly and concisely. One study concluded:

Economists, legislators, and the public generally would like to see pricing decisions by big companies analyzed in logical fashion, with historical comparisons of competitor's prices, cost factors, and profit margins given consistent and quantitative weight in detailed memoranda of officials involved. Unfortunately for those who would insist on fully ordered business behavior, such strategic memoranda summarizing the considerations at an important conference leading to a price decision are rarely found. . . . Repeatedly, reference was made to the "art" or "feel" of pricing rather than observance of a formula.[1]

Clearly, pricing is one of the most discussed yet least formally structured aspects of marketing management.

The first section of this chapter offers a discussion of pricing terminology, an overview of the manner in which the economist approaches the subject of pricing, and a suggested format for systematically dealing with pricing problems from a managerial perspective. This systematic approach to pricing then becomes the framework for the remainder of the chapter—setting pricing objectives, setting pricing policies, and developing pricing procedures. The chapter concludes with a brief discussion of legal considerations.

[1] A. D. H. Kaplan, J. B. Dirlam, and R. F. Lanzillotti, *Pricing in Big Business* (Washington, D.C.: The Brookings Institution, 1959), p. 13.

THE NATURE OF PRICING

Perhaps much of the confusion surrounding pricing practices has evolved from the very narrow context in which the term is typically defined.

Pricing Perspectives

The term price can mean many things, depending on whether it is viewed from a macro or micro perspective. In a macro sense, Backman has described it in the following manner:

To the consumer the structure of prices indicates the terms on which he can acquire the goods for which he spends his money income. To the producer the structure of prices indicates the terms on which he may dispose of his goods and services or acquire the goods and services of others.[2]

In a micro sense, price is generally regarded to be the "money value of a product or service as agreed upon in a market transaction."[3]

It has long been recognized that to completely understand a "price" in any particular transaction one must know much more than the amount of money involved. Both the buyer and seller should be familiar with "the amount and quality of the product or service to be exchanged; the time and place at which the exchange will take place and payment will be made, the form of money to be used, the credit terms and discounts that apply to the transaction, guarantees on the product or service, delivery terms, return privileges, and other factors."[4] That is, the total bundle of satisfactions being obtained at the specified money price is the most relevant measure of value received.

Just as the "total product" is more relevant than merely the physical product, so also is the "total price" more relevant than merely the money price. *Time* expended in the purchase process, and the *convenience* of physical facilities where purchases may be made, are only two of many factors that could conceivably be considered to be just as "costly" to the purchaser as the agreed-upon money price of the total product. Thus, a more managerially relevant definition of price might be stated as follows: *price is the total package of dissatisfactions that a purchaser must be willing to incur in order to obtain some specified package of benefits.*

Nature of Pricing

In an economic sense prices serve to allocate scarce resources among those desiring the resources. Once again, however, this approach is of little practical value to the

[2] Jules Backman, *Price Practices and Price Policies* (New York: The Ronald Press Company, 1953), p. 9.

[3] Donald V. Harper, *Price Policy and Procedure* (New York: Harcourt Brace Jovanovich, Inc., 1966), p. 1.

[4] *Ibid.*, pp. 1–2.

marketing manager. The marketing manager—indeed, almost everyone—concedes that as the price of a product is increased, the quantity sold will usually decline. However, this is an oversimplification of the market process and how buyers behave. A demand curve that slopes downward and to the right may be intuitively acceptable, but the marketing manager can think of many products that are exceptions.

The apparent paradox between expected and actual consumer reaction to price levels is understandable when one recognizes that price is only one element in the firm's total marketing effort. Effective promotional effort, product improvement, or improved customer service may more than offset the negative effect on demand produced by a price increase. Indeed, a price increase may in itself have a salutary effect on demand.[5] Customers may interpret high prices to mean greater quality—as shown, for example, by the price inelasticity of demand for pharmaceutical products, patent medicines, "prestige" products, and professional services.

Importance of Pricing

A study of key marketing executives in successful manufacturing companies concluded that nonpricing strategies were more important than pricing in determining corporate and marketing success. One-half of the respondents did not even select pricing as one of their firm's five most important strategy areas. Thus, companies often appear to consider other elements in the total marketing strategy to be safer, more effective, methods of achieving their objectives.[6] Nevertheless, an appropriate pricing strategy is an important requirement for successful marketing.

Price Theory

Economists have developed a carefully structured body of microeconomic theory that deals with the process of establishing prices to maximize corporate profitability. Although instances in which this theory provides practical solutions to pricing problems are rare, it is helpful in illuminating the nature of the environment in which managers must make pricing decisions.

The technique of marginal analysis is typically employed to illustrate how prices should be established in various kinds of market situations.

BASIC CONCEPTS. Listed below are some of the basic cost concepts, demand concepts, and terms in marginal analysis.[7]

---

[5] Several authors have commented on the fact that price, per se, can be considered as a promotional element in the firm's total marketing effort. For example, see Brian Dixon, *Price Discrimination and Marketing Management*, Michigan Business Studies, Vol. 15, No. 1 (Ann Arbor, Mich.: Bureau of Business Research, University of Michigan, 1960), p. 27.

[6] For a discussion of the reasons why nonprice promotion is typically considered to be more effective than price promotion, see Stewart H. Rewoldt, James D. Scott, and Martin R. Warshaw, *Introduction to Marketing Management* (Homewood, Ill.: Richard D. Irwin, Inc., 1969), pp. 516–518.

[7] Harper, *Price Policy and Procedure*, pp. 3–4.

Average total cost (ATC) represents average total cost per unit and is derived by dividing total costs (which include a "normal" return on invested capital) by the number of units of product or service sold.

Marginal cost (MC) is the change in total costs that results from producing an additional unit of product or service.

Average revenue (AR) is the average revenue per unit sold, derived by dividing total revenue by the number of units of product or service sold.

Marginal revenue (MR) is the change in total revenue that results from the sale of an additional unit of product or service.

Price elasticity of demand is a measure of the responsiveness of the quantity sold to price changes. Mathematically it is the ratio of the percentage response of the quantity sold to a percentage change in price. The demand for a product or service is said to be *elastic* if the total revenue increases as the price is reduced. Demand is *inelastic* if the total revenue decreases when the price is reduced. If there is no change in the total revenue when prices are changed, demand is said to display *unitary elasticity*. In graphic terms, a perfectly elastic demand is illustrated by a perfectly horizontal line, a perfectly inelastic demand by a perfectly vertical line.

PRICING UNDER PURE COMPETITION.[8] The basic conditions required for a market to be purely competitive are:

1. There are a large number of buyers and sellers, none of which is large enough to exert significant pressure on the supply offered on the market.
2. The products and services sold are homogeneous.
3. There is complete freedom for firms to enter or leave the industry.[9]

Perhaps the market situation that most closely approximates this economic model is that which faces the seller of agricultural commodities. Relatively few agricultural producers are large enough to affect the market price of the homogeneous product they sell, and, while capital requirements are often greater than anticipated, freedom to enter or leave the industry prevails. Under these circumstances the market establishes a price that equates demand and supply, and the individual firm must sell its goods at a price over which it has no control. The only choices open to the firm are whether or not to sell at the market price, and, if so, how much to sell.

---

[8] Much of what follows in this and subsequent sections dealing with price theory is based upon material contained in George J. Stigler, *The Theory of Price*, rev. ed. (New York: The Macmillan Company, 1952); and Richard H. Leftwitch, *The Price System and Resource Allocation*, rev. ed. (New York: Holt, Rinehart and Winston, Inc., 1963).

[9] The economist distinguishes between pure competition and perfect competition by adding the requirement of complete market information to achieve perfectly competitive conditions.

Figure 12-1   Price determination in a purely competitive market.

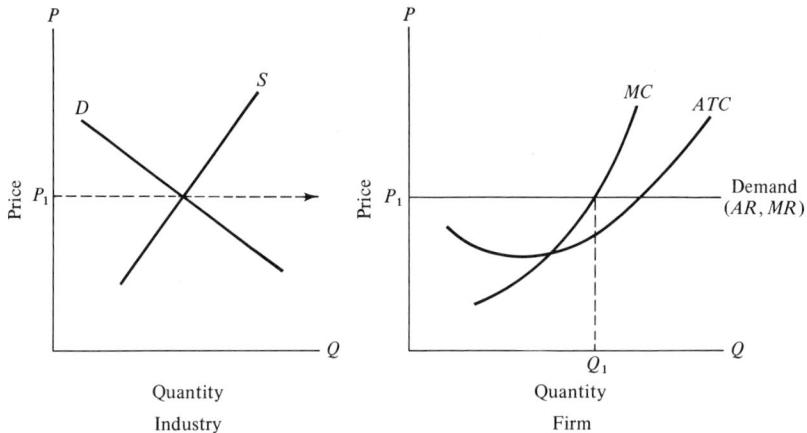

Industry   Firm

The economist would illustrate this process as shown in Figure 12-1.[10] The interaction of industry supply and demand establishes a market price of P_1, and this price becomes the highest price at which an individual firm can sell its product. Consequently, the firm faces a perfectly elastic, horizontal demand curve. Assuming the firm wishes to maximize profits in the short run, it will offer to sell quantity Q_1 at the market price of P_1. At this point the firm's marginal revenue (MR) is equal to its marginal cost (MC).[11]

MONOPOLY PRICING. The opposite extreme is the monopoly model, which assumes the seller has complete control over the entire supply of a unique product, for which there is no substitute so similar that price changes in it would affect his sales. In essence, the monopolist is the industry. If the amount buyers will purchase varies inversely with price, the firm's demand curve will be similar to that shown in Figure 12-2, sloping downward and to the right.

The monopolist would seek to establish the combination of price and output that provides him with the greatest total profit. Figure 12-2 again illustrates application of the profit-maximizing principle of offering that quantity for sale that equates marginal revenue and marginal cost. That is, in order to maximize profits in both the short and long run, the monopolist would offer quantity E for sale at a price of B. This decision would generate total revenues of $OBCE$, average total costs of $OADE$, and total profits of $ABCD$.

[10] The revenue and cost conditions illustrated for the firm in Figure 12-1 could exist only in the short run. The firm is earning profits in excess of a "normal return on capital," which would encourage expansion in the industry and an equating of price and average total cost in the long run.

[11] The firm will always maximize profits by selling that quantity of product which results in equating its marginal revenue and marginal cost. Up to that point, an increase in quantity sold adds more to the firm's total revenue than to its total costs; beyond that point, additional sales would add more to total costs than to total revenue.

Figure 12-2   Determination of price and output under
monopoly conditions.

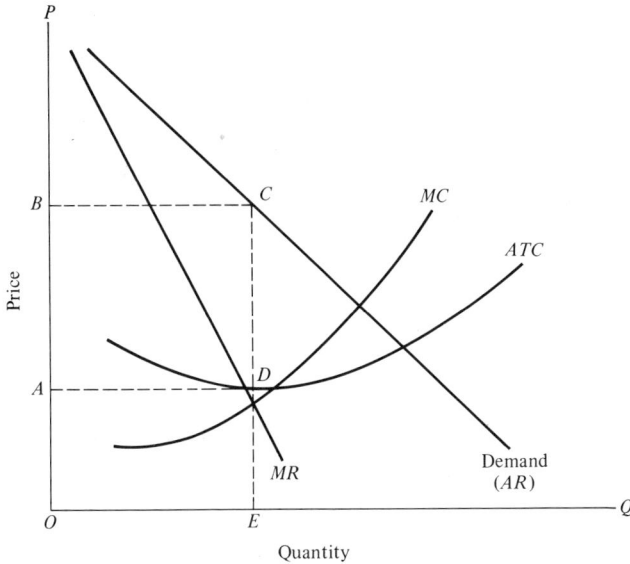

PRICING UNDER MONOPOLISTIC COMPETITION. While the monopolist controls the total supply of an industry's goods, the firm in a monopolistically or imperfectly competitive market controls only a portion of the total industry supply of product. The industry demand schedule is the aggregate of all the individual schedules of member firms. In order to gain a certain degree of independence, however, each firm does attempt to develop certain "unique" product characteristics that differentiate its product offering from those of its competitors. Thus, the industry schedule is made up of many segments, each of which may shift as competition or changes in buyer behavior cause changes in demand for the products of a given firm.[12]

The condition of imperfect competition closely parallels the actual conditions under which most marketing managers must operate. It recognizes that the firm's demand curve may be moved upward and to the right by improved marketing effort or downward and to the left by more effective marketing effort by competitors. Shifting the demand curve upward and to the right increases the firm's profits; the opposite occurs when the demand curve moves downward and to the left.

The graphic representation of conditions facing the firm under conditions of imperfect competition is so similar to Figure 12-2 that a new graph need not be developed. However, it should be emphasized that the demand curve in Figure 12-2 would reflect the position of a firm rather than an entire industry. Procedur-

[12] Rewoldt, Scott, and Warshaw, *Introduction to Marketing Management,* p. 520.

ally, the profit-maximizing price and quantity would be selected in exactly the same fashion as described for the monopolist.

CONTRIBUTIONS OF PRICE THEORY. Price theory is helpful because it carefully examines the interrelationships that exist between several important forces that affect pricing. Moreover, price theory provides a useful standardized terminology for the discussion of cost and demand concepts, and provides a benchmark against which a "real" pricing situation may be compared.[13]

However, while price theory is useful in establishing marketing and pricing objectives, price policies, and pricing procedures, it is not an optimizing, prescriptive tool for management decision making.[14]

A Systematic Approach To Pricing

Figure 12-3 is a diagrammatic summary of a systematic approach to pricing. It begins with corporate and marketing objectives and strategy. Pricing objectives required to achieve marketing and corporate objectives are specified and pricing strategy alternatives are identified; then primary pricing procedure guidelines are identified. These guidelines are used to develop specific prices, which may or may not be pretested for market impact. Results are monitored, evaluated, and compared with pricing objectives. While all of these steps must be dealt with implicitly if not explicitly, the sequence may not always be in the order presented here.

SETTING PRICING OBJECTIVES

Pricing should be consistent with and contribute to the achievement of marketing and corporate objectives and strategies. Unfortunately, many companies do not have integrated, operational pricing objectives. For example, many companies state that the objective of pricing is to maximize profits. However, in almost any firm there are factors that mitigate against, or must be considered in addition to, a goal of profit maximization. For example, the firm may be interested in increasing its market share or its rate of growth, even at the expense of immediate profits; may fear that it would incur adverse public reaction to an attempt to maximize profits; or may feel that ethical considerations prevent it from operating in such a way as to maximize profits.[15]

While some of these considerations may be considered attempts to contribute toward the long-term profitability of corporate operations, most would consider them to be modifications to an objective of profit maximization. Such circumstances are not rare. In one pricing study the authors reported that the major pricing objectives of selected large American businesses were a composite of several factors rather than any one single factor. They concluded that the pricing goals pursued by the twenty firms included in the sample could best be classified as:

---

[13] Harper, *Price Policy and Procedure*, p. 13.
[14] *Ibid.*, p. 11.
[15] *Ibid.*, p. 32.

1. Pricing to achieve a target return on investment.
2. Stabilization of price and margin.
3. Pricing to realize a target market share.
4. Pricing to meet or prevent competition.
5. Pricing subordinated to product differentiation.[16]

Figure 12-3   A pricing planning and control system.

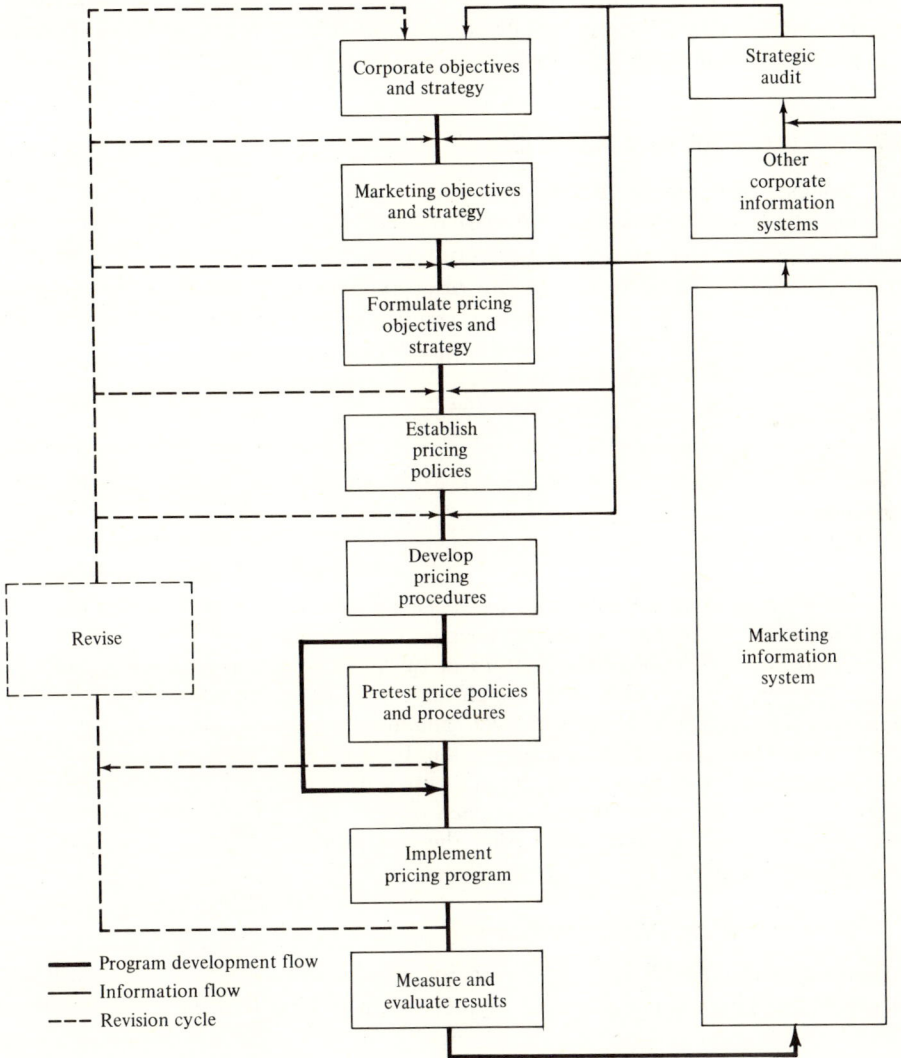

———   Program development flow
———   Information flow
– – –   Revision cycle

[16] Robert F. Lanzillotti, "Pricing Objectives in Large Companies," *American Economic Review*, Vol. 48, No. 5 (December 1958), pp. 921–940; and Kaplan, Dirlam, and Lanzillotti, *Pricing in Big Business*, p. 128.

Though each of the companies examined focused primarily on one of these objectives, each company typically was concerned with all of them, and the primary differences in their operations were based solely on their particular hierarchy of pricing objectives. For example, a company such as General Motors or the Ford Motor Company might seek to maintain or improve its market share and at the same time to increase its target return on invested capital. On the other hand, Esso, while understandably concerned with "meeting competition," is referred to in the Brookings Study as a company that prices to yield a target return on investment.[17] Figure 12-4 illustrates these objectives, those of other firms included in this study, and the relative success of each firm.

SETTING PRICING POLICIES

Price policies are general principles, rules, or action guidelines that the firm endeavors to follow in making daily pricing decisions.[18] These policies must be established within the context of a carefully structured set of pricing objectives, because failure to carefully coordinate price policies with the overall objectives of pricing will almost certainly diminish the probability of successfully achieving the firm's marketing and total corporate objectives.

The Complexity of Pricing Policies

The process of establishing price policies is extremely complex, primarily because it involves the consideration of a vast array of factors external to the firm. Consider:

Pricing policy must somehow touch base with such economic factors as foreign competition, competition of substitute products, industry competition (including price leadership), yield on investment, average cost and marginal cost, product demand, quality and other selling features of the product, and conditions of the market. Further, pricing policy must weigh important governmental or legal elements. . . ; the congressional concern over "administered prices"; the not-always-consistent antitrust policies on pricing of the Justice Department, the Federal Trade Commission, the courts, and the antitrust statutes themselves; and public relations, i.e., the impact of a price advance or cut on public opinion, government, the press, the business community, the company's employees, its unions, customers, and suppliers.[19]

The Anatomy of Pricing Policies

Profit-making remains the guiding principle for most companies in establishing price policies. There is no "formula for success" in pricing that fits every business;

[17] *Ibid.*, p. 156.

[18] Harper, *Price Policy and Procedure*, p. 28.

[19] William H. Peterson, "Divergent Views on Pricing Policy," *Harvard Business Review*, Vol. 41 (March-April 1963), p. 20.

instead, each firm must weigh the facts and decide on pricing policies based upon factors relevant to its own market environment. The following types of decisions must be made:

1. How should our price compare with "average" prices in the industry? Specifically, should we be 2 percent above or 4 percent below the average? and, when we speak of the average, which firms' prices are we going to include in the computation?
2. How fast will we meet price reductions or increases by rivals?
3. How frequently will it be advisable to vary price? To what extent is stability of price advantageous?
4. Should the firm make use of "fair trade" price maintenance?
5. How frequently should the firm run price promotions?[20]

A wide variety of pricing policies are possible;[21] however, they can be synthesized into three critical categories. First, a company can engage in an openly aggressive effort to seize a part of its rival's market share. Cutthroat pricing, advertising wars, excessive product expenditures, and the so-called "unfair methods of competition" that the FTC attempts to police are common ingredients in such an effort. A second alternative might be termed a "conservative marketing policy," which represents an attitude of live-and-let-live. Striving to charge the same price, keeping advertising expenditures at a level that will not invite retaliation in the form of advertising wars, and following common marketing procedures exemplify such a policy. Finally, there may be an implicit or explicit agreement in the industry to behave in some predetermined fashion. Price leadership, market-sharing agreements, various kinds of pooling arrangements, and explicit trade practices or procedures agreements may be indicative of such behavior.[22]

These three approaches can be used simultaneously. For example:

. . . the industry may charge uniform prices but strive to improve its relative position by the most ruthless behavior as far as advertising or trade practices are concerned. In fact, this is probably the typical pattern of behavior. The reason is obvious: everyone is damaged by price rivalry—all of the industry profits may be destroyed by price cutting so that everyone, even the victor (in the sense of the one who is able to improve his market-share position) loses as far as profits are concerned.[23]

---

[20] Alfred R. Oxenfeldt, "Multi-Stage Approach to Pricing," *Harvard Business Review*, Vol. 38 (July-August 1960), p. 131.

[21] For a discussion of alternative pricing policies see Harper, *Price Policy and Procedure*, p. 29.

[22] Lawrence Nabers, "Making Pricing Policies," *The Business Review*, Vol. 7 (May 1960), p. 5.

[23] *Ibid.*

Figure 12-4 Pricing objectives of 20 large corporations.

Company	Principal Pricing Goal	Collateral Pricing Goals	Rate of Return on Investment (After Taxes) 1947–55 Average	Range
Alcoa	20 percent on investment (before taxes); higher on new products (about 10 percent effective rate after taxes)	(a) "Promotive" policy on new products (b) Price stabilization	13.8	7.8–18.7
American Can	Maintenance of market share	(a) "Meeting" competition (using cost of substitute product to determine price) (b) Price stabilization	11.6	9.6–14.7
A & P	Increasing market share	"General promotive" (low-margin policy)	13.0	9.7–18.8
Du Pont	Target return on investment—no specific figure given	(a) Charging what traffic will bear over long run (b) Maximum return for new products—"life cycle" pricing	25.9	19.6–34.1
Esso	"Fair-return" target—no specific figure given	(a) Maintaining market share (b) Price stabilization	16.0	12.0–18.9
General Electric	20 percent on investment (after taxes); 7 percent on sales (after taxes)	(a) Promotive policy on new products (b) Price stabilization on nationally advertised products	21.4	18.4–26.6
General Foods	33⅓ percent gross margin: "⅓ to make, ⅓ to sell and ⅓ for profit"; expectation of realizing target only on new products	(a) Full line of food products and novelties (b) Maintaining market share	12.2	8.9–15.7
General Motors	20 percent on investment (after taxes)	Maintaining market share	26.0	19.9–37.0
Goodyear	"Meeting competitors"	(a) Maintain "position" (b) Price stabilization	13.3	9.2–16.1
Gulf	Follow price of most important marketer in each area	(a) Maintain market share (b) Price stabilization	12.6	10.7–16.7

Company	Principal pricing goal	Collateral pricing goals	Average	Range
International Harvester	10 percent on investment (after taxes)	Market share: ceiling of "less than a dominant share of any market"	8.9	4.9–11.9
Johns-Manville	Return on investment greater than last 15-year average (about 15 percent after taxes); higher target for new products	(a) Market share not greater than 20 percent (b) Stabilization of prices	14.9	10.7–19.6
Kennecott	Stabilization of prices		16.0	9.3–20.9
Kroger	Maintaining market share	Target return of 20 percent on investment before taxes	12.1	9.7–16.1
National Steel	Matching the market—price follower	Increase market share	12.1	7.0–17.4
Sears, Roebuck	Increasing market share (8–10 percent regarded as satisfactory share)	(a) Realization of traditional return on investment of 10–15 percent (after taxes) (b) General promotive (low margin) policy	5.4	1.6–10.7
Standard Oil (Ind.)	Maintain market share	(a) Stabilize prices (b) Target return on investment (none specified)	10.4	7.9–14.4
Swift	Maintenance of market share in livestock buying and meatpacking		6.9	3.9–11.1
Union Carbide	Target return on investment	Promotive policy on new products; "life cycle" pricing on chemicals generally	19.2	13.5–24.3
U.S. Steel	8 percent on investment (after taxes)	(a) Target market share of 30 percent (b) Stable price (c) Stable margin	10.3	7.6–14.8

SOURCE: Robert F. Lanzillotti, "Pricing Objectives in Large Companies," *American Economic Review*, Vol. 48, No. 5 (December 1958), pp. 921–940. Copyright 1958 by the American Economic Association. Reprinted by permission of the author and publisher.

In structuring an individual firm's pricing program specific aspects of the pricing decision must be examined in some detail. These include decisions regarding price levels, competitive pricing considerations, price flexibility, geographic price differentials, discounts, and product-line pricing decisions as well as several others.

Price-Level Policies

Each firm must decide whether it wishes to be the price leader or a follower in its industry. This decision is most often a function of the firm's economic strength relative to that of its competitors. Many firms, some of them quite large, feel they have no alternative but to follow the prices established by one or a few of their larger competitors. Thus:

The pricing policy of National Steel is one of matching the market. It has disregarded costs in pricing, because . . . it has assumed that it is at least as efficient in its field as any of its competitors. Therefore, it is able to meet a competitor's price no matter what that price may be. . . . In summary, the few brief pricing rules enunciated . . . for National Steel were as follows:

- Follow the lead of the price leader, which is U.S. Steel, while sweetening the base price a little when, as in Detroit, the company has a considerable freight advantage.
- Absorb freight if necessary on a single order, but watch closely the annual bill.
- Never manipulate extras to get an order; reduce the base price if necessary to meet a competitive cut.
- Price is never built on cost; pressure is backward on cost.[24]

The behavior exhibited by National Steel and other firms such as Kroger[25] appears to be quite common among firms that find themselves engaged in oligopolistic competition.

Life-Cycle Pricing

It is also useful to establish a policy guiding the pricing of products over their life cycles. During the initial stages of the cycle, as pointed out in Chapter 10, the product is likely to be in its strongest competitive position. As competitive products enter the market in the later stages of the cycle, the product's market strength may decline substantially. The policy that the firm adopts for pricing a new product will significantly affect the speed with which the product moves through this cycle.

Two contrasting pricing policies for new products are "skimming" and "market penetration." The most appropriate will depend primarily upon the

[24] Kaplan, Dirlam, and Lanzillotti, *Pricing in Big Business*, pp. 204–205.
[25] *Ibid.*, p. 206.

Figure 12-5   Skimming and penetration price policies.

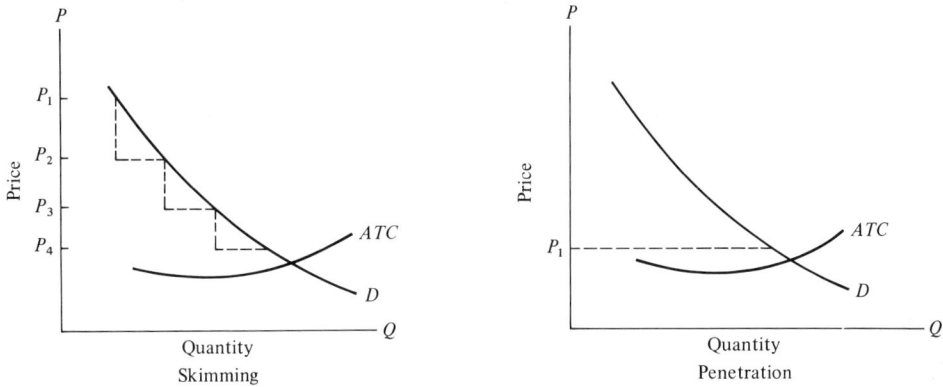

Skimming

Penetration

nature of the product, the degree of protection offered by patents, the elasticity of demand in the target market, and the firm's target rate of capital recovery (Figure 12-5).

A skimming policy, or policy of "sliding down the demand curve," is designed to take the "cream" of the market at each successively lower price level. This "cascading" process is often used to maximize profits on new products. It is especially appropriate: (1) in the product introductory stage when demand is fairly elastic in the upper ranges; (2) when the product is well protected by patents or is difficult to duplicate rapidly; (3) when the firm has established an accelerated target rate of capital recovery; (4) when the firm initiating such a policy is a "leader" in the industry; and (5) when the firm is uncertain of the manner in which the target market may react to alternative price levels.[26] A skimming policy was used successfully for the Polaroid Land Camera and is used widely in the publishing industry.

In contrast, a penetration policy is particularly attractive: (1) when it forces competitors to "stay out" of the market initially, or even indefinitely; (2) when there is no "elite" market for the product, that is, where the entire demand curve is fairly elastic; (3) when the firm wishes to encourage widespread adoption of the product; (4) under circumstances where, as volume expands, economies of scale will reduce costs; and (5) when it is desirable to slow down the passing of the product through the life cycle. DuPont tends to follow such a pricing policy on several of its products;[27] Union Carbide, on the other hand, employs a modified penetration policy.

[26] It seems a better strategy to establish a high price that can be reduced if it meets with unfavorable customer reaction than to start with a low price and then attempt to raise it.

[27] Kaplan, Dirlam, and Lanzillotti, *Pricing in Big Business*, p. 152.

Price Flexibility

A firm can adopt one price or flexible prices. A one-price policy offers the same price to all customers who purchase goods under essentially the same conditions and in the same quantities.[28] Terms of sale are clearly specified and administered on a uniform basis so that all who buy the same quantity pay the same price.[29] Such a policy is commonplace among many producers and most retailers in the United States.

A flexible-price policy indicates that the firm will sell the same products and quantities to different customers at different prices. Prices are varied on the basis of the particular customer's ability to bargain or on competitive factors in the marketplace. While flexible-price policies are not as commonplace as they once were, they may be appropriate under extremely competitive market circumstances where the firm's salesmen may be called upon to make adjustments in price relative to local conditions. However, such policies are not without legal difficulties, and may cause ill-will on the part of customers who learn that others have obtained lower prices for the same "total product."

Geographic Pricing Policies

Perhaps few examples illustrate the interdependencies among pricing policies and other aspects of marketing operations as clearly as decisions regarding geographic pricing policies.[30] Approximately 9 percent of the nation's gross national product consists of charges associated with the movement of freight. Almost every firm incurs some of these charges and consequently must determine to what extent it wishes to recover them through the prices it charges. Measures that might be relied upon in this respect are f.o.b.-origin[31] and delivered-pricing.

F.O.B. PRICING. When the seller quotes a price "f.o.b. origin," "f.o.b. mill," or "f.o.b. factory," this is the price of the product ready for shipment at the plant or warehouse. The buyer pays any freight bills associated with the shipment. Since the burden of shipment rests with the purchaser, it is his responsibility to determine whether to utilize private or public transportation and to specify carriers.

F.o.b.-origin pricing relieves the seller of the burden of transportation and assures him that he will receive the same net return from every sale of the product regardless of where the buyer may be located. However, the most important and often critical limitation of such a policy is that it may make it virtually impossible for the seller to sell his product in distant markets.

[28] E. Jerome McCarthy, *Basic Marketing: A Managerial Approach,* 3d ed. (Homewood, Ill.: Richard D. Irwin, Inc., 1968), p. 562.

[29] A one-price policy should not be confused with a "single-price" policy. A single-price policy means all customers pay the same price regardless of the quantity they may purchase.

[30] For a glossary of terms frequently used in discussions of geographic pricing policies, see Backman, *Price Practices and Price Policies,* pp. 176–177.

[31] F.o.b. is an abbreviation for "free on board.'"

DELIVERED PRICING. Delivered-pricing policies are relied upon by sellers interested in selling in distant markets. The most common of these policies include the uniform delivered price, freight equalization, zone pricing, and basing point pricing.[32] Each contains the same basic ingredients: the price of the product itself and some portion of the transportation costs involved in getting the product to the buyer.

1. *Uniform delivered price.* This approach is exactly the opposite of f.o.b. origin, because the seller assumes all the costs of delivery. The prices customers pay are equal regardless of their location. However, the net prices the seller realizes differ as a function of the location of the various customers being served.

2. *Freight Equalization.* Here the seller absorbs only those transportation costs that he absolutely must in order to compete in distant markets. Freight equalization makes the delivered price of his product equal to or less than that of rivals located closer to the customer.

3. *Other Delivered-Pricing Alternatives.* Zone pricing and basing point pricing are further variations on the basic theme of freight absorption. Such policies are difficult to administer and *may* be illegal. As a consequence, before adopting such policies, the seller is well advised to carefully examine his need to use them.

Discount policies

Many firms elect to offer their customers discounts from list prices. Such discounts are granted in order to compensate resellers for the marketing activities they perform, to encourage them to buy in larger quantities, to stimulate prompt payment, or to obtain better promotional efforts. These techniques are called functional, quantity, cash, and promotional discounts.

FUNCTIONAL DISCOUNTS. These discounts represent a reduction in price to a buyer because of his position in the channel of distribution; they are his compensation for performing various marketing activities. If a manufacturer distributes his products through wholesalers and retailers as well as direct to ultimate consumers, the firm typically establishes a triple scale of prices. Full list price may be charged the ultimate consumer, whereas a discount of 33⅓ percent may be given the retailer and a 10 percent discount allowed the wholesaler.

QUANTITY DISCOUNTS. These discounts are used to increase the quantity purchased and/or improve customer loyalty among buyers. *Noncumulative* quantity discounts are reductions from the established list price for each of the various classes of customers when they buy in excess of certain specified quantities. Such a discount is applied on a per-order basis in order to encourage larger but less frequent orders, buying in anticipation of demand, and full-line purchasing.[33]

---

[32] For a description of the various methods of selling products "freight allowed" and the classes of products typically sold under each, see Backman, *Price Practices and Price Policies,* pp. 182–184.

[33] Rewoldt, Scott, and Warshaw, *Introduction to Marketing Management,* p. 551.

Cumulative quantity discounts are granted on the basis of total purchases over some specified period of time. They offer the buyer an inducement to concentrate his purchases with the seller.

These two types of quantity discounts are occasionally used together to gain the advantages of each. For example, a seller might grant his customers a 1 percent discount on each individual order in excess of $250 and an additional 1 percent discount to those customers whose total purchases exceed $10,000 during a calendar year.

CASH DISCOUNTS. The terms "2/10, net 30" are but one of the literally hundreds of ways in which cash discounts might be specified.[34] These particular terms indicate that the purchaser will be granted a 2 percent discount if he pays his account within 10 days, the full amount without benefit of a reduction being due in 30 days. These discounts are used to accelerate payment and as a promotional tool to gain access to key resellers.

PROMOTIONAL OR SPECIAL DISCOUNTS. These discounts may be granted "for advertising purposes, for special services rendered to the vendor, for the employment of demonstrators in the buyer's store, for so-called 'P.M.'s' ("push" money), and for other sales promotional devices."[35] Along with other techniques they are used to gain distribution through resellers and increase resellers' selling efforts.

Extreme care must be exercised in structuring and granting these discounts. A discount represents a reduction in "price" and as such may be considered discriminatory under the provisions of the Robinson-Patman Act.[36]

Product-Line Pricing Policies

Multiproduct firms usually have products in the line actively competing with one another, and the manner in which they are priced will have a profound effect on their relative success.

One of the basic questions facing a manufacturer of a line of products involves determining the price differentials that should exist among the various substitute items within the product line. This is an important consideration, since buyers often consider the purchase of several closely related items within the seller's line before making their selection. In fact, the seller often encourages such a comparison by the manner in which he presents his sales messages. Consequently, the manufacturer should develop price relationships between the various items in his product line that encourage such a comparison.[37]

---

[34] For an extensive discussion of cash discounts and extended dating, see W. R. Davidson and A. F. Doody, *Retailing Management,* 3d ed. (New York: The Ronald Press Company, 1966), pp. 570–574.

[35] *Ibid.,* p. 512.

[36] The reader is directed to the "Legal Considerations" section of this chapter for a more detailed discussion of the Robinson-Patman Act.

[37] See Alfred R. Oxenfeldt, "Product Line Pricing," *Harvard Business Review,* Vol. 44 (July-August 1966), p. 137.

Other Price Policies

Other pricing policies are important in specific situations. These include price lining, customary pricing, psychological pricing, and promotional pricing.

Price lining is the practice of offering products or services to the market at a limited number of price points. The price-line policy established by Sears in their china department illustrates the concept quite well:

Where a leading department store will stock 250 to 300 china patterns, Sears . . . simply can't afford the duplication. A mere 25 to 30 designs—from Tradition down to plastic at $10.99 a set—must do the job. But the limited selection is carefully planned on a system of price points, or levels, that will cover the whole range and gently, but inexorably, encourage the customer to step up in the spending scale. . . . In the words of Sears' jargon, the customer is moved from "good" to "better" to "best."[38]

When customers expect to pay certain specific prices for products and services, these prices are said to be *customary.* Many convenience goods such as candy, soft drinks, and chewing gum have customary prices, and it is almost impossible for a seller of these products to ignore them. Such a condition is often the result of price lining, since buyers become used to well-accepted price lines.[39]

Customary prices, and price lining to the extent that it creates customary prices, are but two examples of *psychological pricing.* Psychological pricing involves developing prices for products or services that have more "appeal" to customers than do others. Prestige products can often be created by charging very high prices, whereas "bait" pricing involving extremely low prices can be used to lure customers to the point of purchase so that they can later be "traded up" to higher-price merchandise. Odd prices—$.39 instead of $.40 or $9.95 instead of $10.00—also fall into this category; they attempt to create the illusion of low prices. Similarly, "even" prices—$10.00 or $100.00—are often used deliberately to create an image of high quality.

Closely related to psychological pricing is the area of *promotional pricing.* Special sales, premiums, trading stamps, combination offers, free goods, and trade-in allowances are examples.[40] While certain of these efforts may be classified as tools of nonprice competition, to the extent that the net effect is the same as a price reduction, they may well be better classified as promotional pricing.

Resale Price Maintenance ("Fair Trade") Policies

Manufacturers of branded merchandise that is in fair and open competition with other commodities of the same general class produced by others may elect to fix

---

[38] "Why Sears Stays the No. 1 Retailer," *Business Week,* January 20, 1968, p. 66.
[39] Harper, *Price Policy and Procedure,* p. 280.
[40] *Ibid.,* p. 284.

the minimum or actual wholesale and retail price at which distributors sell their products. They are granted this right under provisions of the Miller-Tydings and McGuire acts.

Fair trade may be useful to a producer if his products are clearly differentiated from those of his competitors, demand curves are relatively inelastic, and price maintenance is necessary to maintain the product goodwill and/or the cooperation of resellers. Products that have been and still are marketed to advantage under the provisions of state and federal resale price maintenance acts include certain drugs, cosmetics, and major appliances.

Two major disadvantages are associated with resale price maintenance. First, if the functional discount established to compensate middlemen for their marketing efforts is excessive, it will undoubtedly encourage the more efficient of the discounters to cut price on the item and use it as a promotional item to build in-store traffic. Second, if a manufacturer elects to rely upon such a policy, the burden of enforcing compliance with the policy falls upon him, and this is often impractical if not impossible.[41]

Implementing Pricing Policies

Are the many factors that managers must consider in establishing price policies worth the effort? Are price policies, once established, carried out in practice? The authors of the Brookings study conclude:

Some of the companies successfully carry out their explicit policies. This seems to be true of Johns-Manville, which when it is the price leader and not thwarted by the competition of substitutes, bases price on cost; but, in entering new areas, prices to reach a mass market, as it did with asbestos shingles. And there is little discrepancy between what Swift believes it should do and what it does in the purchasing and pricing of its sensitive product.[42]

However, the study indicates that other, equally large, economically strong companies have not met with the same degree of success in implementing their stated price policies. For example:

. . . Through the years, General Motors has developed an elaborate technique for handling costs, which sometimes has been presented as its basic pricing guide. Yet, the selection of the price, as an examination of the company's earnings statements appears to demonstrate, must deviate by a wide margin from the level that would result from the use of the Donaldson Brown variant of standard cost pricing. . . .

---

[41] For further discussion of the advantages and disadvantages of fair trading as well as its current legal status see T. N. Beckman and W. R. Davidson, *Marketing*, 8th ed. (New York: The Ronald Press Company, 1967) pp. 519–524; Harper, *Price Policy and Procedure*, pp. 261–268; Louis W. Stern, "Economic Factors Influencing Manufacturer's Decisions Concerning Price Maintenance," *Journal of Retailing*, Vol. 41 (Spring 1965), pp. 30–37 ff.

[42] Kaplan, Dirlam, and Lanzillotti, *Pricing in Big Business*, p. 278.

International Harvester, by its own account, has been unable to price as it would like, in an industry in which its sales of specific pieces of farm equipment are often smaller than those of a close competitor.[43]

From such highly respected yet limited evidence, one must conclude that for the most part price policies or guidelines are exactly that, only guidelines. The manager's time is not wasted, however, in carefully preparing a set of price policies, even if they are not followed precisely.

DEVELOPING PRICING PROCEDURES

Even though specific pricing objectives have been established and a body of price policies has been formulated to guide subordinates in attaining these objectives, the marketing manager has not completed his pricing responsibilities. He still must become involved in overseeing the development of pricing procedures capable of establishing specific unit prices that attain these objectives and that are consistent with price policies. These pricing procedures are primarily demand-oriented or cost-oriented.

Demand-oriented Pricing

One of the interesting outcomes of consumer attitude formation is the attitude towards certain levels of price. Chester Wasson attributes "quantum effects" to these attitudes. A given product may not move at $1.05, but a package containing only four-fifths as much, clearly labeled as to quantity, will readily sell at $.98. One dollar is a quantum point as far as customers are concerned.[44]

As pointed out in previous chapters, customers sometimes use price as an indicator of quality. In other words, studies have shown "that demand curves may not invariably be negatively sloped, that price itself may have more than one meaning to the consumer, and that a higher price may sometimes increase, rather than decrease, readiness to buy."[45]

The types of products that can best be priced on the basis of what the market will bear are those that are difficult to judge on bases other than price. Scotch whiskey might be an example. Most consumers cannot distinguish inexpensive and expensive Scotch if all identifying marks have been removed. Johnnie Walker Black Label has been advertised with the phrase: "At $9.40 it's expensive." The same condition exists for many other products.

The goal of demand-oriented analysis is to determine the market's evaluation of product value. Since such a value can only be approximated, the result of such analysis is usually a range of prices acceptable to the market. The top of this

[43] *Ibid.*, pp. 277–278.

[44] S. H. Britt, *Consumer Behavior and the Behavioral Sciences* (New York: John Wiley & Sons, Inc., 1966), p. 402.

[45] Harold J. Leavitt, "A Note on Some Experimental Findings About the Meaning of Price," *Journal of Business*, Vol. 27 (July 1954), p. 210.

range represents the demand "ceiling." The "floor" must be determined through cost analysis.

Cost-oriented Pricing

Many firms set their prices solely on the basis of the cost of manufacturing or, in the case of middlemen, the cost of acquisition. The procedure seems to have found favor because it is simplistic and easily administered. A common example of cost-related pricing is markup or cost-plus pricing, which involves compiling known or projected costs and adding a percentage to direct and indirect costs for the profit factor. The construction contractor who estimates his actual costs of performing a particular job and then adds 15 percent to cover his overhead and perhaps another 10 percent for his profit is using cost-plus pricing.

Similar practices are often relied upon by manufacturers, and they are the rule rather than the exception in almost all forms of wholesaling and retailing. For example, if a retailer purchased from a wholesaler for $5 an item that he and his competitors typically mark up 33⅓ percent on retail, he would set the selling price at $7.50.[46] Thus, he would realize a $2.50 gross margin of profit on the item at the time of sale.

Equity pricing is a slight modification of the cost-plus method. The only procedural difference is that a rate-of-return-on-investment goal is calculated, which then becomes the determinant of the markup to be added to costs. While cost-plus and return-on-investment pricing vary somewhat in procedure, their goal is the same: each seeks to guarantee some predetermined margin of profit on every unit sold.

Cost-based pricing is more complicated than it appears. One difficulty is determining the type and amount of the costs to be included in the base figures. For example, are overhead costs allocated to each product on the basis of standard volumes, or are estimates of future costs or historical costs used? Are research and development costs included? In addition, each of the various classes of costs may change in a different way as the level of output changes. These problems must be carefully analyzed and resolved to insure that the margins established are, in fact, profitable.[47]

Cost-oriented pricing tends to ignore the demand side of the pricing problem. This outlook is typified by the price setter who arbitrarily establishes a markup percentage that he feels is "appropriate." Such practices, focusing exclusively on internal considerations, are just as limited as the obverse, where the

---

[46] The markup percentage may be given as a percent of the retail selling price or of the dollars of cost. The 33⅓ percent markup on retail is the equivalent of a 50 percent markup on cost; that is, $2.50 is 50 percent of the cost price of $5.00. For a detailed discussion of retail pricing practices see Davidson and Doody, *Retailing Management*, pp. 451–497.

[47] This does not mean that the margin on every product in the line must be "profitable." Competitive conditions and promotional considerations may limit this possibility. In the short run, it may even be necessary for the firm to establish a price that fails to cover "full costs."

Figure 12-6   Modified break-even analysis.

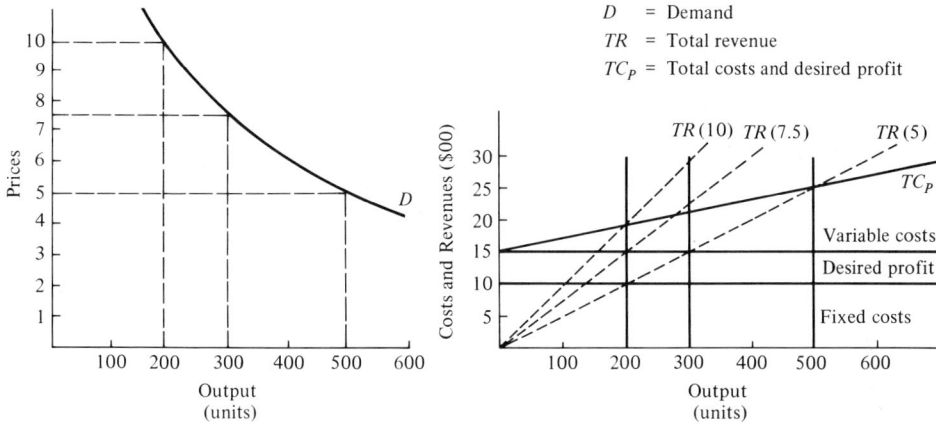

price setter lets the market set the price regardless of costs. The most desirable approach examines the interaction between price and both demand and cost.

Break-even Analysis

Break-even analysis permits an examination of the relationships between fixed costs, variable costs, volume, and price. While far from being an optimizing price-setting technique, it is a useful managerial tool.

Figure 12-6 illustrates how a modified form of break-even analysis can be employed in the examination of several alternative prices. In this example the price setter estimates that if he prices the product at $10, approximately 200 units can be sold. Similarly, at prices of $7.50 and $5 he can expect to sell 300 and 500 units, respectively. Total fixed costs over the relevant range of output are estimated to be $1,000, while variable costs have been estimated at $2 per unit. The firm has established a policy of pricing to obtain a predetermined target rate of return on investment, which, for this product, has been translated into a desired profit margin of $500.

The quantity of product that must be sold to cover total costs and realize the target margin of profit can be determined by setting total revenue equal to total costs plus the desired level of profit. That is:

$$TR = TC + Pr,$$

where TR = total revenue—price times quantity $(P \cdot Q)$,
TC = total costs—fixed costs plus variable costs per unit
times the number of units sold $(FC + VC \cdot Q)$,
Pr = desired profit margin in dollars.

Extending this formula to permit determination of the number of units that must be sold, we have

$$P \cdot Q = FC + (VC \cdot Q) + Pr$$

or

$$Q = \frac{FC + Pr}{P - VC}.$$

This relationship is illustrated graphically in Figure 12-6.[48]

The quantities that must be sold at each of the three alternative prices in order to achieve the target return are 187.5 units at $10, 272.7 units at $7.50, and 500 units at $5. Thus, the target return on investment for this product can be attained by selecting any of the three prices. However, as demonstrated in Table 12-1, the price generating the greatest profit is $7.50.[49]

Table 12-1   Profitability Analysis

Price	Quantity	Total Revenue	Total Cost	Profit	Target Profit	Profits in Excess of Target
$10.00	200	$2,000	$1,400	$600	$500	$100
$7.50	300	$2,250	$1,600	$650	$500	$150
$5.00	500	$2,500	$2,000	$500	$500	0

Integrated Pricing Procedures: An Example[50]

The hypothetical firm in this example makes small hand tools, which are sold through hardware retailers as well as other outlets. The tools are considered as one product line. The total cost for each item was calculated by allowing administrative, research and development, and sales expense to be allocated to product-adjusted costs on a proportional basis and by allowing engineering expense to be allocated to the products that actually required the effort. These costs are shown in Table 12-2.

The company follows a policy of attempting to obtain 30 percent return on average invested capital on an annual basis. The total net investment is $3,000,000, which indicates a goal of $900,000 before taxes. This represents a markup of about 41 percent on cost. When the markup is applied, the prices in Table 12-3 result.

---

[48] Linear cost functions have been assumed in this example for simplicity. However, this is not a requirement for conducting such an analysis. Nonlinear variable costs can be portrayed by an appropriate curved line, whereas fixed costs that change significantly at certain levels of output can be illustrated by means of a step function.

[49] While the price of $7.50 is the best among the three prices under analysis, it may not be the *best* price from among the full range of alternative prices. Further analysis would be required to make such a determination.

[50] This example is adapted from and based largely upon material contained in William J. Riley, "Financial Responsibility and Sales Prices," *Management Accounting*, Vol. 49 (September 1967), pp. 57–62.

Table 12-2   Hardware Tools, Total Cost Calculations, Year 19XX

Description	Pliers	Hammers	Planes	Saws	Hand Drills
Forecasted unit sales (units)	200,000	150,000	75,000	60,000	80,000
Material	$ 24,000	$ 15,000	$ 29,250	$ 54,600	$ 48,000
Direct labor	36,000	18,000	270,000	324,000	230,400
Indirect expenses	70,574	66,287	287,808	287,170	167,161
Subtotal	$130,754	$ 99,287	$587,058	$665,770	$445,561
Selling & administrative	15,900	13,000	76,100	86,500	58,500
Engineering	1,000	800	19,700	25,300	3,200
Total cost	$147,474	$113,087	$682,858	$777,570	$507,261
Unit cost	$ .74	$ .75	$ 9.11	$ 12.96	$ 6.34

Table 12-3   Results of Price Markup

Product	Unit Cost (Including A.S.&E.*)	Profit	Selling Price
Pliers	$ .74	$ .30	$ 1.04
Hammers	.75	.31	1.06
Planes	9.11	3.74	12.85
Saws	12.96	5.31	18.27
Hand Drills	6.34	2.60	8.94

* Administrative, selling, and engineering expenses.

Management compared these proposed selling prices with their current prices. Economic conditions indicated that a 3 percent increase in costs was realistic in view of the level of inflation. In addition, it was felt that demand for several of the products had historically been quite stable and that total sales would be affected only slightly, if at all, by moderate price increases. This analysis indicated that a flexible pricing policy should be established, and the prices for each item were established as shown in Table 12-4.

The following decisions were made:

Pliers

Price to be increased from $.95 to $1.00.
Selling effort to be increased.
Volume to be increased to 220,000 units.

Table 12-4   Economic Analysis of Hardware Tools

Product	Current Selling Price	Proposed Selling Price	Comments
Pliers	$ .95	$ 1.04	Steady market, not significantly influenced by moderate price fluctuations, sales efforts minimum. Generally no special price considerations required. Product quality about equal to competing items. Cost-reduction possibility—not significant.
Hammers	.60	1.06	Same as for pliers except quality slightly below competing products due to the tendency of handles to break because of lower-grade hardwood utilization. Cost-reduction possibility—none.
Planes	13.80	12.85	Widely fluctuating market, difficult to sell high-quality product. Current engineering efforts should increase precision of product. Superior to other items on the market. Cost-reduction possibility—about $.60 each with introduction of new sharpening process.
Saws	15.00	18.27	Increasing market, sales manager feels forecast volume conservative, very high-quality superior product. Cost reductions possible if material bought in larger quantities, but different processing required for better finish on blades.
Hand drills	8.75	8.94	Very competitive market, sensitive to price fluctuations. Sales efforts substantial to maintain volume. Price considerations sometimes given to large retailers. Raw-material costs high and cost reductions impossible.

Hammers

No price change.

Selling effort to be reduced.

It represents the lowest volume of contribution and is least influenced by technological advances, and so on.

Volume is to remain unchanged.

Planes

Price to be slightly decreased from $13.80 to $13.50 each.

National advertising program to be undertaken at an estimated cost of $30,000.

Volume expected to increase in two years but sales budget for 19XX to be held at 75,000 units.

Saws

Prices to be increased by $1.00 each.

Production manager to decrease costs by 50 cents each in material and/or direct labor.

Sales forecast increased to 65,000 units.

Study authorized to examine return from proposed new processing equipment.

Hand drills

It would be best if prices were unaltered. However, since a 19-cents-per-unit deficit has been detected, a price of $8.90 is recommended.

After reviewing the revised price structure and predicted volumes and cost changes, the treasurer recalculated the operating profit for year 19XX. The profit forecast by item is contained in Table 12-5.

This case is oversimplified for the purpose of illustration; however, it demonstrates how costs and prices are related. The company's operating profit is forecast to be $788,800, or $111,200 short of the $900,000 targeted return on equity. It reaffirms that no magic pricing formula exists.

As product lines become more complex and competitive market relationships increase, this type of analysis becomes substantially more complicated but increasingly more important.

LEGAL CONSIDERATIONS

The pricing practices of firms engaged in interstate commerce are closely regulated by federal law. The most important of the several pieces of legislation that affect price-setting is the Robinson-Patman Act.

Price Discrimination

The Robinson-Patman Act "prohibits discriminations in price between different purchasers of commodities of like grade and quality, where any of the purchases involved are in interstate commerce, and where the effect may be substantially to lessen competition or to tend to create a monopoly in any line of commerce, or to injure, destroy, or prevent competition with any person who either grants or knowingly receives the benefit of such discrimination, or with customers of either of them."[51] Thus, it makes unlawful any price discrimination between different purchasers of commodities of like grade and quality[52] that may *tend* to injure competition.

Once the government has proved that discriminatory prices have been quoted, the firm still may be able to justify its actions. Such a justification must

[51] Beckman and Davidson, *Marketing,* p. 78.

[52] Among the many decisions that reflect the court's thinking on what constitutes "like grade and quality," see *U.S.* v. *Borden Co.,* 383 U.S. 637 (1966); *Anheuser-Busch, Inc.,* 54 FTC 277 (1957); and *Standard Oil of Indiana,* 49 FTC 923 (1953).

Table 12-5   Hardware Tools Budget and Profit Forecast, Year 19XX

	Pliers	Hammers	Planes	Saws	Hand drills	Total
Units	220,000	150,000	75,000	65,000	75,000	
Unit sales price	$1.00	$.60	$13.50	$16.00	$8.90	
	$220,000	$ 90,000	$1,002,500	$1,040,000	$667,500	$3,020,000
Cost						
Material	26,400	15,000	29,250	59,150	45,000	174,800
Labor	39,600	18,000	270,000	351,000	211,500	890,100
Cost reductions	0	0	0	(32,500)	0	(32,500)
Factory burden	39,600	18,000	270,000	318,500	211,500	857,600
Unabsorbed burden[a]						11,200
Mfg. cost	105,600	51,000	569,250	696,150	468,000	1,901,200
Selling, admin. & eng.	18,000	9,000	96,000	118,000	89,000	330,000
Total cost	123,600	60,000	665,250	814,150	557,000	2,231,200
Operating profit	$ 96,400	$ 30,000	$ 337,250	$225,850	$110,500	$ 788,800
Percent to sales	43.8%	33.3%	33.6%	21.7%	16.6%	26.1%

[a] Fifty percent of factory burden considered variable.

be based upon differences in its costs of serving different customers or upon meeting prices established by competitors.[53]

COST DEFENSE. The firm can use a "cost defense" if it can prove that the lower price is the result of differences in the costs of serving the various buyers. If the defendant can show that the price differences do not exceed the cost differences, the discriminatory prices are legal regardless of their effect on competition. However, since the FTC and the courts have been reluctant to accept a firm's accounting data to substantiate such a contention, this defense has seldom been used successfully.

GOOD-FAITH DEFENSE. The "good-faith" defense is a second alternative. If the defendant can show that his price was established in "good faith," to meet the equally low price of a competitor and *not* to undercut it, the discrimination is legal.[54] While this defense is considered "absolute," there are circumstances under which the FTC and courts will not permit it to be used.

1. A company generally is permitted to grant discriminatory prices in good faith only to retain old customers, not to acquire new ones.
2. The good-faith defense is applicable only at the primary level of distribution; that is, a seller cannot quote a lower price to a customer in order to help that customer better meet his own competition.
3. A seller cannot grant a discriminatory price in good faith when he knows that the price he is meeting is unlawful.

Discounts and Allowances

The Robinson-Patman Act also restricts the granting of discounts and allowances. It specifies that any advertising allowances or other promotional assistance or services that a seller offers to one buyer must be made available to all other purchasers on "proportionally equal" terms. The only qualification to this provision of the act is that competition must in fact exist between the purchasers. In the same fashion, the Robinson-Patman Act applies to functional discounts only when there is competition among resellers receiving the discounts. When such is the case, functional discounts must be made available equally to all such resellers.

While the issue of quantity discounts is often quite cloudy, one fact is clear: such discounts must reflect cost savings in deliveries made to one place at one time. As long as noncumulative quantity discounts bear such a relationship, they are apparently permissible. On the other hand, cumulative quantity discounts are, at best, *highly* suspect. Further, the degree to which such discounts are suspect

---

[53] The following discussion of the "cost" and "good faith" defenses is based upon material contained in F. D. Sturdivant, L. W. Stern, J. R. Grabner, Jr., et al., *Managerial Analysis in Marketing* (Glenview, Ill.: Scott, Foresman and Company, 1970), pp. 133–134.

[54] *Standard Oil of Ind.* v. *FTC*, 340 U.S. 231 (1951).

increases in relation to the extent to which large companies gain an advantage in purchase price over small ones.[55]

The Robinson-Patman Act also prohibits paying brokerage fees to a brokerage firm that is not independent of both the buyer and the seller.

Delivered Pricing

The Supreme Court has held that delivered pricing systems that result in price matching by all competitors is an unfair method of competition.[56] However, if the delivered pricing system does not involve collusion among competitors and certain other conditions exist, such pricing may be legal. The qualifying conditions are:

1. The seller is willing to sell on an f.o.b. basis when a purchaser so requests.
2. The seller is maintaining a uniform delivered price at all points of delivery —as when he charges nationwide uniform delivered prices.
3. The seller is absorbing freight costs, or some portion of them, in order to meet competition.
4. The buyers and/or their customers are noncompetitive.[57]

SUMMARY

Pricing is one of the most complex aspects of marketing management. A multi-faceted activity, it begins with the establishment of specific, measurable *pricing objectives* that are consistent with, and lead to the attainment of, corporate and marketing objectives. Some of the more common pricing objectives include pricing to achieve a target return on investment, stabilizing prices and margins, achieving some specified market share, meeting or beating competitive prices, and accomplishing some predetermined degree of product differentiation.

The second facet of pricing involves the development of *price policies*. These policies serve as general principles or rules that the firm endeavors to follow in making everyday pricing decisions. The policies can be established only after the pricing objective(s) have been clearly specified. Price levels, competitive pricing considerations, price flexibility, geographic price differentials, discount structures, and product-line pricing are a few of the more important decision areas in which clear guidelines need to be formulated.

It is also necessary to develop *pricing procedures* that establish specific unit prices. While these techniques are typically either demand- or cost-oriented, the best pricing procedure carefully considers both factors.

It is usually desirable to *pretest* prices prior to full-scale implementation. One procedure relies on test markets or simulation to develop probable customer reaction to alternative prices and then utilizes a modified form of break-

[55] See *FTC* v. *Morton Salt Co.*, 334 U.S. 37 (1948).
[56] *FTC* v. *Cement Institute*, 333 U.S. 683 (1948).
[57] Beckman and Davidson, *Marketing*, p. 519.

even analysis to assess the impact of the various prices on corporate profitability. Pretesting techniques are discussed in Chapters 18 and 19.

Finally, it is advantageous to *continuously monitor* the effectiveness of price policies and practices in achieving stated pricing objectives. Comparing actual performance with desired performance permits periodic adjustment in pricing practices to better attain marketing and corporate objectives. These procedures are discussed in Chapter 21.

QUESTIONS FOR REVIEW AND DISCUSSION

1. Compare and contrast the principal pricing goals of Standard Oil (Ind.), Esso, and Gulf Oil (see Figure 12-4). Is there a significant difference between their stated goals, and if so, why?
2. Compare and contrast the stated target rate-of-return-on-investment goals established by General Motors and U.S. Steel (see Figure 12-4). What factors might contribute to such a substantial difference?
3. Distinguish between pricing objectives, pricing policies, and pricing procedures.
4. It has been stated that most firms tend to rely on cost-plus pricing procedures. What factors contribute to the popularity of this approach? What are some of the more pronounced limitations of this technique?
5. Would you classify the pricing procedure employed by the hardware manufacturer in the text example as being primarily cost-oriented or demand-oriented? Why?
6. Figure 12-6 indicates that a price of $6 would generate demand for 400 units. From the standpoint of profitability would a price of $6 be more desirable than one of $7.50? Why?
7. "I don't understand all the confusion surrounding the best way of setting pricing objectives and policies or developing pricing procedures. The firm's overriding goal is to maximize profits, and setting price at a point where marginal revenue is equal to marginal cost insures that this objective will be met." Discuss.

Chapter 13   Channel Programs

Channels of distribution are quietly but perceptibly under-going a series of important changes. The marketing manager, if he is to develop viable channel relationships in the decade of the seventies, must understand the rationale of channel design and the nature of changing channel structures as well as the factors in the marketplace giving rise to the need for such change.

This chapter briefly examines the nature of channel management; it then surveys strategic changes in channel structures, including the increasing importance of vertical marketing systems, intertype competition, the polarization of retail trade, and the emergence of the "free-form" corporation. Next, channel operations are examined in a systematic fashion consistent with these strategic considerations. This systematic analysis involves establishing channel objectives, developing a channel strategy, designing alternative channel configurations, evaluating and choosing among these alternative channel structures, and pretesting, implementing, and controlling the chosen channel or channels.

THE NATURE OF CHANNEL MANAGEMENT

A channel of distribution is the structure of intracompany organization units and extracompany agents and dealers, wholesale and retail, through which a commodity, product, or service is marketed.[1] The channel includes a firm's internal

[1] *Marketing Definitions: A Glossary of Marketing Terms,* Compiled by the Committee on Definitions of the American Marketing Association, Ralph S. Alexander, Chairman (Chicago: American Marketing Association, 1960), p. 10.

marketing organization units as well as the outside business units it uses to serve its target market segments. Moreover, the channel does not end at its juncture with the target market segments, but *includes* them.

The work of these institutions and agencies can perhaps best be explained by examining the various flows they supervise. Goods originate with producers of raw materials and move through a series of processors and middlemen into the hands of ultimate consumers. However, these institutions are concerned with more than the physical movement of goods. They also administer the passage of the rights and responsibilities of ownership as well as the many activities that facilitate the passage of title to the goods they handle.

Channel Structure

Traditional marketing channels are loosely structured networks of vertically aligned firms. The structuring of these networks depends largely upon the nature of the product and the target market the firm is seeking to reach. A few of the numerous channel structures that might be relied upon to effectively distribute goods to ultimate consumers and industrial end-users are illustrated in Figure 13-1.

The various configurations illustrated in Figure 13-1 may help us visualize some of the many ways in which channels might be structured. However, the diagram is deceiving in two respects. First, it does not accurately indicate the many existing forms of each of the various middlemen. For example, as illustrated in Figure 13-2, there are numerous variations in the type and number of organizations at the wholesale level alone. The complexity of channel design is further magnified when the vast number of various types of retail organizations are also taken into consideration. The ways in which these middlemen might be combined to form channels is almost innumerable.

The second area of possible misunderstanding also concerns the number and type of various middlemen. However, in this instance it involves the recognition that not all classes of middlemen are available in every geographic area or line of trade. That is, all classes of wholesalers are not usually available in every trading area to distribute each product line. Thus: "In a product line such as fashion apparel, a garment maker may have an extremely limited choice of types of middlemen: the selling agent, the broker, the direct-buying retailer, or the chain store buying office."[2]

There is no one "best" channel configuration for all firms producing similar classes of products, even though they may be serving the same end-users. Each firm's channel structure must be developed within the framework of the firm's corporate and marketing objectives, its management philosophy, and available resources. Multiple channels of distribution often must be developed, especially when the firm has established multiple target market segments. For example, a

---

[2] Phillip McVey, "Are Channels of Distribution What the Textbooks Say?" *Journal of Marketing*, Vol. 24 (January 1960), p. 62.

Figure 13-1 Alternative channels of distribution.

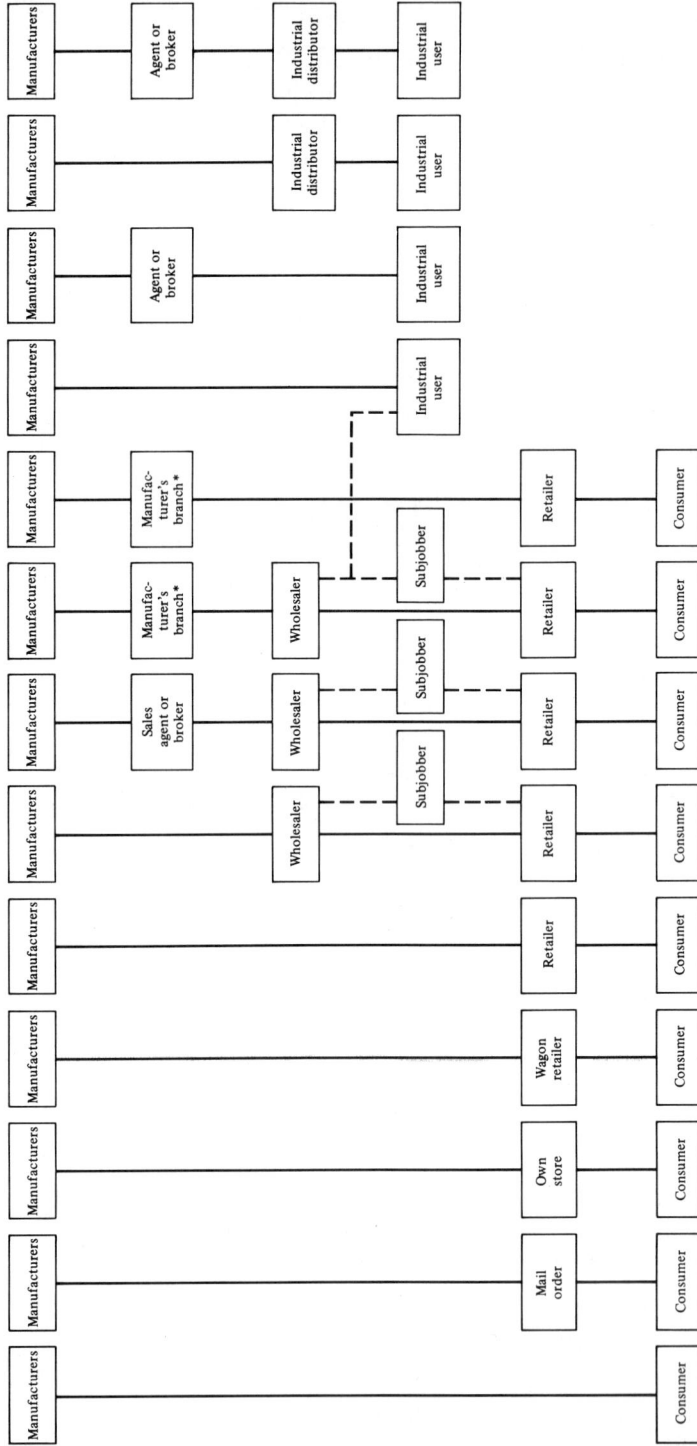

*A manufacturer's branch is owned by the manufacturer.

SOURCE: Adapted from John R. Bromell, *Primary Channels of Distribution for Manufacturers*, Business Information Source, U.S. Department of Commerce (July 1950), p. 3.

284

Figure 13-2   The structure of wholesaling.

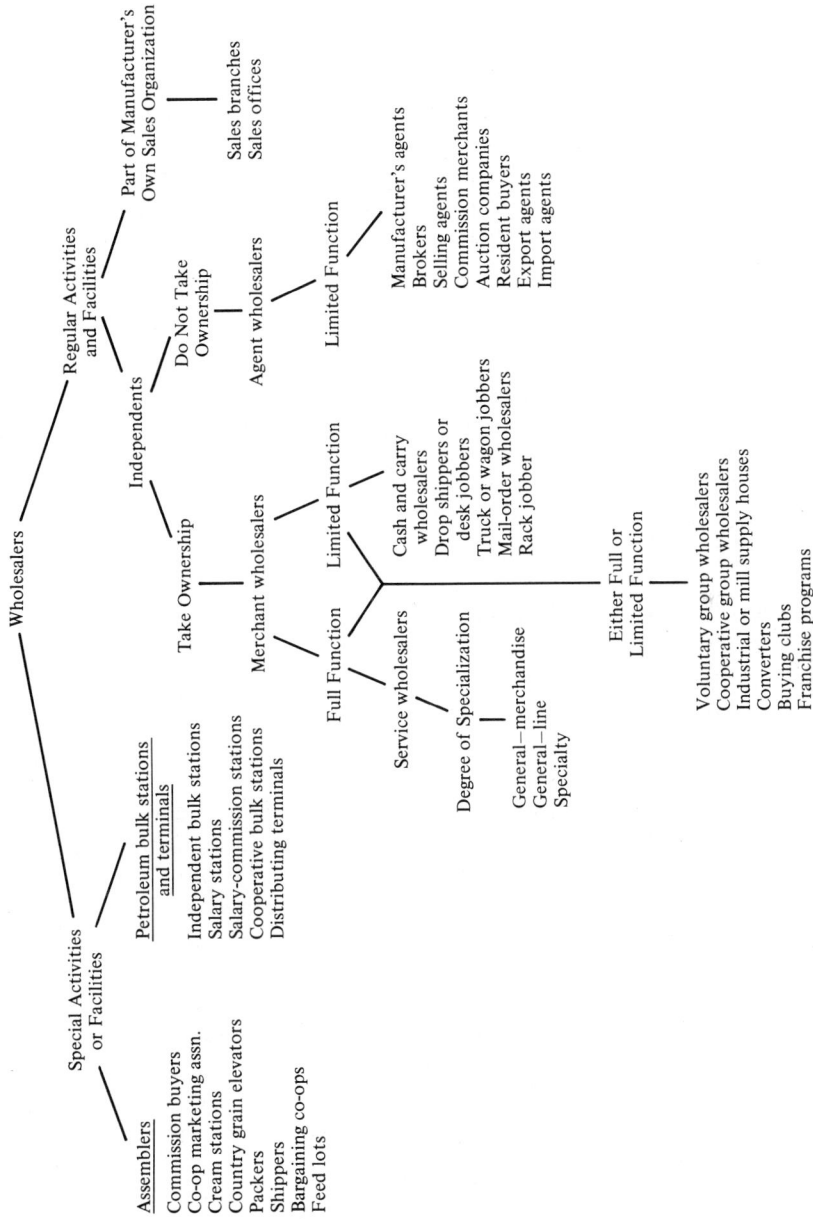

Wholesalers

Special Activities or Facilities

Assemblers
Commission buyers
Co-op marketing assn.
Cream stations
Country grain elevators
Packers
Shippers
Bargaining co-ops
Feed lots

Petroleum bulk stations and terminals
Independent bulk stations
Salary stations
Salary-commission stations
Cooperative bulk stations
Distributing terminals

Regular Activities and Facilities

Independents

Take Ownership

Merchant wholesalers

Full Function

Service wholesalers

Degree of Specialization
General—merchandise
General—line
Specialty

Limited Function
Cash and carry wholesalers
Drop shippers or desk jobbers
Truck or wagon jobbers
Mail-order wholesalers
Rack jobber

Either Full or Limited Function
Voluntary group wholesalers
Cooperative group wholesalers
Industrial or mill supply houses
Converters
Buying clubs
Franchise programs

Do Not Take Ownership

Agent wholesalers

Limited Function
Manufacturer's agents
Brokers
Selling agents
Commission merchants
Auction companies
Resident buyers
Export agents
Import agents

Part of Manufacturer's Own Sales Organization
Sales branches
Sales offices

285

Figure 13-3   Channel geometry.

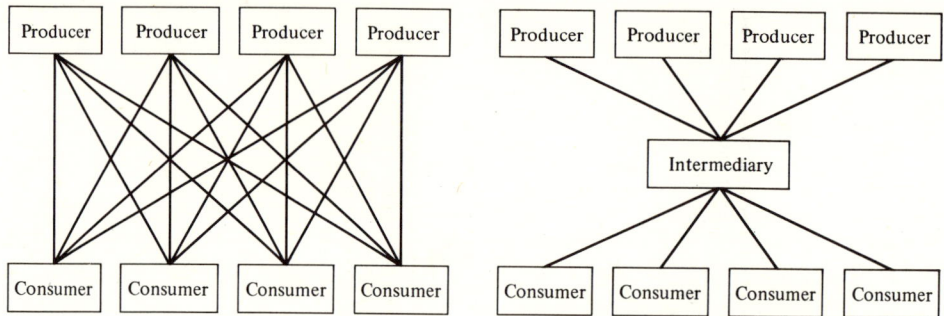

tire manufacturer may sell to wholesalers as well as directly to large retail chains and through his own retail stores.

Channel Geometry

The raison d'être of alternative channel configuration can perhaps best be seen from a geometric perspective. Figure 13-3 illustrates two alternative approaches to structuring product flow from the point of production to that of consumption. The diagram on the left represents "direct" distribution; that on the right demonstrates how an intermediary might be positioned in the channel in order to effect "indirect" distribution.

The geometry of these diagrams clearly illustrates two important structural factors that otherwise might be difficult to fully describe: the principle of minimum total transactions and the concept of sorting. Direct distribution requires 16 transactions to complete the exchange activity between four producers and four ultimate consumers. However, by the employment of an intermediary—perhaps a retailer—the total number of transactions is reduced to eight. In addition, since distribution costs are relatively fixed per transaction, the use of middlemen also *tends* to reduce distribution costs for the channel as a whole.[3]

The concept of sorting was advanced by Alderson as the most essential role of marketing intermediaries.[4] In his treatment, middlemen serve to reconcile a relatively narrow product offering from each of several sources of supply into a wide assortment at the point of final sale. That is, consumer demand is usually for a different, much broader assortment of goods than is usually made available

---

[3] While it is commonly accepted that direct distribution is the most costly form of distribution, this should not be construed as meaning that distribution costs will automatically decline in relation to the number of intermediaries or even that the use of an intermediary will *always* result in lower total distribution costs. A detailed cost/benefit analysis should always be conducted in the course of developing and choosing among alternative channel structures.

[4] Wroe Alderson, *Marketing Behavior and Executive Action* (Homewood, Ill.: Richard D. Irwin, Inc., 1957), pp. 195–227.

by any one producer. In addition, the ultimate consumer typically wishes to buy this broader assortment of products in small quantities. Thus, the intermediary seeks to develop an assortment of merchandise that satisfies the diverse needs of the customers he serves and sells it in the quantities they demand.

THE CHANGING STRUCTURE OF DISTRIBUTION

This section describes some of the limitations that traditional approaches to channel management face in today's dynamic business environment and then examines recent trends and changes designed to overcome these shortcomings.

Conventional Channels

Following the Second World War, the structure of distribution in the American economy was highly stable and relatively atomistic. Small and medium-sized firms dominated most lines of trade, and traditional channel linkages (such as those illustrated in Figure 13-1) were the dominant means of distribution and were expected to perform a conventionally defined set of marketing functions. Small retailers, for example, typically price-marked merchandise, maintained unit control records, reordered goods, and initiated local promotional campaigns.

While these linkages seemed appropriate when established, many were actually or potentially a source of diseconomies. The need for each member of the channel to establish and maintain a field sales force to repeatedly call on the same accounts resulted in high selling costs. The persistence of many small-scale units resulted in the sacrifice of scale economies. In addition, the autonomy of the operating units frequently resulted in duplicative programming, as when manufacturers, wholesalers and retailers each price-marked merchandise. Finally, and perhaps most importantly, the rigidity characteristic of such channels did not permit economies to be effected even when recognized.

Vertical Marketing Systems[5]

During the last two decades significant changes have occurred in the structure of distribution. New modes of distribution appeared, including the discount department store, the rack jobber, the super drugstore, and the cash-and-carry building-supply wholesaler. Table 13-1 illustrates the rates of growth of certain selected retail establishments. Note especially the increase in sales realized by discount department stores vis-à-vis those of conventional department stores.

Such vertical marketing systems, by contrast with conventional channels of distribution, consist of networks of horizontally coordinated and vertically

---

[5] This discussion of vertical marketing systems is based in large part on material developed by Alton F. Doody of The Ohio State University, William R. Davidson, Chairman, Management Horizons, Inc., and Bert C. McCammon, Jr., Director, Center for Advanced Studies in Distribution, an affiliate of Management Horizons, Inc.

Table 13-1   Annual Sales of Selected Types of Retail Stores in the United States for 1962, 1964, 1966, and 1968

Annual Sales (in billions of dollars)

Type of Store	1962	1964	1966	1968	Percent Change (1962–1968)
Supermarkets	$39.1	$ 43.0	$ 48.4	$ 53.8	37.6%
Conventional department stores (adjusted sales figure)	13.1	14.3	16.3	15.3	16.8
Drug stores	7.7	7.8	9.8	11.5	49.4
Women's apparel stores	5.5	5.2	7.2	7.4	34.5
Discount department stores	6.9	10.8	15.0	19.4	181.2
Furniture stores	5.1	7.6	6.9	7.7	50.9
Variety stores	4.4	4.3	4.3	4.9	11.4
Appliance, radio, and television dealers	3.8	4.6	5.0	5.2	36.8
Men's and boys' clothing dealers	2.7	3.0	3.5	4.4	62.9
Hardware stores	2.7	2.8	3.0	3.2	18.5
Automotive supply stores	2.6	2.9	3.4	4.6	76.9
Shoe stores	2.6	2.7	2.8	3.2	23.1
Total	$96.2	$109.0	$125.6	$140.6	46.2%

SOURCE: *The True Look of the Discount Industry (1963–1969 Editions),* Super Market Publishing Company, Inc., New York, and authors' calculations.

aligned establishments managed as a total system.[6] They no longer require each channel member to perform an historical set of marketing functions but rely upon the concept of functional shiftability to improve total system performance. That is, establishments of each level are reprogrammed so that marketing functions within the system are performed at the most advantageous level or position.[7] The salient characteristic of these forms of distribution networks (Figure 13-4) are summarized in Figure 13-5.

This activity led to the development of three major types of vertically aligned networks—corporate, contractual, and administered systems.

CORPORATE SYSTEMS. The vertically integrated corporate distribution system has an extended history. Singer, for example, operated company-owned warehouses and stores in the 1870s. However, vertically integrated corporations did not become a decisive factor in distribution until the mid-1950s. Since that

[6] Bert C. McCammon, Jr., Albert D. Bates, and Joseph P. Guiltinan, "Alternative Models for Programming Vertical Marketing Networks," a paper presented at the 1968 Fall Conference of the American Marketing Association, Denver, August 30, 1968, p. 25.

[7] William R. Davidson, "Changes in Distributive Institutions," *Journal of Marketing,* Vol. 34 (January 1970), p. 7.

Figure 13-4   The concept of functional shiftability.

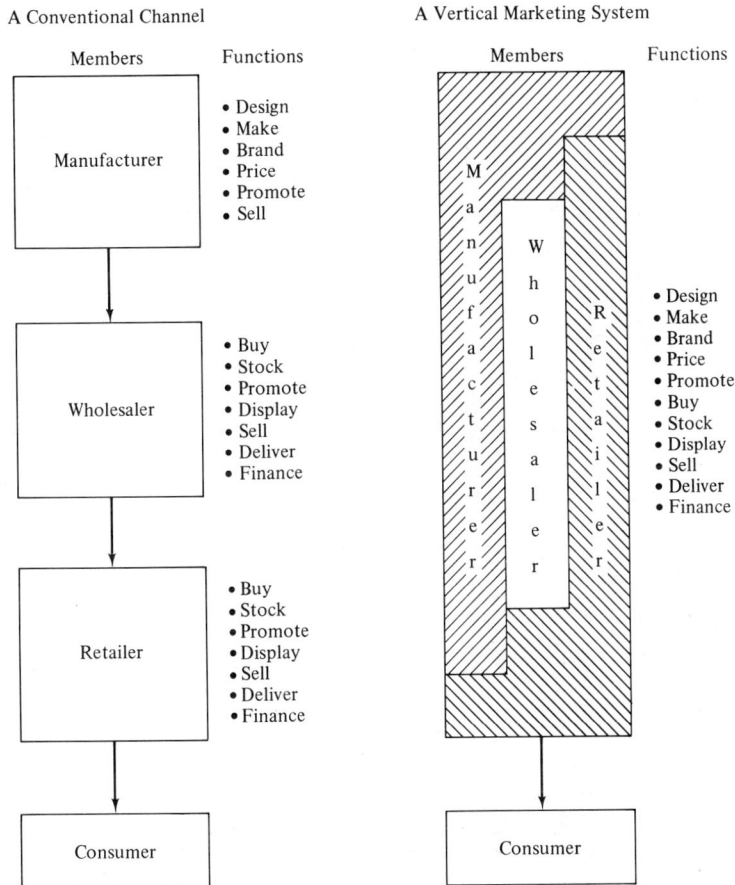

A Conventional Channel

A Vertical Marketing System

Members   Functions

Members   Functions

Manufacturer

- Design
- Make
- Brand
- Price
- Promote
- Sell

Manufacturer

Wholesaler

Retailer

- Design
- Make
- Brand
- Price
- Promote
- Buy
- Stock
- Display
- Sell
- Deliver
- Finance

Wholesaler

- Buy
- Stock
- Promote
- Display
- Sell
- Deliver
- Finance

Retailer

- Buy
- Stock
- Promote
- Display
- Sell
- Deliver
- Finance

Consumer

Consumer

time they have experienced rapid growth, and today many distribution networks are partially or fully integrated corporate complexes.

Sherwin-Williams, for instance, now operates over 2,000 retail outlets, while Hart Schaffner & Marx owns more than 200 stores. In addition, large food chains now obtain 15 to 20 percent of their requirements from company-owned manufacturing and processing facilities. Sears reportedly obtains 50 percent of its throughput from manufacturing facilities in which it has an equity interest, and Holiday Inns is rapidly evolving into a self-supply network that includes a carpet mill, a furniture manufacturing plant, and numerous captive redistribution facilities. In short, these and similar organizations are massive, vertically integrated corporate systems.

CONTRACTUAL SYSTEMS. The three principal versions of contractual systems are wholesaler-sponsored voluntary groups, retailer-owned cooperatives, and

Figure 13-5   Salient characteristics of competing distribution networks.

Network Characteristics	Type of Network	
	Conventional Marketing Channel	Vertical Marketing System
Composition of network	Network composed of isolated and autonomous units, each of which performs a conventionally defined set of marketing functions. Coordination primarily achieved through bargaining and negotiation.	Network composed of interconnected units each of which performs the most desirable combination of marketing functions. Coordination achieved through the use of detailed plans and comprehensive programs.
Economic capabilities of member units	Operating units frequently unable to achieve systemic economies.	Operating units *programmed* to achieve systemic economies.
Organizational stability	Open network with low index of member loyalty and relative ease of entry. Network therefore tends to be unstable.	Open network but entry rigorously controlled by the system's requirements and by market conditions. Membership loyalty assured through the use of ownership or contractual agreements. As a result, network tends to be relatively stable.
Number and composition of decision makers	Large number of strategists supported by a slightly larger number of operating executives.	Limited number of strategists supported by a significantly larger number of staff and operating executives.
Analytical focus of strategic decision makers	Strategists preoccupied with cost, volume, and investment relationships at a *single* stage of the marketing process.	Strategists preoccupied with cost, volume, and investment relationships at *all* stages of the marketing process. Corresponding emphasis on the "total cost" concept accompanied by a continuous search for favorable economic tradeoffs.
Underlying decision-making process	Heavy reliance on judgmental decisions made by generalists.	Heavy reliance on "scientific" decisions made by specialists or committees of specialists.
Institutional loyalties of decision makers	Decision makers committed to traditional forms of distribution.	Decision makers committed to marketing concept and viable institutions.

franchised store programs. Firms operating in these configurations "pool" their resources to achieve operating economies and market impact that are difficult, if not impossible, to achieve through independent action. More specifically, such vertically aligned enterprises contribute to a common advertising fund, adhere to compatible merchandising programs, share computer and warehouse facilities, and combine their purchases to achieve effective buying power.

Voluntary, cooperative, and franchise networks are more formidable today than they were a decade ago. Consider a few dramatic examples:

- In the food field, IGA now operates more stores than A&P, while Super Value outlets generate higher annual sales than Kroger. Southland, a franchising organization founded in the late 1950s, is now the eighth largest food distribution network in the country, largely because of the success of its "7-11" stores.
- In the hardware field, wholesalers affiliated with the Pro, Liberty, and Sentry networks now supply thousands of "independent" stores with supporting services that are comparable, or in some cases superior, to those enjoyed by chain outlets.
- In appliance distribution, MARTA (Metropolitan Appliance Radio Television Association) has a total membership of 250 stores accounting for sales of more than $200,000,000.
- In the furniture industry, Baumritter's vertical marketing program involves hundreds of outlets, while retailers franchised as Ethan Allen "Carriage Houses" often achieve sales per square foot twice the national average.
- Midas, Muffler King, Milex, and AAMCO are only a few of the many networks specializing in the field of automotive repair services.[8]
- In the "away from home" food market, McDonald's, Burger Chef, Kentucky Fried Chicken, and other organizations that were obscure or nonexistent a decade ago now dominate the industry.

ADMINISTERED SYSTEMS. Administered programs affect a particular line of merchandise in a store rather than the store's entire operation. Such programs go beyond traditional store-vendor compacts into joint ventures that involve the development of comprehensive programs for a specified line of merchandise.

Programs of this type have been developed by both manufacturing and wholesaling organizations. Common manufacturer examples are the programs developed and administered by the O.M. Scott & Sons Company in lawn products, by Villager in women's apparel, by Magnavox in the home entertainment field, and by Kraft foods in supermarkets. Within wholesaling, administered systems are found in drug, hardware, sporting goods, and phonograph records as well as many other merchandise classifications.

---

[8] AAMCO expanded from a pilot operation to more than 500 outlets with annual sales substantially in excess of $100 million in only six years.

SIGNIFICANCE. How important are these systems in the American economy at the present time? In the 1960s the market share held by firms operating 10 or more stores soared to 30 percent of total retail volume. And if present trends continue, by 1975 chains with 10 or more units will have twice as large a share of the total retail market as they had as recently as the late 1950s. In addition, stores affiliated with voluntary, cooperative, and franchise networks currently account for 35 to 40 percent of total retail sales. When these figures are combined, it is apparent that roughly two-thirds of total retail sales are generated by outlets affiliated with some type of vertical marketing system.[9] Moreover, these statistics do not take into direct account the impact of administered systems, about which very little is known statistically.

Intertype Competition and the Polarization of Retail Trade

As manufacturers, wholesalers, and retailers seek to satisfy the unique needs of more narrowly defined market segments, they have had to abandon "line of trade" conventions and offer a much wider variety of merchandise. This phenomenon, known as *scrambled merchandising*, is becoming increasingly apparent at all levels in the channel of distribution. For example, it has been estimated that about one-fourth of all retail stores—or as many as 450,000 retail establishments—are involved to some degree in selling tires, batteries, or other automotive parts, supplies, or accessories. In addition, as many as 200,000 outlets are believed to be involved to some degree in marketing housewares.[10] This trend has substantially intensified competition of an intertype character. Thus:

Today, retailers sell wholesale, wholesalers sell retail, hardwares sell soft goods, department stores sell food, food stores sell appliances, they all sell toys and discount stores sell everything. Finished goods often move to the same retailer from wholesalers, distributors, jobbers, assemblers and direct from producers. In some cases, goods by-pass the retailer altogether moving directly to consumers. In short, traditional classifications of middlemen, trade channels, and goods have lost considerable validity.[11]

Another factor of increasing importance is the degree to which retail trade is becoming polarized. At the one extreme is the group of mass merchandisers characterized by the 70,000-square-foot stores of Central Hardware Company of St. Louis, the home-modernization stores of the Wickes Corporation, Lowe's Companies, Inc., and a large-mass appeal drug store such as Super X, a relatively new division of The Kroger Company. Diametrically opposed are the specialized

[9] B. C. McCammon, Jr., A. D. Bates, and J. P. Guiltinan, "Alternative Models for Programming Vertical Networks."

[10] Davidson, "Changes in Distributive Institutions," p. 8.

[11] Donald J. Bowersox, "Changing Channels in the Physical Distribution of Finished Goods," in *Marketing and Economic Development* (Chicago: The American Marketing Association, 1965), p. 711.

boutique-type stores that rely upon a deep assortment of a specialized line, often limited to a concept or a "look". The Villager specialty shops and Ethan Allen stores also illustrate such operations.[12]

The "Free-form" Corporation

Intertype competition, the polarity of retail trade, the impact of vertical marketing systems, and market opportunity have interacted in such a manner as to permit and stimulate the development of free-form corporations. These corporations are willing to go anywhere and do anything in distribution. Consider:

The J.C. Penney Company, Inc., is now an example of a free-form corporation. Ten to fifteen years ago, Penney's was a chain of small town, limited service, general merchandise stores. It has now evolved to an aggressive free-form operation consisting of full-scale urban Penney Department Stores, Penney Auto and Truck Service Centers, Treasure Island Discount Stores, The Thrifty Drug Company Chain, a large catalog sales division, a financial subsidiary for accounts receivable funding, a life insurance marketing program, and European stores through an equity interest in Sarma S.A., a Belgian company with 100 stores and 270 franchised units.[13]

This trend is likely to significantly enlarge concentration ratios at all levels within the channel of distribution. This will affect the options available to the marketing manager in designing channel strategies and programs.

Strategic Implications

The emergence and growth of professionally managed and centrally programmed distribution networks during the past decade represents major *strategic* realignments in the field of distribution. These systems have rapidly and deeply penetrated the core markets of conventionally structured channels of distribution, with the result that individual firms and entire networks are threatened.

Conventional organizations—relying on traditional responses—cannot compete effectively against marketing systems or free-form corporations.[14] Independent motel operators, for example, inevitably experience severe difficulty in nullifying the competitive advantages of the Holiday Inn network. The small, independent appliance dealer recognizes daily his limitations in effectively competing against the Sears organization. Similarly, the independent hardware wholesaler and retailer cannot *tactically* offset the *strategic* maneuvers of integrated networks. In short, the ascendancy of large, strategically potent networks

[12] Davidson, "Changes in Distributive Institutions," *op. cit.*, p. 8.
[13] *Ibid.*, p. 9.
[14] See Frank F. Gilmore, "Strategic Planning's Threat to Small Business," *California Management Review,* Vol. 9 (Winter 1966), pp. 43–50.

has created an environment in which tactics must irretrievably be subordinated to strategy in the structure of distribution.[15]

A SYSTEMATIC APPROACH TO CHANNEL MANAGEMENT

Figure 13-6 summarizes the steps involved in systematically approaching the problem of channel management. As indicated in the schematic, channel decisions are deeply rooted in corporate-level objectives and strategies. Consequently, an analysis of channel operations first requires a careful analysis of each of these factors. This analysis, coupled with a thorough understanding of the nature of the target market segments, leads to the identification of specific channel objectives and a strategy capable of achieving them.

Next, the manager must design, evaluate, and choose among alternative channels in order to develop a product flow consistent with the channel strategy. Though it is not mandatory, the manager is always well advised to pretest the chosen channels and reseller-support programs prior to full-scale implementation. Finally, the effectiveness of the channel programs must be measured and evaluated against channel goals on a continuous basis. Each of these aspects of channel management is analyzed in greater depth in the sections that follow.

Channel Objectives

Channel objectives are inexorably tied to corporate objectives and strategy. In this respect, it might be appropriate to state that the objectives of channel management involve achieving some target rate of return on investment. However, it is difficult for a channel, per se, to earn a return on dollars invested. Such a measure is the result of the firm's total marketing effort—the nature of the product offered for sale, the price charged, and all other aspects of the market offer.

Consequently, it is desirable to develop a more carefully circumscribed set of objectives to guide channel operations. One method involves establishing a share of the market goal to be obtained in each of the firm's several target market segments. The market-share goals should be stated in terms of (1) dollars or units of sales, and (2) the profits that each target is expected to produce. These objectives might be stated in the following manner.

Corporate objective: To achieve an 18 percent after-tax rate of return on net worth.

Marketing objective: To obtain total sales of $10 million and a 5 percent after-tax net profit margin.

Channel objective: To obtain $5 million in sales in the industrial market with a 6 percent realized net profit margin and $5 million in sales in the consumer market with a 4 percent realized net profit margin.

[15] McCammon, Bates, and Guiltinan, "Alternative Models for Programming Vertical Networks," p. 26.

Figure 13-6   A channel planning and control system.

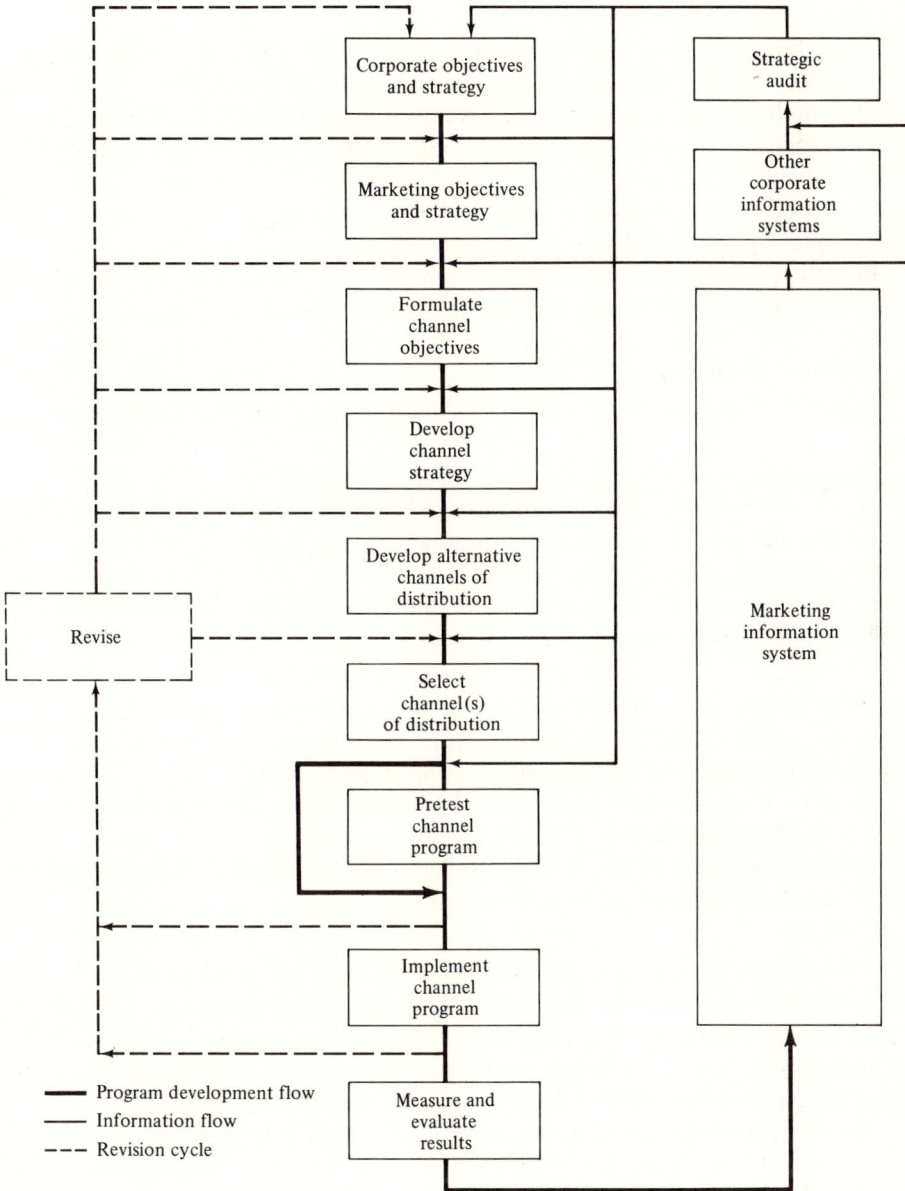

Program development flow
Information flow
Revision cycle

Once these or similar objectives have been established, the marketing manager may also wish to establish a series of secondary, supportive channel objectives. These objectives identify the activities necessary to achieve the sales and profit goals in each target market. Illustrative objectives are:

1. Ratios of the coverage desired in each class of wholesale or retail institution through which the firm may distribute its products.
2. The level and composition of inventory in each type of institution.
3. The quantity and type of advertising and sales support that each reseller should perform.
4. Specific sales promotion goals, including the amount and location of display space that should be made available at the retail level.
5. Other market and customer development activities necessary to increase reseller effectiveness and ultimate consumer demand.

Channel Strategy

As Figure 13-7 indicates, the essence of channel strategy involves developing programs that profitably satisfy the needs of all channel members—ultimate consumers, resellers, and seller. The seller's channel strategy should be based upon a careful and complete assessment of the needs and expectations of two customer groups—the ultimate consumers of the product and the various classes of resellers through which the products may be marketed. Their needs largely determine how channel strategy *must* be developed. Consequently, developing a channel strategy entails seeking answers to four important questions:

1. Is it most desirable to distribute the product line directly or indirectly?
2. If indirect distribution is preferable, what types of resellers or reseller systems can best achieve channel objectives?
3. How many resellers are required by geographic region for each target market segment?
4. What needs of these various resellers must be satisfied if their cooperation and support are to be enlisted?

UTILIZATION OF INTERMEDIARIES. The first step in developing a channel strategy is to decide upon the degree to which direct distribution is desirable. If the firm decides upon direct distribution, it has, in fact, established its strategy, and questions 2, 3, and 4 become irrelevant. However, if it elects to rely upon indirect distribution, these latter three issues must also be resolved.

Direct distribution permits the seller to maintain a high degree of control over the manner in which his products are marketed, including to whom the product will be sold as well as how it will be priced and promoted. Fuller Brush and Avon, as well as several firms engaged in the production and distribution of encyclopedias and vacuum cleaners, rely upon this form of distribution.

Figure 13-7   A frame of reference for channel strategy.

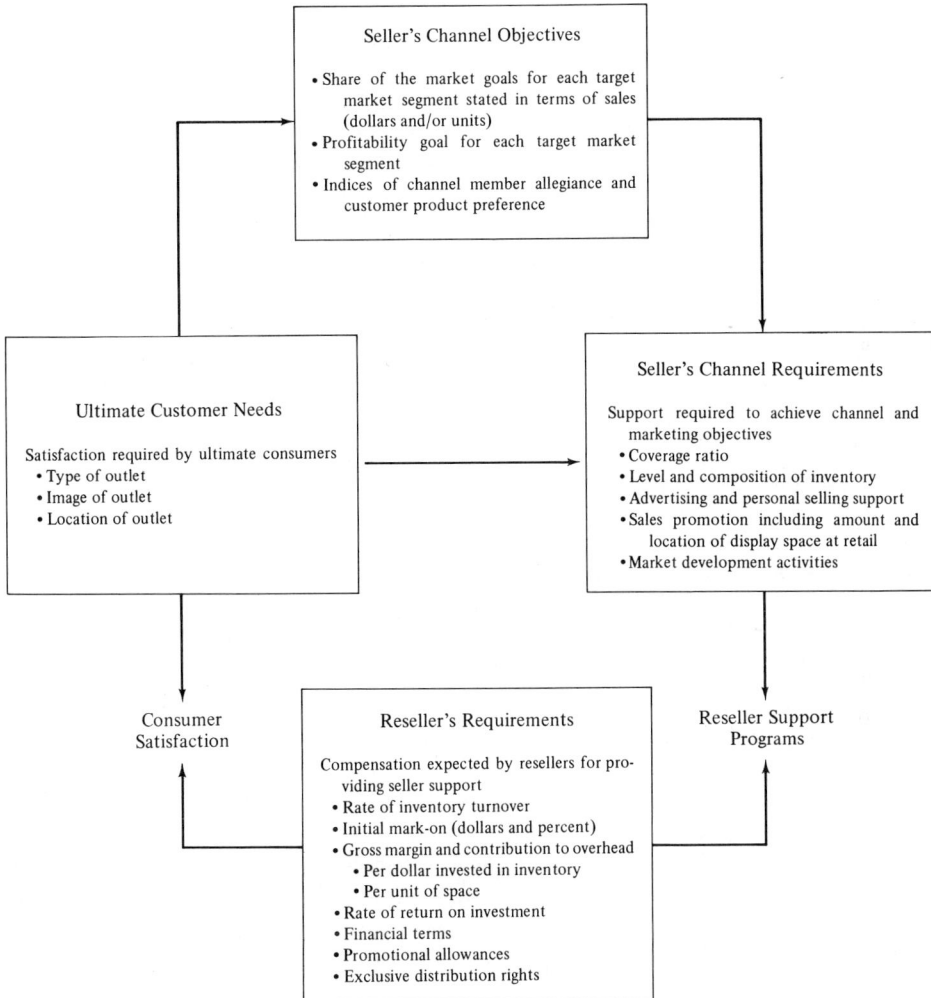

Seller's Channel Objectives

- Share of the market goals for each target market segment stated in terms of sales (dollars and/or units)
- Profitability goal for each target market segment
- Indices of channel member allegiance and customer product preference

Ultimate Customer Needs

Satisfaction required by ultimate consumers
- Type of outlet
- Image of outlet
- Location of outlet

Seller's Channel Requirements

Support required to achieve channel and marketing objectives
- Coverage ratio
- Level and composition of inventory
- Advertising and personal selling support
- Sales promotion including amount and location of display space at retail
- Market development activities

Consumer Satisfaction

Reseller's Requirements

Compensation expected by resellers for providing seller support
- Rate of inventory turnover
- Initial mark-on (dollars and percent)
- Gross margin and contribution to overhead
  - Per dollar invested in inventory
  - Per unit of space
- Rate of return on investment
- Financial terms
- Promotional allowances
- Exclusive distribution rights

Reseller Support Programs

However, such distribution is extremely expensive and requires a substantial resource base. In addition, few sellers produce a product of sufficiently high unit value, or a wide enough product line, to permit them to distribute directly to the ultimate consumer and still achieve the efficiencies associated with mass distribution.

Relying upon some combination of middlemen to accomplish product distribution is one means of overcoming these limitations. Middlemen are specialists at performing the various distribution functions. This specialization, together with their years of experience and numerous contacts, often results in significant economies of operation. In short, distributing through certain classes of wholesalers and/or retailers may be the only efficient means of effectively reaching certain target market segments.

Indirect distribution also has disadvantages—primarily, a reduction in direct control over marketing activities and increased difficulty in obtaining current market information regarding markets and products.

STRUCTURE. Once a decision has been reached on the degree to which middlemen will be employed in product distribution, the firm must determine whether it wishes to rely upon a conventional channel configuration or a vertically aligned channel structure. This decision revolves around two basic considerations—the effectiveness and the efficiency of each alternative.

The question is whether traditional channels or vertically aligned systems can best achieve the two primary channel objectives of market share and profitability. Vertical marketing systems are typically capable of achieving the same or better sales volume than traditional channel arrangements but with substantially lower costs. As described earlier, these economies are achieved by shifting marketing functions to the point in the channel at which they can be performed most efficiently. For example, repositioning of the data-processing activities, the price-marking of merchandise, and/or promotional programming often results in substantial savings.

Additional economies may be realized through simplifying and synchronizing channel operations. Simplification economies might include utilization of pre-printed order forms, routinized billing procedures, and telephone selling. Synchronization economies entail vertically coordinating systems and procedures throughout the length of the channel, standardizing inventory assortments and layouts at multiple levels of the distribution process, and vertically integrating fractionalized information systems into integrated, total management information systems. In addition, to the extent that these efforts result in improved utilization of production, warehousing, and data-processing facilities, each member of the channel may also realize substantial improvements in costs.

INTENSITY. When the extent to which middlemen are to be used and the manner in which they will be structured have been decided upon, the seller must determine the number of intermediaries to use at each stage or level in the channel of distribution.[16] Three major alternative courses are open to him—intensive, selective, or exclusive distribution.

The goal of *intensive distribution* is to achieve maximum market exposure of the product or product line. This involves having the product stocked in as many outlets where consumers would expect to find the product as possible, and typically requires the utilization of both wholesalers and retailers. Producers and resellers of consumer convenience goods almost always adopt a policy of intensive distribution. In addition, producers of widely used raw materials, as well as some

---

[16] This, of course, assumes that the seller has decided upon some form of indirect distribution; otherwise, as previously noted, he would not have to deal with the issues of channel structure and intensity of distribution.

industrial products such as operating supplies or perishable hand tools, also rely upon such a strategy.

In contrast, *selective distribution* refers to the use of a limited number of wholesalers and/or retailers. Some consumer shopping and specialty products, and certain classes of industrial equipment for which customers have a strong brand preference, are often distributed in this manner. Most sellers who elect selective over intensive distribution do so in order to gain better control over reseller marketing activities. In addition, it often permits the seller to substantially reduce his selling costs and cultivate key customers more aggressively. The major limitation is that selective distribution usually lessens the product's market exposure.

Exclusive distribution is the most extreme form of selective selling. It refers to the supplier's granting wholesalers or retailers exclusive rights to distribute the company's products in a given geographical market. The supplier may also elect to require that the distributors (wholesalers) or dealers (retailers) enter into exclusive dealing arrangements, whereby they agree not to carry competing lines of merchandise. Such arrangements are common at the retail level for the distribution of furniture, certain major appliances, and new automobiles. This strategy is commonly adopted when the producer is willing to reduce market exposure in order to gain more aggressive selling effort on the part of his resellers and greater market penetration in his target market segments.

RESELLER-SUPPORT PROGRAMS. The producer must also develop appropriate methods of compensating intermediaries for performing the activities that the seller considers necessary for marketing success. As illustrated in Figure 13-7, this requires programs that effectively couple the interests of the seller and the various classes of resellers in a mutually beneficial manner.

The seller's interests relate to his channel objectives—that is, they encompass his goals of market share and profitability as well as the goals he establishes for resellers, such as coverage ratios, inventory levels, promotional, and market-development activities. On the other hand, resellers are not averse to helping the seller achieve his goals as long as they can achieve their own. Some of the more important interests of the reseller include some target rate of return on investment; adequate financial terms, functional discounts, and promotional allowances; satisfactory rates of inventory turnover; and, perhaps, protected distribution rights.

Three distribution policies are commonly used by sellers to effect channel linkage—price concessions, financial assistance, and protective provisions. The producer must develop from among the numerous alternatives within each of these policy areas a package that attracts, retains and properly motivates each of the various middlemen he wishes to utilize. Figure 13-8 contains a partial listing of some of the many factors that might be considered in structuring such a program.

Channel Design

The third step in managing channel operations entails designing a channel of distribution that is consistent with the channel strategy and capable of achieving

Figure 13-8   Developing reseller support programs:
selected distribution policy alternatives.

I. "Price" Concessions
  A. Discount Structure
    trade (functional) discounts
    quantity discounts
    cash discounts
    anticipation allowances
    free goods
    prepaid freight
    new product, display, and advertising allowances
      (without performance requirements)
    seasonal discounts
    mixed carload privilege
    drop shipping privilege
    trade deals
  B. Discount Substitutes
    display materials
    premarked merchandise
    inventory control programs
    catalogs and sales promotion literature
    training programs
    inventory maintenance programs
    advertising matrices
    management consulting services
    merchandising programs
    sales "spiffs"
    technical assistance
    payment of sales personnel and demonstrator
      salaries
    promotional and advertising allowances
      (with performance requirements)

---

channel objectives. Typically there are many ways of combining middlemen to achieve channel objectives. However, strategic decisions concerning the extent to which intermediaries are to be employed, the intensity of product distribution, the extent to which the channel is to be vertically programmed, and the manner of compensating middlemen all serve to limit the number of combinations that are appropriate. For example, a decision to distribute the product line through wholesalers and retailers on a selective basis on a highly programmed basis, utilizing a specific reward system, substantially reduces the number of options available to the seller.

Other factors that should be considered include the nature of the market to be served, product characteristics, the quality and quantity of available middle-

II. Financial Assistance
   A. Conventional Lending Arrangements
      term loans
      inventory floor plans
      notes payable financing
      accounts payable financing
      installment financing of fixtures and equipment
      lease and note guarantee programs
      accounts receivable financing
   B. Extended Dating
      E.O.M. dating
      seasonal dating
      R.O.G. dating
      "extra" dating
      postdating
III. Protective Provisions
   A. Price Protection
      premarked merchandise
      fair trade
      "franchise" pricing
      agency agreements
   B. Inventory Protection
      consignment selling
      memorandum selling
      liberal returns allowances
      rebate programs
      reorder guarantees
      guaranteed support of sales events
      maintenance of "spot" stocks and fast delivery
   C. Territorial Protection
      selective distribution
      exclusive distribution

men, and the strengths and weaknesses of the company itself.[17] Each of these factors will be examined briefly.

NATURE OF THE MARKET. A larger market potential, such as that available for many consumer convenience goods, almost requires the use of middlemen to effect distribution. However, as customers become more highly concentrated, it may be possible to distribute relatively high-value products more directly, as is the case for many industrial items.

[17] A thorough discussion of these considerations may be found in E. Jerome McCarthy, *Basic Marketing:A Managerial Approach* (Homewood, Ill.: Richard D. Irwin, Inc., 1968), pp. 417–422; S. H. Rewaldt, J. D. Scott, and M. R. Warshaw, *Introduction to Marketing Management* (Homewood, Ill.: Richard D. Irwin, Inc., 1969), pp. 274–285; and W. J. Stanton, *Fundamentals of Marketing*, 2d ed. (New York: McGraw-Hill, Inc., 1967), pp. 348–353.

In addition to market size and concentration, the frequency, regularity, and size of customer purchases also affect the length of the channel and types of intermediaries to be employed. Channel practices in the distribution of groceries illustrate this point. Dairy products and baked goods purchased regularly and frequently may be distributed on a door-to-door basis. In addition, however, the firm producing or merchandising these items typically seeks distribution through retailers as well, selling directly to large grocery chains while at the same time it sells to smaller stores through wholesalers.

Another market consideration in channel design involves customer preferences. "The buying habits of ultimate consumers and industrial users, the amount of effort the consumer is willing to expend, the desire for credit, the preference for one-stop shopping, and the desire for the services of a personal salesman significantly affect channel policies."[18] The substantial increase in "convenience" food store sales indicates that consumers are willing to pay more for selected items such as dairy products, baked goods, and party supplies when the location of these outlets is in closer proximity than traditional grocery outlets.

PRODUCT CHARACTERISTICS. Unit value, perishability, bulkiness, and the technical nature of the product also affect the number and type of middlemen to be used. Products with a low unit value are typically distributed through long channels relying upon both wholesalers and retailers. On the other hand, companies can better afford to distribute products with a high unit value through shorter channels. Highly perishable items, such as refrigerated dairy products, baked goods, and fresh produce are often distributed through short channels to facilitate speedy delivery and minimize delay.

Extremely bulky items such as coal are difficult to handle and costly to transport; consequently they are often distributed on a direct basis. Other, more complicated technical products, such as electronic data-processing equipment, also are frequently distributed on a direct basis, but for different reasons. In this case direct distribution by the producer's own sales force may be necessary to satisfy requirements for highly technical selling knowledge, expert installation, and servicing.

MIDDLEMAN CONSIDERATIONS. Enlisting the support of certain specific middlemen is often the key to gaining access to the firm's target market segments. The preceding section discussed the structuring of reseller-support programs for this purpose. However, certain other factors should also be recognized. Regardless of the reseller support he offers, the marketing manager may not be able to find the exact kinds of middleman specialists he desires in every geographic area. For example, the market specialist available in metropolitan centers may not be available in rural areas. If the marketing manager is fortunate enough to find the type and number of middlemen he wishes in each market area, there are almost certain to be significant differences in levels of performance of the intermediaries.

When the right type of middleman support is available, other problems may arise. Competitors may already have established relationships with the best

[18] Stanton, *Fundamentals of Marketing*, p. 349.

middlemen—perhaps including exclusive dealing arrangements—and it is usually difficult to convince them of the propriety of adding another line.

In other situations, certain long-established, traditional relationships between various middlemen such as wholesalers and retailers may virtually "dictate" the types and number of middlemen that must be employed. For example, grocery, hardware, and drugs are distributed almost exclusively through a broad network of wholesalers and retailers. To violate these "established" channels may insure defeat of the firm's total marketing program.

COMPANY STRENGTHS AND WEAKNESSES. Large firms often enjoy a strong marketing position compared to other channel members. While middlemen may be able to perform certain marketing functions more efficiently, the large, financially strong company tends to be less totally dependent upon these services. The large firm also tends to be well established in certain channel systems and, in most cases, distributes a relatively wide product line or lines through the resellers it has chosen. Middlemen dealing with such a firm find it difficult not to comply with their requirements concerning additions to the product line, promotional effort, sales terms, and periodic performance of special services.

SELECTING INDIVIDUAL MIDDLEMEN. The process of choosing among available middlemen is a difficult but critically important process. The seller's efforts to maximize marketing effectiveness at the point of final sale is largely dependent upon how well he selects individual middlemen and then administers the system of which they are a part.

Objectives of individual firms vary too much to allow an exhaustive listing of criteria for evaluating middlemen. However, the following considerations are appropriate in most cases.[19]

1. Does he now, or is it likely that he will in the *near* future, sell to the target market segment I am attempting to reach?
2. Is his sales force of adequate size and well enough trained to generate the level of sales desired in the geographic territory he serves?
3. Is he properly located with respect to trading areas, shopping centers, and competitive outlets?
4. Are his promotional policies and activities adequate in terms of my requirements?
5. Does he normally offer the types of services to his customers that are consistent with the needs of the target market segment? That is, what type of reputation does he have among the customers he now serves?
6. Are his product policies consistent with our needs? That is, does he now or will he carry competing products detrimental to the sales of our product lines? Are his policies concerning variety, assortment, and depth of inventories consistent with our requirements?

[19] Many of the questions that follow have been developed from material contained in Stanton, *Fundamentals of Marketing*, pp. 360–362.

7. Are his physical plant and equipment adequate to insure proper levels of service to the target market?
8. Does he have adequate financial strength to pay his bills promptly and extend necessary financial support to his customers?
9. Is the management of the firm progressive and capable of properly implementing the activities that will ensure marketing success?
10. Is the firm receptive and eager to work with us within the conditions we have established for other, similar classes of middlemen?

Evaluation, Implementation, and Control

So far the seller has established channel objectives, developed a strategy to achieve these objectives, and critically evaluated the various middlemen that might be utilized. The next step involves evaluating the ways the chosen middlemen may be combined to achieve channel objectives. This requires determination of which channel structure(s) can best achieve target levels of sales consistent with the firm's profit objectives.

The channel that produces the highest sales volume may not be the most profitable channel configuration. It is also quite possible that the channel that produces the greatest profit in the short run may not have the greatest potential for long-term profitability. The marketing manager must seek to resolve these conflicting points of view by selecting those channels that offer the greatest long-run profitability while producing acceptable short-run profits consistent with the firm's more immediate marketing and channel objectives.

Additional factors to be considered include channel conflict and flexibility. The channel should be structured and administered in such a way that the self-interests of members at various levels (vertical conflict) are recognized and satisfied by various reseller-support programs. Territorial boundaries and exclusive selling arrangements should be carefully defined to reduce conflict among members at the same level in the channel (horizontal conflict). Moreover, channels should be established with the realization that few business arrangements are permanent; the seller should seek to convey to his resellers the philosophy that change is inevitable, that the flexibility to react to this change is critical, and that when changes become necessary they will be made to the mutual advantage of all channel members.

Unfortunately, it is never possible for a seller to know in advance that he has selected the "best" channels. Consequently, it is strongly advisable to pretest the chosen channels prior to full-scale implementation.[20]

The last, and perhaps most important step in managing channel operations is to implement the chosen program and continuously evaluate its performance over time. This entails developing standards of channel performance and then devising measurement techniques that will permit proper evaluation of the various

[20] The procedures for conducting such a pretest are discussed at length in Chapters 18 and 19.

members of the channel. The seller may establish sales quotas for each inter-mediary as well as for the entire channel. Quotas may be developed for each territory, product line, and customer group for a specified period of time, and actual performance can then be evaluated by continuous examination of orders, invoices, and reseller inventories. Other measures that may be utilized include indices of reseller and ultimate-consumer satisfaction, quantity and quality of advertising performed, promptness in paying bills, and the amount of new business acquired.

LEGAL IMPLICATIONS

This section deals with the legality of vertical mergers, dealer selection, exclusive dealing arrangements, territorial restrictions, full-line forcing, and brokerage fees. Under varying conditions, these may be subject to one or more of three federal laws—the Sherman Antitrust Act, the Clayton Act, and Section 5 of the Federal Trade Commission Act.

Vertical Mergers

Vertical mergers or integration may be perceived as undesirable from an anti-trust perspective when the companies being merged operate in vertically related markets. The vulnerability of this action is heightened if either market is highly concentrated and there is a history of vertical mergers that have increased the risks for independent third companies—especially where these independent third companies find it increasingly difficult to find suppliers or outlets who are not also competitors.[21] Thus:

. . . the FTC has made it mandatory that all Portland cement companies notify the Commission at least 60 days prior to the consummation of any merger or acquisition involving any ready-mix concrete producer, so that they may institute action blocking the proposed merger if it appears to have anticompetitive over-tones.[22]

. . . in relation to the Brown Shoe Company/G. R. Kinney Company merger . . . the court held that the acquisition of Kinney by Brown would foreclose other shoe manufacturers from Kinney's outlets, thus increasing barriers to entry and concentration of the retail shoe market.[23]

Dealer Selection

The guiding principle in the right of a supplier to select dealers to whom he will sell is the so-called "Colgate doctrine." The Supreme Court decided in 1919[24]

---

[21] For a more detailed discussion of the legality of vertical mergers see Frederick D. Sturdivant, et al., *Managerial Analysis in Marketing* (Glenview, Ill.: Scott, Foresman and Company, 1970), pp. 118–119.

[22] *Ibid.*

[23] *Ibid.*

[24] *United States* v. *Colgate & Co.*, 250 U.S. 300 (1919).

that the Sherman Act "does not restrict the long recognized right of a trader or manufacturer engaged in an entirely private business, freely to exercise his own independent discretion as to parties with whom he will deal. And, of course, he may announce in advance the circumstances under which he will refuse to deal." This prerogative is also formally recognized in Section 2(a) of the Robinson-Patman Act, which states that "nothing herein contained shall prevent persons engaged in selling goods, wares, or merchandise in commerce from selecting their own customers in bonafide transactions and not in restraint of trade." Thus, with certain exceptions including exclusive arrangements, territorial restrictions, and full-line forcing, the Colgate doctrine appears to stand, so long as the refusal to deal or the threat to do so does not involve an illegal conspiracy or is not used as an instrument to achieve an otherwise illegal end, such as price-fixing or monopolization.[25]

Exclusive Dealing

Exclusive dealing involves an arrangement between a supplier and dealer whereby the dealer agrees not to handle directly competing products offered by his supplier's competitors. Such an arrangement grants the dealer the right to sell a given product or product line exclusively in a specified territory and it offers the supplier the advantage of receiving the dealer's intensive sales efforts. These types of arrangements are governed mainly by Section 3 of the Clayton Act.

While there is no hard and fast rule relative to the legality of exclusive dealing arrangements, it appears they are perfectly legal when they are not related to competition. For example, oil companies clearly have the right to require their dealers to refrain from selling competing brands of gasoline in pumps and storage facilities supplied to the dealer by the manufacturer. However, when such a decision would have an adverse effect on competition by foreclosing competitors from market outlets, they have generally been held to be illegal.[26]

Territorial Restrictions

Limitations on the territory in which a dealer must concentrate his efforts are common to almost all exclusive dealing arrangements. And, in general, it is well established that manufacturers have the legal right to sell through one dealer in a given territory. Such restrictions may become illegal, however, "in cases where

[25] T. N. Beckman and W. R. Davidson, *Marketing*, 8th ed. (New York: The Ronald Press Company, 1967), p. 412.

[26] *Ibid.*, p. 406–407. For more detailed interpretations of the legality of exclusive dealing see: *Standard Oil Company of California and Standard Stations, Inc.* v. *U.S.*, 337 U.S. 293, 69 Sup. Ct. 1051 (1949); *Thomson Mfg. Co.* v. *FTC*, 150 F.2d 952 (1st Cir. 1945), cert. denied 326 U.S. 776 (1945); *FTC* v. *Sinclair Refining Co. et al.*, 261 U.S. 463 (1923); and *Brown Shoe Co., Inc.* v. *FTC*, 339 F.2d 45 (8th Cir. 1964) (U.S. Sup. Ct. June 6, 1966).

it can be shown that they have been used in such a manner that the effect was or tends to restrain competition or to monopolize commerce in the commodity."[27]

Full-line Forcing

Requirements contracts involve a dealer's purchasing all or some specified portion of his requirements of a particular product for a stipulated period of time from a single supplier. Such contracts may be a part of exclusive dealing arrangements or, in some instances, may be used as a substitute for exclusive dealing.

The requirement that a dealer handle a full line of the supplier's goods is not generally considered to be illegal as long as there is no requirement that the dealer not handle competitive products. Full-line forcing without an exclusive dealing arrangement is considered to be legal because it does not preclude the dealer from also handling a portion or the full line of a competitor's products.[28]

Brokerage Fees

The Robinson-Patman Act prohibits the payment or receipt of brokerage fees except for brokerage services actually rendered. The intent of this provision is to prevent sellers from granting brokerage fees to large-scale buyers who purchase directly from producers or through a "dummy" brokerage office operated by the regular employees of the purchasing company.

SUMMARY

A channel of distribution is the path that a firm's products follow as they move from the producer or seller to the ultimate consumer of the product. The firm may rely upon one or several different channels of distribution. It can distribute its products directly or it may elect to rely on any of a great number of various specialized intermediaries to accomplish product distribution.

The distribution sector of the economy is undergoing a series of critical changes. The most important developments include the growth of vertically integrated distribution channels, a dramatic increase in intertype competition, the increasing polarization of retail trade, and the emergence of "free-form" corporations.

To effectively adapt to these changes, the marketing manager must approach channel management in a systematic manner. The first step involves setting objectives that channel operations are expected to achieve. Most important among these objectives are sales and profit goals for each of the firm's target market segments. The next step is to develop a strategy to achieve these objectives. Strategic issues include whether to distribute on a direct or indirect basis, whether conventional channels or vertically programmed networks are most desirable, the

[27] Beckman and Davidson, *Marketing*, p. 408.
[28] *United States* v. *J. I. Case Co.*, 101 F. Supp. 856 (1951).

number of middlemen to utilize, and the development of effective reseller support programs. Various channel alternatives must then be evaluated on the basis of their relative profitability, and the most desirable channel or channels must be selected. Multiple channels may be required to effectively reach each of the firm's target market segments.

Channel configurations and reseller-support programs should be pretested in a controlled test market or through the technique of simulation to determine whether they will achieve channel objectives. If objectives are not attained, necessary changes should be made prior to full-scale implementation.

Once implemented, the effectiveness of the channel programs must be measured and evaluated against channel goals on a continuous basis. This last step completes the systems approach to marketing management. It constitutes a feedback mechanism that tells the marketing manager how well his decisions are succeeding and affords him the opportunity of making changes as they become necessary.

QUESTIONS FOR REVIEW AND DISCUSSION

1. It has often been said that "you can eliminate the wholesaler but you can't eliminate his function."
   (a) Do you agree with this statement? Why or why not?
   (b) What does this statement imply about the continued, accelerated growth of vertical marketing systems in the United States?
2. Compare and contrast conventional channels of distribution with vertical marketing systems.
3. Explain the concept of functional shiftability.
4. "The ascendancy of large, strategically potent networks has created an environment in which tactics must irretrievably be subordinated to strategy in the structure of distribution." Discuss.
5. Differentiate between primary and secondary channel objectives. Can you think of instances when "secondary" objectives might be more important and take precedence over primary objectives? Cite examples.
6. Explain the major differences between intensive, selective, and exclusive distribution. Are decisions as to the intensity of distribution more relevant when formulating channel strategy or when designing the structure of the channel?
7. Can you think of circumstances under which criteria other than sales volume, cost, or profitability might be used to better advantage in evaluating alternative channel designs? What are some of these criteria?
8. Do you think it necessary for a seller to fully understand the nature of his resellers' business prior to the time he establishes his various reseller-support programs? Why or why not?

Chapter 14   Physical Distribution

The manager responsible for physical distribution must develop an efficient, effective means of moving various sized shipments of products by any of a great number of transportation agencies from several sources of supply to an almost unlimited number of points of destination. He is actively involved in plant and warehouse site selection, choosing among alternative transportation agencies, warehouse supervision, inventory control, materials handling and packaging, and many other activities.

The inherent difficulty of the task is complicated further by the fact that the purchasing function is traditionally responsible for raw materials; production is responsible for packaging, inventory control, and plant warehousing of finished products; and marketing is responsible for the management of field inventories of finished goods. This fragmentation of the distribution function leads to inefficiency and interdepartmental conflicts in the definition and performance of the firm's distribution mission.[1] Clearly, *the physical distribution function can and should be viewed as an integrated system of activities whose main purpose is to plan for and control raw-material and finished-goods flows.*

The marketing manager should approach the physical distribution function in a systematic manner to ensure that this integration takes places. The approach suggested—and followed throughout this chapter—begins with an analysis of the critical nature of physical distribution systems, examines alter-

[1] The organizational aspects of physical distribution management are discussed in Chapter 17.

native approaches to managing distribution activities, and then carefully develops a procedure for such management. This approach includes a careful analysis of corporate objectives and strategy, the development of distribution objectives, and the design, evaluation, and implementation of distribution systems. The chapter concludes with a brief example of how alternative distribution systems may be evaluated.

A SYSTEMATIC APPROACH TO PHYSICAL DISTRIBUTION

The importance of distribution, or logistics, has been well recognized for centuries. As early as 1915 the two functions of marketing were identified as (1) demand creation and (2) physical supply.[2] What does appear to be a post-Second World War phenomenon is the emphasis upon developing integrated distribution systems.[3]

The Criticality of Physical Distribution Systems

During the 1950s and 1960s four major factors contributed to interest in integrated distribution systems and shaped the development of distribution thinking.[4] In the mid-fifties the American Businessman found himself in a situation where production technology was well advanced but marketing costs were increasing rapidly. In order to stay competitive in the marketplace he knew he must reduce these costs, and physical distribution represented one of the last remaining frontier areas for significant cost savings.[5]

As indicated in Table 14-1, physical distribution costs represent from 9 to 25 percent of total costs, *excluding the costs associated with carrying inventories.* Inventory carrying costs (Figure 14-1) constitute the largest single cost of distribution. Thus, the total costs of physical distribution may realistically range between 20 and 50 percent of the firm's *gross sales.*[6]

[2] Arch W. Shaw, *Some Problems in Market Distribution* (Cambridge: Harvard University Press, 1915).

[3] For a discussion of the historical growth of physical distribution management see Donald J. Bowersox, Edward W. Smykay, and Bernard J. LaLonde, *Physical Distribution Management: Logistics Problems of the Firm* (New York: The Macmillan Company, 1968), pp. 8–15. Also see James L. Heskett, Robert M. Ivie, and Nicholas A. Glaskowsky, Jr., *Business Logistics: Management of Physical Supply and Distribution* (New York: The Ronald Press Company, 1964), pp. 38–39.

[4] Bernard J. LaLonde, remarks made at the James R. Riley Symposium on Business Logistics, The Ohio State University, Columbus, Ohio, March 11, 1969.

[5] See Paul D. Converse, "The Other Half of Marketing," *Twenty-Sixth Boston Conference on Distribution* (Boston, 1954), pp. 22 ff.; John F. Magee, "The Logistics of Distribution," *Harvard Business Review,* Vol. 38 (July-August 1960), pp. 89–101; Peter F. Drucker, "The Economy's Dark Continent," *Fortune,* April 1962, pp. 265–270; Donald D. Parker, "Improved Efficiency and Reduced Cost in Marketing," *Journal of Marketing,* Vol. 26 (April 1962), pp. 15–21. In addition see Robert P. Neuschel, "Physical Distribution—Forgotten Frontier," *Harvard Business Review,* Vol. 45 (March-April 1967), pp. 125–134.

[6] Bowersox, Smykay, and LaLonde, *Physical Distribution Management,* p. 13. Converse, in "The Other Half of Marketing," has estimated that the costs associated with the physical handling and distribution of goods may easily approximate one-half the total costs of marketing.

Table 14-1   Physical Distribution Costs in Six Selected Industries[a]

Industry	Percent of Total Costs (1962)
1. Food and kindred products	24.80
2. Machinery (electric and nonelectric)	9.34
3. Chemical, petroleum, and allied products	21.53
4. Paper and allied products	14.66
5. Primary and fabricated metal	21.82
6. Wood products (including furniture)	16.69

SOURCE: Richard E. Snyder, *Distribution Age*, December 1963, "Physical Distribution Costs in Six Selected Industries."
[a] *Note:* Does not include inventory carrying costs.

Figure 14-1   Logistics costs of a typical consumer-goods manufacturer.

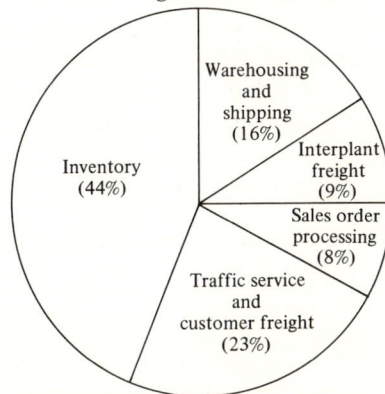

SOURCE: B. J. LaLonde, "Integrated Distribution Management—The American Perspective," *Journal of Long Range Planning*, Vol. 2 (December 1969), p. 64. Reprinted by permission.

Another major influence was the growing recognition of the profit leverage available from these reduced logistics costs. For example, if the firm makes 2 percent net profit on each dollar of sales, then a savings of 2 cents in distribution costs is equivalent to a $1 expansion in sales, and a $2 savings is equivalent to $100 in sales expansion. Such profit leverage makes a persuasive argument for reviewing the opportunities to reduce costs by integrated distribution management.

A third major factor was the advent of technological improvements in data processing. Historically the quantity of distribution data had often exceeded data-processing capabilities. New technology, however, relying on magnetic tape, optical scanning, and random-access files, made it possible to handle these large masses of data in an efficient, integrated fashion.

Finally, there was growing awareness of the importance of distribution in providing customer satisfaction. Management realized that selling the product is only half the job.[7] Getting the product to the customer at the right time in the right quantity and with the right logistical support (parts and service) is the other half.

Approaches to Distribution Management

No single "best" distribution system can be prescribed for all business firms. The distribution function, like other functions of the firm, must be developed within the framework of the firm's management philosophy and available resources. However, three rather distinct, identifiable approaches to integrated distribution management emerged during the 1960s. They are: (1) materials management, (2) physical distribution management, and (3) business logistics.[8] The distinctions among these three approaches are illustrated in Figure 14-2.

The materials-management approach usually evolves out of a traditional purchasing orientation to materials flow. This approach focuses on the acquisition of raw materials, supplies, and goods-in-process inventories. Many of the firms that take this approach are involved in industrial markets where the range of potential customers is limited and the value added by manufacturing is relatively high.

The physical distribution-management approach, on the other hand, is con-

Figure 14-2   Alternative approaches to integrated distribution management.

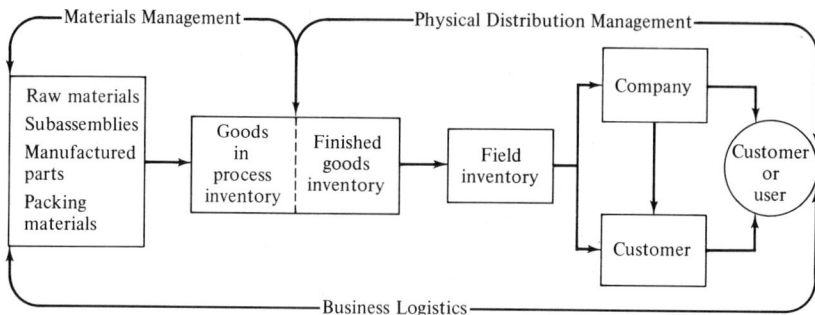

SOURCE: B. J. LaLonde, J. R. Grabner, Jr., and J. F. Robeson, "Integrated Distribution Systems: A Management Perspective," *International Journal of Physical Distribution*, Vol. 1 (October 1970), p. 43. Reprinted by permission.

[7] "Boosting Sales Through Customer Service," *The Management Review*, Vol. 51 (March 1962), pp. 76–79; H. J. Bullen, "New Competitive Selling Weapon: Physical Distribution Management," *Sales Management*, Vol. 94 (May 7, 1965), pp. 41–52; "Case for 90% Satisfaction," *Business Week*, January 14, 1961, pp. 82 ff.

[8] Bernard J. LaLonde, James F. Robeson, and John R. Grabner, Jr., "The Business Logistics Concept," *Bulletin of Business Research, The Ohio State University* (May 1969), pp. 1–3 ff.

cerned with the integration of finished-goods distribution. The National Council
of Physical Distribution Management defines physical distribution management as:

"a term employed in manufacturing and commerce to describe the broad range
of activities concerned with the efficient movement of finished products from the
end of the production line to the consumer, and in some cases includes the movement of raw materials from the source of supply to the beginning of the production line. These activities include freight transportation, warehousing, materials
handling, protective packaging, inventory control, plant and warehouse site selection, order processing, market forecasting, and customer service."[9]

Many firms that have taken this approach are in the high-volume consumer-
packaged-goods areas or in businesses where the sales or marketing department
has traditionally been responsible for the distribution task.

The most comprehensive approach to integrated distribution systems is
business logistics—"a total systems approach to the management of the distribution process including all of those activities involved in physically moving raw
material, in-process inventory, and finished-goods inventory from point of origin
to point of use or consumption."[10]

The total logistics approach has been utilized by firms with multiple production points, wide product lines, and a wide range of potential customers or
users. It is particularly appropriate when the firm is multinational, having raw-
material, assembly, distribution, and export networks reaching into different
countries.[11]

A Physical Distribution Planning and Control System

Figure 14-3 presents a physical distribution planning and control system. The
starting point is a detailed understanding of corporate and marketing objectives
and strategy for the long run as well as for the budget period in question. The
analysis of these and other considerations permits the development of specific
distribution objectives and budgets. This objectives-budgeting process is circular,
in the sense that revisions of objectives and expenditures are usually required.

Alternative physical distribution systems capable of achieving the designated
objectives are developed and evaluated, and the most appropriate is selected. This
is an extremely complex procedure; therefore it is usually desirable to pretest the
chosen system and modify it if necessary. The final step is to monitor the distribution system to ensure that actual performance meets planned performance requirements.

[9] This definition obtained from the National Council of Physical Distribution Management, 307 N. Michigan Ave., Chicago, Ill.
[10] Bernard J. LaLonde, "Integrated Distribution Management—The American Perspective," *Journal of Long Range Planning*, Vol. 2 (December 1969), pp. 61–71.
[11] The necessity for firms involved in international trade to adopt the logistics concept
is treated in Robert E. McGarrah, "Logistics for the International Manufacturer," *Harvard
Business Review*, Vol. 44 (March-April 1966), pp. 154–166.

Figure 14-3   A physical distribution planning and control system.

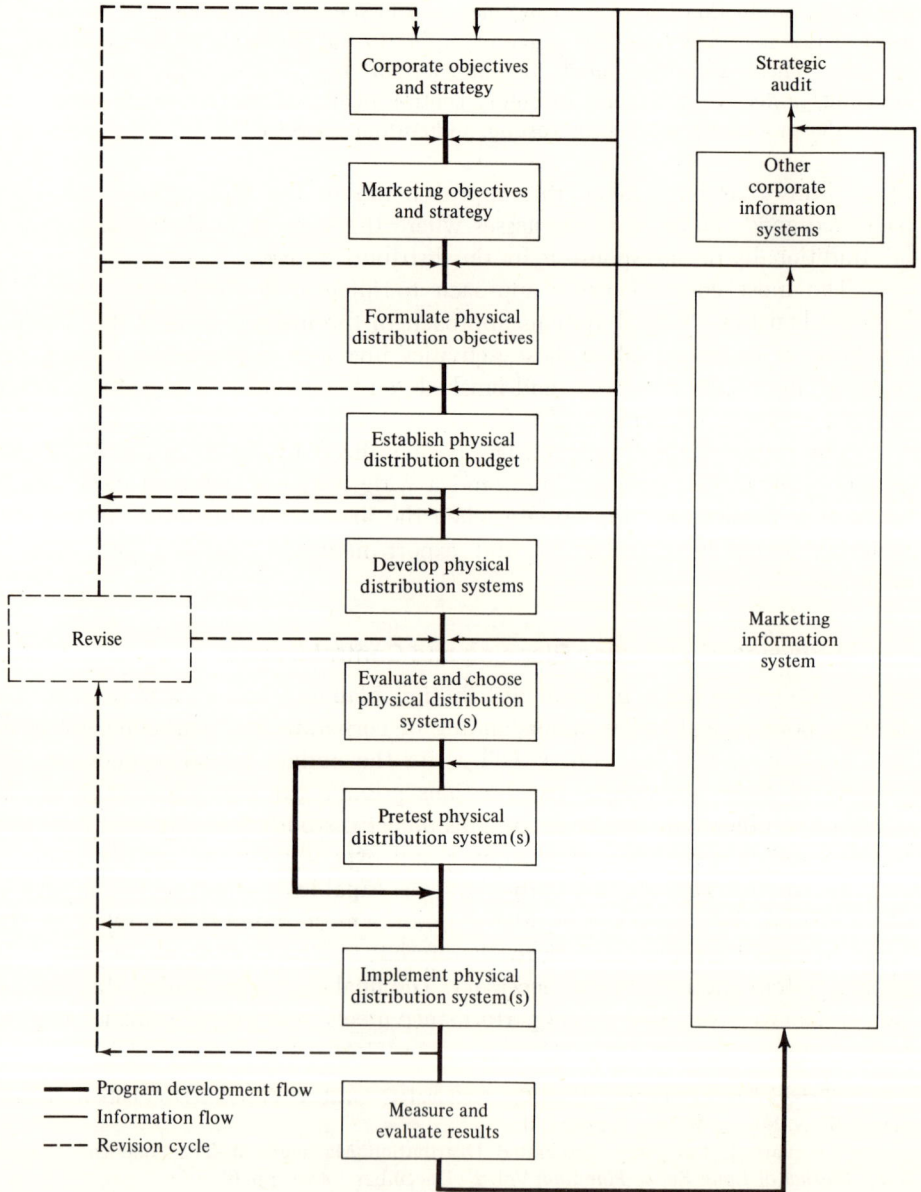

ESTABLISHING PHYSICAL DISTRIBUTION OBJECTIVES AND BUDGETS

A sophisticated physical distribution system accomplishes physical distribution objectives that in turn contribute to the achievement of marketing and corporate objectives. This section discusses the nature of physical distribution objectives and identifies alternative objectives that might be developed.

The Nature of Physical Distribution Objectives

Physical distribution systems are concerned primarily with supporting product-flow activities in marketing and production, and distribution objectives specify the support that the distribution system will be called upon to provide to these two functional areas.[12] This support involves two factors: (1) delivery-service performance level and (2) cost expenditure. The goal is to establish a balance between performance and cost that will result in the desired return on investment for the firm. This balance becomes the objective to be satisfied by physical distribution activities and provides guidance in the design and evaluation of alternative physical distribution systems.

When developing delivery-service standards, it is necessary to consider both time and consistency of performance. Cost considerations, on the other hand, center on the dollar requirements for alternate levels of the following services:

Time—lead time between order and delivery (often referred to as the order-cycle time).

Dependability—consistency and reliability in meeting delivery-date schedules; in sending the right amount and type of merchandise, damage free; and in following special instructions.

Communications—in feedback on deviations from the norm or what's expected, in information flow from order through invoice.[13]

Physical Distribution Objectives

Specific physical distribution objectives are itemized in Figure 14-4. Clearly, physical distribution should be viewed as a mutually interdependent set of functions. They must be examined together as a total system in order to determine how each one should be operated in the best interests of the customer and the firm. Customer orientation is of critical importance: "It is important that these objectives start with the customer, not with the end of the company's distribution

[12] For a more complete treatment of the process of developing physical distribution objectives see Bowersox, Smykay, and LaLonde, *Physical Distribution Management*, pp. 114–116. The discussion that follows is based largely on this treatment of the subject.

[13] John F. Gustafson and Raymond F. Richard, "Customer Service in Physical Distribution," *Transportation and Distribution Management*, Vol. 4 (April 1964), p. 20.

Figure 14-4   Physical distribution objectives.

Service Factor	Objectives
	To develop a physical distribution system:
Order-cycle time	Capable of effecting delivery of the product within 8 days from the initiation of a customer order: • transmission of order—1 day • order processing (order entry, credit verification, picking and packing)—3 days • delivery—4 days;
Dependability of delivery	Which insures that 95 percent of all deliveries will be made within the 8-day standard and that under no circumstances will deliveries be made earlier than 6 days nor later than 9 days from the initiation of an order;
Inventory levels	Which maintains inventories of finished goods at levels which will permit • 97 percent of all incoming orders for class A items to be filled • 85 percent of all incoming orders for class B items to be filled • 70 percent of all incoming orders for class C items to be filled;
Accuracy in order filling	Capable of filling customer orders with 99 percent accuracy;
Damage in transit	Which insures that damage to merchandise in transit does not exceed 1 percent;
Communications	With a communication system which permits salesmen to transmit orders on a daily basis and which is capable of accurately responding to customer inquiries on order status within four hours.

facilities. This implies an understanding of where the customer buys, how much, how often, and what kind of service he expects for specific products in specific geographic markets."[14]

Many companies have improved their performance by viewing physical distribution from a total-system perspective when establishing objectives. For example,

[the E. F. MacDonald Co.] reduced inventory by 40%, cut . . . warehouses from seven to three, cut nonproductive movements between stores by 90%, and is giv-

[14] F. R. Denham, "Making the Physical Distribution Concept Pay Off," *Handling and Shipping*, Vol. 8 (October 1967), pp. 54–59.

ing higher merchandise performance at greater consistency with less inventory but more items.[15]

"International Minerals and Chemical Corp. . . . speeded up its customers' order cycle by five days through the use of electronic data processing, thereby allowing them to keep lower inventories. It also adopted an electronic freight car tracking system called Tels-Car to allow still lower customer inventories by reducing the number of "lost" shipments. While it was doing this, it reduced the number of its warehouses from 44 to 13.[16]

DEVELOPING ALTERNATIVE PHYSICAL DISTRIBUTION SYSTEMS

The physical distribution concept requires that the various distribution activities be viewed from a total-system perspective rather than as a series of fragmented, independent operations. This section will discuss the systems concept as it applies to physical distribution systems.

The Systems Concept in Physical Distribution

Figure 14-5 illustrates how a general systems approach can be used to schematically represent the essential operations of a highly simplified direct system of distribution. A more realistic, yet still rather simple system of distribution, involving two distribution centers as well as direct distribution from the plant, is illustrated in Figure 14-6.

These two flow diagrams provide insight into the conceptual manner in which physical distribution systems should be viewed.[17] That is, *physical distribution systems should be thought of as a system of inventories in motion.* The critical characteristics are:

First, it is the performance of the total system which is singularly of importance. Components only exist and find justification to the extent that they enhance total system performance. Second, components need not have optimum design on an individual basis, because emphasis is based upon their integrated relationship with other components in the system. Third, there exists between components a functional relationship, which may hinder combined performance. This relationship is commonly called trade-off. Finally, it is explicit that components linked together as a system can, on a combined basis, produce a result greater than that possible

---

[15] "The Next Place for Paring Costs," *Business Week*, May 1, 1965, pp. 132–136.

[16] *Ibid.*

[17] For a more detailed discussion of the systems concept and systems analysis see T. B. Glans, B. Grad, D. Holstein, W. E. Meyers, and R. N. Schmidt, *Management Systems* (New York: Holt, Rinehart and Winston, Inc., 1968). Also see Stanford L. Optner, *Systems Analysis for Business Management*, rev. ed. (New York: Prentice-Hall, Inc., 1968). In addition, see Paul M. Stokes, *A Total Systems Approach to Management Control* (New York: American Management Association, 1968); and Claude McMillan and Richard F. Gonzalez, *Systems Analysis*, rev. ed. (Homewood, Ill.: Richard D. Irwin, Inc., 1968).

Figure 14-5   A simple system of
direct distribution.

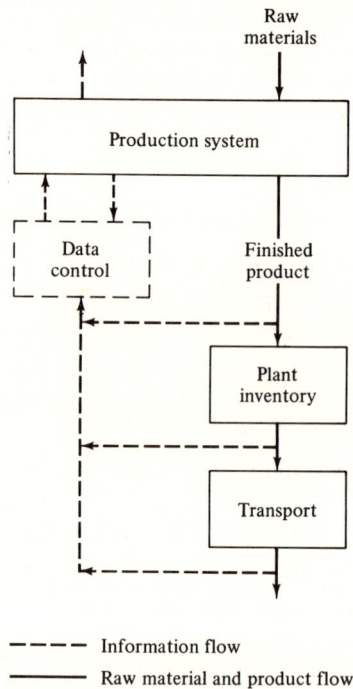

- - - -   Information flow
———   Raw material and product flow

by individual performance. In fact, the desired result may not be attainable without integrated performance.[18]

Components of the Physical Distribution System

The major components of a firm's physical distribution system can be grouped into four broad areas, which we list below together with some attendant considerations:

1. Fixed facilities
   (a) Types of plants and warehouses
   (b) Number of plants and warehouses
   (c) Location of plants and warehouses
   (d) Warehousing operations
2. Inventory allocations at fixed facilities
   (a) Inventory levels
   (b) Point (level) at which each item of inventory should be reordered
   (c) Quantities of each item in inventory that should be reordered

[18] Bowersox, Smykay and LaLonde, *Physical Distribution Management,* p. 103.

3. Transportation
    (a) Materials handling within fixed facilities
    (b) Transportation between the firm's fixed facilities
    (c) Transportation from the firm's fixed facilities to middlemen or ultimate consumers
4. Logistical support systems
    (a) Number, type, and location of repair parts within the system
    (b) Packaging
    (c) Information flow

The fixed facilities—plants, warehouses and markets—are often referred to as the *nodal* points in the physical distribution system. They represent the reposi-

Figure 14-6   A distribution system: two distribution centers and direct distribution.

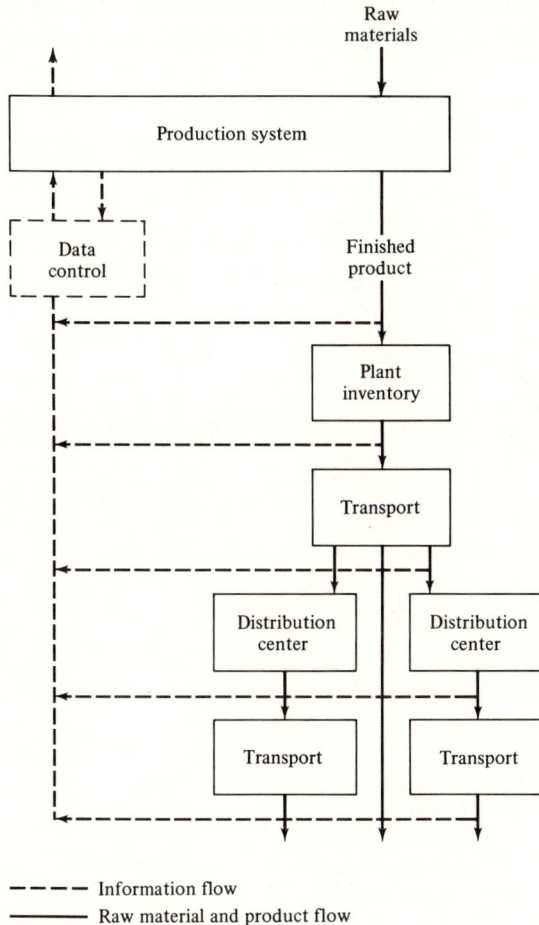

- - - - Information flow
———— Raw material and product flow

tories for the various levels of inventory. The transportation network represents the linkage between the *nodal points* of inventory, and the entire system is dependent on efficient information flow to effectively maintain operations. Such a distribution system is illustrated diagrammatically in Figure 14-7. Each component of the system is discussed below.

FIXED FACILITIES. A firm's products increase in value as they move toward the ultimate customer. Physical distribution systems must overcome spatial separations while accomplishing the firm's marketing objectives. An important part of this effort involves determining how many fixed facilities the firm should have and where they should be located.

The nodes in Figure 14-7 represent fixed facilities—in this illustration, plants, factory warehouses, company-owned distribution centers, and public warehouses. While all of these facilities are classified as "fixed," some are obviously more fixed than others. For example, while the firm has a sizable investment and relatively long-range commitment in plants, factory warehouses, and distribution centers, it has considerable flexibility in deciding to use more or less public warehousing.

The importance of selecting the best possible network of fixed facilities is

Figure 14-7   Schematic representation of a physical distribution process.

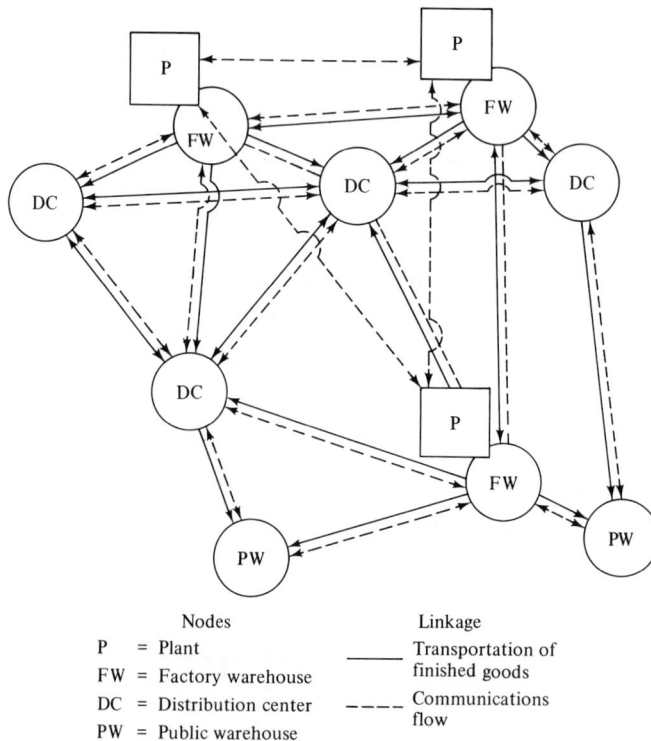

Nodes		Linkage	
P	= Plant	———	Transportation of finished goods
FW	= Factory warehouse		
DC	= Distribution center	- - - -	Communications flow
PW	= Public warehouse		

critical, and an important aspect of this selection involves specifying the location of these facilities. Studies in location theory are often classified as either land-utilization analyses or facility-location analyses.[19] Land-use studies focus upon the competition among producers for space on which to operate, and upon land rent as the price that allocates the available space.[20] In contrast, facility-location analysis is most commonly used to determine the best location for a specific kind of activity.[21] Of the two, facility-location studies probably offer the best guidance to managers interested in solving problems associated with plant or warehouse location.[22] The location of retail stores, while further complicated by demographic factors and consumer behavior, has received rather substantial attention.[23]

Plant locations represent the originating point of the value-creation process, while retail or customer locations represent its terminus. Warehouses or distribution centers connect these other two forms of fixed facilities and perhaps are justified only to the extent that they increase sales impact at the point of final

[19] Von Thunen is generally credited with the original work in location theory. For a concise English translation of von Thunen's work see Arthur H. Leigh, "Von Thunen's Theory of Distribution and the Advent of Marginal Analysis," *Journal of Political Economy*, Vol. 54 (December 1946), pp. 481–502. For a description of the differences between land-utilization analyses, facility-location analyses, areal theorists, and point theorists see Gilbert A. Churchill, Jr., "Plant Location Analysis: A Theoretical Formulation," in *Science, Technology, and Marketing*, 1966, Fall Conference Proceedings, The American Marketing Association, pp. 649–652.

[20] For a state-of-the-art overview of land-use studies see William Alonso, *Location and Land Use* (Cambridge, Mass.: Harvard University Press, 1964).

[21] See Alfred Weber, *Theory of the Location of Industries*, trans. Carl J. Friedrich (Chicago: University of Chicago Press, 1929); Edgar M. Hoover, *Location of Economic Activity* (New York: McGraw-Hill, Inc., 1948); Walter Isard, *Location and Space Economy* (Cambridge, Mass.: The M.I.T. Press, 1956); August Losch, *The Economics of Location*, trans. William H. Woglom (New Haven: Yale University Press, 1954); and Melvin L. Greenhut, *Plant Location* (Chapel Hill: University of North Carolina Press, 1956).

[22] A few of the important publications dealing with the general subject of warehouse location are Alfred A. Kuehn and Michael J. Hamburger, "A Heuristic Program for Locating Warehouses," *Management Science*, Vol. 9 (July 1963), pp. 643–666; Harvey N. Shycon and Richard B. Maffei, "Simulation—Tool for Better Distribution," *Harvard Business Review*, Vol. 38 (November-December 1960), pp. 65–75; Donald Bowersox, "The Distribution Center Location Problem," *Business Review*, Vol 11 (Winter 1964–1965), pp. 39–54; and Ronald H. Ballou, "Dynamic Warehouse Location Analysis," *Journal of Marketing Research*, Vol. 5 (August 1968), pp. 271–276.

[23] See Eugene J. Kelley, *Locating Controlled Regional Shopping Centers* (Sagutuck: The Eno Foundation for Highway Traffic Control, 1956); Richard L. Nelson, The Selection of Retail Locations (New York: F. W. Dodge Corp., 1958); William J. Reilly, *The Law of Retail Gravitation* (New York: Pillsbury Publishers, Inc., 1963). [For a complete treatment of the various laws of retail gravitation see George Schwartz, *Development of Marketing Theory* (Cincinnati: South-Western Publishing Company, 1963), pp. 9–34.] Also see Bernard J. LaLonde, *Differentials In Supermarket Drawing Power*, Marketing and Transportation Paper No. 11 (East Lansing: Bureau of Business and Economic Research, Michigan State University, 1962); and Saul B. Cohen and William Applebaum, "Evaluating Store Rents," *Economic Geography*, Vol. 36 (January 1960), pp. 1–35.

product transfer.[24] Sales impact can be increased by improving the service level by adding warehouses. However, as the number of warehouses continues to increase, their average size decreases, and their efficiency and service to customers also begin to decrease. For example, "increasing the number of warehouse facilities means carrying field inventories in more locations, and the total quantity of goods in the distribution pipeline will increase, thereby increasing inventory investment and carrying costs. Transportation costs may also increase because of the decreasing ratio of carload to less-than-carload tonnage."[25]

Thus, while extremely important, fixed facilities represent only one segment of the firm's total distribution system. Their impact on and interdependence with inventories, transportation, and support systems cannot be overemphasized.

INVENTORIES. Inventories serve to uncouple successive stages in the manufacturing-distribution process by making it unnecessary to gear production directly to consumption or, alternatively, to force consumption to adapt to the necessities of production.[26] In this way inventories permit the various stages to operate more economically and with greater autonomy. This decoupling causes inventories to be accumulated for one of four basic reasons:

1. *Movement inventories* are inventory balances needed because of the time required to move stock from one place to another. . . . Movement inventories are usually thought of in connection with movement between distant points—plant to warehouse. However, any plant may contain substantial stocks in movement from one operation to another.
2. *Lot-size inventories* are probably the most common in business. They are maintained wherever the user makes or purchases material in larger lots than are needed for his immediate purposes.
3. *Fluctuation stocks*, also very common in business, are held to cushion the shocks arising basically from unpredictable fluctuations in consumer demand.
4. *Anticipation stocks* are needed where goods or materials are consumed on a predictable but changing pattern through the year, and where it is desirable to absorb some of these changes by building and depleting inventories rather than by changing production rates with attendant fluctuations in employment and additional capital capacity requirements.[27]

The objective is to allocate these inventories among the fixed facilities within the production-distribution system efficiently and effectively. Should the firm stock every item it carries at every location? How many of each item should

[24] Bowersox, "The Distribution Center Location Problem," p. 40.

[25] Raymond LeKashman and John F. Stolle, "The Total Cost Approach to Distribution," *Business Horizons,* Vol. 8 (Winter 1965), pp. 34–35.

[26] John F. Magee, "Guides to Inventory Policy: Functions and Lot Sizes," *Harvard Business Review,* Vol. 34 (January-February 1956), p. 51.

[27] *Ibid.,* pp. 52–53.

Figure 14-8   A perspective on profit/inventory effectiveness.

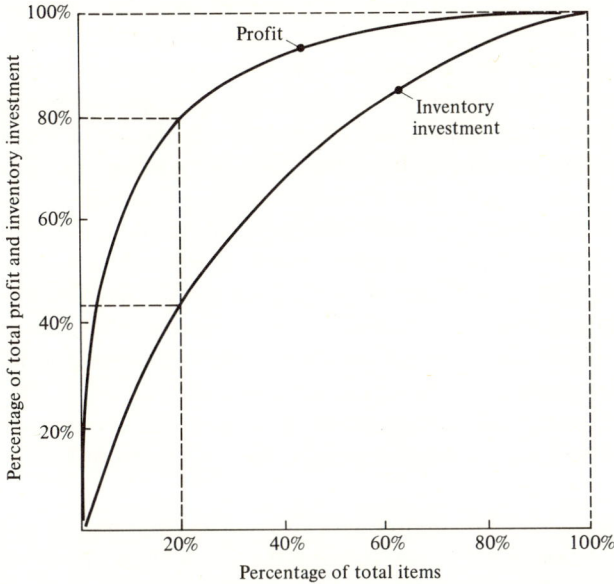

be stocked in each location? As Figure 14-8 indicates, a firm carrying a wide
assortment of a given product line usually discovers that approximately 20 percent of the items account for 80 percent of the profit and probably less than 50
percent of the dollar investment in inventory. Given this situation, the firm must
carefully evaluate significant additions to field inventories above the 20 percent
of the items generating the bulk of the profit. Many companies have found it to
their advantage to centralize inventories on the slow-moving, low-profit items and
utilize the fastest form of transportation available to satisfy demand for these
products. In several instances this has proven to be more profitable than dupli-
cating inventories of these same items in several inventory locations.

INVENTORY CONTROL.[28] The effective control of inventory requires that each
item in the product line be viewed individually with respect to two key considerations. The first involves determining the reorder point, or *when* to replenish the
stock of an item; the second concerns determining the reorder quantity, or by
how much stocks should be replenished.[29] The following example illustrates in
highly simplified terms how each of these calculations might be made.

[28] This discussion of inventory control is based on material contained in *Basic Principles
of Wholesale IMPACT* (White Plains, N.Y.: International Business Machines Corporation,
1967), pp. 9–14, and Max D. Richards and Paul S. Greenlaw, *Management Decision Making*
(Homewood, Ill.: Richard D. Irwin, Inc., 1966), pp. 470–475.
[29] The determination of exact reorder points can become an extremely complex procedure
and is not within the scope of this discussion. For further information dealing with this subject
see R. G. Brown, *Decision Rules for Inventory Management* (New York: Holt, Rinehart and
Winston, Inc., 1967), and *Basic Principles of Wholesale IMPACT*, pp. 22–50.

Consider an item with a *constant* average monthly usage of 100 units. If we assume there are the equivalent of 300 working days per year, then the daily usage would be four units. Further, if the supplier of this item consistently delivers merchandise in two weeks, a decision rule can be developed that will minimize the likelihood that the firm will experience lost sales because of its inability to meet demand. The rule would be: *when inventory on hand reaches a two-week supply (48 units), place an order.* Thus, 48 units represents the reorder point. However, the reorder quantity remains to be determined, based upon economic considerations.

One approach to solving this problem is to calculate the most economical order quantity (EOQ). This methodology seeks to determine the reorder quantity that will minimize the total costs of placing an order (acquisition costs) and of carrying the item in inventory (inventory carrying costs). Figure 14-9 illustrates the manner in which these two sets of costs react to alternative order sizes (Q). As the order size increases, the carrying costs will increase, but, since fewer orders will be placed, ordering costs will decrease. The components of carrying, ordering, and total costs can be described in the following fashion.

1. *Carrying costs.* The annual cost of carrying one unit of inventory is frequently calculated by multiplying the value of the item under consideration (C) by a percentage figure (I) that represents management's estimate of opportunity costs, taxes and insurance on the items being

Figure 14-9   Opposing cost analysis.

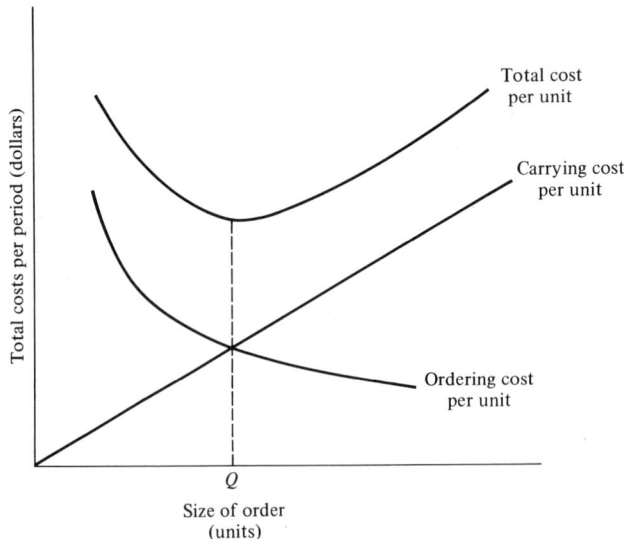

carried, and so on, per year as a percentage of the value of the inventory.[30] Total carrying costs are equal to the cost of carrying one unit (CI) multiplied by the average inventory, which is equal to $Q/2$. Thus, total annual carrying costs are $(Q/2) CI$, and will increase as Q, the reorder quantity, increases.[31]

2. *Ordering costs.* The number of orders that will be placed during any given period is equal to the demand for the period (R) divided by the size of each order (Q). Total ordering costs per period are equal to the cost of placing each order (S) times the number of orders per period, R/Q or $(R/Q)S$. As the order size increases, fewer orders will be required to meet demand and thus the ordering costs will decrease.[32]

3. *Total costs.* Total costs are the sum of carrying and ordering costs and may be expressed in equation form as

$$TC = \frac{Q}{2} CI + \frac{R}{Q} S.$$

Fortunately, a formula has been developed to determine the quantity that will minimize these total costs.[33] This equation, the first derivative of total costs with respect to Q, takes the following form:

$$Q = \frac{\sqrt{2RS}}{CI}.$$

[30] Several estimates of the costs of carrying inventory are available in the literature. They range from a low of 20 percent per year of the value of the item(s) being carried to a high of 35 percent.

[31] Richards and Greenlaw, *Management Decision Making*, p. 471.

[32] *Ibid.*

[33] Total costs are minimized when the slope of the total-cost curve is zero. Therefore, the EOQ formula may be obtained by setting the first derivative of total costs with respect to Q equal to zero, and solving for Q as follows:

(1) $TC = \dfrac{Q}{2} CI + \dfrac{R}{Q} S$

(2) $\dfrac{dTC}{dQ} = \dfrac{CI}{2} - \dfrac{RS}{Q^2}$

(3) Setting the first derivative equal to zero: $Q^2 CI = 2RS$; and $Q = \sqrt{\dfrac{2RS}{CI}}$.

That this represents a minimum point rather than a maximum is indicated by the positive sign of the second derivative:

$$\frac{d^2 TC}{dQ^2} = \frac{2RS}{Q^2}.$$

In the example under consideration, if we further assume that the cost value of the item (C) is \$1, that it costs \$1 every time an order for the item is processed (S), and that the imputed inventory carrying cost is 10 percent per year (I), we can rely upon the preceding equation to determine the most economical quantity to order.

$$(1) \qquad Q = \sqrt{\frac{2RS}{CI}},$$

$$(2) \qquad Q = \sqrt{\frac{2(1200)(1)}{1(.10)}},$$

$$(3) \qquad Q = \sqrt{2400},$$

$$(4) \qquad Q = \quad 155 \text{ units.}$$

The decision rule formulated earlier would now be modified to state: *when inventory on hand reaches a two-week supply (48 units), place an order for 155 units.*

The effective control of inventories usually becomes substantially more complex than this brief discussion would indicate. The uncertainty of demand and lead time adds a new dimension to the analysis in the form of a need to establish safety stocks. However, the fundamental aspects of calculating reorder points and reorder quantities form the basis for almost all the more sophisticated manual and computerized inventory control systems currently in use.

TRANSPORTATION. A firm has three basic alternatives available in developing its transport capability. It can purchase point-to-point transportation at specified charges from any legally authorized transportation company; it may enter into contractual arrangements with individuals or firms for specialized, exclusive movement services; or the firm may elect to purchase or lease its own fleet of equipment. These three forms of transport are typically referred to as common, contract, and private carriage. Figure 14-10 illustrates some of the ways these methods can be combined.

In choosing between transportation alternatives, three factors are of primary importance—cost of service, speed of service, and consistency of service. These factors are interrelated:

The cost of transport results from the actual payment for a movement between two points plus the expense related to having inventory committed to transit. . . . Speed of service relates to the actual time required to complete a transfer between two facilities. Speed of service and cost of service are related in two ways. First, those transport specialists capable of providing fast service normally charge higher rates. Second, the faster the service the shorter is the interval that materials and inventories are frozen in movement between facilities (with a resultant decrease in total system inventory investment).

Consistency of service refers to measured performance over a range of transfers between two facilities. In essence, how dependable is a given method of trans-

Figure 14-10   Modes, legal forms, auxiliary users, and principal coordinated systems of transportation.

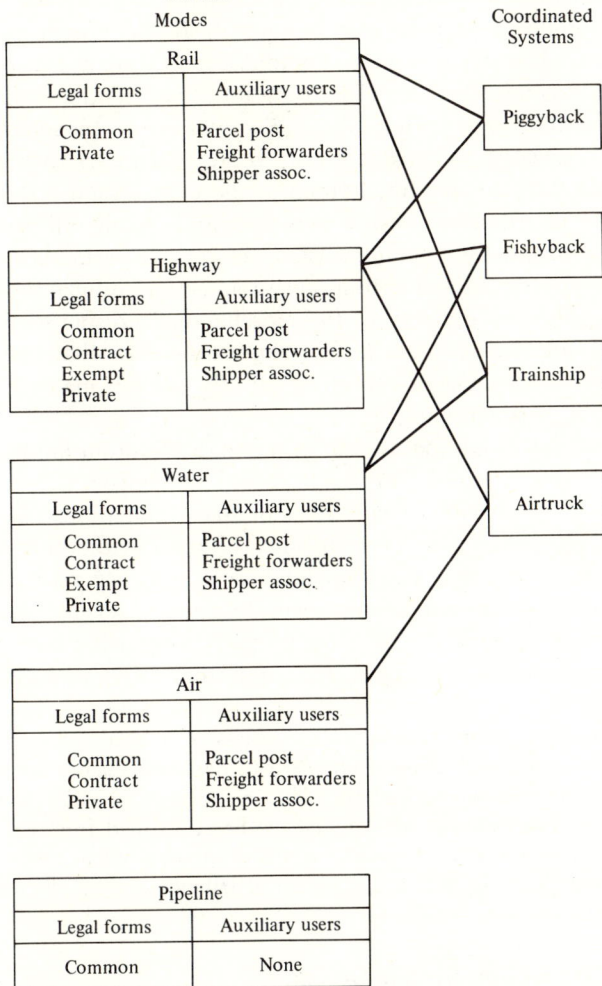

SOURCE: J. L. Heskett, R. M. Ivie, and N. A. Glaskowsky, Jr., *Business Logistics: Management of Physical Supply and Distribution,* copyright © 1964 by The Ronald Press Company, New York.

fer with respect to time? In many ways consistency of service is the most important characteristic of a transportation system. If a given movement takes two days one time and six the next, serious bottlenecks can develop in the flow of goods within the physical distribution system.[34]

---

[34] Bowersox, Smykay, and LaLonde, *Physical Distribution Management,* p. 106.

Developing the firm's transport capability involves arriving at a balance between speed of service and transfer cost. This balance can be determined only after the total distribution system has been reviewed. Under certain circumstances high-cost, fast methods of transfer may be most desirable. Under other conditions a slower, less costly transfer may be preferable. Integrating a transportation capability within the existing structure of fixed facilities is essential if the total system is to operate effectively and performance objectives are to be achieved.

LOGISTICAL SUPPORT SYSTEMS. Logistical support refers to activities undertaken to facilitate the effective functioning of the distribution system. It includes packaging, parts distribution, and communication. While all such supportive activities are important, the communication network is particularly critical. One of the primary purposes of the distribution system is to minimize time from receipt of an order (impulse) to delivery of the merchandise (response);[35] such a goal can be achieved only by a system of communication flow that complements the product flow and is capable of reporting rapidly on the manner in which the distribution system is functioning.

The criteria that should be used to evaluate distribution information systems include: (1) maximum usable information and flexibility; (2) minimum cost, bias, and error; (3) provision of flow data in space and time; (4) geographical homogeneity of data; and (5) compatibility of data with other information.[36]

Distribution information has two dimensions. *Quality* refers to the degree to which distribution communications accurately report events, correctly reflect customer needs, and provide the basis for properly appraising emerging trends in distribution. *Speed* depends on the degree of system integration. Thus:

It makes little sense for a firm to accumulate orders at a local sales office for a week, mail them to a regional office, send them to data processing, finally assign them to a distribution warehouse, and then ship air express in order to give fast delivery. Perhaps a direct phone call would have been justified from the customer's office, if such speedy order transmittal would have resulted in faster delivery at a lower total cost. Once again it is a question of balance among all components of the physical distribution system.[37]

Physical Distribution System Design

A distribution system links fixed facilities, inventories, transportation, and support systems in a manner that will achieve a predetermined level of distribution performance. As Figure 14-11 illustrates, four major factors affect the structure of the system: (1) the distribution audit; (2) performance standards; (3) market characteristics; and (4) constraints.

[35] Donald J. Bowersox, "Total Information Systems In Logistics," *Transportation and Distribution Management*, Vol. 4 (October 1964), p. 25.

[36] Allan D. Dale and Richard J. Lewis, "GEMNI—A Corporate Information System for Distribution Management," *Business Review*, Vol. 11 (Winter 1964–1965), p. 11.

[37] Bowersox, Smykay, and LaLonde, *Physical Distribution Management*, p. 109.

Figure 14-11   A framework for physical distribution system design.

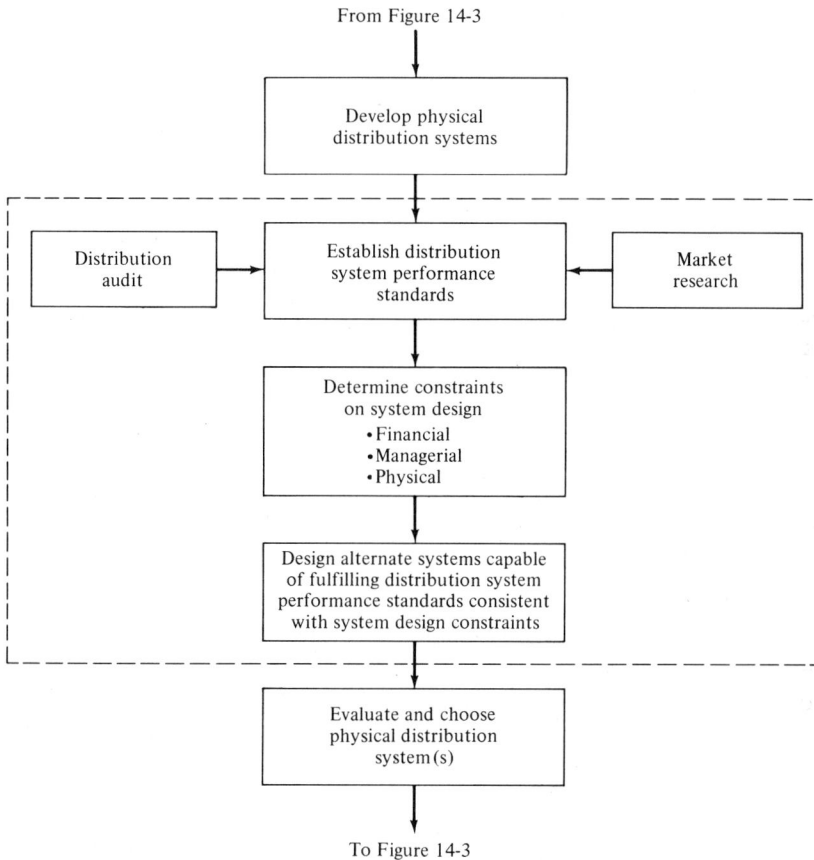

From Figure 14-3

```
        ┌─────────────────────────┐
        │  Develop physical       │
        │  distribution systems   │
        └─────────────────────────┘

┌ ─ ─ ─ ─ ─ ─ ─ ─ ─ ─ ─ ─ ─ ─ ─ ─ ─ ─ ─ ─ ─ ─ ─ ─ ┐
│                                                  │
│ ┌──────────────┐  ┌─────────────────┐ ┌────────┐│
│ │ Distribution │→ │ Establish       │←│ Market ││
│ │ audit        │  │ distribution    │ │research││
│ │              │  │ system          │ │        ││
│ │              │  │ performance     │ │        ││
│ │              │  │ standards       │ │        ││
│ └──────────────┘  └─────────────────┘ └────────┘│
│                                                  │
│                 ┌──────────────────┐             │
│                 │ Determine        │             │
│                 │ constraints      │             │
│                 │ on system design │             │
│                 │  • Financial     │             │
│                 │  • Managerial    │             │
│                 │  • Physical      │             │
│                 └──────────────────┘             │
│                                                  │
│       ┌──────────────────────────────┐          │
│       │ Design alternate systems      │          │
│       │ capable of fulfilling         │          │
│       │ distribution system           │          │
│       │ performance standards         │          │
│       │ consistent with system        │          │
│       │ design constraints            │          │
│       └──────────────────────────────┘          │
└ ─ ─ ─ ─ ─ ─ ─ ─ ─ ─ ─ ─ ─ ─ ─ ─ ─ ─ ─ ─ ─ ─ ─ ─ ┘

        ┌─────────────────────────┐
        │  Evaluate and choose    │
        │  physical distribution  │
        │  system(s)              │
        └─────────────────────────┘
```

To Figure 14-3

THE DISTRIBUTION AUDIT. This procedure develops profiles of: (a) the nature of the product or products to be moved through the system, (b) the nature of the fixed facilities being utilized in the existing distribution system, (c) the manner in which the actual output of the distribution system will be measured in order that it can be compared to distribution-system performance standards, (d) the costs associated with performing existing activities in the physical distribution system.

DISTRIBUTION-SYSTEM PERFORMANCE STANDARDS. These standards specify the objectives the physical distribution system should be designed to achieve. The form these standards might take was presented in Figure 14-4.

THE MARKET AND COMPETITIVE PROFILE. This analysis specifies current and potential customer demands for individual products. Who are current customers? How much do they buy of each product? What is a reasonable estimate of future requirements? What special services do they require? Where are they located from a physical distribution viewpoint?[38] In addition, the nature and the quality of the physical distribution services being offered by competitors are analyzed.

CONSTRAINTS. The firm's financial, managerial, and physical limitations must be taken into consideration, for they specify how the distribution system *can* be designed. It is unrealistic for a firm to design a system that adequately meets its distribution needs but that cannot be implemented because of inadequate financial, managerial, or physical resources.[39]

EVALUATING PHYSICAL DISTRIBUTION SYSTEMS

Three general approaches can be used to select a physical distribution system that satisfies performance standards and is consistent with resource capabilities. These approaches are: (1) micro-functional cost analysis, (2) macro-functional cost analysis, and (3) macro-functional profit analysis.[40]

Micro-functional Cost Analysis

The first and simplest level of analysis involves measuring and analyzing the costs *within* each of the many activity centers in the distribution system.[41] This approach requires the analyst to:

1. Select the single activity center that is to be analyzed.
2. Establish the level of distribution performance that is to be the standard for this activity center.
3. Determine which alternative methods of performing this activity are capable of achieving the required distribution performance standards and thus are to be included in the analysis.
4. Identify the level of costs associated with performing the various tasks within the activity center by each of the alternative methods.
5. Analyze the cost tradeoffs between the alternative methods of performing this activity.
6. Select the approach that minimizes costs and achieves the desired standard of performance.

Micro-functional cost analysis is very simplistic. It provides useful cost information relative to the alternative methods of performing the tasks within the

[38] *Ibid.*, p. 103.

[39] For additional information on distribution system design see William B. Saunders, "Designing a Distribution System," *Distribution Age*, Vol. 64 (January 1965), pp. 32–36.

[40] The scope of the analysis described in this section is limited to a discussion of physical distribution systems. In most instances, however, the analyses apply equally well to similar aspects of systems of physical supply.

[41] The term "activity centers" refers to the activities described in the section entitled "Scope and Structure of Physical Distribution Systems"—that is, transportation, materials handling, inventory, and so on.

various activity centers; however, it is of extremely limited value, primarily because it is a suboptimizing approach. While it may analyze alternative costs within an activity center, it does not consider the impact these alternatives might have on the costs of accomplishing tasks in other activity centers. Since physical distribution is a highly interdependent system of activities, such effects must be taken into consideration in order to minimize suboptimization.

Macro-functional Cost Analysis

Macro-functional cost analysis, or the so-called total-cost model,[42] is probably the model most widely used for evaluating alternative distribution systems. This technique examines the interdependence which exists between the costs in each activity center. It is a useful method for approximating the magnitude of change that might take place in total physical distribution costs as various elements in the systems are altered. These might include the mode of transportation; type of transportation (public or private); inventory levels; and the types, locations, and number(s) of plants and warehouses.

Macro-functional cost analysis involves:

1. Establishing the distribution performance standards for the total distribution system.
2. Determining which distribution systems are capable of achieving the required distribution performance standards and thus are to be included in the analysis.
3. Identifying the level of costs associated with performing the various tasks in each of the activity centers for each of the distribution systems under consideration.
4. Analyzing the cost tradeoffs associated with each of the alternative distribution systems.
5. Selecting the distribution system that provides the requisite level of performance at the lowest total cost.

The total-cost model, though useful, has several inherent limitations. It assumes that fixed and variable costs can be clearly identified, that there is a straight-line relationship between costs and volume, and that there is a constant average shipment size for goods moving between two points.[43] Moreover, it does

[42] The description of the methodology that follows is based largely on material found in the following sources: H. T. Lewis, J. W. Culliton, and J. D. Steele, *The Role of Air Freight In Physical Distribution* (Boston: Division of Research, Graduate School of Business Administration, Harvard University, 1956); Bowersox, Smykay, and LaLonde, *Physical Distribution Management*, pp. 299–322; and J. L. Heskett, R. M. Ivie, and N. A. Glaskowsky, *Business Logistics* (New York: The Ronald Press Company, 1964), pp. 454–469. Also see Marvin Flaks, "Total Cost Approach to Physical Distribution," *Business Management*, Vol. 24 (August 1963), pp. 55–61.

[43] Heskett, Ivie, and Glaskowsky, *Business Logistics*, p. 468.

not consider the magnitude and timing of capital investments required or the cost and revenue streams associated with a particular system.

Macro-functional Profit Analysis

Macro-functional profit analysis closely parallels, and is a natural extension of, the preceding analysis. Instead of concluding the analysis on the basis of cost minimization, it enlarges the analysis to include an explicit consideration of: (1) the effects the various levels of customer service provided by each physical distribution system might have on demand, (2) the different levels of investment that may be required to implement each physical distribution system, and (3) the time value of the savings generated by these various investment outlays.

An Illustrative Comparison of the Macro-functional Cost and Profit Analyses[44]

To demonstrate the similarities and differences of the macro-functional cost and profit techniques as they apply to the evaluation of alternative distribution systems, consider the case of the Apex Company. Apex presently maintains field stocks at 30 public warehouses scattered throughout the country. The public warehouse stocks are replenished from the company's main warehouse located at its only plant. Shipments are made in truckload lots to public warehouses, and deliveries are made from the warehouses either by local cartage firms or by l.t.l. shipments. When an item ordered is not in stock at a particular warehouse, the item is back-ordered and shipped to the warehouse either from the plant warehouse or from stocks at one of the other public warehouses.

The company's distribution manager is considering two proposals for restructuring the present distribution system. Proposal A involves establishing three strategically located distribution centers and eliminating the stocks held at public warehouses. These centers would be served by rail from the plant warehouse, and shipments to customers would be made via motor carrier. A new order-processing system would also be installed in conjunction with the new centers in order to reduce the order cycle between the distribution centers and the plant warehouse.

Proposal B is identical except it uses four distribution centers rather than three. The effects of the present and proposed systems are shown in Table 14-2.

Table 14-3 gives a five-year projection of operating results. Apex executives estimate that the improved customer service resulting from fewer backorders and shortened times for filling backorders in proposals A and B will generate an increase in sales over those that can be expected if the present system is retained. During the first two years under proposal A they estimate that gross orders will be

[44] This comparative analysis is based upon material contained in John R. Grabner, Jr., and James F. Robeson, "Distribution Systems Analysis: A Problem in Capital Budgeting," in David McConaughy, ed., *Business Logistics: Problems and Perspectives* (Los Angeles: University of Southern California Research Institute for Business, 1969), pp. 143–156.

Table 14-2   Operating Characteristics of Apex's Present and Proposed Physical
Distribution Systems (all dollar figures in thousands)

Characteristics	Present System	Proposed Systems	
		A	B
Warehouse replenishment time	16 days	8 days	8 days
Average customer order cycle time from warehouse stocks	5 days	5 days	4 days
Average customer order cycle time for backorders	25 days	18 days	16 days
Proportion of total orders backordered	25%	10%	8%
Proportion of backorders cancelled	20%	20%	20%
Lost sales (percent of total orders)	5%	2%	1.6%
Annual operating expenses: Production, sales, and general administration expenses	$2,000+.80NS[a]	$2,000+.80NS	$2,000+.80NS
Physical distribution expenses: Transportation and warehousing	$ 285+.052NS	$ 310+.038NS	$ 325+.030NS
Inventory carrying costs[b]	60+.005NS	40+.003NS	50+.004NS
Depreciation (buildings and equipment)	10	40	52
General physical distribution administrative expense	25	35	40
Order handling	15	40	50
Total physical distribution expenses	$ 395+.057NS	$ 465+.041NS	$ 517+.034NS
Investment required: Inventories	$ 300+.025NS	$ 200+.015NS	$ 250+.020NS
Warehouses (new)		500	600
Equipment (new)		300	400
Land		75	100

[a] NS = net sales. Net sales = total orders received − cancelled backorders.
[b] Annual inventory carrying costs are assumed to be 20 percent of the book value of inventory.
The inventory carrying cost equation was derived by multiplying the inventory figure (found
in the investment-required part of the table) by .20.

2 percent greater than under the present system and about 1 percent greater during each succeeding year. The decrease in orders after the second year reflects
Apex management's belief that their competitors will initiate retaliatory measures.

Table 14-3   Total Cost and Total Profit Analysis of Apex Company's Present and Proposed

	Present System				
	Year				
	1	*2*	*3*	*4*	*5*
Total orders received[a]	$20,000	$21,000	$22,000	$23,000	$24,000
Orders cancelled	1,000	1,050	1,100	1,150	1,200
Net sales	$19,000	$19,950	$20,900	$21,850	$22,800
Production, sales, and general administrative expenses	17,200	17,960	18,720	19,480	20,240
Total physical distribution costs	1,478	1,532	1,586	1,640	1,695
Net profit before tax	$ 322	$ 458	$ 594	$ 730	$ 865
Tax (50 percent)	161	229	297	365	432
Net profit after tax	$ 161	$ 229	$ 297	$ 365	$ 433

[a] Total orders received for System A are assumed to be 2 percent greater than present system in years 1 and 2 and 1 percent greater each year thereafter. Total orders received for system B are assumed to be 2.5 percent greater than present system in years 1 and 2 and 1 percent greater each year thereafter.

SOURCE: Derived in part from Table 14-2. Order cancellations, production, sales and general administrative expenses, physical distribution costs, and the investment required in inventories were obtained by multiplying net sales volume (by the equation shown in Table 14-2) for the relationship between these factors and net sales volume.

Under proposal B, sales would be 2.5 percent greater during the first two years and 1 percent greater during the remaining three years of the planning period. The cost figures shown in Table 14-3 were projected on the basis of the relationships among the various types of expenses and net sales shown in Table 14-2.

If either total costs or total profits are used to decide among the three alternatives, the results are as follows:

	Total Costs over 5 Years (000)	Total Profits over 5 Years (000)
Present system	$7,931	$1,484
Proposal A	6,806	2,514
Proposal B	6,322	2,832

Based on this analysis, either proposal A or B would be preferable to the present system over the next five years. Further, proposal B appears preferable to A because the firm will realize greater profits over the duration of the planning period owing to lower operating costs, an increased level of gross sales due to better service, and a smaller proportion of lost sales.

However, management wants to consider three additional factors: (1) the

Physical Distribution Systems (thousands of dollars)

		A			Proposed Systems		B		
		Year					*Year*		
1	*2*	*3*	*4*	*5*	*1*	*2*	*3*	*4*	*5*
$20,400	$21,420	$22,220	$23,230	$24,240	$20,500	$21,525	$22,220	$23,230	$24,240
408	428	444	465	485	328	344	356	372	388
$19,992	$20,992	$21,776	$22,765	$23,755	$20,172	$21,181	$21,864	$22,858	$23,852
17,994	18,794	19,421	20,212	21,004	18,138	18,945	19,491	20,286	21,002
1,285	1,326	1,358	1,398	1,439	1,203	1,237	1,260	1,294	1,328
$ 713	$ 872	$ 997	$ 1,155	$ 1,312	$ 831	$ 999	$ 1,113	$ 1,278	$ 1,442
356	436	494	572	656	416	500	556	639	721
$ 357	$ 436	$ 493	$ 573	$ 656	$ 415	$ 499	$ 557	$ 639	$ 721

investment required to implement each of the proposed systems, (2) the net cash flows generated by the present and proposed systems, (3) the present value of the estimated savings to be realized by implementing the proposed systems.

Each of the proposed systems requires a certain initial investment for warehouses, equipment, and land. The investments required to implement proposals A and B are $875,000 and $1,100,000, respectively.

As shown in Table 14-4, both proposed systems increase profits by reducing distribution costs and increasing sales volume.[45] However, profits are only one aspect of the returns to be realized from an investment. Equally important are the differences that will be realized in net cash flows in each year of the planning period.

The net cash flow realized from a project in a given year is composed of the after-tax profits it generates plus the sum of any noncash expenses charged against it for tax purposes and any changes it makes possible in the amount of funds invested in assets. In the case of the Apex Company, the noncash expenses consist of the depreciation on the new buildings and equipment required to implement the proposed changes. The depreciation is charged as an operating expense for tax purposes but does not actually result in a cash outflow. Therefore, the depreciation charges represent funds that are actually available for other uses.

Either of the proposed systems will enable the company to reduce its investment in inventories. Since these funds are available for other uses, they should also be counted as part of the returns realized from changing the distribution sys-

---

[45] The sources of the increased profitability are summarized in the first five lines of Table 14-3.

Table 14-4 Return on Investment Analysis of Apex Company's Proposed Physical Distribution Systems (thousands of dollars)

	Proposed System A					Proposed System B				
	Year					Year				
	1	2	3	4	5	1	2	3	4	5
Physical distribution cost savings[a]	$193	$206	$228	$242	$256	$275	$295	$326	$346	$367
Contribution margin on sales gained by better service[b]	158	166	139	145	152	195	205	160	167	175
Total increase in before-tax profits due to improved physical distribution service	351	372	367	387	408	470	500	486	513	542
Tax (50 percent)	175	181	184	194	204	235	250	243	256	276
Net increase in after-tax profits due to improved physical distribution service	$176	$181	$183	$193	$204	$235	$250	$243	$257	$276
Add:										
Depreciation and capital recovery[c]	40	40	40	40	715	52	52	52	52	836
Difference in average annual inventory levels[d]	275	279	290	298	309	122	120	130	134	138
Annual net increase in funds available if system adopted	$491	$500	$513	$531	$1,228	$409	$422	$425	$443	$1,250
Discount factor (20 percent annual rate of return required on this type of investment)	.833	.694	.579	.482	.402	.833	.694	.579	.482	.402
Present value of annual net increase in funds available	$403	$347	$297	$256	$494	$341	$293	$246	$214	$502

Present value of total increase in funds available[e]	$1,797	$1,596
Total initial investment required	875	1,100
Profitability index[f]	2.05	1.45

SOURCE: Derived from Tables 14-2 and 14-3.

In the following footnotes let i = any year in the planning period, j = any one of the proposed distribution systems, and p = the present distribution system.

[a] $TDCS_{ij} = TDC_{ip} - TDC_{ij}$, where $TDCS$ = total distribution-cost savings and TDC = total distribution costs.

[b] $CMSG_{ij} = (NS_{ij} - NS_{ip})(1 - x_j NS_{ij})$, where $CMSG$ = contribution margin on sales gained by better service, NS = net sales, x = sum of variable portions of production, sales, general administrative and physical distribution costs, and $(1 - x_j NS_{ij})$ = contribution margin, i.e., the percentage of net sales that is available for covering overhead expenses and contributing to profit. In this particular example: $CMSG_{iA} = (NS_{iA} - NS_{ip})(1 - .841) = (NS_{iA} - NS_{ip})(.159)$ and $CMSG_{iB} = (NS_{iB} - NS_{ip})(1 - .834) = (NS_{iB} - NS_{ip})(.166)$. This factor measures the opportunity cost of retaining the present system. It indicates the amount of funds each of the proposed systems will make available that will not be available if the present system is retained. This amount is measured by the increased sales volume expected less the variable expenses that will be incurred in generating the additional volume.

[c] The warehouses, equipment, and land purchased for the new system will have economic value at the end of the planning period. Therefore, we have assumed that these assets can be resold, if need be, for their depreciated book value at the end of the five-year planning period. This element of capital recovery accounts for the large increase in cash flow in year 5.

[d] $DAAI_{ij} = I_{ip} - I_{ij}$, where $DAAI$ = differences in average annual inventory investments and I = average annual inventory investment. I, for each system, present and proposed, was computed using the relationship between inventories and net sales shown in Table 14-2.

[e] Sum of present values of annual net increases in funds available.

[f] Profitability index = $\dfrac{\text{present value of total increase in funds available}}{\text{total initial investment required}}$

tem. The differences between the total funds available if one or the other of the proposed systems is adopted, and those available if the present system is retained, are summarized on the line entitled "Net increase in funds available" in Table 14-4.

The Apex Company has a variety of other possible uses for its investment funds in addition to the revamping of its distribution system. After considering the risk involved in changing distribution systems, and the returns that might be realized from other investment projects, top management has determined that the company must realize at least a 20 percent after-tax return on any major investment in its distribution system.

Considering the time value of money, and a 20 percent return on investment requirement, returns of $1,000 realized in one year would presently be worth $833, while returns of $1,000 in five years would be worth $402 at present. Stated differently, the company is willing to invest $833 today in order to realize $1,000 one year from now and $402 today in order to realize $1,000 five years from now. The discounted value of the savings generated by each of the proposed systems is shown on the line titled "Present value of net increases in funds available" in Table 14-4.[46]

The final step involves the determination of a profitability index. This is a ratio of the present value of the stream of funds that will become available as a result of the change in distribution systems to the present value of the total investment required to implement the change. Any system with an index greater than 1.00 satisfies the return criterion.

On the basis of the foregoing analysis, the desirability of the two proposed changes in distribution systems is calculated as follows:

	Proposal A	Proposal B
(1) Present value of total increase in funds available over the planning period	$1,797,000	$1,596,000
(2) Total initial investment required (obtained from Table 14-2)	$ 875,000	$1,100,000
(3) Profitability index (1÷2)	2.05	1.45

Both projects have a profitability index greater than 1.00. System A's index is 2.05, which indicates a return in excess of 40 percent per year after taxes, and system B's index is 1.45, a return of approximately 29 percent per year after taxes. Its higher return makes system A the preferred system.

SUMMARY

Integrated distribution begins with the establishment of specific, measurable physical distribution objectives. These objectives are established after careful

---

[46] For a detailed explanation of present-value theory see J. Fred Weston and Eugene F. Brigham, *Managerial Finance,* 2d ed. (New York: Holt, Rinehart and Winston, Inc., 1966), pp. 167–173.

analysis of the firm's corporate and marketing objectives and strategy, customer distribution needs, and competitive offerings. Next, the objectives of physical distribution must be reconciled with the physical distribution budget in order to insure that the objectives are attainable and internally consistent.

Once objectives have been established, the physical distribution manager should seek to develop alternative distribution systems that are capable of achieving these objectives. Then alternative systems must be evaluated and the most desirable one(s) chosen. Three procedures are available to evaluate distribution systems—micro-functional cost analysis, macro-functional cost analysis (total-cost analysis), and macro-functional profit analysis. The first two rely upon some form of cost minimization for the objective function, while the latter is based upon maximizing the firm's return on investment in distribution operations.

It is often advisable to pretest the chosen distribution system(s) prior to full-scale implementation. These procedures are described at length in Chapters 18 and 19. Finally, the actual performance of the distribution system should be measured and compared with the distribution performance standards (objectives) on a continuing basis so that the system can be adjusted in accordance with changes in the marketplace.

QUESTIONS FOR REVIEW AND DISCUSSION

1. Which factors historically have caused physical distribution activities to assume increasing importance in American business operations?
2. How would you evaluate the relative importance of fixed facilities, transportation, inventory management, and logistical support systems in the decade of the seventies?
3. Compare and contrast systems of product flow with those of information flow.
4. Evaluate the realism of the physical distribution objectives cited in Figure 14-4 for a full-service hardware wholesaler with a three-state marketing area and a fleet of private trucks.
5. Summarize the strengths and weaknesses of macro-functional cost analysis (total cost) as a means of evaluating alternative physical distribution systems. Can you develop advantages and disadvantages in addition to those cited in the text?
6. To what extent does macro-functional profit analysis utilizing return on investment overcome the disadvantages associated with macro-functional cost analysis?
7. What disadvantage do you see in the *practical* application of macro-functional profit analysis?
8. Should physical distribution systems be pretested prior to full-scale implementation? Why?
9. Which elements in the physical distribution system (fixed facilities, inventories, and so on) will be seriously affected if and when the supersonic transport comes into widespread use by the nation's airlines?

Chapter 15   Advertising Programs

How much should a firm spend on advertising? What types of media should be used? What kinds of advertisements should be run? Has the campaign been successful?

The role and the importance of advertising vary considerably from one company to another. Regardless of its role, however, advertising is generally agreed to be one of the most difficult components of the marketing program to manage effectively. Among companies that have overcome or learned how to deal with these problems, advertising has often been a key factor behind marketing success.

THE NATURE AND SCOPE OF ADVERTISING PROGRAMS

Nature of Promotion and Advertising

The promotional activities of companies are usually classified into four basic categories:

>*Advertising*: Any paid form of nonpersonal presentation and promotion of ideas, goods, or services by an identified sponsor.
>
>*Personal selling*: Oral presentation in a conversation with one or more prospective purchasers for the purpose of making sales.
>
>*Sales promotion*: Those marketing activities, other than personal selling, advertising, and publicity, that stimulate consumer purchasing and dealer effectiveness, such as displays, shows and exhibitions, demonstrations, and various nonrecurrent selling efforts not in the ordinary routine.

Publicity: Nonpersonal stimulation of demand for a product, service, or business unit by planting commercially significant news about it in a published medium or obtaining favorable presentation of it on radio, television, or stage that is not paid for by the sponsor.[1]

This chapter is concerned with advertising, and, to a limited extent, sales promotion. Personal selling is discussed in Chapter 16.

An Advertising Planning and Control System

Figure 15-1 summarizes the advertising planning and control system that will be discussed in the remainder of this chapter. The process begins with advertising objectives, which specify the role of advertising in achieving those marketing objectives required to satisfy corporate objectives. A tentative advertising budget is established, and a creative strategy, advertisements, and media strategy are formulated. The complete advertising campaign is tested and/or implemented and the results are subsequently measured and evaluated. Each of these steps is discussed in greater detail below.

SETTING ADVERTISING OBJECTIVES

Several studies indicate that relatively few companies have specific, measurable advertising objectives.[2] Yet such objectives are critically important, for they form the foundation for an effective advertising program. This section discusses the nature of advertising objectives and alternative ways of formulating them.

The Nature of Advertising Objectives

Advertising objectives specify the contribution that advertising is expected to make to the achievement of marketing objectives. To be managerially useful, they must be stated in specific measurable terms. This means that an advertising objective must have four major components: (1) *a specific sales or communication task*—in other words, *what* is to be accomplished; (2) *a defined audience*—or who should do the task; (3) *a defined degree*—or the extent to which the audience is to do the task; and (4) *a defined period of time*—or the time period when the results are to be achieved.[3]

To illustrate, here is the advertising objective for one of Oscar Mayer's meat products:

---

[1] *Marketing Definitions: A Glossary of Marketing Terms*, Compiled by the Committee on Definitions of the American Marketing Association, Ralph S. Alexander, Chairman (Chicago: American Marketing Association, 1960).

[2] See, for example, Russell H. Colley, ed., *Defining Advertising Goals* (New York: Association of National Advertisers, 1961); and Saul S. Sands, *Setting Advertising Objectives* (New York: National Industrial Conference Board, Business Policy Study No. 118, 1966).

[3] Colley, *Defining Advertising Goals*.

Figure 15-1   An advertising planning and control system.

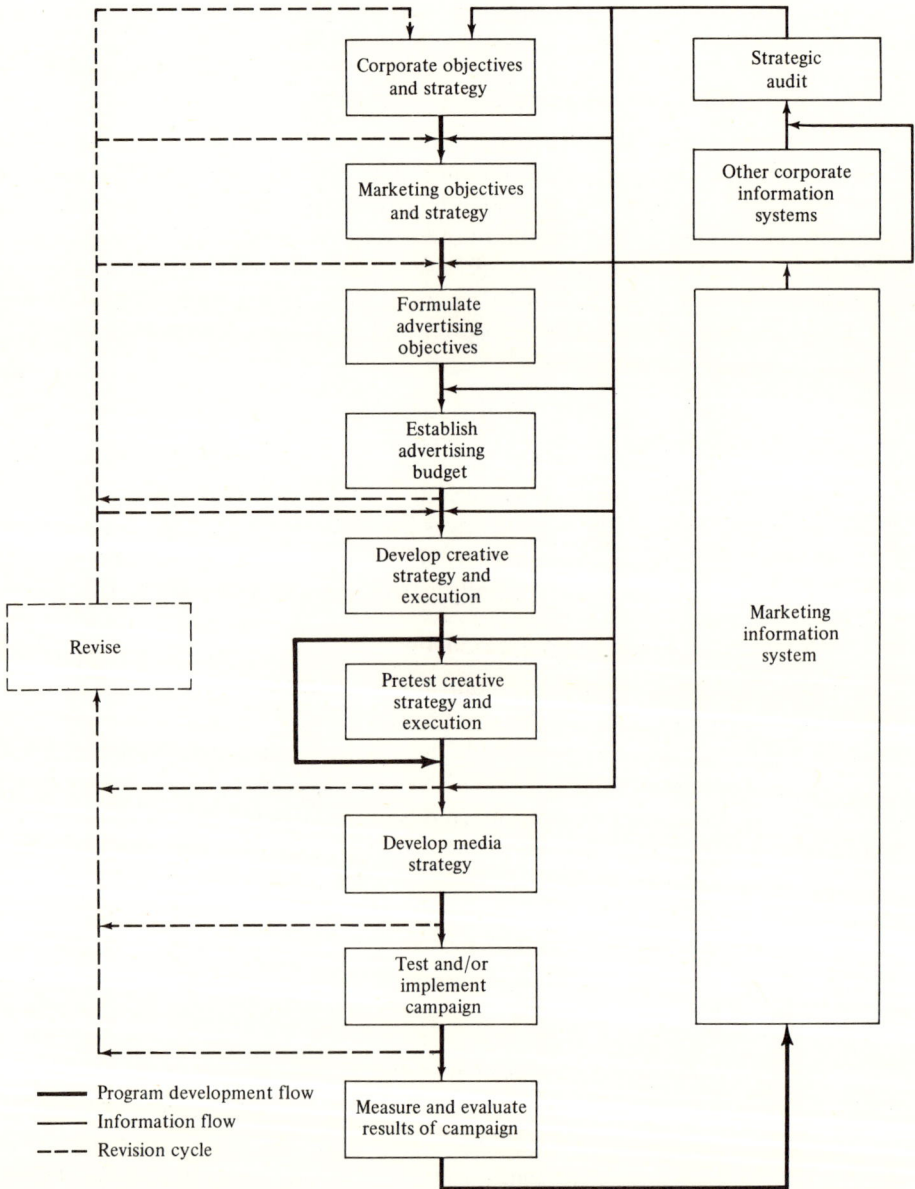

The *task* was to communicate the fact that Oscar Mayer cold cuts were available in a new easy-open, reclosable, full-view package. The *audience* was all U.S. housewives who buy two or more packages of cold cuts a month. The *degree* was 30 percent of the defined audience. The *time period* was one year.[4]

The Task Controversy

For over a decade there has been heated debate over whether the task of advertising should be to generate sales or achieve certain prerequisite communication effects, such as brand awareness, knowledge, preference, or conviction to purchase. In 1961, The Association of National Advertisers endorsed the need for communication tasks. They argued that sales cannot serve as an objective, because they are affected by all marketing efforts, but that communication effects can be measured using existing research techniques. Hence proponents of this view—known as DAGMAR (Defining Advertising Goals, Measuring Advertising Results) —contend that advertising tasks should be stated in terms of communication effects rather than sales.[5]

Many advertising experts disagree with the DAGMAR philosophy. They point out that both communication effects and sales are caused by many factors[6] and that it is not always correct to assume that the better advertising communicates, the more it will sell. In other words, without specific evidence, it is not safe to conclude that higher levels of awareness and knowledge, or more favorable attitudes toward a brand, will result in increased sales. Sometimes it happens, other times it does not.[7]

Thus it is not possible to generalize about the relative desirability of sales and communication tasks. If a company empirically determines that communication effects are functionally related to sales, communication levels can be used as advertising tasks. If these relationships do not exist, then both sales and communication tasks can be used.[8]

Establishing Specific Tasks

Since advertising objectives must be tailored to accommodate a company's specific corporate and marketing objectives and the conditions it faces in

---

[4] Dik Warren Twedt, "How to Analyze your 1966 Advertising Budget . . . Before You Approve It?" *Business Management*, September 1965, pp. 38–43 ff, at p. 40.

[5] Colley, *Defining Advertising Goals*, p. 21.

[6] A. J. Vogl (quoting from Charles A. Raymond), "Advertising Research—Everybody's Looking for the Holy Grail," *Sales Management*, November 1, 1963, p. 43.

[7] See, for example, Jack B. Haskins, "Factual Recall as a Measure of Advertising Effectiveness," *Journal of Advertising Research*, Vol. 4 (March 1964), pp. 2–8; *Attitude Research at Sea* (Chicago: American Marketing Association, 1966); Joel N. Axelrod, "Attitude Measures that Predict Purchase," *Journal of Advertising Research*, Vol. 8 (March 1968), pp. 3–17; and Roger Barton, "ARF Asks: Are Awareness, Attitude, and Behavior Related?" *Media Scope* (January 1968), pp. 53–68.

[8] For further discussion see Charles K. Raymond, "Must Advertising Communicate to Sell?" *Harvard Business Review*, Vol. 43 (September-October 1965); and Colley, *Defining Advertising Goals*.

achieving them, it is not possible to specify specific advertising tasks. However, it is possible to present a framework that can be used by individual companies.

The procedure is first to understand company and marketing objectives and then to develop an inventory of ways the company's marketing program differs from those of competitors. Points of difference that are relevant and meaningful to customers in the target market segment, and that are amenable to advertising, become potential candidates for specific communication tasks. These may include product attributes, price, retail availability, service, warranty, and so on. Consumption-system analysis, preference-distribution analysis, and similarity and preference mapping are particularly useful in choosing advertising tasks (see Chapter 9).

Determining the Defined Audience

The defined audience component of the advertising objective is usually the target market segment for the overall marketing program. Alternative ways of segmenting markets and estimating the sales potential of alternative market targets were discussed in Chapter 9.

Determining the Degree of Task Accomplishment

The third component of the advertising objective specifies the target degree of accomplishment for whatever is selected as the task. It is desirable to state the degree in "from-to" terms—for example, to increase awareness *from* 10 percent *to* 60 percent. The reason is that the difficulty of achieving whatever is specified depends not only on the absolute increment of improvement but also the base level. For example, it is a different problem to increase awareness from 10 to 40 percent than from 50 to 80 percent, even though the increment in both cases is 30 percentage points.

To be able to put advertising objectives in these terms it is first necessary to determine the "from," or current level. This requires research to identify how many prospects already know about or believe whatever communication task is selected—if a communication task is used. If the task is sales-oriented, then it is necessary to determine the current level of sales and market share.

Given the current level of whatever is specified as the task, the next problem is to determine what the target improvement increment should be. If the task is sales, then the target improvement increment will be that amount required to achieve the level of sales volume and/or market share stated in the general marketing objective.

If a communication task is used, the problem is more difficult. The challenge is to determine what level of communication is required to achieve the sales objective of marketing. For example, assume the communication task is brand preference and the marketing objective is a 30 percent market share. Then the question is, what preference share is required to achieve a 30 percent market share? Or, if the communication task is awareness, then what awareness share is required to achieve a 30 percent target market share? In order to answer these types of questions, it is necessary to determine the functional relationship between communication levels and sales. This usually requires sophisticated controlled experiments on a periodic basis.

Determining the Specified Time Period

In most instances the time period for accomplishing the advertising objective(s) will be one year. The reason, of course, is that this period is most commonly used to plan, budget and control marketing and other functional areas of the business.

In a growing number of instances, however, the time period is being extended beyond one year. For new products, often one year is not enough time to accomplish objectives. Frequently it is desirable to overspend in one period and maintain or reduce expenditures in subsequent periods. This extension of the planning period is commonly referred to as "payout planning."

DETERMINING THE ADVERTISING INVESTMENT

The amount of money to be spent on advertising is one of the most difficult and often one of the most important decisions facing a marketing executive. This section reviews and critically evaluates alternative approaches to this important decision area.

Keyed-to-Sales Approach

There are two varieties of this approach. One approach—the percent-of-sales method—involves a calculation of the percentage of the sales dollar allocated to promotion in the past and applies this percentage either to past or forecasted sales to arrive at the budget. The other approach is to allocate a fixed amount per unit for advertising; the budget is then accumulated by forecasting unit sales.

These approaches have several weaknesses. First, although advertising must ultimately be justified in terms of its contribution to sales, under this method sales determine advertising. Second, sales cannot be forecasted without some assumption about the level of advertising. Third, the approach does not focus on the objectives of the campaign; therefore, the amount allocated bears no necessary relationship to the expenditure level required to achieve objectives.

Despite these problems, this approach is widely used. One reason is that it is simple to calculate. Because it appears definite and can be compared to the percentage being allocated by competitors, it is said to be easier to justify to top management. Moreover, since expenditures are keyed to anticipated revenues, it is often perceived as a financially safe solution to a complex problem.[9]

The Return-on-Investment Approach

This approach argues that advertising is not an expense but rather an investment that should compete for funds with alternative investments. The present worth

[9] For further discussion see Sands, *Setting Advertising Objectives*, Chap. 3.

of the stream of profits generated by advertising should be compared with the cost of funds and the present worth of the stream of profits that could be obtained by the best alternative use of funds. In rationing capital among advertising and competing investment alternatives, the cutoff point should be the firm's cost of capital.[10]

The major problem in using this approach is to determine the effect of advertising on sales so the return can be estimated. Since progress is being made in this area, this approach may enjoy more widespread acceptance in the future.

All-You-Can-Afford Approach

Sometimes management spends as much as it feels the company can afford without jeopardizing its financial position. This is often calculated by determining the residual amount remaining from the selling price after reseller margins, non-marketing costs, and profit margins are subtracted.

It is apparent that an advertising budget derived in this manner (by multiplying the residual amount per unit times estimated sales in units) bears no necessary relationship to the effort required to achieve advertising objectives. For this reason, this approach is rarely used except where sales are strongly responsive to the level of advertising expenditures. Some new products have this characteristic.

Objective and Task Approach

This technique, used mainly by larger companies, is the second most common method of establishing the advertising budget. After objectives have been specified, it is necessary to determine what tasks and programs are required to achieve them. The costs required to implement these programs are estimated and summed to yield the advertising budget.

The conceptual logic underlying this approach is sound. The problem lies in determining how much it will cost to achieve the objective(s) and in deciding whether an expenditure of this amount will be profitable. In order to overcome these problems it is necessary to determine the functional relationship between advertising expenditures and the sales or communication task. These relationships can be determined empirically, but the effort and expense are such that only larger corporations normally attempt it. In situations where the benefits exceed the costs, this is a sound and preferred approach to the budgeting of advertising expenditures.

The "NEWS" Model

One of the largest advertising agencies in the world, Batten, Barton, Durstine & Osborn, has designed a planning and control system for new products called NEWS (new-product early warning system). Several years of research in more

---

[10] See, for example, Joel Dean, "Does Advertising Belong in the Capital Budget?" *Journal of Marketing*, Vol. 30 (October 1966), pp. 15–21.

than 30 product categories has yielded a series of recursive equations, linking (1) gross rating points to advertising expenditures, (2) expenditures to awareness, (3) awareness to trial, (4) trial to usage, and (5) usage to sales dollars. These relationships are estimated separately, using either linear or nonlinear relationships from data obtained in test-market experiments.

Through this series of relationships it is possible to link advertising expenditures to product sales and market share. Thus, given a sales or market-share objective, it is possible to determine the advertising expenditure necessary to achieve that objective. While several technical inadequacies still exist, the NEWS model has been used successfully to determine advertising expenditure levels for several new packaged goods.[11]

DESIGNING THE CREATIVE APPROACH

Effective advertisements are not necessarily those that executives and customers like or consider to be good. Unfortunately, designing creative approaches is far more difficult than it appears. It is necessary to formulate the creative strategy and then determine the best way of executing it. In addition, legal restrictions must be observed.

Creative Strategy

Creative strategy specifies what advertisements should accomplish. The general nature of the creative strategy should be identified in the communication-task component of the advertising objective. Thus creative strategy will identify those elements of the marketing program that differ from competitors' and are meaningful to customers in the target market segment. We can better understand this process by examining illustrative case histories.

PURINA DOG CHOW.[12] In the middle 1950s, Ralston Purina Company decided to create a new dry dog food. Consumer research indicated that dog owners wanted a dog food to be four things: highly palatable, completely nutritious, economical, and convenient to serve and store. Ralston's research and development came up with a new food, and in taste tests dogs preferred it, six to one.

The initial creative strategy emphasized nutrition, with some stress on palatability. At that time nutrition was the main claim of all dog foods, the key to all animal feeds, and the biggest selling point of all of Ralston's other feeds. Although sales were going well, the creative people were not satisfied. They felt the palatability claim should have dominated.

It was decided to do further research concentrating on how the dog owner felt about his dog rather than what the owner expected of a new dog food. The results indicated the owner's main concern was whether his dog would eat the

[11] See Lawrence Light and Lewis Pringle, "New Product Forecasting Using Recursive Regression," in David T. Kollat, Roger D. Blackwell, and James F. Engel, *Research in Consumer Behavior* (New York: Holt, Rinehart and Winston, Inc., 1970).

[12] Noel Digby, "Purina Dog Chow: All You Add is Love" (Chicago: American Association of Advertising Agencies, Central Region Convention, October 14, 1966).

food. If he did not eat it, nutrition would be valueless. Thus the new creative strategy stressed palatability: "New Purina Dog Chow—Makes Dogs Eager Eaters." With other companies emphasizing nutrition, Purina was able to capture a significant market share and has retained it ever since.

CESSNA AIRCRAFT.[13] In 1964, aircraft and Cessna sales had reached a plateau. Unit sales were not increasing to any great degree; in fact, they were less in 1963 than in 1957. One of the major reasons was fear, particularly among older people. Other factors were fear of cost involvement, distance from the airfield, the unsettled weather conditions in certain parts of the country, and fears held by wives.

Sales analysis revealed that the company was selling more expensive airplanes to the same pilots. The company concluded that if it was going to sell more airplanes, there must be more pilots. Research indicated that out of every 100 new flying students, within a 10-year period, 14 bought a new or used airplane, and four bought new airplanes. Since Cessna had a 50 percent market share, analysts calculated that the company should sell two new airplanes for every 100 new students. Given the marketing objective of doubling unit sales during the next five years—from 3,400 to 7,000—it was determined that the number of flying students would have to increase from 109,000 to 200,000.

The creative question was how to increase the number of flying students to the desired levels. The challenge was to get potential students into an airplane and to make the first ride cheap enough to eliminate, at least in the initial stage, the cost barrier. The strategy: a learn-to-fly campaign featuring a $5 introductory offer to try flying without making a commitment to continue. Dealers were informed of the rationale behind the strategy and given point-of-sale materials and other forms of assistance. In 1968, the number of students was running above the goal. Unit sales doubled in three years, two years ahead of the expected five-year goal.

Creative Execution

The purposes of creative execution are (1) to attract attention, (2) to hold attention, and (3) to accomplish the objectives spelled out in the creative strategy. This can be accomplished by the appropriate use of message themes, headlines, copy, illustration, and layout. Also involved are decisions concerning the size or length of commercials and the use or nonuse of colors and color combinations.

There is almost an infinite number of ways of combining these execution variables into advertisements. Many professionals have advanced guidelines for making these decisions. For example:

1. On the average, five times as many people read the headline as read the body copy. If you haven't done some selling in your headline, you have wasted 80 percent of your client's money.

---

[13] A. Laney Lee, "Cessna's One Hundred Million Dollar Coupon" (Chicago: American Association of Advertising Agencies, Central Region Convention, November 11–12, 1968).

2. Copy should be specific and factual; generalizations and platitudes should be avoided.
3. The best TV commercials are built around one or two forcefully demonstrated ideas.
4. TV commercials are not for entertaining; they are for selling. Persuasive commercials never sing.[14]

Such criteria, though useful as general guidelines, should not be taken as formulas for success in every situation. Advertisements violating these criteria sometimes prove effective, and advertisements consistent with these criteria are sometimes relatively ineffective.[15] The determinants of effectiveness appear to vary from one situation to another as well as across products. Thus, effectiveness criteria must be isolated for specific product categories through appropriate pretesting techniques. These methods are discussed in the next major section of this chapter.

Legal Restrictions on Creative Strategy and Execution

A substantial proportion of the legal environment of marketing applies to advertising. These restrictions are briefly surveyed below.[16]

THE FEDERAL TRADE COMMISSION ACT.   The Federal Trade Commission Act of 1914 and its Wheeler-Lea Amendment in 1938 exert a strong influence on advertising. Section Five prohibits unfair methods of competition in interstate commerce where the effect is to injure competition. This includes false and misleading advertising, which means, among other things, that advertising must be written so as not to deceive "the trusting as well as the suspicious, the casual as well as the vigilant, the naive as well as the sophisticated."

The Commission also (1) is empowered to issue cease-and-desist orders, which become binding after 60 days; (2) has jurisdiction over false advertising of foods, drugs, and cosmetics; and (3) issues injunctions to halt improper food, drug, or cosmetic advertising when it appears the public might be harmed. In order to fulfill these responsibilities the Commission staff continually monitors all forms of interstate advertising.[17]

---

[14] David Ogilvy, "Raise Your Sights! 97 Tips for Copywriters, Art Directors & TV Producers—Mostly Derived from Research" (an internal publication by Ogilvy, Benson, & Mather).

[15] See, for example, "Mini-Sell on Madison Avenue," *Dun's Review*, July 1967, pp. 27 ff.; Dik Warren Twedt, "A Multiple Factor Analysis of Advertising Readership," *Journal of Applied Psychology*, June 1952, pp. 207–215; and John C. Maloney, "Is Advertising Believability Really Important?" *Journal of Marketing*, Vol. 27 (October 1963), pp. 1–8.

[16] For a more detailed discussion of legislative and regulatory restrictions on advertising see "How the U.S. Regulates Advertising," *The World of Advertising* (Chicago: Advertising Publications, Inc., 1962), pp. 182 ff.

[17] *The World of Advertising*, p. 184. For discussion of what constitutes false and misleading see "Advertising Alert," No. 1 (January 12, 1962), published by the Federal Trade Commission.

THE FEDERAL FOOD, DRUG, AND COSMETIC ACT. The Food and Drug Administration is empowered to investigate and litigate advertising claims appearing on the label or package of food, drug, and cosmetic items. In addition, it is authorized to require full disclosure of side effects and complications in the advertising and labeling of prescription drugs. It is authorized to seize illegal shipments upon evidence of violation.

STATE AND LOCAL REGULATIONS. In addition to Federal restrictions, a variety of state and local regulations affect advertising. In 1911 Printers' Ink proposed a "model statute," which has been adopted or adapted by the majority of states. This statute specifies what constitutes deceptive advertising.

PRETESTING CREATIVE APPROACHES

Because the effectiveness of various execution techniques varies from one setting to another, whenever possible it is desirable to pretest alternative advertisements before deciding which ones to use in a campaign. A firm should insist that its advertising agency document the effectiveness of the advertisements they propose. This testing should be done by an outside organization and paid for by the agency. This section describes and evaluates some of the most common pretesting techniques.

Opinion-Measurement Techniques

ORDER-OF-MERIT RATINGS. This procedure requires each respondent to rank-order a number of advertisements according to such criteria as: (1) which of these advertisements would you most likely read? (2) which of these advertisements interest you the most? (3) which of these advertisements would be most effective in causing you to buy? That advertisement receiving the greatest number of "number one" ratings is presumably the most desirable.

PAIRED COMPARISONS. This technique asks respondents to evaluate each alternative advertisement under consideration against all others, one pair at a time. Any evaluation criterion can be used—for example, which would you most likely read, which interests you the most, which would most likely cause you to buy. As before, the advertisement receiving the highest rating is presumably the most effective.

RATING SCALES. The semantic differential is one of the most widely used scaling techniques. This technique requires respondents to evaluate advertisements in terms of paired polar adjectives, such as expensive-cheap, shy-aggressive, low class-high class. Using appropriate research designs, respondents are given advertisements and asked to mark the space on paired polar adjective scales that most nearly corresponds to their opinion. That advertisement that most nearly corresponds to the adjective profile desired is judged most desirable.

EVALUATION OF OPINION-MEASUREMENT TECHNIQUES. The order-of-merit and paired-comparison methods have several drawbacks. One is the "halo effect," or the tendency for some people to rate an advertisement high on many attributes because they like some aspects of it. Another problem is that some respondents play the expert and evaluate advertisements as they think others would. Third, these two methods yield only relative rankings; all advertisements may be poor in absolute terms. Finally, the ranking of a large number of advertisements can be onerous and exceedingly difficult when the differences between them are relatively minor.[18]

Rating scales overcome the "relatively good-absolutely poor" problem in that they can measure intensity of preference. Other advantages are that the rating scale is standardized and allows temporal comparisons, is reliable and repeatable, and lessens biases resulting from question phrasing.[19] For these reasons, rating scales are typically more useful than the other two approaches.

Readership and Recall Measurement Techniques

PORTFOLIO TESTS. This technique exposes a group of respondents to a group of test and control advertisements. The test advertisement that induces the most recall of relevant content is judged most effective in capturing and holding attention.

DUMMY ADVERTISING VEHICLES. Dummy advertising vehicles are realistic-appearing, but bogus, advertising vehicles designed for the purpose of pretesting advertisements. Test advertisements as well as other advertisements are inserted in the vehicle along with editorial or program materials. Test advertisements are evaluated on the basis of a number of criteria, including recall, copy readership, and the extent of product interest.

These two approaches have the same basic limitation—recall scores can vary as a result of the consumer's interest in the products being advertised. This can be overcome by developing norms, or, in the case of portfolio tests, by including only products in the same generic category. Of the two approaches, dummy vehicles are preferable because they more nearly simulate the normal viewing environment.[20]

Preference- and Attitude-Change Measurement Techniques

Since the objective of advertising is frequently to change attitudes and preferences, changes in these phenomena are often used to pretest competing advertisements. The Schwerin Theatre Testing System is one of the most widely used techniques in this category.

Under the Schwerin method, tickets are mailed to households in a few

[18] Darrell B. Lucas and Stewart H. Britt, *Measuring Advertising Effectiveness* (New York: McGraw-Hill, Inc., 1963), pp. 105–108.

[19] William A. Mindak, "Fitting the Semantic Differential to the Marketing Problem," *Journal of Marketing*, Vol. 25 (April 1961), pp. 28–33.

[20] John C. Maloney, "Portfolio Tests—Are They Here to Stay?" *Journal of Marketing*, Vol. 25 (July 1961), pp. 32–37; Alvin A. Achenbaum, Russell I. Haley, and Ronald Gatty, "On-Air vs. In-Home Testing of TV Commercials," *Journal of Advertising Research*, Vol. 7 (December 1967), pp. 15–19.

major cities inviting people to view new television shows with commercials inserted in the usual place. Before the showing each respondent is asked to select, from a brand list for the product category to be tested, the brand he would prefer if successful in a drawing. After the showing (which includes the test advertisement), each respondent is asked to indicate the brand he would prefer if successful in another drawing. The Schwerin "Relative Competitive Preference," or RCP, score for the test commercial is calculated by subtracting the percentage of respondents preferring the brand *before* the commercial from the percentage preferring the brand *after* the commercial, and then subtracting the average before-after differences found in the pretesting of other brands in the product field (RCP = After-Before-Norm).

Although many advertisers and advertising agencies have criticized the Schwerin technique, it has been successfully used by many firms, including some of the nation's leading advertisers.[21]

Laboratory Measurement Techniques

During the last decade several so-called laboratory techniques have enjoyed growing acceptance as pretesting tools. Some of the most widely used methods are discussed below.

THE TACHISTOSCOPE. This instrument presents stimuli, such as test advertisements, under various conditions of speed, exposure, and illumination. It has been used to determine the rate at which different advertisements convey information. Speed of recognition has been found to correlate with readership scores.[22]

THE PSYCHOGALVANOMETER. This device measures the amplitude or height of sweat-gland activity (called GSR or galvanic skin response). The intensity of GSR is thought to measure viewer interest, and, although it has been criticized, it has been successfully used to pretest advertisements.[23]

PUPIL-DILATION MEASUREMENT. This type of instrument measures the diameter of the pupil at frequent intervals, such as twice per second. It is used to evaluate the effectiveness of different creative approaches, measure interest in different parts of a commercial, and select advertisements for a campaign. Although this technique has also been criticized, it has reportedly been used to

[21] See, for example, A. R. Dodd and P. J. Kelly, "New Study Tells TV Advertisers How Advertising Builds Sales and Share of Market," *Printers' Ink,* May 1964, pp. 27–38; Robert D. Buzzell, "Predicting Short-Term Changes in Market Share as a Function of Advertising Strategy," *Journal of Marketing Research,* Vol. 1 (August 1964), pp. 27–31; and J. E. Fothergill and A. S. C. Ehrenberg, "On the Schwerin Analyses of Advertising Effectiveness," *Journal of Marketing Research,* Vol. 2 (August 1965), pp. 298–306.

[22] Clark Leavitt, "Intrigue in Advertising—The Motivating Effects of Visual Organization," *Proceedings: 7th Annual Conference* (New York: Advertising Research Foundation, Inc., 1961), pp. 19–24.

[23] John M. Caffyn, "Psychological Laboratory Techniques in Copy Research," *Journal of Advertising Research,* Vol. 4 (December 1964), pp. 45–50.

select some of the most successful advertisements run by several advertising agencies in the Interpublic Group of Companies.[24]

SALIVATION MEASUREMENT. This device measures the rate of salivation. It is used primarily to pretest food advertisements, since saliva flows vary widely when consumers view food products.[25]

EVALUATION OF LABORATORY TECHNIQUES. Laboratory pretesting techniques are becoming increasingly popular. Since many do not rely on verbal reporting by the respondent, they are free from response bias. Moreover, compared to many other techniques, they can often be conducted more quickly, less expensively, and more covertly.

On the other hand, there are several problems. In many cases it is not clear what these techniques actually measure. Often too, there is some question as to biases resulting from the apparent artificiality of the testing environment. Finally there is controversy over the sample sizes and selection procedures used. Despite these limitations, many experts expect laboratory techniques to be used more widely in the future.[26]

MEDIA STRATEGY

While the creative aproach is being developed, it is necessary to select the best communication channels to carry the advertising message to the target-market audience. As Table 15-1 indicates, the use of media varies widely across industries and companies. The reasons for these differences will become apparent as we discuss the factors influencing the selection of general media and specific vehicles within a medium.

Selecting Major Media Types

The first step in media strategy is to select the general types of media that will be used in the campaign (major types are itemized in Table 15-1). One factor that should be considered is the target market segment. The objective is to select those media that reach customers in the target segment with the minimum waste (minimum coverage of people or organizations not in the target segment).

Creative strategy is also considered. Which media allow the creative strategy to be executed most effectively? If visual demonstration is needed, then print

---

[24] Herbert E. Krugman, "Some Applications of Pupil Measurement," *Journal of Marketing Research*, Vol 1 (November 1964), pp. 15–19.

[25] See, for example, Paul Schwerin and Malcolm Murphy, "The Development of Salivation Measurements as a Possible New Technique for Objectively Determining Consumer Reactions to Pictorial Advertisements," *Schwerin Research Corporation Technical and Analytical Review*, May 1963, entire issue.

[26] For a description and evaluation of other laboratory pretesting techniques see Roger D. Blackwell, James S. Hensel, Michael B. Phillips, and Brian Sternthal, *Laboratory Equipment for Marketing Research* (Dubuque, Iowa: Kendall-Hunt Publishing Company, 1970).

Table 15-1 Advertising Expenditures of the Top 25 National Advertisers, 1969[a]

	Adv. Expend. as Percent of Sales	Total Advertising Expenditures (000)	Percentage Distribution of Advertising Expenditures								
			News-paper	Gen. Mag.	Farm Pub.	Bus. Pub.	Spot TV	Network TV	Spot Radio	Network Radio	Out-door
Procter & Gamble Co.	9.2	$275,000	1.0	5.4	—	0.5	29.7	63.2	0.2	—	—
General Motors Corp.	0.7	171,500	14.5	25.0	0.5	3.6	7.9	25.7	15.9	2.2	4.6
General Foods Corp.	8.5	151,000	1.8	18.0	—	4.5	16.7	53.6	4.3	1.0	—
Sears, Roebuck & Co.[b]	1.4	125,000	0.8	51.7	0.1	—	2.8	18.7	25.1	0.2	0.6
Colgate-Palmolive Co.	22.9	121,000	2.7	3.3	—	0.1	29.2	54.1	7.6	3.0	0.1
Bristol-Myers Co.	12.5	115,800	1.8	18.0	—	4.5	16.7	53.6	4.3	1.0	—
Ford Motor Co.	0.8	112,132	10.7	22.3	1.6	2.5	8.0	30.7	16.6	3.4	4.3
American Home Products	9.8	97,000	3.1	6.9	0.1	0.5	23.4	48.8	14.6	2.4	0.3
Warner Lambert Pharmaceutical	17.0	92,000	1.4	8.7	—	8.0	21.6	60.1	0.2	—	—
American Tel. & Tel.	0.6	85,808	12.3	27.3	—	6.6	7.9	28.8	12.7	1.9	2.6
R. J. Reynolds Industries	3.8	85,000	2.6	9.8	0.4	0.2	15.6	64.4	5.9	1.0	0.1
General Electric Co.	0.9	77,500	15.1	35.6	0.1	15.2	7.1	22.0	3.0	1.5	0.5
RCA Corp.	2.4	77,000	26.0	30.1	—	4.5	17.2	19.4	2.0	—	0.7
American Brands	2.8	74,400	8.3	17.8	—	0.3	15.0	56.5	1.1	—	0.7
Sterling Drug Co.	19.5	73,000	2.2	15.0	0.2	0.8	15.8	57.4	4.5	4.2	—
Coca-Cola Co.	5.3	72,000	8.8	10.6	—	1.0	44.6	12.7	19.4	—	3.0
Distillers Corp.—Seagrams, Ltd.	4.9	65,699	27.4	54.9	—	1.6	0.5	—	—	—	15.6
Chrysler Corp.	0.9	64,292	11.0	13.4	0.3	1.0	8.5	39.6	21.3	2.9	2.0
Gillette Co.	10.3	62,800	1.8	10.0	—	0.2	25.2	60.9	1.4	0.4	0.2
Kraftco	2.4	62,500	18.3	20.8	0.1	3.7	23.4	31.7	1.1	0.2	0.7
Lever Bros.	12.6	62,000	3.8	7.1	—	0.1	40.8	46.4	1.6	—	0.1
General Mills	6.0	61,000	3.3	11.0	0.1	0.7	29.1	55.5	0.2	—	0.1
Standard Brands, Inc.	5.8	60,000	10.9	17.0	0.7	2.1	38.4	13.9	12.3	0.5	4.3
Rapid-American Corp.	2.8	58,000	10.5	30.7	—	1.9	2.0	43.0	0.8	—	11.1
Philip Morris, Inc.	5.0	57,200	1.5	18.2	—	0.2	13.6	62.7	2.5	0.6	0.8

SOURCE: Reprinted with permission from the August 24, 1970 issue of *Advertising Age*. Copyright 1970 by Crain Communications, Inc.
[a] In measured media only.
[b] Does not include $200 million in local advertising.

media or television may be preferable. If the objective is to maintain a high level of awareness, then radio may be appropriate.

Distribution is another consideration. If the product is available only in local or regional areas, then media with national coverage will ordinarily not be used, unless the company plans to expand distribution.

The need for speed and flexibility should be determined. Media vary in terms of how far in advance advertisements must be submitted. Newspapers and radio usually have the shortest closing period, so, if the creative approach uses current events, these media are preferable (unless arrangements can be made with other media).

The advertising budget should also be considered, particularly when it is relatively small. The cost of one advertisement on television or in national magazines may exceed $30,000. With a budget of $300,000 or less, these costs become a major consideration, because the success of the entire campaign becomes dependent on a few advertisements.

Legal and ethical considerations may be important. For example, it is illegal to advertise liquor or cigarettes on television. Commonly accepted standards of taste may also influence media choice.

Finally, the media that competitors are using should be considered. The usual tendency is to duplicate the media choices of others. However, in some situations companies have achieved notable success by an innovative media strategy that allowed them to dominate product-category advertising in a medium. In the early 1960s, for example, Shell improved their market share substantially by advertising heavily in newspapers while competitive oil companies were fragmenting their investments in traditional media.

Selecting Media Vehicles

The next step in media strategy is to select specific vehicles within each medium. For example, if magazines and television are chosen as media, then it is necessary to select specific magazines and television programs or time slots.

One factor to consider in selecting a specific vehicle is the role it plays in the lives of its audience—the needs it fills and audience attitudes toward it. The objective is to select vehicles that have an image and mood that enhances, or at least is compatible with, the product or service being advertised.

The amount and type of assistance needed from a vehicle is another consideration. For example, the availability of special editions of national magazines that reach only certain geographic areas or demographic groups is often important. Another type of service is the "split run," presenting different versions of the same advertisement to matched groups so that advertising effectiveness can be measured. Also important is the availability of research on the characteristics of the vehicle's audience. When these types of services are desired, they are an important consideration in selecting media vehicles.

Another consideration is the ability of the vehicle to reach the target market segment with a minimum of waste coverage. Some vehicles provide these data,

Table 15-2   Major Information Sources for
Estimating Vehicle Audiences

Type of Medium	Service
Magazines	Brand Rating Index
	Standard Rate and Data Service
	Daniel Starch and Staff
	W. R. Simmons Associates
Newspapers	Brand Rating Index
	Standard Rate and Data Service
Television	A. C. Nielson Company
	American Research Bureau
	Brand Rating Index
	W. R. Simmons Associates
Radio	American Research Bureau
	Brand Rating Index
	Pulse Inc.
Outdoor	Traffic Audit Bureau

others do not. In the latter case it may be necessary to purchase audience-characteristics data from syndicated services. (See Table 15-2.)

Many sophisticated advertisers select vehicles on the basis of their efficient coverage of heavy users of the product category, because heavy users may constitute only 20 percent of the market but account for 80 percent of total volume. Since one heavy user buys as much as eight regular users, vehicles that reach a higher proportion of these heavy users are usually more efficient. Generally, socio-economic characteristics are poor predictors of heavy users. Therefore, typically, it is more efficient to first identify heavy users and then determine which specific vehicles are seen or heard by them. Often this approach dramatically increases the efficiency of a media plan.[27]

Space and time costs are often the most important factor in vehicle selection. These costs can be obtained in Standard Rate and Data volumes—although for some vehicles, particularly television, these amounts are often misleading, because the final cost is determined through negotiation. Except for advertisers with small budgets, absolute costs are not an appropriate measure. The most commonly used criterion relates cost to exposure in terms of cost per thousand readers for print media, cost per thousand homes for television, and comparable measures for other media. These cost-per-thousand (CPM) rates are used to compare and select specific vehicles.

There is, however, growing discontent with the CPM criterion. CPM's for various vehicles have to be evaluated in terms of their qualitative characteristics

[27] See, for example, Twedt, "How to Analyze Your 1966 Advertising Budget," p. 43.

and the services they provide. Moreover, the denominator of CPM formulas is circulation, readership, or viewing audience, all of which include members and nonmembers of the target market. Consequently many advertisers cost compare vehicles on such bases as cost per thousand prospects reached, or cost per thousand heavy buyers reached. These qualified measures are more precise and are preferable when the data required for their calculation can be obtained at a reasonable cost.

Media Scheduling

After media and specific vehicles have been selected, it is necessary to determine how much and when each will be used. This is the complicated area of media scheduling, which involves decisions concerning reach, frequency, and continuity.

REACH. The total number of prospects reached is a major criterion in selecting the combination of media and vehicles for the final media schedule. The starting point is the "degree-of-accomplishment" component of the advertising objective(s). Suppose this is "an increase from 20 to 80 percent." We can restate this objective in absolute terms by multiplying the target-market size by the target percentage. Thus, if the target market consists of 10 million prospects, then the accomplishment objective is an increase from 2 million to 8 million, or an increment of 6 million.

It is then necessary to translate the degree-of-accomplishment objective into the reach objective. The latter will be larger or higher than the accomplishment objective, since all people reached will not respond in the desired way that is spelled out in the communication component of the advertising objective. In other words, it is necessary to determine the functional relationship between reach and degree of accomplishment. At the present time no generalizations can be advanced concerning the specific parameters of this relationship; rather they need to be derived from research and experience.

FREQUENCY. Frequency refers to the average number of times the average member of the target market will be reached by a media schedule during a specified time period, usually four weeks. The question is: how many times during the time period must a media schedule reach target customers in order to achieve the communication task or sales objective?

Unfortunately it is not possible to specify optimum frequency rates, for studies indicate that they vary by product, type of communication task, and medium.[28] Therefore optimum frequency rates must be determined by the individual advertiser based on specific research and experience.

ESTIMATING REACH AND FREQUENCY. After reach and frequency targets have been specified, it is necessary to determine the total reach and frequency delivered by alternative combinations of media vehicles. Several factors complicate this estimating problem. Audience accumulation is one such factor. The audience of a

[28] See, for example, "Frequency in Broadcast Advertising," *Media/Scope*, March 1962.

vehicle changes over time as the result of additions and deletions to the initial reading or viewing audience. In the past there has been little basis for dealing with this problem. In the 1960s, however, Agnostini found in the case of magazines that each new issue added to existing coverage adds a decreasing fraction of the non-covered population in a manner similar to N^{-a}, where N is the number of issues published and a is calculated from the average audience of one issue and the accumulative audience of two issues.[29] Formulas have also been developed for estimating the accumulative audiences of broadcast vehicles.[30]

Duplication is the other major complication. The difficulty is that prospects exposed to one vehicle are often exposed to others. Therefore we must subtract this duplication in estimating reach and take it into account when estimating frequency. Agnostini has isolated a constant that, when applied to the total audience reached by several vehicles, determines the nonduplicated audience reasonably accurately up to about five or six combinations.[31] Refinements in this procedure, as well as other techniques, have been advanced in recent years.[32] In addition, the *Starch Consumer Magazine* Report and the Simmons Reports measure duplication between pairs of magazines.

Recently, several techniques have been advanced that purport to simultaneously estimate the reach and frequency of combinations of vehicles. These include probability-of-exposure indices, combination simulation and panel-data approaches, and other techniques. These approaches are beyond the scope of this text; however, illustrative references are provided for the interested reader.[33]

CONTINUITY. Continuity refers to the temporal aspect of a media schedule. One type of continuity is concerned with the relationship between advertising and sales in situations where the product has a seasonal demand pattern. Kuehn has suggested that advertising carryover (the residual effects of past advertising) and habitual brand choice are two fundamental considerations in adapting to seasonal fluctuations. When there is no carryover and no habitual choice, the

[29] J. M. Agnostini, "Analysis of Magazine Accumulative Audience," *Journal of Advertising Research,* Vol. 2 (1962), pp. 24–27. For other empirical tests of this formula see John Bower, "Net Audiences of U.S. and Canadian Magazines: Seven Tests of Agnostini's Formula," *Journal of Advertising Research,* Vol. 3 (March 1963), pp. 13–21.

[30] Paul Keller, "Patterns of Media-Audience Accumulation," *Journal of Marketing,* Vol. 30 (January 1966), pp. 32–37.

[31] J. M. Agnostini, "How to Estimate Unduplicated Audiences," *Journal of Advertising Research,* Vol. 1 (1961), pp. 11–14.

[32] See, for example, Pierre Hofmans, "Measuring the Cumulative Net Coverage of Any Combination of Media," *Journal of Marketing Research,* Vol. 3 (August 1966), pp. 269–278. Also see the articles by Bower, Marc, Gaffyn and Sagovsky, and Kuhn in the *Journal of Advertising Research,* Vol. 3 (March 1963).

[33] Jack B. Landis, "Exposure Probabilities as Measures of Media Audiences," *Journal of Advertising Research,* Vol. 5 (September 1965), pp. 24–29; Marcel Marc, "Combining Simulation and Panel Data to Obtain Reach and Frequency," *Journal of Advertising Research,* Vol. 8 (June 1968), pp. 11–16; and Oddvar Bie Mevik and Niels Vinding, "Two Dimensions of Media Selection: Coverage and Frequency," *Journal of Advertising Research,* Vol. 6 (March 1966), pp. 29–34.

level of advertising should coincide with the seasonal pattern of sales. In cases where there is carryover and/or habitual purchasing, peaks in advertising expenditures should precede anticipated peaks in sales, and troughs in advertising expenditures should precede troughs in sales. The greater the carryover, the greater the lead time; and the greater the degree of habitual purchasing, the less variation in the temporal investment in advertising. Further refinements of this approach appear to offer promise for dealing more effectively with seasonal sales patterns.[34]

The other dimension of continuity is concerned with advertising density, or the extent to which the media schedule concentrates expenditures during given time periods. For example, is it more desirable to equalize the insertion of advertisements throughout the year, or should they be concentrated in certain periods and omitted in others? There is some evidence that concentration is best if high impact is desired in a particular short-run period; if continuity of impact is desired, a less concentrated schedule is preferable.[35] The evidence is inadequate to support generalizations; hence, once again it is desirable to formulate a density strategy on the basis of individualized research.

The Media Plan

The end result of this type of media analysis and planning—aided perhaps by the use of various media-selection models (see Chapter 19)—is a master schedule indicating for each day of the year the advertising media and vehicles that will be used, the locations of these insertions, and the time and place of their appearance. This plan becomes the central document for media control and evaluation.

MEASURING ADVERTISING EFFECTIVENESS

Successful advertisers generally pursue a sophisticated program designed to measure the effectiveness of advertising campaigns. This practice, known as *posttesting*, differs from the *pretesting* of advertisements before they are used in a campaign. The posttesting procedure is to select one or more techniques by which the advertiser can determine whether he has accomplished the advertising objective(s). This section discusses illustrative techniques.

Techniques for Measuring Awareness and Knowledge

These types of techniques are used when the advertiser is trying to achieve a defined level of awareness and/or knowledge in a selected target market segment (or segments).

[34] Alfred A. Kuehn, "How Advertising Performance Depends on Other Marketing Factors," *Journal of Advertising Research*, Vol. 2 (March 1962), pp. 2–10; also see Jay W. Forrester, "Advertising: A Problem in Industrial Dynamics," *Harvard Business Review*, March–April 1959, pp. 100–110.

[35] Hubert A. Zielske, "The Remembering and Forgetting of Advertising," *Journal of Marketing*, Vol. 23 (January 1959), pp. 239–243.

ADVERTISING-RECOGNITION MEASURES. Several techniques are used to measure the degree to which prospects recognize advertisements. One of the methods most widely used was developed by Daniel Starch for printed advertisements. The Starch approach uses a national sample to evaluate advertisements in approximately 1,000 newspapers and magazines. Readers of a given issue are questioned concerning their readership of advertisements as well as parts of the advertisements. Responses are expressed in several ways: (1) *noted*—the percent of readers that remember seeing the advertisement; (2) *seen-associated*—the percent of readers that recall seeing or reading any part of the advertisement identifying the product or brand; (3) *read most*—the percent of readers reading at least one-half of the advertisement; (4) *readers per dollar*—the number of readers attracted by the advertisement for each dollar invested in space; and (5) *cost ratios*— expressing the relationship between readers per dollar and the median readers per dollar for all half-page or larger advertisements in the issue.[36]

Investigations of the Starch approach have isolated several problems. First, interest in the product category results in a substantial inflation of readership. Second, some types of people have a tendency to overclaim readership. Third, some studies have shown that interviewing styles distort outcomes although there are contradictory findings on this subject. Another researcher concluded that this type of technique measures interest more than anything else.[37]

Despite these problems, the Starch method is widely used. Starch scores are at least a rough indication of the power of advertisements in a campaign to attract and hold attention. Moreover, the data are useful in assessing the pulling power of competitors' campaigns, and they allow evaluation of the relative pulling power of creative variations.

ADVERTISING-RECALL MEASURES. Recall-measurement techniques also attempt to assess the level of awareness generated by advertising campaigns. We outline here two illustrative variations of this type of technique.

1. *Unaided recall.* The unaided-recall technique uses no cuing devices. For example, respondents might be asked, "What advertisements have you seen lately?" Since it is difficult to obtain useful and meaningful responses with this approach, an aided technique is more commonly used to measure advertising recall.

2. *Aided recall.* There are many varieties of aided recall. For example, respondents might be asked, "What advertisements for (*insert product category*) have you seen lately?" This technique usually produces more meaningful answers than unaided recall. The percentage of respondents recalling the brand of interest,

---

[36] "Brief Description of the Scope, Method and Technique of the Starch Advertisement Readership Service," published by Daniel Starch and Staff, Mamaroneck, N.Y.

[37] Valentine Appel and Milton L. Blum, "Ad Recognition and Response Set," *Journal of Advertising Research*, Vol. 1 (June 1961), pp. 13–21; D. Morgan New, "Measuring Advertising Recognition," *Journal of Advertising Research*, Vol. 1 (1961), pp. 17–22; and William D. Wells, "Recognition, Recall, and Rating Scales," *Journal of Advertising Research*, Vol. 4 (September 1964), pp. 2–8.

when compared to precampaign levels, is used as a measure of the effectiveness of the campaign.

Of the several syndicated services that use aided-recall techniques, the Gallup Robinson Impact Test is one of the most widely used. Qualified issue readers are given a group of cards bearing the names of several brands and asked to indicate which of the brands are advertised in the issue being tested. The issue is then opened for each brand the respondent recalls, and he is asked whether this is the advertisement he was thinking of. A "proven name registration" figure is calculated, using the percentage who correctly relate the brand name and the advertisement. Studies investigating this technique have generally concluded that it measures memory with a minimum of distortion from other factors.[38]

BRAND AWARENESS. Brand awareness, as opposed to advertising awareness, is another commonly used method of measuring advertising effectiveness. For example, respondents might be asked, "Considering (*product class*), please tell me all the brands you can think of." The measure of effectiveness may be the percentage of respondents mentioning the brand first or second. The difference between the precampaign and postcampaign percentage (preferably adjusted by the pre-post differences in the control group)is used as a measure of effectiveness. There is evidence that in some situations "first brand awareness" is a useful predictor of brand switching.[39]

BRAND KNOWLEDGE. Although a campaign may have produced the desired level of awareness, it may or may not have communicated the desired product benefits or other aspects of the creative strategy. Consequently, it is common to test prospects' knowledge of key copy points. Pre-post campaign shifts in the percentage of prospects having the desired knowledge are used as a measure of advertising effectiveness.

Preference-Measurement Techniques

These techniques are used when the advertising objective is to achieve a target increment in the percentage of prospects preferring the advertiser's brand. Preference is also used as a criterion variable when the advertising objective is a certain level of sales but the decision to purchase does not occur until a subsequent time period. There are several ways of attempting to measure preference:

1. *Paired comparisons.* For example, respondents might be asked: "I'm going to name some brands of (*insert product class*). I'd like you to tell me which of each pair you would be more likely to purchase."
2. *Buying game.* Respondents are asked: "I am going to give you some cards showing different situations you might run into if you were shopping for (*insert product class*). In each case I would like you to tell me which brand you would be most likely to purchase."

---

[38] Lucas and Britt, *Measuring Advertising Effectiveness*, Chap. 4. For a somewhat different perspective see Wells, "Recognition, Recall, and Rating Scales," pp. 2–8.

[39] See, for example, Axelrod, "Attitude Measures that Predict Purchase," pp. 3–17.

3. *Rating scale.* Respondents are told: "I would like you to rate some brands
   of (*insert product class*) from +5 to −5. The more you think a brand
   is above average, the higher the plus number you should give it, up to
   +5. The more you think a brand is below average, the bigger the minus
   number you should give it, all the way down to −5."

Pre-post campaign shifts (corrected for control-group differences) in a
brand's relative position can be used to measure advertising effectiveness.
Evidence to date indicates that the paired-comparison and buying-game approaches are preferable to rating scales because in some situations they have
been found to predict purchase behavior.[40]

In some cases, the advertising objective may be to move prospects closer to
purchase. Several techniques can be used to estimate how effective the advertising
campaign has been in achieving this objective. For example, respondents can be
asked the following both before and after a campaign:

Now I would like you to tell me about your interest in purchasing various brands
of (*insert product class*). Tell me which statement best describes your feelings
about each brand as I name them:
    I will definitely buy the brand next time.
    I will probably buy the brand in the near future.
    I might buy the brand in the future.
    I don't know whether or not I will buy the brand.
    I will probably not buy the brand.
    I will certainly not buy the brand.
    I would not use this brand under any circumstances.

Using appropriate experimental controls, pre-post campaign differences in the
position of the advertiser's brand can be used as a measure of advertising
effectiveness.[41]

Sales-Measurement Techniques

Where advertising objectives are stated in terms of sales, it is desirable to measure
the effect of the advertising campaign on sales. Until recently, the general consensus was that this relationship could not be measured since sales are affected
by a host of factors—the product, pricing, channels, the sales force—in addition
to advertising. In recent years, however, there has been growing acceptance that
the sales effects of advertising campaigns can be measured in many situations,
if the appropriate controls and research designs are used. Where a substantial
percentage of prospects make a buying decision after the campaign and after
the period during which effectiveness is measured—as is the case with many
durable goods—it is, at best, difficult and probably impossible to measure sales
effects. In these situations, measures of preference or conviction-to-purchase are

[40] *Ibid.*
[41] *Ibid.*

usually used as criteria. But in other situations it is possible to estimate the sales effects of advertising campaigns. This section describes and evaluates some of the measurement techniques most commonly used for this purpose.

BEFORE-AFTER WITH CONTROL-GROUP DESIGN. This classic design uses several test and control cities (Figure 15-2). The normal level of sales is calculated for both types of cities prior to the campaign, and then the campaign is presented to the test cities but not the control cities. The level of sales is then calculated for both control and test cities. The effect of the campaign is calculated by subtracting precampaign from postcampaign sales in the control cities and then subtracting that amount from the difference between post- and precampaign sales in the test cities.

Figure 15-2   A before-after with control group design for measuring the effectiveness of advertising campaigns.

	Test Cities	Control Cities
Precampaign measure of sales	Yes	Yes
Advertising campaign	Yes	No
Postcampaign measure of sales	Yes	Yes

The difference between the post- and precampaign sales in test cities is a function of advertising plus all other factors. The post-precampaign difference in sales in the control cities is a function of all other factors. By subtracting the sales differences in control cities from those in test cities, a tolerably accurate estimate of the effect of advertising is obtained, providing the test and control cities are reasonably comparable.

MULTIVARIABLE EXPERIMENTAL DESIGNS. While the experimental design above yields a reasonably accurate estimate of the effect of the advertising campaign on sales, it does not generate explanations for the success or failure of the campaign. Multivariable designs produce these explanations, and hence are used by some very large advertisers because of their superior diagnostic value.

Figure 15-3 presents a classic multivariable design that has been used by the

Figure 15-3   A multivariable experimental design for measuring the effectiveness of advertising campaigns.

	No Newspapers				Newspapers			
	No Radio		Radio		No Radio		Radio	
	No TV	TV	No TV	TV	No TV	TV	No TV	TV
No Outdoor	(1)	(2)	(3)	(4)	(5)	(6)	(7)	(8)
Outdoor	(9)	(10)	(11)	(12)	(13)	(14)	(15)	(16)

SOURCE: Reprinted from the *Journal of Advertising Research*. Copyright © 1961 by the Advertising Research Foundation.

Ford Motor Company. The power of this factorial design is explained by George H. Brown, Ford's former director of marketing research:

. . . for any single medium, eight geographic areas have been exposed and eight have not been exposed. Thus it is possible to observe how each medium behaves alone and in all possible combinations with other media.

If identical dollar expenditures (at national rates) are established for each medium, area 1 will receive no advertising expenditures, areas 2, 3, 5, and 9 will receive advertising at the same dollar rates, areas 4, 6, 7, 10, 11 and 13 will receive advertising at twice this dollar rate; areas 8, 12, 14, and 15 at three times as much dollar advertising and area 16 at four times this dollar expenditure.[42]

Thus this type of factorial design is capable of measuring the effectiveness of all combinations of media used, as well as four different levels of advertising expenditures. For these reasons it is a very efficient design. However, the complexity and cost involved make it impractical for all but very large advertisers.[43]

SUMMARY

Advertising is one of the most important elements in the marketing strategies of many companies. A sophisticated approach to advertising begins with the establishment of specific, measurable advertising objectives based on corporate and marketing objectives and strategy, buyer behavior, and competitive analysis. Also involved is the establishment of an advertising budget via the use of such methods as keyed-to-sales, ROI, objective and task, and payout planning.

Designing a creative approach involves the formulation of creative strategy and plans for its creative execution. Since there are few concrete guidelines in preparing advertisements, it is usually desirable to pretest them before using them in the actual campaign.

It is also necessary to design a media strategy to carry the message to potential prospects. This involves the selection of general as well as specific media vehicles. These vehicles are scheduled using the criteria of reach, frequency, and continuity, and perhaps computer media models.

Finally, it is usually advantageous to measure the effectiveness of the advertising campaign. The procedure is to match the measurement technique with the

[42] George H. Brown, "Measuring the Sales Effectiveness of Alternative Media," *Proceedings of the 7th Annual Conference* (New York: Advertising Research Foundation, 1961), pp. 43–47.

[43] For a discussion of other techniques see Irwin M. Grossack and Robert F. Kelly, "Measuring Advertising Effectiveness: Use of PTM," *Business Horizons* (Fall 1963), pp. 83–88; Richard E. Quandt, "Estimating the Effectiveness of Advertising: Some Pitfalls in Econometric Methods," *Journal of Marketing Research*, Vol. 1 (May 1964), pp. 51–60; Roy H. Campbell, "A Managerial Approach to Advertising Measurement," *Journal of Marketing*, Vol. 29 (October 1965), pp. 1–6; and Peter Langhoff, "Options in Campaign Evaluation," *Journal of Advertising Research*, Vol. 7 (December 1967), pp. 41–47.

advertising objective. Several techniques were presented and evaluated for each major type of objective.

QUESTIONS FOR REVIEW AND DISCUSSION

1. Select three advertisements that frequently appear on television and identify the underlying creative strategies.
2. "Advertising forces people to buy things they do not need." Discuss.
3. A regional bottler of soft drinks enjoys considerable success in his market area. His objective for the forthcoming budget period is to maintain 70 percent awareness among households in his market area. What type(s) of media should he use?
4. A large furniture company has designed a line of water beds and wants to market them nationally. Recommend an advertising objective(s).
5. Last year a large firm introduced a men's hair spray. This year they want to increase brand preference from 3 to 10 percent of U.S. males aged 15 to 34. Their advertising agency has prepared several advertisements. What pre-testing technique(s) should be used?
6. In the December 21, 1970, issue of *Advertising Age*, an advertising agency criticized Miles Laboratories for spending $23 million in advertising to sell $60 million worth of Alka-Seltzer. The agency suggested that Miles would be better off putting some of the money into research to develop new products that are worth advertising. Discuss.

Chapter 16   Sales-Force Programs

Personal selling is the focal point of marketing effort[1] and the major promotional activity in most businesses. Personal selling expenses are often two or three times as high as advertising expenditures.[2] Thus, sales management is a critical activity having dramatic impact on profitability as well as significant strategic implications.

This chapter examines the nature of personal selling, discusses recent changes in the selling function, and analyzes the role of personal selling in developing and accomplishing corporate objectives and strategy.

A SYSTEMATIC APPROACH TO PERSONAL SELLING

After reviewing basic sales terminology, this section examines the nature of personal selling and then overviews the approach to sales management that will be discussed in the remainder of the chapter.

The Nature of Personal Selling

As described in Chapter 15, personal selling is one of four basic means of communicating the firm's total product offer. It was defined as the oral presentation in a conversation with one or more prospective purchasers for the purpose of making sales.

[1] "Top Executives Rank Salesmanship Tops, Study Shows," *Sales Management*, Vol. 96 (March 18, 1966), p. 120.

[2] See T. N. Beckman and W. R. Davidson, *Marketing*, 8th ed. (New York: The Ronald Press Company, 1967), pp. 591–592; and William J. Stanton, *Fundamentals of Marketing*, 2d ed. (New York: McGraw-Hill, Inc., 1967), pp. 519–520.

Dividing the market into three buying segments—*pretransactional, transactional*, and *posttransactional*—we find that advertising, sales promotion, and publicity are most commonly used to cultivate the market during the pretransactional phase. Advertising may also be used during the posttransactional phase to reduce postpurchase dissonance. In contrast, as indicated in Figure 16-1, selling is important in all three phases.[3]

Advertising is a one-way form of communication that frequently must compete with other messages in the same medium. In addition, the message is designed to appeal to a large number of people in the target market. While expensive per insertion, the cost of advertising per copy-reader, listener, or viewer is quite reasonable. For example, it has been estimated that a full-color page advertisement in *Life* magazine provides exposure for about 1/6 cent per copy-reader.[4]

In contrast, personal selling is a two-way form of communication, which makes it a far superior means of selling. The sales message is more flexible and personal and often more powerful than an advertisement. The salesman, using his in-depth product knowledge, can adapt his message to meet the immediate needs of the buyer and deal with his objections in an appropriate manner. Perhaps most important, the salesman can *ask* for the order. However, the cost of this flexibility and impact is quite high. When all sales-related expenses are considered, the cost of a typical sales call has been estimated to be in excess of $31.[5] Thus, while advertising is usually more *efficient*, sales effort is typically more *effective*.

Figure 16-1   Relative importance of advertising and selling market place.

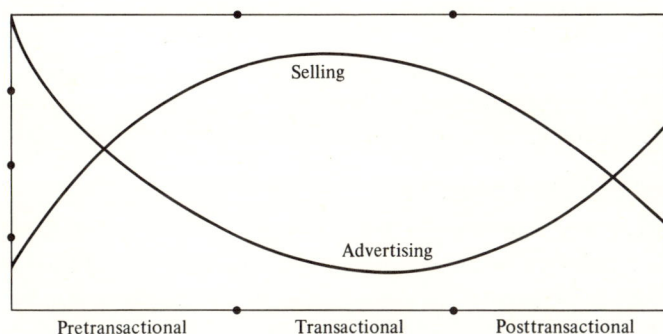

SOURCE: H. C. Cash and W. J. E. Crissy, "Comparison of Advertising and Selling," in E. J. Kelley and W. Lazer, eds., *Managerial Marketing: Perspectives and Viewpoints*, 3d ed. (Homewood, Ill.: Richard D. Irwin, Inc., 1967), p. 556.

[3] Harold C. Cash and W. J. E. Crissy, "Comparison of Advertising and Selling," in *Managerial Marketing: Perspectives and Viewpoints*, Eugene J. Kelley and William Lazer, eds., 3d ed. (Homewood, Ill.: Richard D. Irwin, Inc., 1967), pp. 555–556.

[4] *Ibid.*, p. 550.

[5] *Ibid.*

Types of Selling

Most sales organizations engage in several types of selling. These are trade, missionary, technical, and new-business selling.[6]

TRADE SELLING. The trade sales force seeks to build up the volume of the company's sales to its customers by providing them with promotional assistance. If the customer is a manufacturer, this involves helping him to be a more effective seller; if an intermediary in the channel of distribution, helping him become a more effective reseller. Thus, the trade sales force "sells through" rather than "sells to" its customer. Trade selling predominates in food, textiles, apparel, and wholesaling.

MISSIONARY SELLING. The responsibility of the missionary salesman is to increase company sales by providing customers with personal selling assistance. This involves persuading indirect customers to purchase company products through direct customers. The "medical detail man" who calls on doctors as the representative of a pharmaceutical house typifies this kind of selling. Whereas the trade force "sells through" customers, the missionary force "sells for" them. Missionary selling is common in foods, chemicals, transportation, warehousing, wholesaling, and the utilities.

TECHNICAL SELLING. The technical salesman provides customers with technical advice and assistance. He sells directly to user or buyer, perhaps to the customer's purchasing agent. Chemicals, machinery, and heavy equipment often require this type of selling.

NEW-BUSINESS SELLING. The new-business salesman seeks to obtain new accounts for the company. This kind of selling is also referred to as "canvassing," "bird-dogging," and "cold-calling." While new-business selling is part of almost every salesman's activities, salesmen specializing in it are found commonly in door-to-door selling, capital-goods selling, and the selling of intangibles such as insurance, advertising services, and consulting services.

The Anatomy of Personal Selling

Different market segments require specific types of sales effort, but all salesmen tend to follow similar procedures in accomplishing their task. These steps are (1) prospecting, (2) preapproach, (3) approach, (4) demonstration, (5) overcoming objections, (6) closing, and (7) follow-up.

PROSPECTING. The first step in selling, assuming the salesman has already been adequately trained and provided with product knowledge, is locating customers. This involves developing a profile of the ideal customer and then searching available sources of information to locate accounts that match this profile.

PREAPPROACH. This phase relates to the salesman's learning all he can about

---

[6] This classification and the description of each that follows are based upon material contained in Derek A. Newton, "Get the Most Out of Your Sales Force," *Harvard Business Review*, Vol. 47 (September-October 1969), pp. 130–143.

the company or person upon whom he will be calling, including personal characteristics, needs, and—of critical importance—the person or persons within the organization who make purchase decisions.

APPROACH. This step refers to the methods the salesman relies upon to gain access to the purchase decision maker and the way in which he begins his presentation. Cold canvassing, referral, and repeat calls are the most common approach situations.

DEMONSTRATION. In this phase, the salesman presents the want-satisfying characteristics of his product or service. Many procedures have been suggested for effectively demonstrating the product, but perhaps the most universal is referred to as the AIDA approach—that is, presenting the product in a way that gains the customer's Attention, holds his Interest, builds his Desire for the product, and ends in purchase Action.

HANDLING OBJECTIONS. A singular advantage of personal selling is that it permits the salesman to react to and overcome objections that arise during the presentation. Effectively overcoming customer objections or questions is critical to successful selling.

CLOSING. It is difficult to choose one aspect of the selling process as more important than another. However, asking for the order is certainly of paramount importance. Once again, the salesman is uniquely positioned to actually ask for an order. Without this step the sale cannot be brought to fruition.

FOLLOW-UP. Sales success usually depends upon repeat business. Consequently, the sale is not completed when the order is taken. To insure repeat business the salesman must follow up to see that the product has been delivered and that its want-satisfying characteristics have been thoroughly understood.

The Changing Nature of Personal Selling

The fabled *Willie Loman* and *Professor Harold Hill* are salesmen of another era. These salesmen sought sales success largely on the basis of personality, emotion, friendship, and loyalty. This orientation to selling has been displaced by the need to better understand the product being sold and evaluate it in terms of how it can satisfy customer needs.[7] As Rieser has said, "The Salesman Isn't Dead—He's Different."[8]

The new approach to personal selling was explained by one executive in the following manner:

In the course of a day, one of our salesmen may be called upon to be a business adviser, advertising counselor, accountant or economist.

. . . The variety of problems encountered by the men who sell our products

---

[7] J. N. Bauman, "Rebirth of the Salesman," *Dun's Review and Modern Industry*, Vol. 87 (March 1968), p. 45.

[8] Carl Rieser, "The Salesman Isn't Dead—He's Different," *Fortune*, Vol. 66 (November 1962), p. 124.

is endless. We expect them to be able and willing to counsel with their customers on all these problems. That is their job.[9]

This attitude is the result of several changes that have taken place recently in the business environment. These include (1) an increase in the concentration of important customers, (2) the centralization of purchase decision making, (3) increasingly more complex, broadly based customer needs that require the selling of systems rather than products, and (4) a desire on the part of both buyer and seller to conserve time and reduce expenses by establishing a continuous, programmed relationship.[10]

CUSTOMER CONCENTRATION. Loosely aligned and otherwise autonomous business units are rapidly being integrated into larger and more disciplined complexes. Traditionally, most business was conducted on a local basis, with buying decisions made by local decision makers. However, the vast proportion of business today is simply not done on such a small scale or in such an independent fashion.[11] The increasing importance of a few pivotal customers poses a decisive, crucial new challenge to sales management.[12]

CENTRALIZED PURCHASING. An increasing proportion of major buying decisions are being made at points far removed from the place of ultimate use or resale, and many buying decisions that were once made on an atomistic basis by people of lower organizational rank are being made at higher levels on a more formalized basis. Thus, an increasing number of salesmen are finding their markets shrinking, as the key buying influences for the firms operating in their territories are simply not in the territory. Consider the following examples.

- A motor-freight salesman is assigned the Cleveland waterfront, which houses the shipping operations of numerous firms. When he canvasses his territory, he discovers that the motor-freight buying decisions in all but three of the firms are made at offices in New York and San Francisco.
- An office machine salesman in Memphis persuaded the office manager of a large oil company's local bulk plant to submit a proposal for new accounting machines. Both are confident that the proposal is sound and fully justified. However, when the salesman calls back to close the order, he is told: "Philadelphia says to hold up on office mechanization because they are working with a consulting firm in Washington on a company-wide system."
- An insurance broker in Seattle worked hard to develop a "total insurance

[9] E. B. Weiss, "The New Rules of Personal Selling," *Dun's Review and Modern Industry,* Vol. 82 (February 1963), pp. 49–50.

[10] See the discussion of vertical marketing systems in Chapter 13.

[11] "The Demise of the Geographically Structured Sales Force: A Management Report," Management Horizons, Inc., Columbus, Ohio.

[12] W. Cameron Caswell, "Marketing Effectiveness and Sales Supervision," *California Management Review,* Vol. 6 (Fall 1964), p. 39.

program" for a small electronics firm. His program, which was in effect for eight months, was abruptly canceled. The electronics firm had been acquired by a larger corporation, and the policy of the new parent company was to handle the "management of risk" on a corporatewide basis.[13]

SYSTEM SELLING. The oil-company example illustrates another important development—the changing character of the product itself. The company was not interested in buying office machines *per se* but was concentrating on a total activity—a companywide system. Increasingly, businesses today are not buying units of merchandise, but are becoming oriented to what may be termed a "product package" or total system concept.

The need to sell systems has produced a clearly recognizable trend toward strategic selling techniques. One such approach is the development of specialized selling teams for sales to key accounts such as government, schools, and export markets.[14] Some companies have added national account managers to negotiate with important accounts.[15] Selling by top executives is also becoming quite common, especially for sales to large accounts or potentially important customers.[16]

The International Minerals and Chemical Corporation's "full orbit "marketing program has been so successful that the firm has reorganized its entire sales force around the new service concept. Where three different groups were selling phosphate minerals, phosphate chemicals, and potash, now every man sells service. "Full orbit" includes:

. . . courses in sales training and sales and production management, as well as periodic management seminars and customer advisory panels. At times, customers are flown to company headquarters to consult specialists in marketing, engineering, public relations and finance. And transportation engineers constantly roam the field, showing how costs can be chopped. In 1962 . . . customers who attended the management seminar increased their purchases by more than 50% over the previous year. All others increased their purchases by less than 10%. . . . Overall, those customers who availed themselves of at least 5 of the 42 separate services offered increased their purchases by more than 20%.[17]

PROGRAMMED MERCHANDISING. Programmed merchandising is an enduring vendor-customer relationship that is rapidly emerging in the distribution industries. It takes maximum advantage of the product knowledge and general market-

---

[13] "The Demise of the Geographically Structured Sales Force," p. 6.

[14] Leon Morse, "The Sound of a Different Drummer," *Dun's Review and Modern Industry*, Vol. 82 (August 1963), p. 27.

[15] Thomas J. Murray, "New Man In Selling," *Dun's Review and Modern Industry*, Vol. 85 (February 1965), p. 39.

[16] "How Five Different Companies Handle the Unclear Role of Top Management in Selling," *Business Management*, Vol. 33 (July 1966), pp. 32–40.

[17] "The 'Something Extra' In Selling," *Dun's Review and Modern Industry*, Vol. 82 (September 1963), p. 34.

ing skill of the manufacturer and the merchandising and reselling capabilities of the wholesaler or retailer. It is a carefully developed total program in which vendor and customer responsibilities are carefully spelled out in great detail.[18] Some of the more common components of such programs include a dollar merchandise budget plan, basic stock plan, agreements on space or display assistance, inventory maintenance, sales training, and promotion.

From the seller's standpoint, the objectives of such a program are the development of the maximum sales and profit potential without competing for it on a day-to-day basis. It eliminates the order-taking role of the salesman and makes the salesman a "customer assistant." From the reseller's point of view these programs are desirable because:

1. He becomes more important to a resource.
2. He is able to develop more preferred resources.
3. He obtains better service.
4. He receives top-management attention from the seller.
5. He is often able to merchandise on a price-maintained basis.

The relationships under programmed merchandising compared with traditional territorial selling are illustrated in Figure 16-2.[19]

A Systematic Approach to Sales-Force Management

Figure 16-3 presents a systematic approach to sales-force management. Management of the selling function is rooted in the firm's corporate and marketing objectives and must be coordinated with the strategies and objectives of each of the other functional areas of marketing activity. These and other considerations permit the development of specific sales-force objectives as well as a sales strategy.

Once the role of the salesman has been established, important administrative aspects of the job emerge. Sales personnel must be recruited, selected, trained, and compensated. In addition, they must be assigned specific tasks within some specified area of operations—often a geographic sales territory. Finally, the sales program must be implemented and monitored in order to adjust organizational efforts to achieve sales objectives.

ESTABLISHING SALES OBJECTIVES AND STRATEGY

Sales objectives are the goals that the sales force and the sales managers are seeking to achieve, while the sales strategy represents the manner in which they

[18] Programmed merchandising is often the vehicle by which reseller support programs are implemented (see Chapter 13, "Developing Reseller Support Programs").

[19] For a more extended treatment of programmed merchandising see "Programmed Merchandising: The New Way to Work with Key Resources," *Department Store Economist*, October 1964, pp. 22–27.

Figure 16-2   Programmed merchandising: comparison of characteristics of vendor-store relationships under programmed merchandising and traditional territorial selling.

Characteristics	Traditional Selling Relationships	Programmed Merchandising Relationships
Time and location of contacts	Vendor control by routing of salesman	Often reseller control or initiation
Information considered	Vendor's sales presentation data	Reseller's merchandising data
Vendor participants	Vendor's territorial salesman	Salesman and major regional or headquarters executives
Reseller participants	Buyer	Various executives, perhaps top management
Reseller's goal	Sales gain and percent markup	Programmed total profitability
Vendor's goal	Big order on each call	Continuing profitable relationship
Nature of performance evaluation	Event-centered: primarily related to sales volume	Specific performance criteria written into the program

SOURCE: Management Horizons, Inc., Columbus, Ohio. Reprinted by permission.

operate to achieve them. The basic, most important objective of the sales force is to achieve the highest level of market response (sales) that the firm is able to satisfy from the expenditure of available marketing resources. That is, all marketing activities—product development, promotion, price, and distribution—should be programmed to produce *profitable* sales by offering want satisfaction to the target market segments over the long run. In most instances, the salesman in his pivotal position at the vendor-customer interface is of critical importance in achieving that long-run profitability.

Corporate Sales Objectives

Sales objectives are frequently stated in terms of sales volume, market share, profit, and expenses.[20] Each of these objectives is coordinated and consistent with the overall corporate objectives discussed in Chapters 1 and 2.

VOLUME GOALS. These objectives are a gross measure of sales effectiveness. They are commonly established in both dollar and unit terms. In aggregate form they are the measures utilized to evaluate the effectiveness of sales managers. When further broken down for each salesman, they are frequently referred to as sales quotas and are effective measures of individual performance.

Volume goals are quite important. However, in an aggregate form, such as

[20] Beckman and Davidson, *Marketing*, p. 600.

Figure 16-3   A sales planning and control system.

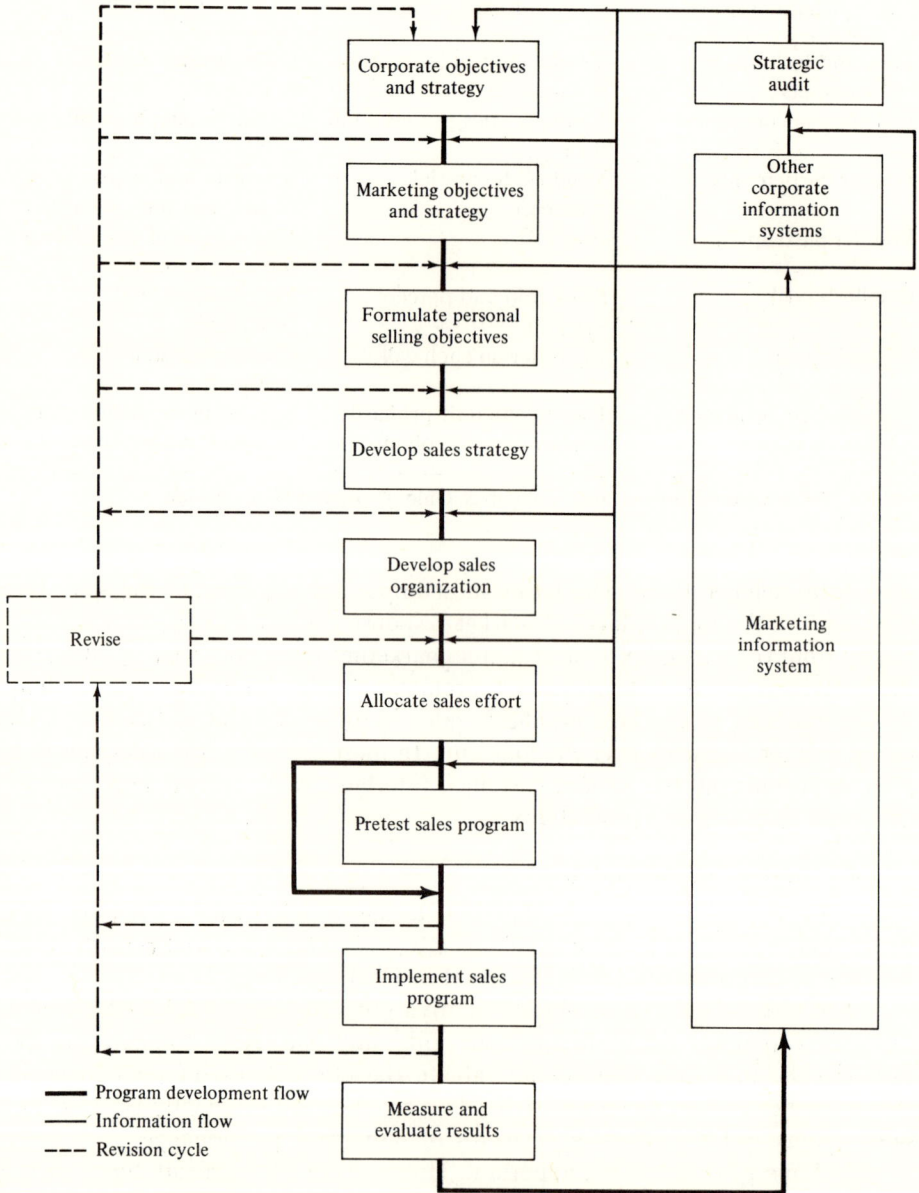

total sales, they do not offer the degree of direction necessary for effective analysis and control of selling efforts. A hierarchy of objectives proceeding from total sales volume to sales by target market segment, salesman, product class, or even individual product should be developed. Table 16-1 illustrates such a hierarchy of objectives.

While volume goals are important, they must be used in conjunction with other, more refined measures. These refinements include share of the market, the profitability of sales produced, and sales expenses.

MARKET SHARE. These targets must be established to further guide sales effort. That is, the volume goal should be refined to indicate the market segments from which the sales should come. Market-share targets are expressed as desired percentages of industry sales, and their hierarchy should proceed in much the same fashion as illustrated in Table 16-1—from the company's share of total industry sales, to the desired level of sales by market segment and, perhaps, by class of products or even individual product.

PROFIT GOALS. Profit goals are typically specified in terms of the gross margin to be attained. Such goals may be established for total sales, individual products, groups of products, sales territories, individual salesmen, certain types of customers, specified time periods, or any combination of these factors.[21] Just as for other sales objectives, the more completely profit goals are assigned to each market segment, salesman, product class, or product, the more likely it is that the goal will be both understood and achieved.

EXPENSE OBJECTIVES. These objectives are a corollary of profit goals. They refer to maximum allowable direct-selling costs including such items as salaries, travel, and entertainment. Both gross-margin profit goals and expense objectives must be met if the firm is to achieve its net-profit goals.

Objectives for the Individual Salesman or Sales Manager

Just as corporate sales objectives are important in guiding corporate marketing efforts, objectives for the individual salesman are important in directing his efforts. The importance and the methodology of setting individual performance standards are discussed at length in Chapter 17. In the present chapter we shall briefly describe performance standards, or objectives for individual salesmen, to complete the hierarchy of sales objectives. Five interrelated objectives are frequently established for salesmen—number of calls per day, order-call ratio, average number of orders per man-day, average order size, and production per man-day.

NUMBER OF CALLS PER DAY. One indication of a salesman's performance is provided by the number of calls he makes each day. To this end, several companies establish a sales-call objective for each salesman. While this objective is not necessarily conclusive evidence of salesman performance, substantial discrepancies from it should be carefully analyzed. Clearly, this objective should not be overemphasized lest it become an end in itself rather than the means to profitable sales.

[21] *Ibid.*

Table 16-1 Sales Volume Objectives (thousands of dollars)

Target Market Segments by Product Class

Salesman	Retail										Industrial		Totals	
	Department stores		Mass merchandisers		T.B.A. stores		Hardware stores		All other					
	Hose	Fittings	Hose	Fittings	Hose	Fittings	Hose	Fittings	Hose	Fittings	Hose	Fittings	Hose	Fittings
Brink	250	50	500	175	175	35	200	25	310	35	420	60	1,855	380
Larson	200	40	—	—	120	20	310	40	400	120	350	45	1,380	265
Murphy	320	45	610	200	140	25	240	45	300	35	380	50	1,990	400
Pike	280	50	520	180	135	22	300	37	410	112	—	—	1,645	401
Wilson	342	47	542	192	147	30	292	35	400	125	412	57	2,135	486
Totals	1,392	232	2,172	747	717	132	1,342	182	1,820	427	1,562	212	9,005	1,932
													10,937	

ORDER-CALL RATIO. A second, interconnected objective is the number of orders received as a percentage of sales calls made. Whereas number of calls relates directly to how hard a salesman is working, the ratio of orders to calls indicates how effective his work is.

AVERAGE NUMBER OF ORDERS PER MAN-DAY. An extension of the order-call ratio is the average number of orders received per man-day spent in the field. This measure, or objective, is valuable in evaluating the effectiveness of sales managers when calculated on a districtwide basis for comparison of districts.

AVERAGE ORDER SIZE. Counting of the number of orders reveals nothing about variations in the average size of the orders. Establishing an objective for average order size overcomes this deficiency.

PRODUCTION PER MAN-DAY. All of the preceding measures or objectives are important in directing sales-force efforts, but each is an indirect measure. The primary goal of selling is sales. An objective that evaluates the overall performance of the firm and its sales management is sales production per man-day.

INTERDEPENDENCE OF INDIVIDUAL SALES OBJECTIVES. These five objectives are highly interrelated. Number of calls can be increased by calling on a small number of accounts more frequently, but this will almost always reduce the order-call ratio. The order-call ratio can be improved by obtaining a large number of small orders rather than a smaller number of large orders, but this will reduce the average order size. In short, no single measure can be used to the exclusion of all others. Objectives should be established in each of the five areas, giving the salesman a clear understanding of exactly what he must accomplish if the firm is to achieve its objectives.

The Sales Strategy

A sales strategy identifies the role personal selling is to play in communicating the firm's total product offer to selected target market segments. It also requires decisions concerning whether to emphasize trade, missionary, technical, or new-business selling, as well as the means by which it will be accomplished—a geographic orientation to sales, team selling, system selling, or a highly programmed approach to merchandising.

Eight basic sales strategies are summarized in Figure 16-4. First, a firm may elect to employ a traditional vendor-customer approach. If it elects this alternative, it then must determine the basic role the salesman is to play in carrying it out— that is, whether the primary sales-force responsibility involves a trade, missionary, technical, or new-business orientation.

Should the firm choose to adopt a strategy of system selling or a highly programmed approach, the type of selling becomes more delimited. These strategies are most appropriate in technical and new-business selling, and they require that the salesman be extremely knowledgeable about the way the target market conducts its business operations. As described earlier, the emphasis is on fully understanding the nature of the customer's needs and showing how the vendor's total product offer or "system" can satisfy those needs. Thus, the salesman must fully

Figure 16-4   Alternative sales strategies.

Types of selling \ Sales Strategies	Traditional vendor-customer relationship	System selling	Programmed selling
Trade		/////	/////
Missionary		/////	/////
Technical			
New-business			

understand the technical characteristics of his customer's problems, whether they be product-oriented (as when he is selling heavy construction equipment) or operations-oriented (as when he seeks to become the sole supplier of consumer convenience goods to a wholesaler or retailer). Programmed selling is often the vendor's means of maintaining the ongoing operation of a total system once it has been sold.

The criteria used to determine which strategy is most appropriate for a particular firm, or for the product class a firm is selling, include the nature of the product, the nature of the market being served, and the sales objectives established by the firm. Thus, if a firm selling fabricated metal products to manufacturers of consumer durable goods has established sales objectives that include high sales volume, high market share, high gross margin, and low sales expenses, it will probably find itself choosing between two alternatives—technically oriented system selling or a highly programmed approach to the market. On the other hand, a manufacturer and seller of vacuum cleaners with the same sales objectives might sell its products directly, door-to-door, to ultimate consumers, at the same time selling on a programmed basis to large mass merchandisers.

MANAGING THE SELLING FUNCTION

The effectiveness of a sales organization is a direct function of its size and capabilities. Furthermore, capability can be developed only after the sales-force objectives and strategy have been established. Thus, the role of sales management is to carefully study the sales objectives and strategy in order to comprehend their implications for recruiting, selecting, training, compensating, allocating, and controlling the sales force.

Recruiting and Selecting Salesmen

Recruiting and selecting good salesmen is one of the most important functions of sales management. Unless the proper individual salesmen are obtained, it will be difficult to achieve profitable sales. Consider:

. . . it costs an average of $10,593 to search out, select, train and supervise one industrial salesman *until he is productive.*[22] That average figure resulted by combining companies which reported "less than $1,000" with companies reporting expenditures ranging up to "$30,000 to $50,000."[23]

Companies that do not recruit and select salesmen effectively also experience very high turnover rates. For example, one major consumer-goods company reported that "of the 1,380 college men hired since 1962, 1,102 have already left. . . . While this company's turnover experience is extreme, there are many that lost half or more of each year's incoming recruits over a three-year period."[24] Thus, many industrial- and consumer-goods companies face a serious problem. They need an upgraded, expanded sales force but have inadequate, ineffective techniques to develop this manpower.[25] One solution lies in more carefully determining specific sales-force needs and then recruiting and selecting men who possess those attributes.

The first step is to develop a profile of attributes that indicate sales success. Some companies have developed lists of characteristics by which they evaluate application blanks; these include age, height, appearance, education, previous business experience, and so on. Others develop lists of desirable personality traits, measured by aptitude tests, including such factors as aggressiveness, dominance, extroversion, optimism, competitive spirit, and so on. In addition, more sophisticated traits such as "empathy" and "ego drive" are frequently included.[26] These criteria are often useful. In this book, however, rather than trying to develop a list of generally wanted traits, it seems more useful to suggest a major set of categories and then let each company establish norms appropriate to its needs. Such a classification might include:

1. Mental (intelligence, planning ability).
2. Physical (age, appearance, health, speaking ability).
3. Experience (education, sales experience, other business experience).
4. Environmental (membership in organizations, amount of insurance owned, marital status, number of dependents, own or rent a home, length of residence in community, religion, race, family and social background).
5. Personality (ambition, interest, enthusiasm, tact, resourcefulness, emotional stability, persuasiveness, dominance, self-confidence, self-reliance, initiative).[27]

---

[22] Emphasis added.

[23] Results of the Sales Manpower Foundation study reported in Henry R. Bernstein, "How to Recruit Good Salesmen," *Industrial Marketing* (October 1965), p. 70.

[24] Andrall E. Pearson, "Sales Power Through Planned Career," *Harvard Business Review,* Vol. 44 (January-February 1966), p. 105.

[25] *Ibid.,* p. 106.

[26] Frederick E. Webster, Jr., "Interpersonal Communication and Salesman Effectiveness," *Journal of Marketing,* Vol. 32 (July 1968), p. 7.

[27] William J. Stanton and Richard H. Buskirk, *Management of the Sales Force,* 3d ed. (Homewood, Ill.: Richard D. Irwin, Inc., 1969), p. 125.

One author has suggested that such an approach is unidimensional, bearing no necessary relationship to the intellectual dimensions that such selection devices are designed to measure.[28] Instead, he indicates that job success may depend much more upon the match between the incumbent's personality and the temperamental demands of the job.

Empirical evidence also tends to verify what might be called the *characteristic-similarity hypothesis*.[29] That is, the more a salesman possesses the same characteristics as his customer(s), the greater the probability of his success. Clearly, this hypothesis has significant implications for recruiting: an approach that considers the interaction of customer-salesman characteristics would be preferable to one that considers only the characteristics of the salesman.[30]

DETERMINING MANPOWER NEEDS. A total recruiting and selection system is illustrated in Figure 16-5. It indicates that the firm's manpower requirement for salesmen depends upon three factors—a job analysis and description of the position to be filled, the qualifications needed to fill that position, and the number of salesmen needed.

Each firm's recruiting efforts typically include a rather consistent set of steps or stages. These include: developing leads on available sales candidates, inviting the candidates for an interview, conducting the interview, extending an offer to applicants adjudged desirable and qualified, and hiring those who accept the offer. Since there is some attrition at each stage, the firm usually must begin with a substantially greater number of leads than the number of salesmen actually required. Figure 16-6 is a diagrammatic representation of the recruiting yield process. It illustrates that the firm in this example must begin with 100 leads in order to meet its goal of hiring 15 salesmen.

Sales Training

Sales training is aimed at two groups: the inexperienced and the inept.[31] The inexperienced must be trained, because the demand for good salesmen is increasing rapidly. And, since it is frequently estimated that about 75 percent of all

---

[28] James A. Belasco, "The Salesman's Role Revisited," *Journal of Marketing*, Vol. 30 (April 1966), pp. 6–11.

[29] See Franklin B. Evans, "Selling as a Dyadic Relationship—A New Approach," *American Behavioral Scientist*, Vol. 6 (May 1963), pp. 76–79; M. Zuckerman and H. J. Grosz, "Suggestibility and Dependency," *Journal of Consulting Psychology*, Vol. 26 (October 1958), pp. 32–38; James E. Stafford and Thomas V. Greer, "Consumer Preference for Types of Salesmen: A Study of Independence-Dependence Characteristics," *Journal of Retailing* (Summer 1965), pp. 27–33; and Gilbert Burck, "What Makes Women Buy?" *Fortune*, August 1956, pp. 93–94, 174–194.

[30] For a series of "knock-out factors" that the Klein Institute for Aptitude Testing recommends employers use to disqualify applicants for a selling job see, Bernstein, "How to Recruit Good Salesmen," p. 72.

[31] "How to Create a Salesman," *Dun's Review and Modern Industry*, Vol. 82 (December 1963), p. 46.

Figure 16-5   A total recruiting and selection system.

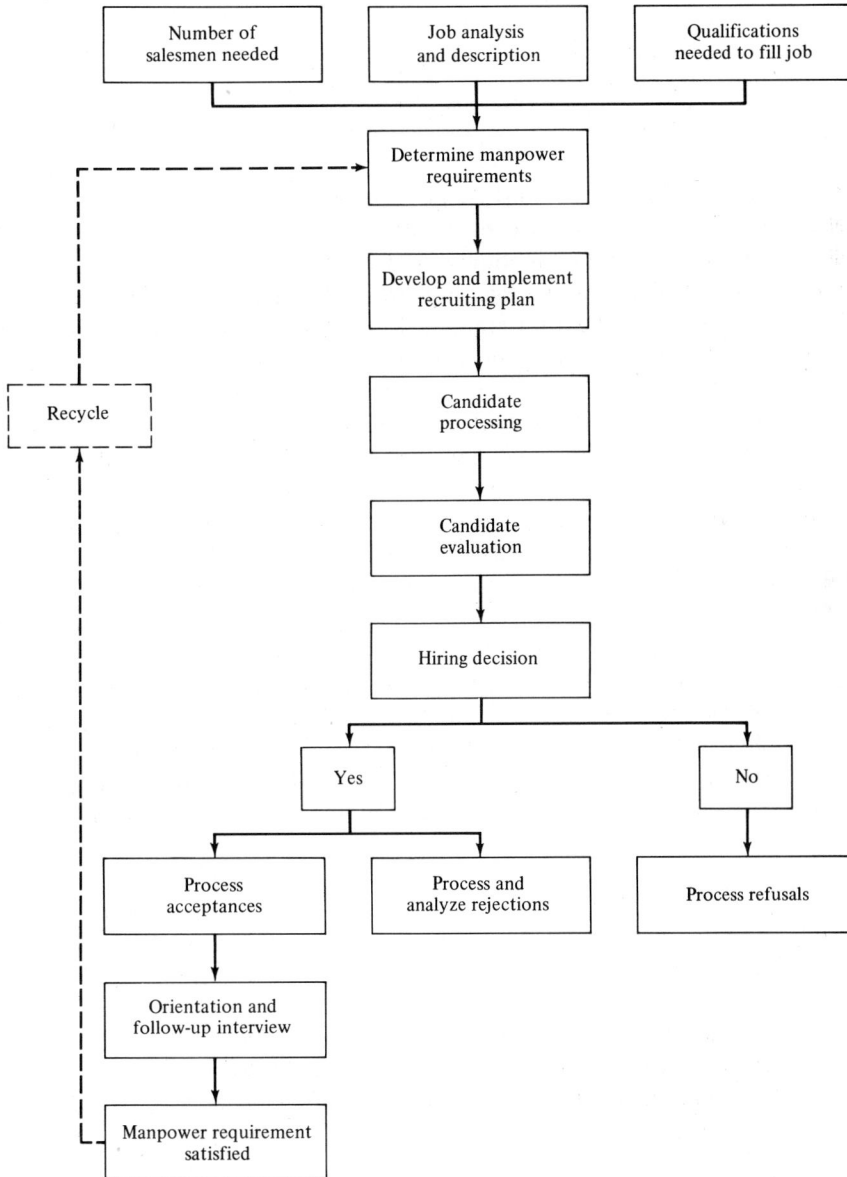

Figure 16-6 Recruiting yield pyramid.

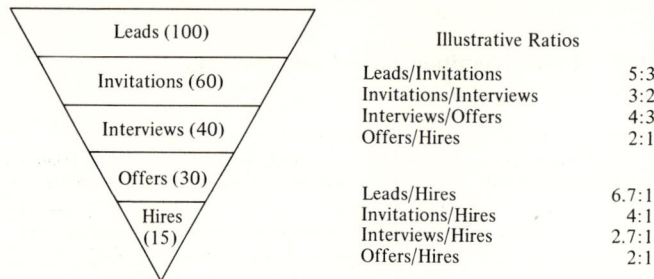

	Illustrative Ratios	
Leads (100)		
Invitations (60)	Leads/Invitations	5:3
	Invitations/Interviews	3:2
Interviews (40)	Interviews/Offers	4:3
	Offers/Hires	2:1
Offers (30)		
Hires (15)	Leads/Hires	6.7:1
	Invitations/Hires	4:1
	Interviews/Hires	2.7:1
	Offers/Hires	2:1

orders are brought in by the top 25 percent of the sales force, it is imperative that the lower 75 percent be made more effective.

Sales training can be divided into two phases—initial training and continuing training. Initial training may last from a few days, as it does in some consumer-goods sales training programs, to several years, as it does when capital goods such as business machines or machine tools are involved. Continuing training, by definition, is a periodic, ongoing process.

Topics usually taught during the initial phase of sales training include product familiarity, company sales policies and procedures, terms of sale, advertising and promotional programs and tools, territorial description, customer potentials, and "craft" qualities or selling techniques. The devices used to impart this knowledge include texts, manuals, films, hypothetical classroom situations or "role playing," simulation games, and supervised on-the-job experience.[32] In recent years the old, too often dull lectures have largely been replaced by sales development sessions designed to hone analytical and evaluation skills. These sessions usually require individual participation and involvement. In addition, trainees appear to be spending more time in the field, earlier in their training than before. For example: "After one week's initiation, Pitney-Bowes sends its trainees into the field. After four-and-a-half weeks, new 'hires' in the electronic data-processing division at Minneapolis-Honeywell move on to the firing line for on-the-job training."[33]

Salesman Compensation

The following procedure has been suggested as appropriate for developing a well-structured sales-compensation plan.

1. Establish clear and consistent compensation objectives.
2. Determine the level of income desired for the salesmen.
3. Determine the relative portion of each of three elements:
    (a) Base salary.

[32] Beckman and Davidson, *Marketing*, p. 601.
[33] "How to Create a Salesman," p. 46.

(b) Individual incentive.

(c) Group incentive.

4. Establish the measurement criteria to be used to evaluate performance.

5. Relate the method of incentive payment to the measurement criteria to establish the compensation "formula."

6. Apply the "formula" to the past experience of several individuals and groups, to test results on historical performance.

7. Make a field test of the new compensation plan, to determine its acceptability to the sales force and to measure its influence on sales performance.[34]

While there are many variations, most compensation programs are based upon one of three basic plans—straight salary, straight commission, or some combination of salary and commission. Each of these plans is illustrated in Figure 16-7.

Figure 16-7   Basic types of compensation plans, assuming that the average salesman will earn $800 per month on sales of $20,000.

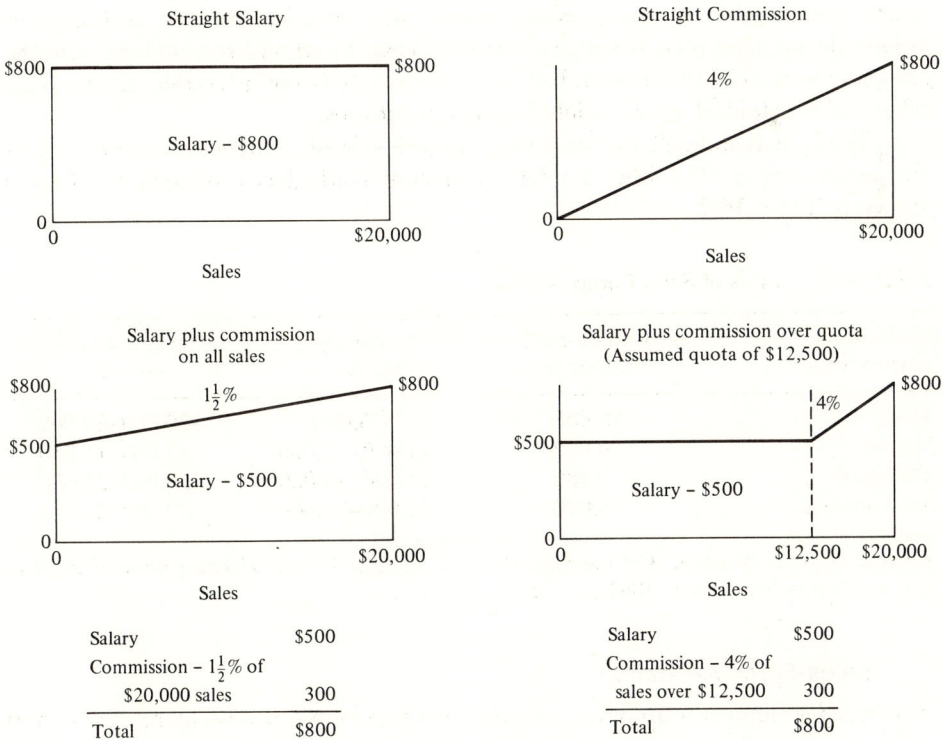

Straight Salary

Straight Commission

Salary plus commission on all sales

Salary	$500
Commission – 1½% of $20,000 sales	300
Total	$800

Salary plus commission over quota (Assumed quota of $12,500)

Salary	$500
Commission – 4% of sales over $12,500	300
Total	$800

[34] Frederick E. Webster, Jr., "Rationalizing Salesmen's Compensation Plans," *Journal of Marketing*, Vol. 30 (January 1966), p. 55.

Salary plans pay the salesman at a fixed rate, and any supplemental income (such as annual or semiannual bonuses, prizes, or merchandise offers) is not directly related to his individual sales record. Such a plan gives the salesman security and permits the manager a certain degree of control over his activities. The major disadvantage of salary plans is that they often offer the salesman little incentive.

Commission plans include those programs in which compensation is paid in proportion to sales. Plans that offer a draw or guarantee against commission would also fall into this category. Straight commission plans seem most appropriate where the salesman is capable of operating independently, as is the case with insurance and automobile salesmen. While these plans offer an incentive for increased sales output, they do not permit the manager to control the salesman's activities very closely. In addition, the sales manager must be sure that the sales produced in this way are consistent with objectives and profitability requirements.

Combination plans include all those in which part of the salesman's compensation is fixed and another part is paid in proportion to sales volume. The salary-plus-commission plan normally pays about two-thirds of total compensation in salary and one-third in commissions, which may vary by product, customer, or volume level. This plan is simple, effective, easy to administer, and permits the company to deal with a known business expense. It is not advisable in situations where sales potential varies widely between territories.

While it is difficult to estimate average levels of compensation for each of the various types of selling, a relatively recent study has produced the figures shown in Table 16-2.

Table 16-2   Levels of Sales Compensation

Sales-force classification	Lowest-paid salesman	Average salesman	Highest-paid salesman
Trade	$8,000	$13,000	$20,000–26,000
Missionary	8,000	11,000–12,000	17,000–18,000
Technical	9,000	12,000–13,000	20,000–26,000
New-business	8,000	12,000–13,000	19,000–24,000

SOURCE: Derek A. Newton, "Get the Most Out of Your Sales Force," *Harvard Business Review*, Vol. 47 (September-October 1969), p. 142.

Sales-Force Allocation

Territorial assignments are often a point of conflict between sales management and salesmen—a conflict which must be resolved to their mutual satisfaction. The company must have effective coverage of its accounts, and the salesman must have the opportunity to earn an adequate living.

Conceptually, each salesman should be assigned to a territory whose size, customer mix, and market potential are consistent with his capabilities—that is, a territory in which he can maximize profitable sales volume relative to his efforts while also maximizing his own income.

The Celanese Plastics Company thoroughly revised its sales territories a few years ago based upon three factors—number of calls, call hours, and travel hours.[35] Each district manager listed every account that was currently using Celanese plastic resins or that might conceivably do so in the future, and then figured out the number of calls needed to cover each account adequately. Next, each salesman was asked to plot his average call time per account and his average travel time to the account. Using these three factors, the total time to be spent on each account per year was estimated and all the accounts in each territory totaled. Fifteen hundred man-hours per territory was used as a bench mark. Territories that came close to this figure were equalized, while those that varied sharply from the norm were revised.[36]

Implementing, Administering, and Controlling the Sales Program

Objectives are set, plans are developed, and performance is measured, but all too often performance goes on as in the past, largely unchanged. As one executive said: "What good is . . . top-level planning if the salesmen won't change their ways? We plan until we are blue in the face, but it just doesn't seem to motivate the fellows on the firing line."[37]

In many instances failure to bring about desired changes in sales-force performance can be attributed to a breakdown in implementation and control. In addition to objectives for the sales division, objectives or standards of performance must be established for each manager and each salesman.[38] Only then can their efforts be adequately and accurately controlled.[39] One approach for implementing and controlling sales programs is summarized in the following four steps.

1. The first step is to translate corporate sales goals into meaningful, specific performance criteria for the upper level of sales management. A set of quantitative criteria of outstanding performance should also be developed.
2. The next step involves sending special teams of sales and marketing per-

[35] "The Art of Dividing Sales Territories," *Dun's Review and Modern Industry*, Vol. 86 (May 1967), pp. 47 ff.

[36] Other, more scientific approaches to the salesman allocation problem have been developed. For example, see Paul E. Green, Michael H. Halbert, and Patrick J. Robinson, "A Behavioral Experiment in Sales Effort Allocation," *Journal of Marketing Research*, Vol. 3 (August 1966), pp. 261–268.

[37] Jon R. Katzenbach and R. R. Champion, "Linking Top-Level Planning to Salesman Performance," *Business Horizons*, Vol. 9 (Fall 1966), p. 91.

[38] The subject of performance standards is discussed at length in the next chapter.

[39] Control of marketing programs is described in detail in Chapter 21.

sonnel into the field to determine the gap between actual and potential gross-profit performance for each major account. Working with specially selected management and staff advisors, the account salesman and his sales supervisor should establish realistic first-year and fifth-year gross-profit potentials for each account. The latter become the basis for territory alignment; the former, for current performance measurement.

3. Subsidiary performance targets should be set up for sales-expense control and small-order reduction for each account. These targets should be based on companywide standards for different types of accounts, modified where necessary to fit special account situations.

4. Finally, to encourage balanced-line selling, product-mix percentage goals should be established for each major product category.[40]

SUMMARY

There is little doubt that the salesman is the focal point of marketing effort. The firm's product, pricing, promotion, and distribution efforts are all designed to facilitate the attainment of corporate objectives through the medium of sales.

The four basic types of personal selling are trade, missionary, technical, and new-business selling. While each salesman must develop his own approach, there does appear to be a rather common series of steps that all salesmen go through to effect profitable sales. These include prospecting, preapproach, approach, demonstrating, handling objections, closing, and following up to insure customer satisfaction.

Today's salesman is quite different from his predecessors. In many lines of trade he is becoming increasingly expert in solving his customer's product and merchandising needs. The factors behind this change include an increase in the concentration of important customers, the centralization of purchase decision making, increasingly more complex customers needs, and the need to conserve the salesman's time and reduce selling expenses.

Sales management involves generating profitable sales that satisfy and are consistent with the firm's corporate strategies and objectives. The managerial activities that must be performed—and performed effectively—to accomplish this end include recruiting, selecting, training, and compensating sales personnel. In addition, salesmen must be assigned specific tasks, and the sales programs should be pretested, implemented, and continuously monitored to adjust sales efforts to achieve the various sales objectives.

QUESTIONS FOR REVIEW AND DISCUSSION

1. Describe the four basic types of personal selling. Are these classifications of personal selling activities mutually exclusive, or might some aspect of each type be found in almost all salesmen's efforts?

[40] Based upon Katzenbach and Champion, "Linking Top-Level Planning to Salesman Performance," p. 92.

2. Distinguish between "system selling" and "programmed merchandising."
3. In what ways do objectives for sales managers and individual salesmen differ from corporate sales objectives?
4. What implications does the *characteristic-similarity hypothesis* have for recruiting salesmen?
5. In what ways have corporate sales training activities been modified in recent years? Why have they been modified?
6. Using the ratios in Figure 16-6, determine the number of leads you need and the number of offers you should make to hire 25 new salesmen.
7. Describe the three basic salesman compensation plans. What are the advantages and limitations of each?
8. Describe the benefits that might result from a good sales compensation plan.

Chapter 17   Managing Market Personnel

The preceding chapters have emphasized the critical importance of strategic planning, programming, and execution. The success of these activities depends, at least in part, on how effectively marketing personnel perform.

Managing is often defined as the process of getting things done through others.[1] This obvious oversimplification does capture the essence of the manager's task—to develop an organization of people committed to achieving corporate and marketing objectives.

This chapter begins with an overview of a professional approach to managing marketing personnel. Then it describes important traditional organization principles and applies them to various marketing activities as well as the entire marketing division. It also discusses some of the factors that motivate individual behavior and develops an appropriate approach for the marketing manager. The chapter concludes with a discussion of techniques for controlling marketing personnel.

A PROFESSIONAL APPROACH TO MARKETING MANAGEMENT

Figure 17-1 illustrates the stages in the professional management process. It illustrates a management-by-objectives approach to marketing management, which can be summarized as follows:

[1] For a detailed discussion of the functions or processes of management see Ernest Dale, *Management: Theory and Practice,* 2d ed. (New York: McGraw-Hill, Inc., 1969), esp. Chaps. 10 through 23.

388

Figure 17-1   The marketing management process.

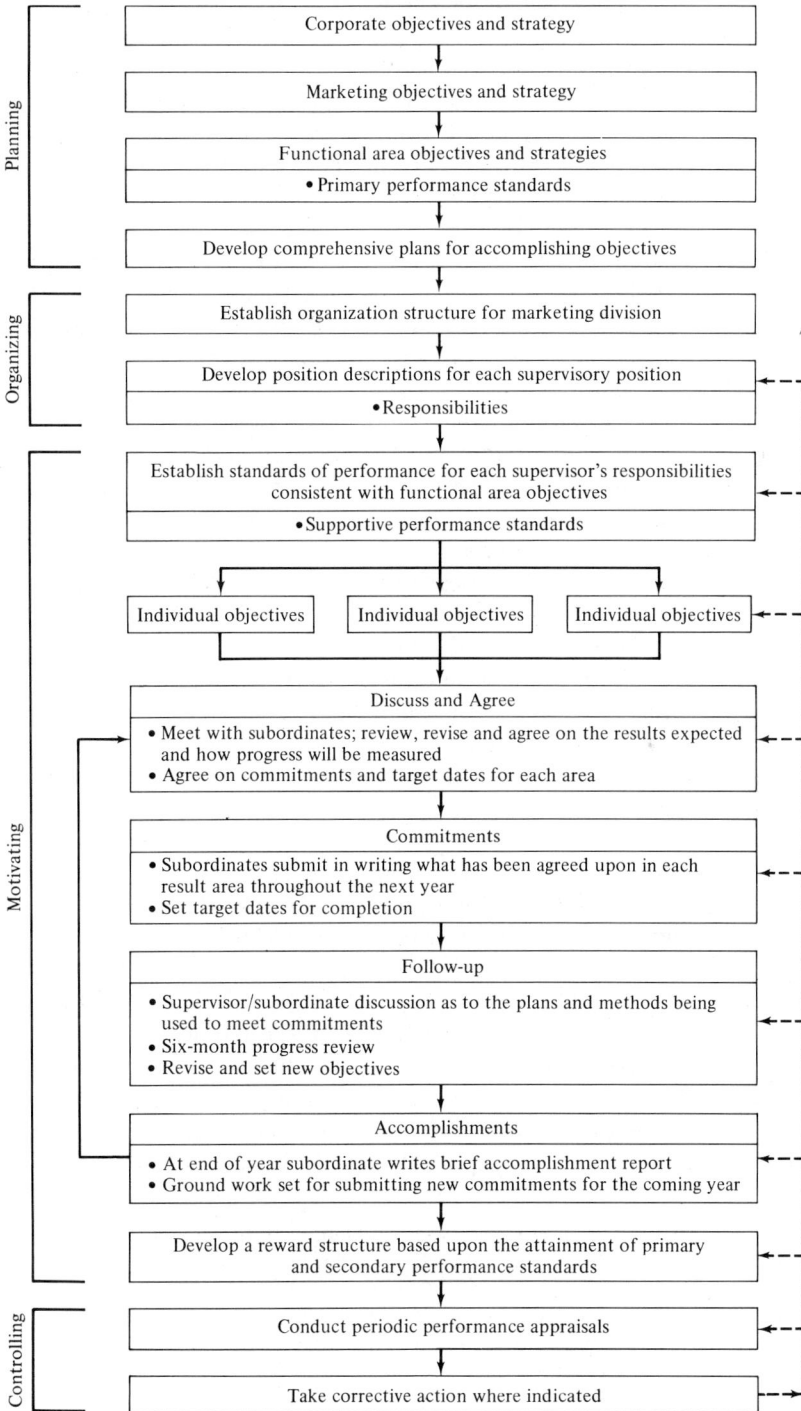

Planning

Corporate objectives and strategy

Marketing objectives and strategy

Functional area objectives and strategies
• Primary performance standards

Develop comprehensive plans for accomplishing objectives

Organizing

Establish organization structure for marketing division

Develop position descriptions for each supervisory position
• Responsibilities

Motivating

Establish standards of performance for each supervisor's responsibilities consistent with functional area objectives
• Supportive performance standards

Individual objectives	Individual objectives	Individual objectives

Discuss and Agree
• Meet with subordinates; review, revise and agree on the results expected and how progress will be measured   • Agree on commitments and target dates for each area

Commitments
• Subordinates submit in writing what has been agreed upon in each result area throughout the next year   • Set target dates for completion

Follow-up
• Supervisor/subordinate discussion as to the plans and methods being used to meet commitments   • Six-month progress review   • Revise and set new objectives

Accomplishments
• At end of year subordinate writes brief accomplishment report   • Ground work set for submitting new commitments for the coming year

Develop a reward structure based upon the attainment of primary and secondary performance standards

Controlling

Conduct periodic performance appraisals

Take corrective action where indicated

——— Program development glow

- - - - Revision cycle

389

1. At the beginning of the planning period, top management establishes overall goals or objectives for the entire organization. These overall objectives are then translated into action plans for every manager in the organization, so that each has clear, unambiguous objectives for his particular area of responsibility—objectives in keeping with the overall organizational objectives.

2. Next, an organizational structure consistent with and capable of achieving these objectives must be established. Whereas objectives represent the "end," organization represents the "means," or the vehicle by which objectives will be achieved.

3. Position descriptions, which clearly define the responsibilities of each individual in the organizational structure, must then be developed.

4. The next phase involves establishing performance standards to guide and direct each individual's activities. These performance standards must be supportive and consistent with functional area and overall corporate objectives.

5. This step involves developing a reward structure that fairly and adequately compensates each individual when he achieves the performance standards established for his position.

6. Finally, and perhaps most importantly, each individual's success or failure in achieving his standards of performance *must* be appraised and corrective action taken where necessary. This represents the key to management. Without it, the preceding activities become just more "paperwork."[2]

For a number of years similar approaches have been used by such successful firms as General Motors, Minneapolis-Honeywell, and General Electric. In general, these approaches have been successful because:

1. People tend to work more effectively if they know what they are expected to do and have knowledge of their effectiveness.

2. By participating in the setting of objectives, subordinates become committed to achieving the desired results.

3. Results can be better achieved when the methods to be used in measuring performance are clearly defined and understood by all parties involved.[3]

---

[2] For a more complete, detailed description of the management-by-objectives process see Peter Drucker, *Managing for Results* (New York: Harper & Row, Publishers, 1964); George Odiorne, *Management Decisions by Objectives* (Englewood Cliffs, N.J.: Prentice-Hall, Inc., 1969); Dale D. McConkey, *How to Manage by Results* (New York: American Management Association, 1967); and J. D. Batten, *Beyond Management by Objectives* (New York: American Management Association, 1966).

[3] Not all references to management by objectives are entirely favorable. Some of the limitations as well as the advantages of this approach may be found in Harry Levinson, "Management by Whose Objectives," *Harvard Business Review*, Vol. 48 (July-August 1970),

ORGANIZING FOR EFFECTIVE MARKETING MANAGEMENT

The first four steps in Figure 17-1 relate to planning activities. They should be familiar from preceding diagrams that illustrated the planning and control system for managing each of the various marketing activities. These steps include the determination of objectives and the development of ways in which those objectives can be achieved. They give direction and purpose to the organization.

If plans represent a course of action for the future, the organizational structure represents the design or the blueprint for action by which these courses of action will be implemented.[4] Thus, organization means: "a system of structural interpersonal relations . . . individuals are differentiated in terms of authority, status, and role with the result that personal interaction is prescribed. . . . Anticipated reactions tend to occur, while ambiguity and spontaneity are decreased."[5]

Once corporate objectives have been determined and a plan of action has been developed, a chart of the type of organization that can best implement the plan and achieve the stated objectives should be drawn. Developing such a chart involves the application of the concept of specialization or division of labor. Thus:

The job of dividing up work starts with a recognition of the tasks to be done. Patterns of activity are then identified, and basic functions are represented on an organization chart. The typical organization chart shows how specific jobs are grouped into departments, and then, into jobs within given departments. Once work is assigned to departments, specific job requirements must be developed. When these specifications are drawn clearly, the positions shown on the chart must be staffed.[6]

The remainder of this section is divided into three parts. The first examines traditional principles of organization. The second discusses alternative approaches to organizing the marketing division as well as certain marketing activities within it. The final section describes and illustrates the process of developing position descriptions.

Traditional Principles of Organization

Organizational "principles" should be viewed as guidelines—not unalterable laws. The primary, overriding consideration in developing an effective marketing

pp. 125–134; Anthony P. Raia, "A Second Look at Management Goals and Controls," *California Management Review*, Vol. 8 (Summer 1966), pp. 49 ff.; and George H. Dixon, "An Objective Look at Management by Objectives," *Managerial Planning*, Vol. 18 (January-February 1970), pp. 19–32.

[4] John G. Hutchinson, *Organizations: Theory and Classical Concepts* (New York: Holt, Rinehart and Winston, Inc., 1967), p. 156.

[5] Robert V. Presthus, "Toward a Theory of Organizational Behavior," *Administrative Science Quarterly*, Vol. 3 (June 1958), p. 50.

[6] Hutchinson, *Organizations*, p. 157.

organization is that the organizational structure should be tailored to meet the needs of the particular markets the firm seeks to serve.

We list below some important "guidelines" that have often proved to be of value in the organizing of marketing activities:[7]

1. *There should be clear lines of authority running from the top to the bottom of the organization.* Clarity is achieved through delegation by steps or levels from the highest executive to the employee who has least responsibility in the organization. It should be possible to trace such a line from the president or whoever is top coordinating executive to every employee in the company. This is known as the "scalar principle" or, following military parlance, "the chain of command."

2. *No one in the organization should report to more than one line supervisor. Everyone in the organization should know to whom he reports, and who reports to him.* This is the "unity of command" principle. Stated simply, everyone should have only one boss. The harassed individual who receives orders from several superiors must continuously decide whose orders to follow first, how to allocate his time so as to displease none and satisfy all, and what to do if he receives conflicting orders from different sources.

3. *The responsibility and authority of each supervisor should be clearly defined in writing.* Putting his responsibilities into writing enables the supervisor, himself, to know what is expected of him and the limits of his authority. It prevents overlapping of authority and lessens confusion. It avoids gaps between responsibilities and enables quick determination of the proper point for decision making.

4. *Responsibility should always be coupled with corresponding authority.* Persons who are being held responsible for achieving certain results should be given the authority necessary to achieve them. Executives must be careful not to delegate authority and then undermine it by making decisions that belong to the individual who is being held responsible.

5. *The responsibility of higher authority for the acts of its subordinates is absolute.* Although a supervisor delegates authority, he still remains responsible for what is done by those to whom he has delegated it. In accord with this principle, an executive cannot disassociate himself from the acts of his subordinates. He is as responsible as they for what they do and what they neglect to do.

6. *Authority should be delegated as far down the organization as possible.* Permitting decisions to be made at the lowest possible level releases the

---

[7] These guidelines or principles of organization are based largely upon material contained in S. Avery Raube, *Company Organization Charts* (New York: National Industrial Conference Board, 1953), pp. 5–13.

energies of those at higher levels for the matters that only they can attend to.

7. *The number of levels of authority should be kept at a minimum.* The greater the number of levels, the longer is the chain of command, and the longer it takes for instructions to travel down and for information to travel up and down within the organization.

8. *There is a limit to the number of positions that can be coordinated by a single executive.* The span of control is seldom uniform throughout an organization. At the upper levels, where positions are interdependent and dissimilar, many organization specialists urge that the span of control embrace not more than five or six subordinates. In some decentralized companies, however, in which the operating units are practically autonomous, the top executive may successfully coordinate as many as 12 or 15 positions.

9. *The organization should be flexible, so that it can be adjusted to changing conditions.* The organization plan should permit expansion and contraction without disrupting the basic design. Good organization is not a straightjacket.

10. *The organization should be kept as simple as possible.* Too many levels of authority make communication difficult. Too many committees impede rather than achieve coordination.

Evolving Patterns of Organization

Traditional organization theory places heavy emphasis on the standardization of activities, a relatively narrow span of control, and the primacy of the line organization and vertical authority. In certain instances such emphasis is appropriate. However, in the field of marketing another pattern of management and organization appears to be emerging. For the most part, it does not supplant traditional organizational principles, but rather places the emphasis differently.

The traditional and evolving patterns of marketing organization are summarized in Figure 17-2. Whereas the traditional approach is concerned with internal processes, the newer model concentrates far more on problems of external adjustment. The organization is viewed as an *ad hoc* arrangement that can always be adjusted and changed if need be. In addition, there is frequent overlapping of job responsibilities and acceptance of the idea of stepping across traditional lines to achieve the overall task.

The newer mode of management also accepts decentralized decision making and therefore has broader spans of control and fewer layers of supervision. Finally, emphasis is on the whole man—his motivation, character, personality, general knowledge, and intelligence—rather than on his special skills and technical know-how.[8]

[8] David G. Moore, "Marketing Orientation and Emerging Patterns of Management and Organization," in William Lazer and Eugene J. Kelley, eds., *Managerial Marketing: Perspectives and Viewpoints*, rev. ed. (Homewood, Ill.: Richard D. Irwin, Inc., 1962), pp. 351–356.

Figure 17-2   Patterns of organization.

Traditional	Evolving
1. Concern with system and internal processes	1. Concern with external environment
2. Logic of the system—"one right way"	2. Subordination of system to overall results
3. Insuring adherence to the system	3. Decentralization
4. Centralization of authority	4. Overlapping responsibility
5. Multiple layers of supervision	5. Reliance on men rather than systems
6. Specialization	
7. Subordination of human values to the machine	
8. Job-oriented rather than results-oriented	

SOURCE: Based on material contained in David G. Moore, "Marketing Orientation and Emerging Patterns of Management and Organization," in William Lazer and Eugene J. Kelley, eds., *Managerial Marketing: Perspectives and Viewpoints*, rev. ed. (Homewood, Ill.: Richard D. Irwin, Inc., 1962), pp. 351–356.

The Anatomy of Formal Organization

No one form of marketing organization is appropriate for all companies, since the organization should be tailored to meet the needs of each. Consequently, several alternative approaches to organizing marketing activities will be presented here and their respective strengths and weaknesses examined.

Specialization or the division of labor is the cornerstone of most organizational structures.[9] Though it has its limitations,[10] this approach appears to be the most widely used in American industry.

There are four principal bases for organizing the firm's marketing activities —by function, region, customer, or product. When the primary basis for delegating responsibility and grouping major marketing activities is by function—such as advertising, sales, physical distribution, and marketing research—the firm may also be referred to as nondivisionalized. The divisionalized company, on the other hand, is typically broken into separate operating divisions on the basis of region, customer, or product groupings.

THE NONDIVISIONALIZED MARKETING ORGANIZATION. The nondivisionalized or functional grouping of marketing activities, as illustrated in Figure 17-3, is a common method of structuring the marketing organization. Each functional manager carries out his responsibilities through a group of specialists, which may or

[9] See William G. Scott, "Organization Theory: An Overview and An Appraisal," *Journal of the Academy of Management*, Vol. 4 (April 1961), pp. 7–26.

[10] See Rocco Carzo, Jr., "Organizational Realities," *Business Review*, Vol. 4 (Spring 1961), pp. 95–104.

Figure 17-3   Functional organization.

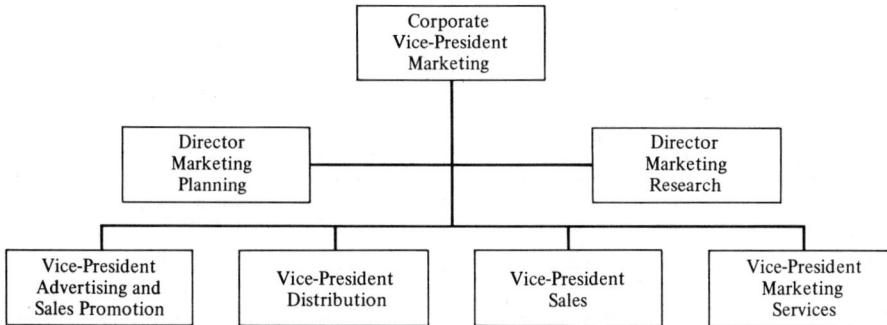

```
                    ┌──────────────┐
                    │  Corporate   │
                    │Vice-President│
                    │  Marketing   │
                    └──────────────┘
        ┌──────────────┐      ┌──────────────┐
        │   Director   │      │   Director   │
        │  Marketing   │      │  Marketing   │
        │  Planning    │      │  Research    │
        └──────────────┘      └──────────────┘
┌──────────────┐ ┌──────────────┐ ┌──────────────┐ ┌──────────────┐
│Vice-President│ │Vice-President│ │Vice-President│ │Vice-President│
│Advertising and│ │ Distribution │ │    Sales     │ │  Marketing   │
│Sales Promotion│ │              │ │              │ │   Services   │
└──────────────┘ └──────────────┘ └──────────────┘ └──────────────┘
```

may not be organized on a functional basis. For example, each of the departments might be further organized on a functional basis except for sales, which might be organized on a regional basis.

Grouping tasks according to similar work characteristics seems most appropriate where the performance of marketing functions is of unusual importance. Such an organization improves coordination and cooperation, because marketing personnel in each department are dealing with similar problems.[11] As firms increase in size, expand geographically, and substantially enlarge their product line, however, regions, customers, or products may become more appropriate bases for marketing organization.

THE DIVISIONALIZED MARKETING ORGANIZATION. A divisionalized marketing organization frequently develops to meet special needs that cannot be met effectively by a functional structure. When a company sells its products over a wide geographical area, it often relies upon regional specialization at some level within the marketing organization—commonly in field sales. Such an organizational structure increases the likelihood that differences in customer needs within each geographical region will be recognized and dealt with effectively.

1. *Regional Organization.* Where substantial regional differences exist, it may be appropriate to organize all marketing activities on a regional basis. Figure 17-4 illustrates this type of structure. The directors of the staff activities of marketing planning and marketing research report directly to the corporate vice-president of marketing as do the vice-presidents of advertising and sales promotion and of marketing services. In addition, three regional vice-presidents have complete responsibility for promotion, sales, distribution, and marketing services within their respective geographical areas. The dotted lines in the diagram indicate that the regional managers of advertising and sales promotion and of marketing services are supported by and their activities coordinated through the corporate managers of each of these functions.[12]

---

[11] Ralph C. Davis, *Industrial Organization and Management* (New York: Harper & Row, Publishers, 1957), p. 70.

[12] See Michael Schiff and Martin Mellman, *Financial Management of the Marketing Function* (New York: Financial Executives Research Foundation, 1962).

Figure 17-4   Regional organization.

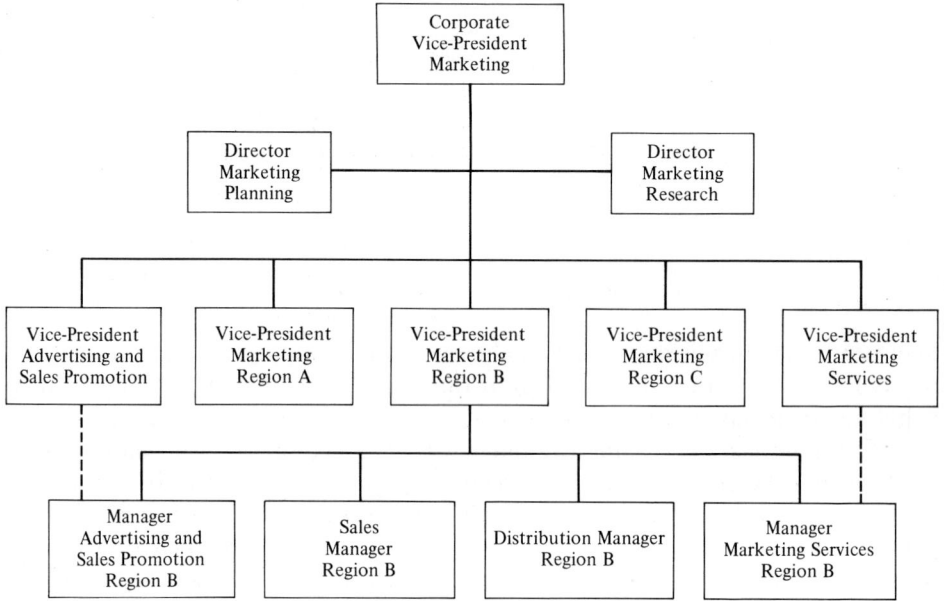

Corporate
Vice-President
Marketing

Director
Marketing
Planning

Director
Marketing
Research

Vice-President
Advertising and
Sales Promotion

Vice-President
Marketing
Region A

Vice-President
Marketing
Region B

Vice-President
Marketing
Region C

Vice-President
Marketing
Services

Manager
Advertising and
Sales Promotion
Region B

Sales
Manager
Region B

Distribution Manager
Region B

Manager
Marketing Services
Region B

Figure 17-5   Customer organization.

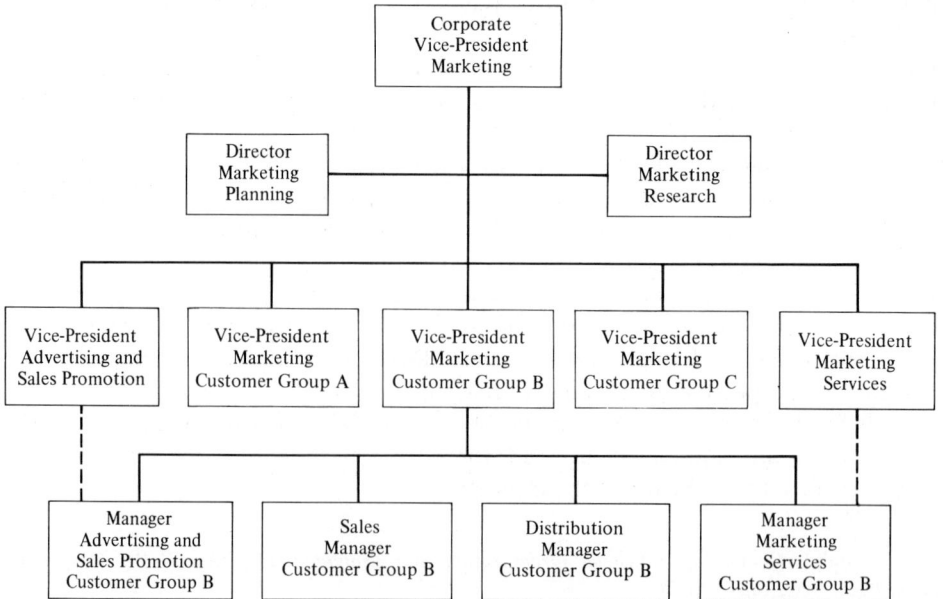

Corporate
Vice-President
Marketing

Director
Marketing
Planning

Director
Marketing
Research

Vice-President
Advertising and
Sales Promotion

Vice-President
Marketing
Customer Group A

Vice-President
Marketing
Customer Group B

Vice-President
Marketing
Customer Group C

Vice-President
Marketing
Services

Manager
Advertising and
Sales Promotion
Customer Group B

Sales
Manager
Customer Group B

Distribution
Manager
Customer Group B

Manager
Marketing
Services
Customer Group B

2. *Customer Organization.* This type of organization is often a desirable means of dealing with distinctly different groups of customers with highly individualized sets of needs (Figure 17-5). Organizing on the basis of customers contributes to a greater understanding of various customer needs and permits the marketing department to tailor its product offerings and approach to market requirements.

3. *Product Organization.* Originating in consumer-goods industries,[13] the product-management concept has rapidly spread to other industries.[14] For example:

- At *Pillsbury,* the man who bears the title, brand manager, has total accountability for results. He directs the marketing of his product as if it were his own business.
- Each of *Kimberly-Clark's* brand managers is responsible for drawing up complete marketing programs for his brand.
- At *Colgate-Palmolive,* product managers are responsible for developing plans and programs that will establish brand leadership and enlarge the current and long-range share of market and profits for their brands.
- Men employed for this work at *Procter & Gamble* are trained to accept the responsibility for the effectiveness of the overall advertising and promotion effort on an important nationally advertised brand.[15]

One study disclosed that three out of four companies in its sample rely on some form of product-oriented organization in their marketing departments.[16]

This trend appears to have developed because the manifold problems of marketing diverse product lines in dynamic markets are too heavy a burden for traditional organizational structures. Product management is a preferred organizational alternative in multiproduct companies where physically separated operating divisions, marketing groups, or sales units are not practical. In these cases the product manager provides a means of insuring individual attention for all major products.[17]

The dimensions of the product manager's job vary widely from company to company, sometimes embracing all the activities of product management and sometimes being limited to sales promotion.[18] Regardless of these variations, the

[13] Robert M. Fulmer, "Product Management: Panacea or Pandora's Box?" *California Management Review,* Vol. 7 (Summer 1965), p. 65.

[14] B. Charles Ames, "Keys to Successful Product Planning," *Business Horizons,* Vol. 9 (Summer 1966), p. 51.

[15] Fulmer, "Product Management," p. 66.

[16] David J. Luck and Theodore Nowak, "Product Management—Vision Unfulfilled," *Harvard Business Review,* Vol. 43 (May-June 1965), p. 144.

[17] B. C. Ames, "Payoff from Product Management," *Harvard Business Review,* Vol. 41 (November-December 1963), p. 143.

[18] R. H. Buskirk, *Principles of Marketing* (New York: Holt, Rinehart and Winston, Inc., 1961), p. 623.

product manager's basic responsibility is the effective planning and coordination of the activities that are vital to his product's success. This involves:

1. Developing written plans for the product line that explicitly define product and market needs and opportunities and indicate what can be done to meet and exploit them.
2. A planning emphasis focused on relatively few areas—those that can make or break the product.
3. Ranging across organization lines, focusing on the activities crucial to product success wherever these activities may be located functionally.[19]

The product-manager approach violates a proven management precept—that responsibility should always be matched by equivalent authority. He has complete responsibility for effectively marketing a product line but seldom has line authority over the full range of activities required to get the job done.[20]

There are several organizational variations of the product-manager concept. Figure 17-6 illustrates one such alternative. In this example the corporate level is organized functionally, as is each of the various marketing functions. In addition, a product manager is given the responsibility of planning and coordinating all of the activities necessary to successfully market each of the key products. This is done to ensure that each product receives the attention and support it merits from manufacturing as well as promotion and field sales.

Other alternatives are illustrated in Figure 17-7. Chart (a) illustrates an organizational approach frequently employed when each product group represents a distinct business large enough to support its own production and marketing operations. The structure outlined in chart (b) may be utilized to advantage when complete divisionalization is not feasible but the marketing requirements are significantly different for each product. Finally, chart (c) illustrates a desirable approach when separate customer groups must be served, when the business of each product is too small for divisionalization yet too unique for consolidation, or when product specialization is important and practical only in the sales area.[21]

Organizing Marketing Activities

NEW PRODUCTS. For companies operating in industries characterized by rapid technological and market change, new and improved products represent the key to corporate success. Two organizational methods are frequently used to achieve that success. The first is the use of teams or committees with representatives from each critical area of the business—marketing, manufacturing, and R&D. The mem-

---

[19] Ames, "Keys to Successful Product Planning," p. 51.

[20] Ames, "Payoff from Product Management," p. 142.

[21] *Ibid.*, p. 143. For an excellent discussion of the use of the product manager, his working relationships, and other aspects of his job as well as selected position descriptions and organization charts see *The Product Manager System*, Experiences In Marketing Management, No. 8 (New York: National Industrial Conference Board, 1965).

Figure 17-6   Product-manager organization.

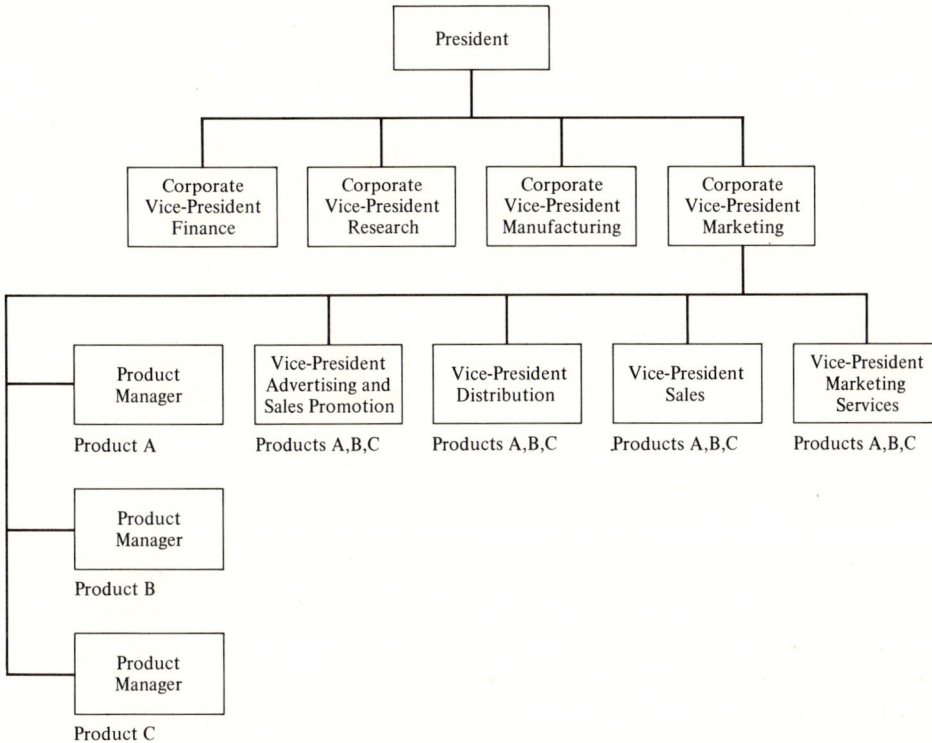

SOURCE: Based upon B. Charles Ames, "Payoff From Product Management," *Harvard Business Review,* Vol. 41 (November–December 1963), p. 142.

bers of these committees should be sufficiently low in the company structure to have detailed technical or market knowledge, and the chairman of the group must have true decision-making authority.[22]

The second alternative involves establishing a separate department to deal with new products. General Foods, General Electric, International Business Machines, and Burroughs are a few of the companies that have adopted this approach.[23] The new-product department might be organized as shown in Figure 17-8.[24]

[22] Jay W. Lorsch and Paul R. Lawrence, "Organizing for Product Innovation," *Harvard Business Review,* Vol. 45 (January-February 1967), pp. 110–111.

[23] S. C. Johnson and C. Jones, "How to Organize for New Products," *Harvard Business Review,* Vol. 35 (May-June 1957), p. 50.

[24] For an alternative approach to organizing new-product activities see Mack Hanan, "Corporate Growth Through Venture Management," *Harvard Business Review,* Vol. 47 (January-February 1969), pp. 43–61. For an extended discussion of new-product organization see *Organization for New Product Development,* Experiences In Marketing Management, No. 11 (New York: National Industrial Conference Board, 1966).

Figure 17-7 Some alternatives to the product-manager approach: (a) separate divisions for complete product specialization, (b) separate product marketing groups, and (c) separate product sales forces.

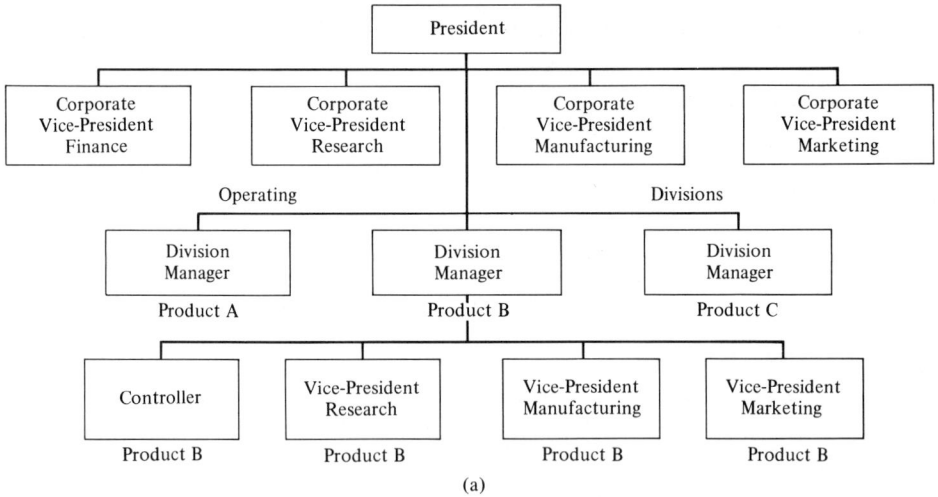

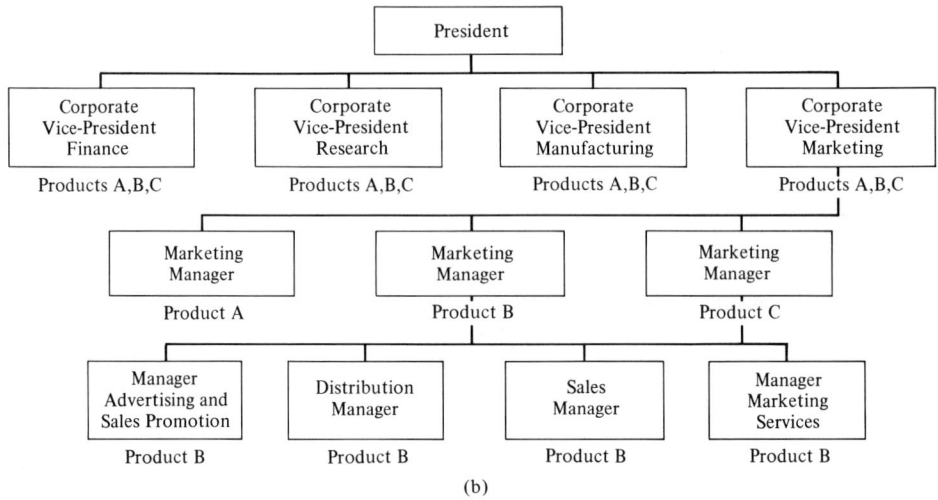

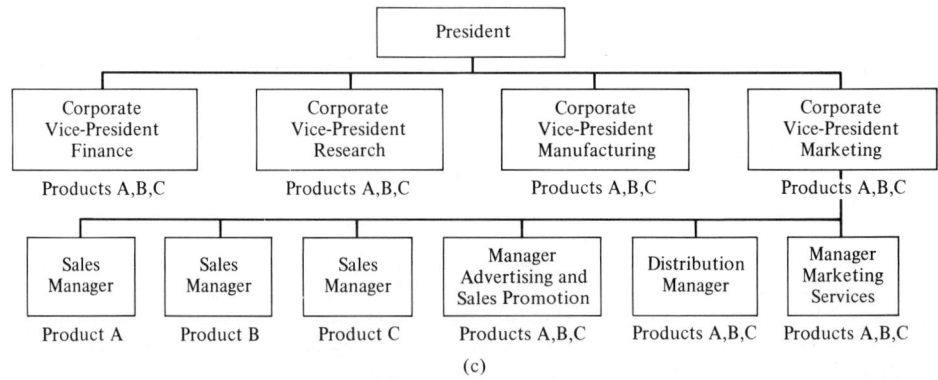

SOURCE: Based upon B. Charles Ames, "Payoff From Product Management," *Harvard Business Review*, Vol. 41 (November–December 1963), p. 142.

Figure 17-8   New-product organization.

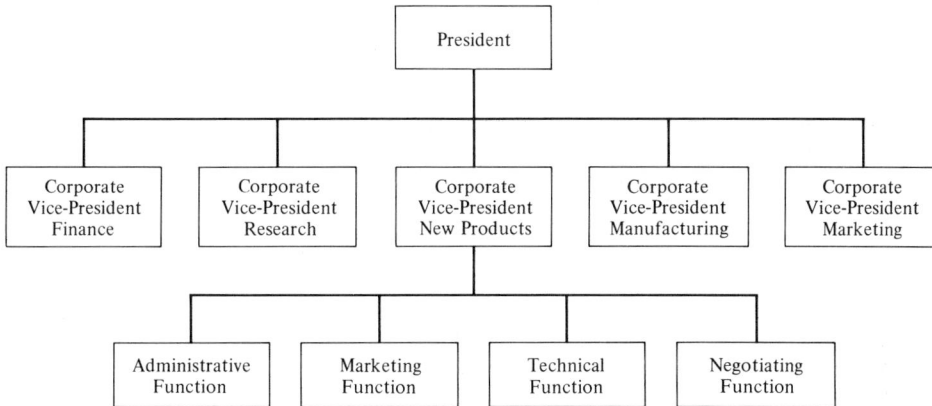

SOURCE: Adapted from S. C. Johnson and C. Jones, "How to Organize for New Products," *Harvard Business Review,* Vol. 35 (May–June 1957), p. 57.

SALES. The selling function is typically organized around function, product, region, or customer. Each of these forms is illustrated in Figure 17-9.

The functional-type organization in chart (a) illustrates an orientation that places all marketing activities under the sales manager's control. This structure is not as common today as it once was. With an increasing reliance on the marketing concept, several of these departments are now on an equal level with sales.[25]

More typical are structures oriented to product, region, or customer. Perhaps most common is a regional-type structure. However, when separate, unique customer needs must be satisfied, or the company sales force must possess highly specialized product knowledge, a customer or product organization may be more desirable. These organizational forms have become more popular as companies have recognized the need to structure their selling activities in ways that most closely correspond to the manner in which they have identified their target markets.

While it is not clear which form of sales organization is in most widespread use, combination-type structures are as common as any other. Figure 17-10 depicts a sales organization that is departmentalized on a functional, product, regional, and customer basis. Examples of this type are numerous. A national food company is organized primarily along regional lines but also has a separate chain-store division. Some pharmaceutical houses maintain regional sales organizations, but within these departments they may also have a chain-store division, wholesale division, and so on.[26]

[25] Hector Lazo and Arnold Corbin, *Management In Marketing* (New York: McGraw-Hill, Inc., 1961), p. 233.

[26] *Ibid.,* p. 238.

Figure 17-9 Alternative approaches to organizing the selling function: (a) functional-type sales organization, (b) product-type sales organization, (c) regional-type sales organization, and (d) customer-type sales organization.

(a)

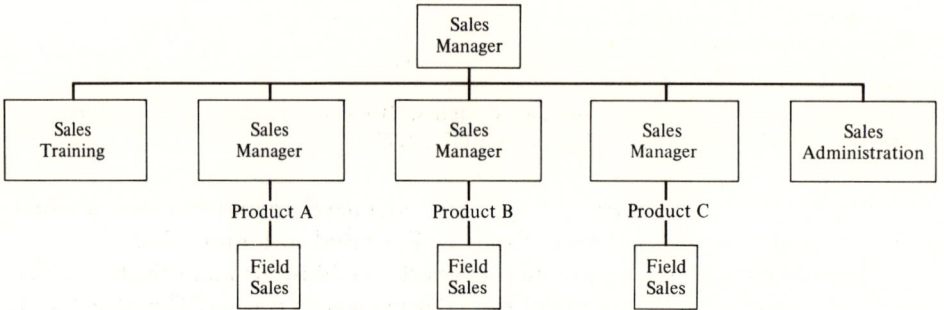

(b)

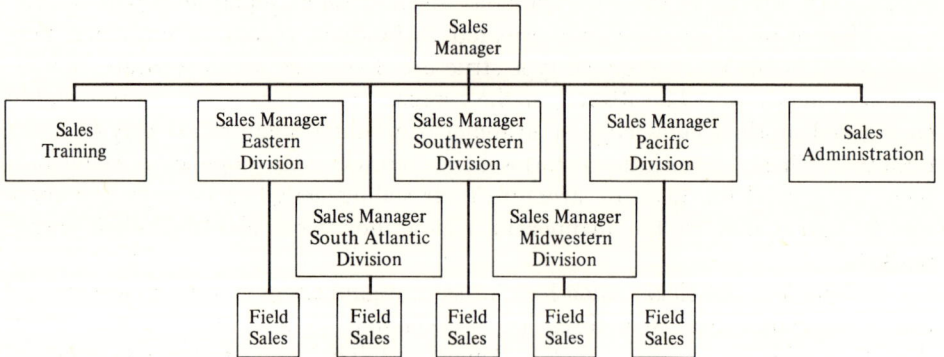

(c)

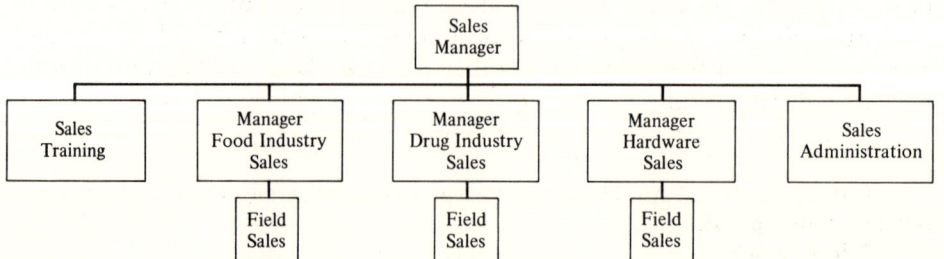

(d)

Figure 17-10   Combination-type sales organization.

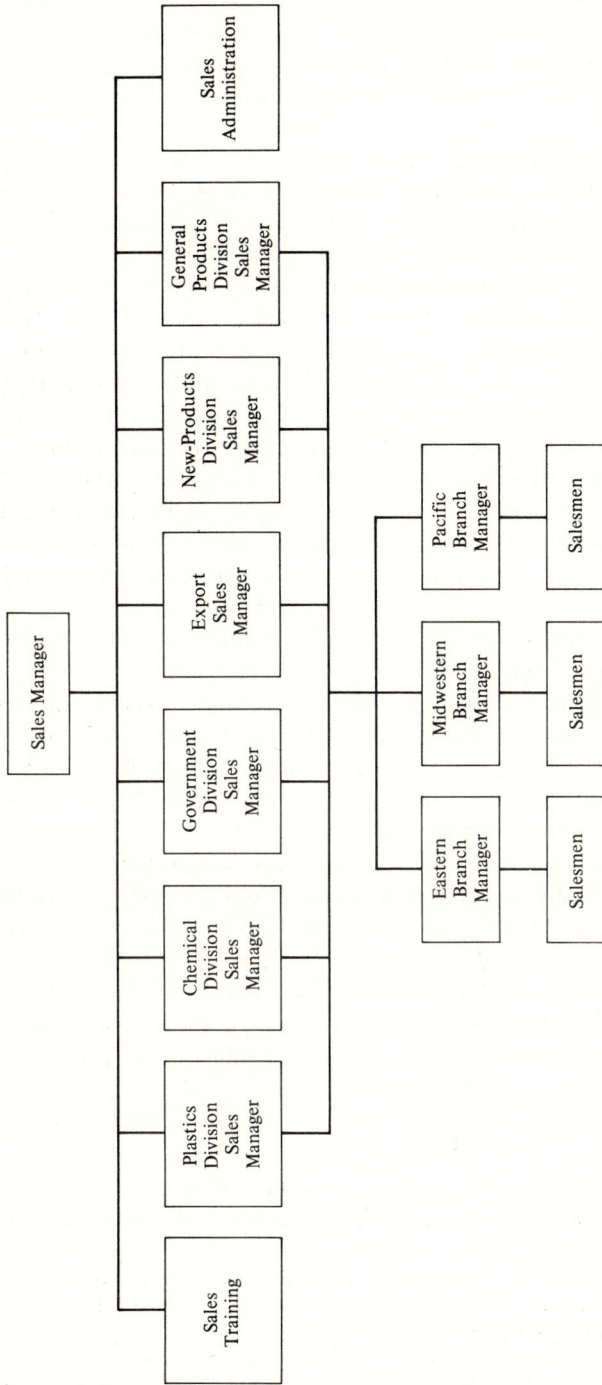

SOURCE: Adapted from examples given in *Charting the Company Organization Structure*, Studies in Personnel Policy, No. 168 (New York: National Industrial Conference Board, 1959).

PROMOTION. Because promotion has become increasingly important, the advertising manager, once subordinate to the sales manager, is approaching a position of equal standing. In many cases, as illustrated in several of the preceding organization charts, he reports directly to the corporate vice-president of marketing.

The nature of the advertising manager's job is also changing. Traditionally responsible only for advertising activities such as artwork, advertising production, and special publications, in many cases his scope is expanding to include the functions of sales promotion and public relations.[27]

Promotional activities are usually organized on the basis of products, functions, or some combination of the two. Chart (a) of Figure 17-11 illustrates a product-type organization. The advertising department contains account managers responsible for the copy, art, production, and distribution operations associated with each product in the product line they have been assigned. They, in turn, report directly to the advertising manager. In the functional-type structure [chart (b)] responsibilities are broken down according to the advertising activities that must be performed. Chart (c) in Figure 17-11 illustrates how these two alternatives can be combined. The latter type organization is found almost exclusively in large industrial organizations with a substantial advertising commitment.

DISTRIBUTION. Responsibility for distribution activities has historically been fragmented among different functional areas of the firm. Some firms are beginning to realize that total costs can be reduced, customer service improved, and interdepartmental conflicts substantially lessened if distribution activities are more closely coordinated and centrally programmed. These firms are developing integrated distribution systems designed to provide predetermined customer-service levels at the lowest possible total distribution costs.

A significant part of this trend involves consolidating distribution activities and organizationally positioning them in a single department. However, since the nature and extent of distribution activity varies widely, and since the organizational repositioning of these activities is a recent phenomenon, there are few established patterns. One approach is illustrated in Figure 17-12. The operations-services dichotomy is a familiar application of the line-staff concept. It is particularly appropriate in overcoming the problems of coordinating the firm's diverse distribution activities.[28]

Developing Position Descriptions

Organization charts represent an orderly allocation of the jobs that must be performed in order to accomplish corporate and marketing objectives. Most

[27] David L. Hurwood and Earl L. Bailey, *Advertising, Sales Promotion, and Public Relations—Organizational Alternatives*, Experiences In Marketing Management, No. 16 (New York: National Industrial Conference Board, 1968).

[28] Bernard J. LaLonde and James F. Robeson, "Organizing and Managing the Corporate Distribution Function," *The Journal of Business Policy*, Vol. 3 (Spring 1972), pp. 21–35.

Figure 17-11   Alternative approaches to organizing promotional activities: (a) product type, (b) functional type, and (c) combination type.

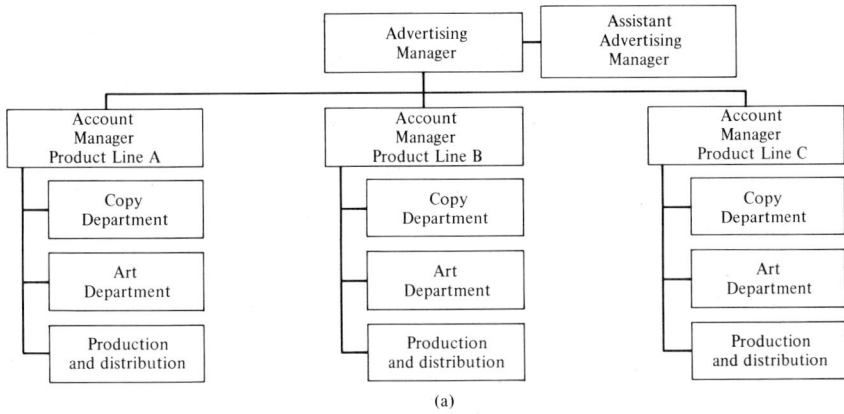

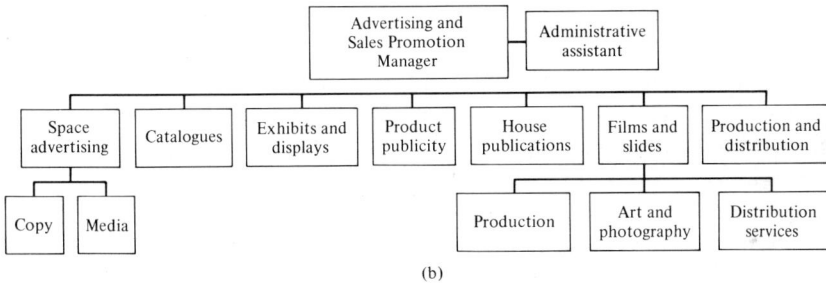

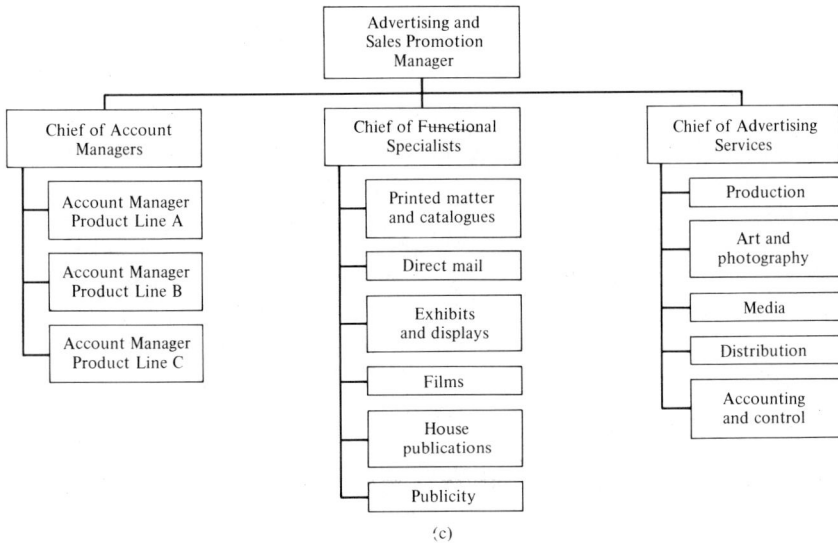

SOURCE: From *Marketing Communications Research Center Report #5*, "Organizing and Controlling Industrial Advertising Operations." Copyright 1956 by Marketing Communications Research Center. Reprinted by permission of Marketing Communications Research Center.

Figure 17-12   Distribution organization.

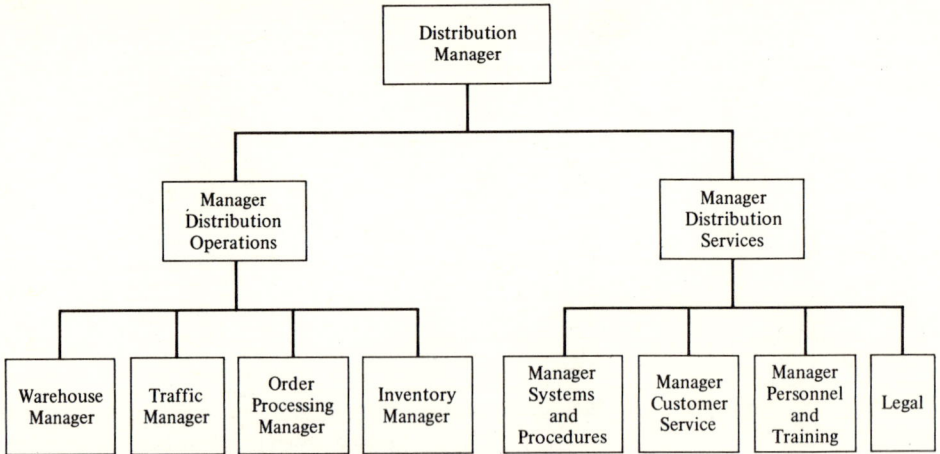

charts show the jobs to be done, their interrelationships, and contain a brief description of the functions of each position. However, these documents are not sufficiently detailed to guide individual activity within the organization, and so position descriptions must be developed to specify the objectives and responsibilities of each position.

A position description should delineate "the basic functions and duties, specific responsibilities, organizational relationships, authority, and accountability assigned to a particular position."[29] Figure 17-13 contains an illustrative position description for a district sales manager in an equipment manufacturing firm.

MOTIVATING AND CONTROLLING MARKETING PERSONNEL

While the position description describes individual duties and responsibilities, it does so in a very general sense. It does not state how the individual's performance will be measured, what standards of performance are desirable, or how his performance will be formally appraised. This section discusses the process of setting and gaining commitment to individual goals. It begins with an examination of some fundamental aspects of motivation, applies these fundamentals to the goal-setting process, and concludes with a discussion of controlling marketing personnel.

Traditional Concepts of Motivation

Most psychologists agree that all behavior is motivated toward satisfying certain needs. One of the most widely accepted treatments of the needs that motivate human behavior has been developed by A. H. Maslow.[30] As was discussed in

[29] Lazo and Corbin, *Management in Marketing*, p. 98.
[30] A. H. Maslow, *Motivation and Personality* (New York: Harper & Row, Publishers, 1954).

Figure 17-13 An illustrative position description: district sales manager—an equipment manufacturer.

TITLE:
District Sales Manager

DIVISION:
Industrial Marketing Department

FUNCTION:
Field Sales Management

RESPONSIBILITIES:
Administrative, Supervisory, and Staff

DUTIES:

General:

To be responsible for the planning and implementation of marketing programs in his assigned district.

Specific:

A. Administrative:
1. Will be responsible for the preparation and implementation of marketing plans for his district. These plans are to be completed and submitted for review by his Area Sales Manager no later than July 15 of each year.
2. Will be responsible for the preparation of the budget for his district and for obtaining approval from his Area Sales Manager.
3. Will be responsible for the preparation of the annual district sales forecast and for obtaining its approval from his Area Sales Manager.
4. Will be required to act as the coordinating point for Marketing Services programs when they affect or concern his district.
5. Will keep informed of market conditions and the competitive situation regarding products, pricing, and procedures, and recommend changes in policies, procedures, or program direction to effectively maintain marketing momentum.
6. Will be responsible for planning, coordinating, and participating in district sales meetings to implement marketing programs.
7. Will be responsible for informing Marketing, Customer Service, and Production Management personnel of trend data taken from district day-to-day activities so proper service and communication can be maintained for and with district customers.
8. Will issue or review all action requests and decisions concerning marketing activities and Industrial Marketing Department policy when these requests or decisions concern people in his district.
9. Will be responsible for prudent administration and implementation of pricing authority given him.

B. Supervisory:
1. Will be specifically responsible through Sales Engineers for the marketing performance of his district.
2. Will make sales calls with the Sales Engineer on a regular scheduled basis to familiarize himself with his accounts, to assure sales and service continuity.
3. Will be responsible for the sales motivation, direction, and supervision of the personnel assigned to his district under his control.
4. Will be required to give performance appraisals to Sales Engineers and make salary and promotion recommendations for the personnel in his district.
5. Will be responsible for approval of Sales Engineers' expenses and for total expense control in his district.
6. Will be responsible for maintaining a high degree of morale by providing the climate for individual personal development and job satisfaction.

C. Staff:
1. Will be required to coordinate special marketing projects and studies as assigned by his Area Sales Manager.
2. Will be a key advisor to marketing management on matters concerning planning, implementation, and evaluation of programs in his district.
3. Will be required, with reasonable notice, to present the status of marketing programs under his control to marketing management.

GENERAL REMARKS:

The District Sales Manager will have a strong sales background, preferably in the company's products and with the Industrial Division's sales force. He will be capable of positively motivating and directing others and of demonstrating the techniques of successful field industrial selling. He should, with proper training, be capable of performing an Area Sales Manager's function. He will report directly to the Area Sales Manager and derive his authority in the performance of his duties from that office.

SOURCE: Morgan B. MacDonald, Jr., and Earl L. Bailey, *The First-Line Sales Supervisor* (New York: The National Industrial Conference Board, 1968), pp. 46–47. Reprinted by permission.

Chapter 6, Maslow's theory identifies five classes of needs. In order of prepotence they are:

1. *Physiological needs*—survival and reproduction needs such as hunger, thirst, sex, and reproduction of the species.
2. *Safety needs*—the avoidance of physical harm, illness, economic disaster, and so on.
3. *Social needs*—belongingness and love needs, the need to associate with like beings.
4. *Esteem needs*—self-respect, respect of others, recognition.
5. *Self-fulfillment needs*—the need to have pride in individual accomplishment or to possess a sense of importance.

Maslow contends that lower-order or physiological needs must be satisfied before the next higher level of needs emerges. Once a need has been satisfied, it ceases to motivate behavior.

Douglas McGregor's theory describes contrasting sets of assumptions management makes in viewing individuals in their work setting.[31] Under "Theory X," management makes these assumptions about behavior:

1. The average human being has an inherent dislike of work and will avoid it if he can.
2. Therefore, most people must be coerced, controlled, directed, and threatened with punishment if management is to get them to put forth adequate effort toward the achievement of organizational objectives.
3. The average human prefers to be directed, wishes to avoid responsibility, has relatively little ambition, and wants security above all.

The assumptions of "Theory X" are giving way to those of the newer concept, "Theory Y". Here it is assumed that:

1. The expenditure of physical and mental effort in work is as natural as play or rest.
2. External control and the threat of punishment are not the only means of bringing about effort toward organizational objectives. Man will exercise self-direction and self-control in the service of objectives to which he is committed.
3. Commitment to objectives is a function of rewards associated with their achievement.
4. The average human being learns, under proper conditions, not only to accept but to seek responsibility.

[31] Douglas McGregor, *The Human Side of Enterprise* (New York: McGraw Hill, Inc., 1960).

5. The capacity to exercise a relatively high degree of imagination, ingenuity, and creativity in the solution of organizational problems is widely distributed but uncommon in the population.
6. Under the conditions of modern industrial life, the intellectual potentialities of the average human being are only partially utilized.

Motivating Marketing Personnel

"Theory Y" and Maslow's explanation of the factors that motivate human behavior offer the marketing manager valuable insights into how he can effectively motivate marketing personnel. These insights are especially valuable in determining how individual performance measures should be selected, performance standards set, and actual performance evaluated.

SELECTING PERFORMANCE MEASURES. If the objectives of the firm are to be achieved, individuals within the firm must know what those objectives are. In similar fashion, if individuals are to achieve their own objectives, they must know specifically what they are. Thus:

- All supervisors should set objectives for the current year and, where appropriate, three- and five-year goals.
- Departmental objectives should be coordinated with company objectives and should clearly identify the contribution that the department will be expected to make for the period of time involved.
- Objectives should include subobjectives, checkpoints, and concrete plans for the achievement of all objectives.

When the company's and marketing department's objectives have been further subdivided into objectives for each individual, the marketing manager must determine how he will measure the individual's progress toward achieving his objectives. If, for example, he wants to be able to assess a salesman's progress toward achieving his annual sales quota, he might select the individual's "total dollar sales-to-date" as the relevant performance measure.

ESTABLISHING PERFORMANCE STANDARDS. Once the performance measure has been selected, the manager must determine the standard or level of performance that is expected. Thus, in our sales example, he must decide what each individual salesman's sales quota will be. However, since each position description typically includes more than one responsibility, and since there are often several ways to measure how well each responsibility is being accomplished, several performance standards must be established for each individual. Figure 17-14 illustrates the performance standards that might be used to evaluate a district sales manager's performance in one of several assigned areas of responsibility.

The process of setting performance standards is outlined in Figure 17-1. It involves agreement by the manager and subordinate upon a set of objectives,

Figure 17-14   Performance standards—district sales manager.

Main Work Elements	What Is Standard Performance?	Performance Is Measured by These Supervisory Techniques and Yardsticks	Examples of What Would Be Generally Regarded as Above Standard Performance	Examples of What Would Be Generally Regarded as Below Standard Performance
1. Analyzes sales, markets, profitability, costs and budgets established for his District and acts in accordance with his findings.	a. Meets yearly sales quota in all markets within ± 5%.	a. Monthly Sales Control Report comparing District current sales with assigned quota.	a. More than 5% over quota for all markets.	a. Under quota in sales, more than 5% on all markets.
	b. Increases sales in all markets by at least 1% over previous year.	b. Monthly Sales Control Report comparing current sales with same period of previous year.	b. Increases sales over previous year by more than 1% in each market.	b. Decreased sales in all markets by more than 1% compared with previous year.
	c. Does not exceed expense budget for District Sales by more than 1%.	c. Monthly Sales Control Report comparing District current expenses with assigned budget.	c. Actual expenses of District less than budgeted expenses.	c. Expense budget for District sales more than 1% high.
	d. Meets estimated quarterly per cent gross contribution by ± ¼%.	d. Quarterly Sales Control Report comparing District current per cent gross contribution with estimated.	d. Per cent gross contribution 0.25% or more than estimated.	d. Quarterly estimated % gross contribution more than 0.25% low.
	e. Meets estimated quarterly dollars gross contribution by ± 1%.	e. Quarterly Sales Control Report comparing District current dollars gross contribution with estimated.	e. Dollars gross contribution 1% or more higher than estimated.	e. Quarterly estimated dollars gross contribution more than 1% low.
	f. Sales in District tend to show less variation than Industrial Indexes for his District but tend to follow over-all trend. Also follow Company's national averages.	f. Monthly Sales Control Report giving Company's national averages plus use of other published indexes.	f. Sales for District greater than published indexes for District or better than rate shown by Company's national averages.	f. Sales in District show more loss than published indexes for District and show more loss than indicated by Company's national average index.

SOURCE: Morgan B. MacDonald, Jr., and Earl L. Bailey, *The First-line Sales Supervisor* (New York: The National Industrial Conference Board, 1968), p. 68. Reprinted by permission.

410

target dates for their completion, and the activities that must be undertaken in order to accomplish the objectives by the established date. It involves mutual planning and problem solving rather than the autocratic establishment of objectives by superiors for their subordinates. This process is accomplished at General Mills in the following manner:

For each position, a statement of accountabilities is included as part of the position guide. The statement sets forth, in general terms, the results that a specific position should produce. In preparing what is called his "Action Plan of Objectives," a manager consults this statement of his accountabilities. He writes the first statement of accountability on the Action Plan and writes under it one or more specific results that he plans to achieve in the year ahead to fulfill that accountability. In similar fashion he continues to note on the Action Plan the remaining statements of accountabilities, following most of them, but not necessarily all, with one or more specific objectives. The manager and his boss then discuss the Action Plan, perhaps modifying specific objectives until both can agree that it is a meaningful and attainable yet challenging plan of action for the year ahead.[32]

A similar approach is followed at Aluminum Company of America:

1. An individual writes down his major performance objectives for the coming year and his specific plans (including target dates) for achieving these objectives.
2. He submits them to his boss for review. Out of the discussion comes an agreed-upon set of objectives.
3. On a quarterly basis he verbally reviews progress toward these objectives with his boss. Objectives and plans are revised and updated as needed.
4. At the end of the year, the individual prepares a brief "accomplishment report," which lists all major accomplishments, with comments on the variances between results actually achieved and the results expected.
5. This "self-appraisal" is discussed with the boss. Reasons for goals not being met are explored.
6. A new set of objectives is established for the next year.[33]

This approach permits subordinates to participate in the establishment of their own objectives or performance standards. As a result, they are likely to become more committed to achieving these objectives.

DEVELOPING A REWARD STRUCTURE. Individuals should be rewarded for accomplishing their objectives, and corrective action should be taken when they fail. This reward can take several forms. An individual committed to achieving a

---

[32] Walter S. Wikstrom, *Managing by—and With—Objectives*, Studies in Personnel Policy, No. 212 (New York: National Industrial Conference Board, 1968), p. 7.

[33] *Ibid.*, p. 3.

particular objective will be compensated in one sense when he does, in fact, achieve or exceed that objective. In addition, it is recommended that his monetary compensation and career progression be based upon his ability to accomplish his objectives.

Controlling Marketing Personnel: The Performance Appraisal

Performance appraisal entails evaluating individual performance and taking corrective action when necessary. This is the process that should be used to control personnel.

The performance appraisal tends to function as a periodic correction of a subordinate's activities when they are not directed toward, or are ineffective in, achieving his performance standards. This process is important because it tells the employee exactly where he stands with his superior and permits him to concentrate his efforts more effectively. The approach used by Eastern Airlines both to establish objectives and to evaluate individual progress toward them is shown in Figure 17-15. Note that it provides for quarterly evaluations.

Interviews at General Electric have provided valuable insights into how this process both should and should not be conducted. For example:

- Criticism has a negative effect on achievement of goals.
- Praise has little effect one way or the other.
- Performance improves most when specific goals are established.
- Defensiveness resulting from critical appraisal produces inferior performance.
- Coaching should be a day-to-day, not a once-a-year activity.
- Mutual goal setting, not criticism, improves performance.
- Interviews designed primarily to improve a man's performance should not at the same time weigh his salary or promotion in the balance.
- Participation by the employee in the goal-setting procedure helps produce favorable results.[34]

SUMMARY

The professional approach to marketing management described in this chapter closely parallels the steps that Ralph J. Cordiner, former head of the General Electric Company, recommends for developing an effective organizational structure. They are:

1. Determine the objectives and the policies, programs, plans, and schedules that will best achieve those objectives for the company as a whole and, in turn, for each component of the business.

---

[34] H. H. Meyer, E. Kay, and M. R. P. French, Jr., "Split Roles in Performance Appraisal," *Harvard Business Review*, Vol. 43 (January–February 1965), p. 123.

Figure 17-15   Eastern Airlines goal-setting worksheet.

	Goal Code: _____
Goal – Setting Work Sheet Eastern Airlines, Inc.	Participant: Name: _____ Title: _____ Organization: _____

Statement of Goal:

List of Basic Assumptions:

Criteria for Evaluating Results:

Result Definition	Quantitative Criteria	Qualitative Criteria	Accomplishment Time Criteria
Target Level			
Minimum Acceptable			

Goal results will be rated: unacceptable, minimum acceptable, target level, above target

Approved:	_____	_____	_____
	Participant	Superior	Date

SOURCE: Reprinted by permission of the publisher from AMA Research Study No. 81, *Marketing Planning.* © 1967 by the American Management Association, Inc.

Figure 17-15   Eastern Airlines goal-setting worksheet (*continued*).

Action Program		Quarterly Progress Report			
Steps	Timing	1st quarter	2nd quarter	3rd quarter	4th quarter
		☐ on target ☐ off target ☐ goal or program revised Comments	☐ on target ☐ off target ☐ goal or program revised Comments	☐ on target ☐ off target ☐ goal or program revised Comments	☐ on target ☐ off target ☐ goal or program revised Comments

Comments by superior

1st quarter	3rd quarter
2nd quarter	4th quarter

414

2. Determine the work to be done to achieve those objectives under such guiding policies.

3. Divide and classify or group related work into a simple, logical, understandable, and comprehensive organizational structure.

4. Assign essential work clearly and definitely to the various components and positions.

5. Determine the requirements and qualifications of personnel to occupy such positions.

6. Staff the organization with persons who meet these qualifications.

7. Establish methods and procedures that will help to achieve the objectives of the organization.[35]

The chapter discussed traditional and emerging concepts of management and organization and described alternative approaches to organizing marketing activities, as well as the entire marketing division. It also described motivational concepts and specified procedures for using these concepts, including the processes that should be used to both set individual performance standards and gain commitment to them.

QUESTIONS FOR REVIEW AND DISCUSSION

1. In what ways does the marketing management process described in this chapter differ from traditional approaches?

2. The fourth principle of organization states: "Responsibility should always be coupled with corresponding authority." Yet, in describing the product manager's role, we noted: "He has complete responsibility for effectively marketing a product line but seldom has line authority over the full range of activities required to get the job done." Discuss.

3. Discuss the relative advantages and disadvantages of the "traditional" and "evolving" patterns of organization enumerated in Figure 17-2.

4. What are the principal bases for organizing the firm's marketing activities? Under what circumstances might each be employed to advantage?

5. Describe the nature of the product manager's job.

6. Why does the professional approach to marketing management include the development of position descriptions?

7. In what ways are performance standards related to position descriptions?

8. "McGregor's 'Theory Y' is what one would expect from someone who 'talks' about workers rather than 'supervises' them. Six months in a line supervisor's position is all it takes to convince any true manager that 'Theory X' is a *far* more representative description of the vast majority of today's hourly employees." Discuss.

[35] Ralph J. Cordiner, *New Frontiers for Professional Managers* (New York: McGraw-Hill, Inc., 1956).

PART IV

PRETESTING MARKETING PROGRAMS

The development of marketing programs involves judgments concerning the sales, cost, and investment consequences of alternative courses of action. Since these judgments may be wrong, and since they often involve substantial amounts of money, it is often desirable to pretest marketing programs before they are used on a large scale. Pretesting techniques are discussed in the two chapters comprising Part IV.

Chapter 18 is concerned with the conventional form of pretesting— test marketing. This chapter examines alternative ways of conducting and evaluating test marketing of total marketing programs.

Since test marketing usually consumes substantial money and time, and often alerts competitors to a company's future marketing strategy, it is desirable to use less costly and more covert techniques whenever possible. Chapter 19 discusses the current status of simulation techniques designed to overcome these problems.

Chapter 18   The Testing of Marketing Programs

"Yes, Orville, but will it fly?" This question may or may not have been tossed at Mr. Wright as he explained his plans and program for manned flight; nonetheless, it is precisely the type of question faced by marketing executives after they have carefully planned an integrated program of marketing action.

One way of answering the question is described by Arthur S. Pearson, director of marketing planning for Bristol-Myers Products, in the following terms:

It is expensive, it is time-consuming, and it gives competition a window on your activities. At best it provides only gross measures, when you would like precision. Everybody talks about its limitations and yet everybody does it—i.e., all successful marketing organizations use it as a basic marketing tool. What is it? As if you didn't know—it is test marketing.[1]

Test marketing (or market testing, or pretesting of integrated marketing programs) is the subject for analysis in this chapter. There are enormous problems and limitations in test marketing, yet most large successful marketing organizations *do* employ it regularly.

This chapter describes the weaknesses in test marketing along with its strengths, analyzes ways test markets can be used to project total market positions, and discusses analytical frameworks with which to obtain solution for the problems of test marketing as it is currently practiced.

[1] National Industrial Conference Board, *Market Testing Consumer Products* (New York: National Industrial Conference Board, 1967), p. 5.

NATURE AND PURPOSE OF TEST MARKETING

At first glance it might seem a simple thing to try out a new marketing program, or an alteration in an existing strategy, on a small scale to see if the product will sell, or sell better. Many complexities arise, however. The pages that follow describe the current state of knowledge about the form of marketing experimentation called test marketing. The discussion applies both to industrial and consumer marketing programs.

Test Marketing Defined

Test marketing is a rigorous attempt to determine the nature of sales response to a set of marketing plans and programs. Ideally, it differs from full-scale application of the marketing program only in volume. In this sense, the emphasis is on the word "test" in test marketing. The German marketing analyst Ulrich Jetter explains the origin of the word *test*: ". . . the test was originally the small crucible in which a small ore sample was examined. One therefore obtains with the test, so to speak, under laboratory conditions, a verdict as to whether the metal sought for, and how much of it, is contained in the ore."[2]

Test marketing is sometimes called market testing (that is, testing the total marketing program in the market) or pretesting of the marketing program. Pretesting is also used as a descriptive phrase to refer to various types of marketing research *preliminary* to the preparation of the marketing program of action. In this chapter, however, *pretesting* will refer to the testing of the marketing program or major elements of the program *after planning* but preliminary to full-scale application.

Narrowing the definition of test marketing, a consultant in this field gives the following description:

Market testing is a research technique in which the product under study is placed on sale in one or more selected localities or areas, and its reception by consumer and trade is observed, recorded, and analyzed. Performance in these test markets is supposed to give some indication of the performance to be expected when the product goes into general distribution. "Performance" includes two aspects: (a) the likely sales and profitability of the product when marketing on a national scale, and (b) "feasibility" of the marketing operation. By "feasibility" I mean the soundness and integration of all the elements that enter into the marketing operation.

Traditional market testing is conducted in localities which are, in theory, representative samplings of the broader area in which it is planned to market the product—the United States as a whole, or a large region of it.[3]

---

[2] Ulrich Jetter, "Werbestrategie" ("Advertising Strategy"), in VBM, Vereinigung Marktforscher Deutschlands, e.V.: *Der Markt heute und morgen* (*The Market Today and Tomorrow*), Hamburg, 1958, p. 165.

[3] Jack A. Gold, in *Market Testing Consumer Products*, p. 11.

Purpose of Test Marketing

Testing of marketing programs results in two basic activities: (1) modification of the marketing program before large-scale application, (2) prediction of eventual market volume and profitability.

At a more basic level, the purpose of test marketing is *to reduce the risk in managerial decisions* about modifying the marketing program at a preintroductory stage and about ultimate volume and profitability. Test markets, it will be obvious before the end of this chapter, *do not replace managerial judgment* concerning the introduction or modification of marketing programs. Like all forms of marketing research, test marketing is *an aid* to managerial judgment—not a replacement.

Test marketing can be an important element in sophisticated efforts to program marketing actions and to evaluate the quality of the programming before large losses are incurred or irreversible errors made. Sittenfeld describes some of the forces that make test marketing necessary:

There is much talk today about "scientific management," by which is meant not only the team of highly qualified specialists who nowadays frequently form the highest level in important undertakings, but also their specialized activities and their co-ordination. In particular this conception embraces those strategical deliberations, systematic preparations, and organizational measures demanded by the modern mass market with its manifold competing offers, its high investments and the risk connected with them. In view of the size of this risk, it is a stark necessity for the company to use all possible means to reduce, and so far as may be, eliminate it.[4]

MODIFICATION OF MARKETING PROGRAM. It is essential to recognize that test marketing is a *pretesting of the total marketing program*. In the past, executives have sometimes viewed it only as a test of the product programs or advertising programs; this view is inadequate. Every element of the integrated program of marketing action should be tested for the purpose of deciding what modifications should be made before final introduction, or whether the program should be dropped completely.

Traditionally, test marketing has often been thought of in terms of a go/no-go decision process. It was a kind of final stage of deciding whether to introduce or kill a new product or a new modification of an old program. That purpose still exists, but increasingly the question is not "Will it sell?" but "With which alternative strategy will it sell best?"

Test markets are most valuable in revealing not what the firm has done *right* in the development of a marketing program but rather what the firm has done *wrong*. The president of Warner-Lambert Pharmaceutical Company describes this purpose of the test market:

[4] Hans Sittenfeld, *Test Marketing* (London: Business Publications Limited, 1967), p. 11.

Your testing operation should be your Cassandra, your prophet of doom. A new-product plan of operation usually looks like a football coach's game strategy. Every play goes for a touchdown. Unfortunately, when the other team gets in there—your competition, and the eminently dispassionate consumer—all your great plays can fall apart. So test everything. Test even your tests.[5]

PREDICTING MARKET OUTCOME. Test markets focused on customer acceptance of a new or altered marketing program may provide data of sufficient quality to support estimates of total market volume, costs, and profitability. Test markets are fairly well accepted as reliable indicators of the ranking of alternative strategies, but there is considerable doubt about their validity as a basis for predicting ultimate national market share (especially for new products);[6] this problem is discussed in a later section. Frequently simulation is a better technique for predicting outcomes, although the data from test markets are useful for simulation models (see Chapter 19).

A Systematic Approach to Test Marketing

Effective test marketing begins with an understanding of the corporate objectives and strategies. Thus, on a global basis of evaluation, the test market is analyzed from the standpoint of how a specific marketing program contributes to the corporate objectives, to marketing objectives, and to programming objectives (such as product objectives and so on). Executives must evaluate the results of test markets with some type of analytical framework, comprised of the firm's objectives at each level and activity of managerial decision making.

This systematic approach to test marketing is shown in Figure 18-1. The test market should pretest each of the functional programs that make up the integrated marketing program of action. The test market should provide adequate data, therefore, for evaluating product programs (including packaging, branding, product features, and so on), alternative prices, alternative advertising and sales promotion programs, sales programs to be used for this product, channel programs, the physical distribution program, and the marketing organization that will be responsible for attaining programmed results. Although each of these elements is evaluated in a test market, there may be no manipulation of the variable identifiably exclusive to the marketing program being tested. That is, if the marketing organization that will be used for a new product is the same as that used by existing programs, no specific manipulation of marketing organization is included in the test program. Typically, marketing organizations, physical distribution systems, and sometimes channel programs are treated as a "constant" in the test program.

[5] Robert B. Kyle, in *Market Testing Consumer Products,* p. 14.

[6] Jack A. Gold, "Testing Test Market Predictions," *Journal of Marketing Research,* Vol. 1 (August 1964), pp. 8–11. But also see replies to this article by Edwin M. Berdy and by Victor L. Cole (and reply by Jack Gold) in "Comments," *Journal of Marketing Research,* Vol. 2 (May 1965), pp. 196–200.

Figure 18-1 A systematic approach for testing marketing programs.

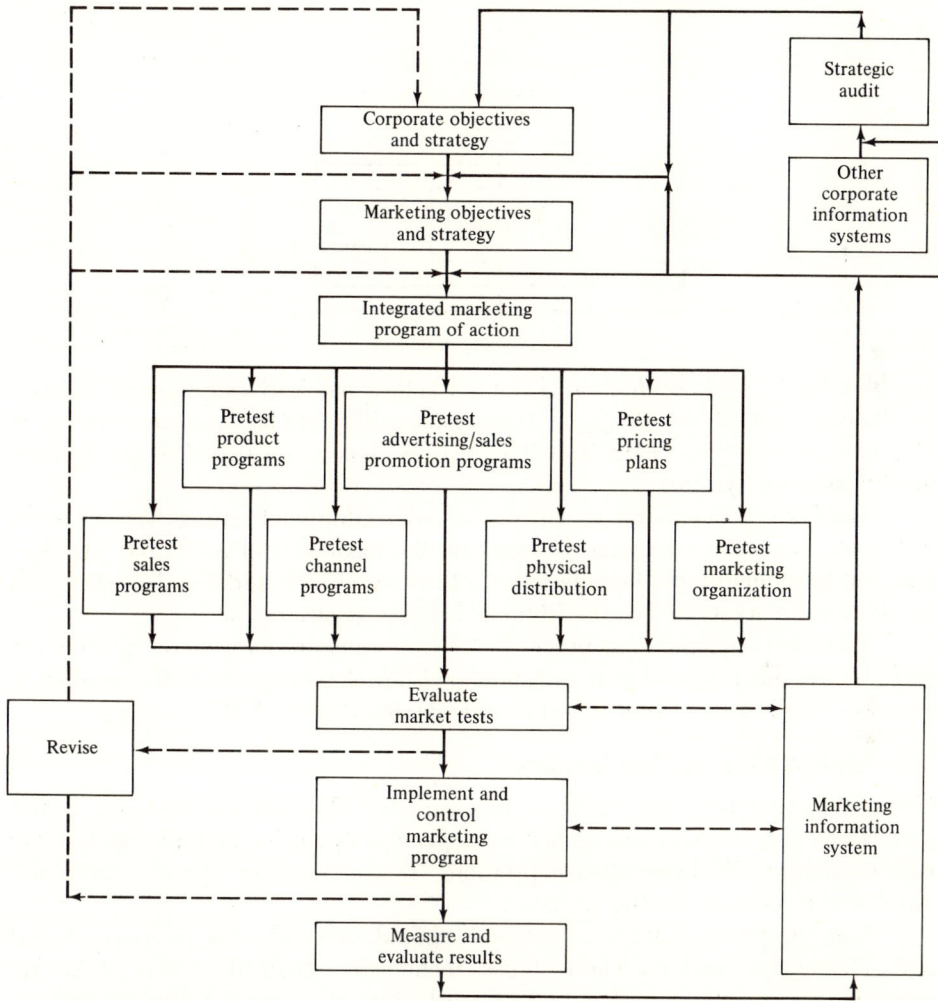

Strategic audit

Corporate objectives and strategy

Other corporate information systems

Marketing objectives and strategy

Integrated marketing program of action

Pretest product programs

Pretest advertising/sales promotion programs

Pretest pricing plans

Pretest sales programs

Pretest channel programs

Pretest physical distribution

Pretest marketing organization

Evaluate market tests

Revise

Implement and control marketing program

Marketing information system

Measure and evaluate results

Information with which to evaluate data from test markets is obtained from the Marketing Information System (MIS). With such data, the analyst can assess the usefulness of the current test-market experience and determine probabilities that data from the current test can be projected to ultimate introduction. Similarly, Figure 18-1 (by the bidirectional arrow to MIS) indicates that data from a specific test market are always stored in the MIS for evaluation of future test markets. Also, decisions to implement the program and the results from that implementation are stored in the MIS; it is through such a process of accumulating information relating test-market results to ultimate market results that a firm is able to assess the reliability, validity, and general usefulness of test markets.

The three major outcomes of test marketing are shown in Figure 18-2, which

Figure 18-2   Outcomes of market-test evaluation (amplification of Figure 18-1).

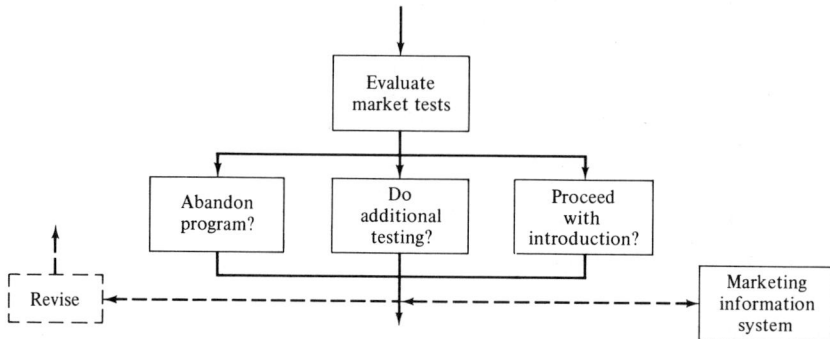

amplifies Figure 18-1. Evaluation of test marketing may lead, as Figure 18-2 shows, to abandonment of the program; that result will probably require revision of objectives or strategies of the firm. The test results are also stored in the Marketing Information Systems.

Another outcome is for executives to order additional testing. When results of the test market are marginal yet indicate the possibility of profitable introduction, not infrequently the best decision is to proceed with additional market tests in additional markets, or to test additional alternative strategies.

The third outcome is to proceed with introduction. Even here, information probably has been gained that indicates revision of some parts of the marketing program. In all cases, of course, test results are stored in the MIS.

Research Before Test Markets

Complete research programming is necessary for the most effective use of test marketing. Test markets should not be depended upon, for example, to test out minor variations in the marketing program. Test markets are too expensive and unreliable to be used for this purpose.

Various types or stages of research should be conducted to insure useful and efficient test markets. These stages, technically classified as nontest market research, are essential to effective test marketing; they are described briefly in Figure 18-3. (Also review Chapters 3, 4, and 10.)

TEST-MARKET OPERATIONS

The conducting of test-market operations and the evaluating of results call for sophisticated skills and careful design and implementation. Essential phases of these operations include (1) establishing test-market objectives, (2) selecting model markets, (3) determining the length of test markets, (4) determining information to be collected, and (5) projecting test-market results. Each of these phases is described below, followed by a discussion of some of the dangers in test-market operations.

Figure 18-3   A complete research program culminating in a market test.

The Conference Board panel identified several stages of research leading up to a full-scale market test. Not every stage was considered necessary in the case of every new product or marketing approach. Terminology used sometimes differed in minor ways, and some of the phases may overlap. But for discussion purposes, the panel members thought in terms of these broad research phases.

Research Activity	Purpose
Continuous working contact between marketing and R&D personnel	(a) To focus R&D on market needs and wants. (b) To keep marketing personnel informed of company's technical capabilities.
Continuous surveillance of market developments and consumer desires	To uncover needs not being fully met by existing products, thereby indicating an opportunity for the company to offer a new or improved product.
Concept test	(a) To see whether the idea for a specific new or improved product favorably impresses the potential consumer. (b) To get a preliminary idea of volume possibilities.
Prototype test	To make a concept test more concrete by using a preliminary sample or model of the product.
Product test	(a) To see whether the product embodying the concept proves satisfactory and desirable under conditions of normal use. (b) To get a preliminary indication of repeat purchase rate probabilities.
Simulation of purchase decision process	(a) To combine all elements, and test the "total concept." (b) To achieve as much realism as possible short of going on sale in a store. (c) To obtain a better indication of repeat-purchase rate.
Miniature market test (Distinction sometimes made between testing in just a few stores, and securing broader distribution in a small town.)	(a) To subject all elements in combination to a realistic test—i.e., to see whether and to what extent people will buy the product in a store. (b) To obtain still better indications of consumer satisfaction with product, and volume probabilities. (c) To permit final modifications in product and other elements before going into full market test.
Market test (Varieties include a "zoned market test" and a "multimarket test.")	"The final step before national introduction." (a) To obtain best indication of consumer satisfaction with product and volume probabilities. (b) To correct flaws in product or in any other element in marketing plan. (c) To decide whether to drop product, revise it, or place it in general distribution.

SOURCE: Conference Board, *Market Testing Consumer Products* (New York: National Industrial Conference Board, Inc., 1967), p. 36. Reprinted by permission.

Establishing Test-Market Objectives

Deciding *what to test* is an essential and often overlooked stage of test-market operations. The selection of all aspects of test-market operations depends upon a good conceptualization of the elements about which data are needed. As a general starting point, the executive in charge of implementing the marketing program should examine each element to determine which should be specifically included in the test market and which included only as "constants."

The best way to determine what information is needed is to pose a comprehensive list of questions about each of the functional programming areas to be pretested (displayed in Figure 18-1) and determine which questions can best be answered in test markets and which need other forms of marketing research. For example, an executive might look at the area described as channel programs (and perhaps physical distribution) and develop the following list:

1. Can the product be shipped through to retail stores without breakage?
2. Is the product properly classified by the trade and placed in the section(s) of the store where it was intended to be?
3. How many units does the average outlet take? ("Does its opening order come up to our expectations?")
4. Is the display material being put to use properly?
5. How is the product priced by retailers in relation to competition?
6. Do the product and package hold up satisfactorily under actual retail shelf conditions?
7. How does the trade react to the item and to its trade discount structure?[7]

This list of questions could be greatly expanded, but it serves to illustrate the process of identifying objectives for test-market operations. It also illustrates the fact that few questions or answers fit neatly into a single area of the marketing program. The answers to questions about channel decisions, it is obvious, are closely related to pricing, product, and sales-promotion decisions, among others. This is one of the justifications for test marketing as opposed to survey research or other methods that investigate one variable at a time. Test marketing develops the potential to investigate the effect of *interrelationships among marketing variables in the realities of a competitive marketplace.*

Selecting Model Markets

A critical issue in designing test-marketing operations is which city or cities are to be used as a model market. Two goals may be operative in this decision: either the city is chosen to be "representative" of the national market or it is chosen for some special characteristic of interest in the specific test operation. In the latter case, a city with heavy usage of the product might be chosen in order to

---

[7] Jack A. Gold in *Market Testing Consumer Products*, pp. 89–90.

generate larger amounts of data. Perhaps a particularly "difficult" market might be chosen if the product involves a high risk of failure. This is sometimes done on the grounds that if the product is successful in the most difficult segment of the market it is bound to be successful in the total market.

The process of selecting model cities ordinarily is a matter of judgment rather than statistical inference. Cities *could be* selected through random sampling procedures, but unless the model market is going to include 30 or more cities, random selection is more likely to produce disastrous results than judgmental selection. Typically, a test market will include two to three cities.

Where the purpose of test marketing is the evaluation of alternative marketing strategies, it is common to select test cities with similar characteristics, and ordinarily these cities will be sought as microcosms of the United States market. Where the purpose of test marketing is to project market share or volume for the United States and there is evidence of variability in the market, the two or three cities may be selected because they reflect *differences* among regions in customer response:

If by way of example there is evidence that three sections of the country react differently to a specified product, then it may be desirable to have test markets in each of the regions. Since the test results for the group of markets in each region will be compared in deriving a national estimate, the markets in each region should be as similar as possible in size, income, competitive activity, trade factors, and media facilities. The differential responses by region can be used for a synthetic estimate of expected national share.[8]

The major areas of checking for representativeness are identified in Figure 18-4 as demographic validity, behavioral validity, and competitive validity.[9] This figure is a description of the major operations in a test market related to selecting model markets. The number of cities to be included depends upon the objectives of the testing operation, but these guidelines can be used:

1. There should not be fewer than two markets for each variation to be tested. This does not include control markets—markets in which the variables to be tested are held constant or allowed for.
2. Where the purpose of the test is to estimate the sales potential of a product which is to be distributed nationally, markets in at least four geographic areas should be used.
3. As the significance of the variables to be tested decreases, the number of markets necessary to reflect the effect of these variables increases. Thus, it is likely that where variations are minor, it may not pay to test-market them. The determination of which of two secondary copy phrases

---

[8] Benjamin Lipstein, "The Design of Test Marketing Experiments," *Journal of Advertising Research*, Vol. 5 (December 1965), pp. 2–7 at p. 3.

[9] A fairly good treatment of selection of model markets is also found in Robert Ferber, Donald F. Blankertz, and Signey Hollander, Jr., *Marketing Research* (New York: The Ronald Press Company, 1964), pp. 521–523.

Figure 18-4   Operations in a test market.

Operation	Purpose
Selection of test market	Utilize a restricted geographical area, which is representative of the national market, in which to test-market new products.
Projection	Observe the marketing achievements in the test area and project them nationwide. For example, if monthly volume in 2 percent of the country is $500, then the total volume projected is $500/0.02 = $25,000.
Check of demographic validity	From careful review of all available data, assure that the test area is generally representative of the broad-scale market in terms of social class, age composition, and other demographic conditions.
Check of behavioral validity	Assure that area is representative in terms of consumption of similar or substitute products.
Check of competitive validity	Assure that competitive strengths in area are approximately similar to those in market as a whole. Also check that no "jamming," as a result of competitors' promotional campaigns for their products, invalidates test results.
Check of marketing mix	Test many factors, such as sizes, prices, promotional method, and size-price-promotion combinations.
Filtering	Use sophisticated statistical methods to filter out the effects of "jamming" and other factors affecting the validity of results.
Final evaluation	Answer these questions: (1) Will the product sell? (2) At what probable volume rate will the product sell?

SOURCE: Norbert Lloyd Enrick, *Market and Sales Forecasting: A Quantitative Approach* (San Francisco: Chandler Publishing Company, 1969), p. 139. Reprinted by permission.

is more effective in building volume is an example of the type of variable it probably would not pay to market-test.[10]

Some of the cities most frequently used to project national sales results are Columbus, Albany, Syracuse, Denver, Des Moines, Dayton, and Peoria.[11]

[10] Frank Ladik, Leonard Kent, and Perham C. Nahl, "Test Marketing of New Consumer Products," *Journal of Marketing*, Vol. 24 (April 1960), pp. 29–34. Also see this reference for a helpful discussion of criteria for selecting test markets.

[11] There is also a position that using "normal" cities is dangerous because of great natural variability between cities. Market Facts, Inc., provides Erie, Wichita, and Fresno for store audits because they can tightly control conditions in each city for clients. See Bud Sherak, "Control and Reduction of Error in Marketing Tests," in John S. Wright and Jac L. Goldstucker, eds., *New Ideas for Successful Marketing* (Chicago: American Marketing Association, 1966), pp. 433–439.

Determining Length of Test Market

Test markets typically run from two months to two years, depending on the objectives and problems of the marketing program. The difficulty is in finding a balance between sufficient length to *collect repurchase data* and sufficient brevity to avoid giving *unreasonable opportunity to competitors* to counteract the program innovation. It has happened more than once that a firm kept a new product in test market long enough for a competitor to copy it and introduce it before the original firm. In other situations, a competitor may not wish to copy the originator but it can collect data on the original firm's test market (probably the same data as the test market firm) and plan changes in its strategy to mitigate the effects of the innovation.

Executives experienced with test markets generally agree that a test should be long enough to accomplish three main objectives:

1. Reveal the product's sales level after initial abnormal influences have run their course (such as curiosity buying).
2. Establish the fact, in the case of a nondurable product, that a satisfactory portion of this sales volume is accounted for by repeat purchases.
3. Bring to light any product or merchandising deficiencies that should be corrected before national introduction.[12]

Information Obtained in Test Markets

Data obtained in test markets are of various types. The variables that determine what data are collected include the quantity and quality of research preceding test marketing, the risk and cost of introducing the program innovation, analytical capacity (mathematical models, simulation, and so on), probabilities of competitive reaction, and data availabilities.

Data typically collected from test marketing include retail sales, patterns of customer usage, reseller behavior and attitudes, market-structure variables, and internal marketing variables operative during the test. These variables and the most common techniques of collecting data are described in Figure 18-5. In the past, researchers have frequently focused attention upon only a few variables, overlooking the richness of data that test markets could yield. This problem has been caused by inability to handle large amounts of data and by narrowness of vision. The first problem is being solved by mathematical models and large-scale computer capacity. The second will be solved by executives who demand more information for the dollars they spend on test markets.

Data-gathering techniques used in test marketing (listed in Figure 18-5) are

[12] *Market Testing Consumer Products,* p. 100.

Figure 18-5   Information obtained in test markets.

Data Subject	Data-Gathering Technique
Retail sales including competitive brands	Store audits
Comparative and historical sales	Internal records
Customer usage patterns including competitive products and brands	Customer panel, interviews
Repurchase patterns	Panel, coupons
Brand awareness	Interviews (probably telephone)
Media influence	Interviews, possibly panel
Reseller behavior (including in-store displays, shelf position, etc.)	Observation, sales-force reports
Competitive advertising	Observation of insertions, content analysis
Pricing	Store audits, sales-force reports
Reseller attitudes and opinions	Sales-force reports, possibly interviews
Physical distribution problems and successes	Internal records
Marketing organization requirements	Internal records, sales-force reports

not fundamentally dissimilar from those discussed in Chapter 3 or in the section on measuring advertising effectiveness in Chapter 15. It is useful, though, to review here in somewhat more detail the subject of store audits as a source of test-market data.

STORE AUDITS. Store audits are systematic attempts to record and report sales that occur at the retail level on a periodic basis.

The basic idea of a store "audit" is very simple. An employee of the research firm visits a store at fixed intervals, usually every two months. With the consent of the retailer, he counts the store's inventory of each item being audited, including stocks on display and in stockroom areas. He also examines copies of the store's purchase invoices or shipment records and determines how many units of each item were received by the store during the period since his last visit—net of any merchandise returns, interstore transfers, etc. From these data, together with the inventory figures obtained on the previous visit, it is possible to compute how many units of each item the store has sold. For a given item, Beginning Inventory *plus* Receipts, *minus* Ending Inventory, adjusted for Returns, etc., *equals* Retail Sales during a given period. The time required to collect such information for 50 items is not much greater than for five or six, so there are obvious advantages in using a syndicated service. (Some companies do operate their own store auditing programs from time to time, either as supplements to a syndicated service or for specific temporary purposes such as test marketing.)[13]

The two largest store-audit services are A. C. Nielsen Company and Audits and Surveys, but there are a number of small services including Ehrhart-Babic Associates, Inc., which specializes in store auditing and related studies in test markets only. Nielsen store audits are known primarily for the Nielsen Retail Index, which gives national estimates of retail sales for grocery, drug, pharmaceutical, photographic, appliance, perfume, liquor, and confectionery products in the United States. It also operates in Canada, the United Kingdom, Ireland, Japan, and major Western European countries. Of primary interest here, though, is the Nielsen Test Marketing Service, which customizes the concept of the national audit to individual metropolitan areas or regions.[14]

Store audits have some limitations. Although retail firms are paid from $10 to $50 per store per audit for cooperation, some refuse to cooperate. In the Nielsen Retail Index, for example, the Great Atlantic & Pacific Tea Company (A&P) is not included. With some syndicated services, questions can be raised about the quality of the personnel used to record sales and therefore about the reliability of the data. Finally, even when data are recorded accurately, retail sales in the test-market area may distort analysis of test-market results because of out-of-stock situations, transshipping, and other aberrations in sales data.

In addition to retail audits, many new services are arising that provide data on inventory shipments from wholesalers and warehouses or large retailers. The relative ease of retrieving data with computerization stimulates the growth of these data services. Such data may be less useful in test marketing than in other applications, though where the test market extends over a large area and a considerable length of time, data on warehouse shipments are valuable.

Projecting Test-Market Results

After a test-marketing project is underway and data begin to be collected, the executive must begin to use the data to make decisions. Presumably he trusts the reliability and validity of the data or he would not have originally approved the design of the test market. In recent years, a number of mathematical tools have been developed to assist executive strategists in their decisions concerning test-market operations.

BRAND-SHARE PREDICTION MODELS. A powerful tool for predicting ultimate brand-share are mathematical models such as those using consumer-panel data. A typical model[15] relates the following variables to brand-share: cumulative growth in the number of new buyers of the brand or product being studied, how often

---

[13] Robert D. Buzzell, Donald F. Cox, and Rex V. Brown, *Marketing Research and Information Systems* (New York: McGraw-Hill, Inc., 1969), p. 222.

[14] An excellent summary of standardized data services for test marketing and other purposes is found in *ibid.*, pp. 218–248.

[15] This model and the illustrative case that follows are adopted from J. H. Parfitt and B. J. K. Collins, "Use of Consumer Panels for Brand-Share Prediction," *Journal of Marketing Research*, Vol. 5 (May 1968), pp. 131–145.

these new buyers buy the brand or product again after their first recorded purchase (repeat purchases), and the rate of total product category purchasing of
these particular buyers compared with the average of all buyers in the product
category (heavy or light usage).

The application of brand-share prediction may be seen in the introduction
of Signal toothpaste in the United Kingdom. The basic model is expressed in the
following manner:

$$\left(\begin{array}{c} \text{predicted ultimate} \\ \text{brand-share} \end{array} \right) = \left(\begin{array}{c} \text{estimated} \\ \text{penetration} \end{array} \right) \times \left(\begin{array}{c} \text{repeat-purchasing} \\ \text{rate} \end{array} \right) \times \left(\begin{array}{c} \text{buying-rate} \\ \text{index} \end{array} \right)$$

Estimated penetration is obtained from consumer-panel data in the test market.
As each new buyer is picked from panel records, she is recorded on a cumulative
penetration curve such as the one displayed in Figure 18-6. Total *estimated*
ultimate penetration can be calculated as soon as the shape of the curve is
determined and a declining rate of increase is observed. For Signal toothpaste, the
ultimate penetration was reached after 36 weeks, although the estimate was
made after 16 weeks.

Much of the success of a brand depends upon the customer's willingness,
once having tried a product, to continue purchasing it. In this model, this is
defined as the repeat-purchasing rate. That statistic also must be taken from
panel data but may be estimated after it levels off. In the Signal case, the ultimate

Figure 18-6   Cumulative penetration of Signal.

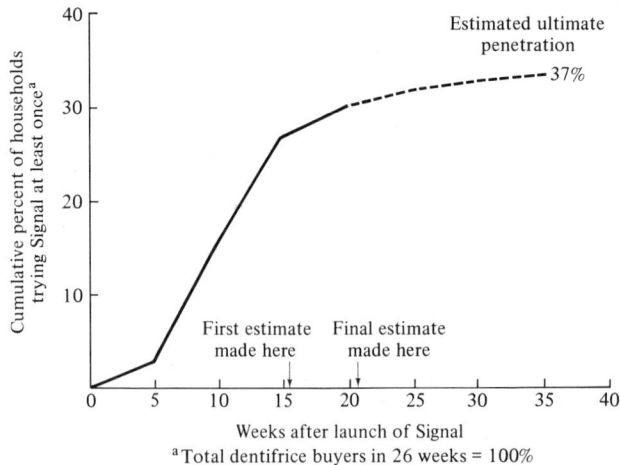

Weeks after launch of Signal

ª Total dentifrice buyers in 26 weeks = 100%

SOURCE: Reprinted from J. H. Parfitt and B. J. K. Collins, "Use
of Consumer Panels for Brand-Share Prediction," *Journal of
Marketing Research*, Vol. 5 (May 1968), pp. 131–145 at 134,
published by the American Marketing Association. Data supplied by Attwood Consumer Panel, Great Britain.

Figure 18-7   Repeat-purchasing rate of Signal buyers.

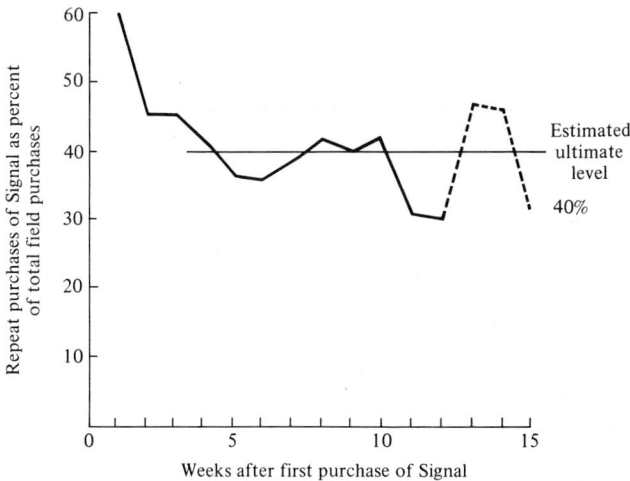

SOURCE: Reprinted from J. H. Parfitt and B. J. K. Collins, "Use of Consumer Panels for Brand-Share Prediction," *Journal of Marketing Research,* Vol. 5 (May 1968), pp. 131–145 at 134, published by the American Marketing Association. Data supplied by Attwood Consumer Panel, Great Britain.

level of repeat purchasing was 40 percent, which was predicted after 12 weeks (see Figure 18-7). With those data, it is possible to estimate ultimate market share of Signal as 40 percent × 37 percent = 14.8 percent.

The third variable in the brand-share model is usage, referred to as a buying-rate index. If the buyers of Signal purchase an average volume, the buying-level index = 1.00 (or 100 percent of average volume of toothpaste bought in a household). Heavy users might have a buying level index of 1.2 or more and light users might have an index of, say, .8 percent The buying-level index is a refinement that was added to the model after Signal toothpaste went on the market; thus actual data are not available here. Assuming, however, an average index of 1.00, the prediction of Signal brand-share would be:

$$\text{Signal brand-share} = 37\% \times 40\% \times 1.00$$
$$= 14.8\%$$

After forty weeks in the market, Signal was actually in the 14 to 15 percent range, and it stayed in that range for over two years, indicating the efficacy of the brand-share model.

Many limitations can be applied to the simple illustration described here. Test-market data must be representative of total market data. Also, market-structure variables such as retail distribution and advertising influences must remain much the same as they were in the prediction period. Also, it should be recognized that the model works best where the average frequency of purchase in the product category is high and where initial penetration responds well to advertising and promotion. Both of these conditions held in the Signal case.

Despite the simplicity of the example given here, many more refinements are possible. It is sometimes possible to make earlier predictions of the ultimate level of penetration, to handle entry into newer product categories, and to handle certain aberrations in the market.[16]

Many approaches are now available to marketing executives to solve the problem of projecting national or ultimate market performance of the marketing program of action from initial data (which may be test-market data or may be initial total market data). Many of these models are based upon early work by Fourt and Woodlock[17] and other simple probability models.[18] Glen Urban developed the SPRINTER model for evaluating new products—a macro behavioral process model employing a network process that is useful, among other things, in evaluating sequential market-testing information.[19] The advertising agency of Batten, Barton, Durstine, & Obsorne has achieved significant advances in understanding how test-market information can be projected for evaluation of total market opportunity, originally with a model called DEMON[20] and more recently with NEWS (New-product Early Warning System).[21] The alert executive finds many useful approaches emerging in this area of analysis, including the use of multiple discriminant functions for the interpretation of test-market data,[22] attempts to forecast demand without test-market data,[23] and various systems for monitoring the progress of new-product introduction[24] and using the Marketing Information System for managerial decision making and control.

[16] See *ibid.* Also see Philip C. Gruber, "Developing Forecasting Models for New Product Introductions," in Robert L. King, ed., *Marketing and the New Science of Planning* (Chicago: American Marketing Association, 1968), pp. 112–118.

[17] Louis A. Fourt and Joseph W. Woodlock, "Early Prediction of Market Success For New Grocery Products," *Journal of Marketing*, Vol. 25 (October 1960), pp. 31–38.

[18] William D. Barclay, "A Probability Model for Early Prediction of New Product Market Success," *Journal of Marketing*, Vol. 28 (January 1963), pp. 63–68.

[19] For an introduction to this type of model, see Glen Urban, "Market Response Models for the Analysis of New Products," in King, *Marketing and the New Science of Planning*, pp. 105–110. Also see, however, David B. Montgomery and Glen L. Urban, *Management Science in Marketing* (Englewood Cliffs, N.J.: Prentice-Hall, Inc., 1969), esp. pp. 333–338.

[20] Abraham Charnes, W. W. Cooper, J. K. DeVoe, and D. B. Learner, "DEMON: Decision Mapping Via Optimum GO-NO Networks—A Model for Marketing New Products," *Management Science*, July 1966, pp. 865–887.

[21] Larry Light and Lewis Pringle, "New Product Forecasting Using Recursive Regression," in David T. Kollat, Roger D. Blackwell, and James F. Engel, eds., *Research in Consumer Behavior* (New York: Holt, Rinehart and Winston, Inc., 1970), pp. 702–709.

[22] William R. King, "Early Prediction of New Product Success," *Journal of Advertising Research*, Vol. 6 (June 1966), pp. 8–13.

[23] Walter B. Wentz and Gerald I. Eyrich, "New Product Forecasting Without Historical, Survey, or Experimental Data," in King, *Marketing and the New Science of Planning*, pp. 215–222.

[24] C. Merle Crawford, "The Trajectory Theory of Goal Setting for New Products," *Journal of Marketing Research*, Vol. 3 (May 1966), pp. 117–125.

Dangers of Test Marketing

Test markets often produce misleading results. If the basic data are misleading even sophisticated analytical models will lead to unprofitable executive decisions. In fact, the application of sophisticated analytical models usually depends upon high-quality data more than do simple approaches.

Often products are successful in test markets but fail miserably in national markets. In other cases (although fewer data support this position) products are killed in test markets when in fact they would have been successful in national markets. The major reasons for inadequate or misleading testing of the marketing program of action are summarized in Figure 18-8.

Test Marketing and Simulation

There is growing dissatisfaction with test marketing. This provides an impetus toward increasing use of simulation techniques. Test marketing is very expensive, requires long periods of time to yield reliable data, and exposes a firm's marketing plan to competitive scrutiny. All of these problems create expanded interest in a substitute for test marketing that can be completed internally and allows a richer spectrum of alternative strategies for analytical review.

The next chapter describes modern approaches to simulation. It should be viewed therefore as a natural progression of the present discussion of test marketing. Simulation techniques encompass many problems other than those traditionally treated with test-marketing approaches. A major value of simulation, however, is the ability to do with mathematical models what test marketing attempts in field tests. Neither approach should be viewed in isolation, however. Increasingly, test marketing and simulation are viewed as complementary, with test marketing emerging as a source of data for manipulation and analysis by simulation techniques (and other programming approaches).

SUMMARY AND CONCLUSIONS

Test marketing is a rigorous attempt to determine the nature of sales response that will be generated from a set of marketing plans and programs. The purpose of test marketing is to reduce risk in managerial decision making about the introduction of a new marketing program or a major alteration in an existing program. Specifically, the results of test marketing are used to modify a marketing program that has been developed before large-scale application (with attendant large-scale risks) and to predict the eventual market volume and profitability it may yield.

Test marketing is used to evaluate the programs that have been developed for all major activities in marketing including product programs, pricing programs, advertising and sales promotion programs, sales programs, channel programs, physical distribution programs, and programs for the marketing organiza-

Figure 18-8   Major dangers in test-market operations.

1. Failure to decide what is to be tested—each test should aim to find an answer to one major question, for example the most effective weight of advertising, a new creative approach, a new price structure or simply product acceptance. The more elements which a manufacturer tries to test at the same time in a single test area, the more difficult it becomes to identify the real causes of success or failure.

2. Failure to base the test market plan on an overall national marketing plan which is both realistic and affordable—the sales target in the test area should be proportionate to the expected national target, and the marketing "mix" (or alternative "mixes" if more than one test area is being used) should duplicate as closely as possible that which is proposed for the national launch.

3. Failure to make comparative tests—no single test permits the comparative evaluation and choice of the best plan from among a number of possible alternatives.

4. Failure to establish benchmarks in the test area—before any test begins it is necessary to establish individual and total sales and/or market penetration of competitive brands (and, where necessary, customer attitudes and preferences) so that subsequent changes can then be compared and evaluated against this base.

5. Failure to select representative test areas—the areas selected must be representative as possible of the country as a whole in terms of geographic location, trade and customer characteristics, media facilities of the type to be used later, in order that the test will serve as a "projection" model for future national operations.

6. Failure to adhere to the test market plan—this applies particularly to changes in advertising weight or content, the media used and pricing; "changing horses" in mid-market can lead to confusion when it comes to analyzing the test results (the need to test the effect of changes in the plan in response to strong competitive counter-measures can be allowed for by choosing another test town within the larger test area for this specific purpose at the outset, in order that results of both the original plan and the changed plan can be compared).

7. Failure to consider and get objective and reliable data on all factors influencing sales results in the test area—such as the calibre of salesmen used, seasonal influences, weather conditions, economic conditions, levels of shop distribution, stock levels and stock cover, out-of-stock ratios, competitors' activities, etc.

8. Failure to stay in the test market long enough to get a clearcut stop-or-go decision —slower-moving products require longer test periods than fast-selling products and the temptation to jump the gun and take a final decision should be resisted by the manufacturer until he can be reasonably sure that the sales pattern has stabilized and the results have been properly analyzed.

9. Reading into test market results more than is supportable by the objective facts— an apparent initial success in test market can all too rapidly turn into a comparative failure as the test market "matures" due to an over-optimistic reading of the situation based on considerations other than those directly related to the test market findings or due to the failure to recognize danger signals from the test.

SOURCE: Leslie Rodger, *Marketing in a Competitive Economy* [London: Hutchinson & Co. (Publishers) Ltd., 1965], pp. 125–127. Reprinted by permission.

tion. Test markets provide data for each of these programs, although some may be regarded as a "constant" in specific tests.

Successful test-market operations require careful planning. This includes establishing test-market objectives to be used in evaluation of results, selecting model markets that meet needs of the test, determining the duration of tests, determining the information to be collected, and projecting test-market results. In recent years there has been a significant increase in the use of mathematical brand-share models in the interpretation of test-market results. There is also a growing belief that some test marketing can and should be replaced with simulation techniques.

QUESTIONS FOR REVIEW AND DISCUSSION

1. What is the purpose of test marketing?
2. Discuss how test marketing is related to other stages in the development of marketing programs.
3. "If test marketing is used, most other forms of marketing research can be eliminated, because the test marketing can be used to ascertain any problems that exist in the marketing program." Evaluate this statement.
4. What factors should be considered in the selection of a model market to be used in test-marketing operations?
5. What are the major considerations to be considered in determining the length of test markets?
6. Prepare a research paper on mathematical models that are useful for analyzing and interpreting data from test markets, summarizing recent developments.
7. This chapter describes basic principles of test marketing that apply to both industrial and consumer marketing programs. Many test-marketing programs have been for consumer products. As a special assignment, prepare a research paper that reviews current books and articles, describing test marketing of industrial products. Analyze major differences that you observe between industrial and consumer test marketing.

Chapter 19   Simulation

What impact will the proposed sales training program have on salesman productivity? Will an increase in advertising expenditures significantly increase sales? If prices are reduced, how will that affect corporate profitability?

The marketing manager may rely upon intuition and experience as he seeks to foresee the impact his decisions might produce. Or, he may rely on test marketing. This chapter discusses a third alternative—simulation. The first section develops a systematic approach to the application of simulation methods; the second describes the ways simulation has been used to analyze marketing problems.

NATURE OF SIMULATION

The Anatomy of Simulation

To simulate is to duplicate the essence of a system or activity without actually attaining reality itself.[1] More precisely:

. . . simulation refers to the operation of a numerical model that represents the structure of a dynamic process. Given the values of initial conditions, parameters, and exogenous variables, a simulation is run to represent the behavior of the process over time. This simulation run may be considered to be an experiment on the model. A set of variables are used in the model together with any exogenous inputs to generate the

---

[1] George W. Morgenthaler, "The Theory and Application of Simulation in Operations Research," in Russell L. Ackoff, ed., *Progress in Operations Research*, Vol. I (New York: John Wiley & Sons, Inc., 1961), pp. 366–372.

behavior of the system during a time interval. The results are values of the variables that describe the state of the system at the end of the time interval. This process is repeated until the desired length of time has been represented.[2]

. . . If a distinction is to be drawn between simulation and the use of other mathematical or symbolic analytic techniques, it is the emphasis on description of the behavior of the system or phenomena over time and the ability to observe this behavior that most clearly distinguishes simulation as a separate technique.[3]

Simulators (models upon which simulation experiments can be performed) can be divided into two basic categories: deterministic or stochastic (probabilistic).[4] A *deterministic model* is an analytical representation of a concept, system, or operation in which there are unique outcomes for a given set of inputs.

A *nondeterministic* or *stochastic model* is one in which the functional relationships depend on chance parameters. The outcomes for a given set of inputs can be predicted only in a probabilistic context.[5]

It is possible to have a deterministic simulator of a probabilistic real system and vice versa. Similarly, it is possible to develop a deterministic model of a deterministic system or a probabilistic model of a probabilistic system.[6]

The methodology usually used to incorporate probability distributions in a simulation study is the *Monte Carlo technique.* This is a method of selecting numbers randomly from one or more probability distributions for use in a particular trial or run in a simulation study.[7]

Another simulation term is *heuristic programming,* which seeks "to understand the process of solving problems, especially the mental operations typically useful in this process."[8] In essence, this term is used to describe the efforts involved in developing and computerizing the "rules of thumb" an individual relies upon to solve complex, ill-structured problems.[9]

[2] Robert C. Meier, William T. Newell, and Harold L. Pazer, *Simulation in Business and Economics* (Englewood Cliffs, N.J.: Prentice-Hall, Inc., 1969), p. 1.

[3] *Ibid.*, pp. 2–3.

[4] Dimitris N. Chorafas, *Systems and Simulation* (New York: Academic Press, Inc., 1965), p. 22.

[5] Francis F. Martin, *Computer Modeling and Simulation* (New York: John Wiley & Sons, Inc., 1968), p. 5.

[6] Chorafas, *Systems and Simulation,* p. 23.

[7] Meier, Newell, and Pazer, *Simulation in Business and Economics,* p. 3. For a more detailed discussion of the Monte Carlo technique see Martin, *Computer Modeling and Simulation,* pp. 31–35. This same source also contains an excellent glossary of terms relating to computer modeling and simulation in Appendix A, pp. 251–258.

[8] G. Polya, *How to Solve It* (Garden City, N.Y.: Doubleday & Company, Inc., 1957), pp. 129–130.

[9] See Herbert A. Simon and Allen Newell, "Simulation of Human Thinking," in Martin Greenberger, ed. *Management and the Computer of the Future* (New York: John Wiley & Sons, Inc., 1962), p. 113.; and Alfred A. Kuehn, "Hueristic Programming: A Useful Technique for Marketing," in Charles H. Hindersman, ed., *Precision and Executive Action* (Chicago: American Marketing Association, 1962), pp. 162–170.

Benefits, Limitations, and Uses of Simulation

The major reason for the growing popularity of simulation is that it does not require all the simplifying assumptions required by more traditional mathematical techniques, such as linear programming, Markov analysis, and regression analysis.[10] A second reason is that recent improvements in computer hardware and software have made it possible to simulate large and complex business systems.

For these and other reasons, simulation is often a realistic way of approaching marketing problems. To date simulation models have been used:

1. *For purposes of experimentation or evaluation*—that is, in trying to predict the consequences of changes in policy, conditions, or methods without having to spend the money or take the risk of actually making the change in real life.
2. *As a means of learning about new systems in order to redesign or refine them.*[11]

While simulation is being relied upon increasingly to examine marketing problems, the technique is not without its limitations. The primary, incompletely resolved problems of both a practical and theoretical nature involve the validation of models and the interpretation of experimental results. Thus:

. . . a simulation model is a numerical representation of a system and is not governed by any physical laws that make it similar in operation to the system being modeled. A valid simulation model should behave in a manner similar to the underlying phenomena. This is a necessary validation criterion, but alone may not be sufficient to permit us to rely on its predictive abilities.

In contrast to analytic methods that yield solutions to problems, simulation experiments yield results that must be treated as experimental data. Procedures for inferring relationships from data obtained from simulation runs are much the same as those employed in any experimental situation, although the inclusion of time as a principal feature of simulation models raises some particular problems with regard to length of run, starting conditions, and so forth.[12]

A Systematic Approach to Marketing Simulation

Figure 19-1 illustrates the role of simulation in evaluating marketing programs. As often mentioned in preceding chapters, it is desirable to pretest the entire marketing program or program components prior to implementation. Simulation

---

[10] Harold Weitz, "The Promise of Simulation in Marketing," *The Journal of Marketing*, Vol. 31 (July 1967), pp. 28–33.

[11] Chorafas, *Systems and Simulation*, p. 17.

[12] Meier, Newell, and Pazer, *Simulation in Business and Economics* pp. 22–23.

rather than intuitive judgment or test marketing is a realistic pretesting device, provided that the following conditions exist:

1. Are we reasonably certain that we can obtain an exact solution or a satisfactory approximation to the solution of our problem through simulation?
2. Is simulation the lowest-cost procedure for solving the problem?
3. Is the particular simulation technique easy to interpret by those likely to use the results of the study?

If simulation is appropriate, then a model is developed following the process summarized in Figure 19-1. Certain steps in this process require clarification before we consider the procedure in greater detail.

PROBLEM FORMULATION. The most common error in simulation studies is an incomplete and/or inadequate specification of the problem and the purpose of the study. Simulation cannot be accomplished unless the objectives of the study have been clearly, carefully, and completely specified.

MODEL BUILDING. The modeling of marketing systems requires the model builder to both conceptualize and document the uncertain, probabilistic relationships that exist among key variables. The model must reduce a complex system to manageable proportions, while, at the same time, replicating the interactions found in the real system. The model must link the firm to its resource base and its markets in a meaningful fashion.

Such a complicated procedure poses problems in determining to what extent the simulation model should be abstracted from reality. Chorafas has summarized a set of guidelines for determining the proper degree of abstraction: "Basically, a mathematical model should be (i) simple enough for manipulation and understanding by those who would use it, (ii) representative enough, in the total range of the implications it may have, and (iii) complex enough to accurately represent the system under study."[13]

In Figure 19-1 the steps in the simulation process from *formulation of the problem* through *analysis of simulation* data are all concerned with various aspects of model building. Developing a marketing model requires first that the relevant portion of the marketing system be examined in terms of its *components, variables, parameters,* and *relationships*.

. . . *Components* are expressed, usually quantitatively, in terms of their significant attributes. *Variables* are expressed within functional relationships. *Parameters* are expressed as constants that can be changed only at the command of the experimenter. *Relationships* are expressed as mathematical and logical statements. Collectively, these expressions comprise . . . mathematical model(s) of the system being investigated.[14]

[13] *Ibid.*, p. 31.
[14] J. H. Mize and J. G. Cox, *Essentials of Simulation* (Englewood Cliffs, N.J.: Prentice-Hall, Inc., 1968), pp. 146–147.

Figure 19-1 A systematic approach to marketing simulation.

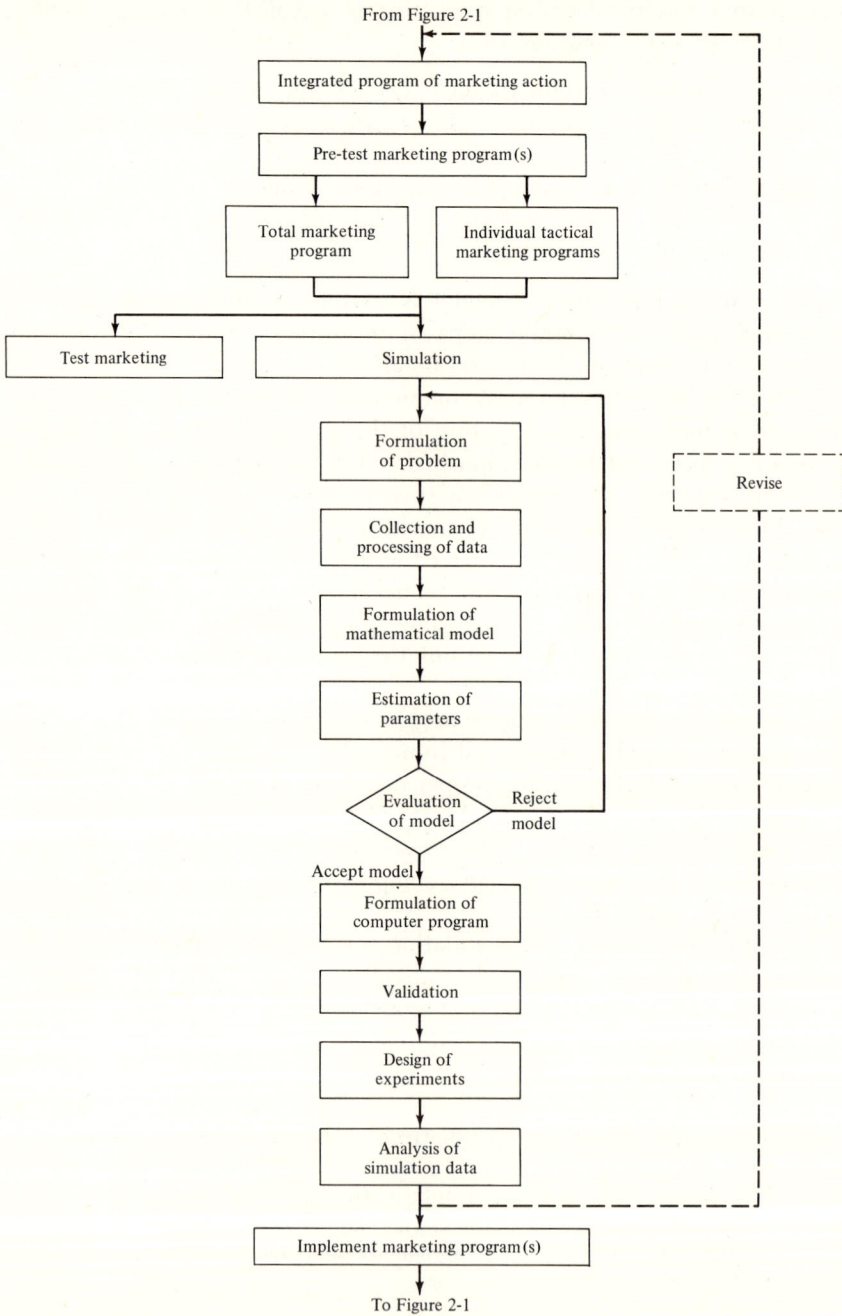

SOURCE: Adapted from T. H. Naylor, J. L. Balintfy, D. S. Burdick, and Kong Chu, *Computer Simulation Techniques* (New York: John Wiley & Sons, Inc., 1966), p. 24.

There are many ways to classify models, but perhaps one of the most relevant for simulation purposes is based upon the objectives to be served in utilizing the model. This approach produces three main classes of models—*descriptive, predictive,* and *prescriptive.*

A *descriptive* model attempts to "paint a picture" of the actual system under study. These models are intended to illustrate or merely describe a real-world process with relatively little abstraction. Thus:

Descriptive models are relatively easy to construct but difficult to manipulate. For this reason, the descriptive model is limited in application to the paraticular situation which it portrays and does not have general applicability to other situations. For the same reason, descriptive models usually do not lend themselves to portraying dynamic situations or causal relationships between variables, although they may sometimes do so. Descriptive models, however, are valuable for obtaining a "feel" for a situation and for providing a stepping stone for the development of other models with more abstract representation.[15]

The objective of the *predictive* model is to aid in predicting the behavior of a system under the influence of several interacting variables. These models predict the behavioral change in a system resulting from a change in one of the variables. For example, a predictive inventory model might predict the change in finished-goods inventory resulting from a delay in raw-material shipments from a supplier. Although useful, these models are limited in that they do not indicate what procedure should be followed to correct an undesirable system response.[16]

The *prescriptive* model is the ultimate in model design and sophistication. If the marketing manager can develop a model that closely represents certain aspects of his operations, he may be able to experiment with the model to generate predictions of probable outcomes under specified competitive market conditions and to evaluate implications of alternative marketing strategies.

Simulation: An Example

In this section a simplified inventory model is utilized to illustrate how the simulation technique might be used to assist the marketing manager in pretesting marketing decisions. In Chapter 16 it was pointed out that if demand and lead time were both known with certainty, then an EOQ model could be relied upon for optimally controlling inventories. However, demand and lead time are more commonly represented by probability distributions of what each is *likely* to be, rather than by a definitive statement of exactly what each *will* be.[17]

[15] M. D. Richards and Paul S. Greenlaw, *Management Decision Making* (Homewood, Ill.: Richard D. Irwin, Inc., 1966), p. 65.

[16] Arnold E. Amstutz, *Computer Simulation of Competitive Market Response* (Cambridge, Mass.: The M.I.T. Press, 1967), p. 93.

[17] This example is based largely on material found in Richards and Greenlaw, *Management Decision Making*, pp. 512–518; and Claude McMillan and Richard F. Gonzalez, *Systems Analysis: A Computer Approach to Decision Models* (Homewood, Ill.: Richard D. Irwin, Inc., 1965), pp. 91–92.

Assume the marketing manager would like to develop an inventory ordering rule for a product for which consumer demand and supplier lead time are variable. He might establish probability distributions for demand and lead-time variability based upon historical records and his own subjective estimate of what he expects the future variability to be, such as those given in Table 19-1. By simulating numerous days of experience based on the probabilities contained in Table 19-1, the manager can determine the impact of various decision rules upon inventory levels, number of orders placed, and lost sales. Then, by assigning costs to each of these variables, he will have a basis for choosing among the proposed decision rules.

Table 19-1   Demand and Lead-Time Probabilities

Daily Demand (Units)	Probability of Occurrence[a]	Lead Time (Days)	Probability of Occurrence
30	.10	1	.20
35	.20	2	.55
40	.40	3	.25
45	.15		1.00
50	.15		
	1.00		

[a] These probabilities are assumed to be the same regardless of day of week for purpose of simplification.

To "simulate" lead times and demand it will be necessary to develop a model that will generate values for these two variables that mirror the probabilities assumed to exist in the real system. That is, as the model is iterated, lead times from one to three days and demand from 30 to 50 units/day should be utilized *in proportion to* the frequency with which each of these conditions is expected to occur in the real system. This can be accomplished by taking numbers from 1 to 100 and assigning the occurrence of an event to a proportion of these numbers equal to the probability of the event's occurrence. The 100 numbers are assigned to lead times and daily demand as shown in Table 19-2. Then, a number

Table 19-2   Assignment of Lead Times and Daily Demand Levels

Daily Demand (Units)	Probability of Occurrence	Occurrence Assigned to Numbers	Lead Time (Days)	Probability of Occurrence	Occurrence Assigned to Numbers
30	.10	1–10	1	.20	1–20
35	.20	11–30	2	.55	21–75
40	.40	31–70	3	.25	76–100
45	.15	71–85			
50	.15	86–100			

Table 19-3 Monte Carlo Generation of Demand Levels and Lead Times

	Demand Levels			Lead Times	
Day	Random Number Chosen	Represents Demand Level of	Order	Random Number Chosen	Represents Lead Time of
1	17	35	1	89	3
2	56	40	2	11	1
3	31	40	3	17	1
4	23	35	4	68	2
5	61	40	5	57	2
6	73	45	6	07	1
7	20	35	7	69	2
8	61	40	8	04	1
9	56	40	9	72	2
10	49	40	10	33	2
11	65	40			
12	45	40			
13	29	35			
14	58	40			
15	71	45			

from 1 to 100 is generated randomly for each demand and lead-time iteration, and the event assigned to the number generated is considered as having occurred in the simulation. This assignment process is illustrated in Table 19-3.

Assume that the manager is interested in testing only two ordering rules over a 15-day simulated period of time.[18] The two rules the manager wants to evaluate are:

1. Whenever the inventories at the beginning of a day have fallen to a level of 80 or below (reorder point), place an order for 80 units (reorder quantity).
2. Whenever inventories at the beginning of a day have fallen to 160 or below, place an order for 160 units.

The data for demand and lead times contained in Table 19-3 would be used to simulate the inventory system for 15 days. The 80-unit reorder rule would produce the results shown in Figure 19-2, while results based upon the 160-unit reorder rule are illustrated in Figure 19-3.[19] With the 160-unit reorder rule: (1)

[18] This example is highly simplified for purposes of illustration. In actual application the 15-day period would undoubtedly be extended and a far greater number of decision rules would be tested. And, of course, the reorder point and reorder quantity need not be equal as shown here.

[19] It is assumed that no order will be placed while any previous order is still outstanding.

Figure 19-2   Inventory simulation with 80-unit reorder rule.

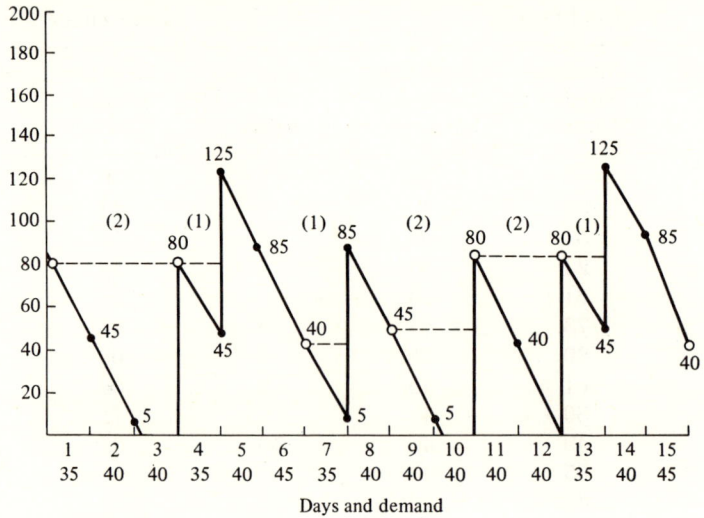

Days and demand

○ Time of order placement
--- Lead time
( ) Lead time in days
Orders placed = 7
Lost sales = 70 (35 in day 3 and 35 in day 10)
Average inventory = 49.7

Figure 19-3   Inventory simulation with 160-unit reorder rule.

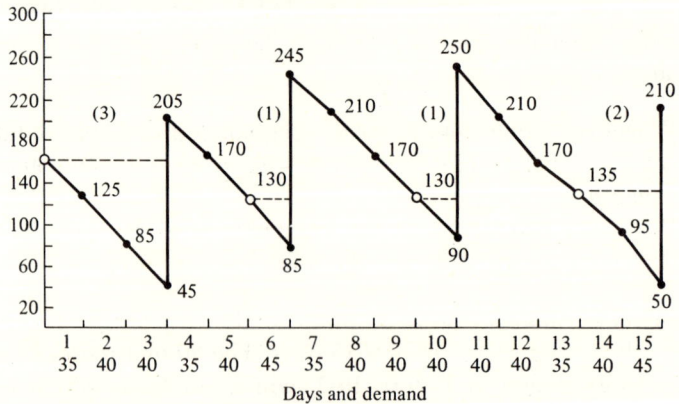

Days and demand

○ Time of order placement
--- Lead time
( ) Lead time in days
Orders placed = 4
Lost sales = 0
Average inventory = 146.3

average inventories are considerably higher (146.3 units as opposed to 49.7 units with the 80-unit rule), (2) fewer orders are placed (4 as opposed to 7), and (3) no sales are lost, as compared with lost sales of 70 units with the 80-unit rule.

While these comparisons are informative, they do not provide adequate information for choosing between the two ordering rules. The manager also needs to view the costs associated with each ordering rule. Assume it costs $5 to place each order; that the cost of each "lost sale" is estimated to be $2; and that, for a 15-day period, as simulated, inventory carrying costs are believed to be about $.50 for each unit of average inventory carried. In such a case, the total costs expected for each ordering rule would be computed as illustrated in Figure 19-4.

The economic results of this example clearly indicate to the manager that the 160-unit reorder rule is preferable to the 80-unit reorder rule. However, they do not say it is the *best* rule that could conceivably be developed. Several additional rules would have to be tested, the 15-day period extended (since it is not of sufficient length to assure "stochastic convergence"), and several iterations of each rule would also have to be conducted before a *best* rule could be selected with any degree of confidence.

SIMULATION IN MARKETING

Simulation models of marketing processes are quite numerous. They can be classified as being either tactical or strategic in their orientation. *Tactical* simulation models are those which deal with specific marketing activities such as pricing, advertising, physical distribution, and so forth. *Strategic* simulation models, often a combination and outgrowth of one or more tactical models, combine the firm's various marketing activities in such a manner that they represent its total marketing program. In addition, since the marketing activities of the firm are not conducted in isolation from other corporate activities, strategic models often include the interdependencies that exist among marketing, production, finance, and personnel.[20]

Figure 19-4   Computation of costs for two ordering rules.

	80-Unit Reorder Rule	160-Unit Reorder Rule
Lost sales	70×$2=$140	0×$2=$ 0
Ordering costs	7×$5= 35	4×$5= 20
Inventory costs	49.7×$.50= 24.85	146.3×$.50= 73.15
Total costs	$199.85	$93.15

[20] A substantially different definition of the nature of tactical and strategic simulation models is contained in Weitz, "The Promise of Simulation in Marketing," p. 29.

This section will briefly examine simulation models that illustrate both tactical and strategic applications. Tactical models will be examined first, since they are often components of the larger, more complex strategic simulation models.

Tactical Simulation Models

During the past 15 years simulation has been applied to a large number of specific types of marketing problems. Some of these problem areas include demand analysis, pricing, channel management, physical distribution, advertising, and consumer behavior.[21] A few of the more noteworthy of these applications are discussed briefly below.

PRICING MODELS. Howard and Morgenroth developed a simulation that replicated the manner in which one executive in a large manufacturing firm set prices on the firm's products. Their model described the way the executive utilized several pieces of information in order to arrive at a specific price. The model was validated by having the executive make 31 pricing decisions and then comparing those prices with prices specified by the simulation model. In each case the model accurately predicted the executive's decision. In another set of 130 pricing decisions made by other executives in the same firm, the model also predicted prices accurately.[22]

Cyert and March developed a model of the organizational behavior of a buyer in a single department within a large retail department store.[23] The model was a complex undertaking that encompassed much more than the buyer's pricing decisions; however, its ability to accurately predict markups, markdowns, and sale prices is impressive. It predicted with perfect accuracy 188 of 197 markups, 140 of 159 markdowns, and 56 of 58 sales prices.

Cohen's simulation describes the aggregate pricing behavior of one large sector of the economy between 1930 and 1940, the shoe, leather, and hide sequence.[24] This sequence is divided into five major segments: hide dealers, cattle hide leather tanners, shoe manufacturers, shoe retailers, and consumers. The model relies heavily on the use of statistical methods such as regression and single-equation least-squares estimation to obtain values for the parameters of the study. It contains over sixty equations that relate in aggregate the significant variables in the shoe, leather, hide sequence. The results indicate that the model is capable of simulating certain aspects of the market process quite well.

[21] For an excellent discussion of simulation studies in marketing see Harold Weitz, *Simulation Models in Marketing*, IBM Technical Report 17–192 (Yorktown Heights, N.Y.: IBM Advanced Systems Development Division, 1966).

[22] John A. Howard and William M. Morgenroth, "Information Processing Model of Executive Decision," *Management Science*, Vol. 14 (March 1968), pp. 416–428. Also see W. M. Morgenroth, "A Method for Understanding Price Determinants," *Journal of Marketing Research*, Vol. 1 (August 1964), pp. 17–26.

[23] Richard M. Cyert and James G. March, *A Behavioral Theory of the Firm* (Englewood Cliffs, N.J.: Prentice-Hall, Inc., 1963).

[24] Kalman J. Cohen, *Computer Models of the Shoe, Leather, Hide Sequence* (Englewood Cliffs, N.J.: Prentice-Hall, Inc., 1960).

CHANNEL MODELS. The Cohen and Forrester[25] models have significant implications for channel management. However, by far the best known simulation study of channel relationships is that done by Balderston and Hoggatt.[26] They developed an extensive model[27] of the way in which individual firms in the West Coast lumber market behave. The basic elements in the model are manufacturers, wholesalers, and retailers linked together by flows of goods, cash, and information; these relationships are illustrated in Figure 19-5.

The objective of the study was to examine market processes. However, the authors claim that with minor modifications their model could be used by market strategists to forecast the effect of short-run price changes on demand, and the profitability of various alternative patterns of vertical integration.

PHYSICAL DISTRIBUTION MODELS. The DYNAMO[28] language devised by Forrester is particularly appropriate for investigating problems associated with inventory flows through the marketing-production-distribution system. Models using this language emphasize the effects that alternative forms of information flow, management decisions, and time delays might have on the firm's total system of inventories.[29] That is, the manager can determine the "sensitivity" of the firm's inventory system to alternative decision rules. Figure 19-6 illustrates such a system. Given a certain set of decision rules, this graph illustrates that the system is quite sensitive to a step increase in sales. Moreover, it takes approximately one year for the system to once again achieve stable conditions.[30]

The simulation studies of the Heinz and Nestlé companies by Gerson and Maffei[31] are also extensive physical distribution studies:

The general aim of the simulation models was to design a least cost system for distributing products from a set of factories through a system of warehouses to the ultimate customer. More specifically, the simulation study permitted the specifications of the optimum number and location of the warehouses for delivery purposes, the specification of which factories should supply a particular warehouse, and a determination of the distribution cost associated with various geographic

---

[25] J. W. Forrester, *Industrial Dynamics* (M.I.T. Press and John Wiley & Sons, Inc., New York, 1961).

[26] Frederick E. Balderston and Austin C. Hoggatt, *Simulation of Market Processes* (Berkeley: Institute of Business and Economic Research, University of California, 1962).

[27] The Balderston and Hoggatt study reportedly cost some $100,000 to conduct.

[28] DYNAMO is a simulation language developed by Professor Forrester specifically for business-oriented problems.

[29] See Forrester, *Industrial Dynamics.* For an excellent overview of the Industrial-dynamics approach see Donald J. Clough, *Concepts in Management Science* (Englewood Cliffs, N.J.: Prentice-Hall, Inc., 1963), pp. 372–393.

[30] Such graphs can be developed directly from simulation runs by using a computer-driven plotting device such as the Calcom plotter.

[31] Martin L. Gerson and Richard B. Maffei, "Technical Characteristics of Distribution Simulators," *Management Science*, Vol. 10 (October 1963), pp. 62–69.

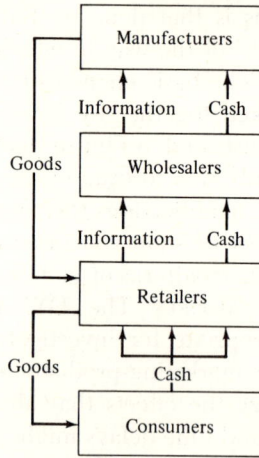

Figure 19-5   The market
              structure in
              simulation
              of market
              processes.

SOURCE: Frederick E. Balderston and Austin C. Hog-
gatt, *Simulation of Market
Processes* (Berkeley: Institute of Business and Eco-
nomic Research, University
of California, 1962). Re-
printed by permission.

Figure 19-6   Industrial dynamics: effects of an abrupt
              change in retail demand.

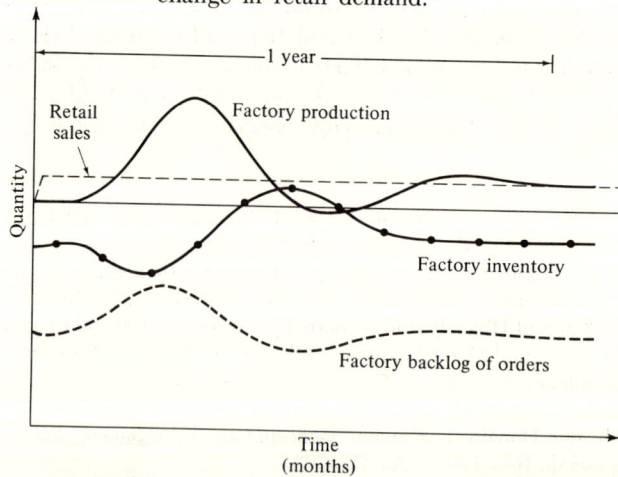

SOURCE: Harold Weitz, *Simulation Models in Marketing,* IBM
Technical Report 17-192 (Yorktown Heights, N.Y.: IBM Advanced Systems Development Division, 1966), p. 41. Reprinted
by permission.

regions, particularly classes of trade (e.g., jobbers, wholesalers, etc.), or particular product lines. Having a detailed and accurate model of the distribution system, the simulation also provides a low-cost method of exploring proposed alterations in the distribution system.[32]

The Gerson and Maffei model is capable of evaluating a system of up to 40 warehouses, 4,000 customers, and 10 factories.[33]

Other physical distribution simulation studies include those by Kuehn and Hamburger[34] (warehouse location) and by Maffei[35] (local delivery-route design). Each is a significant study in its own right and affords the marketing manager new insights into the decision-making process in each of these specific problem areas.[36]

ADVERTISING MODELS. Early attempts to model media evaluation and selection used the mathematical technique of *linear programming*. The solution of such models is accomplished by a mathematical process called the *simplex* method. This method involves a systematic search among all solutions permitted by the constraints until the optimum combination of advertising vehicles is determined.

Basic models of this type have been used by one of the large advertising agencies (Batten, Barton, Durstine, & Osborn) and by several other organizations.[37] BBDO's revised media model calls for the establishment of goals and objectives stated in terms of gross impressions, reach, average frequency of exposure, and frequency distribution of the number of occasions members of the target audience are to be exposed to the client's advertising. The model uses linear programming, but its purpose is to design a media plan that will come

---

[32] Weitz, *Simulation Models in Marketing*, p. 42. For a somewhat less technical discussion see Harvey N. Shycon and Richard B. Maffei, "Simulation—Tool For Better Distribution," *Harvard Business Review*, Vol. 38 (November-December 1960), pp. 65–75.

[33] For an overview of how the technique of simulation can be used in designing the total distribution system see B. Corbishley and F. R. Denham, "Simulation . . . Dynamic Approach to Distribution System Design," *Handling and Shipping*, Vol. 10 (August 1969), pp. 68–72.

[34] Alfred A. Kuehn and Michael J. Hamburger, "A Heuristic Program for Locating Warehouses," *Management Science*, Vol. 9 (July 1963), pp. 643–666.

[35] Richard B. Maffei, "Modern Methods for Local Delivery Route Design," *Journal of Marketing*, Vol. 29 (July 1965), pp. 13–18.

[36] Additional simulation studies of a tactical nature include Edgar A. Pessemier, "Forecasting Brand Performance Through Simulation Experiments," *Journal of Marketing*, Vol. 28 (April 1964), pp. 41–46; William D. Wells, "Computer Simulation of Consumer Behavior," *Harvard Business Review*, Vol. 41 (May-June 1963), pp. 93–98; and Charles S. Mayer, "Pretesting Field Interviewing Costs Through Simulation," *Journal of Marketing*, Vol. 28 (April 1964), pp. 47–50.

[37] See, for example, Harry D. Wolfe, James K. Brown, G. C. Thompson, and Stephen H. Greenberg, *Evaluating Media* (New York: The National Industrial Conference Board, Business Policy Study No. 121, 1966), Chap. 8.

as close as possible to achieving the stated goals (instead of maximizing exposures to the most effective vehicles, which original models do).[38]

Young and Rubicam's "High Assay" procedure is one of the most popular attempts to utilize *iteration* models. The basic procedure is to begin with the media available in the first week and select the single best buy. After this choice is made, all remaining media vehicle candidates are reevaluated, taking into consideration audience duplication and potential media discounts. If the achieved exposure rate is below the optimal rate, a second selection is made for the same week. This process continues until the optimal exposure rate for the week is reached, at which point new media vehicle alternatives are considered for the following week.[39]

The models discussed thus far all attempt to find the optimum media vehicles. Simulation models have different objectives: they determine the reach and frequency of media schedules and in some cases design schedules. The model developed by the Simulmatics Corporation performs both of these functions,[40] while the other most widely used model—the London Press Exchange's CAM Model—estimates reach and frequency but does not construct media schedules.[41] Simulation, then, complements linear programming and iteration models in that each attempts to deal with different problems.

The major limitations of media simulation are: (1) it lacks a procedure for finding better schedules; (2) it does not include an overall effectiveness function —rather it produces a multidimensional picture of impact; and (3) the representativeness of the hypothetical populations underlying the calculations is always suspect.[42]

---

[38] For other types of linear models see James F. Engel and Martin R. Warshaw, "Allocating Advertising Dollars by Linear Programming," *Journal of Advertising Research*, Vol. 4 (September 1964), pp. 42–48; and Stanley F. Stasch, "Linear Programming and Space Time Considerations in Media Selection," *Journal of Advertising Research*, Vol. 5 (December 1965), pp. 40–46.

[39] William T. Moran, "Practical Media Decisions and the Computer," *Journal of Marketing*, Vol. 27 (July 1963), pp. 26–30.

[40] See *Simulmatics Media-Mix: Technical Description* (New York: The Simulmatics Corporation, October 1962).

[41] For a description of the CAM model see Harry Wolfe et al., *Evaluating Media*, Chap. 8.

[42] Philip Kotler, "Computerized Media Planning: Techniques, Needs and Prospects," *Occasional Papers in Advertising* (Urbana, Ill.: American Academy of Advertising, 1965). For descriptions and discussions of other media models see Philip Kotler, "Toward an Explicit Model for Media Selection," *Journal of Advertising Research*, Vol. 4 (March 1964), pp. 34–41; D. M. Ellis, "Building Up a Sequence of Optimum Media Schedules," *Operational Research Quarterly*, Vol. 17 (December 1966), pp. 413–424; Alex M. Lee, "Decision Rules for Media Scheduling Dynamic Campaigns," *Operational Research Quarterly*, Vol. 14 (December 1963), pp. 365–372; Douglas B. Brown, "A Practical Procedure for Media Selection," *Journal of Marketing Research*, Vol. 4 (August 1967), pp. 262–269; Willard J. Zangwill, "Media Selection by Decision Programming," *Journal of Advertising Research*, Vol. 5 (September 1965), pp. 30–36; John Little and Leonard Lodish, "A Media Selection Model and its Optimization by Dynamic Programming," *Industrial Management Review*, Vol. 8 (Fall 1966), pp. 15–23.

Strategic Simulation Models

Strategic simulation models are designed to help the marketing manager define the proper level, mix, allocation, and timing of the firm's total marketing effort. Several companies have constructed elaborate computerized models of their markets in order to test and predict probable responses to alernative marketing programs. Among these companies are Pillsbury (cake market),[43] Lever Brothers (detergent market),[44] and General Electric (flashbulb market). General Electric's simulation model was constructed to determine why similar promotions yielded substantially different sales results at different times.[45] The Lever Brothers simulation was initially constructed as a marketing game to be used in training marketing executives. However, as it was periodically revised and updated, it grew more complex and truly representative of the firm's actual market environment, becoming a valuable research tool.

These and similar simulation models have been described by Kotler as "microbehavioral market simulators," which consist of

1. A representative set of final customers who are distributed geographically,
2. A representative set of marketing channel members, such as retailers and wholesalers, and
3. Specific competitors.[46]

These simulators are extremely helpful to managers as they seek to develop and pretest the effects of alternative marketing strategies.[47]

THE KOTLER MODEL. Kotler developed a model that permits the manager to investigate nine different classes of marketing strategy.[48] His model deals with "the problem of formulating a long-run competitive marketing strategy for a new product introduced into the market with classic growth, seasonal, and merchandising characteristics."[49] The kinds of questions the model seeks to answer include:

---

[43] "Pillsbury Finds a New Mix That Pays," *Business Week*, June 26, 1966, p. 178.

[44] Alfred A. Kuehn and Doyle L. Weiss, "Marketing Analysis Training Exercise," *Behavioral Science*, Vol. 9 (January 1965), pp. 51–67.

[45] Philip Kotler, "Operations Research in Marketing," *Harvard Business Review*, Vol. 45 (January-February 1967), p. 44.

[46] *Ibid.*

[47] For additional discussion of the use of simulation in evaluating alternative strategies see Arnold E. Amstutz, *Management Use of Computerized Micro-Analytic Behaviorial Simulations*, Working Paper 169–66 (Cambridge: Alfred P. Sloan School of Management, M.I.T., March 1966); Philip Kotler, "The Competitive Marketing Simulator: A New Management Tool," *California Management Review*, Vol. 7 (Spring 1965), pp. 49–60; and Frank J. Charvat, "Simulation Model for Marketing Management," *Marketing and the New Science of Planning*, Proceedings, American Marketing Association, 1968, pp. 253–255.

[48] Philip Kotler, "Competitive Strategies for New Product Marketing over the Life Cycle," *Management Science*, Vol. 12, No. 4 (December 1965), pp. 104–119.

[49] Weitz, *Simulation Models in Marketing*, p. 81.

1. Which long-run strategy is the best to adopt if the firm wants to guarantee a minimum return regardless of what its competitor does?
2. Which long-run strategy subjects the firm to the greatest amount of risk?
3. Which strategy offers the chance of greatest profit?
4. If the rival strategy is known in advance with certainty, which is the best adaptive strategy?[50]

THE TUASON MODEL. Roman Tuason developed a model of the household coffee market, consisting of a number of coffee manufacturers.[51] The model permits the "simulated" manufacturers to make decisions regarding price, deals, and cost control on a weekly basis. Thus:

The decisions made are designed to test the efficiency of a particular adaptive, diagnostic strategy. Essentially the firm considers whether the last period results satisfy its market share and profit goals, and if either or both are unsatisfied, the firm makes marketing mix adjustments. The retailers set the final prices on the basis of their desired gross margin. Competitors' behavior in pricing and dealing is generated stochastically. All of the inputs enter seven empirically derived equations for different segments of the coffee market to determine sales and profit results.

Given a model which described the elements of the household coffee market, Tuason tested the effectiveness of the strategy . . . under different conditions of variability in the size of the total market and in the company cost. He also examined the effect of giving different relative weights to the companies' two objectives of profit and market share. One of the conclusions he reached, for example, was that this particular adaptive strategy is significantly more effective in an environment of high sales variability than of low variability.[52]

THE BONINI MODEL. One of the most ambitious strategic simulation models to date has been developed by Charles P. Bonini.[53] The formal structure of the "firm" in Bonini's simulation is depicted in Figure 19-7. Decisions are made at eight points, or decision centers. These decision centers, illustrated in Figure 19-8, are executive committee, manufacturing vice-president, general sales manager, plant supervisor, industrial engineering department, district sales managers, foremen, and field salesmen.

[50] *Ibid.,* p. 84.

[51] Roman V. Tuason, "Experimental Simulation of a Predetermined Marketing Mix Strategy," unpublished Ph.D. dissertation, Northwestern University, 1965.

[52] Weitz, *Simulation Models In Marketing,* p. 79.

[53] Charles B. Bonini, *Simulation of Information and Decision Systems in the Firm* (Chicago: Markham Publishing Company, 1967). For an excellent summary treatment of the Bonini model see Claude McMillan and Richard F. Gonzalez, *Systems Analysis: A Computer Approach to Decision Models* (Homewood, Ill.: Richard D. Irwin, Inc., 1965), pp. 241–262. The Systems Development Corporation Model, another large-scale strategic simulation effort, is described in the same source, pp. 232–241.

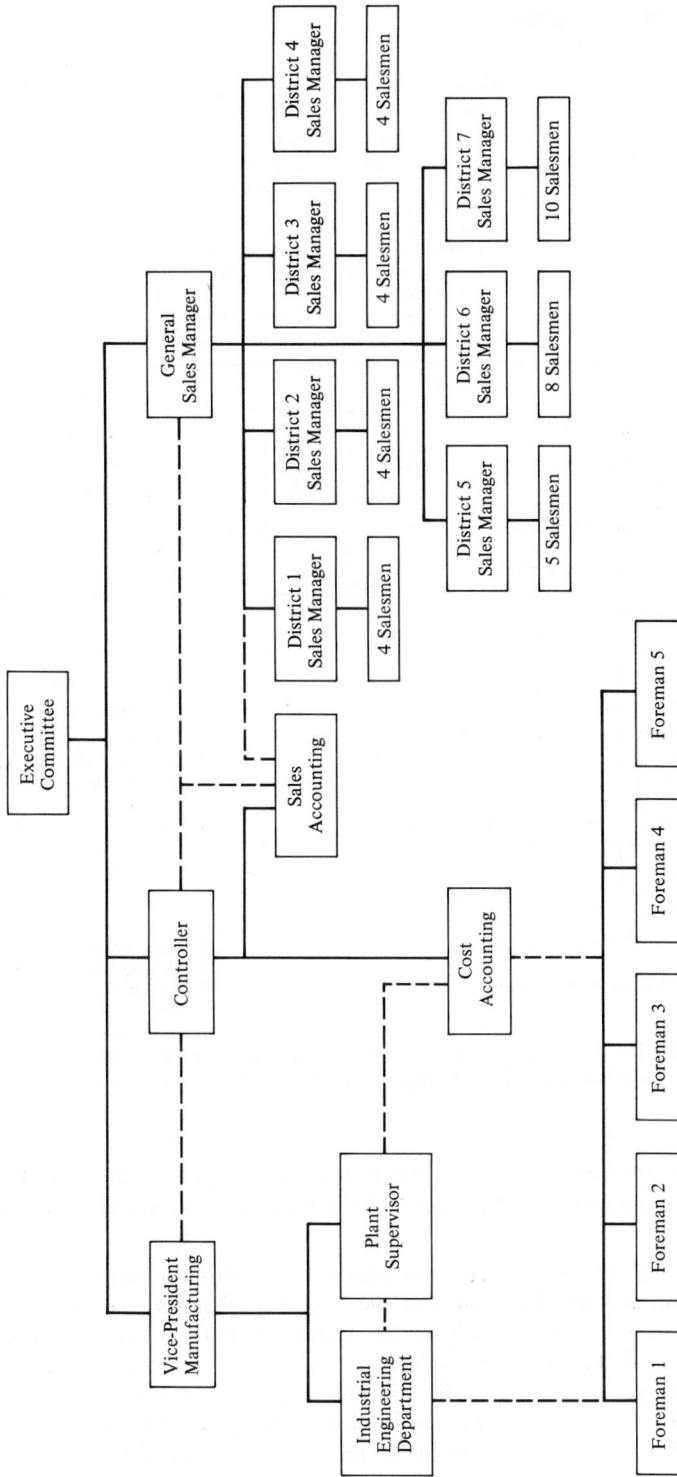

Figure 19-7   Formal organization of the simulated firm.

SOURCE: Charles P. Bonini, *Simulation of Information and Decision Systems in the Firm* (Chicago: Markham Publishing Company, 1967), p. 30. Copyright © 1967 by Charles E. Bonini.

Figure 19-8   Decisions made at various levels in the firm.

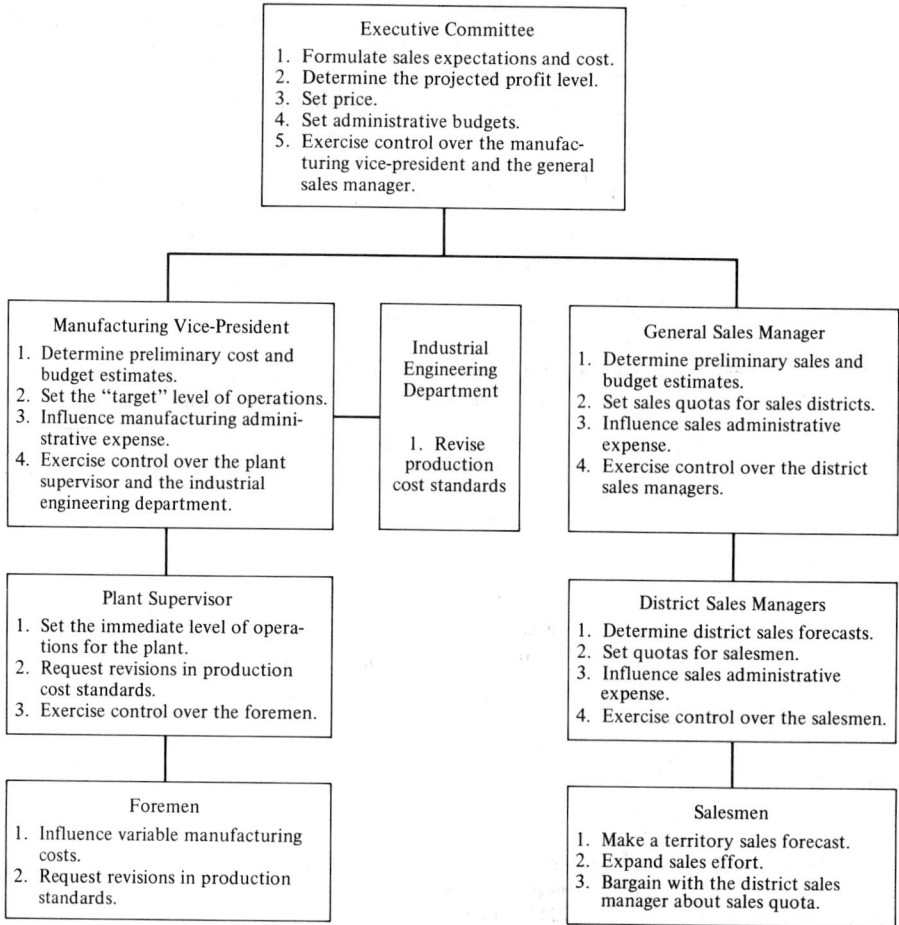

SOURCE: Charles P. Bonini, *Simulation of Information and Decision Systems in the Firm* (Chicago: Markham Publishing Company, 1967), p. 31. Copyright © 1967 by Charles E. Bonini.

The Bonini model was built for purposes of experimentation. McMillan and Gonzalez, commenting on the nature of the experiments Bonini performed, stated:

Changes in eight factors were carefully planned to modify the environment, information system, and decision system of the firm. The changes were introduced to test the parameters, and generally to test existing hypotheses about behavior of the firm. Each of the eight factors had two values, a normal and an alternative value. . . . There were 2^8 (or 256) possible experiments, but the number was reduced to 64. Each experiment simulated activity in the firm for 108 months.

Observations of the values of a set of system variables tracked were recorded, summarized and evaluated statistically to measure the effects of the changes. The system variables tracked were price, cost, pressure, inventory, sales and profit. The two values for each of the factors were:

Factor	Standard	Alternative
1. Environment	Stable	Variable
2. Market growth	2% per year with moderate cycle	10% per year (irregular)
3. Industrial engineering	Loose	Tight
4. Contagious pressure	Slight	Much
5. Sensitivity to pressure	High	Low (insensitive)
6. Inventory valuation	LIFO	Average cost
7. Sales force knowledge of inventory	Knowledge	No knowledge
8. Past vs. present information in control	Present information	Past information

The first two factors change the firm's environment. Modifying the probability distribution for the variable demand is all that is involved when modeling the alternate to relatively stable environment. The next three factors modify decision parameters. Factor 6 changes a decision rule, while the last two factors model different amounts of available information and its content; i.e., whether historical data is reported or merely current data.[54]

The extensive results of the experiments just described are not discussed here; however, the results were satisfactory.

SUMMARY

One of management's most important tasks is to develop a means-end-means chain of corporate objectives and strategy, marketing objectives and strategy, and an integrated program of marketing action. The interdependency of each of these factors implies that a successful marketing program is a *means* of achieving the *end* of marketing objectives, which in turn is one *means* of achieving corporate objectives.

Simulation can be used in structuring the hierarchy of objectives and action-oriented programs in two ways. First, it is often a valuable tool in actually developing marketing strategy and integrated marketing programs. It can be used to arrive at satisfactory solutions to otherwise seemingly insoluble problems. Second, once an integrated marketing program has been developed, the marketing manager may elect to rely upon simulation as a means of pretesting the total marketing program or individual tactical marketing programs.

Simulation is a nonanalytic technique that can be used to experiment upon various aspects of the marketing system over time. It requires that a model of relevant portions of the marketing system be constructed and, in most circum-

[54] *Ibid.*, pp. 261–262.

stances, computerized. After repeated iterations of the model it is usually possible to arrive at satisfactory conclusions relative to the efficiency of various decision rules or marketing programs.

Simulation overcomes many of the deficiencies associated with other problem-solving techniques. First, simplifications and assumptions are not required for simulating *to the extent* that they are demanded by analytic solutions. Second, simulation is a relatively inexpensive method of experimenting with marketing systems. Moreover, once marketing models have been developed for simulation studies, they often can be extended into models capable of yielding optimum solutions. While these models typically are rather extensive, line managers can usually understand them because of the logical, straightforward manner in which they are constructed.[55]

QUESTIONS FOR REVIEW AND DISCUSSION

1. How would you describe the nature of the technique of simulation to someone completely unfamiliar with the term?
2. In which areas of corporate operations do you feel the technique of computer simulation might be applied to greatest advantage?
3. (a) Describe the problems you would foresee in "selling" a sophisticated computer simulation model to corporate line executives.
   (b) What plan of action would you develop to overcome each of these problem areas?
4. Compare and contrast the EOQ model described in Chapter 14 and the inventory simulation model described in this chapter as a practical means of managing a firm's inventories.
5. What advantages do you feel might accrue to a line manager relying upon the technique of simulation for the first time?
6. Discuss the following comment. "Relying on the technique of simulation as a means of developing managerially relevant decisions is nonsense. Simulation requires developing a probability distribution of expectations regarding some future set of events which is nothing more than pure speculation. Flipping a coin or throwing darts would probably be just as reliable."

[55] Weitz, "The Promise of Simulation in Marketing," p. 30.

PART V CONTROLLING AND EVALUATING MARKETING PROGRAMS

After a marketing program has been implemented, the firm must continuously monitor its effectiveness in achieving marketing and corporate objectives. Part V is concerned with this monitoring process.

Chapter 20 examines marketing information systems that generate the data required to determine whether the marketing program is producing the results required to achieve the strategic plan; if it is not, then new action programs are required. Chapter 21 examines the procedures and techniques involved in controlling and evaluating the results of marketing programs.

Chapter 20   Information Systems
for Marketing Management

A customer of Owens-Illinois Glass Company ordered some
containers from the Libbey Products Division. A short while
later he changed his mind and called the O-I representative to
cancel the order. He could not cancel; the shipment was already
in his plant.

Woodward and Lathrop, Inc., in Washington, D.C., provides its management with an 81-page daily report that gives
the previous day's sales by store, by department, and by dollar
amounts, together with a comparison with the previous year-to-
date and the trend of sales for each of the company's nine
outlets.

Macy's of New York has found a profitable merchandising
weapon by computerizing its 1.3 million charge accounts. The
computer can break out accounts in numerous ways—by alpha-
bet, by house number, by size of average charge, and other
categories. Macy's applied the system to a merchandising plan
by asking the computer to print out a list of customers of the
Herald Square store who lived in four counties and inviting
them to a special after-hours sale of furniture and home furnishings.

Chrysler Corporation queried its information system to
determine the future market for heavy trucks. From an analysis
of significant components of the heavy-truck market since the
Second World War, they were able to formulate a predictive
within *one month* to answer management's question.[1]

---

[1] "Computers Begin to Solve the Marketing Puzzle," *Business
Week*, April 17, 1965, pp. 114 ff.

These are just a few of the many ways in which marketing executives are using marketing information systems. Such examples, however, can hardly do more than hint at the nature of marketing information systems, the complexities of designing and implementing such systems, or the problems frequently encountered by firms that do not adequately prepare for the institution of a new system.

This chapter is divided into six major sections. The first presents the basis and rationale of marketing information systems; design considerations are discussed in the second. The third section describes the components of the system. The fourth and fifth sections analyze basic considerations in implementing the marketing information system and discuss bases useful in the evaluation of the system. The final section is a summary-prototype of the way a sophisticated marketing information system might be used in managerial decision making.

Throughout this chapter the abbreviation MIS is used. This abbreviation is sometimes used for a management information system, but in this book MIS refers to a subset of the total management information system—the marketing information system.

BASIS AND RATIONALE OF THE MIS

It is popular for major firms to state that they have or are building a marketing information system. The great surge of demand for such systems implies a great need for them. Some firms, however, may have instigated development of an MIS primarily as a symbol of a progressive, well-managed company. Too frequently, systems developed on such a basis have never become fully operative or, if operative, have not been fully utilized by the executives to whom they were supposed to be helpful. It is important, therefore, to analyze carefully the basis and rationale of the MIS in the strategic programming of successful organizations in the seventies.

The Information Paradox

At all levels of management, there is an increasing and unrelenting demand for additional information. At the same time, the amount of data available is mushrooming. There is no scarcity of data; they are available in many forms and from many sources (many of these sources were described in Chapters 4 and 18). The wide variety of data inputs generate massive quantities of information about changes in the competitive environment, legal issues, economic trends, value shifts, population characteristics, technical advances, internal abilities, and many other variables that influence management decisions for marketing programming. Data are available in rapidly accelerating quantities from government, academic, and trade publications, from marketing research firms, and from internal data-generating organizations.

It is paradoxical, therefore, to find managers frequently complaining about the lack of suitable information for decision making. How can managers beg for additional information and at the same time be in the midst of an information inundation? The reasons might be summarized as follows:

- There is too much marketing information of the wrong kind, and not enough of the right kind.
- Marketing information is so dispersed throughout the company that a great effort is usually necessary to locate simple facts.
- Important information is sometimes suppressed by other executives or subordinates for personal reasons.
- Important information often arrives too late to be useful.
- Information often arrives in a form that leaves no idea of its accuracy and there is no one to turn to for confirmation.[2]

All of this suggests that management needs a system to consolidate the information available for decision making. Further, managers must identify information that is not routinely available and devise a method for gathering that information.

Need for Systems Approach to Information

Every firm in existence collects information about the environment and the potency of the firm in its operations; the need is to *systematize* that information to be sure that the collection, handling, and dissemination profitably affect the decision making of appropriate executives.[3] Several specific problems that arise in modern business firms (and most other types of organizations[4]) make critical a systematized approach to information. These information pressures are described briefly below.

SWIFTNESS OF ENVIRONMENTAL CHANGE. The swiftness of environmental change is forcing firms to generate information that permits executives to anticipate environmental change, rather than merely react to environmentally forced crises within the firm. Increasing pressures from intertype and intratype competition, proliferation of product technology, increasing complexities of organizational structure, and dramatic shifts in resource availability all contribute to the need for increasing ability to monitor and anticipate environmental change. The increased complexity of information technology itself, through breakthrough discoveries in electronic data processing, operations research, simulation, and systems analysis, has put tremendous pressure on the marketing executive for more meaningful information to facilitate decision making.

---

[2] Philip Kotler, "A Design for the Firm's Marketing Nerve Center," *Business Horizons,* Vol. 9 (Fall 1966), p. 63.

[3] Richard L. Pinkerton, "How to Develop a Marketing Intelligence System," *Industrial Marketing,* Vol. 54 (April 1969), p. 63.

[4] For examples outside traditional marketing organizations, see Philip Kotler and Sidney J. Levy, "Broadening the Concept of Marketing," *Journal of Marketing,* Vol. 33 (January 1969), p. 10.

EFFICIENT USE OF MANAGEMENT TIME. Managers recognize the need for additional information. Yet, if they spend additional time collecting and analyzing information, they must take time from other management activities. More time spent in gathering information means that less time available for reaching decisions. This condition dictates that greater efficiencies be achieved in gathering and disseminating information.

Marketing managers often collect information in a relatively unplanned manner or in response to specific problems confronting them. They read journal articles that interest them or happen to come to their attention rather than having a system that insures their seeing the ones they need to see. They read some or *all* of the salesmen's reports rather than only the ones that truly need management's attention. They spend large amounts of time plowing through reports of market conditions and internal performance, with the result that by the time all the information is absorbed, little time is left for thoughtful decision making. Without a systematized approach to information, the alternatives are either *inefficient time usage* by management in absorbing information, or the making of decisions *without* information.

INFORMATION DEFICIENCIES. Information in many firms is never assimilated into the organization or is lost before it reaches decision-making executives.

A study by Gerald Albaum illustrates how information is lost before it reaches decision-making executives. Albaum investigated how well information flowed from customers of a large decentralized firm through their salesmen to the marketing executives. A sample of customers was enlisted to pass on six fabricated pieces of marketing information that would be of interest to firm's marketing executives. The information concerned the changing requirement of customers, the building of a new factory by a competitor, the price being quoted by a competitor, the availability of new material that could be used in making the product, and the development of a competitive product made from a new material.

Albaum wanted to determine how far, how fast, and how accurately information would travel within the firm. Four of the six bits of information never got beyond the salesman. Of the two remaining bits of information, one arrived three days later but was distorted, and the last arrived ten days later with reasonably good accuracy.[5]

Three primary information deficiencies arise in an unmanaged information system:

> *Information loss* may result from employees' simply forgetting or neglecting to pass on information to those who could use it. They may not realize that the information is useful to others in the organization, and in some instances they deliberately suppress information for personal reasons.

[5] Gerald S. Albaum, "Horizontal Information Flow: An Exploratory Study," *Journal of the Academy of Management*, Vol. 7 (March 1964), pp. 21–23.

Information distortion may result from poor listening and collecting or from changing the information to fit one's biases. Furthermore, information is likely to be distorted the more times a message is encoded, transmitted, and decoded.

Information delay may result from the intervention of a large number of relay points between the source and the user, as well as from the manner of reporting.

Benefits of Systems Approach to Information

The problems described above may be overcome by an information system designed to collect, evaluate, and report marketing information in a format that is usable, understandable, timely, and accurate to those who must make decisions.

The benefits of the MIS are many and varied. Primarily, an MIS should result in improved decision making relating to marketing. The time horizons of the firm should be expanded beyond the day-to-day problem level, information should be filtered sufficiently that managerial morale and efficiency will be improved, a broader managerial perspective should replace the "tunnel" vision of executives with only specialized information, synthesis should be facilitated to yield a more strategic perspective, duplication of effort should be reduced, and overreaction to startling news should be moderated.[6]

Specifically, elements of the marketing program should benefit directly from a sophisticated, systematized approach to marketing information. Some examples of typical marketing program variables and the benefits that are associated with an MIS are described in Figure 20-1.

DESIGNING THE MIS

The central function of the MIS is to provide communication between elements of the firm and elements of the environment. Since communication is a two-way process, it is important to understand that both the transmitter and the receiver are integral parts of the communication system. Thus, if the needs and competencies of the receivers are not a central part of the MIS, the system is unlikely to be effective.[7]

Boundary-Spanning Qualities of Information

An effective MIS is designed in such a way that information becomes the boundary-spanning agent between the firm and its environment. Figure 20-2

---

[6] For amplification of these benefits, see William T. Kelley, *Marketing Intelligence* (London: Staple Press, 1968), pp. 25–31.

[7] R. A. Johnson, F. E. Kast, and J. E. Rosenzweig, "Communications and Systems Concepts," in Samuel V. Smith, Richard H. Brien, and James E. Stafford, *Readings in Marketing Information Systems: A New Era in Marketing Research* (Boston: Houghton Mifflin Company, 1968), pp. 98, 106.

Figure 20-1 Benefits possible with a sophisticated MIS.

	Typical Applications	Benefits	Examples
Control Systems	1. Control of marketing costs.	1. More timely computerized reports.	1. Undesirable cost trends are spotted more quickly so that corrective action may be taken sooner.
	2. Diagnosis of poor sales performance.	2. Flexible on-line retrieval of data.	2. Executives can ask supplementary questions of the computer to help pinpoint reasons for a sales decline and reach an action decision more quickly.
	3. Management of fashion goods.	3. Automatic spotting of problems and opportunities.	3. Fast-moving fashion items are reported daily for quick reorder, and slow-moving items are also reported for fast price reductions.
	4. Flexible promotion strategy.	4. Cheaper, more detailed, and more frequent reports.	4. On-going evaluation of a promotional campaign permits reallocation of funds to areas behind target.
Planning Systems	1. Forecasting.	1. Automatic translation of terms and classifications between departments.	1. Survey-based forecasts of demand for complex industrial goods can be automatically translated into parts requirements and production schedules.
	2. Promotional planning and corporate long-range planning.	2. Systematic testing of alternative promotional plans and compatibility testing of various divisional plans.	2. Complex simulation models both developed and operated with the help of data bank information can be used for promotional planning by product managers and for strategic planning by top management.
	3. Credit management.	3. Programmed executive decision rules can operate on data bank information.	3. Credit decisions are automatically made as each order is processed.
	4. Purchasing.	4. Detailed sales reporting permits automation of management decisions.	4. Computer automatically repurchases standard items on the basis of correlation of sales data with programmed decision rules.

Research Systems		
1. Advertising strategy.	1. Additional manipulation of data is possible when stored for computers in an unaggregated file.	1. Sales analysis is possible by new market segment breakdowns.
2. Pricing strategy.	2. Improved storage and retrieval capability allows new types of data to be collected and used.	2. Systematic recording of information about past R&D contract bidding situations allows improved bidding strategies.
3. Evaluation of advertising expenditures.	3. Well-designed data banks permit integration and comparison of different sets of data.	3. Advertising expenditures are compared to shipments by county to provide information about advertising effectiveness.
4. Continuous experiments.	4. Comprehensive monitoring of input and performance variables yields information when changes are made.	4. Changes in promotional strategy by type of customer are matched against sales results on a continuous basis.

SOURCE: Donald F. Cox and Robert E. Good, "How to Build a Marketing Information System," *Harvard Business Review* Vol. 45 (May–June 1967), p. 140. Reprinted by permission.

Figure 20-2   Information vacuum between
firm and the environment.

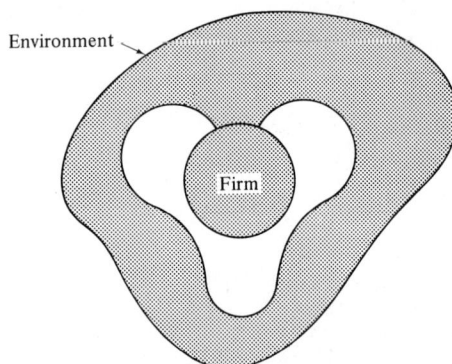

represents this boundary-spanning process by viewing the boundary as one of
information exchange, where the level of the firm's output is governed by the
effectiveness of information exchange between the firm and the customer. Where
perfect exchange of information does not occur, the point of contact between the
firm and its environment is small. This situation, illustrated in Figure 20-2, probably typifies many firms.

Figure 20-2 shows a "vacuum" between the firm and its environment except
at one area of contact. This is a vacuum in the information system, which must
be remedied for effective communication. In the case illustrated, there is little or
no communication between the firm and the environment. When the situation is
viewed in this way, some obvious questions arise. What is the point of contact?
Is this a prime area for communication? Why does the vacuum exist? Why is the
distance between the firm's boundaries and those of the environment not constant? Could other linkages or contact points be established? What is needed to
bridge the gap? Is it worth bridging? Does the distance fluctuate? The answers to
these questions provide a conceptual basis for designing the type of information
system needed for any specific marketing organization.

Marketing Information System Defined

We can obtain a more precise definition of the MIS by defining the central concepts of information and systems. Information can be defined as "data of value in
decision making."[8] Information has value only when it is transferred[9] and is a
major input to decision making.[10] A useful definition of a "system" in the MIS is

[8] M. C. Yovits and R. L. Ernst, "Generalized Information Systems," a paper presented
at the Second Conference on Electronic Information Handling, Pittsburgh, Pa., April 1967, p. 3.

[9] John W. Murdock and David M. Liston, Jr., "A General Model of Information Transfer:
Theme Paper," 1968 Annual Convention, American Documentation Institute, Vol. 18, No. 4,
p. 197.

[10] Howell M. Estes, "Will Managers Be Overwhelmed by the Information Explosion?"
in Smith, Brien, and Stafford, *Readings in Marketing Information Systems*, p. 184.

"an organized or complex whole; an assemblage or combination of things or parts forming a complex or unitary whole."[11] The essential condition in the design of the MIS is that the system be relevant to all the important elements in the marketing program and that there is some orderly way of collecting, describing, and analyzing their interaction.[12] The system that is properly designed aids in conceptualizing complex situations, allows executives to spot inconsistencies or areas of inadequate information, and directs managerial attention to outputs rather than inputs.

Marketing information systems differ from traditional marketing research in scope and unity of design. Lee Adler observes that traditionally, market research has been:

(a) preoccupied with the gathering of unrelated facts,
(b) reactive to day-to-day business pressures,
(c) insistent on rigorous methodology,
(d) highly specialized,
(e) overcome by new techniques.[13]

A marketing information system, in contrast, is described by Uhl as an organized entity: "A fundamental requisite for better managed marketing is that the scattered information activities be both perceived and managed as an entity. That is, these activity components must be (1) identified throughout the organization, (2) thought of as being parts of a whole, and (3) managed as an information unit."[14]

Decision-Oriented Marketing Information Systems

The purpose of the MIS is to improve decisions necessary for planning, implementing, and controlling the marketing function of the firm. The relationship between information and the marketing program is shown in Figure 20-3. The MIS is designed to facilitate information gathering, verification, classification, combination, summarization, and analysis, storage, retrieval, and reporting in satisfactory formats to ensure effective use by marketing management. The MIS does not *make* decisions but it *supports* effective decision making by structuring a problem, searching for alternative courses of action, and assists in the evaluative process of choosing among alternative courses of action.[15]

[11] Johnson, Kast, and Rosenzweig, "Communications and Systems Concepts," p. 45.
[12] Thomas Prince, *Information Systems for Management Planning and Control* (Homewood, Ill.: Richard D. Irwin, Inc., 1967), p. 7.
[13] Lee Adler, "Phasing Research into the Marketing Place," in Smith, Brien, and Stafford, *Readings in Marketing Information Systems*, p. 163.
[14] Kenneth Uhl, "Better Management of Marketing Information," in *ibid.*, p. 36.
[15] Paul Green, "Uncertainty, Information and Marketing Decisions," in J. Kernan and M. Sommers, eds., *Perspectives in Marketing Theory* (New York: Appleton-Century-Crofts, 1968), p. 229.

Figure 20-3   A marketing information system for developing a marketing program.

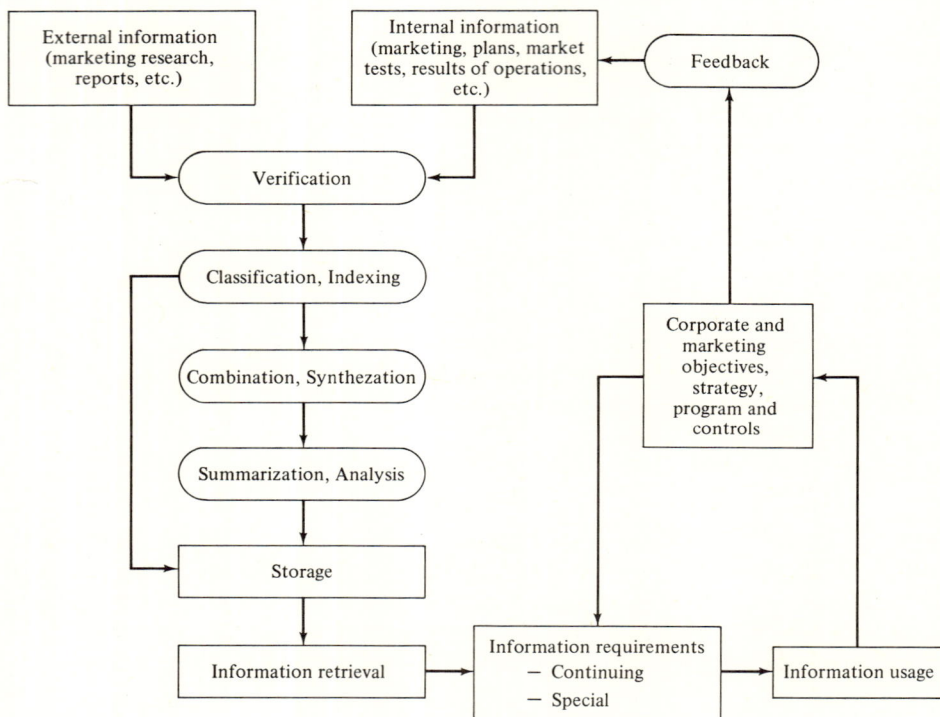

COMPONENTS OF THE MARKETING INFORMATION SYSTEM

Marketing information systems may be manual, semiautomated, or computerized. Regardless of which technology is employed, four basic components are needed in most marketing information systems. They have been described by David Montgomery and Glen Urban as: (1) a data bank, (2) a model bank, (3) a measurement-statistics bank, and (4) a communications capability. These internal components interact with two external elements: (1) the manager or user, and (2) the environment.[16] See Figure 20-4 for a description of these components.

The Data Bank

Decisions about what types of data to include in the MIS are of enormous consequence. Of importance also are decisions about the computer or manual systems to be used for data storage, retrieval, manipulation, and transformation.

[16] David B. Montgomery and Glen L. Urban, "Marketing Decision-Information Systems: An Emerging View," *Journal of Marketing Research,* Vol. 7 (May 1970), pp. 226–234. Also see David B. Montgomery, "Developing a Balanced Marketing Information System," Working Paper of the Marketing Science Institute, July 1970.

Figure 20-4   Decision-information system structure.

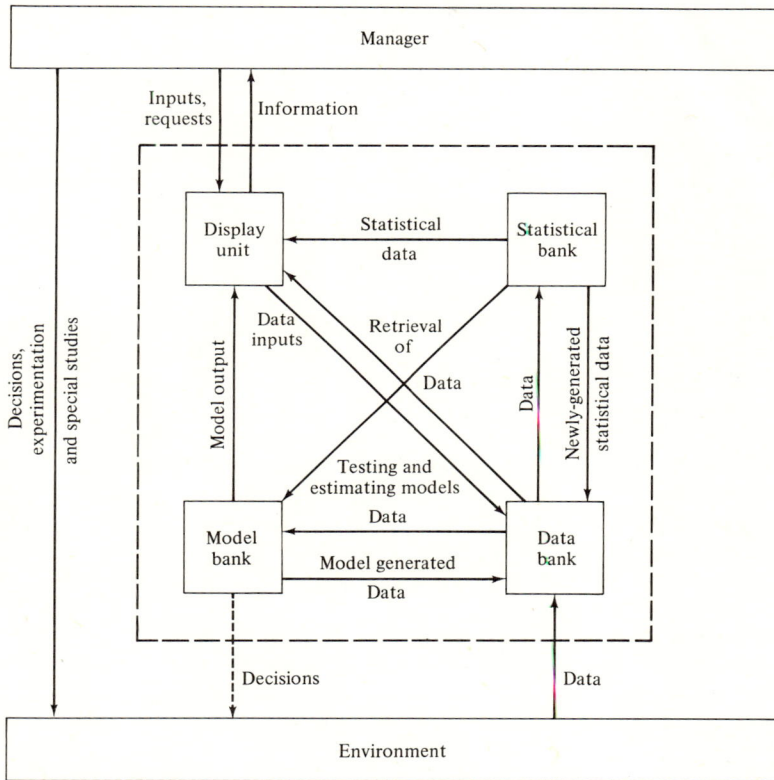

Information system boundaries — — —

SOURCE: Reprinted from David B. Montgomery and Glen L. Urban, "Marketing Decision-Information Systems: An Emerging View," *Journal of Marketing Research,* Vol. 7 (May 1970), pp. 226–234, at 227, published by the American Marketing Association.

DATA. Considerable thought and research are required to determine the types of data needed by present systems, and even greater insight is required to anticipate what types of data are not currently needed but should be included to allow historical comparison in the future. Usually, designers and users of the MIS are under great pressure to include "everything" that might possibly be needed. The problem here, of course, is that the costs of data collection may lead to neglect of other elements of the MIS. Also, the firm may spend so much time and energy in data collection that users are distracted from interpretive functions.

There is no uniform categorization of the data that should be included in an MIS. Design of the data requirements is a highly individualized process. As an example, Figure 20-5 describes the data that might be collected and stored in an MIS for a hypothetical consumer goods company.

Figure 20-5   Data categories for a hypothetical consumer-goods company MIS.

I. *Internal Corporate Records*
   A. Financial and cost data by product and time period
   B. Internal report data:
       1. Salesman's call reports.
       2. Marketing-mix data by product, time period, and market.
       3. Sales performance information on previously implemented new products.
       4. Life-cycle information on products in the line.
       5. Copy and format data on company advertisements.
   C. Judgmental inputs:
       1. Forecasts by product, time, and forecaster.
       2. Estimates of market sensitivity to company and competitive marketing activities.
II. *External Data*
   A. Secondary sources:
       1. Government (e.g., population demographic data, ZIP-coded area).
       2. Commercial (e.g., M.R.C.A. panel data, Nielsen store audits, B.R.I. data).
       3. Freight rate.
   B. Primary sources:
       1. Test-market information.
       2. Market experiments.
       3. Market structure analysis.
       4. Competitive marketing activity.
       5. Advertising performance measures (e.g., Schwerin, Gallup-Robnison, Starch).

SOURCE: David B. Montgomery, "Developing a Balanced Marketing Information System," working paper of the Marketing Science Institute, July 1970, p. 5. Reprinted by permission.

LEVEL OF AGGREGATION. A fundamental question concerns the level of aggregation to be used in the data bank. A tradeoff is sometimes made between the desire for disaggregated data and the reduced storage and handling costs of aggregated data. With increased need for historical comparison, increased analysis of varied units (products, sales territories, departments, and so on), and increased utilization of data for model building and other integrated analytical procedures, a key concept in the design of the data bank should be to *maintain data in their most elemental, disaggregated form.*

PROCESSING. Many types of systems are in common use for processing of data. The key characteristics of any system are flexibility and modularity. Because a useful MIS is an evolving system, it is essential to design maximum flexibility to handle changes, both anticipated and unanticipated. Storage of the data in modules (compartments) facilitates maximum flexibility.

The simplest of systems may store data in the form of original reports, books, and other printed materials. More sophisticated systems use microfilm or various forms of plastic or other storage and retrieval technologies.[17] Even more sophisticated systems, relying upon computerized data processing, usually store data in punched cards, discs, or magnetic tape.

TELEPROCESSING. A recent development of great value to medium-sized and even many large firms is the emergence of on-site teleprocessing terminals, which communicate with a massive central computer shared by various users. The on-site terminal, which might be regarded as a small computer itself, consists of a reader, a line printer, and communication adaptors and data sets. The reader transmits data to the central computer, and the printer later prints reports from the MIS or control messages from the central computer.

PROCESSING ACTIVITIES. With so many data processing systems available for use in contemporary marketing information systems, the proper choice calls for high degrees of technological and economic knowledge as well as very specific understanding of the decisions to be handled using the MIS. The final selection or combination must be capable, however, of performing the following seven basic operations on the data:

1. *Data preprocessing.* (The ability to clean and edit data.)
2. *File creation, reorganization, and deletion.*
3. *File maintenance and updating.*
4. *Information retrieval.*
5. *Logical operations on data.* (Useful when a file is being prepared for statistical analysis.)
6. *Data transformation.* (The ability to perform arithmetic operations on data—crucial to simple analysis, such as computation of market shares, as well as to more complex statistical analysis.)
7. *Report generation.* (The ability to generate reports readily in nearly any desired format.)[18]

The Model Bank

The model bank of the MIS provides capability to structure the effects of alternative strategies and programs and to assist in the evaluation of alternative courses of action. Models may be *predictive* in that they project potential results from courses of action, they may be *search* models that develop or display alternatives and search for the optimum solution, or they might be *behavioral simulations* that comprehensively describe the results of specified programs.

Many of the early models used in marketing have been described as techniques looking for problems; they have been of little immediate relevance in managerial decision making. The future is likely to bring to the typical MIS, how-

[17] A useful description of the noncomputerized data bank of Coca-Cola is found in Malcolm McNiven and Bob D. Hilton, "Reassessing Marketing Information Systems," *Journal of Advertising Research,* Vol. 10 (February 1970), pp. 3–12.

[18] Montgomery, "Developing a Balanced Marketing Information System," pp. 6–7.

ever, models that are problem-centered rather than technique-centered. Although optimization techniques are improving, the mainstream of marketing models is still in nonalgorithmic techniques, such as heuristic programming and simulation.

Perhaps the most frequently used models are those relating to advertising decisions, such as MEDIAC,[19] or ADFORS.[20] Other models, such as SPRINTER,[21] provide predictions of market response to a wide range of variables in the total marketing program.

Model banks need models of a variety of types, although the models should be compatible with each other and should offer the relative strengths of both simplicity and complexity. For maximum effectiveness, they must relate ultimately to a return-on-investment model employed by the firm in the development and implementation of its marketing strategy.

The Measurement-Statistics Bank

The MIS includes a variety of subsystems to provide a basis for measurement and estimation and methods for testing response functions and models. This is a rapidly evolving technology; new techniques are appearing continuously.

Both data-based and judgment-based estimation methods should be a part of the measurement-statistics bank. Bayesian techniques, especially, require the latter. Judgmental assessments of future sales by salesmen and subjective estimates of product acceptance are examples of data resulting from judgmental technology. A suggested design for the measurement-statistics bank of the MIS is presented in Figure 20-6.

The Display Capability

The display capability of the MIS may be either manual or computerized. If the latter, it may be batch-processed or processed on-line. Batch-processing operations are dominant in current computerized marketing information systems, but they may eventually be replaced by on-line systems. The actual output in the past has normally been printed, either typed or electronically processed to yield various forms of hard copy. The future, however, is likely to bring a rapid increase in video display units (cathode-ray tube or other technologies), especially in systems that contain on-line operations.

It is difficult to overemphasize the need to provide MIS output to manager-users in a manner that is timely and understandable. Montgomery and Urban conclude: "As the only direct contact between the user and the system, it is crucial that this interface be designed to provide for convenient, efficient user-

[19] John D. C. Little and Leonard M. Loclish, "A Media Planning Calculus," *Operations Research*, Vol. 17 (January-February 1969), pp. 1–35.

[20] Daniel S. Diamond, "Quantitative Approach to Magazine Advertisement Format," *Journal of Marketing Research*, Vol. 5 (November 1968), pp. 376–387.

[21] Glen Urban, "SPRINTER Mod. III: A Model for the Analysis of New Frequently Purchased Consumer Products," *Operations Research* (forthcoming).

Figure 20-6   Methods incorporated in a measurement-statistics bank.

I. *Data-Based Methods*
   A. Analysis of variance and other parametric procedures
   B. Multivariate procedures:
      1. Regression analysis.
      2. Discriminant analysis.
      3. Factor analysis.
      4. Cluster analysis.
   C. Nonparametric statistics:
      1. Cross-classification.
   2. Goodness-of-fit-measures.
      3. Rank-order measures.
      4. Nonparametric analysis of variance and multivariate procedures.
   D. Time-series analysis
   E. Numeric estimation techniques
   F. Nonmetric scaling
II. *Judgment-Based Methods*
   A. Decision-theory program
   B. Methods for obtaining judgmental assessments
   C. Bayesian multivariate analysis

SOURCE: David B. Montgomery, "Developing a Balanced Marketing Information System," working paper of the Marketing Science Institute, July 1970, p. 12. Reprinted by permission.

system interaction if the marketing information system is to have impact on management."[22]

IBM EXAMPLE. IBM's Commercial Statistics Department collects information from their vast sales force concerning any competitive or customer-related problem.[23] Marketing representatives (salesmen) submit reports describing the problems customers are having with any of IBM's hardware or software, the appeals used by competing computer firms, and the circumstances surrounding the sale of IBM equipment or the loss of a sale to competition.

When this information is received, it is combined with information from trade publications and other intelligence sources and redistributed to salesmen in the form of *Weekly Flashes* and *Industry Newsletters*, which inform the salesmen about the environment, IBM's competitors, and effective ways to combat the competition. Also, from technical sources within IBM, each salesman has access to a *Computer Description Manual*. This closely guarded document candidly describes competing equipment and compares it to IBM equipment.

In this basic MIS, information gathered from salesmen can be combined with information from other sources and returned to salesmen in a form that can

---

[22] Montgomery and Urban, "Marketing Decision-Information Systems," p. 232.

[23] Information gathered from an interview with a former computer sales representative for International Business Machines.

enhance their competitive situation. This information can also be forwarded with necessary transformations and analyses to specified decision centers within the firm for planning and implementing of marketing strategy.

IMPLEMENTING THE MIS

Marketing information systems often provide more potential than profit. Though they profoundly alter the decision-making capabilities of management, they are expensive to develop; firms often spend many years and dollars before attaining successful implementation of the MIS. The following pages describe some of the parameters involved in the development and operation of the MIS as a means to increased profitability of marketing operations rather than merely as a symbol of progressiveness.

Fundamental problems to be overcome when implementing the MIS are listed by Smith as follows:

1. Design of the MIS is organization specific.
2. There is no one proper organizational structure for the firm. It is dependent on the decision-making structure and the environment which the firm deals in.
3. The MIS must be formulated in terms of user requirements, but users do not normally know what they need.[24]

Sequential Levels of Sophistication

Effective systems development typically proceeds in manageable stages of increasing sophistication rather than attempting to develop a "total" system all at once. The fundamental reason for this approach is inadequate understanding of the total system environment or decision processes. Consequently, the efficient strategy is to develop a total *subsystem* that performs to specifications and add, sequentially, additional subsystems.

The sequential development of subsystems proceeds from those areas that yield most readily to analysis and systematization and those which display the greatest potential for increased profitability payout. Frequently, the marginal value of the initial information subsystems is very high, and dollars invested are leveraged effectively toward obtaining profitability goals. As the firm proceeds in developing additional systems—toward its total systems goal—marginal productivity usually decreases until the firm sequentially reaches its optimal information system.

The goal of a *total* information system should not immediately be expected to be achieved. One systems analyst comments:

[24] Wendell R. Smith, "The Role of Planning in Marketing," in Smith, Brien, and Stafford, *Readings in Marketing Information Systems,* p. 217.

I am afraid we are being misled by all this talk about "total systems." The present quest for total should be recognized as a hazardous quest for the "ideal." . . . We cannot design systems boundaries that go beyond our ability to define our problems.[25]

SYSTEM COSTS. With a sequential system design and a few thousand dollars, almost any firm can begin the development of its MIS. Systems at much more sophisticated levels have cost several million dollars. A large company with sales in the $500 million range should expect to invest several hundred thousand dollars in addition to equipment leasing or purchase charges to develop a relatively sophisticated, computer-based MIS.[26]

Involvement of Top Management

Almost every successful system of marketing information has extensively involved the firm's top executives in its design, implementation, and use. If executives are not involved from the beginning, they are unlikely to develop the understanding of the system's capabilities that they need in order to rely upon its outputs. Of practical consequence, also, is the fact that unless top management understands and believes in the value of the MIS, they are unlikely to authorize the money or time horizon necessary to implement an effective MIS.[27]

Security Systems

Implementing an MIS requires careful attention to preserving the system's security in at least three ways. First, the security of the data themselves must be guaranteed; users of the data must be prevented from inadvertently destroying data or altering system programs. Secondly, users in different departments or organizational levels must be prevented from obtaining access to data that would be distracting to them or confidential to other departments. In time-shared information systems, particularly, this requires complex passwords and identification systems to prevent unauthorized release of data. Finally, in the contemporary environment the system's physical security is a condition to be programmed rather than left to chance. It should be protected against both espionage by competitors and sabotage by revolutionary or discontented individuals.

REQUIREMENTS FOR SYSTEMS SUCCESS

The acquisition and installation of a sophisticated information system does not, by itself, guarantee improved marketing performance. Too many company case

[25] Adrian M. McDonough, "Keys to a Management Information Systems in Your Company," in Smith, Brien, and Stafford, *Readings in Marketing Information Systems*, p. 321.

[26] Donald F. Cox and Robert E. Good, "How to Build a Marketing Information System," *Harvard Business Review*, May-June 1967, p. 154.

[27] For additional helpful information concerning the effective implementation of the MIS see Conrad Berenson, "Marketing Information Systems," *Journal of Marketing*, Vol. 33 (October 1969), pp. 16–23; and Joel N. Axelrod, "14 Rules for Building an MIS," *Journal of Advertising Research*, Vol. 10 (June 1970), pp. 3–12.

histories heavily underline this point. Superior performance results only when an advanced MIS is employed by management groups who have an *intensive understanding* of the new technology of marketing management and who know how to apply it in the development and implementation of high-yield marketing programs.

The lessons of the past indicate that too frequently companies have programmed for mediocre system payout by:

1. Trying to graft a sophisticated information system onto a conventionally managed marketing organization.
2. Not getting line managers involved in the new information system until it is an accomplished fact.
3. Assuming that *more* information is *better* information.
4. Assuming that better information, once available, will be readily accepted and used in the organization.
5. Assuming that *better* information will automatically yield *better* results.
6. Delegating the development and implementation of the information system to a specialized staff that is insulated from the mainstream of marketing management.
7. Assuming that the new system does not affect the way marketing programs should be managed.

The important point to be made here, of course, is that high-yield payout comes not merely from the availability of more or better information, but rather from the *effective use* of better information. How effectively the information is used depends, in turn, upon how well the firm's line executives understand the system's application. Thus, the key to superior performance with any advanced information system is *system-oriented education for line management.*

SUMMARY

Marketing information systems are growing in number and importance at an accelerating rate. This growth can be attributed to the unrelenting demand for management information to increase effectiveness of marketing strategies. The swiftness of environmental change and the proliferation of data of many types provide the impetus for management to seek the benefits offered by a marketing information system.

The marketing information system (MIS) is an assemblage of information activities perceived and managed as an entity. These activity components must be (1) identified throughout the organization, (2) thought of as being parts of the whole, and (3) managed as an information unit for the purpose of increasing the effectiveness of decision making.

David Montgomery and Glen Urban have identified the major components of the MIS as (1) the data bank, (2) a model bank, (3) a measurement-statistics bank, and (4) a communications capability. These internal components interact with two external elements: (1) the manager or user and (2) the environment.

Implementation of an MIS must be organization-specific and must be formulated in terms of user requirements. The most efficient development of an MIS usually proceeds from the development of working information subsystems, which sequentially are expanded to a total system. The total involvement and the abilities of top management are essential if an MIS is to lead to improved decision making and not merely to more or better information.

QUESTIONS FOR REVIEW AND DISCUSSION

1. What is meant by the term "information paradox"?
2. Describe the environmental and organization conditions that might indicate the need for an MIS in a large consumer-goods manufacturing firm.
3. Describe the benefits that might reasonably be expected in the planning, control, and research functions of a marketing organization after the implementation of a sophisticated MIS.
4. Define a marketing information system and distinguish it from traditional marketing research.
5. Describe and analyze the major components of a sophisticated and balanced marketing information system.
6. "Data stored in an MIS ordinarily should be aggregated at the highest possible level in order to provide system efficiency, expedite information delivery, and minimize costs." Comment on this statement.
7. Prepare a report on recent developments that might improve the model bank available in a sophisticated MIS.
8. Analyze the position stated in this chapter that top management must be involved in the design and implementation of an MIS if it is to be effective.
9. Describe the educational or retraining system for a firm's top management that should be undertaken before the implementation of a new MIS.

Chapter 21   Controlling and Evaluating Marketing Programs

The Aluminum Supply Company offers a notable example of a system to control elements in the marketing program. This company was started in 1959 in the founder's home with $2,000 of capital. Less than 10 years later the company was selling over $1,000,000 a year and on its way to being one of the largest aluminum distributors in the United Kingdom. A sales control system is credited with much of the success in making each account as profitable as possible.

The control system provides for a daily review of accounts, noting purchases, deviations from normal expectations and comments of sales representatives about the account. It also measures the cost of servicing the account (including sales representatives' calls, amount of advertising allocated to account, and number of personal letters to the account). Every three months the value of the account is audited, and the number of sales calls or other marketing activities is adjusted to reflect the actual needs and profitability in servicing the account.

Based upon the control system of Aluminum Supply Company, eight calls per day are programmed for each sales representative, including order of call and a map for reference. This is done to control travel cost and the valuable time of the sales representative.

To test the value of this control system, the chief executive of Aluminum Supply tried an experiment with new sales representatives. One salesman was controlled; the other was left to work completely on his own initiative, to go where he wanted. Both salesmen were matched for ability. In the first month the uncontrolled salesman produced $720 of business compared to the controlled man's $3,120. The controlled man's sales rose to $4,080 the second month and $5,280 the third month, completely outstripping the uncontrolled salesman's performance.[1]

Large companies such as General Foods, DuPont, Johnson & Johnson, Trans-World Airlines, and American Cyanamid have instituted sophisticated systems of control over marketing activities, participating in a trend toward giving much more attention to this vital phase of marketing management. This chapter describes the basic elements of a marketing control and evaluation system that completes the management cycle of decision making and operation described in this book.

THE NATURE OF MARKETING CONTROL

It is important that executives have a clear conception of what is meant by marketing control. Without an understanding of control, a manager can hardly be expected to exercise it in the most efficient and effective manner. Even though control procedures may be designed and largely monitored by staff personnel, they are unlikely to be effective unless a clear understanding of the nature of control is possessed both by the designers of control systems and *by the persons being controlled.*

Marketing Control Defined

Marketing control can be defined as a systematic effort to compare marketing performance to predetermined standards, plans, or objectives in order to take any remedial action required in the marketing program to see that marketing resources are being used in the most effective and efficient way possible in achieving corporate and marketing objectives.[2] An executive of Phillips Chemical Company explains that control procedures are the means for making operations of the marketing program a dynamic process: *"The essence of control is action which adjusts operations to predetermined standards, and its basis is information in the hands of managers."*[3]

Purpose of Control

The purpose of controls is to let the manager know how things are going in time so that he can do something about it. Control procedures allow taking corrective action in such a way as to attain the firm's marketing objectives. Part of the purpose of control is to regulate the organization in such a way that it reaches and

---

[1] This case is adapted from James Dening, *Marketing Industrial Goods* (London: Business Publications Limited, 1968), pp. 159–160.

[2] Adapted from William Travers Jerome III, *Executive Control—The Catalyst* (New York: John Wiley & Sons, Inc., 1961), p. 24, and Robert N. Anthony, *Planning and Control Systems: A Framework for Analysis* (Boston: Division of Research, Graduate School of Business Administration, 1965), p. 17.

[3] Douglas S. Sherwin, "The Meaning of Control," *Dun's Review and Modern Industry,* Vol. 67 (January 1956), pp. 45–46 ff.

maintains a state of equilibrium that is adaptive and sensitive both to changes in the external environment (consumption markets, resource markets, wholesale markets, cultural and life-style forces, and so on) and to changes in the firm's resource base (production capacities, marketing resources, personnel, and so on).

Specifically, control systems most frequently are used for the following purposes:

1. Projecting desired results accurately.
2. Identifying and forecasting major trends.
3. Detecting operating problems in time to take corrective action before they become critical.
4. Determining the need for changes in the marketing program.
5. Providing continuous guides for improving performance.

Relation to Planning

There is frequently some confusion about the difference between the marketing plan and the marketing control system. Though related, they occur at different ends of the management spectrum. Plans provide the basis of the marketing program, and control attempts to insure that the program achieves the plan. Good planning, alone, does not guarantee attaining objectives: "The manager who believes he has provided for control when he has established objectives, plans, policies, organization charts, and so forth, has made himself vulnerable to really serious consequences."[4]

Annual marketing plans have been described in many ways,[5] but most have the following common elements:

1. Specific objective(s) of the plan.
2. Relationship between the specific objective(s) and the objective of the firm, or an explanation of the extent to which this plan will advance the higher-level and longer-term objectives of the firm. Quantitative measures should be included, if possible.
3. Other specific objectives considered, and the planner's opinion of the relative values of these specific objectives. This evaluation should also include quantitative measures, if possible.
4. Costs of executing the plan.
5. Forecasts of the firm's environment.

---

[4] *Ibid.*

[5] Ernest C. Miller, *Marketing Planning* (New York: American Management Association, Inc., 1967); John M. Brion, *Corporate Marketing Planning* (New York: John Wiley & Sons, Inc., 1967); Wroe Alderson, "Theory and Practice of Market Planning," *Cost and Profit Outlook*, Vol. 2 (July-August 1958); Clarence E. Eldridge, *The Role and Importance of The Marketing Plan* (New York: Publications Department, Association of National Advertisers, Inc., 1966); Everett C. Horne, "Developing a Marketing Plan," in Frederick E. Webster, Jr., *New Directions in Marketing* (Chicago: American Marketing Association, 1965), pp. 80–87.

6. Course of action recommended: first briefly, then in detail.
7. Alternative courses of action and reasons why they were considered inferior to the action recommended.
8. Projected results of the plan, if it is executed.
9. Listing of control standards and procedures to be used for controlling execution of the plan.[6]

It might appear that element 9 of the list above is the one that is essential to controlling the plan. Actually, the other elements are essential also. The objectives (both general and specific) provide the "standards" or norms by which control procedures check performance to determine whether deviations require remedial action. Estimated costs in the plan also provide norms with which to evaluate performance. If patterns of actual costs begin to deviate significantly from the costs estimated in the marketing plan, not only are remedial cost controls indicated, but the objectives or nature of the marketing mix may need to undergo substantial alteration. The control procedures must take this possibility into account. Control procedures may reveal significant differences in the environment from what was forecast in the firm's marketing plan; these deviations may call for revision of the marketing plan.

The plan also reveals the alternative courses of action that were considered and rejected. However, if the firm's environment or performance differs significantly from what was planned for, the alternative courses of action may be more advantageous. They may form the basis of the contingency programs developed in the control process. Finally, it is possible for the control process to reveal no significant deviants from the firm's marketing plan in its specific elements but for profitability and market performance to fall short of (or surpass) the projected productivity. In such instances, a flaw has been revealed in the assumptions or basic development of the marketing plan. The control process, by revealing this at the earliest possible date, permits reappraisal and correction of flaws in the basic planning process. A good plan has good controls built into it.

The remaining portion of this chapter is directly related to the first two chapters, since the control process is designed for use in attaining objectives such as those outlined in Chapters 1 and 2. The reader probably will find it useful to skim over those two chapters before studying the specific nature of the control process, described in the following pages.

THE CONTROL PROCESS

Developing a control process for the marketing program consists of analyzing the critical elements of the process and developing procedures or "routines" to insure satisfactory performance. The critical elements of this process are shown in Figure 21-1, which is a flow chart of the marketing planning and control process that

[6] Leon Winer, "Are You Really Planning Your Marketing?" *Journal of Marketing*, Vol. 29 (January 1965), pp. 1–8.

Figure 21-1   A system for controlling and evaluating marketing programs.

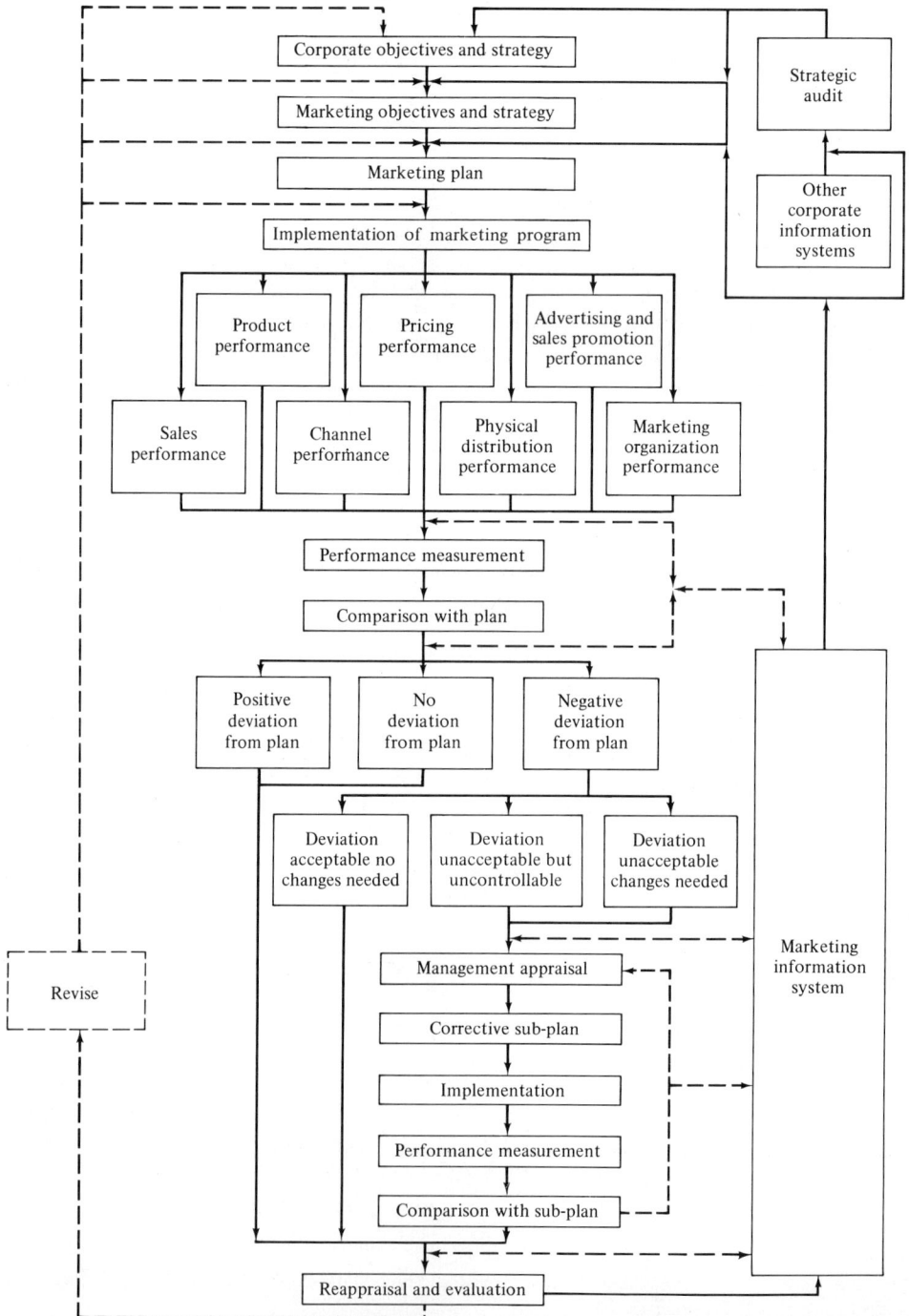

highlights some details of the control process. The major stages of control are identified in Figure 21-1 as defining control objectives (from the marketing plan), performance measurement and comparison with norms, management appraisal, implementation of corrective action, and reappraisal and evaluation. Those stages in the control process are amplified in the pages that follow.

Control by Objectives

The objectives stated in a marketing plan are the explicit basis for control of the plan. To the degree that objectives are measurable and are related to the broader objectives of the firm (see Chapter 1), a control system is able to be a challenging guide to action in management by objectives. A common *fallacy* in the development of control systems is to *include only part of the firm's objectives*—namely, to include specific operational objectives but omit the broader objectives of the firm's marketing plan. One authority on management control systems summarizes the nature of this problem:

> . . . a management control system cannot be developed, nor can management control be exercised effectively, unless the company has a specific objective and overall plan for reaching that objective. For example, in building a control system, one must know not only what kind of business the company is in now, but also the kind of business it plans to be three, five, or even ten years from now.[7]

Unfortunately, many control systems are entirely too narrow in their definition of objectives, permitting evaluation of executive performance only in a very limited time frame and neglecting the (often) more important executive function of adapting the firm's resources to the opportunities provided by a changing environment. Figure 21-1 shows that objectives for the control process should evolve from the corporate mission and strategic plan as well as the marketing plan.

Performance Measurement with an MIS

The "guts" of a control system is measurement of marketing performance with the firm's marketing information system. The MIS must be developed and operated in such a way that it provides information that is *accurate, timely, and relevant* to the needs of the control process. Designing a performance measurement system for control purposes typically involves exception reporting, selecting efficient control units, provision of integrated program information inputs, elemental program information inputs, and control of information delivery. Each of these considerations is described below.

EXCEPTION REPORTING. Most control systems, rightly or wrongly, are being developed to provide reports primarily on an exception basis. This development is a function of the rise of management by exception, defined by Lester Bittel in the following way: "Management by exception, in its simplest form, is a system

---

[7] Robert J. Mockler, "Developing the Science of Management Control," *Financial Executive* (December 1967), pp. 80–93.

of identification and communication that signals the manager when his attention is needed; conversely, it remains silent when his attention is not required."[8]

An example of exception reporting applied to product programs is provided by the SCM Corporation. Here, products are classified annually according to their sales potential. One group contains products expected to hold their own in the coming year; this group gets only limited attention from executives as long as performance monitoring in the control system indicates that the pattern is continuing. A second group of products contains those that exhibit substantial unrealized potential. The control system provides more detailed reports (including special "request" reports) in order that executives can devote greater attention to developing the potential of these products. The third group of products contains those with dwindling markets. To these, management gives substantial and frequent attention, seeking improvement or replacement.[9]

The principle of exception reporting is excellent, since it permits executives to concentrate their energies and limited time on thos projects and problems most likely to provide high yields for the firm. Routine problems are solved at appropriate lower levels. In practice, exception reporting works well only when the *objectives are defined broadly* enough to insure that the company exploits *total and future market opportunities* as well as past and present markets.

SELECTION OF CONTROL UNITS. Effective performance measurement depends upon efficient selection of control units—or determining *what* and *who* are to be measured. The firm might focus performance measurement upon *internal* variables (measuring costs, activities, and so on) or upon *external* variables (sales, market share, and so on). In order to control *productivity*, however, it is necessary to measure the performance of internal variables as they *relate* to external variables. For control purposes, the three most common[10] external reporting bases are (1) product groups, (2) accounts (customers by size or type), and (3) sales territories.

Because costs and activities are measured internally and revenue or results are measured externally, some very great problems arise in attempting to measure *productivity performance* on the basis of products, accounts, or sales territories. These problems are best resolved by a control system that permits the allocation of functional (internal) costs to external (revenue) control units. One of the leading authorities in marketing productivity measurement, Charles Sevin, has determined a system for allocating activity costs to revenue-producing control units[11]; this system is shown in Figure 21-2.

[8] Lester R. Bittel, *Management By Exception* (New York: McGraw-Hill, Inc., 1964), p. 5. Also, see pp. 35–145 for discussion of the measurement—observation—comparison cycle used in management-by-exception control systems.

[9] The SCM case is described in Gordon H. Smith, "Direction and Control of Expansion," in H. B. Maynard, ed., *Top Management Handbook* (New York: McGraw-Hill, Inc., 1960), pp. 1026–1029.

[10] Thomas J. McGann, "Yes! The Controller Belongs on the Marketing Team," *The Controller* (August 1961), pp. 377–387.

[11] Charles H. Sevin, *Marketing Productivity Analysis* (New York: McGraw-Hill, Inc., 1965).

Direct cost reporting systems are helpful in implementing control systems when using either product, account, or sales-territories reporting bases. The term *variable costing* is perhaps more descriptive than direct costing.[12] Under historical, full-costing techniques, the fixed element of manufacturing and marketing overhead was allocated to the cost of producing and distributing the products in the product mix and consequently was reflected in cost of goods manufactured and cost of goods sold. This tends to hide valuable information about the marginal income of each product and the product mix in general. Under direct costing, only variable costs are charged to the cost of manufacturing and distributing the product, while fixed overhead costs are deducted along with general administration costs in determining net income before taxes.[13] Although neither the Internal Revenue Service nor the American Association of Certified Accountants will allow direct costing for external reporting,[14] the process is valuable in control processes in a variety of ways,[15] including control of productivity associated with expanded capacity[16] and evaluation of contemplated changes in the marketing program requiring changes in sales volume to maintain or increase productivity.[17]

Along with its many advantages, direct costing has some disadvantages. First, a cost is fixed only in the short run; over the long run all costs are variable, and decisions relying on variable costs can be misleading for evaluation of long-run objectives. Second, a misdirected emphasis on volume instead of profitability can be destructive to a business if it leads to preoccupation with uneconomical products. Third, pricing decisions based upon direct costing can lead to serious errors in the optimization process. Fourth, contribution margin may be measured even more meaningfully on a per-hour or per-day basis rather than a product basis. Fifth, direct costing as a planning tool depends upon accuracy of projected demand schedules. When they fail to be achieved, results can be misleading— although an adequate control system should determine such deviation.[18]

The selection of optimally useful control units probably dictates that performance measurement be conducted on the basis of *all three* external bases and with as much detail on internal costs as is practicable. With manual accounting systems this was nearly impossible, but now, with storage of computerized cost

[12] See Richard E. Williams, "Converting to a Direct Costing System," *Management Accounting* (January 1968), pp. 23–34.

[13] Frank H. Mossman and Malcolm L. Worrell, "Analytical Methods of Measuring Marketing Profitability: A Math Approach," *Business Topics*, August 1966.

[14] Julius W. Phoenix, "Direct Costing—A Challenge to Traditional Inventory Pricing?" *The New York Certified Public Accountant*, Vol. 36 (May 1966), pp. 379–382.

[15] John R. Patterson, "Decision Making Applications of Direct Cost Information," *Management Accounting* (January 1960), pp. 11–22.

[16] For an example, see Charles T. Horngren, "A Contribution Margin Approach to the Analysis of Capacity Utilization," *The Accounting Review*, Vol. 42 (April 1967), pp. 254–264.

[17] Sam R. Goodman, "Improved Marketing Analysis of Profitability: Relevant Costs and Life Cycles," *Financial Executive*, June 1967.

[18] These limitations are summarized from Herson and Hertz, "Direct Costing in Pricing: A Critical Reappraisal," *Management Service*, March-April 1968.

Figure 21-2   A control system for measuring marketing productivity.

Functional-Cost Groups and Bases of Allocation

Functional-Cost Group	To Product Group	To Account Group	To Sales Territory
1. Selling-direct costs: Personal calls by salesmen and supervisors on accounts and prospects. Sales salaries, incentive compensation, travel, and other expense.	Selling time devoted to each product, as shown by special sales-call reports or other special studies.	Number of sales calls times average time per call, as shown by special sales-call reports or other special studies.	Direct.
2. Selling-indirect costs: Field supervision, field sales-office expense, sales-administration expense, sales-personnel training, sales management. Market research, new product development, sales statistics, tabulating services, sales accounting.	In proportion to direct selling time, or time records by projects.	In proportion to direct selling time, or time records by projects.	Equal charge for each salesman.
3. Advertising: Media costs such as TV, radio, billboards, newspaper, magazine, etc. Advertising production costs; advertising department salaries.	Direct, or analysis of space and time by media; other costs in proportion to media costs.	Equal charge to each account; or number of ultimate consumers and prospects in each account's trading area.	Direct, or analysis of media circulation records.
4. Sales promotion: Consumer promotions such as coupons, patches, premiums, etc. Trade promotions such as price allowance, point of purchase displays, cooperative advertising, etc.	Direct, or analysis of source records.	Direct, or analysis of source records.	Direct, or analysis of source records.
5. Transportation: Railroad, truck, barge, etc., payments to carriers for delivery of finished goods from plants to warehouses and from warehouses to customers. Traffic department costs.	Applicable rates times tonnage.	Analysis of samplings of bills of lading.	Applicable rates times tonnage.

Functions, costs			
6. Storage and shipping: Storage of finished goods inventories in warehouses. Rent (or equivalent costs), public warehouse charges, fire insurance and taxes on finished goods inventories, etc. Physical handling, assembling and loading out of rail cars, trucks, barges for shipping finished products from warehouses and mills to customers. Labor, equipment, space, and material costs.	Warehouse space occupied by average inventory. Number of shipping units.	Number of shipping units.	Number of shipping units.
7. Order processing: Checking and processing of orders from customers to mills for prices, weights and carload accumulation, shipping dates, coordination with production planning, transmittal to mills, etc. Pricing department. Preparation of customer invoices. Freight accounting. Credit and collection. Handling receipts. Provision for bad debts. Salary, supplies, space and equipment costs (Teletypes, Flexowriters, etc.).	Number of order lines.	Number of order lines.	Number of order lines.

SOURCE: From *Marketing Productivity Analysis* by Charles H. Sevin. Copyright © 1965 by McGraw-Hill, Inc. Used with permission of McGraw-Hill Book Company.

and sales information in a firm's MIS becoming routine, such measurement is becoming much more feasible. Computerized systems require that data from invoices be stored in desegregated form (so that retrieval can be accomplished on the basis of *products within invoices*, for example) to permit maximum reporting and control flexibility.

INTEGRATED PROGRAM INFORMATION INPUTS. Information inputs used for comparison with the marketing plan may be of two basic types. Information inputs may reflect the performance of the total or *integrated* marketing plan, or they may reflect the performance of the *elements* that contribute to the plan, listed in Figure 21-1. The former type is discussed first.

Integrated program information inputs reflect the cumulative effect of the planning and execution of the marketing program.[19] It is a measure, therefore, for controlling and evaluating performance of top general management of a firm and the chief marketing executives.

Specifically, information inputs are based upon sales or one of many derivatives of sales. Integrated information inputs, therefore, include the following:

1. Gross revenue from sales.
2. Unit volume of sales.
3. Marketing contribution to profit and overhead.
4. Gross profit.
5. Market share (by volume or revenue).
6. Sales change.
7. Sales backlog.
8. Market expansion.
9. Other results of the integrated marketing program (such as inventory turnover, asset turnover, return on net worth, and so on).
10. Combinations of the above.

It is still common to use total performance measures in marketing control systems, but this practice has come under serious criticism in recent years as a measure of dynamic control. The inadequacies of integrated program information inputs are summarized in the following statement:

In a marketing control system where the variable controlled is such a final performance criterion, three main problems arise. These might be termed the *problems of timeliness,* of *diagnosis,* and of *detection of market opportunity.* Assume, for example, that the control variable is profit rate, as defined by the principles of accounting, which govern the firm's accounting system. It is evident that the con-

---

[19] For a thorough discussion of measurement of factors affecting marketing performance, see Richard Jay Lewis, "A Business Logistics Information and Accounting System for Marketing Analysis," unpublished D. B. A. dissertation (East Lansing, Mich.: Michigan State University, 1964). Also see E. R. Hawkins, "Distribution Cost Analysis," *Industrial Distribution,* Vol. 47 (April 1957), pp. 82–84.

trol procedure will *detect problems only after their effects have so permeated the system as to have generated an out-of-control condition.* Early detection of a decision situation appears to be a rather neglected criterion for the choice of a control system. Consider the popularity of costs per unit sold, per customer, or per sales territory as a control basis. The fact that these problem indicators make it easy to set control standards appears for many marketing practitioners to be more important than the disadvantages of late detection of marketing problems. Approaches of this type do not seem to recognize that it can be very difficult and costly to change adverse trends once they become established. The underlying behavior or buying patterns which produced the change may have become customary or habitual.[20]

PROGRAM-ELEMENT INFORMATION INPUTS. The most useful diagnostic information inputs in the control process are those that measure performance of each element in the firm's marketing program. The firm's MIS and other corporate information systems should provide inputs with which to compare actual results with planned results. Where deviations exist, changes can be made in the marketing program, and/or planned objectives may be revised (in instances where changes in environment or incorrect assumptions about program effectiveness prohibit attaining original objectives). Thus, the information inputs needed for control of elements in the marketing program include the following:

1. Actual results of product programs compared to planned results.
2. Actual results of pricing programs compared to planned results.
3. Actual results of advertising and sales promotion program compared to planned results.
4. Actual results of sales program compared to planned results.
5. Actual results of channel program compared to planned results.
6. Actual results of physical distribution program compared to planned results.
7. Actual results of marketing organization and personnel program compared to planned results.

In addition to direct comparisons of program objectives with actual results, various derivative information inputs are needed for diagnostic purposes. An exhaustive list of such information inputs would be impossible, since they depend upon the marketing objectives, strategies, programs, and managerial styles of specific firms. The nature of diagnostic information inputs, however, is revealed in this sample description by Mark Stern:

1. *Sales expense to sales revenue.* This is clearly a most important ratio and

[20] William S. Peters and Richard Kuhn, "A Bayesian Approach to the Construction of Marketing Control Systems," in Robert L. King, ed., *Marketing and the New Science of Planning* (Chicago: American Marketing Association, 1968), pp. 79–84. (Italics added.)

warrants constant observation. It is easily calculated by taking the output of the sales organization model and dividing it by net sales revenue. Sales expense should cover the branch office overhead, salesmen's salaries, travel expenses, customer entertainment, commissions, and so forth. The expense-to-revenue ratio is a reasonable measure of the efficiency of the sales organization.

2. *Advertising expense to sales revenue.* This ratio is quite similar to the previous one and is determined by taking the output of the advertising model and dividing it by net sales revenue. Although in most firms the amount spent on advertising is usually a fixed percentage of sales, this is not the recommended approach. Setting the level of the advertising budget was not done on that basis in the total marketing system.

3. *Sales force productivity.* This may be in terms of average personal selling man-hours expended per dollar of sales revenue, or in terms of the number of units (or dollars) that the average salesman sells per week, month, or year. An implicit assumption regarding reasonable values was made when the sales organization model was designed. Consequently, salesman productivity is an important measure because it monitors the continuing validity of the sales organization model.

4. *Physical distribution cost per unit.* The physical distribution system can be used to calculate the cost of moving each unit as the ratio of the total physical distribution cost and units shipped. Clearly, this is a measure of the effectiveness of the physical distribution model.

5. *Service expense ratio.* Each unit sold may be guaranteed to function properly when installed in the customer's office. Furthermore, a guarantee may be given to protect customers against defects in workmanship and materials. The service expense ratio is calculated as the repair costs divided by net sales revenue.

6. *Average sales per order.* A range of reasonable values of this ratio must be assumed in calculating the sales parameters of the sales organization model. The average sales revenue resulting from each order should be known, so that the model can be revised (or at least retested for validity) as the ratio changes.[21]

Analysis of these diagnostic inputs on a periodic basis may generate requests to the MIS for additional information inputs about program elements in the marketing plan. One function of the ratios above, however, is to indicate which of the elements of the marketing program deserve *highest priority* for intensive investigation and corrective action.

INFORMATION DELIVERY. A final consideration in performance measurement with the firm's MIS and other corporate information systems is to insure that

[21] Mark E. Stern, *Marketing Planning: A Systems Approach* (New York: McGraw-Hill, Inc., 1966), pp. 134–135.

information needed for control purposes is delivered to the individuals who need it and in a form that they will use. In many firms, information already exists that would be useful in the control process but the right people are not getting it. Gerald Albaum observes: "When a company analyzes its methods for handling the vital flow of information to its decision makers, it may be shocked to realize that it is not even using effectively the marketing information it already has."[22]

In designing the nature and format for delivery of control information to appropriate executives, two considerations apply:

1. Information should be excluded that is extraneous to the problem of control.
2. Information should be delivered to the executive quickly, so that operations do not deviate any further from the plan or any longer than can be avoided.

It should be apparent that marketing executives increasingly need to understand financial and other analytical information. At the same time, there is increasing concern among financial and accounting executives to understand marketing programs and to provide the types of information that can be used in their planning and control. A recent study concluded that accounting information for decision making is in the midst of two major trends. One is toward greater selectivity of what is reported—to provide information that is actually useful for decision making. The other trend is toward quantitative reporting, by an information system, of matters that have traditionally been evaluated exclusively in qualitative terms.[23]

Management Appraisal of Marketing Performance

A properly functioning control process will deliver information for management appraisal indicating one of three things is happening to marketing performance. One, positive deviations from the marketing plan are occurring (overperformance). Two, the marketing program is operating with no significant deviations from plan. Three, the marketing program is operating with negative deviations from plan. These possibilities are shown in Figure 21-1 along with possible outcomes. It is the first and last types of deviation with which the marketing executive must be concerned, and these are discussed below.

CONTROL OF OVERPERFORMANCE. Positive deviation from the marketing plan is one of the more pleasant problems that an executive must appraise; however, it would be a mistake to assume that no further action is necessary. The executive's

[22] Gerald Albaum, "Information Flow and Decentralized Decision Making in Marketing," *California Management Review*, Vol. 9 (Summer 1967), pp. 59–70, at p. 59.
[23] Thomas J. Burns, ed., *The Use of Accounting Data in Decision-Making* (Columbus, Ohio: College of Commerce and Administration, The Ohio State University, 1967).

appraisal is immediately used for reappraisal and evaluation of the marketing program to see whether corporate or marketing objectives should be revised. Similarly, the condition that caused overperformance (such as lowering of cost for an element of the marketing program, or a greater than anticipated market enlargement) needs careful analysis. It may be of such significance that it can compensate for limitations recognized in other elements of the marketing program. Consequently, it may be to the firm's advantage to revise the firm's objectives, its marketing program, or both.

If a firm finds that one product or sales territory is particularly successful in relation to competition, this may be a good time to devote additional resources to this area of high productivity before competitors take action.

The control process is intended not only to detect and correct difficulties and shortcomings, but—just as important—to detect significant market opportunities that have been underevaluated in earlier marketing plans.

UNCONTROLLABLE NEGATIVE DEVIATION. Management appraisal of a negative deviation from marketing objectives may reveal that the magnitude of the deviation is greater than can be accepted without concern but that the causes are uncontrollable by executive action. Common situations of this sort include adverse economic conditions in the market, breakthrough discoveries by competitors, internal difficulties, and the like.

It is desirable that the control system reveal significant negative deviations from plan even though they are uncontrollable. This information permits reappraisal of the marketing program with an eye to possible revision in later planning periods. It is also essential for other functional areas of the firm. For example, the controller needs to know of significant deviations in market performance for his own cash-flow control process, and the production department needs to know in order to minimize inventory costs and production scheduling.

The danger in labeling a negative deviation as uncontrollable is that new objectives will be established that will be lower than what actually could be obtained. A kind of "negative synergy" frequently operates among the sales force and other groups when they are allowed to change original objectives. A recession or major competitive discovery often provides an "excuse" for failure to attain results that actually are attainable. Most firms find it best to operate under the original marketing plan and objectives, even though they are not attained, unless there is clear evidence that revision could permit the firm to reprogram marketing activities for increased effectiveness.

CONTROLLABLE NEGATIVE DEVIATION. Management must appraise indicators of negative deviation from planned results to determine whether or not the deviation is significant. Within certain limits of deviation, the costs involved in management control and programming activity may outweigh the incremental profitability to be derived from attempting to achieve planned results. Additionally, some random variation in market performance indicators is expected and should not be viewed as a signal for action.

The management appraisal system may use Bayesian techniques or other

Figure 21-3   Control chart for appraising performance deviation from planned results.

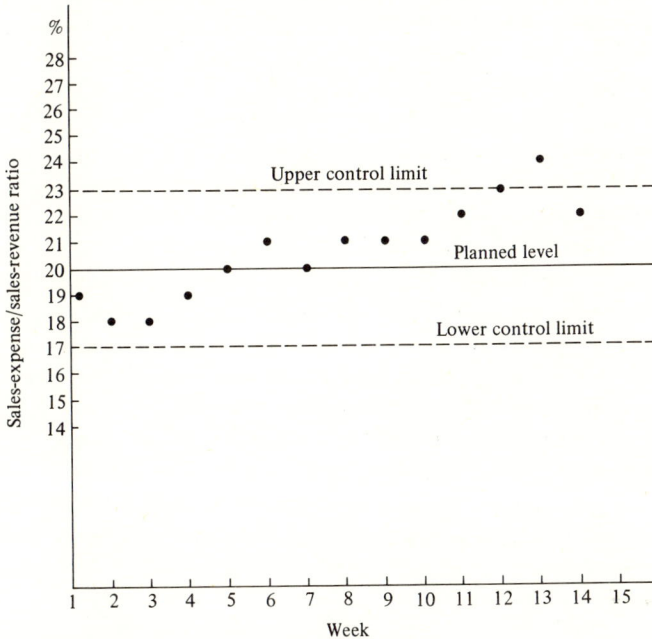

approaches for sorting out optimal control limits.[24] Figure 21-3 shows a simple statistical control chart for appraising the sales-expense/sales-revenue ratio. As long as the ratio is within predetermined control limits, no corrective action is required. In week 12, however, Figure 21-3 shows that this ratio went above the upper control limit, and it appears that correction action was taken to achieve a decrease the following week.

Many forms of control mechanism, such as Gantt charts, PERT charts, and other models, are used for appraising performance.[25] Standard financial ratios and analyses of many types are also appropriate.[26]

CORRECTIVE SUBPLANS. The consequence of management appraisal of performance deviation from planned standards is the development of a corrective subplan (shown in Figure 21-1). This is needed when negative deviation is

[24] Peters and Kuhn, "A Bayesian Approach to the Construction of Marketing Control Systems." Also see Wroe Alderson and Paul E. Green, *Planning and Problem Solving in Marketing* (Homewood, Ill.: Richard D. Irwin, Inc., 1964), Chap. 12.

[25] See Earl P. Strong and Robert D. Smith, *Management Control Models* (New York: Holt, Rinehart and Winston, Inc., 1968). This is an introductory treatment but it contains an extensive bibliography of more advanced methods.

[26] J. Fred Weston and Eugene F. Brigham, *Managerial Finance* (New York: Holt, Rinehart and Winston, Inc., 1966), esp. pp. 67–184.

beyond acceptable limits and it appears that corrective action can profitably reverse the situation.

The corrective subplan may be designed to control elements of the marketing program in such a way that the original plan is achieved, or it may result in substantial revision of the marketing program. Here are some examples of situations that might be encountered:

1. The marketing budget for a single product is too large. The present level of expenditure results in such sharply diminishing returns that substantial gains would be obtainable through shifting efforts to other products (where the rate of diminishing returns is not so great).
2. The marketing budget for a single product is too small. Either added expenditures would bring increasing returns, or the rate of diminishing returns is still low as compared with that for other products.
3. The marketing mix is inefficient. Either not enough or (more likely) too much is being spent, for example, on advertising a product as compared with personal efforts to sell it. Changes in the marketing mix would increase the product's sales or profit-contribution dollars.
4. Marketing efforts are grossly misallocated, as among products, customers, and territories. If the allocations among products were changed, even though the total level of expenditure remained the same, sales or net profits would be increased.[27]

Implementing Corrective Action

Implementing a corrective subplan requires disciplined exercise of control. In some instances the exercise of control is part of the mechanics of the control system; in others, specific executive judgment and action are required. Insofar as possible the principles of action (timing, responsibility, and so on) and attitudes and procedures should be preprogrammed.

SECURING ACCEPTANCE OF CONTROL PROCEDURE. People usually do not like to be corrected or "controlled." Thus, this aspect of management is often more demanding of executive skill than some others.[28] Management can merely emphasize compliance—protecting market share, maintaining control limits on sales and travel expenses, reprimanding for low productivity, and so on. However, that approach is a stifling one. A more viable solution is to attain personnel participation in the development of marketing plans and goals to the extent that *marketing control procedures are accepted because marketing goals are accepted*. In such an organizational environment, employees may correctly view control systems as enabling tools rather than restrictive procedures.

CONTINGENCY PLANS. Corrective subplans are implemented most rapidly

---

[27] Sevin, *Marketing Productivity Analysis*, pp. 6–7.

[28] For helpful suggestions in accomplishing this task, however, see Martin L. Bell, *Marketing Concepts and Strategy* (Boston: Houghton Mifflin Company, 1966), pp. 629–673.

and perhaps most easily if they are developed before they are needed. Control systems can be used to indicate changes in the market that signal the implementation of an alternative strategy—one that has already been carefully planned, tested, and perhaps partially programmed.[29] If the changes that cause negative deviation from planned results are environmentally determined, it is likely that competitors are facing the same problem. The firm that has a control system that detects the changes first and has a contingency plan that allows the firm to be the first to make alterations in the marketing program may be in a position to increase by several points its market share or profitability. This may have a significant long-run effect upon a firm's relative market strength.

Reappraisal and Evaluation

The final stage in a marketing control system is one of reappraisal and evaluation of the marketing plans and program (see Figure 21-1). This is based upon the premise that anything worth planning is worth reviewing.

The reappraisal and evaluation stage is devoted to careful analysis of the firm's performance in order to determine how it is related to the firm's marketing program. Were the assumptions about advertising effectiveness correct? Was the allocation of sales resources an optimal one based upon performance? Did stresses develop in the marketing organization that inhibited effectiveness of the program? These and many other questions should be raised both to gain generally improved understanding of the nature of marketing relationships and specifically to assist in the development of future plans and programs. Marketing research should be used to assist in the evaluation[30] along with appropriate theoretical and analytical models that illuminate the critical relationships.[31]

Reappraisal and evaluation of marketing performance includes attention to favorable deviation from the marketing plans as well as negative deviation. In some ways, it is more important to know what causes *favorable* results than the converse. After the H. J. Heinz Company introduced their new control system, one of their executives explained their analysis of favorable as well as unfavorable variances:

The line of thinking, of course, is that something caused the favorable variance— either unexpected effectiveness of factors of production or some reduction in standard cost which needs reexamination. If the causes of improvement are positive and can be identified, their possible permanence can be appraised; and if the development, whatever it is, can be passed on to other factories or departments,

---

[29] B. Charles Ames, "Marketing Planning for Industrial Products," in George Schwartz, ed., *Science in Marketing* (New York: John Wiley & Sons, Inc., 1965), pp. 100–111.

[30] Harper W. Boyd, Jr., and Steuart Henderson Britt, "Making Marketing Research More Effective by Using the Administrative Process," *Journal of Marketing Research*, Vol. 2 (February 1965), pp. 13–19, esp. p. 18.

[31] L. A. Williams, *Industrial Marketing Management and Controls* (London: Longmans, Green & Co., Ltd., 1967), pp. 197–252.

it will improve the over-all company profit picture. There are frequent improvements in the company's products, recipes, processes, and costs, and some of these are directly traceable to properly investigated variances from standards and budgets.[32]

THE MARKETING AUDIT

An important activity of top management of the marketing function is to assume responsibility for the marketing audit—a structured study of the firm's marketing activities that goes well beyond the reappraisal and evaluation stages of normal marketing control processes described above.

Nature of the Marketing Audit

The marketing audit can be defined as ". . . a systematic, critical, and impartial review and appraisal of the total marketing operation: of the basic objectives and policies of the operation and the assumptions which underlie them as well as of the methods, procedures, personnel, and organization employed to implement the policies and achieve the objectives."[33]

The basic purpose is not to determine how well the firm's marketing organization has performed in the past but, rather, to search for marketing opportunity in the future. It is an attempt to break away from the problem of everyday operations and to enlarge the firm's vision of the opportunities presented to it and of the potential strengths or weaknesses of its marketing resource base in exploiting those opportunities.

Total Evaluation Program

The marketing audit is a comprehensive and penetrating analysis of six major areas of a firm's marketing function. The six areas of a firm's marketing activities that should be appraised are: (1) objectives, (2) policies, (3) organization, (4) methods, (5) procedures, and (6) personnel.[34]

Management by objectives has become common in contemporary business practice, but it appears that rather limited attention has been given to *the source of objectives*. Because of the marketing function's direct interaction with the firm's environment, it is likely that marketing factors increasingly influence the objectives of the firm and thus must be monitored and intensively evaluated.

Objectives represent the goals and targets of the firm, but *policies* are the broad, fixed guidelines that provide principles for achieving objectives. These

[32] Controllers Institute Research Foundation, Inc., *Management Planning and Control: The H. J. Heinz Approach* (New York: Controllers Institute Research Foundation, 1961), p. 55.

[33] Abe Shuchman, "The Marketing Audit: Its Nature, Purposes, and Problems," *American Management Association Report No. 32* (New York: American Management Association, 1959).

[34] Alfred R. Oxenfeldt, *Executive Action in Marketing* (Belmont, Calif.: Wadsworth Publishing Company, Inc., 1966), p. 746. See pp. 745–757.

need to be challenged to determine their validity in a rapidly changing environment. The organization of a firm in contemporary society is often undergoing change, and the marketing audit needs to assess these changes to determine guiding principles if not specific formats.

The *methods* and *procedures* of a firm need to be examined on the basis of the rigorous quantitative and behavioral-research and analytical models. Methods and procedures are examined in a marketing audit on the basis of alternatives that have been considered or should be rejected.

Finally, the *personnel* of a firm must be audited—especially from the perspective of resource planning, updating of executive skill, and basic performance factors.

Frequency of Marketing Audits

A controlled plan for the timing of marketing audits should be standard practice in a well-managed marketing organization. Oxenfeldt has outlined criteria for determining the frequency of various elements in the marketing audit:

1. Those appraisals that are easiest and least costly should be conducted most frequently; and conversely, those that are most complex and most disturbing to the organization should be conducted least frequently.
2. Those appraisals that promise the greatest benefits—judged on the basis of previous experience, the speed with which changes have been taking place, and other factors—should be conducted most frequently.
3. There probably is a time limit beyond which no part of the total evaluation should be delayed. It is suggested that every aspect of most companies' marketing activities should be appraised rigorously at least every three years.
4. One should conduct appraisals no more frequently than the fundamental circumstances justify. Daily evaluations of market-share changes, for example, would be palpably foolish; monthly comparisons might be too frequent and lead to unfounded conclusions; yet annual comparisons would probably be too infrequent.[35]

Selecting the Auditors

Sources of auditors are of three basic types. One group can be classified as internal line officers of a firm. These are individual executives who, as part of their regular duties, perform the audit at specified periods (or when some crisis arises!). Such auditors, however, find it difficult to devote sufficient time to the audit and to maintaining impartiality. Another source of auditors is internal staff—perhaps a central marketing auditing staff, which might serve various divisions and subsidiaries of a firm and still maintain balance between impartiality and in-depth knowledge of the firm's operations.

[35] *Ibid.*, p. 756.

A third source of marketing auditors is outside management consulting firms. Such firms are frequently selected because of their ability to maintain impartiality and a detached perspective on the client firm's present involvement in markets, procedures, organization, and personnel. Also the consulting firm is more likely than the client to be able to assign to the audit a variety of personnel with in-depth knowledge of specialized evaluation procedures.

The marketing audit differs from the control process in a very significant way. The control process is concerned with operations on a short-term basis and asks primarily: "Are we doing things right?" A marketing audit includes this question but goes well beyond it to ask: "Are we doing the right things?"

AN INTEGRATED MARKETING PLANNING AND CONTROL SYSTEM—THE CELANESE CORPORATION

We can perhaps best summarize the material in this chapter by showing how one company integrates planning and control. Figure 21-4 diagrams the entire process. The corporate objectives and strategies are direct influences upon operations under the direction of the marketing vice-president. It is his responsibility to analyze major industry and company trends and secure agreement on planning assumptions for an upcoming period. On the basis of these assumptions, objectives and programs for obtaining them are established.

The control process at Celanese includes provisions for measuring overall results against planned sales objectives as well as control procedures for measuring and correcting each of the major elements of the marketing program. The system includes information feedback loops to deliver information to each appropriate managerial control point in the system. A system of this type can increasingly be expected to be a requirement of high-yield management of the marketing function.

Marketing control systems, of course, do not replace creative managerial activity. No matter how mechanical or programmed a control system might become, the attainment of high-yield managerial results will require management ability to look beyond the figures at the assumptions, the purposes of the system, the objectives of the corporation, the basis of the standards, and the methods of collecting and disseminating information. The intelligent marketing manager is skeptical; he questions the accountants, statisticians, and other individuals responsible for providing information upon which the executive must base decisions determining the ultimate performance fate of the firm.

SUMMARY AND CONCLUSIONS

Marketing control is a systematic effort to compare marketing performance to predetermined standards, plans, or objectives in order to take any necessary remedial action in the marketing program to see that marketing resources are

Figure 21-4 Marketing planning and control process for the operating companies of Celanese Corporation of America.

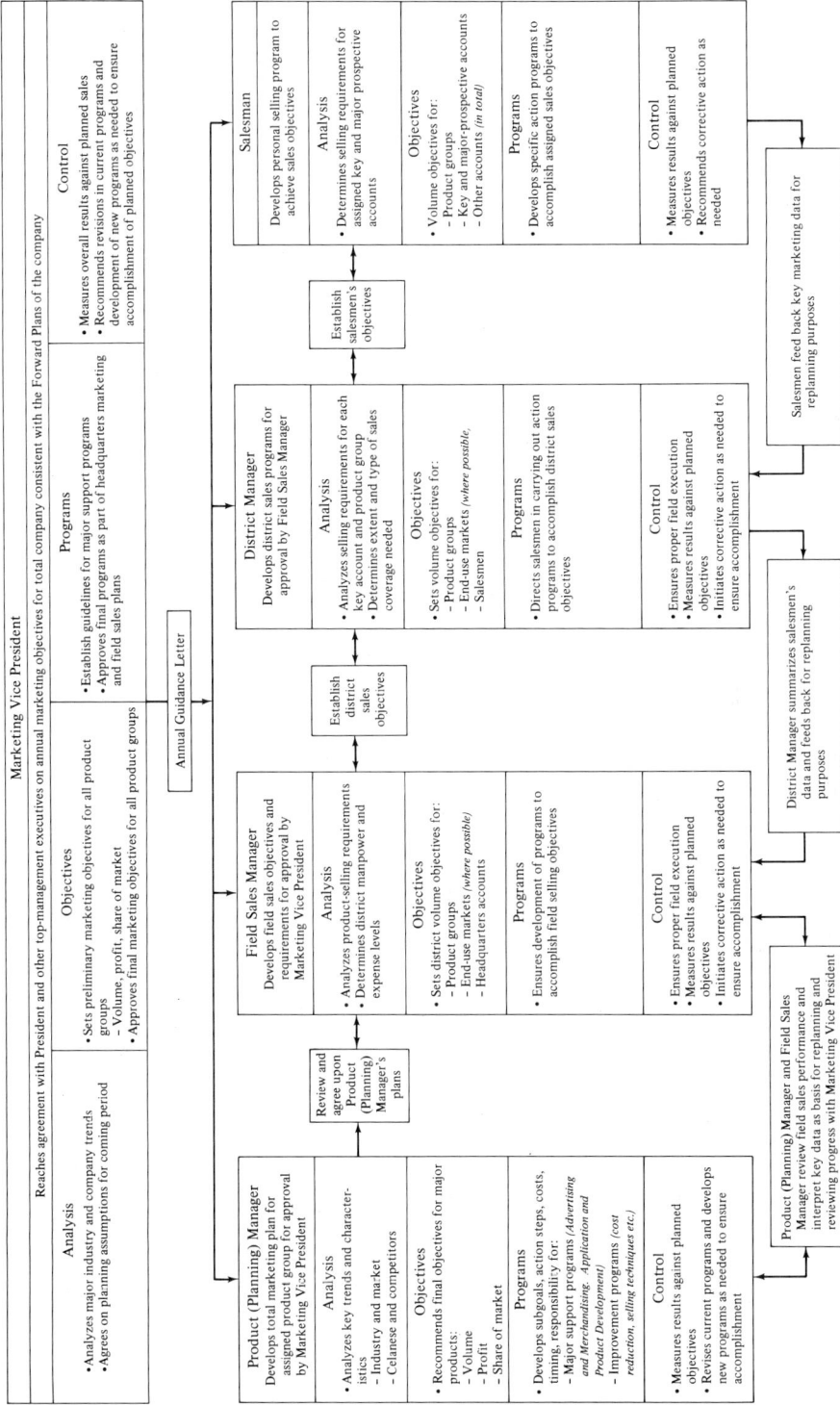

Marketing Vice President

Reaches agreement with President and other top-management executives on annual marketing objectives for total company consistent with the Forward Plans of the company

Analysis	Objectives	Programs	Control
• Analyzes major industry and company trends • Agrees on planning assumptions for coming period	• Sets preliminary marketing objectives for all product groups – Volume, profit, share of market • Approves final marketing objectives for all product groups	• Establish guidelines for major support programs • Approves field programs as part of headquarters marketing and field sales plans	• Measures overall results against planned sales • Recommends revisions in current programs and development of new programs as needed to ensure accomplishment of planned objectives

Annual Guidance Letter

Product (Planning) Manager

Develops total marketing plan for assigned product group for approval by Marketing Vice President

Review and agree upon Product (Planning) Manager's plans

Analysis
• Analyzes key trends and character-istics
  – Industry and market
  – Celanese and competitors

Objectives
• Recommends final objectives for major products:
  – Volume
  – Profit
  – Share of market

Programs
• Develops subgoals, action steps, costs, timing, responsibility for:
  – Major support programs *(Advertising and Merchandising, Application and Product Development)*
  – Improvement programs *(cost reduction, selling techniques etc.)*

Control
• Measures results against planned objectives
• Revises current programs and develops new programs as needed to ensure accomplishment

Product (Planning) Manager and Field Sales Manager review field sales performance and interpret key data as basis for replanning and reviewing progress with Marketing Vice President

Field Sales Manager

Develops field sales objectives and requirements for approval by Marketing Vice President

Analysis
• Analyzes product-selling requirements
• Determines district manpower and expense levels

Objectives
• Sets district volume objectives for:
  – Product groups
  – End-use markets *(where possible)*
  – Headquarters accounts

Programs
• Ensures development of programs to accomplish field selling objectives

Control
• Ensures proper field execution
• Measures results against planned objectives
• Initiates corrective action as needed to ensure accomplishment

Establish district sales objectives

District Manager summarizes salesmen's data and feeds back for replanning purposes

District Manager

Develops district sales programs for approval by Field Sales Manager

Analysis
• Analyzes selling requirements for each key account and product group
• Determines extent and type of sales coverage needed

Objectives
• Sets volume objectives for:
  – Product groups
  – End-use markets *(where possible,*
  – Salesmen

Programs
• Directs salesmen in carrying out action programs to accomplish district sales objectives

Control
• Ensures proper field execution
• Measures results against planned objectives
• Initiates corrective action as needed to ensure accomplishment

Establish salesmen's objectives

Salesmen feed back key marketing data for replanning purposes

Salesman

Develops personal selling program to achieve sales objectives

Analysis
• Determines selling requirements for assigned key and major prospective accounts

Objectives
• Volume objectives for:
  – Product groups
  – Key and major-prospective accounts
  – Other accounts *(in total)*

Programs
• Develops specific action programs to accomplish assigned sales objectives

Control
• Measures results against planned objectives
• Recommends corrective action as needed

Must work closely with Advertising and Merchandising and Application and Product Development to ensure that all these plans are fully integrated

SOURCE: George B. Moseley in *The Development of Marketing Objectives and Plans* (New York: National Industrial Conference Board, 1963), p. 35. Reprinted by permission.

being used in the most effective and efficient way possible in achieving corporate and marketing objectives.

The purpose of control systems is to provide a basis for action in implementing the firm's marketing plan. The control process is composed of several stages, in which control objectives are defined (from the marketing plan), performance is measured and compared with norms, and then management appraises performance to determine necessary actions, implements corrective action, and provides for reappraisal and evaluation of the marketing program.

The marketing audit, a special form of reappraisal and evaluation consisting of a periodic, in-depth analysis and appraisal of the total marketing operation, is becoming an important part of high-yield managerial performance.

QUESTIONS FOR REVIEW AND DISCUSSION

1. Delineate what types of marketing executives should be informed about the nature of the marketing control system used in a firm.
2. What are the purposes of marketing control systems?
3. How are marketing control systems related to the plan for a firm's integrated marketing program?
4. Describe what information inputs should be expected from a firm's marketing information system for control purposes.
5. Develop a position that information for a marketing control system should be based upon performance indicators for the total marketing program or for specific elements of the marketing program. Defend your position.
6. "The purpose of a marketing control system is to determine when performance is below planned results. When results surpass objectives, the marketing control system is not necessary." Comment on this statement.
7. Describe a marketing audit and its role in high-yield management.

PART VI SOCIAL
AND ETHICAL
PERSPECTIVES

The United States is experiencing the pains of an era of uncom-
fortable discontinuity. The values
and tested procedures of the past
are being questioned, not only by
radicals, but also by moderates
and some conservatives. Though
the future is vague, apparently it
will be less like the past than
ever before. Chapter 22 explores
corporate and marketing responsibilities during the decade
ahead.

Chapter 22 Social and Ethical Perspectives for Corporate Marketing Executives

We have also come to this hallowed spot to remind America that the fierce urgency is now. This is no time to engage in the luxury of cooling off or to take the tranquilizing drug of gradualism. Now is the time to make real the promise of democracy.

We must forever continue our struggle on the high plane of dignity and discipline.

Even though we face the difficulties of today and to-morrow, I still have a dream. It is a dream deeply rooted in the American dream. I have a dream that one day this nation will rise up and live out the true meaning of its creeds . . .

Dr. Martin Luther King, Jr.,
at the steps of the Lincoln
Memorial in Washington, 1963

Outcries for corporate sensitivity to human and social needs may soon become a major input into the strategic planning process of all but the most inhumane American firms. Executives who once asked why students were not spending more time studying instead of getting involved in social causes now find themselves forced by those same students to plunge headlong into the search for decency and responsibility in the midst of a confusing and sometimes overwhelming environment.

Profit once reigned unchallenged as the sole rationale for the existence of the corporation and as the basis for strategic marketing planning. In truth few executives honestly believed profit to be the *only force* worth considering in the firm's operations. Within themselves, executives probably welcome the pressures from outside the firm that have forced them to reveal their innermost thoughts. Thus, they have been able to verbalize their convictions that other motivations are indeed relevant forces that help shape the corporation's strategies.

Profit is a necessary but not a sufficient rationale for business. This statement is being increasingly recognized by business leaders. The President of the Ohio Bell Telephone System recently told employees, "I recognize that there are many who say that the only job of business is business. I cannot agree. The crisis in our cities cannot be met without business involvement." The President of the Polaroid Corporation stated that the function of industry is the development of people, and the Chairman of Bell and Howell—a man who later left business to become a United States Senator—stated that the basic objective of the firm is the development of individuals.

This chapter does not describe the specific ways that marketing executives and their firms should operationalize social and ethical responsibility. That changes year by year. Instead, this chapter presents an analytical description of the variables that firms and individuals can use in seeking their own interpretation of social and ethical responsibility. Some students of marketing might correctly prefer that this chapter begin the book. There is logic, however, in its being a concluding chapter, since in many ways it is the departure point for personal career decisions. It should help one relate the technology that has now been mastered to a philosophy of personal and corporate concern that will allow each to survive in the transitional environment that characterizes United States society.

This chapter emphasizes the environmental responsibilities that a variety of forces are dramatically revealing to the corporation. The chief executive officer of Cummins Engine Company summarized the need for this revolutionary role of business in a speech to the Institute for Urban Development:

The changes in attitude, thought, custom, and action which are now called for may well be unprecedented in history. It is not clear that we shall make them in time. If we do, it will be because we in business made accurate appraisal of what is required of us, and led the reform, the revolution, and neither opposed it, nor left it to others.

SOCIAL AND ETHICAL RESPONSIBILITY

Marketing, because it is the primary interface of business with society, should be more vitally concerned about its social and ethical responsibility than any other field in business. Its concern should be one of active involvement rather than passive interest. Social responsibility is important to marketing and other executives today, not so much because marketing itself is threatened by detractors, but rather because the society in which marketing functions is in jeopardy. Businessmen today realize there is more to corporate activity than the last line of the profit and loss statement. Marketing should be in the vanguard of this realization.

Environmental pollution is one of the social problems facing businessmen most directly. Other problems that marketing executives face include racism and the role of minorities, the marketing of products that are socially disruptive, harmful, or to some degree fraudulent. The existence of poverty, inadequate nutrition and housing, low-grade mass media, and rising rates of theft and pilferage are glaring indicators that marketing has failed as well as succeeded. When people fail to understand each other and each other's way of life so that war is necessary, questions arise whether communications arts are very advanced at all. When marketing executives claim expertise in communications and personal understanding and at the same time war and personal alienation are omnipresent, questions arise. Do marketing men lack sufficient expertise in the art of communications or is their expertise not being directed at the more pressing problems of society?

Two types of responsibility impinge upon the planning of marketing strategy. The first is social responsibility, which can be defined simply as accepting an obligation for the proper functioning of the society in which the firm operates. This involves the firm's accountability for the activities through which it can reasonably contribute to the proper functioning of the society.

Ethical responsibility is the other factor affecting strategic marketing. Ethical responsibility is even more fundamental than social responsibility in that it exists without the firm or without a well-developed society. Ethical responsibility is concerned with the determination of how things should be, human pursuit of the right course of action, and the individual's doing what is morally right. Much of the basis for social responsibility is derived from the ethical aspect of responsibility.

When an executive is acting in an ethical manner he is also being socially responsible, but the converse is not always true. An executive can be socially responsible to his community (that is, participate in many worthwhile civic activities) but at the same time lead a dissolute life. This points out the essential difference between social and ethical responsibility. To be socially responsible, it is sufficient to act in a responsible manner to society regardless of intent. Actions alone determine social responsibility, and a firm can be socially responsible even when doing so only under extreme coercion. The government may pass laws that *force* firms to be socially responsible in matters of water and air pollution. Militant pressure groups may *force* firms to be socially responsible in employment and training practices. Consumers may *force* marketers to be socially responsible in presenting product information on packages or in advertising.

An executive or his firm is socially responsible by his actions alone. To be ethically responsible, it is not sufficient to act correctly; ethical intent is also necessary. Since it is far easier to view a man's actions than to know his innermost thoughts, social responsibility is easier to assess. The difficulty of measurement tends to exclude ethical responsibility from discussions of business strategy. This is unfortunate, since of the two, ethical considerations are more important. They determine what is socially responsible and the resolve of individuals within the society to do it.

In this chapter, ethical responsibility is not discussed explicitly, but it is implicit in the conceptual framework, since it is the ultimate focal point for the development of a viable perspective on the firm's and the individual's obligations to society.

CORPORATE SOCIAL RESPONSIBILITY

The initial focus of this section will be on the social responsibility of the corporation as a complete entity. The emphasis will then shift to more specific marketing activities. However, in an era of consumer orientation, considerations of total corporate strategy usually apply directly to functions of marketing.

Social Responsibility Defined

A more rigorous definition of social responsibility, provided by Howard Bowen, underlies this discussion. The social responsibility of businessmen ". . . refers to the obligations of businessmen to pursue those policies, to make those decisions, or to follow those lines of action which are desirable in terms of the objectives and values of our society."[1] The most important aspect of this definition is its focus on society and not on elements within the firm.

The social responsibility of the firm and the social responsibility of the executive are not one and the same. The businessman can be socially responsible as he personally interacts with his own environment, while at the same time his firm may be socially irresponsible. An executive may be very active in worthwhile civic affairs directed at the betterment of the community while at the same time his firm is polluting the rivers and atmosphere. Clearly, this individual is not being totally socially responsible; either he is ignoring one sphere of his social responsibility or he is unaware that damage is being done. If total responsibility to society is to be honored, the social responsibility of the individual and that of the firm must be congruent.

Spheres of Social Responsibility

The firm has six primary spheres of social responsibility. Those of the individual will not be discussed separately, since his responsibility is implicit in the firm's. We shall focus upon activities that directly affect strategic marketing considerations.

Underlying this discussion is the assumption that being socially responsible is the correct course of action for the firm to pursue. Such an assumption is, of course, desirable from a societal standpoint but also, hopefully, from the firm's standpoint. An implicit assumption underlying such a philosophy is that long-run multiple goals of survival and growth in the environment, individual fulfillment, and profit are optimally achieved in a firm that is being socially responsible. The

[1] Howard R. Bowen, *Social Responsibility of the Businessman* (New York: Harper & Row, Publishers, 1953), p. 6.

six spheres of responsibility include the firm itself, employees, the consumer, other firms, the community, and the society.

THE FIRM'S SELF-RESPONSIBILITY. The most basic responsibility the firm has is to itself. A firm must make a profit in order to stay in business. Survival is paramount, because only an extant firm can even think about its social responsibility.

A fundamental social responsibility is to those members of society who are stockholders or owners of the firm and vitally concerned about the survival of the firm. A firm is conceived and allowed to become an entity in society for some expressed purpose. In meeting this purpose, the firm meets its initial social responsibility. Even though this is the most basic form of social responsibility, it is not sufficient or without limit. A firm may, for example, in its own fight for survival, imperil other firms that society also needs, or it may imperil individuals within society. When this happens, the total effect of the firm's existence may be negative even though the firm survives. In such an instance, the self-social responsibility of the firm must become subservient to the greater good of society.

For example, a firm may be very profitable but practicing a socially disruptive practice such as racial discrimination. Society—even though it needs the firm's product—may deem the negative effect of the firm's operations so detrimental that the firm must either stop its detrimental practices or cease to exist. On the other hand, society may elect to allow a paper company to survive, even though it practices socially harmful activities such as water pollution, because the papers are essential for magazines and school supplies. In such an instance society allows the polluter to survive but only so long as no other alternative exists for solving the real needs of the society. If the firm can no longer produce the required profit for survival, however, it should and will cease to exist.

RESPONSIBILITY TO EMPLOYEES. In honoring its self-social responsibility, the firm cannot neglect its social responsibility to employees. American social norms are such that social responsibility of the firm includes, at the minimum, a just wage and working conditions that allow employees to express their humanity. A firm might be socially responsible to stockholders by fostering subsistence wages and sweatshop working conditions, but contemporary norms do not permit this within the definition of responsible behavior in the society as a whole.

There has been a tendency to justify decency to workers on the basis that it is profitable to do so. The cliche, "Happy workers are productive workers," can be used to justify to stockholders higher wages and improved fringe benefits. The cliché may be true (or it may not be!), but *social responsibility dictates that decency to employees and encouragement of individual fulfillment be practiced even if the result is reduced profitability in both the short and long run.*

RESPONSIBILITY TO CONSUMERS. The marketing orientation of the modern corporation increases the importance of consumer social responsibility. The resources of the firm are massively coalesced for the purpose of satisfying consumers at a profit. In a seller's market, producing firms can react passively to consumer needs; the consumers must actively seek out their purchases. In contemporary industrialized societies, the tide has turned and the consumer is besieged by producers actively and aggressively courting his patronage. The producer assuming this posture has a greater social responsibility to the consumer than one who lethargically sells all that he can produce.

Survival of the firm may be paramount, but the firm's *raison d'etre*—as defined both by governmental policies and by modern managerial philosophy—is to service adequately the satisfactions desired by consumers. Certain extinction faces the firm that displays a patent disregard of its responsibility to consumers. Some time ago, a leading retailer articulated six areas of responsibility to the consumer and they remain relevant today:

1. Know the consumer. Find out what he wants to buy, at what price, and his attitudes toward your product or service.
2. Restudy your business on the basis of what the consumer thinks of you and wants from you.
3. Be certain you have adequate devices to protect the consumer from the human failings of your business.
4. Review your advertising to be certain that it is accurate, honest, and useful to the consumer.
5. Consider what you are doing to educate the consumer on your product or service.
6. Examine carefully long-range objectives in terms of price, good quality, good taste, safety, *et cetera* vis-à-vis the consumer.[2]

The nature of the firm's responsibility to consumers has been the concern of many government leaders. Perhaps the most concise statement is that of President John F. Kennedy in his 1962 declaration of rights for the consumer:

1. The right to safety.
2. The right to be informed.
3. The right to choose.
4. The right to be heard.[3]

These rights have been reaffirmed by every United States president since Kennedy. President Richard M. Nixon explained in a public speech how these rights relate to consumerism: "Consumerism in the America of the 70s means that we have adopted the concept of 'buyer's rights.' . . . The buyer has the right to accurate information on which to make his free choice."

The challenge to executives responsible for marketing strategy is to institute

---

[2] Jack I. Straus, President, R. H. Macy and Co., "The Responsibility of the Businessman to the Consumer," in Harwood F. Merrill, ed., *The Responsibilities of Business Leadership* (Cambridge, Mass.: Harvard University Press, 1949), pp. 54–55.

[3] E. B. Weiss, "Marketers Fiddle While Consumers Burn," *Harvard Business Review,* July-August 1968, p. 45.

controls over marketing tactics that insure that these rights are upheld—and that do so in ways consistent with the firm's other responsibilities. Some firms have created within the firm a position for a person to assume the role of advocate for the consumer. It is his (or, typically, her) task to make the firm constantly aware of practices that potentially violate the rights of the consumer.

With widespread attention being given to the "marketing concept" or increased consumer orientation, it is perhaps easier for executives to be aware of and practice responsibility to the firm's consumers. To remain viable, it is becoming recognized, a firm must be aware of and responsive to its responsibility to the consumer. For the firm to do otherwise is economic suicide.

RESPONSIBILITY TO OTHER FIRMS. A firm must act responsibly in its dealings with three types of other firms: (1) firms that are customers, (2) firms that are suppliers, and (3) firms that are competitors. The first type of relationship differs little from the responsibility due individuals who are customers. This discussion, therefore, focuses upon responsibilities to the latter two types of firms.

Responsibility toward supplier firms demands consideration of the effect of buying transactions on the fate of the supplier. This does not imply altruistically keeping an inefficient supplier in business. Rather, it means that the buyer will not unduly exercise his power over the supplier and will make reasonable efforts to schedule purchases or communications in such a way that the supplier is encouraged to operate effectively. This norm of behavior has been codified in the credo of the National Association of Purchasing Agents, who request their members to act with loyalty to the purchasing firm but also "with justice to those with whom he deals."[4] More specifically, the buying agent should "buy without prejudice, work for honesty in buying and selling, and denounce all forms and manifestations of commercial bribery."[5] The purchasing agent is merely an instrument of the firm, so if he is to act responsibly, the firm must have policies that foster this type of behavior.

Responsibility to competitive firms is more difficult to ascertain in the American economic system. The right to put competitive firms out of business or at least to gain an advantage over them is essential to the concept of free enterprise. Basically, irresponsible behavior toward competitors fosters irresponsible behavior towards consumers. If deception, fraud, or similar practices are used to injure a competitor, they are likely also to injure the consumer. Practices (such as monopoly or other malfeasances that restrain competition) that deceive the consumer or limit his freedom of choice among competitive suppliers are the ones that are usually classified as irresponsible to competitors as well. The difficulty of establishing a basis for socially responsible behavior in this area is verified, it seems, by the existence of laws such as the Sherman Act and regulatory bodies such as the Federal Trade Commission. If it were not so difficult to

---

[4] Robert J. Holloway and Robert S. Hancock, *Marketing in a Changing Environment* (New York: John Wiley & Sons, Inc., 1968), p. 214.

[5] *Ibid.*

distinguish with clarity between right behavior and wrong, there would not exist such an abundance of legislation and adjudication on the subject.

RESPONSIBILITY TO THE COMMUNITY. In recent years, the responsibility of the firm to the community in which it operates has become more obvious. Frequently, the business firm has the capacity to be a decisive influence in a community. It is this sphere of influence that is in desperate need of assistance. Firms have found that developing a prospering and friendly community is often in the firm's self-interest as well as part of its responsibility. Conversely, the lack of responsibility exercised by some firms has sometimes created a hostile and detrimental environment. Businessmen in the ghettos of Watts, Newark, and Detroit have found out just how detrimental a hostile community can be. Social responsibility to the community should have been learned in business school years ago instead of forced upon the firm by riots, protests, and the sufferings of distressed community members.

The degree of social responsibility a firm has to a given community is a function of the extent of dependency. Clearly, the sole employer in an area has a greater individual responsibility to the community than if there are a multitude of employers. The aggregate social responsibility, however, may be the same.

There are two aspects of the firm's social responsibility to the community: (1) what the firm ought to do and (2) what the firm ought not to do. In the first category are civic activities such as Junior Achievement, training programs, encouragement of United Fund, development of recreational and educational facilities, support of the chamber of commerce, encouragement of good government and adequate taxation bases. Under the second category are such misdeeds as air pollution, water pollution, discrimination in employment, and careless deployment of resources.

As an example, consider the case of a firm in Los Angeles that located its garage for a large fleet of trucks adjacent to the sole playground for a housing development containing 750 families—most of them with several small children. There were no curbs on the street and hundreds of children played on the same street the large trucks drove on when returning to the garage. The only entrance the company provided for the garage required the trucks to drive through the middle of the playground area, at about the peak usage time of the playground. At the time of this writing, no children had been killed by the trucks, but a number had been struck and injured.

The apparently irresponsible action of this firm probably was not one of malicious intent. It could well be a matter of executives' failure to consider such factors in their decision to locate the garage in the area.

Situations such as the above indicate the need for increased awareness of total responsibility by business executives in their planning. In discussing community social responsibility, Paul Langdon has suggested three guidelines to help direct the firm. He states:

1. Get all the information you can concerning a situation.

2. Ascertain who would be affected by a decision and whether anyone would be hurt by it.
3. Base a decision on the long-run effects and implications.[6]

These guidelines do not in themselves provide correct courses of action but they suggest what one should consider before embarking on any course of action that might affect the community. Such considerations make unintentional breaches of social responsibility less likely.

RESPONSIBILITY TO SOCIETY. Societal responsibility is all-encompassing; it is the ultimate criterion against which the responsibility of the firm can be measured. It represents more than the sum total of the other spheres of responsibility, since it goes beyond the immediate task environment of the firm. No firm in today's world can afford to lead an insular existence. To survive, the firm must meet not only the product needs of a population, but societal needs as well.

The all-encompassing nature of societal responsibility is shown in Figure 22-1. The firm must honor all the spheres that comprise its immediate milieu. When all spheres are considered together, the net effect of the firm's actions can be determined. Only when the firm has met this final test can it be considered truly socially responsible.

HOW BUSINESSMEN FEEL ABOUT THEIR RESPONSIBILITY

"Are businessmen aware of the social responsibility they and their firms have?" That is a question often asked of the young executive, who lives in a world that views businessmen with open hostility or at least suspicion. How aware are businessmen of the needs for responsibility to society?

Historical Attitudes Toward Responsibility

In 1946, *Fortune* magazine conducted a management poll on the topic of social responsibility.[7] The first question posed was the following:

A few years ago it was frequently said that businessmen ought to acquire a "social consciousness." What was usually meant was that businessmen were responsible for the consequences of their actions in a sphere somewhat wider than their profit-and-loss statements. Do you think that businessmen should recognize such responsibilities and do their best to fulfill them?

An overwhelming 93.5 percent responded "yes" while only 1.6 percent responded "no." The rest either didn't know (.2 percent) or said it depends (4.7 percent).

---

[6] Paul R. Langdon, "Ethics in Management-Community Relations," in Robert Bartels, ed., *Ethics in Business* (Columbus, Ohio: Bureau of Business Research, 1963).

[7] "Fortune Management Poll," *Fortune*, March 1946, pp. 197–198.

Figure 22-1   Spheres of social responsibility.

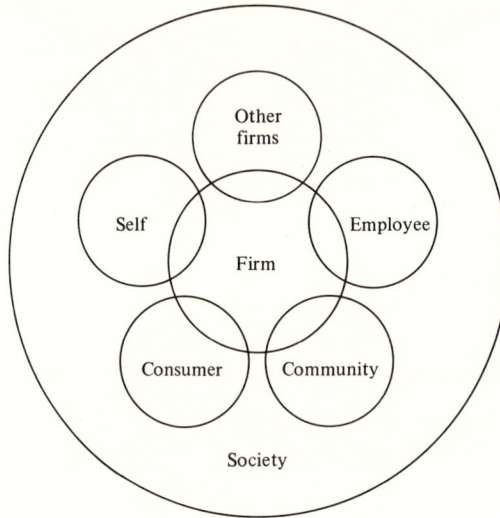

When asked what proportions of the *businessmen they knew* had a "social consciousness" of this sort, the percentages were considerably different. The responses to that question were as follows:

None	.4%
Less than 10%	11.8
About a quarter	22.2
About a half	29.2
About three-quarters	26.7
All	3.0
Don't know	6.7

The number of businessmen who actually are responsible appears, in that survey, to be much less than the number who feel they should be.

Recent Attitudes Toward Responsibility

More recent studies indicate that businessmen believe other goals than profit are important. A *Harvard Business Review* survey presented executives the following statement:

. . . the businessman exists for only one purpose, to create and deliver value satisfaction at a profit to himself. . . . If what is offered can be sold at a profit (not necessarily a long-term profit), then it is legitimate. . . . The cultural, spiritual, social, and moral consequences of his action are none of his occupation concern.

In this study, 94 percent of the executives disagreed with the above statement.[8]
Another statement was given to the same group of executives:

For corporation executives to act in the interest of shareholders alone, and not in
the interest of employees and consumers, is unethical.

Over 80 percent of the executives surveyed agreed with the above statement.[9] As
encouraging as these responses might appear, their luster is dimmed some by a full
15 percent of the executives who agreed with the statement, ". . . whatever is
good business is good ethics."[10] Evaluating these views of executives, Baumhart
summarizes with a note of hope:

These executives see a business enterprise as a society of human beings—a society
with obligations not only to the people who provide capital, but also to employees,
customers, suppliers, government, and even at times competitors.[11]

BUSINESS INTEREST IN RESPONSIBILITY. In another survey—one of the classic
works on social responsibilities of businessmen—Bowen found businessmen
interested in social responsibility.[12] His major conclusions include the following:

1. Businessmen manifest widespread and sincere interest in the subject.
2. Their pronouncements regarding their general responsibilities are frequent and eloquent.
3. Businessmen are unanimous in their belief in the need for public education (this suggests a realization that the required adjustments are
   bilateral, that is, businessmen must adjust their operations to the needs
   of society but society must also develop attitudes and policies more
   favorable to business).
4. Businessmen are concerned about better public relations, which they
   hope to achieve by educating the public and adopting socially oriented
   goals.[13]

ATTITUDES TOWARD SPECIFIC ISSUES. One of the most recent and useful
studies is John W. Clark's *Religion and the Moral Standards of American Busi-*

---

[8] Theodore Levitt, "Are Advertising and Marketing Corrupting Society? It's Not Your
Worry, Levitt Tells Business," *Advertising Age*, October 6, 1958, p. 89. Cited in Raymond
C. Baumhart, "How Ethical Are Businessmen?" *Harvard Business Review*, July-August 1961,
p. 7.

[9] Paraphrase of Robert N. Anthony's thesis advanced in "The Trouble with Profit
Maximization," *Harvard Business Review*, November-December 1960, p. 126. Cited in
Baumhart, "How Ethical Are Businessmen?" p. 10.

[10] *Ibid.*, pp. 10–12.

[11] *Ibid.*, pp. 12–16.

[12] Bowen, *Social Responsibility of the Businessman*.

[13] *Ibid.*

nessmen.[14] Rather than survey attitudes toward social consciousness in general, Clark surveyed executives on specific issues. Only a few illustrative issues are discussed here.

In this study, only 15 percent of executives surveyed *disapproved* of the refusal of U.S. Steel to exert pressure for racial integration. However, 96 percent *approved* of a firm's decision to install a costly filter to reduce air pollution. Among the executives, 18 percent *disapproved* of an accounting firm's decision not to hire foreign students as apprentices for the summer months, while 95 percent *approved* of a company president's community activities on company-paid time.[15] These answers are not necessarily polar or even necessarily inconsistent. They do illustrate that norms of social responsibility vary according to the specific issue. It is also clear that there are definite limits to the social responsibility businessmen perceive to exist.

Conclusions

A businessman's attitude toward social responsibility reflects how he feels about social responsibility, not necessarily what he will do. Nevertheless, a positive attitude toward social responsibility presumably increases the probability that he will act in a responsible manner. It is apparent that businessmen are becoming keenly aware of their social responsibility and that most have a positive attitude toward it. However, there is far from unanimity as to the specific nature of the social responsibility.

The decade of the seventies appears to be one of increasing or renewed social consciousness—or at least the latent awareness is being made more manifest. Several reasons appear to explain increasing social consciousness:

1. Society is aware that businessmen have been derelict in certain areas and consequently is making demands.
2. In other areas where society has not yet realized business' omissions or commissions, businessmen are taking corrective action to avoid a direct confrontation.
3. The ignored and oppressed are screaming for attention. Part of their clamor is directed at society in general and a portion is aimed directly at business.
4. Business is responding to these cries in both areas, since the government has achieved only limited effectiveness in coping with the ills of the society.

A rationale that could underlie the four reasons stated above (particularly 2 and 4) is enlightened self-interest. Many executives take undue pride in their social consciousness, which is actually enlightened self-interest under the guise

[14] John W. Clark, *Religion and the Moral Standards of American Business* (Cincinnati: South-Western Publishing Company, 1966).

[15] *Ibid.*, pp. 109–110.

of social responsibility. This is not to condemn their behavior—the behavior may be exemplary. It does question motives. Motives vis-à-vis social responsibility are not as crucial as motives with regard to ethical behavior. Motives, in fact, determine whether ethical-appearing behavior is actually ethical. The subject of motives is broached here so that the executive does not indulge in self-deception and accord himself undue piety for his selfless acts.

Recent events that vividly portray society's plight have contributed most to the executive's increased awareness of social responsibility. Protest and violent rioting provide a rude awakening to the napping corporation. Forced to view rural poverty and urban slums, the businessman sees elements of the great society that lack greatness. Struck by this stark reality, the rightly disturbed executive asks:

"What can a marketing executive do?"

MARKETING AND SOCIAL RESPONSIBILITY

Marketing has a special role in attaining corporate social responsibility. To see it, let us recall the central role of marketing as the corporate interface with environmental systems. This centrality is evident when marketing is defined as:

. . . the process in a society by which the demand structure for economic goods and services is anticipated or enlarged and satisfied through the conception, promotion, exchange and physical distribution of such goods and services.[16]

This global view of marketing entails a need for:

1. An understanding of the entire marketing system, its historical development, and the forces within it that spell its dynamics, which may be useful for the purposes of making appropriate choices and decisions, *recognizing its contribution to the social order* or developing the knowledge and perspective.
2. An *understanding of the environment within which the marketing process is being performed* as illuminated by other social disciplines.
3. Duly considering all points of view, with *emphasis on consumer or social welfare,* on the maximization of optimization of profit or efficiency in individual enterprise and on *relationships between social and acquisitive efficiency.*[17]

The Marketing Interface

Marketing provides the primary interface with environmental systems. If marketing, as the interactive organ of the firm, does not honor social responsibility, it is

[16] Marketing Staff of the Ohio State University, "A Statement of Marketing Philosophy," *Journal of Marketing,* January 1965, p. 43.

[17] *Ibid.,* p. 44. Italics added.

unlikely that the corporate social responsibility of the firm will be carried out.

Three aspects of the marketing interface have been identified by C. W. Cook, Chairman of General Foods. These special responsibilities of marketing are:

1. to offer a *social product,*
2. to make it available at a *social price,*
3. to make a *social profit* in the process.[18]

A social product is "one with value transcending intrinsic or strictly utilitarian qualities,"[19] a social price is simply "the lowest price at which it can be offered,"[20] and a social profit is a profit consistent with the contribution to social welfare. Granting certain ambiguities in these definitions, they still serve to highlight societal aspects in marketing's primary activities.

The Challenge of Change

Marketing activities are crucially intertwined with the dynamism of the American society. To be socially responsible, increased understanding is needed of the relationship of marketing to social and technological change. Marketing affects and is affected by change. This relationship is described by Robert W. Austin:

1. *Marketing* is responsible today for incredible technological change.
2. Technological change will continue to cause social change.
3. Social change brings demands for action to meet or mitigate the effects of social change.
4. The job of *marketing* today must be broadened to include an awareness of the social change it causes. And that awareness will place new responsibility on *marketing* management for intelligently, carefully thought-out decisions as to the basic responsibility for meeting such change.[21]

The challenge of marketing is to adapt creatively to these changes and also to direct them.

Marketing strategy has often ignored a subtle but important change in consumer demand—a demand for a better life. Malcolm P. McNair wonders why our consumeristic economy "has failed to sense a growing social dimension of demand, a demand for a better life for the community."[22] Marketing executives, chief proponents of the consumeristic society, will increasingly face not only the

---

[18] C. W. Cook, "The Social Value of Marketing," *The Conference Board Record,* February 1967, p. 32.

[19] *Ibid.,* p. 33.

[20] *Ibid.,* p. 34.

[21] Robert W. Austin, "Responsibility for Social Change," *Harvard Business Review,* July-August 1965, p. 52. Marketing has been substituted for his references to business in general.

[22] Malcolm P. McNair, "Marketing and the Social Challenge of Our Times," American Marketing Association, June 1968 Conference Proceedings.

recognition of a growing demand for a better life but also a *responsibility* for seeing that the demand is satisfied.

Reasons for Marketing Responsibility

There are two main reasons that marketing should be socially responsible: (1) because it is the right thing to do, and (2) because it serves the firm's enlightened self-interest. A General Electric executive amplifies the latter when he affirms ". . . a fabulous opportunity to forge new growth through making a business of development, and broadening the focus to comprehend basic social problems."[23] Marketing planning is concerned more with economic growth than with social progress, it is true, but the relationship between social and economic malaise makes progress in one impossible without progress in the other.[24]

Five specific reasons why business executives can and should be responsible are clearly stated by the chairman of the Whirlpool Corporation:

1. Business has most of the jobs available under its jurisdiction and the ability to create new jobs and train people to fill them.
2. Business enjoys a degree of flexibility and independence that permits it to change policy and practice rapidly to adjust to new circumstances as they arise. It does not have to wait for the voters to make up their minds or submit its plans to the city council for approval. *It has command.*
3. Business has the manpower and the management skills to develop workable programs for solving the various problems that exist and the money and facilities to implement them.
4. Business is in a position to function at the local level where, in the final analysis, the job has got to be done.
5. Business can master more sheer power for social action than all the rest of the elements of the community combined. It has the ability to get things done and that is what is needed.[25]

Having primary responsibility for the interface and communications of the business firm, marketing assumes primary responsibility for social improvement.

Marketing's Accomplishments

The accomplishments of marketing are, for the most part, the accomplishments of the total business firm. Companies have made major advances in rehabilitating blighted urban areas. Countless companies have started programs to hire and train hard-core unemployed, making them productive members of society again.

---

[23] M. B. McKitterick, Vice-President of Corporate Planning, General Electric, "Planning the Existential Society," American Marketing Association, Fall 1968 Conference Proceedings.

[24] W. Leonard Evans, Jr., "Ghetto Marketing: What Now?" American Marketing Association, Fall 1968 Conference Proceedings.

[25] Elisha Gray II, "Changing Values in the Business Society," *Business Horizons*, August 1968, p. 23.

The sense of identity and the purpose this provides an individual goes far beyond the pure economic worth of such programs.

Executives of many firms advise struggling ghetto entrepreneurs. As consultants, they provide a valuable service to those who lack practical business experience. In helping to solve the problems of fledgling firms, they are ensuring a strong base for continued social and economic growth. Franchising organizations such as International Industries have developed programs for minority-group members to obtain franchises and special training without the normal capital investment. Other firms are building new plants in ghetto areas where employment is badly needed or, if unable to move plant sites, are providing transportation from the center city to their plants.

PUBLIC COMMUNICATIONS. Two important aspects of social programs are: (1) doing them, and (2) having people aware of what is being done. Some maintain that the former is sufficient. That is only partly true. Effectiveness is limited when public mistrust and misinformation are allowed to develop. When a firm's social involvement is not communicated to the public, people with negative attitudes may assume inaction and initiate programs that limit the firm's ability to be responsible. Programs undertaken by a firm that make positive contributions often receive only limited attention, while acts of irresponsibility frequently gain extensive exposure.

CASE EXAMPLE—CIRCLE F. The experience of a medium-sized firm in Trenton, New Jersey, illustrates the beneficial effects of marketing activities directed at informing the public of community concern. Circle F, a $30 million manufacturer of electric products, even though the largest employer in Trenton, was virtually unknown. A new president took over and decided the company's community responsibility had been ignored too long. To change this, he started a program to improve the company's relationships and image with the community. He took the following steps:

1. The company's advertising agency prepared a series of advertisements to run in local newspapers . . . to make the company better known.
2. The company bought radio time. Advertising on the program was similar in content to that in its printed advertisements.
3. The company compiled a list of 6,000 persons of influence in their area. A month after each of its printed ads appeared, it mailed reprints to these persons.
4. The company sought and obtained considerable publicity in the local newspaper.
5. The company drew up a list showing its employees' membership in local organizations and also showing which of them they could belong to.
6. The company is about to set up a formal speakers bureau.
7. The company is involved in community projects. They sponsor an essay writing contest for high school students and an art exhibit.[26]

---

[26] "How to Make an Impact in Your Community," *Business Management*, December 1967, pp. 52–53.

The program resulted in five immediate benefits:

1. The company is obtaining a slightly bigger response to its help wanted ads than it used to.
2. Higher caliber workers are responding.
3. The company has received hundreds of unsolicited letters from business, civic, and government leaders complimenting the company on its program.
4. The program has had an effect on the company's local sales.
5. The program has had a good effect on employee morale; the company reports reduced absenteeism and lower employee turnover.[27]

The company did not initiate dramatic new community involvement, but it did make the community aware of what it was already doing. The efforts were directed at the well-being of the community, not toward sales activities—but there were multiple goal utilities for the company.

Marketing's Challenge

The number of critics of marketing activities leads one to conclude there must be something wrong, or as yet unresolved, about the responsibility of marketing activities. Perhaps marketing usually acts responsibly, yet something must account for the persistent perception of marketing's behavior by its critics. These charges by critics present a challenge to management in the seventies. The major areas of criticism or challenge have been identified as: (1) the economic order, (2) advertising and selling, (3) products, and (4) prices.[28]

CONSPICUOUS CONSUMPTION. Critics of marketing claim that it not only perpetuates an unfair economic system but also fosters conspicuous consumption and encourages waste. They further maintain that marketing directs people toward the more material aspects of our society—a process made even more heinous by the plight of the have-nots in our society.

Claims about an unfair economic system require more attention than the present discussion can allow. In the past, businessmen felt no need to concern themselves with such discussions; the economic system or the role of marketing in it was not seriously questioned. That era, however, has passed. The well-informed marketing analyst can adequately defend a marketing-oriented economic system. Unfortunately, however, many analysts have been ill-equipped. Evidence indicates that the imperfections of the existing system—although real—are no greater than those of alternative forms of economic order. Alternative economic orders, such as those which are more socialistic, are even more materialistic in their rationale. Judged from a historical perspective, they are usually transitional to the type of consumer-oriented enterprise system presently attacked by critics of marketing.

[27] *Ibid.*
[28] Holloway and Hancock, *Marketing in a Changing Environment*, pp. 206–211.

The charge that marketing directs attention to attaining material goods is probably valid. In the past, businessmen could ignore those persons who did not attain the rewards of the marketing system—and no serious problems were caused by ignoring them. That era, also, has passed. Marketing men, whether they like it or not, have to do something about the clamor of the have-nots—who are as enticed by marketing strategy as those for whom the marketing messages were primarily intended.

ADVERTISING AND SELLING. The American Association of Advertising Agencies has adopted a code outlining ethical standards. Some of the more salient points of the code are:

1. The public is entitled to expect that advertising will be reliable and honest in presentation.
2. A prohibition against knowingly producing advertising which contains:
   (a) False or misleading statements or exaggerations, visual or verbal.
   (b) Testimonials which do not reflect the real choice of a competent witness.
   (c) Price claims which are misleading.
   (d) Comparisons which unfairly disparage a competitor's product or service.
   (e) Claims insufficiently supported, or which distort the true meaning or practicable applications of statements made by professional or scientific authority.[29]

Granting that the above statements are open to interpretation, adherence to the spirit of the standard would give advertising's critics little to criticize. The problem—one not uniquely associated with business relationships—is how to cause people to adhere to the creeds to which they subscribe.[30]

PLANNED OBSOLESCENCE. Time and time again the charge of planned obsolescence has been leveled at marketing. To be honest, it sometimes happens—but deliberate attempts to build products that will wear out sooner than necessary are rare. The charge of planned obsolescence has substance only when the product is viewed myopicly as a physical entity. In contemporary society, a product is far more than its physical attributes. A change in any of the product dimensions enhances its value to the consumer, and if he has the money—which he often does in industrialized economies—he chooses to buy the improved product. The naïve social critic sometimes assumes that this results in waste—basing his criticism upon the assumption that the original product is then discarded by the person with money who purchased the improved product. The naïveté of the criticism, of course, is in ignoring the fact that the original product moves through a chan-

<hr>

[29] Joseph W. Towle et al., *Ethics and Standards in American Business* (Boston: Houghton Mifflin Company, 1964), pp. 285–286.
[30] *Ibid.*

nel of reuse, permitting people to have clothes, cars, and appliances who in other economies would be denied even the reused product.

HIGH PRICES. Apart from sweeping charges of too high prices or flagrant price-fixing antitrust violations, social critics usually have little to recommend to marketing strategists about pricing. Everyone wants lower prices, but when one considers the question in terms of value added and resources with which to buy the products, the masses of consumers empirically appear to accept marketing policies on pricing of most products. An area of increased need for responsibility in the seventies will most likely center on pricing of selective services and products essential to the welfare of the society—such as drugs, hospital and medical care, education, and other sensitive products.

Public Expectations of Business Responsibility

One reason marketing must meet the challenge of responsibility is the public's faith in the ability of business to remedy social ills. Two polls seem to show that people believe business firms can and should attack social problems. One poll conducted for a national news magazine showed that of those questioned:

92 percent wanted business to help eliminate depressions,
87 percent wanted business to help rebuild cities,
72 percent wanted business to help find cures for diseases,
83 percent wanted business to aid colleges,
80 percent wanted business to contribute resources to the war against poverty,
83 percent wanted business to help eliminate racial prejudice,
90 percent wanted business to become involved in controlling pollution.[31]

In another poll, 62 percent felt it would be better if private enterprise were doing more of what government does now, while only 21 percent felt that it would not.[32] Clearly business has been given approval to act. When he was vice-chairman of Ford Motor, Arjay Miller suggested how business might accomplish its social tasks:

The corporation must go beyond its traditional role of business enterprise and seek to anticipate, rather than simply react to, social needs or problems. This may require the establishment of a long-range planning function to make sure a firm

[31] Survey conducted by Louis Harris and Associates published in *Newsweek*, May 2, 1966, p. 84, cited in George Champion, "Creative Competition," *Harvard Business Review*, May-June 1967, pp. 61–67.
[32] Richard Cornuelle, *Reclaiming the American Dream* (New York: Random House, Inc., 1965), p. 10, reporting a poll conducted by Belden Associates cited in Champion, "Creative Competition."

will be able to respond to what society wants to do. It may involve not only changed "products" but also changed internal organization.[33]

SYMBIOTIC MARKETING. Creative synergism is required to solve the social tasks of marketing. Lee Adler suggests an effective solution to be "symbiotic marketing."[34] Symbiotic marketing is defined as "the alliance of resources or programs between two or more independent organizations, designed to improve the marketing potential of each."[35] To solve the problems the nation faces, business must unite and bring together their resources. Individual firms lack direction and can tackle only small portions. An alliance for social progress among businessmen would require devoting some of their time and energy to the ills of society, guided by planning and vision that would maximize the energies exerted for the greater good.

DEPARTMENT OF CORPORATE-SOCIETAL AFFAIRS. One proposal for improving business strategy to achieve more effective social involvement is to form a new department of corporate-societal affairs. This should involve a high-level vice-presidency logically organized under marketing or corporate planning. The vice-president of corporate-societal affairs would meet with community leaders and similar executives in other firms to plan and enact corporate-community projects. Far more would be accomplished by many firms in a unified action than by a few crusaders struggling to stem the tide of unrest and malaise. Such an executive is also in a position to draw together the resources available for action within his own firm and coordinate them with those of others.

This executive would help society and the firm by creating new markets and new products to serve existing markets and future markets. This goes one step beyond the marketing concept where the consumer is king; in this perspective society is king.

The essence of the challenge for marketing is summarized by Walter L. Jeffrey:

It appears rather apparent that the American economy is rapidly moving to the point where it will make increased demands upon the discipline of marketing.

In the decades ahead the marketing challenge will be far greater than conception of a philosophy of growth. The challenge will rest solely upon the development of executive techniques to manage the continued growth of the most abundant economy ever known to mankind.

Finally, marketing's changing responsibility will have social implications. . . . Marketing can work as a persuasive force in guiding the development of natural

---

[33] Arjay Miller from a speech delivered at a University of Illinois Symposium, April 21, 1967 quote in Weiss, "Marketers Fiddle While Consumers Burn."

[34] Lee Adler, "Symbiotic Marketing," *Harvard Business Review*, November-December 1966, pp. 59–71.

[35] *Ibid.*, p. 60.

resources and human capabilities into the most socially desired and accepted channels of growth.[36]

CONSEQUENCES OF INACTION

If the firm does not respond to the needs of society, society will turn elsewhere. In the short run, the consequence of inaction is government intervention. Historically, when business has failed to act when it should have, the state or federal government has interceded. Legislation, regulation, and coercion may be poor substitutes for a firm's own purposeful strategy honoring its social responsibility, but they are very likely to occur.

In the long run, the consequence of inaction is extinction of the firm. For a free-enterprise system to flourish, its members must contribute not only to their own health but also to the well-being of the system that supports them. Where they do not, the system will replace (through evolution or revolution) the irresponsible institutions or member firms with more responsive ones. If firms fail to act, elements of incipient decay will flower. In the United States, the seeds of destruction have been planted; only time will tell whether they will grow and be harvested or whether they will be weeded out by business involvement in the problems of the environmental system that houses it. The firm is an integral part of society and as such depends on the well-being of society for its own well-being. To take from society and give nothing in return weakens both the system and the member components. It is, however, the sensitive, aggressive new leadership that is emerging on the business horizon that will determine the ultimate outcome. Will they be given an opportunity by existing leaders to meet the challenge? Will they have the ability and the personal commitment to become involved in the important concerns of the society?

In the oft-quoted words of Edmund Burke: "All that is required for the triumph of tyranny is for good men to do nothing."

QUESTIONS FOR REVIEW AND DISCUSSION

1. Distinguish between business responsibility and business ethics.
2. "Profit is a necessary, but not sufficient, rationale for business." Write a short essay analyzing the meaning of this statement. Does it appear that this position is commonly accepted by American business firms?
3. Summarize the major events of the past two to three years that you interpret as important indicators or signals of problems in the society with which businessmen should plan strategic action.
4. Conduct a survey among business and other students to determine what they consider the most pressing problems of the country. How does business contribute to the cause of these problems?

[36] Walter L. Jeffrey, "The Conglomerate Corporation and Marketing in a Changing Society," American Marketing Association, Winter 1967 Conference Proceedings.

5. Prepare a list of the most pressing problems in society that business might reasonably help solve. Analyze in detail how business is most likely to exercise responsibility in these matters.
6. Choose a firm about which you can obtain substantial information. Analyze the issues they face in fulfilling their responsibility to the firm itself, the employees, consumers, other firms, the community, and society. Prepare a program for corrective action where it may be needed.
7. The text describes some specific actions that businessmen consider improper for the business executive. Prepare an additional list of actions that you consider improper but frequently violated. Justify your choices on the basis of your own ethical code.
8. Why does marketing have a central role in exercising the social responsibility of a business firm? Discuss.
9. Prepare a report on recent efforts of marketing organizations to take a more positive stance in meeting their responsibility to the community or society. Do these efforts appear to be successful? Analyze the reasons for success or failure.
10. "The well-informed marketing analyst can adequately defend a marketing-oriented economic system." Assume that you are asked to defend such a system to a person who is advocating a revolutionary system much different from the system in this country. Prepare a logical outline of such a defense.
11. The text describes part of the code of ethics of the American Association of Advertising Agencies. Apparently people believe there are violations, even though the code exists. What is your explanation of such violations? How would you recommend that society prevent such violations in the future?

AUTHOR INDEX

Abrams, Dorothy, 245n
Achenbaum, Alvin A., 351n
Ackoff, Russell L., 438n
Adler, Lee, 3n, 11n, 15, 31n, 40n, 209n, 242n, 469, 524
Agnostini, J. M., 358
Albaum, Gerald, 184n, 464, 493
Alcott, James, 149n
Alderson, Wroe, 33n, 35n, 138n, 187n, 286, 482n
Alevizos, John P., 69n
Alexander, Ralph S., 137n, 221–223n, 225n
Allen, Irving L., 85n
Allen, J. Knight, 14n
Alonso, William, 321n
Ames, B. Charles, 36n, 39n, 397n, 398n, 497n
Amstutz, Arnold E., 443n, 453n
Andreasen, Alan R., 108n
Angelus, Theodore L., 299n, 232n, 241n
Ansoff, H. Igor, 7n, 18n, 19n, 21n
Anthony, Robert N., 481n, 515n
Appel, Valentine, 360n
Applebaum, William, 321n
Armstrong, J. Scott, 65n
Assael, Henry, 190n
Austin, Robert W., 518
Axelrod, Joel N., 343n, 361n, 477n

Backman, Jules, 253, 266n, 267n
Backstrom, Charles H., 69n
Bailey, Earl L., 41n, 43n, 183n
Balderston, Frederick E., 449
Bale, Maurice E., 191n
Ballou, Ronald H., 321n
Banks, Seymour, 89n, 196n
Barclay, William D., 434n
Barnett, Norman L., 191n
Bartels, Robert, 28n, 170n, 172n, 173, 513n
Barton, Roger, 343n

Bass, Frank M., 189n
Bates, Albert D., 288n, 292n, 294n
Batten, J. D., 390n
Batthof, C. Larry, 179n
Bauer, Ray, 192n
Bauman, J. N., 369n
Baumhart, Raymond C., 515
Beckman, Theodore N., 157n, 270n, 277n, 280n, 306n, 307n, 366n, 373n, 382n
Beik, Leland L., 56–57n, 59n, 60n, 69n
Belasco, James A., 380n
Bell, James E., Jr., 108n, 191n
Bell, Martin L., 496n
Belson, William A., 85n
Bender, Wesley C., 123n
Bendix, R., 97n
Bengston, Roger, 245n, 246n
Bennett, Peter D., 122n, 202n
Berdy, Edwin M., 422n
Berenson, Conrad, 223n, 477n
Berg, Thomas L., 7n, 235n, 236n
Bernstein, Henry R., 379n
Berry, E. Janet, 235n
Bieda, John C., 200n
Bittel, Lester R., 485–486
Blackwell, Roger D., 60n, 76n, 88n, 114n, 115n, 132n, 175n, 190n, 244n, 347n, 353n, 434n
Blankenship, A. B., 51n, 246n
Blankertz, Donald F., 84n, 427n
Blood, Robert O., Jr., 95n
Blum, Milton L., 360n
Boddewyn, J., 171n
Bogue, D. J., 165n
Bonini, Charles B., 454–456
Borden, Neil H., 39n
Bowen, Howard R., 508n, 515
Bower, John, 358n
Bowersox, Donald J., 292n, 310n, 315n, 321n, 322n, 327n, 328n, 331n

527

SUBJECT INDEX